Cognition

Cognition
The Thinking Animal
Second edition

Daniel T. Willingham

University of Virginia

PEARSON
Prentice
Hall

Upper Saddle River, NJ 07458

Library of Congress Cataloging-in-Publication Data

Willingham, Daniel T.
  Cognition : the thinking animal / Daniel T. Willingham.—2nd ed.
    p. cm.
  Includes bibliographical references and index.
  ISBN 0-13-182447-3
  1. Cognitive psychology. I. Title.

BF201.W56 2004
153—dc21

2003040505

Editor in Chief: Leah Jewell
Senior Acquisitions Editor: Jayme Heffler
Managing Editor: Joanne Riker
Editorial Assistant: Jennifer Conklin and Kevin Doughten
Executive Marketing Manager: Sheryl Adams
Production Editor: Laura A. Lawrie
Permissions Research: Amy Goldberger
Manufacturing and Prepress Buyer: Tricia Kenney
Art Director: Jayne Conte
Cover Design: Bruce Kenselaar
Cover Illustration: Auguste Rodin/Explorer, Paris/Superstock, Inc.
Line Art Manager: Guy Ruggiero
Illustrator (Interior): Maria Piper
Composition: This book was set in 10/12 Trump Mediaeval by Laserwords
  Private Limited.
Printer/Binder: Interior printed by R. R. Donnelley/Harrisonburg, cover printed by
  Phoenix Color Corp.

Credits and acknowledgments borrowed from other sources and reproduced, with
permission, in this textbook appear on pages 589–593.

10 9 8 7 6 5 4 3 2 1

ISBN 0-13-182447-3

*This book is dedicated
to my parents*

Contents

8   Motor Control   286

9   Visual Imagery   328

12   Language   456

Preface

A long-standing goal of human enquiry is to understand ourselves. How can we characterize the human species? Here are some well-known definitions of "man."

> Man is by nature a political animal. —Aristotle
>
> Man is a noble animal. —Sir Thomas Browne
>
> Man is a tool-using animal. —Thomas Carlyle
>
> Man is a reasoning animal. —Seneca
>
> Man is a social animal. —Benedict Spinoza
>
> Man is a rational animal who always loses his temper when he is called upon to act in accordance with the dictates of reason. —Oscar Wilde

All these proposals are, in a sense, correct, but are all rooted in another characteristic. We are able to act politically, use tools effectively, understand nobility, and so on because of our ability to think. The book you are reading is a study of cognition—of how humans think.

READABILITY

Cognitive psychology does not seem to have the intrinsic interest of some other areas of the field. Textbook authors are aware of this problem, but to be honest, I've never cared much for their remedies. The usual strategy is to include "real world" examples and demonstrations, usually found in little boxes that appear every few pages. This strategy seems to confirm the reader's growing suspicion that they are bored by sending the implicit message. "Yes, yes, I know this stuff is boring, but hang in there, and every few pages I'll toss in one of those boxes with a demonstration or real-world application to keep you going."

I've done three things in this book to try to arouse readers' interest in the material.

- I have explicitly stated the questions that motivate cognitive psychologists. These questions we ask are of general interest, but psychologists don't always do the best job of explaining the questions in any detail. We plunge right into the answers, which seem arcane. Each chapter in this book is organized around two or three straightforward questions that are easy to appreciate and explained in detail.
- To the extent possible, I have used a narrative structure. By that I mean that there are causal links within and across chapter sections, so that it

is clear why you are reading something. Nothing is more boring than a list of unconnected facts.

- I have tried to write in a non-stilted, not-especially-academic style.

Despite the light tone, this book is not light in content. An easy way to check the coverage is by examining the key terms section at the end of each chapter.

PEDAGOGY

Readability is fine, but the goal of a textbook is, after all, that students learn the material. Different students like and use different pedagogical features, so I've included a few different ones to help them learn.

- A brief preview poses the broad questions and provides the broad answers covered in each section.
- Key terms are identified by boldface type and are defined immediately thereafter. They are also collected in a glossary.
- Each section closes with a series of questions. The "stand-on-one-foot" summary questions ask students to summarize what they learned in the section they just read. The name comes from the Talmudic story of the heretic who went to great sages, asking each to summarize all of the Torah during the time he could stand on one foot. (He finally found a willing sage in Hillel, who quoted from Leviticus: "What is hateful to you, do not to others.") The idea is simply to get readers to pause for a moment and make sure they understood the major points.
- The end of each section also includes questions that require considerably more thought; the student will need to apply what he or she has just learned to new situations, or go beyond the material in some way. I call these "questions that require two feet." Answers to all questions are provided at the back of the book.

I've also included an appendix containing background information and explanations of several concepts, such as statistical significance, that will be familiar to students who have taken other psychology courses but that beginning students may not know.

THE BRAIN

The influence of neuroscience on cognitive psychology is substantial and increasing. This trend poses two problems for teachers of cognitive psychology courses: how much of this material to include (given that it could support a semester-long course) and how to deal with the fact that understanding cognitive neuroscience requires some background knowledge of the brain.

With regard to background, there is a section of the book titled "Interlude: The Brain" after chapter 1. Other cognitive textbooks include some description of neuroscience, but I handle this topic a bit differently. I don't think it's optimal to try to present the basics of neuroscience in a dozen pages. The truth is that much of the basic material (such as the workings of an action potential) is not needed for beginning cognitive neuroscience. Instead, I focus on three points: (1) Why do cognitive psychologists want to learn about the brain? (2) How do they gather information about the brain? (3) What are the brain structures that cognitive neuroscientists frequently refer to?

How much cognitive neuroscience should be in a cognitive psychology textbook? My goal is to give the instructor some flexibility. Certain findings have had such an impact on cognitive psychology that they simply must be part of any course. I have tried to describe these findings in a way that assumes no background on the part of the student. For the instructor who prefers a greater emphasis on cognitive neuroscience, I have included additional materials. Besides the "Interlude," key studies from cognitive neuroscience are discussed in supplemental boxes set off from the main text. Those instructors who place less emphasis on cognitive neuroscientific approaches can, of course, instruct students to simply skip over this material.

I hope that I have written a textbook that will make students enthusiastic about this field and will make them want to know more than they can find in this book. Hillel's answer to the impatient heretic is not always quoted in full; after providing the summary of the Torah, Hillel added, "Now go and study," acknowledging that a one-sentence summary was bound to be lacking and that the heretic should learn more. I have not succeeded in summarizing cognitive psychology in a sentence, but I hope that this book will serve as a starting point for students who will then want to learn more about the field.

Supplement Program

Web site—www.prenhall.com/willingham

Prepared by Glenn E. Meyer, Trinity University includes an online study guide for students, chapter objectives, web links, flashcards of key terms, and much more!

PowerPoint slides

Prepared by Glenn E. Meyer, Trinity University includes selected art from the text available in a chapter-by-chapter lecture format. These slides can be accessed on the text web site: www.prenhall.com/willingham and can be customized to fit your lecture style.

Instructor's Manual with Tests

includes chapter outlines, suggestions for demonstrations, classroom activities, research and discussion questions, and more. The testing portion of the manual has approximately 65 questions per chapter.

TestGen Software

Prepared by John Philbeck, George Washington University Computerized version of the test questions, which operates on both PC and MAC systems, includes 65 questions per chapter.

Research Navigator

Is there a writing requirement to your course? Prentice Hall's new Research Navigator helps students conduct online research. Research Navigator provides students with extensive help on the research process and gives the students access to three exclusive databases full of relevant and reliable source material including EBSCO's **ContentSelect** Academic Journal Database, *The New York Times* Search by Subject Archive, and the Best of the Link Library. FREE when packaged with any Prentice Hall text. Contact your local Prentice Hall sales representative for more details or take a tour at www.researchnavigator.com.

WHAT'S NEW IN THE SECOND EDITION?

Needless to say, all chapters have been updated as appropriate. I have tracked all of the relevant journals to be sure the book is as up to date as possible. In some cases, new material represents true breakthroughs that have been made in the last few years; in other cases, the new material supports the central points of the story told in the last edition. Likewise, there have been numerous small changes that I hope will make things clearer to the student; I've expanded important points that seemed unclear, changed examples, and dropped a few discussions that seemed more distracting than enlightening. Still other changes are more revolutionary than evolutionary.

- A new chapter on motor control discusses perception, attention, memory, problem solving, and other aspects of cognition that have an impact on the world only if the perceiver or attender makes some motor movement. Despite the centrality of motor control to mental life, most cognitive psychology textbooks don't cover the topic. This new chapter will make it easier for instructors to include this topic in their courses.
- The brief introduction to brain anatomy in the "Interlude" is handled differently than it was in the first edition. Many books, including my first edition, begin with a high-level description of brain anatomy. But for a course in cognitive psychology, most of this material needs to be understood at only the most basic level. At the same time, continued and repeated reference is made to particular cortical areas, with the mad-tea-party approach to nomenclature that marks that field. Thus in this edition I pass over most of the brain in silence and focus on three things: first, what cognitive psychologists learn from studies of brain localization; second, how brain localization information is obtained;

and third, the names of the cortical areas to which repeated reference will be made.

- In chapter 3, "Attention," greater coverage is given to attentional blink, psychological refractory period, and inhibition of return. The final section, "Why Does Selection Fail?" now includes logical subsections to make clear how this material relates to the rest of the chapter.
- In chapter 10, "Decision Making," I've expanded coverage of the work of Gigerenzer, Hoffrage, Tooby, and Cosmides and others as a viable alternative to the framework of Kahneman and Tversky. This work is discussed in two sections: "Probabilities versus Frequencies" and "Social Factors."

I would greatly appreciate feedback and suggestions regarding this text. It is easiest to reach me via electronic mail: willingham@virginia.edu.

ACKNOWLEDGMENTS

I am grateful to the team of people at Prentice Hall who worked so hard to bring this book to professors and students. I'm especially grateful to Jayme Heffler, who has been such a hardworking and responsive editor, and to my production editor, Laura Lawrie.

I also offer sincere thanks to my colleagues who reviewed the first edition: John Philbeck, George Washington University; Patty O'Neil, University of Mississippi; Erik Altmann, Michigan State University; Ruth Spinks, University of Iowa; Kenneth Milles, Edinboro University; and Stan Klein, University of California, Santa Barbara. Their suggestions were invaluable in this revision. I particularly thank Erik Altmann of Michigan State University for his remarkably thorough feedback.

I have had the remarkable good fortune to learn from and work with some great cognitive psychologists, all of whom are also gentle, warmhearted people. My thanks to my graduate school advisors—Bill Estes, Steve Kosslyn, and Mary Jo Nissen—who were so generous with their time and wisdom. John Gabrieli has also been an enduring influence as a colleague and friend. I'm also grateful to my cognitive colleagues at the University of Virginia—Chad Dodson, Michael Kubovy, Denny Proffitt, Tim Salthouse, Jackie Shin, and Bobbie Spellman—for their helpfulness with particular questions, for their encouragement in all matters, and for making it fun to come to work.

My thanks to my daughter Rebecca for her understanding on the days and evenings missed as Dad sat hunched over the word processor.

My thanks to my wife Trisha, for her unfailing love and support in this project and in all other projects that we undertake together or separately.

Finally, my special thanks to my parents, who have been patient and supportive guides throughout my life. I dedicate this book to them, for the advices.

Daniel T. Willingham
University of Virginia

1

Cognitive Psychologists' Approach to Research

WHY MAKE ASSUMPTIONS?

HOW DID PHILOSOPHERS AND EARLY PSYCHOLOGISTS STUDY THE MIND?

Philosophical Underpinnings
The Beginnings of Modern Psychology
The Response: Behaviorism
Behaviorism's Success

HOW DO COGNITIVE PSYCHOLOGISTS STUDY THE MIND?

What Behaviorism Couldn't Do
Failures of Behaviorism to Account for Human Behavior
The Computer Metaphor and Information Processing
The Behaviorist Response
Abstract Constructs in Other Fields
So What, Finally, Is the Cognitive Perspective?

Have you ever wondered how we see or how we remember things? Have you ever contemplated the strange nature of attention?

I didn't think so.

Most of the people I know do contemplate how the mind works, but only when their mind lets them down. They contemplate memory ("Why can't I find my keys?"), attention ("I *want* to find my keys, so why can't I concentrate?"), and vision ("How could I not see my keys when they were right in front of me the whole time?"). Questions such as "How does vision work?" seem somewhat interesting, but no more interesting than thousands of other questions. It's like someone asking you whether you want to know about the history of guitar making. "I don't know; maybe. Is it interesting?"

Truthfully, "How does vision work?" is a bad question because it's too general. In cognitive psychology, as in most fields, the devil is in the details, but that's where the fun is, too. Vision, attention, and memory become interesting only when you pose more specific questions about them.

This book poses questions about the mind and describes the answers cognitive psychologists have uncovered. The first thing we have to decide, then, is which questions to ask—how to get more specific than "How do we see?" You'll find that the questions we ask are deeply influenced by assumptions we make about the mind and, indeed, assumptions about what it is to be human. It seems obvious that it would be better not to make assumptions when we are just starting to study the mind. Therefore, the first question to take up is **Why make assumptions?** As we'll see, the answer is that it is difficult or impossible to avoid making assumptions. If that's true, we should at least be clear about the assumptions cognitive psychologists make. If you know the assumptions, it will be clearer to you why cognitive psychologists ask the questions they do, and if you understand why they ask a particular question, it will be much easier to understand the answer.

But the approach of cognitive psychologists developed in part as a response to other approaches that people had tried but that seemed to have flaws. Thus our second question is **How did philosophers and early psychologists study the mind?** As we'll see, a number of different approaches have been tried in the last 2,000 years, but it was only about 125 years ago that a serious, systematic effort began to apply the scientific method to human thought. That date is some 200 years or more after the scientific method had been used in other domains of knowledge. Furthermore, cognitive psychology was not the first scientific approach to studying the mind; it arose in response to the flaws in other methods.

Finally, our third question is **How do cognitive psychologists study the mind?** As we'll see, the cognitive approach is informed largely by an analogy of the mind to a computer; like a computer, the brain takes in information, manipulates it, and then produces responses. The truth is more complicated than that, of course, and we will elaborate on this metaphor later.

WHY MAKE ASSUMPTIONS?

> ➤ *Preview* People make two types of assumptions when they study the mind. The first assumption concerns what the important questions are. We can't study everything at once, so we must pick some aspect of the mind as a starting point for study. What we perceive to be the starting point is biased by our assumptions about the mind. The second type of assumption concerns beliefs about the mind (even very general, vague beliefs) that affect how everyone thinks about vision, attention, or memory before really knowing anything about them. In this section we look at examples of these assumptions in the study of vision.

Psychologists typically make two types of assumptions in studying the mind. First, we make assumptions about what aspects of the mind are important enough to explain. We can't say, for example, "This study will explain everything about vision." Of course we want to do that eventually, but we have to start somewhere. So what aspect of vision will we tackle first?

The second type of assumption is more obviously an assumption in that it is something we believe (maybe for good reason, maybe not) that affects our ideas about vision before we even start trying to learn about it.

Here's an example of each type of assumption. To begin with, we make an assumption about what it is that needs to be explained. For most of the last 2,000 years, people interested in vision have wanted to explain the conscious experience of visual perception, asking, "How do we consciously perceive the qualities of an object—its shape, size, and distance?" Unconscious processes involved in vision were not considered. Cognitive psychologists also seek to explain conscious visual perception, but they are more interested in the unconscious processes that eventually lead to conscious perception. In some ways, visual information in consciousness is the endpoint of vision; we need to explain the many steps that lead to this endpoint. Indeed, it has recently become obvious that some types of vision never become conscious. For example, some parts of the visual system help you move your body, but you are never aware of any aspect of this type of vision; I explain how this is possible in chapter 2.

The second type of assumption involves the beliefs that influence the questions we pose when we study something. For example, one dilemma about vision was this: The lens of the eye inverts the image of the world so that the image is projected onto the back of the eye upside-down. We obviously don't see the world upside-down, so how does the image get turned right side up? (See Figure 1.1.)

This question was posed in 1604 after Johanes Kepler speculated that the crystalline body of the eye functions as a lens does and therefore inverts the image. (René Descartes put the idea to the test some 20 years thereafter,

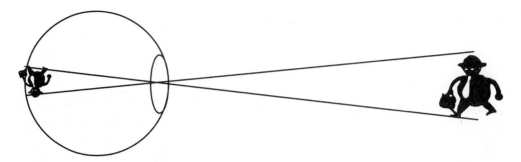

Figure 1.1.   *Light falling on the eye is inverted by the lens. Therefore, the image on the retina is upside-down compared with objects in the real world.*

conducting an experiment with the eye of a bull.) This question bothered philosophers until the early 19th century, even though William Molyneux, writing in 1692, gave the correct answer to this problem: it's not really a problem. It doesn't matter that the top of the world is represented on the bottom of the retina (the light-sensitive cells at the back of the eye). But the idea of the inverted retinal image was so troubling that Johanes Mueller, a famous physiologist, felt compelled to address it as late as 1826.

Why was the inversion of the retinal image so disturbing? Because of a background assumption about vision everyone was making. It seemed reasonable to assume that the conscious perception of the visual world was not in the retina but in some part of the brain. The assumption was that the retina presents an image to the part of the brain that handles conscious perception. You might think of the back of the eye as a screen on which another part of the brain watches the world go by—upside-down. So the natural question to ask is, "How does the mind perceive the world right side up?" But this assumption is wrongheaded because the conscious visual part of the brain is not a little person watching the retina.

Mueller proposed instead that everything the mind perceives is a function of the state of the nerves coming into the brain. (He called it the theory of specific nerve energies.) The pattern of neural activity *is* perception; perception is not the product of someone watching the pattern of neural activity. Therefore, it doesn't matter whether the top of the world is represented in the top or the bottom of the retina as long as there is a consistent relationship between what is in the world and the pattern of neural activity to which it leads. If the top of the world could be represented anywhere in the retina, that would be a problem, but with the top of the world consistently in the bottom of the retina, we understand what we are seeing.

Here's another way to think about it. As you might know, a computer graphic file is stored as a series of 1s and 0s. When they are interpreted by the software in your computer, they form an image of ... let's say a cat. You would not expect that if you printed out the 1s and 0s on a piece of paper, they would form the image of a cat; the 1s and 0s are a different representation of

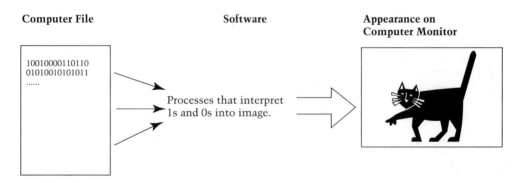

Figure 1.2.   *A computer can represent the image of a cat in a format that looks nothing like a cat. The representation is interpreted by software in the computer and displayed as an image on the screen that is recognizable as a cat.*

the image of the cat (see Figure 1.2). In the same way, the pattern of neural activity on the retina doesn't have to look like the thing it's representing. Once you drop the belief that the pattern of neural activity on the retina must look like what is out in the world, you realize the inverted image is not a problem.

If making assumptions gets you in trouble, it appears that what you need to do is avoid making assumptions. But it's much harder than you might think not to assume anything. Many of our assumptions are hard to spot because we take them for granted. Had I lived in the 17th century I don't think I would have been smarter than everyone else. I would have been scratching my head with the rest of them.

Now we need to ask what assumptions cognitive psychologists make. How do they view the mind? What questions seem natural to ask if you're a cognitive psychologist? We'll get to that later in the chapter. In fact, we're not going to start our discussion with cognitive psychology. The field of cognitive psychology is only about 45 years old, yet people have been thinking about how the mind works for more than 2,400 years. It is misleading to wrench cognitive psychology out of that historical context. Many of the ideas in cognitive psychology grew out of older ideas, or in some cases in direct opposition to older ideas. So we start with the older ideas, which set the stage for cognitive psychology.

Stand-on-One-Foot Question

1. *What two types of assumptions usually are made when we study the mind?*

Question Requiring Two Feet

> 2. *When we study the mind, we can't observe it directly. We can observe what people do and we can observe the environment around them, but we can't observe thought directly. What do you think this fact will mean for theories of the mind?*

HOW DID PHILOSOPHERS AND EARLY PSYCHOLOGISTS STUDY THE MIND?

➤ *Preview* We can identify three waves in the history of the study of the mind before the advent of cognitive psychology. In the first wave, philosophers considered the workings of the mind. They were interested primarily in the acquisition of knowledge in all its forms. During the Renaissance many issues were approached via the scientific method, which stresses observation, not reason alone. The scientific method was not applied to the study of the mind until the late 19th century, however, mostly because of assumptions people held about how the mind was likely to work. This application of scientific method to the study of the mind is the second wave. Initially, psychology was largely the study of conscious experience, but it took a radical turn between 1910 and the 1920s, when consciousness was expunged and psychology became the science of overt behavior. This movement, called behaviorism, was the third wave. Behaviorism was ascendant until the late 1950s, when mental life reasserted itself as an important part of any explanation of human behavior.

In this section we cover three basic trends in the history of the study of the mind before the development of cognitive psychology. The first trend concerns the philosophical background of the study of the mind. We discuss only Western philosophy because that is the philosophical tradition that influenced early psychologists and, eventually, cognitive psychologists. The second concerns the application of the scientific method to the study of the mind. The third concerns the abandonment of the study of the mind in favor of the study of behavior.

Philosophical Underpinnings

ANCIENT GREECE.   Approximately 2,400 years ago, the philosophers of ancient Greece left the first written record displaying consistent curiosity about and speculations on the workings of the mind (although there are bits and pieces scattered through earlier documents).

Philosophy is the pursuit of knowledge in all its forms, although over time many philosophical questions have been co-opted by the sciences. Because knowledge is central to philosophy, philosophers have been especially interested in how knowledge is acquired. There are three ways of asking how knowledge is acquired, and these three questions were later asked by cognitive psychologists.

- **Perception**. How do we gain access to knowledge about the world immediately around us?
- **Memory**. How do we retain knowledge about the world for later use?
- **Nature and nurture**. What is the origin of knowledge? Is knowledge gained through experience, or is it largely innate, with experience serving to release or activate knowledge we are born with?

The Greek philosophers posed questions about the mind that were relevant to their broader interests about knowledge. How accurate were their answers? They weren't even close. In fact, the Greeks were usually incorrect both in outlook and in detail. For example, Plato proposed that the eye emits some sort of beam, which combines with an essence of the object and then projects back to the eye. Incidentally, many adults today hold similar erroneous views. Studies show that, depending on exactly how you phrase the questions, as many as 86% of adults believe that vision involves some type of emission from the eye (Winer, Cottrell, Gregg, Fournier, & Bica, 2002).

We can see that the answers that Greek philosophers came up with were not accurate. But were their questions at least good ones? Many books will tell you that the Greeks' lasting contribution lies in the questions they raised, which set the agenda for future philosophers and eventually for cognitive psychology. I don't think that's quite accurate, though. Their real contribution lay not in their specific questions but in three assumptions they made that allowed them to pose those questions.

- The world can be understood and predicted because it works in systematic ways. If events occurred randomly or at the whim of capricious gods, trying to predict events would be hopeless.
- Humans are part of the physical world, and as for other entities in the world, we can potentially understand and predict how they will operate. If humans were qualitatively different from physical objects and animals, we could never hope to predict what people might do or what they will think.
- Explanations of events in this world should rely on other events within this world instead of invoking magical or mystical happenings. For example, Hippocrates proposed that epilepsy was a disease of the body (as other diseases were understood to be), thereby rejecting earlier views that it resulted from direct intervention of a god.

These beliefs feel so natural to us today that it is hard to remember that they are assumptions. Indeed, these three assumptions are critical to all of the sciences. Experience tells us that these assumptions are helpful in trying to explain things around us; at the time the Greeks first made them, however, they were quite bold. Once you assume that the world is predictable, that you can understand it, and that humans have no special place in this world (meaning that human behavior can be explained just like anything else), it is natural to take the next step and ask a few questions about how the human mind works, such as how it perceives and remembers things. Again, it's the assumptions of the ancient Greeks that are most impressive rather than the questions or the answers they posed.

THE DARK AGES AND MIDDLE AGES.   Few contributions were added to the philosophy of mind between the time of Aristotle, who died in 322 B.C., and the birth of Descartes at the end of the 16th century. How is this possible?

Several factors contributed to the lack of progress. By 146 B.C. Greece was dominated by the Romans, who had a more practical mindset than the Greeks. Pursuit of knowledge for its own sake was not especially esteemed, so no one was asking where knowledge comes from, as the Greeks had. After the fall of the Roman Empire in 476 A.D., Europe was dominated by various Germanic peoples, usually called barbarians. Although *barbarian* has unpleasant connotations that probably aren't fairly applied to these people, it's doubtful that they were sitting around contemplating the workings of the mind. In addition, feudalism and the decline of urbanism did little to help intellectual life. Nor did the ascendance of the Christian church around the year 400 make for a favorable climate for philosophy of mind. The church was interested in the soul, not in scholarly pursuits unrelated to theology.

You shouldn't have the impression that intellectualism was dead during this age, but it was definitely channeled in certain directions, and those directions were not toward study of the human mind.

THE RENAISSANCE THROUGH THE NINETEENTH CENTURY.   *The Advent of the Scientific Method.*   The Renaissance refers to a time in Europe (the 13th through 17th centuries, very broadly) marked by the rise of humanism, a subsequent flowering of literature and the arts, and the beginnings of modern science. Humanism emphasizes secular concerns and the individual (as opposed to religious concerns and the religious community). From the viewpoint of a cognitive psychologist, a critical feature of the Renaissance was the return of one of the assumptions characteristic of ancient Greece: that the world can be understood and predicted, and even more, that trying to understand the world is a worthwhile pursuit. Thus the literal meaning of *Renaissance* ("rebirth") is appropriate. The Renaissance also saw a birth: the birth of modern science.

What makes something scientific? We often think of science as being associated with white coats and antiseptic laboratory equipment. In fact, science is not characterized by the people who do it or by subject matter. Science is simply a *method* of finding out new things. The scientific method is well suited to some questions ("What does the heart do?") and poorly suited to other questions ("What makes a novel great?").

What made the scientific method new in the Renaissance was its emphasis on observation as a route to knowledge. How do you know something is true? There are two possible roads to the truth: you can sit in your armchair

Figure 1.3. *The two main methods of inquiry: reasoning and observation.*

and reason about <u>what you think must be true, or you can go out and observe</u> <u>what happens in the world.</u> For example, you might reason that planetary orbits must be circles because a circle is a perfect shape, and it would make sense for the universe to be organized in terms of perfect shapes (see Figure 1.3). Or you might get a telescope and make observations of the planets and try to figure out what orbital shape is consistent with your observations. Before the Renaissance, people did some observation, but contemplation and logic were more often considered the best route to knowledge.

There are two things to bear in mind. <u>First,</u> scientists have always used both methods. After you've made your observations, you still go back to your armchair to try to make sense of them, using reason. But the key is that then you go back out into the world again, armed with new predictions (the product of your armchair reasoning), which you will test with new observations. The <u>second</u> thing to bear in mind is that the fact that you're observing doesn't mean that you won't make (occasionally colossal) mistakes. Aristotle concluded that the mind must be located in the heart, not the brain, on the basis of the observation that people sometimes survived severe injury to the brain, but they never survived serious injury to the heart.

Renaissance scientists made mistakes of interpretation (like Aristotle and like scientists today), but they were sound in their emphasis on observation. The attempt to understand nature through observation had a number of dramatic successes during the Renaissance. Copernicus asserted that the earth revolves around the sun and not vice versa; Galileo formulated the law relating distance, time, and the speed of free-falling bodies; Isaac Newton discovered that gravity rules both heavenly bodies and the humble apple; and William Harvey learned that blood circulates and that the heart functions as a pump. All these advances were triumphs of the observational method as a path to knowledge.

Why Didn't Psychology Start Until 1879? The pace of science picked up in the 17th century as advances were made in astronomy, physics, chemistry, and biology. So why did it take another 200 years for scientists to apply the scientific method to the study of the mind? You might imagine that it was an equipment problem—scientists needed computers, sophisticated timing devices, and so forth. In fact, fascinating and revealing experiments on the workings of the mind can be done with a deck of playing cards (cards were invented in about the 10th century).

No, the problem was still one of assumptions. The Renaissance brought back two of the assumptions the Greek philosophers made: that the world can be understood and predicted and that explanations should be of this world (that is, we can't invoke ghosts or gods in our explanations). But the third assumption—that humans have no special status—was difficult to resurrect.

Suppose we assume that humans have no special status in the world, so our behavior is as predictable as the behavior of physical bodies (such as a falling apple). Humans are more complex, obviously, but they are still predictable. What does being predictable imply? It implies that the mind follows a set of rules. When you're in Situation A, your mind follows Rule 1; when you're in Situation B, it follows Rule 2; and so on. In saying that behavior is predictable, we are essentially saying, "It is possible to have a complete understanding of human behavior such that I can know what a person will do before he or she does it." This view is called **deterministic**.

The alternative is a **nondeterministic** view. This view says, "No, there is something else that guides our thoughts and determines our actions. Call it a soul, if you like. It's the working of this other agent that gives us free will. We are free to act as we please, so you will never be able to predict another person's behavior accurately."

Under the nondeterministic view—accepting the belief that people have free will—studying the mind seems futile. Psychology tries to understand why people act as they do. But if they act as they do because of the vagaries of free will, which is by definition not bound by rules, how will psychologists ever understand human behavior? They won't.

During the Renaissance, most people probably assumed that free will existed. They would have recognized that the scientific method could analyze the behavior of inanimate bodies such as planets and falling rocks, but they would have believed that humans are wholly different. The idea of applying the scientific method to studying the mind probably would have seemed as ridiculous to them as it would seem to you if I suggested that we apply the scientific method to evaluating literature.

The foregoing discussion does not mean that scientists believe that there is no such thing as a soul or that there is no such thing as free will. Whether there is a soul is a question that science is not well suited to answer. Many scientists believe that humans have a soul and have free will. Yet we cannot use these concepts in scientific theories and explanations of human behavior. Even if they exist, they are not understood in a scientific sense, so they don't mesh well with other scientific concepts.

The great philosopher Immanuel Kant raised a different objection to a science of the mind. He concluded that mental processes take place in time, but they don't take up any space and therefore can't be measured. Thus the scientific method could not be applied to mental processes. Many people were persuaded by this argument and concluded that there was no point in trying to use the scientific method to understand mental processes.

During the Renaissance, then, there was no science of the mind because of a background assumption that the scientific method would not work on the mind, that the mind was inherently unpredictable. But smart people were still contemplating the workings of the human mind. In the 300 years or so between Descartes and the beginnings of scientific psychology, many topics were debated that were rooted in one question: Where does knowledge come from? Like the Greeks, Renaissance philosophers were interested in memory and perception, but these interests often developed from the question of the origin of knowledge.

On the Origin of Knowledge. Descartes is usually credited with the first modern extended treatment of philosophy of mind, written in the early 17th century. He set forth a fairly moderate view on the origin of knowledge, saying that there are ideas that come from experience as well as innate ideas that everyone is born with. The position that ideas are innate came to be known as **nativist** because ideas were seen as native to every human. Another group of philosophers who came to be known as **empiricists** (Thomas Hobbes, John Locke, George Berkeley) argued that all of our knowledge comes from experience impinging on an impressionable mind. Later empiricists (David Hume, James Mill, John Stuart Mill) argued that the mind is more active in learning from experience, whereas the earlier empiricists had painted a picture of a rather passive mind being shaped by experience.

Gottfried Leibniz, in a direct response to Locke (but published much later), wrote that innate ideas are very important. He believed that experience serves only to liberate ideas that were in the mind already, presumably because one is born with such knowledge.

Immanuel Kant offered a compromise between nativist and empiricist views that was similar in spirit to Descartes's view, arguing that experience is the teacher, but *how* people experience things depends on native categories. For example, your perception of time and space does not depend on experience. You are born with the ability to perceive them; you don't need to be exposed to time and space the way you *do* need to be exposed to a language in order to learn it. Furthermore, how you perceive time and space does not depend on your experience. All humans experience time and space the same way because they are human.

Nativist and empiricist views had been set forth by the Greeks, most forcefully by Plato and Epicurus, respectively, but philosophers in the Renaissance and beyond furthered these views, considered new arguments, and formulated compromise positions.

Perception. Descartes discussed perception for the same reason as the Greeks: to understand where knowledge comes from. Other philosophers, notably George Berkeley, discussed perception as part of the empiricist versus nativist argument. Berkeley was an extreme empiricist. In *An Essay Towards a New Theory of Vision*, he set out to show that even basic perceptual experience is learned. Berkeley argued that even something that feels as natural as the perception of distance actually requires experience. He discussed some cues to the perception of distance that are still recognized as important, but he discussed them to emphasize that there are no native, inborn ideas and that everything must be learned.

Memory. The empiricists were also associationists. **Associationism** holds that knowledge originates from simple information from the senses and that this sensory information can be combined into more complex ideas. You know what an apple looks like because you have seen an apple before. But some complex ideas, such as the concept of democracy, clearly are not sensations. So where does this sort of knowledge come from? A complex idea such as democracy is the product of a number of simpler ideas that are joined together (associated). Things become associated if they occur at the same time.

Aristotle described the process of association, proposing several principles or rules by which associations are formed: ideas would be associated if they were similar, or if they were very dissimilar, or if they were contiguous in space or time. All of the empiricists (Hobbes, Locke, Berkeley, Hume, James Mill, and John Stuart Mill, to name the best known) agreed that contiguity, or an association in time or place, was important. If a clown appears every time you go to a particular shopping mall, you'll come to expect to see the clown when you enter the mall. Experimental work in the 20th century showed that the empiricists were correct in stressing time as a critical factor in associations. Locke and Hobbes were also correct when they stressed that repeating an association would make it easier to learn, and Locke added the (mostly correct) idea that learning associations also depends on whether they lead to pleasure or pain.

SUMMARY. This discussion has merely introduced the ideas of Renaissance and post-Renaissance philosophers. What's important to know is what they were trying to do. For the most part, they were arguing about the origin of knowledge. Renaissance philosophers also made observation part of their method, although they rarely conducted experiments as such. We might infer that they began to include more observation in their arguments about cognition because of the success of the scientific method in other fields. Many Renaissance philosophers borrowed metaphors from other sciences in discussing the mind. Locke talked about consciousness as a chemical compound, perhaps because he had been at Oxford University, where Robert Boyle had demonstrated that chemical compounds are composed of elements. John Stuart Mill also used the chemistry analogy. Hobbes was influenced by Galileo's movement studies and believed that thought was motion of the nervous system. Hume also discussed Newton and the possibility of finding basic laws of thought that would correspond to the laws of motion. Thus, in their use of scientific metaphors and their increasing use of observation in the world to support their ideas, we can see the creeping influence of the scientific method on Renaissance philosophers.

The Beginnings of Modern Psychology

In the last section we saw that the intellectual apparatus was in place to start a science of the human mind as early as the 17th or 18th century, but background assumptions about the nature of thought led people to conclude that it would not be worthwhile to apply the scientific method to this field. The first investigators who made the attempt would launch a new science.

Wilhelm Wundt usually gets credit for founding modern psychology in 1879, though he was not the first to publish a scientific psychological work. Gustav Fechner and Ernst Weber had performed landmark experiments years earlier. Why, then, aren't Fechner and Weber called the first psychologists? The reason you usually hear is that Wundt was the first to establish a laboratory devoted to psychology. It's not actually true. Wundt started his lab in 1879 at the University of Leipzig. William James started a lab in 1875 at Harvard. But James apparently used it only for demonstrations in teaching, so that lab is deemed not to count. Actually, the year doesn't matter so much because Wundt founded the discipline of psychology not because he started a lab but because he did what was necessary to get the science going.

Imagine for a moment that you have invented a new scientific field. For example, suppose you think the field of ethics needs your help because there is little agreement about what is ethical and what isn't. You think that if only people would apply the scientific method to the study of ethics, we would eventually home in on the one true set of ethical principles that all humans should use to guide their concepts of right and wrong. How will you launch your new science of ethicology? Here are some things you might do.

- Start journals devoted to ethicology to show that the field is making progress.
- Train students who can go out and teach ethicology.
- Write a textbook of ethicology to make it easier to teach others.
- Organize symposia on ethicology to gain publicity.
- Try to get universities to organize departments of ethicology.
- Spend a fair amount of time persuading people that the whole enterprise is possible because initially they'll think it's a crock.

Wundt did all these things for psychology. The idea of studying the mind using scientific method seemed as improbable to a lot of people in the late 19th century as studying ethics using the scientific method does right now.

Another important thing you must do if you are starting a science is define its domain. What does the science seek to explain? There were two slightly different answers to this question around the turn of the century. Wundt was inspired by the success of chemistry. The periodic table had just been worked out, and Wundt thought it was a realistic and worthwhile goal to try to work out a periodic table of the mind. What are the basic elements of consciousness, out of which more complex thoughts are constructed? Although Wundt later denied the chemistry analogy, his writings are suffused with the idea. This viewpoint came to be known as **structuralism** because the goal was to describe the structures that make up thought. (We can recognize the associationism of Locke and others in this approach of combining simple concepts.)

Meanwhile, William James, the one who started the laboratory that didn't count, was inspired by developments in evolutionary theory. A guiding principle for James was that mental processes must have a purpose; they must be *for* something. This viewpoint came to be known as **functionalism** because the emphasis was not on mental structures but on the function of mental processes.

The emphasis on what was to be explained differed between Wundt and James, but there was a common thread. Both sought to explain how thought worked, and for them thought was nearly synonymous with consciousness. Structuralism and functionalism had different ways of framing this question, however, and they had different methods of gathering evidence. Wundt championed **introspectionism**, a method of study in which people tried to follow their own thought processes, usually as they performed some simple task such as listening to a metronome. The trick was that such introspection was said to require training. A person couldn't just listen to the metronome; someone more experienced had to teach the "right" way to listen, telling the trainee what he or she should be experiencing. If that sounds odd to you, it should. This method turned out to be a big problem. Because people were trained to report what they were thinking about, the trainer played a big role in shaping what people said they experienced. Five people may have had five different experiences when they looked at an apple, but after they had been trained they would all report the same experience, which was pretty much whatever the trainer thought they should say. I'm making the problem a bit extreme to illustrate the point, but that is the heart of it.

James also used introspection but of a different sort. He followed his own mental processes as a way of learning about them, but he was much less dogmatic about how introspection should be done. He frowned on dogma in psychology, and he had a healthy respect for objective experiments, which do not rely on introspection, though he disliked doing them himself. Perhaps because he later lost interest in psychology, or perhaps because James's distaste for dogma was not conducive to starting a movement in the field, functionalism never became a prominent school of psychology. Still, James had a more lasting impact on experimental psychology than any other 19th century figure. His *Principles of Psychology* (1890) is still a source of ideas for cognitive psychologists.

Wundt's legacy is quite different. Although he worked out a detailed theory of psychology and published prolifically, little of his thinking remains influential. Still, he is duly credited with starting the field, and because he trained so many students, many of today's psychologists can trace their academic lineage to Wundt (including me; I was a student of W. K. Estes, who was a student of B. F. Skinner, who was a student of E. G. Boring, who was a student of E. Titchener, who was a student of Wundt).

The Response: Behaviorism

There was one big problem with Wundt's introspectionism: it didn't work. There was the problem of training people to introspect—a problem of the method they used—and there were other methodological problems. A more basic problem was that the introspectionists didn't come up with any interesting results. In the end, you can make all the arguments you want for why your method is the best, but if you don't learn something using the method, the whole enterprise begins to look silly. Between 1879 and 1913, the introspectionists had few results they could point to.

In 1913, John Watson published a paper titled "Psychology as the Behaviorist Views It." The first paragraph of that paper is remarkable.

> Psychology as the behaviorist views it is a purely objective experimental branch of natural science. Its theoretical goal is the prediction and control of behavior. Introspection forms no essential part of its methods, nor is the scientific value of its data dependent upon the readiness with which they lend themselves to interpretation in terms of consciousness.

Watson was throwing down the gauntlet, calling for a complete shift in psychology. By 1913 psychology was considered a full-fledged science. Wundt had trained many students, and they in turn had founded psychology departments in academic institutions all over the world. Most of them remained introspectionists of one sort or another. They were the establishment of psychology in 1913, and Watson challenged their assumptions with his four basic principles of **behaviorism**.

1. Psychologists should focus only on that which is observable. Watson emphasized that objective measurement is crucial, and introspection obviously can't be measured objectively. If you were introspecting in front of a metronome, you could say that you're thinking about anything and nobody could prove you wrong.
2. Psychologists should explain behavior, not thought or consciousness. Because objective measurement was so important, Watson maintained that consciousness was not a suitable subject for psychology. In other words, Watson was saying that the subject matter of the science should change.
3. Theories should be as simple as possible. Everyone agreed on this basic principle of the scientific method; Watson raised the issue because the psychological theories of the time were becoming convoluted.
4. The overarching goal of psychology is to break down behavior into irreducible constructs. Structuralists had been trying to find the basic building blocks of consciousness. Watson suggested instead that the search be for the basic building blocks of *behavior*. (His candidate for the basic building block was the conditioned reflex.)

Backtrack just a second. We said that Renaissance philosophers were concerned primarily with the origin of knowledge, and they addressed questions of memory and perception as part of that issue. The introspectionists were not really concerned with the origin of knowledge but instead were trying to explain the workings of the mind. What did they mean by *mind*? They meant *conscious thought*. Recall that Wundt was trying to do mental chemistry, to figure out the basic elements that compose consciousness.

Now Watson was saying, "Throw the mind out the window." Remember Kant's position that mental processes could not be measured, so applying scientific methods to them is impossible. Watson agreed with him! He was saying that introspectionism hadn't made progress because trying to deal with mental processes was hopeless. Instead, psychology should be redefined. It was not a science of mental processes but a science of behavior. The impasse psychologists faced was this: How can we explain the workings of mental processes, which are so complicated and elusive? Watson cut the Gordian knot by declaring that mental processes were irrelevant, and instead behavior should be the subject matter of psychology. This point of view was indeed tempting. Many of the problems that stumped researchers of the mind for centuries would simply disappear if instead of thought we studied behavior.

And psychologists went for behaviorism. It's fair to say that behaviorism was the dominant point of view in the United States from the 1920s through the 1950s (Gardner, 1985). It wasn't just a matter of expedience. Behaviorism offered the interesting results that introspectionism lacked, and it looked as if behaviorism had a great deal of promise. In the end, however, behaviorism was found lacking and was replaced by cognitive psychology. Before I explain what went wrong with behaviorism, let me tell you why it looked good for a while.

Behaviorism's Success

The philosophy underlying behaviorism was appealing because it was so straightforward. Psychologists could feel they were being scientific when they emphasized behavior because it is observable. Everyone can agree on what a person does, but it is much more difficult to say anything about a person's mental processes (see Figure 1.4). Everyone can agree that Joe hit Bill, but it's much harder to agree on what Joe's thoughts were when he hit Bill: Was Joe angry or frustrated, or was he just having a bad day?

Behaviorism also seemed to offer a promising start on the framework of a grand theory of behavior. Behaviorism, like almost every other science, sought to simplify complex subject matter by finding basic, irreducible units. Chemistry has the element; biology has the cell; physics has the atom; and psychology has ... what? Behaviorists proposed that the basic unit of behavior is the reflex, an automatic action by the body that occurs when a particular stimulus is perceived in the environment.

You are born with many reflexes. If you touch something hot, you will jerk your hand away. You don't need to learn that reflex; you're born with it. Other reflexes are learned. For example, if every day I ring a bell and then give you a sour ball, in time the sound of the bell will elicit the responses usually elicited by the sour ball (such as salivation).

Figure 1.4. *It is difficult to agree on what a rat is doing if you try to guess the rat's internal states; it's much easier to agree on the rat's behavior. The same is true of humans.*

Does that example make you think of Pavlov's dogs? Watson proposed that the basic unit of behavior might be the conditioned reflex, as described by Pavlov. You are born with some innate reflexes (such as withdrawing your hand from pain) and others are the product of experience (perhaps salivating when you hear a bell). These learned reflexes are called **conditioned reflexes**. The training procedure (and the resultant learning) that produces conditioned reflexes is called **classical conditioning** (see Figure 1.5).

Classical conditioning begins with an **unconditioned stimulus**, which elicits an **unconditioned response**. *Unconditioned* means that the animal comes to the experiment with the predisposition to respond in a particular way. Food is an unconditioned stimulus leading to the unconditioned response of salivation because before the experiment is conducted, the unconditioned stimulus (food) leads to the unconditioned response (salivation). A **conditioned stimulus** evokes little or no response. If you ring a bell, a dog might turn toward the sound; if you ring the bell several times, the dog stops turning its head.

If you pair the conditioned stimulus (bell) with the unconditioned stimulus (food) enough times, the conditioned stimulus (bell) comes to elicit a **conditioned**

Before training	Training	After training
Bell → no response Food → salivation	Bell, followed by food	Bell → salivation

Figure 1.5. *Pavlov's classical conditioning procedure.*

response. The conditioned response is similar to (but not always identical to) the unconditioned response. In this case, the conditioned response would be salivation, but the animal might not salivate as much.

The idea that the conditioned reflex might be the building block of all thought and behavior sounds reminiscent of the empiricist philosophers: simple associations build up to produce more complex thoughts. Indeed, the basic idea was very old. Aristotle noted that if two things happen at the same time often enough, they become associated.

So why is Pavlov famous? The difference between Pavlov's work and previous observations is that Pavlov was specific about how the learning takes place and therefore could speculate about the mechanism. Pavlov performed a simple operation to relocate one of the dog's salivary glands on the outside of its cheek so that the number of drops of saliva it secreted could be measured accurately. Thus he could get a precise measure of how much the dog salivated, which in this case is essentially a measure of the dog's expectation of being fed. Having this good experimental setup allowed Pavlov to ask other questions: How many times must the bell and food be paired for the animal to learn? What happens if I ring a different bell? What happens if sometimes I ring the bell and don't provide food? What happens if I ring the bell and give the dog a different type of food? Being able to ask (and answer) such specific questions allowed behaviorists to start thinking about a general theory of behavior, with the conditioned reflex at its center.

It wasn't long before people noticed that the conditioned reflex can't account for all of behavior. In the conditioned reflex, two stimuli are presented to the animal, and the animal responds to stimuli, but animals also can actively do things that have important consequences. For example, suppose you try a new Chinese restaurant in town, and the food is awful. You figure that the cook may have had a bad night, or that you ordered something that happened to be bad, so you try again. Again, it's awful. So you don't go back. This experience obviously entails learning, but it is not classical conditioning. You actively made a choice (you went to the restaurant) and your choice had consequences (you got a lousy meal). The consequences of your choice influence the likelihood that you will make the same choice again. This type of learning is called **operant conditioning**. It occurs when the animal actively makes a response (the operant) and the probability of making that response in the future changes depending on the consequences the animal encounters. Operant conditioning was seen to be different from classical conditioning. In classical conditioning, a neutral stimulus (such as a bell) comes to have meaning. In operant conditioning, an initially neutral response (such as selecting a particular restaurant) comes to have meaning.

Edward Thorndike (1911) did some work in this vein in the early 20th century. He put a cat in a slatted box that had a door operated by a lever inside. Thorndike timed how long it took the cat to make its escape over a number of trials and discovered a systematic learning curve. On the basis of this and other experiments, Thorndike proposed the law of effect, which basically said that if you do something and good consequences follow, you're more likely to do it again, whereas if bad consequences follow, you're less likely to do it again. Still, it wasn't until the 1930s that the importance of this type of learning was fully appreciated, largely through the work of B. F. Skinner (1938).

Instead of following the story of behaviorism, I want to push ahead to cognitive psychology. Suffice it to say that from the 1920s until the early 1960s virtually all experimental psychologists in the United States were behaviorists. Behaviorism dominated American psychology because, to a large extent, it worked. Behaviorists could make many good predictions about behavior. Most of their experiments were with animals, but there was a good reason for that choice. From the behaviorist perspective, behavior was mostly the product of what had happened to you, meaning what sorts of conditioned reflexes you had acquired through the environment and what sorts of behaviors had been rewarded or punished over the course of your lifetime. It was therefore difficult to conduct experiments on humans because the experimenter had no way of knowing what their history was and therefore what they already knew coming into the experiment. Investigators could raise an animal from birth and know exactly what its history was, so they used animals. But were animals really like people? Behaviorists figured that humans were much more complex, but the basic laws of learning probably were the same. They also noted that every science starts with simple situations. When Galileo wanted to investigate how objects move, he started with spheres rolling down planes, not leaves blowing in a high wind. Once you understand the simple situation you can move on to more complex situations.

In the late 1950s behaviorism began to crumble. There were a number of reasons, but they fall into two categories. (1) People started to doubt that behaviorism could do what it had promised. (2) It became obvious that eliminating any discussion of mental processes from psychology was hurting more than it was helping. The replacement for behaviorism was cognitive psychology, and so our story begins.

Stand-on-One-Foot Questions

3. *Why was scientific method not applied to the human mind before the 19th century?*

4. *What psychological questions did philosophers address during the Renaissance?*

5. *What change did scientific psychology undergo in terms of what it sought to explain?*

Questions Requiring Two Feet

6. *One of the assumptions that the Greeks made was that explanations for events in the world should be "of this world." In other words, there is not much point in proposing explanations of observable events in terms*

of unobservable forces. To what extent do you think people you know hold this assumption?

7. *Behaviorism swept away the introspective method. But should people's introspections be of any interest to psychology?*

How Do Cognitive Psychologists Study the Mind?

> ➤ *Preview* The impetus for a new way to study the mind came from several sources. Among psychologists there was increasing dissatisfaction with the behaviorist position because it seemed unable to account for some important human behaviors, such as language. Scientists in other fields (including artificial intelligence and neuroscience) made great use of abstract constructs—hypothetical representations and processes—in accounting for intelligent behavior, although these were anathema to behaviorists. In moving away from behaviorism, cognitive psychologists needed to move toward something, and artificial intelligence offered a ready model. One could conceive of the human mind as similar in some respects to a computer. Both manipulated information as a way of generating intelligent behavior. This computer metaphor has remained influential, although it can be taken too literally. In the last part of this section, I show how a cognitive psychologist would analyze one very simple bit of behavior: answering the question "What is your hometown?"

What Behaviorism Couldn't Do

One small bump in the road for behaviorism came as early as World War II. The armed forces became interested in problems of human performance—what humans can do well and what they can't. A great deal of military equipment was operated by humans, and when operators made mistakes, the results could be catastrophic. For example, people had to sit in front of radar screens trying to sort out what the little green lights meant; some identified enemy planes and some didn't, and it was not easy to differentiate them. Obviously a mistake by the radar operator could be very costly. The army quickly found out that technicians occasionally made mistakes no matter how much training they had undergone. So the army wanted to know (and in a hurry) why there was a limit to human performance. Why could performance get very good but not become perfect? Behaviorists were supposed to be the experts on behavior, but they had little to say on this topic. Behaviorism could explain how certain things are learned (if you start with no knowledge, you can get better) but it didn't have much to say about the endpoint of learning (why you don't eventually become perfect). This limitation wasn't a problem for behaviorism, exactly, but it did make clear that there were some things behaviorism couldn't explain.

Much more serious were problems raised in the 1950s. Behaviorism was perceived by psychologists as proposing that the experiences of an animal during its lifetime completely determined its behavior—in other words, that the animal's genetic inheritance counted for nothing and that what the animal did was a function of what it had been rewarded and punished for doing.

Strictly speaking, that is not what behaviorism proposed, and indeed such a proposal could only be called silly. Obviously it is easy to train a pigeon to peck something and very difficult train a rat to peck something; the predisposition to peck or not peck is a product of the animal's genetic inheritance. But it is true that behaviorists did not emphasize the possibility of important genetic contributions to behavior. Almost everything they studied was the learning that took place during the lifetime of the animal, and so it seemed as though they were saying that when an animal is born it is a clean slate, a blank tablet, waiting to be written on by the environment.

In the 1950s a number of important papers were published in ethology showing that the clean slate idea could not be true. Ethologists do not study animals in laboratory settings; they go into the wild and study animals in their natural habitat. Ethologists described **fixed-action patterns**, complex behaviors that animals engage in though they have little opportunity for practice or reward. For example, the male stickleback fish performs a series of stereotyped mating behaviors, including establishing a territory, building a nest, luring a female into the nest with seductive wagging motions, and inducing the female to lay eggs in the nest by prodding her tail (Tinbergen, 1952). Behaviorist accounts do not offer a ready explanation for such stereotyped, complex behaviors. According to behaviorist principles, these actions should require more practice and their performance should require reward.

Another dramatic finding from ethology was that of a **critical period**, a window of time during which an organism is primed to learn some particular information. If the organism doesn't learn the information within the critical period, later it may be unable to acquire the information. For example, there is a critical period during which chicks learn who their mother is (Hess, 1958). The first large object a chick sees during this time period is taken to be its mother, and the chick follows the object around thereafter. If a few days pass before chicks see a large object, the learning is more difficult to obtain. If the first object that chicks see is a large ethologist—for example, Konrad Lorenz— then the ethologist is taken to be Mom (see Photo 1.1). (For a review of this work, see Bolhuis & Honey, 1998; see also Berardi, Pizzorusso, & Maffei, 2000.)

As with fixed-action patterns, the results supporting critical periods indicate that the nervous system is not a learning machine that responds only to reward or punishment following an action. Rather, organisms seem to come into the world with a nervous system that is primed to learn particular things; it is part of their genetic heritage. This explanation sounds obvious, but it did not fit into the behaviorist theory in any obvious way.

The first problem with behaviorism, then, was that it could not account for some elements of animal behavior. The second problem was that people became uneasy about whether behaviorism could account for human behavior in all cases.

Photo 1.1.   *Konrad Lorenz with goslings.*

Failures of Behaviorism to Account for Human Behavior

The study of language was a dark cloud looming on the behaviorist horizon almost from the beginning. Keep in mind that behaviorists conducted almost all their experiments on animals. They were essentially offering a promise: "Don't worry, all our work with animals will apply to humans." Some people did worry, and their chief worry was that behaviorist principles derived from experiments with animals would not be able to account for human language. B. F. Skinner (1984) recounts in his autobiography that as a newly minted Ph.D. in the mid-1930s, he had such a discussion with the great philosopher Alfred North Whitehead.

> Here was an opportunity which I could not overlook to strike a blow for the cause, and I began to set forth the principal arguments of behaviorism with enthusiasm. Professor Whitehead was equally in earnest—not in defending his own position, but in trying to understand what I was saying and (I suppose) to discover how I could possibly bring myself to say it. Eventually we took the following stand. He agreed that science might be successful in accounting for human behavior provided one made an exception of *verbal* behavior. Here, he insisted, something else must be at work. He brought the discussion to a close with a

friendly challenge: "Let me see you," he said "account for my behavior as I sit here saying, 'No black scorpion is falling upon this table.'"

The next morning I drew up the outline of a book on verbal behavior. (pp. 149–150)

Skinner may have outlined the book the next morning, but it was not until 1957 that he published *Verbal Behavior*. His analysis of language was straightforward behaviorism. How does a child learn language? Through reward in the environment. The infant learns that saying "Da" elicits excitement from the parents, which is very rewarding. But the parents get used to the child saying "Da," and soon the child must produce a more complex utterance, such as "Dad," to be rewarded. Through reward, the child learns ever more complex utterances. The analysis was more sophisticated than that, but it did not stray far from the behaviorist line.

Two years after Skinner's book was published, a review came out that soon attracted more attention than the book, although the review was not published in a major journal. It was written by a young linguist named Noam Chomsky and can be summarized this way: "Not only is Skinner's account wrong, but a behaviorist explanation cannot, in principle, ever account for language" (1959). Chomsky argued that Skinner had grossly underestimated the complexity of language. First, he attacked Skinner's account of the scorpion-on-the-table problem. To account for why a person utters a remark at any given time, Skinner could only say that the behavior was under stimulus control, meaning that some subtle property of the stimulus (combined with the individual's history) had elicited this verbal response. Chomsky pointed out that this explanation is really no explanation at all. If you see a painting and say "Dutch," it is presumably due to some subtle property of the painting. But you might just as well have said "Stinks," "Nice," or "Too much red." And in each case, Skinner could only say that, because of the comment you made, he must infer that that particular aspect of the stimulus (stinkiness, niceness, redness) was controlling your behavior. That is no explanation.

A second important point Chomsky made was that language is **generative**, meaning that people can create novel sentences. Behaviorism can explain why you might repeat a behavior (you were rewarded last time), but it's not nearly as good at describing why you do something novel, such as utter a sentence you've never said before. And the ability to generate novel utterances is the heart of language. We seldom say the same thing twice in just the same way.

Indeed, how is it that you can say or comprehend a series of words you've never said or heard before, such as "Banana peels have nothing to do with success as a cab driver"? How do you get the grammar right? It's tempting to say, "There are *rules* for what makes a sentence grammatical. It's like the formula for a line: $y = mx + b$. You put in values for m, which is the slope, and for b, which is where the line runs into the y axis, and you have described a line. In the same way, there might be abstract formulas you use to construct a sentence. You plug in the ideas for the things you want to say, and the formulas turn your ideas into a grammatical sentence." This idea was a big blow to behaviorism. Starting in the 1950s and 1960s psychologists of language proposed such sets of rules (called grammars) and left behaviorist accounts behind.

Convinced that the results of animal experiments did *not* extend to human linguistic abilities, many psychologists, not just those who studied language, were shaken by Chomsky's argument. If behaviorism can't account for language, who knows what else it will fail on?

The impression that behaviorist principles couldn't give a complete account of human behavior was reinforced by studies of memory. Here's an example from a study by Weston Bousfield (1953). Suppose I give you this list of words to remember.

lion, onion, Bill, firefighter, carrot, zebra, John, clerk, Tim, nurse, cow

Ten minutes later I ask you to recall the words. Most people do not recall the words in the order they heard them. They recall all of one category, such as animals, then all of another category, and so on. How can this result be explained? When participants are asked what they are doing in such studies, they say they are using a retrieval strategy: they know that one animal will make them think of other animals, so it's easiest to remember all the animals at once. A behaviorist would shrink from the term *strategy* because a strategy is not observable. But people clearly reorder the words, and they say they are doing that to help them remember better. Can we ignore what the people say they are doing? We can't ignore the fact that people reorganize the word order—that's observable behavior—so how can we account for it? Behaviorism dictated that psychologists shouldn't consider a person's plans, goals, or strategies in accounting for what they do. But the idea of strategy seemed to be a major component of what people did in memory studies such as this one.

Behaviorism did not provide a framework in which to use constructs such as grammars or strategies. But if behaviorism were abandoned, what would take its place? A replacement was found through analogy of the human mind to a computer.

The Computer Metaphor and Information Processing

Metaphors are very important in the study of the mind (Daugman, 1990). No one knows what the mind is or how it works, so people often say, "I think the mind is like...." For example, Descartes was impressed by animated statues in the gardens at the chateau of Saint-Germain-en-Laye, outside Paris. As a visitor strolled through the gardens he or she stepped on hidden plates that set the statues in motion. In one, Perseus descended from the ceiling of a grotto and slew a dragon that rose from the water. The system animating the statues was based on hydraulics—water moving through hidden pipes—and Descartes proposed a hydraulic system of nerve function (1664/1972).

In the 19th century many researchers likened the brain to a telephone switchboard; the criss-crossing pattern of connectivity of neurons is reminiscent of an enormous switching station (von Helmholtz, 1910/1962). And Donald Hebb (1949) proposed a model of neural functioning in the late 1940s that invoked solenoids and capacitors.

In the 1950s a new metaphor became available. Artificial intelligence researchers realized that early computers solved number-crunching problems with symbols. The number 6 was not physically realized with six pieces of something in the computer, the way an abacus represents 6 with six beads. The computer uses a binary code in which the sequence 0-1-1-0 might mean "6," but 0-1-1-0 is just a symbol, one that could just as easily represent "bird" or "twiddling thumbs." So artificial intelligence researchers began speculating on what a computer might be capable of if the symbols it used represented something other than numbers.

Naturally, when 0-1-1-0 means "6" and the goal is to get a computer to manipulate numbers, we have certain expectations. We want to be able to add numbers, subtract them, and so forth, and we expect that the basic laws of addition will be built into the computer. For example, the order in which numbers are added by the computer shouldn't matter: $6 + 3 = 9$ is equivalent to $3 + 6 = 9$. Thus, a computer uses representations (such as 0-1-1-0) and processes that do things to the representations such as addition and subtraction. A **representation** is a symbol (0-1-1-0) for an entity in the real world ("6"). A **process** manipulates representations in some way.

That's clear enough for computers. What if we can approach human thought that way? Suppose that humans, like computers, use representations and processes. If we think of humans as processors of information, we can set up new questions for the study of the mind. What we want to know about humans is (1) what kind of symbols or representations humans use and (2) what processes humans use to manipulate those representations.

Here's another way to use the computer metaphor. Computers have hardware and software. The hardware is the actual physical piece of machinery (the central processing unit, the hard drive, the memory chips, and so on). The software is the set of instructions that tells the hardware what to do. Why not think of humans that way? This approach has been fruitful for neuroanatomists studying the hardware and cognitive psychologists studying the software of the brain. You could say that behaviorists wanted to talk only about what was observable—what was seen on the screen of the computer and what was typed on the keyboard—and therefore were missing most of the interesting information.

This metaphor proved very powerful and became known as the **information processing** model. This approach to studying the human mind is characterized by three assumptions.

- Humans are processors of information, just as computers are processors of information. The processing of information supports human thought and behavior.
- Representations (of objects and events) and processes that operate on these representations underlie information processing.

- Information processing typically occurs within largely isolated modules, which are organized in stages of processing. Thus, one module receives information from another module, performs an operation on the information, and passes the information on to another module.

I provide an example of this information processing perspective toward the end of this chapter. For now, keep in mind that humans take in information from the environment, for example, through sight and hearing, transform that information, for example, by interpreting it in light of memory, and then emit more information, for example, through speech.

The Behaviorist Response

The idea that psychologists could propose hypothetical representations used by the mind is powerful. We've already mentioned the case of language, in which something like sentence grammars seemed necessary to account for the ability to generate novel sentences. Memory is another domain of behavior in which hypothetical processes and representations are potentially useful.

It is easy to keep a small amount of information in mind for a short time (about 30 seconds). You might look up a telephone number and cross the room to the phone, repeating the number to yourself. You dial the number, and then it is gone from your memory. If you are interrupted as you cross the room so that you stop repeating the number, you'll have to look it up again. Clearly, you usually remember things for longer than 30 seconds. Why do you remember the phone number only for that long?

Here's an account you might give. You might say that there are two types of memory: long-term memory, which can keep memories for years, and short-term memory, which is used to maintain information for 30 seconds or so. Short-term memory is useful because it is hard to get material into long-term memory, and you don't always need to remember things for years, anyway.

Short-term memory could be said to contain representations. Just as a computer has a representation (0-1-1-0) for the concept "6," your mind has a way to represent "6." Furthermore, short-term memory uses processes that manipulate representations. For example, if you wanted to remember "6" for several minutes, a process would continually refresh the concept "6" so that it remains accessible.

A behaviorist would object, "Where, exactly, is this mystical representation of '6'? I don't see it." The response is that short-term memory is an **abstract construct**, a theoretical set of processes (such as refresh) and representations (such as 6) that are useful in explaining some data. Any abstract construct you propose is therefore a mini-theory. It is a proposal about the way the mind operates.

A behaviorist would argue that proposing the abstract construct of short-term memory is wrong for these reasons.

- The construct is circular. The behavior that people easily recall information for 30 seconds is explained simply by stating that it occurs because we have a memory system designed to remember things for 30 seconds.
- The concept diverts attention from the important issues. Remember, <u>psychology is a science of behavior, not of thought</u>.
- The proposition is impossible to verify because it is not observable. There is no way to confirm whether short-term memory exists because it can't be seen, touched, or measured in any way.

It was difficult for psychologists to abandon the idea that if they talked about representations and processes, then they were not being scientific. They needed support for the idea that abstract constructs could be scientifically useful. Such support came from two fields: computer science and neuroscience.

Abstract Constructs in Other Fields

It looked as if the information processing perspective might be useful in accounting for human thought, but there was still the issue of whether investigators were being scientific if they used abstract constructs. In both computer science and neuroscience, however, researchers were using abstract constructs freely with no apparent loss of rigor.

ARTIFICIAL INTELLIGENCE. Artificial intelligence is the pursuit of intelligent behavior by a computer. The idea is to get a computer to produce output that would be considered intelligent if a person produced it. Most researchers think that a program that gets a computer to complete a task can be considered a theory of how the human mind completes the task. And these theories rely completely on abstract constructs. These researchers propose that certain information is contained in memory; that this information can be combined or used in specific ways, according to a set of rules; and that these rules and the information in memory drive behavior.

Here's an example. In the mid-1950s Allen Newell and Herb Simon (1956) developed a program that proved theorems in formal logic. The program worked by starting with a list of axioms—statements that it could take as true—and a list of rules for how the axioms could be combined. The program also remembered proofs that it had already discovered so that they could be used as needed. The program had a number of strategies it used to discover proofs; for example, sometimes it tried working backwards by starting with the conclusion and trying to get back to the initial premises.

Three things are critical about this program and what it represents. First, the behavior the program produced was quite impressive. Until that time, behaviorists could more easily ignore artificial intelligence because the artificial intelligence programs didn't do anything sophisticated. Behaviorists could say,

"Computers are nothing but fancy adding machines. What they are capable of is not really behavior." But here was a program constructing logical proofs; that certainly sounds like sophisticated behavior.

Second, Newell and Simon were not simply saying, "Look, we can get a computer to do something that looks like thought; isn't that neat?" To this, a behaviorist might reply, "So what? You programmed the computer to solve proofs, and it solves proofs. *You* are the intelligent agent because you programmed the computer." But Newell and Simon were saying that the method the computer used to solve the problem was like the method humans used. They provided evidence for this by asking people to prove the theorems and to describe what they were doing as they did it. People reported strategies similar to those the program used (such as working backwards).

The third important thing about the program is that it used abstract constructs. You can't see or touch the strategies that the program used. The usual response of behaviorists to a theory that entailed strategies was, "That's not scientific. You can't observe strategies." But there was nothing unscientific or mystical about the program. The artificial intelligence researcher could say, "I'm being quite specific about what I mean by 'strategy.' Look, there's the strategy right there in the program, and here are the rules describing when the strategy is invoked."

NEUROSCIENCE.   Another way to be specific about an abstract construct is to tie it to a brain structure. It's one thing to propose the existence of a short-term memory system. It's something else again to find a short-term memory system located in the dorsolateral frontal cortex of the brain.

The links between brain structure and function have been pursued since the 19th century. One way to do this is by examining people with brain damage caused by stroke, tumor, or disease. Some of these people have quite specific cognitive problems. For example, suppose you find a brain-damaged patient whose cognitive functioning appears completely normal in every other respect but who has no short-term memory—he can't keep a phone number in mind for 30 seconds. If you know where the brain damage is, you might infer that you know where short-term memory is. If this patient has damage to brain area X and no longer has short-term memory, then brain area X must support short-term memory.

This inference is correct up to a point. The problem is, how do we know which part of the brain is damaged? In the 1950s the main way to know where brain damage had occurred was as a consequence of surgery. If a surgeon must go in and remove some tissue (to remove a tumor, for example), we know exactly where the brain damage is: the surgeon caused it. In the late 1950s and early 1960s there were a few cases in which dramatic and important things were learned about cognition from such patients.

Perhaps the most famous patient of this sort is H.M. (Corkin, 1984), who is known by his initials to protect his privacy. H.M. had epilepsy that was unresponsive to even very high dosages of medication. His seizures were frequent and severe and were so debilitating that he could not continue in school. In such cases, surgery may be appropriate. Seizures usually have a focus, meaning that they start in one part of the brain and then spread. If a surgeon can take out the part of the brain that is the focus, the seizures may stop.

H.M. underwent surgery in 1957, in which a number of structures near the center of his brain were removed. At that time, the best knowledge about the function of these structures was that they were important to the sense of smell, so it was thought that H.M. probably would lose his sense of smell. That seemed a small price to pay to eliminate the seizures.

Unfortunately, however, H.M. lost his ability to form new memories. His short-term memory is normal. He can remember a phone number for 30 seconds just as you or I can. His long-term memory is fine, too, if you ask him about events that happened before the surgery. He can remember his friends in high school, what was happening in the world in the early 1950s, and so on. What he can't do is form new long-term memories. Thus, H.M. has learned almost nothing new since 1957. He does not know who the president is now or what year it is. He wouldn't recognize the term *Watergate* or know that the Berlin Wall has fallen. If you spent an hour in pleasant conversation with H.M. and then left the room for a few minutes, upon your return he would not remember having met you.

The point here is that data from H.M. provided dramatic evidence in favor of using an abstract construct such as short-term memory in a theory of how memory works. We can say there is short-term memory and long-term memory. Because of the surgery, we know that the hippocampus and other structures that H.M. lost are important for transferring information from short-term memory into long-term memory. But we know that those structures don't support short-term or long-term memory themselves because these types of memory work fine in H.M. So we need to find which parts of the brain support those other functions.

Suppose now that you're not a neurologist but an experimental psychologist interested in learning and memory. On the one hand, the behaviorists are saying, "You can't use terms such as *short-term memory*. They are not rigorous because they refer to things that cannot be observed." On the other hand, findings such as those from H.M. strongly suggest that the concept of short-term memory would be useful. What would you do?

Box 1–1 Do We Really Need Cognitive Psychology?

In this chapter we've gone over the approach that cognitive psychologists use to study the mind. Part of that approach has been to use the physical structure of the mind—that is, the brain—to help us determine how the mind works. We might ask, therefore, whether we might not be better off studying the brain. If we believe that the workings of the mind depend on what happens in the brain, why not study the brain to start with?

(Continued)

We should recognize that there are often different, but equally valid, ways of describing the same thing. It is sometimes useful to think of *levels* of description. A common example is the relationship of chemistry and physics. Both physicists and chemists agree that most or all of chemistry is reducible to physics. That doesn't mean that chemistry is pointless, or that chemists are merely biding their time until the physicists come along and finish the job. In the same way, we might say that cognitive events are, of course, reducible to brain events, but that doesn't devalue the cognitive level of description.

These different levels of description are particularly important when we're talking about the brain. The reason is that even a simple behavior—for example, seeing and recognizing a friend—calls on many different brain regions. So if we study brain region X, we might understand what it does, but to understand how we recognize a friend, we need to know about brain regions X, B, R, O, and C, and in addition, we need to learn how they communicate and interact. Studying the brain alone will not lead us to examine the interaction of brain areas X, B, R, O, and C. Quite the opposite; it is studying the cognitive level of description that will reveal the importance of a function such as recognizing a friend, and that in turn will motivate us to study complex brain interaction.

Finally, there are important practical results of studying a cognitive level of description of what the brain does. For example, consider cochlear implants (Rauschecker & Shannon, 2002). These are microelectrode arrays implanted in the inner ear to directly stimulate the auditory nerve of the brain. Early versions of cochlear implants attempted to directly replace the input that the cochlea would usually provide. Newer versions take advantage of a psychological principle: so long as a sound contains enough high-frequency harmonics, the fundamental frequency will be "reconstructed" by the mind even if it is not present in the signal. Designers can omit low sound frequencies from a cochlear implant—simplifying the job the implant must perform—at no cost to the perception of important sounds such as speech. Thus, if we are trying to develop electronic devices to replace faulty brain parts, we need to know more than the anatomy and physiology of the brain. It is also useful to have a cognitive description of how the brain works because that can suggest more efficient designs for such devices.

In sum, although neuroscience informs cognitive psychology, and indeed, cognitive psychology informs neuroscience, one is not a replacement for the other.

So What, Finally, Is the Cognitive Perspective?

We have discussed some of the developments that have influenced cognitive psychology.

- Behaviorism could not account for all the experimental data, especially in studies of language and memory.
- It looked as if abstract constructs would help account for the data.
- Neuroscientists and artificial intelligence researchers provided examples of how abstract constructs could be used effectively in a scientific way.

- The interaction of representations and the processes that manipulate them can be likened to the workings of a computer.

This brief overview also makes it obvious what the assumptions of the cognitive perspective are. The chief assumption is that there are representations as well as processes that operate on them. Another assumption is that we can discover what these processes and representations are. There is currently no way to observe these processes directly. We infer the existence of these processes based on people's behavior. For the moment, let's just say that the assumptions of the cognitive perspective appear reasonable, but we should never forget that they are assumptions. (For a perspective on the use of representations in cognitive theory, see Markman & Dietrich, 2000.)

So that's the approach and the assumptions behind it. How is it applied? Here's the way a cognitive psychologist would think about a problem. Suppose you and I meet at a party and we make the usual small talk.

> You: So, how's it going, or something?
> Me: All right. Where are you from?
> You: Pittsburgh. How's your research going?
> Me: Uhh … you don't really care, do you?
> You: No, that was me being polite. I'm going to go to the bar now.

Take one little part of that interchange. I ask where you're from. You answer. It takes you perhaps half a second, but consider all that had to happen during that half a second. My question "Where are you from?" comes to you as a series of sounds. First, these sounds must be interpreted as speech. Speech interpretation, it turns out, is not trivial. Take just one component of speech interpretation: figuring out where the boundaries of words are. You'd think that there should be pauses between words—little breaks where there is no sound—but that's not the case. There are little breaks when people talk, but they don't correspond to the boundaries of words. So the first thing that must be done is to figure out the words of the sentence.

Then you have to assemble the words into something with meaning. Why is this a complex process? The question "Where are you from?" in this context is easy to interpret, but the same utterance could mean something very different in another context. For example, if I said, "Where are *you* from?" right after you spilled your drink all over yourself, it would probably be taken as an expression of scorn, not a polite pleasantry.

Once you know what I'm asking, you have to find the answer in memory. Your memory is loaded with information: what a snowflake looks like, what oatmeal is, the lyrics of many songs you hate but can't forget, where Brazil is located, and so on. Among all the mountains of information in your memory, how can you almost instantly pluck out exactly the right piece of information and ignore everything else?

Once you have the right piece of information ("Pittsburgh") you have to decide what to do with it. I've asked you where you're from and you've retrieved the answer, but are you going to answer my question? Not necessarily.

If you thought I might have something against Pittsburgh, you might be reluctant to tell me you're from there. If you knew that I love Pittsburgh, you might think telling me you're from there would set off a long soliloquy on the beauty of the three rivers, and you might prefer to avoid that. All of us are constantly making social and practical decisions about what to say and what not to say.

Suppose you decide to go ahead and say "Pittsburgh." You still have to decide *how* to say it. You could say "Pittsburgh," or "I'm from Pittsburgh," or "Pittsburgh, Pennsylvania," or "I hail from Pittsburgh," or "Pittsburgh—what's it to you?"[1] Every time you say something, there is more than one way to phrase it, and you have to select which way you are going to use.

Now suppose you know you're just going to say "Pittsburgh." You have to send the proper commands to the muscles of the lips, tongue, and so on to form the word.

Here's the point. I ask you what your hometown is, and in less than a second you say "Pittsburgh." But an amazing amount of cognition (unconscious, of course) had to happen in that brief second (see Figure 1.6). You perceived what I said, looked up the answer in memory, and so on. And each of these processes looks pretty amazing just on its own.

This example outlines how cognitive psychologists think about problems. They look at cognitive tasks and try to figure out which processes are

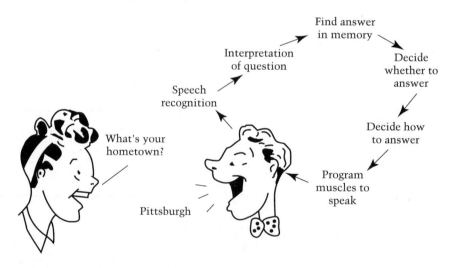

Figure 1.6.   *The processes that might be involved in answering the simple question "What's your hometown?"*

[1]My wife won't let me forget the time I tried to pretend I was Canadian and said, "I'm from Toronto, Canada," whereas a Canadian would say, "I'm from Toronto, Ontario." If you're an American and don't see why this is funny, consider someone saying, "I'm from Philadelphia, USA."

absolutely necessary to getting the task accomplished. Cognitive psychologists tend to think of mental work as being performed in stages (in our example, speech perception, memory, decision making, motor control), and a psychologist usually studies just one of these stages. Each stage is so complex that it's enough of a challenge to understand just one. In trying to characterize these stages, cognitive psychologists devise theories in terms of abstract constructs: hypothetical representations and processes that operate on those representations.

That's the overview of the cognitive perspective. I've tried to give a sense of how cognitive psychologists think about problems. The remainder of the book describes the answers cognitive psychologists have proposed. As described earlier, cognitive psychologists tend to think in terms of stages of information processing. First, information from the environment is perceived, then memory is contacted, and so on. This book follows that stage theory in presenting one cognitive process in each chapter. We begin with the question of how we know what is in the environment—how we perceive.

Stand-on-One-Foot Questions

8. *What problems led to a decline in the influence of behaviorism?*
9. *What is information processing?*
10. *How did cognitive psychologists respond to the protests of behaviorists that references to abstract representations and processes were not scientific?*

Questions That Require Two Feet

11. *Do you think some of the things humans learn might be subject to critical periods?*
12. *At the start of this chapter I mentioned that most of the people I know tend to notice the workings of their mind only when it fails. How often do you think that your mind fails, relative to the number of times it succeeds in carrying out a cognitive process?*
13. *The "What's your hometown?" example emphasized that many cognitive processes are involved in performing what seems to be a simple cognitive task. The basic approach was to figure out processes that had to occur to make the behavior happen. Would that approach apply equally well to the subcomponents we identified, such as identifying words in the sentence and finding the answer in memory?*

KEY TERMS

abstract construct
associationism
behaviorism
classical conditioning
conditioned reflex
conditioned response
conditioned stimulus
critical period

deterministic
empiricist
fixed-action patterns
functionalism
generative
information processing
introspectionism
nativist

nondeterministic
operant conditioning
process
reflex
representation
structuralism
unconditioned response
unconditioned stimulus

Interlude: The Brain

WHERE IS THE DAMAGE?

WHERE IS THE ACTIVATION?

THE BEHAVIORAL SIDE OF THE EQUATION

Lesion Studies
Imaging Studies

PROBLEMS AND LIMITATIONS OF ANATOMICAL STUDIES

WHY DOES LOCALIZATION HELP US?

THE FIVE-MINUTE BRAIN ANATOMY LESSON

We've just gotten started, so why are we stopping for this interlude about the brain? At one level the answer may seem quite obvious: we're studying the mind, so some knowledge of the brain would be useful. Many researchers, however, believe that we can study the mind separately from the brain. To continue the metaphor from chapter 1, we could maintain that it is possible to study the software separately from the hardware. Until the mid-1980s most cognitive psychology textbooks contained little information about the brain, and that choice accurately reflected the research strategy of the field. There were researchers who studied the relationship of the mind and the brain, but their fields remained separate from cognitive psychology.

Neuropsychologists did give the cognitive viewpoint an initial boost, as described in chapter 1, but neuropsychology as a whole was clinically oriented—concerned with the treatment of brain-damaged patients—and less concerned with basic research in how the mind works. Other researchers study the brain and behavior primarily in animals, and many of the questions they pursue are separate from the concerns of cognitive psychologists.

Today, cognitive psychology is greatly informed by neuropsychology. This change has its roots in the mid-1970s, when tools to examine the human brain became available. The information about the brain that has proved most useful to cognitive psychologists is **localization**, which means finding a location in the brain that supports a particular cognitive process or function. We alluded to this goal in chapter 1. Cognitive psychology seeks to describe the representations the brain uses and the processes that manipulate those representations. The assumption is that we should be able to find evidence that these hypothetical processes and representations are localized in the brain. For example, if we propose that people use visual images to solve certain problems, we should be able to find a location in the brain that stores images or a part of the brain that supports a process to manipulate them, perhaps by rotating them or making them larger or smaller.

How can we find evidence of localization? Two families of methods have been used. The logic of each is fairly straightforward.

1. If brain area X supports cognitive function Y, then damage to area X will lead to an impairment in tasks that require function Y. For example, if the temporal cortex of the brain supports the storage of mental images, then damage to the temporal cortex should lead to impairment in the use of mental images.
2. If brain area X supports cognitive function Y, then area X will be active when function Y is engaged. For example, if the temporal cortex of the brain supports the storage of mental images, then the temporal cortex should be active when people use visual images.

These principles seem straightforward enough, and the principles dictate the tools we need. For the first method we need some method of knowing where the brain is damaged. For the second method we need some way of measuring brain activity. We'll examine each in turn.

WHERE IS THE DAMAGE?

Damage to the brain can result from many causes: a stroke, an infection, an operation to relieve epilepsy or remove a tumor, or a degenerative disease such as Alzheimer's disease, to name a few. Examining patients who have some damage to the brain and using that information to infer the function of different parts of the brain has a long history of success. In the early 1860s Paul Broca reported the case of a patient who had damage to the left frontal lobe and had a problem producing speech. The patient could understand language, as long as the grammar was simple, but could produce speech only poorly. A few years later, Carl Wernike reported the case of a patient who had damage to a different part of the brain; this patient could not understand speech, and although he could speak fluently, what he said did not make sense. These observations caused a sensation because they clearly indicated that different functions could be assigned to different parts of the brain. People assumed that these areas handled production and perception of speech, respectively, but that characterization turned out to be oversimplified.

The difficulty in the 1860s and the century that followed was that no technology could localize brain damage adequately. Note that the inference takes this form.

> If the patient cannot understand language, and the patient has damage to ventral lateral frontal cortex, then the ventral lateral frontal cortex supports language.

To make that conclusion, psychologists needed to know the location of the damage, but there were few ways to do that. One method was to wait until the patient died and then physically inspect the brain to see where the damage was, but it might be decades until the patient died. (Broca's patient died young because of an infection.) Another method was to focus on the small population of cases in which the location of the damage was known because it was the result of brain surgery, but most brain damage is the consequence of stroke, not surgery, so the investigator won't get to examine many people.

Much better would be a method by which one could see the brain damage without invading the patient's skull. Why not take an X-ray picture of the brain? X-ray images show internal structure, but they compress the three-dimensional brain into a two-dimensional image. The resulting image not only loses volumetric information; it's a big blur.

A better solution is **computerized axial tomography** (commonly called a **CAT scan**) using X-ray technology to show three-dimensional structure. The patient lies on a gurney with his or her head in the center of a large doughnut-shaped structure. Around the perimeter of the doughnut are X-ray sources and X-ray detectors. As the X rays are directed through the patient's head, some are absorbed by various structures (the skull, blood, the brain itself) and some pass

Figure I.1. *Absorption of light through tinted glass.*

all the way through the head to the X-ray detector on the other side. The denser a structure is, the more X-ray energy it absorbs.

The detector on the other side of the X-ray source can tell you how much of the X ray has gotten through the head, but what absorbed some of the X rays along the way, and where was it? You are left with the average density of the brain. Figure I.1 shows a simple model for how this is done, using visible light and tinted glass. The square represents a cube of tinted glass. If we shine a light through the cube with an intensity of 20 (in arbitrary units), a clear cube absorbs 0 units and a black one absorbs 20 units. If we shine a light through an array of 3 cubes and measure 17 units coming out the other side, how can we determine the tint of each cube?

Figure I.2 shows an array of 9 tinted glass cubes. We know the intensity of light going into each row and column (20 units) and the remaining intensity after the light shines through each row and column, shown at left. Can we derive the value of each individual cube?

If we look at the top row, all we know is that the 3 cubes combined to absorb 3 units of light, but we don't know which cube absorbed how much. But if we look at all the rows and columns simultaneously, the possible values each cube can take are constrained. As shown in the diagram on the right, we can derive the value for each cube.

That is what a CAT scan does. It uses multiple X-ray values, as shown in Figure I.3. Each detector gives the density of the tissue in a single line, but if we combine the densities along intersecting lines, we can derive the density for a single point.

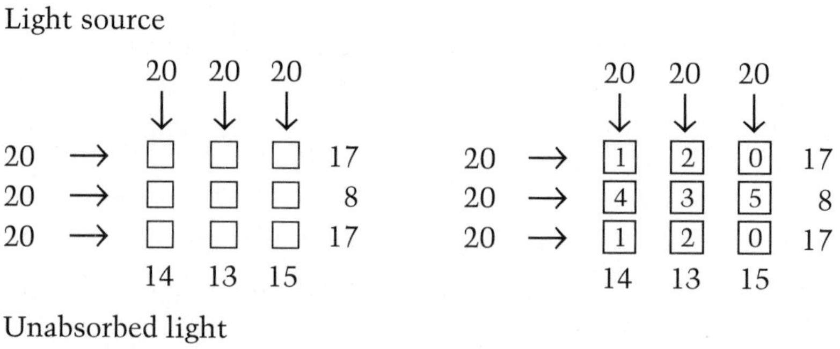

Light source

	20	20	20				20	20	20	
	↓	↓	↓				↓	↓	↓	
20 →	☐	☐	☐	17		20 →	1	2	0	17
20 →	☐	☐	☐	8		20 →	4	3	5	8
20 →	☐	☐	☐	17		20 →	1	2	0	17
	14	13	15				14	13	15	

Unabsorbed light

Figure I.2. *Determining absorption values in an array.*

X-Ray Source

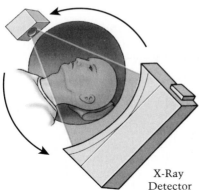

Figure I.3. Setup for a CAT scan.

X-Ray
Detector

We can tinker with the numbers and come up with the values for each cube in our simple example. A CAT scan deals with thousands of values, so the calculations are performed by a computer. The resulting values represent the average density of a cube of tissue; if there are density differences within that tissue, you won't see them. A CAT scan provides a three-dimensional map of values, a sculpture of density values, usually presented in two-dimensional slices.

How do we use these density values? The tissues of interest vary in density. Bone is very dense, blood is not dense at all, and brain cells (the part we care about) are of intermediate density. This technique allows us to see tumors, which differ from surrounding healthy tissue in density, and to see the result of stroke. And so we can localize some types of damage to the brain without opening the patient's head.

A second method using similar logic, **magnetic resonance imaging (MRI)**, provides much better resolution. MRI also yields a tissue density map, but the principle is not X-ray detection. Instead, MRI exploits the magnetic properties of hydrogen atoms, which are plentiful in organic matter. In their normal state, hydrogen atoms spin around an axis, and these axes are oriented randomly. The MRI machine generates a strong magnetic field that causes hydrogen atoms to orient their axes in parallel. A second magnetic wave is then applied in order to make only certain atoms spin, or resonate (just as sound waves of the correct frequency make a tuning fork resonate). The concentration of the hydrogen can be read from the intensity of the resonance. (Localizing these intensity values actually requires a third signal, but you get the idea.)

These methods are of interest because we want to localize function in the brain. One way to do that is to apply the principle that if brain area X is damaged and cognitive function Y is lost, we can infer that area X supports function Y. These methods allow us to make confident statements about which part of the brain is damaged.

Where Is the Activation?

A different approach to localization measures ongoing activity in the brain while an organism engages in a behavior. If brain area X supports function Y, then activity should be observed in area X when function Y is engaged.

How do we know when part of the brain is active? To understand the most commonly used measures of brain activity, you need to know a bit about the basics of brain activity.

As you may know, the cells in the brain that support cognition are called **neurons**. There are approximately 10^{12} neurons in the brain (that's a thousand billion). Neurons are interconnected, and one neuron can "tell" another neuron that it is firing. If enough of a neuron's neighbors are active, that indicates to an individual neuron that it too should be active, and it will, in turn, communicate this activity to its neighbors.

Neural communication is both chemical and electrical. Neurons release chemicals that influence their neighbors. The effect of the chemicals is to change the neighboring neuron's membrane so that electrically charged ions can pass through it. Under normal circumstances, there are more negative ions inside the neuron's membrane than in the fluid surrounding the neural membrane; the charge across the membrane—its membrane potential—is about -70 millivolts (mV). When a neuron fires, the membrane allows positively charged ions to rush into the neuron, changing the membrane potential to $+40$ mV. Thus, the chemical influence of neighboring neurons causes a chemical change in the neural membrane, which results in an electrical change in the neuron.

The firing of a neuron is an all-or-none event. The neuron fires if the influence of its neighbors reaches some threshold. Although the response seems to be "on" or "off," the neuron can communicate a degree of activity by the frequency of firing (in other words, how many of these firings occur per second). Because neural firing is an electrical event, if we can measure electrical activity in the brain, we can measure the activity of neurons.

Neuroscientists have two chief ways to eavesdrop on the electrical conversations of neurons. **Single-cell recording** is a technique that records the number of times per second that an individual neuron fires. Single-cell recording studies are almost always performed on animal subjects. The animal undergoes surgery in which a small hole is drilled in the skull and a plastic anchoring device is attached. An electrode probe can be placed through the anchoring device and directly into the desired part of the brain. The brain does not have pain receptors, so the probe does not hurt the animal. The probe is insulated, except for the tip, so the probe's tip can record electrical activity, specifically, neural firings.

The basic technique in single-cell recording is to have the animal engage in some behavior while the researcher records electrical activity from a brain area of interest. For example, the investigator might record from a cortical area while a monkey is making a reaching movement. The result might be that a particular neuron fires when the monkey reaches in a particular direction but does not fire when the monkey reaches in another direction. By having the monkey engage in many different behaviors, the researcher can investigate the precise conditions under which the neuron fires. By finding an association between a neuron's activity and the behavior, scientists can begin to understand what the neuron contributes to behavior.

The second method, most often used with humans, is an **electroencephalogram (EEG)**. During an EEG electrodes are placed over the participant's scalp. Each electrode reads the electrical activity of the neurons below it. The ability of EEG to localize activity is not as good as that of other methods. The electrical activity is very weak, of course, so the signal must be greatly amplified. Usually 12 to 64 electrodes are used, so each electrode records the summed activity of millions of neurons. Furthermore, the skull and protective tissue covering the brain are fairly good insulators that diffuse the electrical signal. One advantage of EEG, however, is that it can provide precise information about when neural activity takes place (temporal information). In fact, EEG can tell when a neuron fires to an accuracy of a thousandth of a second, or 1 millisecond (abbreviated *msec* or *ms*).

If you simply put electrodes on a person's head, what you would see is not a flat line (representing no electrical activity) and then some activity once he or she does some task. Instead, you would see a wavy line all the time, representing continuous brain activity. Neurons have resting potentials, which means that they are always firing at some rather slow pace (just how quickly or slowly depends on the type of neuron). Thus, each electrode summarizes millions of neurons, each of which is always slightly active. To get around this problem, researchers measure **event-related potentials (ERPs)**. In this technique the researcher administers tens or hundreds of trials that are similar to one another, then averages all of the squiggly EEG waves from these trials (see Figure I.4).

The resulting average wave is smooth. Researchers often compare two types of ERPs that are similar but vary on one dimension. For example, a researcher studying memory might compare ERPs when the participant successfully recalled a word with ERPs when the participant couldn't recall a word (recall vs. no recall) at each of the 64 electrodes. There probably will be no difference in the ERPs of these two types of trials at most of the electrodes, but any electrode sites that do show a difference will help the researcher localize successful recall in the brain.

Again, EEG is not a very good technique for spatial localization, but it is good for temporal resolution. EEG may tell you only that a difference in successful and unsuccessful retrieval appears in the ERP of the right frontal lobe, which is pretty vague, but the technique could tell you very precisely at what time you start to see a difference in successful and unsuccessful recall. Researchers are starting to use EEG in combination with other techniques so that they can get information about activity that is precise both in terms of when it occurs and where it occurs.

The two most important methods of localizing human brain activity are **positron emission tomography (PET)** and **functional magnetic resonance**

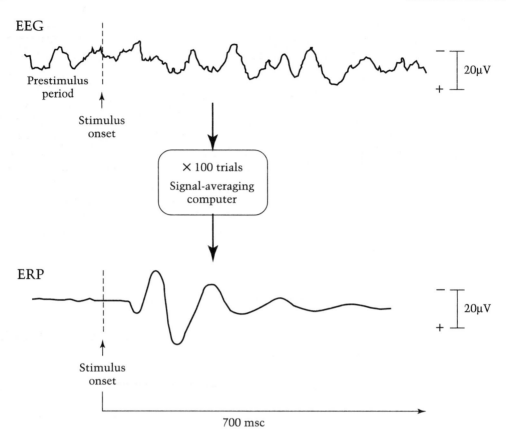

Figure I.4. *Comparison of electroencephalogram (EEG) and event-related potential (ERP) waves.*

imaging (fMRI). Single-cell recording and EEG are both electrical measures and therefore measure a direct product of neural activity. PET and fMRI measure brain activity indirectly. These methods detect changes in metabolism or in blood flow in the brain. One assumption, which appears to be well founded, is that metabolism follows brain activity; when the brain is more active, it demands more glucose (the sugar the brain uses for energy). Another assumption is that if a particular part of the brain needs more glucose, the vascular system will shunt more blood to that part of brain to satisfy the need.

PET measures blood flow with a small amount of a radioactive tracer that has a short half-life. The injected tracer begins to decay immediately, emitting subatomic particles called positrons that collide with nearby electrons and are destroyed. Each collision generates two gamma rays, which are emitted in exactly opposite directions. All this is happening while the patient's head is in (you guessed it) a large doughnut-shaped device that determines where the gamma rays originated. More gamma rays means more positrons, which means more radioactive isotope, which means more blood, which means more neural activity. Although this pattern of inference might seem tortuous, the science behind it is well founded.

The technique of fMRI works much like the type of MRI we've already discussed (which is sometimes called structural MRI to emphasize that it reveals neural structure but not activity). fMRI takes advantage of the magnetic properties of blood hemoglobin, the protein that carries oxygen to all cells of the body. Blood from which the oxygen has been absorbed is called deoxygenated. Oxygenated blood has magnetic properties, but deoxygenated blood does not. fMRI techniques calculate the ratio of oxygenated to deoxygenated blood in a local area. You would think that an active area would have mostly deoxygenated blood because the brain has absorbed all of the oxygen. Actually, the opposite is true; the vascular system floods the active part of the brain with oxygenated blood.

THE BEHAVIORAL SIDE OF THE EQUATION

Recall that there are two inferences we would like to be able to make that will help us localize cognitive function in the brain.

1. If brain area X supports cognitive function Y, then damage to area X will lead to an impairment in tasks that require function Y.
2. If brain area X supports cognitive function Y, then area X will be active when function Y is engaged.

We have discussed ways of figuring out whether area X is impaired (for lesion studies) and whether area X is active, but we have not yet discussed how to isolate cognitive function Y.

Lesion Studies

Suppose we have localized the brain damage in a particular patient. Now we want to discover which cognitive process is damaged in this patient. This is not a trivial problem. For example, in chapter 1 we mentioned patient H.M., who has a severe disability: he cannot learn new information. Suppose you had just conducted the first study of patient H.M. You read a list of words aloud to him and asked him a few minutes later to recall the list, but he was unable to remember any of the words. You are tempted to conclude that H.M.'s memory is impaired. But how do you know it's his memory that is causing the problem? What if he has a problem of attention and ignored the words you read? What if his memory is fine but he didn't understand the words?

How do you decide what is causing the problem? For the example we just gave, you could ask H.M. to immediately repeat the words so you know he's paying attention, and you could test his language ability in other ways to make sure he can understand the words in the memory task. Basically, that's what you do in all lesion experiments. Usually there are many potential reasons someone could be impaired on a task, so you have to administer other tasks to determine the cause.

You also have to keep in mind that the brain damage may not neatly knock out one cognitive function. The part of the brain that is damaged by a stroke or tumor does not depend on the cognitive organization of the brain. A stroke may kill parts of several areas, each of which supports a different cognitive function, leaving the patient partially impaired on a large number of cognitive tasks.

Imaging Studies

PET and fMRI measure brain activity, but much of the brain is active much of the time. If you wanted to know which part of the brain is involved in reading a word, for example, you couldn't simply put people in a scanner and have them read aloud. Instead, you must administer at least two similar tasks that differ in the particular function you want to study. For example, you might conduct a study like this one.

Condition	Description	Hypothetical Processes Involved
1	See fixation point	Attention
2	See random letter strings	Attention + vision
3	Read words	Attention + vision + reading
4	Say related word	Attention + vision + reading + memory

For each task, we have a set of cognitive processes that we think are needed to accomplish the task. We can take a PET scan showing the brain areas that are active for Condition 2 and subtract the activation from Condition 1, and that should subtract out the activations caused by attention, leaving us with just the activations caused by the visual processes engaged when the participant looks at letters. We can do similar subtractions to isolate other cognitive processes because each successive condition adds one cognitive process. Other techniques in fMRI do not use subtractions per se, but they still make use of task comparisons like this one.

PROBLEMS AND LIMITATIONS OF ANATOMICAL STUDIES

Let's summarize what we've said so far. Our ultimate goal is to gain support for hypothetical cognitive processes and representations. One way to do that is to localize these processes or representations in the brain. We do that by two sets of inferences.

> If brain area X is damaged and cognitive function Y is impaired, then X supports Y.
>
> If brain area X is active while cognitive function Y is performed, then X supports Y.

So far we have discussed how we know when brain area X is damaged (localizing the lesion) and how we know when X is active (using single-cell recordings and imaging techniques). We've also discussed how to isolate function Y. Unfortunately, these inferences are not as straightforward as we would like. You may recall that these if–then statements were reversed when we first mentioned them.

> If brain area X supports cognitive function Y, then damage to X will impair Y.
>
> If brain area X supports cognitive function Y, then engaging Y will lead to activity in X.

These statements are true, but that does not mean the reversed statements we've been working with must be true. If you know that P leads to Q, that does not mean Q leads to P. For example, it is true that if you drink beer, you must be 21. That doesn't mean that if you are 21, you must drink beer; you can drink soft drinks, beer, or whatever you want. Have a look at this table.

Rule	Valid Deduction	Invalid Deduction
Beer drinkers must be at least 21 years old.	*Given:* That person is drinking beer. *Conclude:* That person must be at least 21.	*Given:* That person is at least 21. *Conclude:* That person must be drinking beer.
If the hippocampus supports memory, then damage to the hippocampus will impair memory.	*Given:* The hippocampus supports memory. *Conclude:* Damage to the hippocampus will impair memory.	*Given:* The hippocampus is damaged and memory is impaired. *Conclude:* The hippocampus must support memory.

The problem is that the evidence we've been talking about is the type that leads us to the invalid deduction. It might be true that brain area X supports function Y, just as the 21-year-old might be drinking beer, but there are other possibilities, which vary depending on the type of study.

Lesion studies may fail to show cognitive impairment; the brain may have found a new way to support the behavior, or the patient may consciously adopt new strategies for these tasks in order to minimize his or her reliance on the missing cognitive process. Area X may support function Y, there can be damage to area X, and yet you don't observe any deficit.

Another possible source of error in lesion studies is that we may incorrectly assign a cognitive function to a particular brain area that has been lesioned if it is not the brain area itself that supported the function. Fibers connecting two brain areas may have passed through the area that was lesioned, and the loss of this connection might have caused the observed loss of function.

Another problem lies at the very heart of the logic of interpreting lesion studies. Consider this metaphor. Suppose you remove a spark plug from a car, with the result that the engine coughs. You cannot conclude that the spark plug was a cough suppressor. Damage to area X leading to loss of function Y does not allow the conclusion that X supports Y. Just as the interactions among the components of a car are complex and loss does not provide a clear window to function, we can expect the interactions of the components of the brain to be complex.

Functional imaging studies have different problems of interpretation. One potential problem is that of correlated activity. Functional scans show all the brain activity associated with a particular cognitive function. Some of that activity may be reliably associated with the function—every time you perform the function, you get the activity—even if the brain area showing the activity is not crucial to getting the function done. For example, frontal cortical areas reliably show robust activation in memory studies, but if that cortex is damaged or missing, patients do not show a devastating loss of memory.

Another problem in interpreting imaging studies lies in the task analysis. Recall that each participant would perform several tasks, each task adding one cognitive process. If the tasks are not analyzed correctly, the whole enterprise falls apart. But there's an even more subtle problem. What if adding one process changes the others? For example, in one condition the participant might look at letter strings (a task that requires vision and attention), and in another condition the participant might look at words (which requires vision, attention, and reading). But what if looking at words requires attention in a different way, or in a different amount, than looking at letter strings? If that's true, then when the researcher does the subtraction, the activity associated with reading hasn't really been isolated because the attention processes in the two tasks weren't equivalent, so the subtraction didn't remove the activation caused by attention. The assumption that one can selectively add cognitive processes without changing other cognitive processes is called the **assumption of pure insertion**.

What do we do about all these problems? The answer is that we cannot rely on any one method; we must try to use all of the methods simultaneously. If they all point to the same answer, we can have more confidence that we have successfully localized a cognitive process. Notice that the methods have different drawbacks. For example, patients with a lesion might find another way to perform a task, and functional imaging might indicate activity in a brain area that is not crucial for a cognitive process. These drawbacks are mirror images of one another; lesion studies might tell you which brain areas are essential for a cognitive process but might miss areas typically associated with a process, whereas imaging studies show you all areas associated with a cognitive process but not which areas are crucial for getting the job done. The strengths and weaknesses of different techniques complement one another. The strategy of employing multiple techniques to address the same question usually is called using **converging operations**. If different methods converge on one answer, our confidence that the answer is correct greatly increases.

WHY DOES LOCALIZATION HELP US?

Why do psychologists want to know where functions are located in the brain? Why are we better off knowing that vision is in the occipital cortex, not the frontal lobe, or the hippocampus, or for that matter in the big toe? This question is seldom addressed, perhaps because people think that the answer is self-evident—surely it is good to know where cognitive functions are in the brain. But a moment's reflection makes this answer less obvious. Let's discuss four ways in which localization can help psychologists.

REPRESENTATION. As described earlier, single-cell recording studies can indicate what sorts of information a particular neuron codes, revealing what sorts of representations are likely to be useful in psychological theories. For example, classic single-cell recording studies indicated that neurons in primary visual cortex coded lines (Hubel & Wiesel, 1959). This important work led to psychological theories of vision in which lines figured prominently as representations (e.g., Selfridge & Neisser, 1960).

DETERMINING SAME OR DIFFERENT. We assume that if two psychological processes are localized to different parts of the brain, they are different, and if they are localized to the same place, they are probably the same. This principle can be useful when we are in doubt as to whether processes are the same or different. In chapter 3 we'll discuss one such result. If you flash a group of dots on a screen and ask a participant to report the number of dots, people are more or less perfect at this task if there are four dots or fewer. With five dots they start to make mistakes. This difference is so dramatic that researchers thought two different processes might be at work: an error-prone process that counts when there are many dots, and an error-free process that can enumerate a smaller number of dots. Brain imaging data indicate, however, that the same part of the brain deals with the task whatever the number of dots; there are not two separate processes.

PROVIDING A NEW MEASURE.   Another advantage to brain localization is that it provides a new way of ensuring that we know what we're talking about. Here's what I mean by that. In chapter 1 I mentioned that the dorsolateral prefrontal cortex (DLPFC) supports short-term memory. Yet short-term memory can never be observed directly. I can observe *tasks*, but I can't observe short-term memory—that's a theoretical construct. I need to be able to predict when short-term memory participates in cognition by identifying tasks in which short-term memory will be involved.

I have a way to test my prediction of which tasks involve short-term memory. If I claim that a task requires short-term memory, then the DLPFC had better be active in an imaging experiment when participants perform the task. And a patient with damage to the DLPFC had better be impaired on that task. By tying my theoretical construct (short-term memory) to the brain, I gain a new way of verifying whether or not my construct contributes to a task.

BRAIN INFORMS THEORY.   We are fairly confident that we understand at least the basics of what some brain structures do. Primary visual cortex in the occipital lobe is a good example; we don't know exactly how it functions, but we know it supports vision. Sometimes that is enough to help settle debates in psychology. The logic is that when you don't know if a particular task draws on a process such as vision, you can test whether it relies on a part of the brain known to support vision (the occipital lobe). If the occipital lobe participates in performance of the task, then it is a good bet that the task relies on visual processing in some way. An example of this logic is described in chapter 9, "Visual Imagery."

SUMMARY.   Cognitive psychologists study cognitive functions in the brain with techniques used to localize brain activity (PET, fMRI) or brain damage (CAT, structural MRI). In addition, we've discussed methods for isolating cognitive processes—what I've called the behavioral side of the equation. Finally, we've listed four ways in which localizing cognitive functions in the brain can prove useful to cognitive psychologists.

Very useful, in fact. Cognitive neuropsychology, a discipline intersecting mind and brain, is growing at a remarkable rate. This trend makes for exciting science, but it poses a problem for the writer of a textbook. Just how much cognitive neuropsychology should be included in a cognitive psychology textbook? The truth is that the topics should be covered in separate courses. Nevertheless, for a representative view of what's happening in the field, I've included key studies from cognitive neuropsychology in each chapter. These studies are set off in boxes that complement the cognitive work you'll read about. Other studies from neuroscience are so integral to cognitive psychology that they are not set off in boxes but are described the text. My hope is that these studies will help you appreciate how cognitive neuropsychology complements the work of cognitive psychologists and that this material will encourage you to learn more about the field.

THE FIVE-MINUTE BRAIN ANATOMY LESSON

In describing brain structures we often talk about the position of one relative to another. Brain structures are large enough that one might want to refer to only part of it; it's tiresome to refer to "the part of the cerebellum that's closer to the top of the head and toward the back of the head." As shown Figure I.5, toward the top of the head is called **dorsal**; toward the bottom is **ventral**; toward the front is **anterior** or **rostral**; toward the back is **posterior** or **caudal**; toward the middle is **medial**; and toward the side is **lateral**. Thus we could replace the cumbersome phrase "the part of the cerebellum that's closer to the top of the head and toward the back of the head" with "dorsal posterior thalamus."

Cerebral Cortex

The cerebral cortex is the layer of cells that covers the outside of the brain. When you see a picture of the brain, you're typically looking at cerebral cortex. This cell layer is quite thin (about 3 millimeters), but unfolded the sheet of cells would cover about 2.5 square feet. That large sheet is crumpled to fit into the skull; hence the wrinkled appearance of the brain. The valleys are called **sulci** (singular **sulcus**) and the hills are called **gyri** (singular **gyrus**). The brain is

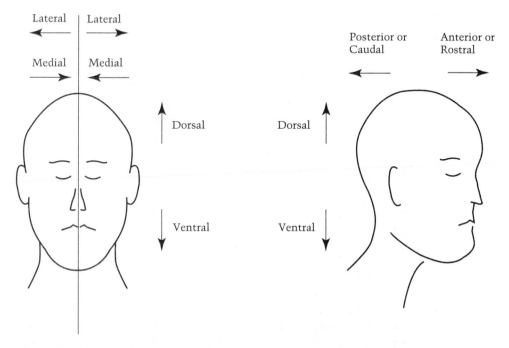

Figure I.5. *Directional descriptors of brain anatomy.*

separated into two hemispheres—left and right—and the cortex folds down into the space between them.

The cortex is not uniform. There are different types of cells in different areas, and most important for our purposes, different parts of the cortex serve different cognitive functions. Researchers refer to different areas of cortex in several ways. We will use three of these naming systems: naming by lobe, naming by function, and naming by landmark. It may seem confusing (or better, stupid) to use three different systems to name the same thing. For example, the primary motor cortex (function) could also be called the precentral gyrus (landmark) or posterior frontal cortex (lobe). (It's also called Brodman's area 4, and M1.) Why not pick one name? I could have translated everything into one system, but doing so would be a disservice to readers because certain structures are very commonly referred to by the name in a particular system. If you referred to the lateral temporal cortex and everyone else is calling it the fusiform gyrus, the other kids would make fun of you.

NAMING BY LANDMARK.   Each gyrus and sulcus in the brain is named, as shown in Figure I.6. A few brain locations are commonly referred to by the

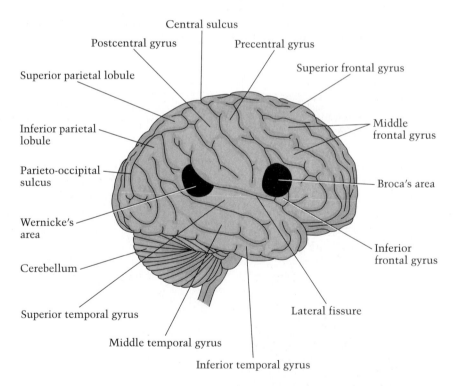

Figure I.6A.   *A lateral view of the brain, showing the names of gyri & sulci, Broca's area, and Wernicke's area. From* Clerical Neuroanatomy for Medical Students, *by R. S. Snell et al., 1980, Boston: Little, Brown, Fig. 1.12, p. 3.*

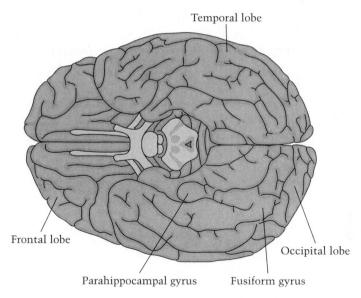

Temporal lobe

Frontal lobe

Occipital lobe

Parahippocampal gyrus   Fusiform gyrus

Figure I.6B. *A ventral view of the brain (i.e., from the bottom.).
From* Foundations of Biological Psychology, *4th ed., by
N. R. Carlson et al., 1999, Boston: Ally & Bacon, Fig.
3.10a, p. 69.*

name of the gyrus: these include the **fusiform gyrus**, the **parahippocampal
gyrus**, and the **cingulate gyrus**. In addition, two regions are referred to by the
names of the researchers who first described their function: **Broca's area** and
Wernike's area.

NAMING BY LOBE.   The cerebral cortex is divided into four lobes, as shown in
Figure I.7. The central sulcus divides the frontal lobe and the parietal lobe. The
lateral fissure (a fissure is a deep sulcus) divides the frontal lobe and the temporal lobe. The occipital lobe is at the most posterior point in the brain (indeed,
much of the occipital lobe is tucked out of sight in the medial walls of each
hemisphere of the brain). Researchers often refer to parts of the cortex by a location within one of the four lobes ("dorsolateral frontal cortex"). *Figure I.8
illustrates the system you will see most often in this book.*

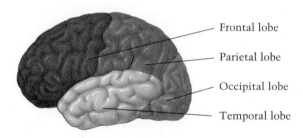

— Frontal lobe

— Parietal lobe

— Occipital lobe

— Temporal lobe   **Figure I.7.**   *The four lobes of the
cerebral cortex.*

NAMING BY FUNCTION.   Some areas of cortex are so well understood that researchers refer to them by their function. This is usually done for **motor cortex, visual cortex, auditory cortex,** and **somatosensory cortex** (concerned with feeling where the body is). In addition, researchers frequently differentiate between structures such as primary and secondary visual cortex. *Primary* usually refers to simpler and *secondary* to more complex processing. For perceptual processes (vision, audition, somatosensation) *primary* means closer to the sense organs; secondary cortex takes the output of the primary cortex and builds more complex meaning from it. In motor cortex, *primary* refers to cortex that is closer to commanding the muscles, whereas *secondary* involves higher-level planning.

The Rest of the Brain

In this book, when we talk about the brain we usually mean cortex. There are just a few other structures you need to keep in mind. The central nervous system is composed of the spinal cord and the brain. The **spinal cord** collects somatosensory information about pressure, temperature, pain, and so on and sends motor information to the muscles. Perched on top of the spinal cord is the brain. The cortex is the outer portion of the brain. Below the cortex are a number of subcortical (below the cortex) structures (see Figure I.9). Here is a list of the subcortical structures we'll talk about and what they are thought to do.

> **Thalamus** A relay station for sensory and motor information. For all senses except smell, the receptors first send information to the thalamus, which passes it on to cortex.
>
> **Amygdala** Thought to be important in processing of emotion (especially fear) and probably information about social functions.
>
> **Caudate and putamen** Separate but related structures important in movement and some poorly understood cognitive functions.
>
> **Hippocampus** Important in memory.
>
> **Cerebellum** Important in motor control and probably in some higher-level cognitive functions, but just what it does is not clear.

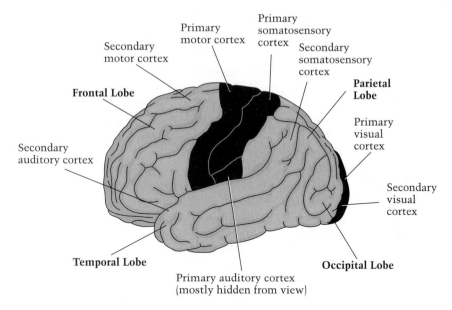

Figure I.8. *Functional areas of the brain. From* Foundations of Biological Psychology, *4th ed., by N. R. Carlson, 1999, Boston: Allya, & Bacon, Fig. 3.10c, p. 69.*

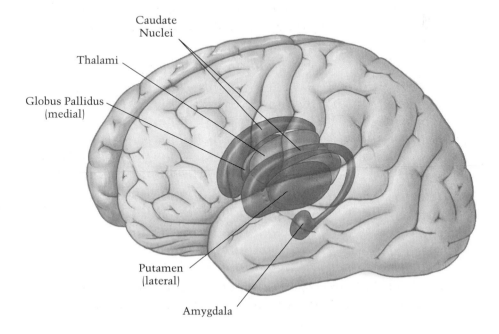

Figure I.9. *The basal ganglia.*

Key Terms

amygdala
anterior
assumption of pure
   insertion
auditory cortex
Broca's area
caudal
caudate and putamen
cerebellum
cingulate gyrus
computerized axial
   tomography (CAT)
converging operations
dorsal
electroencephalogram

(EEG)
event-related potentials
   (ERPs)
functional magnetic
   resonance imaging
   (fMRI)
fusiform gyrus
gyri (gyrus)
hippocampus
lateral
localization
magnetic resonance
   imaging (MRI)
medial
motor cortex

neurons
parahippocampal gyrus
positron emission
   tomography (PET)
posterior
rostral
single-cell recording
somatosensory cortex
spinal cord
sulci (sulcus)
thalamus
ventral
visual cortex
Wernike's area

2

Visual Perception

WHAT MAKES VISUAL PERCEPTION HARD?

HOW ARE VISUAL AMBIGUITIES RESOLVED?

Shape
Brightness
Distance and Size
Top-Down Influences in Vision
An Alternative: The Ecological Approach

WHAT IS VISUAL PERCEPTION FOR?

Identifying Objects
Navigation

Of all the cognitive functions your brain performs, vision is both the most remarkable and the most difficult to appreciate. It is difficult to appreciate vision precisely because it is so marvelous; vision works so efficiently, so effortlessly, that you have no clue what it is doing or how difficult its task is. Consider this: For $5 you can buy a calculator that can perform long division far more quickly and accurately than any human. For $15 you can buy a computer program that can beat 99% of the population in chess. Yet there is no computer that can drive a truck. Why not? It's clear that a robot could turn a steering wheel and press an accelerator; the problem is that there is no computer that can rapidly perceive the road, other cars, pedestrians, and so on.

This example should tell you one thing: vision is hard. The first question we'll take up is **What makes visual perception hard?** We can't simply ask, "How do humans see?" That question is not specific enough. We need to know why it's hard to see—what specific problems must be solved for vision to work—before we can start to think about how the human visual system might solve those problems. As we'll see, vision is hard because the pattern of light that falls on your eye is consistent with many different scenes out in the world; the problem is figuring out which scene is actually out in the world. Here's a simple example. What is the object depicted in Figure 2.1?

You probably said that this object is a square, but it could be a cube, the bottom of a pyramid, or a number of other solids. Thus even this simple picture is consistent with more than one object in the world, and knowing the object's identity for certain is impossible. You may well be protesting, "Dan, we're all very impressed by your square, but the fact is that we do see, and we usually see accurately." That's true, and vision happens quickly and its product (your conscious visual perception) is consistent. When you walk into a room, you immediately perceive the objects that are in the room, their relative positions, their colors, their textures, whether they are moving, and so on. Indeed, everyone would agree on these properties, just as everyone agrees that Figure 2.1 depicts a square.

Why does everyone agree if knowing the identity of the object is impossible? All visual stimuli are inherently ambiguous. The fact that we all see a square in Figure 2.1 tells us that the perceptual system somehow resolves the ambiguities inherent in a two-dimensional representation. The second question we will take up is **How does the visual system resolve ambiguities?** The answer is that the perceptual system makes assumptions about the way

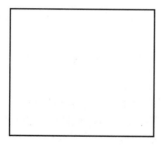

Figure 2.1. *This object appears to be a square, but it could be a cube or any other three-dimensional object with one square face that happens to be oriented toward you.*

objects in the world usually look so we can resolve the ambiguity of figures such as the square. For example, one assumption the visual system makes is that objects are unlikely to be oriented at improbable angles. There are many ways in which a cube could be oriented in space, but very few of those orientations of the cube leave just one face of the cube visible to the observer. It would be like seeing a coin that just happens to be edge-on so that it looks like a line. Such orientations are so rare that your visual system assumes that they don't happen. Figure 2.1 is much more likely to be a square than a just-happens-to-be-oriented-that-way cube, so the visual system gambles that it's a square.

Okay, we can see. But why? **What is vision for?** Broadly speaking, vision serves two goals. First, it allows us to know the qualities of objects at a distance (how big is it, is it moving, and does it have large pointy teeth?). This knowledge helps us behave in appropriate ways (attack small edible-looking things, flee from large aggressive-looking things). The "at a distance" feature is helpful because we can evaluate what something is without having to walk up and touch it. The second function of vision is that it serves action, meaning that we know where things are so that we can move around effectively (pounce with accuracy on the small edible-looking thing, skirt immovable objects as you're fleeing from the aggressive-looking thing). So, briefly put, the function of visual perception is to (1) identify objects and (2) help us navigate in the world. How do we identify objects, and how does vision help us navigate? As we'll see, these two functions actually are handled by separate parts of the brain.

WHAT MAKES VISUAL PERCEPTION HARD?

> ➤ *Preview* As we've just discussed, visual perception is complicated, but it's not easy to appreciate that fact because our cognitive systems are so good at analyzing visual stimuli. In this section we examine more closely what makes visual perception hard. The crucial point is that the image falling on the retina does not fully determine what is in the world. For example, size and distance are indeterminate; if the image of something is small, the object in the world might be either small or far away. Other indeterminisms we'll discuss include shape and orientation (if you see what looks like an ellipse, what's in the world might really be an ellipse, or it might be a circle that is turned slightly to the side) as well as light source, reflectance, and shadow.

The chief problem the visual system faces is the **inverse projection problem,** which relates to the way that light from the world falls on the **retina** (the layer of light-sensitive cells on the back of the eye). How do we recover the three-dimensional shape of a real-world object from a two-dimensional projection on the retina? An infinite number of three-dimensional objects could give rise to a two-dimensional projection. We cannot know what is out in the world solely on the basis of the information source available to us—neural impulses from the retina of the eye—because the world is three-dimensional and the image projected on the retina is two-dimensional.

To get a feel for what this means, suppose you are a painter and I am a sculptor, and you want to paint a picture of my groovy sculpture. How will you go about this? You could put a pane of glass in front of my sculpture and simply trace the form (and background) that you see through the glass, as shown in Figure 2.2. That would work marvelously as long as you didn't move your head. If you moved your head—for example, if you leaned to the right—the location of the sculpture would move relative to the glass, so the painting would be ruined. But if you stick with one point of view you can reliably turn a three-dimensional scene into a two-dimensional scene. There is a single mapping of the three-dimensional scene into two dimensions even if you bring in a different painter as long as the positions of the sculpture, the glass, and the painter stay the same.

But if you show someone else the two-dimensional painting on the pane of glass, could that person know what the sculpture looks like? In other words, could he or she reconstruct the three-dimensional scene? No, because an infinite number of possible scenes are consistent with any two-dimensional picture. That's the inverse projection problem your visual system constantly

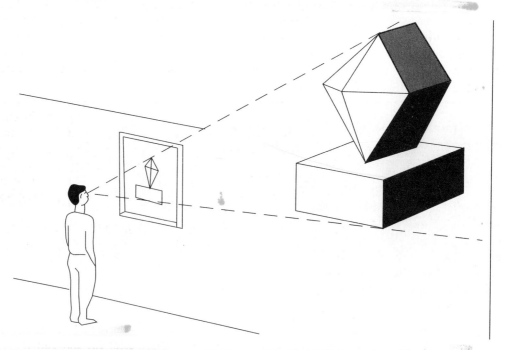

Figure 2.2. *A three-dimensional object seen from a single perspective creates a unique two-dimensional projection. This two-dimensional projection is consistent with an infinite number of three-dimensional objects, however. In this figure, the observer sees the sculpture so that it looks like a kite on a rectangle rather than a diamond on a box.*

faces. In the case of the visual system, the two-dimensional representation is the pattern of light on the retina. Your retina is two-dimensional, and recovering three-dimensional information about objects in the world poses the same problems as described in the sculpture painting example. So the visual system must deal with indeterminacy in **shape** and **orientation**.

A second thing we want to know about an object is its surface features: what color it is, how dark or light it is, and so on. Shape can distinguish a cherry from an apple, but it is color, not shape, that will tell us whether the cherry is ripe.

We run into a problem in trying to determine an object's color and brightness because the only source of information we have about surface features is the light that enters the eye. The technical term for the amount of light the eye receives is **luminance**. Three factors contribute to luminance: the amount of illumination (a 100-watt light bulb, a 25-watt light bulb, the sun), the reflectance of the object (white, black, gray), and whether the object is in shadow. A piece of coal viewed in bright sunlight actually has higher luminance than a snowball viewed in candlelight. Nevertheless, the coal looks black and the snowball looks white. How does the visual system unravel the three factors that contribute to luminance so that it gets the reflectance of objects right?

For an example, look at the Mach card stimulus in Figure 2.3. What does it look like to you? This figure could depict an arrow-shaped object that is white on top and gray on the bottom. Or the object could be an open book, face-down, illuminated from the top, so that the bottom is in shadow. Thus another set of indeterminacies involves **light source, reflectance**, and **shadow**.

Object size and distance also are indeterminate from a two-dimensional representation. Bear in mind that everything you know about objects in the world comes from the image that the object projects onto the retina. In general, larger objects do project larger images onto the retina, but the size of the retinal projection also depends on the distance between the object and the observer. If you see a square that appears small, is it truly a small square, or is it actually a large square that is far away? Thus a third indeterminacy involves **size** and **distance**.

One real-world example of the relationship between object size and distance involves the sun and the moon. Although the moon is much smaller

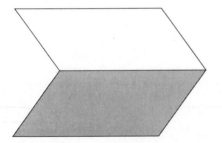

Figure 2.3. *A Mach card. The gray part of the figure could be gray because the surface of the object depicted is gray, or it could be gray because the surface is white but it is in shadow.*

than the sun, it is also much closer. It so happens that these two factors balance out nearly perfectly; the sun and moon project same-sized images on the retina and thus appear to be the same size when viewed from the earth. That's why the moon just covers the sun during a total eclipse. The moon would not appear to be the same size as the sun from a vantage point nearer or farther than the earth.

The main things you would want to know about an object—its shape, the color and brightness of its surface, its size, its distance—are indeterminate from the information that is available to the retina, so that's why vision is hard. How then are we able to see?

Stand-on-One-Foot Question

1. Name the three indeterminacies that make visual perception difficult.

Questions That Require Two Feet

2. Size and distance are indeterminate, so if you see a car that appears small, you can't know whether it is a big car far away or a small car close by. Yet you seem to have no problem figuring that out. Why?
3. The apparent size of the tip of your thumb when held at arm's length is about the same size as the moon, viewed from the earth, as Tom Hanks showed us in the movie Apollo 13. Would it work the same way if you stood on the moon and looked at the earth? That is, would the tip of your thumb appear about the same size as the earth?

Box 2–1 Is Face Perception Special?

One visual problem doesn't seem so difficult: recognizing faces. People are good at recognizing faces, considering that they differ only in subtle ways. We all have two eyes, a nose, a mouth, and so on, yet we can differentiate other people at a glance. Given the importance of social relations in our species, we might propose that evolutionary pressures have favored a special perceptual mechanism for identifying faces.

One bit of evidence supporting this idea is the existence of prosopagnosia, a syndrome that selectively affects a patient's ability to recognize faces. Patients have no difficulty recognizing common objects, but they cannot recognize familiar faces, including the faces of family members or even their own. Patients can still recognize other people by their voices or perhaps by a distinctive feature such as a prominent mustache. These patients typically have suffered bilateral damage to the secondary visual areas and the ventral temporal lobe.

(Continued)

The fact that people can demonstrate a failure to recognize faces but still exhibit normal recognition of other objects is strong evidence for the idea that face recognition and object recognition are supported by fundamentally different processes. However, there is an important difference between recognizing an object and recognizing a face. When you recognize an object such as a car, you simply identify the class of object. You are not asked to differentiate individuals. In face recognition, you must recognize an individual. Thus the problem for prosopagnosic patients may be in recognizing individuals, not in recognizing faces per se.

The evidence on this proposal is mixed. On the one hand, Jane McNeil and Elizabeth Warrington (1993) presented an interesting case study of a sheep farmer (W.J.) who had prosopagnosia. W.J. was shown a series of photos of either unfamiliar sheep or unfamiliar people and was then given a recognition test. He successfully recognized 81% of the sheep but only 50% of the people. Other sheep farmers could recognize 89% of the people and performed a bit worse than

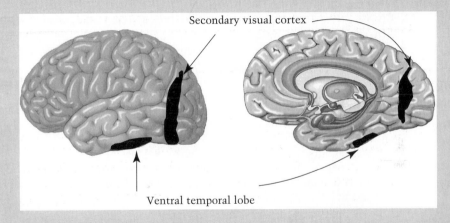

Figure B2.1.   *Two fairly similar Greebles.*

(Continued)

W.J. in recognizing sheep, averaging 69%. These data indicate that it is possible to have intact memory for individuals (such as the faces of individual sheep) and yet be impaired in recognizing people; thus there might be a process in the brain that is specialized for recognizing human faces.

Other data indicate that faces are not special. Functional imaging studies have emphasized the importance of the fusiform gyrus (located in the ventral temporal lobe) in face recognition; this area is sometimes referred to as specialized for face perception. Isabel Gauthier and her colleagues (1999) sought to show that this area is specialized not for face perception but for visual expertise. The researchers used stimuli formed from meaningless but complex figures called Greebles. Greebles are difficult to differentiate at first, but recognition improves with practice.

The researchers were especially interested in what parts of the brain were associated with improvement in Greeble recognition. They found that the fusiform gyrus was a key area showing activation associated with increasing expertise, thus lending support to the idea that the fusiform gyrus may not necessarily be a "face area" per se but rather is associated with visual expertise. In another experiment, Gauthier and her colleagues (2000) imaged the brains of car experts and bird experts as they performed tasks with birds, cars, and other objects. The fusiform gyrus was active for stimuli for which participants were experts, providing further evidence that there is not a part of the brain specialized for faces; rather, the fusiform gyrus is specialized for visual expertise.

Are faces special? In the end, this question has not yet been answered. It's possible that W.J. was using different strategies to recognize sheep and people, such as relying on specific markings in the ovine version of a prominent mustache, so that experiment may not be definitive. On the other hand, perhaps faces really are special and Gauthier's experiments shows only that brain processes that normally handle face processing can be co-opted to deal with other tasks requiring visual expertise.

How Are Visual Ambiguities Resolved?

➤ *Preview* How does our cognitive system resolve the ambiguities inherent in visual perception so that we can accurately interpret what we see? The answer is that we make unconscious assumptions that resolve the ambiguities. Shape and orientation are resolved by assuming that objects are not in unusual orientations. Shape perception is also influenced by the frame of reference in which the object is viewed. Light source, reflectance, and shadow are resolved by making assumptions about the color of objects and typical ambient lighting. Size and distance are usually resolved by using cues to distance in the environment (for example, an object that partially covers another must be closer to the observer).

Ecological psychologists propose that all of these problems and ambiguities may be more in the minds of psychologists than in the visual fields of observers.

(Continued)

They propose that the environment actually provides a variety of cues that make the job of vision much simpler than it first appears. We examine the sorts of cues they claim people use.

The short answer to the question of how visual ambiguities are resolved is that these insoluble problems become solvable if you are willing to make assumptions. Your visual system makes assumptions about the nature of objects in the world and how they are illuminated. You should note that these assumptions are not made by some executive part of the visual system. Rather, they are built into the way the visual system itself is engineered, the same way many cameras are designed with the assumption that pictures will be shot in daylight.

Yet the assumptions built into the visual system do not guarantee a correct solution. Indeed, if you know these assumptions, you can create two-dimensional paintings that look compellingly three-dimensional, or you can induce the visual system to make errors (that's what visual illusions do). The main point is that vision is not a representation of exactly what is in the world; it is a representation of what is probably in the world. It's a construction based on wise gambles. We'll go through the key visual properties of objects—shape, surface, size, and distance—one by one.

Shape

Let's start with the square shown in Figure 2.1. Why do you call the figure a square and not a cube? Your visual system is sensitive to what sorts of objects are likely to have projected a particular image onto your retina. Yes, the object could be a cube, but think of all the different angles at which a cube could be positioned. Only a few views of a cube look like a square, so your visual system assumes that what you're seeing is actually a square. Hermann von Helmholtz, one of the first giants of vision research, called this the **likelihood principle** (1910/1962). This principle has been important in many modern theories of vision, although as some researchers have pointed out, it's hard to distinguish whether the visual system interprets stimuli using likelihood or simplicity as the guide (Chapter, 1996; Pomerantz & Kubovy, 1986; van der Helm, 2000).

We can state generally that the likelihood principle implies that a two-dimensional straight line will be interpreted as being straight in three dimensions and lines that appear parallel in two dimensions will be interpreted as parallel in three dimensions. From most vantage points, lines that are truly parallel (or nearly so) in three-dimensional space will appear that way in a two-dimensional representation, whatever the viewing angle. (This principle works only for short lines, such as those that define the edges of objects.) To see that this is true, take out your wallet or a pen or another object with parallel sides. Watch the opposing, nearly parallel edges of the object as you rotate it, and you'll see that the edges remain parallel even as the angle of viewing changes.

But there is another way in which our square is ambiguous. Couldn't it be a diamond that has been rotated? This question illustrates the importance of **frames of reference** in the perception of shape: the position or orientation or motion of an object is always defined relative to something else. For example, using the earth as a frame of reference, the sun moves around the earth. Using the sun as a frame of reference, the earth moves around the sun. The same relationship is true at smaller scales; if you and I face each other and there is a pencil on the floor to my right, the pencil is to your left. When we locate the pencil relative to a spatial frame of reference centered on me, you don't share that frame of reference. Using the room as the frame of reference, however, we would both think of the pencil as being in the same location.

Much of the time, the perceptual system uses gravity to establish a frame of reference that is independent of the viewer's position. Look at the square in Figure 2.1 again, this time tilting your head 45 degrees. It still looks like a square, right? That's because your frame of reference is still based on the surrounding environment, defined by gravity.

Figure 2.4 shows two versions of the same shape, which looks different in the two panels. At left it looks like a diamond, and at right it looks like a rotated square (Kopferman, 1930). Steve Palmer and his associates (1988) demonstrated that the gravity-based orientation of a diamond or square can be overridden by a purely visual frame of reference, in this case a rectangle. Participants were to report whether they saw a square or diamond (relative to gravity). On some trials there was no reference frame except gravity. On other trials the square or diamond was surrounded by a rectangle that was either upright or tilted at 45 degrees. Thus there were two possible frames of reference, visual and gravitational, which could either agree (as in the left panel of Figure 2.4) or disagree (as in the right panel). Participants were faster to make their decision when the two reference frames agreed than when they disagreed.

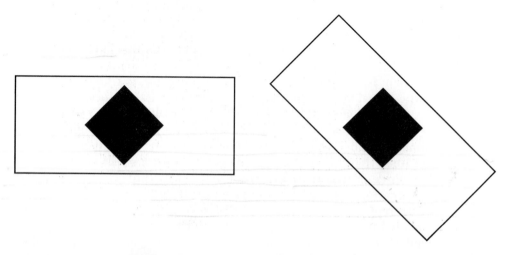

Figure 2.4. *Visual and gravitational frames of reference.*

It is clear that in addition to assumptions based on likelihood, such as whether or not we are viewing an object head-on given particular visual information, frames of reference play a critical role in shape disambiguation and perception of orientation.

Brightness

A change in luminance (the amount of light hitting the retina) can result from a number of factors. For example, the cylinder in Figure 2.5 appears to be uniformly colored, and there is a light shining on it from the right. However, it is possible that the cylinder is illuminated evenly but is colored lighter gray on the right and darker on the left. The visual system makes several simple assumptions to choose between these alternatives.

First, the visual system assumes that surfaces are uniformly colored. That's why shading makes such a difference in the three-dimensional quality of a painting. Changes in shading are assumed by the visual system to reflect shadows caused by hills and valleys in the surface of an object, not variations in the brightness of the object itself. The full moon looks so flat because it is uniformly bright. When the light of the sun strikes the many craters and hills of the moon, it reflects at many angles. Thus, the brightness is even across the entire full moon and it therefore looks like a disk, not a sphere.

The second assumption is that gradual changes in brightness could be caused by shadows. Shadows have fuzzy edges, but changes in the reflectance of a surface typically do not. Hence, it is easy to distinguish the change in brightness caused by the cylinder's shadow from the change in brightness

Figure 2.5. *The three factors that contribute to luminance: light source, shading, and shadow.*

caused by the light and dark square of the checkerboard; the shadow has fuzzy borders. Another important cue to shadows comes from movement. If an object moves, its shadow moves in association with the object.

Nevertheless, there is still ambiguity in decoding information that comes from shape. Look again at the Mach card in Figure 2.3. It could be a book that is open with its spine toward you, with a light source from above, or it could be a book that is open and facing you, with a light source from below. In interpreting shading information, the visual system assumes that light comes from above an object—a sensible assumption because vision evolved in a world where light almost always comes from the sun. The assumption that light comes from above is what makes the crater in Photo 2.1 look concave; turn this book upside-down and see what happens when the pattern of shading changes.

Now let's consider the checkerboard pattern in Figure 2.5. Believe it or not, the white squares that are in shadow are the same shade of gray as the dark squares that are not in shadow. (Cover the surrounding areas and compare the two squares to see that this is true.) The visual system uses **local contrast** to evaluate the likely shade of each square; the perceived surface lightness depends on the light-to-dark ratios of areas that are next to one another in the same plane. Squares surrounded by darker squares (in shadow or not) are considered to be light. The sharp boundaries of the squares also help the visual system determine that the boundaries are likely to be created by paint, not shadows, because shadows usually have fuzzy edges. Thus the checkerboard is easy to interpret as being a field with light and dark squares. Hence, the light squares look light even when they are in shadow.

Photo 2.1. *Light sources are assumed to come from above, so this object appears to be an indentation or crater. See what happens to the figure if you turn the book upside-down.*

The fact that you don't perceive the similarity of brightness between the light squares that are in shadow and the dark squares seen in full light may seem like a failing of the visual system. But as Edward Adelson (1998), who designed this illusion, points out, it does not reflect a failing of the visual system but rather a success. Your visual system does not need to assess the absolute brightness of regions of space. It needs to analyze complex scenes to find simple, meaningful components, such as "checkerboard with dark and light patches, partly in shadow."

Alan Gilchrist (1997) used the three-dimensional visual stimulus in Figure 2.6 to demonstrate the importance of local contrast. Horizontal and vertical surfaces, some painted white and some black, are labeled *W* and *B* in the figure. A light bulb illuminates the horizontal part of the stimulus more than the vertical part. Participants viewed the stimulus **monocularly**—that is, with

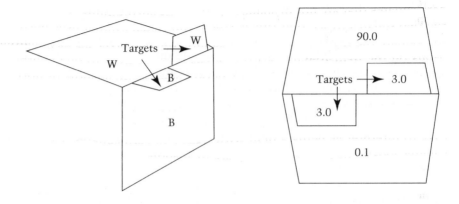

Target	Median Observer Match	
	Monocular	Binocular
Upper Tab	3.75	8.0
Lower Tab	7.75	3.0

Figure 2.6. *At top left is the apparatus participants viewed (W stands for white, B for black). At top right is the stimulus as the participants actually viewed it; because they viewed it with one eye, it looked like a flat surface. It was illuminated with one light bulb from above, so the horizontal surfaces were struck by more light than the vertical surfaces. The numbers in the figure at top right show the amount of light reflected from the surface. The table at the bottom shows brightness ratings (high numbers = brighter) for the targets when the apparatus was viewed monocularly or binocularly. Although the targets have equal luminances, the brightness ratings are heavily influenced by the surrounding field.*

just one eye—through a peephole. The one-eyed viewing and the peephole restricted their viewpoint so that the stimulus looked flat, like a painting hanging on a wall. From the participant's perspective the setup looked like the figure at the top right. The numbers show the actual luminance of each part of the figure. The two tabs had equal luminance (3.0 foot-lamberts) because the upper tab was white but got little light and the lower black tab got a lot of light.

The tabs did not look equal to participants, even though they had equal luminances. At the bottom of the figure you can see the brightness ratings participants gave to the tabs. The upper tab looked much darker than the lower tab. Why? Because the lower tab was surrounded by a much darker field that appeared to be in the same plane. Because the lower tab and the field that seemed to surround it appeared to be in the same plane, the visual system assumed that they must have received the same amount of illumination. The tab lower appeared much brighter than the surrounding field, so participants assumed it must have a lighter surface.

This effect vanished when participants viewed the stimulus **binocularly**, that is, with both eyes. The participants could now see that the tabs were not in the same plane and so could be illuminated differently. (If two surfaces are at right angles, like the front and the top of a desk, they are likely to receive different amounts of illumination from a single light source.) When the stimulus was viewed binocularly, the brightness judgments for the tabs reversed.

How could participants tell that the stimulus was not flat if they viewed it with both eyes? The answer to that question involves depth perception, our next topic.

Distance and Size

Size and distance trade off: when an object is far away it appears small, and when it is near it seems large. How can we determine the true size and distance of the object? There are two classes of answers to this question. One group of strategies is rooted in the visual system, the other in information derived from the environment.

CUES IN THE VISUAL SYSTEM.   There are three cues to depth that are based on properties of the visual system. The first is **accommodation**. The lens of the eye changes shape in order to focus an image on the retina. The shape change of the lens varies depending on how much the muscles that change the shape are flexed. This cue is important only at relatively close ranges (less than a meter or so), where the muscles must work quite hard.

Another cue to depth is **convergence**. As an object gets closer, your eyes "cross" more and more to gaze at it. You point your eyes at an object so that the light reflecting from it falls on the center of the retina, which is called the **fovea**. This part of the retina is the most accurate at seeing small details. Because your eyes are some distance apart, when objects are fairly close to you, your eyes start to cross to keep the image on the fovea of each eye. Convergence is useful as a cue to distance only when objects are fairly close, however. For objects that are moderately far away (say, more than 20 feet), the eyes are nearly parallel, so convergence is not helpful.

Stereopsis is a more important cue to distance. Because the eyes are in different places, they get slightly different views of an object. Hold one finger in front of your face and rapidly open and close your left and right eyes, alternately. Does your finger seem to change positions? This difference in view of the left and right eye is called **retinal disparity**.

Now look at the left part of Figure 2.7. When both eyes are rotated so that points *A* and *B* fall on the fovea, they receive different views. The points seem closer together to the left eye than to the right eye; compare the size of the angles created at the fovea by *A* and *B* in each eye. In the right side of the figure, the difference between the views of the two eyes is not as extreme, so the angles are closer to being the same. Thus the disparity between the views of the left and right eyes is larger for nearby objects. The visual system uses the difference

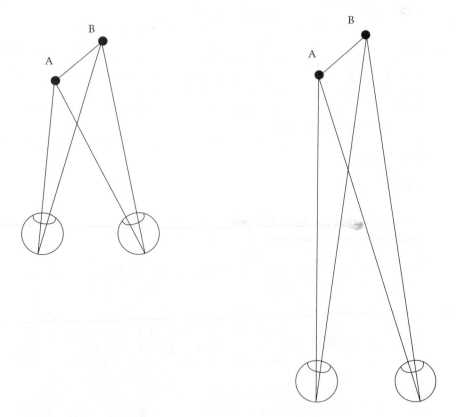

Figure 2.7. *The left and right eye get different views of objects, and this difference is greater when the observer is closer to the object. In the left-hand figure, the distance between A and B seems larger to the right eye than to the left eye. The greater distance is apparent from the greater angle of the two lines going to the right eye. The difference between the left eye and right eye is not as great in the figure on the right, where the distance between observer and object is greater.*

between the left and right eye to figure out how far away an object must be. If a tree appears in roughly the same place on the left and right retinas, it is quite distant. If its position were very different in each eye, the visual system would know the tree was nearby.

Stereopsis probably is the reason some of the effects we've been discussing work only if the stimulus is viewed monocularly. Stereopsis obviously can't be a cue to distance if there is only one retinal image. In Gilchrist's experiment on brightness perception, the illusion depended on participants perceiving the stimulus as a flat plane, and the appearance of flatness vanished when the stimulus was viewed binocularly.

The power of stereopsis as a cue to depth can be observed from the **random dot stereograms** developed by Bela Julesz (1971). These patterns are constructed by taking a grid (say 100×100) and randomly coloring each square white or black. In an identical grid, the investigator defines a square in the center (perhaps 10×10) and moves it to the right one space. Now there is a blank column on the left, which is filled in randomly with white or black squares. The result is two grids that are identical except that a square region in the center has been moved over in one grid. A simpler version is shown in Figure 2.8.

If you present the left grid to the left eye and the right grid to the right eye, there is a disparity at the center of the grid. The participant sees a remarkable image of a square in the center floating above the rest of the picture.

For stereopsis to work, you have to perceive that the same object is on each retina but in different places; that is, there must be retinal disparity. In the left part of Figure 2.9, it is clear that the snowman is in a different position on the left and right retinas. But in the right part of Figure 2.9, it's harder to tell which dot in the left retina goes with which dot in the right retina. How do you match up the dots?

This **correspondence problem** gets worse as objects in the visual field become harder to distinguish. The problem reaches peak difficulty in the random

Figure 2.8. *A 9×9 grid shows how a random dot stereogram is created. The two grids are identical with one exception. The central 3×3 section of the grid on the left (outlined in gray) has been moved one square over in the grid on the right. The resulting three blank squares are filled in randomly.*

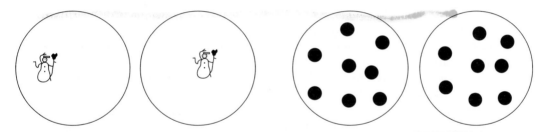

Figure 2.9. *The two circles at left indicate the left and right retinas as we look at a snowman in a field of snow. It is easy to find the snowman in each retina, and it is therefore easy to calculate how different the location of the snowman is on each retina. At right, we might be looking at pieces of coal in a field of snow. To calculate the retinal disparity, we need to know which piece of coal in the right retina matches which piece of coal in the left retina, but the pieces of coal are very similar, making this matchup (the correspondence problem) difficult.*

dot stereogram because the elements to be matched up are identical black dots. Furthermore, in the real world you would have other cues to distance to help you—for example, you would know that a person was far away because she appeared small. In the random dot stereogram there are no cues to depth except retinal disparity, and there are no monocular cues to form (no snowman, for example). Despite the difficulty of the correspondence problem, the visual system does solve it—random dot stereograms show depth, which was Julesz's point in devising them. Precisely how the visual system does this is not fully understood, however. A number of theories have been offered, but they are beyond the scope of this book. For our purposes, it is noteworthy that depth can be perceived in random dot stereograms because this fact indicates that the visual system is very good at using binocular disparity as a cue to distance even when no form information is available.

The cues that we've been discussing—accommodation, convergence, and stereopsis—are all based on properties of the visual system. We now turn to other cues to distance or size that are inherent in the environment.

CUES IN THE ENVIRONMENT. Experience is one thing that tells us the size of objects; this cue is called **familiar size**. When we see a car, we assume it is the size of a normal car, even if it is far away and therefore appears small. Similarly, people should be people-sized, houses house-sized, and so forth. We don't often see an object that we've never encountered before, which would give us no clue as to its likely size.

Bill Epstein (1965) showed the importance (and the limits) of familiar size as a cue to distance. He took photographs of a dime, a quarter, and a half-dollar and then printed each coin as the size of a quarter. Epstein mounted the photographs on black rods and placed them an equal distance from the observer. The room was darkened, and the photographs were illuminated with a spotlight. The participants had to view them monocularly. The participants thought the photographs were real coins, and because they appeared to be the same size, participants judged them to be different distances away (a real dime, for example, would have to be closer than the half-dollar for the coins to look the same size).

Thus familiar size can influence the perception of size and distance. But Epstein's results changed completely when people viewed the stimuli binocularly, seeing the coin photos as they actually were: equidistant and of equal size. Binocular viewing made a difference because participants could use stereopsis, and pitted against familiar size, stereopsis was the clear winner.

Familiar size solves the size–distance trade-off by providing information about size. Other cues in the environment concern distance and are often called **pictorial cues**. Many of these cues are used in a well-known painting by Jean-François Millet, *The Gleaners*, shown in Photo 2.2. One such cue is **occlusion**. An object that is in front of another will partly overlap it. In the painting, the image of the central figure overlaps the figure on the left. That is possible only if she is in front of the figure on the left. Occlusion is a useful cue even with unfamiliar figures because the perceptual system assumes that figures usually are closed; that is, if you see part of an object, the rest of it is still there, occluded by the other object.

The Gleaners provides another cue to distance called **texture gradient**. In the foreground, individual stalks of cut wheat are visible, but higher in the picture plane, they are not. In the real world we can make out more detail when things are nearby, so objects in the lower part of the picture look closer.

Photo 2.2. *Jean-François Millet's painting* The Gleaners *uses many pictorial depth cues.*

It is possible, of course, that the background is not farther away, and there happen to be no individual stalks of wheat in those regions; but again, the visual system assumes that surfaces (in this case, the surface of the field) are uniform, so the lack of detail higher in the picture plane is interpreted as indicating distance.

This picture also gives some sense of **linear perspective**. Lines that are parallel in three-dimensional space converge in two-dimensional space if you extend them far enough; the farther the distance, the closer they are to converging. For example, the sides of a road appear to get closer together in the distance, as shown at the left in Figure 2.10. This is less obvious from our everyday experience but equally true of parallel lines in three dimensions, as shown at the right in Figure 2.10.

There is subtle linear perspective in *The Gleaners* as well. You can see some lines or shadows on the field to the left of the leftmost figure and to the right of the rightmost figure. As in Figure 2.10, these lines converge toward a vanishing point on the horizon.

The **relative height** of objects also is a cue to distance. The rightmost figure in the painting appears closer than the others not because she occludes anyone but because she is lower in the visual field. To her right is a figure on horseback. This figure is very high in the visual field, indicating great distance, which is reinforced by the very small size. This is not a microscopic horse hovering over her shoulder.

The final distance cue used in the painting is **atmospheric perspective**. Objects in the distance look indistinct and often have a hazy, bluish appearance. The air is full of dust and water particles that scatter light, so if you view a distant object, more of the light reflected from the object is scattered by the time it hits your eye. The image of these distant objects is blurred because much of the light has been scattered.

Why are there so many cues to distance? The reason is that they are useful for objects at different distances. It's true that size and distance trade off,

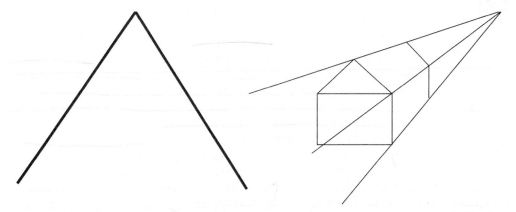

Figure 2.10. *Linear perspective. At left, two parallel lines in a plane (the sides of a road) converge in the far distance. At right, the three parallel sides of a house converge in the distance.*

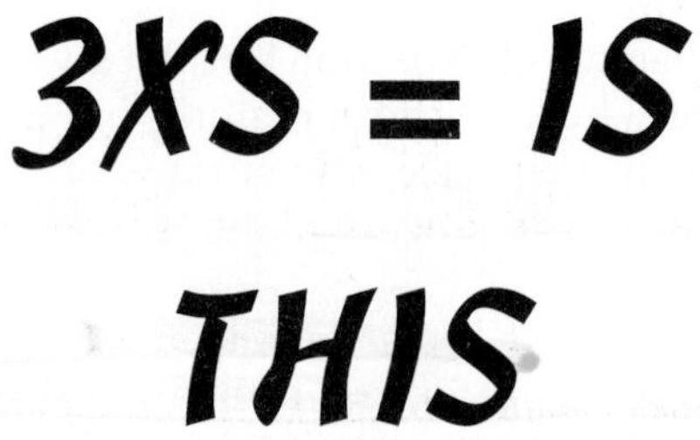

3XS = IS

THIS

Figure 2.11. *Note that the final two characters are identical in the first line and the second line, but they are interpreted differently because of the surrounding context.*

but distance is usually discernible from one of these cues, and knowing distance helps us decide on size.

Top-Down Influences in Vision

We've seen that visual processing is complicated because the two-dimensional image on the retina underspecifies what the three-dimensional world looks like. You can't tell what the shape of an object is from the retinal projection because shape and orientation trade off; you can't tell the size or distance of an object because these two factors trade off; and you can't tell whether an object is white, gray, or black because differences in luminance could result from shading, lighting, or shadows. Yet all these problems can be solved if you're willing to make a few assumptions, taking advantage of cues in the environment.

So far in our discussion, information seems to flow in one direction. This **bottom-up processing** begins with raw, unprocessed sensory information and builds toward more conceptual representations. But bottom-up processing can't handle all of vision alone.

For example, how can the mind arrive at different interpretations of the last two characters in each line of Figure 2.11? This demonstration seems to argue for **top-down processing** in which conceptual knowledge influences the processing or interpretation of lower-level perceptual processes. If you're reading the second line in the figure, the conceptual knowledge that you are reading letters leads you to interpret the ambiguous characters as the letters that complete the word "THIS."

Even with limited perceptual information, you can still figure out what something is if you have good conceptual information. For example, suppose I tell you that Figure 2.12 shows some lowercase letters. The figure doesn't show complete letters; it just tells you whether a letter goes below the line you're writing on (*g, y, j*), above the line (*h, l, k*), or within the line (*e, a, s*). Can you identify the four-word phrase written in this impoverished alphabet?

Now suppose I give you some conceptual information: the phrase is the title of a classic movie. Most people find that the conceptual information makes an otherwise impossible perceptual task possible. With good conceptual information, you can make up for the impoverished perceptual information. But is this really changing the way you see the stimulus? Not really. It's affecting your guesses about what the stimulus is supposed to represent. So the question is whether people actually use conceptual information when

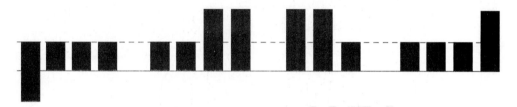

Figure 2.12. *This four-word phrase doesn't depict details of letters; for each letter it shows only whether the letter goes above or below the line. Without any conceptual information, it's hard to know what is spelled; with conceptual information, top-down processing helps you identify what is spelled.*

they see. (The movie, by the way, is *Gone With the Wind*.) It turns out that people do use conceptual information when they see, up to a point.

In a classic experiment showing the effects of conceptual information on vision, Stephen Palmer presented participants with complex scenes. Participants were given 2 s to look at the scene—plenty of time to figure out that it was a kitchen, for example. Next, one of three objects was flashed within the scene very briefly: either a contextually appropriate object (bread), a similarly shaped contextually inappropriate object (a mailbox), or an object that didn't fit the context and wasn't shaped like the target object. The objects were flashed for just 65 ms. Participants correctly identified the contextually appropriate object 80% of the time but were right only 40% of the time for the other objects. Similar effects have been demonstrated by Irving Biederman (1981).

Of course, you would recognize the mailbox eventually, even when it is out of context. However, there are some instances in which you can't identify an object without the context. For example, the third shape from the right at the bottom of Figure 2.13 could be the letter *C*, a hook, or a sideways hill. There's really no telling. Once it is seen in context, as at the top of the figure, it is perfectly recognizable, but in isolation none of the parts is identifiable.

We've been assuming that processing is mostly bottom-up. In that case, you would look at Figure 2.13 and identify the nose, then the ear, then the eye, and so on, and finally put all the pieces together and figure out that it's a face. But we've just said that you can't figure out that an item is a nose (or an ear, or whatever) until you know that it's part of a face. Palmer called this situation the **parsing paradox**. Parsing means figuring out what the pieces of a larger whole are. Thus the parsing paradox is the apparent impossibility of identifying the face in Figure 2.13 until you know it has a nose, a mouth, and so on. But you can't identify the nose, mouth, and so on, until you know it's a face.

Palmer suggested that the resolution to the parsing paradox is that we do both top-down and bottom-up processing simultaneously and each type of processing helps the other, as shown in Figure 2.14.

There is obviously a role for top-down processes in visual perception; vision operates more quickly when contextually consistent information is perceived,

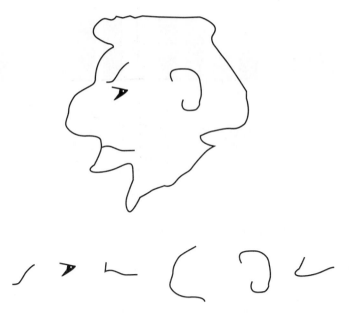

Figure 2.13. *This figure is easy to recognize when the parts are seen together (in a sensible spatial arrangement) even though it is composed of parts that are difficult to recognize alone.*

and ambiguous stimuli are perceived in a way that is consistent with context. But top-down processes must take a back seat to bottom-up processes. When something truly unusual appears in the environment (say, a chimp typing at a computer), you may be slower to perceive it because it is out of context, but you do perceive it.

An Alternative: The Ecological Approach

A second point of view on the whole problem of vision contends that the model posed at the beginning of the chapter is flat-out wrong. (I heard you sigh.) Up until now we have been discussing what is often called the **computational approach**, which assumes that the information in the environment is impoverished—all that the retina has to work with is a series of lines—and therefore the visual system must do a great deal of computing to recover the three-dimensional shapes and movements of the environment.

J. J. Gibson (1979) is considered the founder of the **ecological approach** to visual perception. Gibson thought vision looks so hard because psychologists have done a terrible job of describing the environment. According to Gibson, the environment contains a variety of cues that specify what is out in the world, but psychologists act as though the environment were composed of nothing but lines. If the retina had no information besides lines, it would be extremely challenging to get an accurate representation of what's in the world. Gibson believed that there is much more information in the world that we can

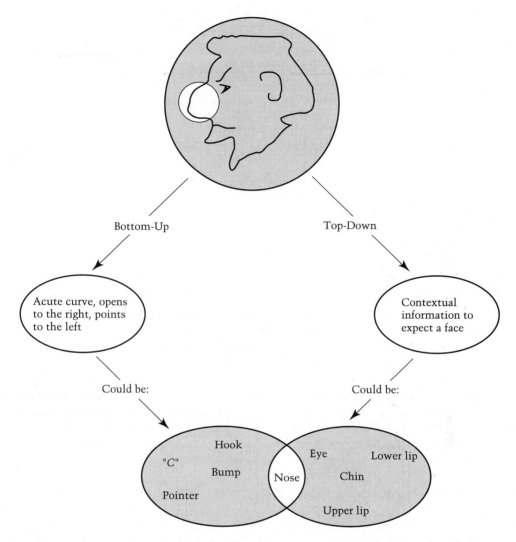

Figure 2.14. *We can use top-down and bottom-up processing simultaneously to identify objects.*

take advantage of. The visual system need not perform elaborate computations because the information in the visual environment is quite rich. Let's go through two examples of these sorts of information sources.

Object Size.   If I see an unfamiliar object (or a familiar object that can take many different sizes, such as a tree), how can I determine its size?

The approach we've been using up until now would say that because it's an unfamiliar object I'd have to first figure out about how far away it is. I could do that from stereopsis. Then I'd note how big the retinal image is (that is, how big it looks) and work back to how big the actual object is, based on its distance.

Other researchers pointed out that better size information was already in the environment (Mark, 1987; Rogers, 1996; Warren, 1984). The horizon line intersects with an object at the **eyeheight** of the observer (at the height of the observer's eyes). Figure 2.15 shows the gray outline of an observer's head—let's say mine. I'm about 6 ft tall, so my eyeheight is around 5 ft 6 in. Therefore, the horizon intersects with the object at 5 ft 6 in. Notice that the horizon intersects with the telephone poles a little below the middle of the pole; the spot where the horizon intersects the pole is 5 ft 6 in (the eyeheight of the observer). Therefore, the pole is a little more than twice 5 ft 6 in, or around 12 ft tall. Notice that even though the poles get smaller and smaller from our perspective, the ratio of the amount of each pole that is above the horizon to the amount below the horizon stays the same. The horizon always intersects the pole a little less than halfway up the pole because each pole is the same size.

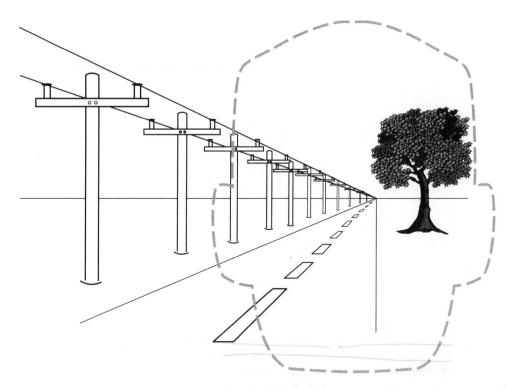

Figure 2.15.   *An example of how eyeheight provides information about object size. Objects meet the horizon at the eyeheight of the observer (outlined in gray). If the observer's eyeheight is 5 ft from the ground, the horizon intersects the telephone pole at 5 ft. The horizon intersects a little less than halfway up the pole, so the pole is somewhat more than 10 ft tall. Adapted from* The Ecological Approach to Visual Perception, *by J. J. Gibson et al., 1979, Boston: Houghton Mifflin, Fig. 9.6, p. 165.*

There is evidence that people use this eyeheight metric. Maryjane Wraga (1999a, 1999b) showed people different-sized steps, and they were to judge the height of each step relative to a standard rod (was the step taller or shorter than the rod?). The tricky part of the experiment was how she manipulated eyeheight. The participants viewed the steps from another room through a small window. On some of the trials, the floor of this other room was about 6.5 in higher than the floor on which they were standing. This difference is small enough that participants didn't notice anything unusual about the floor in the other room. Still, participants judge their eyeheight relative to where they think the floor is, so the false floor effectively changes their eyeheight. (The manner in which Wraga and others hypothesized the eyeheight information is used actually is more complicated than this, but the principle is the same.) The results showed that the false floor did affect size judgments: participants judged steps to be about an inch shorter when the floor was raised.

Eyeheight information is used in the entertainment industry. Things look bigger when your eyeheight is made artificially lower. You might note this next time you are at the movies. A director who wants to make an actor look taller or more impressive will film that actor with the camera held not at eye level, but at perhaps waist level, effectively lowering the eyeheight of the moviegoer and thereby making the subject seem taller (see Photo 2.3).

Photo 2.3. *The Terminator is shot with the camera low to the ground. We assume that the camera is at our eyeheight, so the Terminator appears taller and more intimidating.*

DISTANCE FOR NAVIGATION.   Suppose you're playing left field in a baseball game and someone hits a ball your way. How do you get to the right position to catch it? Well, may be you calculate the trajectory of the ball, judge where it is going to land, and run to that spot. That would take a fair amount of calculation. But it turns out that a simple cue in the environment can be used instead.

Michael McBeath, Dennis Shaffer, and Mary Kaiser (1995) provided evidence that people actually catch a fly ball by running so that the trajectory of the ball looks like a straight line. Imagine a two-dimensional picture in which the baseball goes upward and to the left. If you run in a direction that makes the ball appear to travel in a straight line, you will go directly to the spot where the ball will land. The details of the geometry are complex, but the basic point is quite simple. It's a beautiful example of the ecological approach.

The ecological approach holds that most vision researchers make the problem of visual perception more difficult than it actually is. Once we have fully described all the rich sources of information available in the environment, they argue, many of the problems of visual perception disappear. Are they right?

To a point, I think the answer must be yes. Ecological psychologists have made this point in the experiments described above, and in others. Still, it is not difficult to find common ground between the two perspectives; even the most determined ecological researchers admit that the perceptual system must do some processing on the information in the environment, and even the most determined computational researchers admit that the environment may contain subtle sources of information that the visual system can use. Thus, the difference between the perspectives may best be thought of as one of emphasis.

Stand-on-One-Foot Questions

4. *Can you use your book and the writing on the cover to demonstrate a frame-of-reference effect, in the same way we showed one with the diamond and the rectangle around it?*

5. *What assumptions does the visual system make about luminance?*

6. *Why are random dot stereograms interesting?*

7. *Summarize the differences between the computational and the ecological points of view.*

Questions That Require Two Feet

8. *From a hill overlooking San Francisco on a brilliantly clear day, the city looks like a small model seen at about 30 ft rather than a full-size city seen at a distance. Why?*

> *9. Can you think of a way to use what you know about perceived size and eyeheight to improve your relationship with a young child?*

WHAT IS VISUAL PERCEPTION FOR?

> ➤ *Preview* Vision helps you know what objects are in the world and helps you navigate (move around). For objects to be recognized, there must be some representation in memory of what they look like. But an object such as a car looks very different from the front, back, and side. Does that mean you need three mental representations to be sure you can recognize it from each perspective? One group of theories holds that you have a single mental representation of an object that is suitable from any angle. Another group of theories proposes that you keep several representations of each object in memory. We discuss the merits of each of these ideas. We also discuss navigation and focus on the difference between conscious visual perception and visual perception that supports navigation. One set of visual processes supports our conscious perception of where things are and what objects are out in the world. Another set of processes, privileged to the motor system, help you move, but you can't get conscious access to their contents.

Attributes of objects, such as size, shape, and distance, are not the end of perceptual processing because only occasionally do we want information about a single attribute. More often, we combine attributes in the visual field to achieve one of two goals: we want to know the identity of objects around us, and we want to know their locations. Knowing an object's identity helps us know what to do to it. If it's an apple, eat it; if it's a stapler, squeeze it; if it's a book of "Shoe" comic strips, ignore it. Knowing an object's location is helpful so that you will know where it is relative to you, where the best place to grasp it is, whether there are obstacles in the way should you decide to grasp it, and so on.

One part of the perceptual system is responsible for figuring out what an object is. Another is responsible for figuring out properties of the object (size, orientation, and so on) that are important for interacting with it. Object identity has been much more thoroughly studied, so we can say more about how that might work. Only recently was it concluded that the visual action system is separate from the object identity system; most of our discussion focuses on how researchers drew that conclusion.

Identifying Objects

We have discussed how the visual system determines the attributes of objects (their distance, size, and brightness). But how does it identify what those objects are? Shape is the most obvious characteristic we use to identify objects—for example, a banana is easy to recognize because of its shape—but other properties can be helpful, too. For example, you can identify the handle on a chest of drawers by its location, even if it has a very unusual shape. A piece of cheese and a brick may have similar shapes, but they are distinguishable based on their color and texture. Thus, the first thing we should realize is that many cues contribute to visual object recognition. Most researchers have focused on shape, however, probably because it is the most reliable cue to object identity.

The core question of object identification is this: What does the memory representation that supports object identification look like? Suppose you recognize that an animal is a cat. Some information in memory must enable you to identify that animal. You have to have some information stored about what cats look like. What kind of information is it?

There are two families of answers to this question. First, the representation in memory could be specific to your viewpoint; you store how the object looks to you, not its actual structure. This is called a **viewer-centered representation** because the representation of the object depends on how the viewer sees it. The second family of theories claims that you store how the object looks independent of any particular viewpoint. In **object-centered representation** the locations of the object's parts are defined relative to the object itself, not relative to the viewer. A viewer-centered representation of an airplane might contain the information that its nose is to the left of its tail. That representation won't work, however, if the plane is turned around or if the viewer is looking at the plane from the front. The object-centered representation locates an object's parts relative to its other parts; thus, it would contain the information that the plane's nose is attached to the fuselage.

For both families of theories, a key problem is dealing with rotated objects. You never know in what orientation you'll see a cat; it might be running, climbing a tree, or curled up by a fire. Think of what an odd profile a cat has when it is curled up by a fire. According to object-centered theories, the representation in memory can't be specific to one viewpoint because an object can appear in different orientations. This claim seems self-evident, yet the viewer-centered theories have a response, as we'll see.

OLDER THEORIES.   An early viewer-centered theory of object recognition was the **template** theory, which proposed that we recognize an object by comparing its retinal image to a representation of the object in memory. Basically, this theory held that we store pictures of what objects are supposed to look like, with labels attached, and then compare images with all these templates. If a template matches what we see, we have identified the object. There are many problems with this model. The easiest one to appreciate is depicted in Figure 2.16.

As the figure shows, if the armadillo turned a bit, it wouldn't match the template, so you'd need another template to match that view of the armadillo. Such a system would require an enormous number of templates. The truth is that no one ever took the template-matching idea very seriously, but it remains popular as a whipping boy, especially in cognitive psychology textbooks.

Figure 2.16. *In the top figure, the observer recognizes the armadillo because it matches his armadillo template. If the same armadillo is turned 180 degrees, the observer cannot identify it because it no longer matches the template.*

Template matching does have some practical uses, however. Vending machines use template matching to evaluate paper money. A bill must be inserted in the machine at a particular orientation so that the machine can identify it.

Feature-matching theories put forward in response to the problems of template-matching theories still used a viewer-centered representation, but they avoided many of the problems of template theories by proposing **critical features** of stimuli. For example, the letter *T* could be defined as having two features: a horizontal line and a vertical line. Changing the size or color of the letter won't change its critical features. You can think of a set of critical features as being a set of lines and curves out of which you could create letters, as shown in Figure 2.17.

Feature-matching theories have several important advantages over template theories. First, in our example, letters can still be recognized even after different transformations. For example, all uppercase *A*s share the same set of critical features. Although they may vary in size, and some have extra, non-critical features such as serifs, most capital *A*s have two diagonal lines and one

	Vertical lines	Horizontal lines	Oblique lines	Right angles	Acute angles	Continuous curves	Discontinuous curves
A		1	2		3		
B	1	3		4			2
C							1
D	1	2		2			1
E	1	3		4			
F	1	2		3			
G	1	1		1			1
H	2	1		4			
I	1	2		4			
J	1						1
K	1		2	1	2		
L	1	1		1			
M	2		2		3		
N	2		1		2		
O						1	
P	1	2		3			1
Q			1		2	1	
R	1	2	1	3			1
S							2
T	1	1		2			
U	2						1
V			2		1		
W			4		3		
X			2		2		
Y	1		2		1		
Z		2	1		2		

Figure 2.17. *The top row labels the features of letters in the alphabet. Each letter can be described according to the number of each feature it contains. From* Human Information Process: An Introduction to Psychology, *by P. H. Lindsay and D. A. Norman, 1977, New York: Academic Press, Table 7.1, p. 264.*

horizontal line. Feature theories also appear to be consistent with known neurophysiology. David Hubel and Torsten Wiesel won a Nobel prize for their groundbreaking work showing that brain cells in visual cortex seemed to respond to lines at different orientations. These cells seemed to be acting as feature detectors, bolstering the feature theory. (See Hubel & Wiesel, 1979, for a review.)

There are problems with feature-matching, however. For example, a sideways letter *R* is not hard for people to identify, although it has none of the critical features of an upright *R*. Furthermore, it is hard to see how feature theories can account for the perception of natural objects. Researchers built feature theories that could recognize letters of the alphabet. It's fairly obvious what the features of a letter are, but what are the features of a dog? Can you develop a theory of how a dog could be "broken down" into features?[1]

OBJECT-CENTERED THEORIES.   Feature-matching theories failed because they could not recognize rotated letters (and presumably other rotated objects) and because there was no obvious way in which they could be extended to natural objects. The solutions to these problems were to make the representations object-centered rather than viewer-centered and to show that natural objects can be broken down into features.

The object-centered answer to recognizing a sideways *R*, which is rotated relative to the viewer, notes that the parts of the *R* are not rotated relative to one another. If your frame of reference is the object, then all parts are where they are supposed to be relative to one another. Thus, when you are looking at a natural object like a dog, you shouldn't look for a head at the top and feet at the bottom. You should look for a head connected to a neck, feet connected to legs, a tail connected to the back, and so on. The relationships between the parts do not change depending on whether the dog is facing left or right, running, or curled up.

But using this representation of parts relative to each other relies on your being able to recognize the parts themselves. How do you do that? How do you "decompose" a dog into parts?

Donald Hoffman and Whitman Richards (1984) pointed out that the perceptual principle of **good continuation**, which was first noted in the 1930s, could be applicable to this problem. The visual system interprets lines as continuing along the path they have been following rather than abruptly changing direction, as illustrated in the left panel of Figure 2.18. You can see that good continuation is a variant of the likelihood principle. It's much more likely that these are two crossed lines (for which there are an infinite number of ways that you would get a crossing similar to this one) than that the figure represents two acute angles, just touching (for which there are few ways to get a figure like this one).

Hoffman and Richards pointed out that this principle can be applied to three-dimensional objects. In the right panel of Figure 2.18, it is unlikely that a single object would make a radical turn at the point marked by the arrow. Instead, it is more likely that this radical turn is caused by the junction of two separate parts. The authors speculated that part boundaries are signaled by edges that subtend convex angles. Indeed, if you ask participants to mark the boundary of two parts, they select the point of maximum curvature. The objects at the right in Figure 2.18 are simple cylinders, but the principle works equally well with a dog's leg and body.

---

[1]You may wonder why researchers based their theories on letters of the alphabet. There were good reasons for doing this. First, people wanted to make their theories comparable to one another. If my theory recognizes letters and yours recognizes faces, how can we compare the theories to see which one works better? Letters gave everyone a standard stimulus set to work with. Second, letter recognition was an important applied problem. There are obvious uses to devising a machine that can recognize letters of different fonts and sizes.

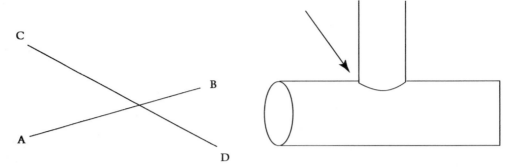

Figure 2.18. *The principle of good continuation is illustrated at left. The visual system sees this figure as two overlapping lines, AB and CD, rather than two angles, AC and BD. The figure on the right shows how good continuation can be used to divide objects into parts. The sudden discontinuity in the edge of the object (indicated by the arrow) makes for poor continuation. Therefore, this location is seen as the place where two parts of the object are joined.*

Thus we may be able to rescue a feature-matching theory. We can solve the rotation problem if we make the representation object-centered instead of viewer-centered, and we can make the representation a collection of parts with their positions defined relative to one another rather than relative to our point of view. Furthermore, it looks as though we can decompose even natural objects such as dogs into component parts.

Several feature theories in this spirit have been offered. An influential one was proposed by Irving Biederman (1987), who argued that object recognition is supported by a set of 36 shapes he called geons (simple shapes that look like bricks, cylinders, and so on) that operate like letters of the alphabet. Complex objects can be built from them, as shown in the left column of Figure 2.19.

A strength of Biederman's theory is that geons are easy to distinguish from one another. For example, from most viewing angles the geon called a brick has three parallel edges and three outer arrow intersections, and a cylinder has two parallel edges, two curved edges, and two line intersections that look like a Y.

Biederman showed participants pictures of objects constructed from geons, similar to those in Figure 2.19. The pictures were degraded in one of two ways. In each case he deleted the same total length of line segments. In the center column the intersections have been left intact, and in the right column many of the intersections have been removed or changed—for example, in some cases one line has been removed so that an intersection could be interpreted as a different type. Biederman showed participants the incomplete drawings for varying amounts of time (as short as 100 ms or as long as 5 s) and asked them to name the objects depicted. If the vertices were present, people were pretty good at this task. They named 90% of the pictures they could see for 750 ms. With the vertices removed, however, participants only got 30% correct even if they saw the pictures for 5 s. These data support Biederman's

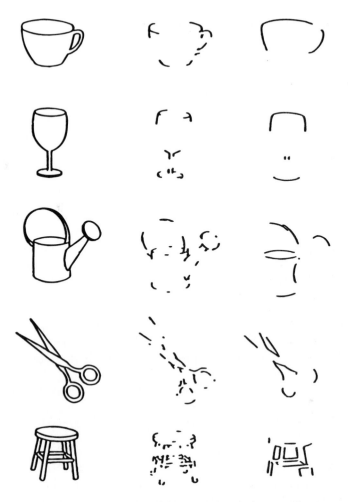

Figure 2.19. *Examples of common objects that can be constructed with the geons proposed in Biederman's theory. The center and right columns show two ways of decomposing the figures: by either retaining line vertices (center) or omitting them (right). In accordance with Biederman's theory, it is easier to identify objects when the vertices are still present. From "Recognition-by-Components: A Theory of Human Image Understanding," by I. Biederman, 1987, Psychological Review, 94(2), Fig. 16, p.135.*

contention that line intersections are crucial for correctly interpreting geometric solids. These geometric solids, according to Biederman, are the building blocks of visual object identification.

Although the Biederman model is appealing, not all evidence supports it. An object like a loaf of bread doesn't have obvious parts, but it does not look like a geon. Other common objects such as shoes have parts, but the parts don't look like any of the geons. The theory cannot readily account for the recognition of such objects.

VIEWER-CENTERED THEORIES.   It seems that object-centered theories would almost have to be right. If the representation of an object is based on your location, you would need a different representation each time you or the object moved.

Alternatively, you could mentally rotate the image of an object to fit your mental representation. Thus a sideways *R* rotated to its normal orientation would match your viewer-centered memory representation of an *R*. The problem with this approach is that it assumes you know how to transform the object so that it matches the representation in memory. Should you rotate it clockwise or counterclockwise? Should you twirl it toward or away from you? Don't you need to know what you are looking for before you know how to transform it? But if you know what you're looking for, you've already identified it and there is no need to rotate it. There are technical solutions to these problems (Ullman & Basri, 1991) but they are beyond the scope of this book.

Another, better solution appears to be a compromise: we store multiple viewer-centered representations of objects (perhaps about 40) and then apply some transformations. There is evidence supporting this multiple-views theory. If you have seen an object from only one point of view, you will have only one representation of that object. So what do you do if you see it from a different point of view? As we said, you rotate your image of the object until it matches the representation. That process of rotating the object takes time. Therefore, if you present the letter *R* rotated 90 degrees from its typical orientation, it should take longer to recognize than if you present *R* in its typical orientation. Note that according to the viewer-independent theory, the orientation of the object shouldn't matter.

Numerous experiments have shown that orientation matters a great deal. Some of the most influential experiments were conducted by Roger Shepard and Lynn Cooper (summarized in Shepard & Cooper, 1986). They often used letters of the alphabet as stimuli; participants had to judge whether the letter was mirror-reversed or not, and the experimenters varied how much the stimulus was rotated from upright.

The more the object has been rotated, the longer a viewer takes to recognize it. That finding makes it sound as if people imagine the object rotating in space until it is upright, whereupon they can recognize it. How do you know which way and how far to rotate a letter so that it is upright? Shepard and Cooper argued that you can identify the letter even when it is rotated—that's how you figure out where the top of the letter is—then you rotate it so that it is upright, and then you can figure out whether the letter is mirror-reversed. So they were arguing that memory representation is object centered; the orientation of the letter doesn't matter when you're trying to identify it.

But letters may not be ideal stimuli for this sort of experiment because there's no telling how many letters people have seen at different angles. What would happen if you used unfamiliar stimuli instead of letters? What would happen if you let people see just one orientation of the stimulus? How about several orientations? The answer is that people seem to form a representation for each of the orientations with which they have a lot of experience. Michael Tarr (1995) showed participants slides of objects made out of cubes; the objects could look quite different from one viewpoint or another, as shown in Figure 2.20.

Tarr trained participants to recognize different objects that were always presented from the same point of view. Later he presented the objects from a novel point of view to see whether participants could recognize them. They could, but the more an object was rotated from the view in which they had seen it during training, the longer participants took to recognize it. It was as if participants' memory of what the object looked like was rather two-dimensional—they knew what the object looked like from one point of view—and identifying the object from another point of view required mentally rotating the stimulus. In another experiment, Tarr presented objects from several points of view during training. In that case, the time it took people to recognize the object was consistent with their imagining the object rotating to the nearest position they had seen during training.

Does this mean that the multiple-view researchers are returning to a template theory in which a nearly infinite number of templates is needed to

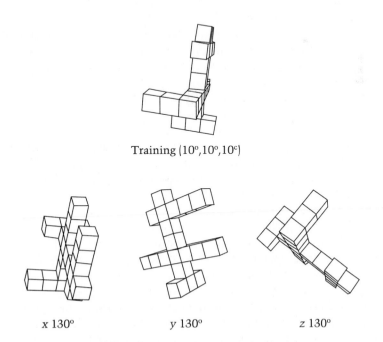

Training (10°, 10°, 10°)

x 130°   y 130°   z 130°

Figure 2.20. *Stimuli of the sort used in Tarr's (1995) experiment. The top figure shows a stimulus participants might see at training; the bottom figures show three rotations of this figure in three different planes.*

recognize objects as they rotate through minute angles? Clearly not. Multiple-view theories acknowledge that some process must be available to regularize the image of the object, but that problem becomes much easier to deal with if several views of a complex object may be stored; its appearance will never be too far from one of the stored images.

So which type of theory is correct: decomposition in parts (object centered) or viewer centered? A number of researchers have suggested that the mind may use two methods of recognition, one from each basic approach (Cooper, Schachter, Ballesteros, & Moore, 1992; Farah, 1990; Jolicoeur, 1990; Tarr & Pinker, 1990) and there is some evidence that there are two such separate processes in the brain (Burgund & Marsolek, 2000). The decomposition-into-parts approach may work well to distinguish between a car and a truck, for example, but it can't make finer-grained distinctions between a Ford and a Chrysler. The decomposition-into-parts idea seems to work well for objects that have some telltale geons that make it easy to identify the object no matter what the orientation. The multiple-view approach seems to retain more information about details and thus may be effective for recognizing objects that don't have telltale parts and for distinguishing between closely related objects such as different varieties of cars.

Navigation

The second function of vision is to help us move around in the world. When you reach out to grab a coffee cup, how do you know where the cup is? If you're like me, your intuition is that you are conscious of the cup's location, and you guide your hand to that location. Strangely enough, the evidence indicates that your conscious awareness of the cup's location is not important in guiding your hand. There is another visual system of which you are unconscious that operates in parallel with the conscious one, and that drives movements.

A key finding came from visual researchers examining the primate brain. Leslie Ungerleider and Mortimer Mishkin (1982) proposed that there are two visual pathways in the brain. One pathway figures out what objects are, and the other figures out where objects are. They proposed this hypothesis after studying brain anatomy and tested it in monkeys. They had two tests: one for object identity and one for object location. The object identity test is called nonmatching to sample. Here's what happens. A sliding door rises, and the monkey sees an object. The monkey knocks the object aside to find a reward such as a peanut. Then the door goes down and comes back up, and the monkey sees two objects: the one it just saw and a new object. If the monkey knocks aside the new object, it will find another peanut reward. If it knocks aside the object it just saw, it gets nothing. That's how the task got its name; the first object is the sample, and the monkey is supposed to pick the nonmatching object. Note that the monkey doesn't need to know anything about object location to perform the task well; all it needs to do is recognize the object it just saw.

The object location task is called the landmark task. In this task, the monkey sees two trapdoors. Under each trapdoor is a well containing either a peanut reward or nothing. A landmark (usually a cylinder) lies closer to one trapdoor than the other, and the monkey should simply choose the trapdoor closer to the cylinder. Thus for this task object identity is irrelevant; the monkey merely needs to know where in space the trapdoors and the cylinder are.

Ungerleider and Mishkin trained some monkeys until they were very good at each task. Next, the researchers lesioned (cut out) part of the monkeys' brains. One group of monkeys had part of the temporal lobe removed (that's near the side and toward the bottom of the brain), and the other group had part of the parietal lobe removed (that's near the back and toward the top). The results were dramatic. The group with the temporal lobe lesion performed well on the landmark task but could no longer succeed at nonmatching to sample. The group with the parietal lesion showed just the opposite pattern of results. Ungerleider and Mishkin interpreted their results as showing that there are two streams of processing in the visual system: a "what" stream that identifies objects and a "where" stream that determines where objects are located. This model can be called the **what/where hypothesis**.

This result was very influential in vision research, but there have always been one or two oddities in this interpretation. For example, how can all the spatial information be separate from the processes that identify objects? Don't you need to know where an object's parts are in order to identify it?

Mishkin and Ungerleider's findings have been reinterpreted in an interesting and convincing way. Melvyn Goodale and David Milner (1992) suggested that it is better to think of them as "what" and "how" streams (which we'll call the **what/how hypothesis**). They argue that spatial information is present in both streams, but its function differs. The "what" stream in the temporal lobe identifies objects and is associated with consciousness. The end product of this processing stream is the conscious perception of where objects are, what they are, their colors, and so on. The "how" stream handles information that helps us move. Thus the "how" stream knows the shape and location of objects so that we can grasp them effectively and reach to the right spot. But all of this knowledge is unconscious. Most of the time there would be no way of knowing that there are two such visual streams because they are in agreement. But Angela Haffenden and Melvyn Goodale (1998) have shown that under some circumstances researchers can fool one system and not the other.

Consider the visual illusion shown in Figure 2.21, which you've probably seen before. When asked to compare the sizes of the circles in the center of the figures at the left and right, most people say that the one on the left appears larger, although both circles are actually the same size. We might propose that this illusion affects the "what" system because it is associated with consciousness. Is the "how" system fooled? The answer is no. Haffenden and Goodale conducted a similar experiment with disks like poker chips, asking participants to judge the size of the center circle by showing its size using their index fingers and thumbs. The experimenters attached infrared light–emitting diodes (IREDs) to each participant's wrist, index finger, and thumb, and a series of

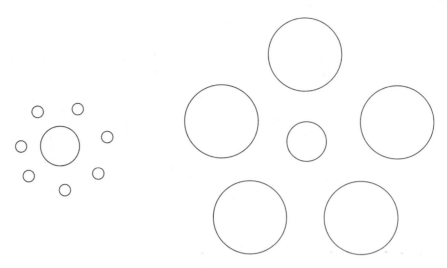

Figure 2.21.   *In this familiar visual illusion, the center circle at the left appears bigger than the center circle at the right. This illusion applies only to conscious visual perception, however. Visual perception that is used to drive motor behavior (such as reaching) is not susceptible to the illusion.*

cameras measured how far apart the finger and thumb were. As expected, people estimated the circle on the left to be bigger. However, when the experimenters asked participants to pick up the poker chips on each side, the illusion didn't hold. A person reaching for an object such as a poker chip prepares the index finger and thumb to grasp the object while the arm is moving into position. The bigger the object, the further apart the index finger and thumb will be; this is called grip size. The researchers found that participants' grip size didn't differ for the left and right circles, even though the circle on the left appeared bigger. This result indicates that the conscious "what" system (which judges how big the objects look) is susceptible to this illusion, but the unconscious "how" system (which supports reaching) is not susceptible to it. This illusion and similar ones have been actively researched in the last few years (see Aglioti, DeSouza, & Goodale, 1995; Bartelt & Darling, 2002; Bridgeman, Gemmer, Forsman, & Huemer, 2000; Franz, Gegenfürtner, Bülthoff, & Fahle, 2000; Gentilucci, Chieffi, Daprati, Saetti, & Toni, 1996; Haffenden & Goodale, 2000; Pavani, Boscagli, Benvenuti, Rabuffetti & Farnè, 1999; Vishton, Rea, Cutting, & Nuñez, 1999). There is some contention over whether these illusions affect the "what" system but not the "how" system, but at this point the evidence favors this interpretation.

Here's another example of the difference between the "what" and "how" systems. What was the steepest hill you've ever driven on? How steep was it, in terms of degrees? (A flat road is 0 degrees, and a vertical cliff would be 90 degrees.) Most people guess that the steepest hill they've ever seen might be 45 or 50 degrees. In fact, the steepest street in San Francisco, a city renowned for its steep hills, is only 18.5 degrees; in my home state of Virginia, no public

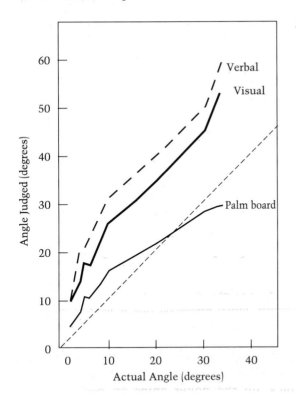

Figure 2.22. *Graph showing judgment of the steepness of nine hills compared with the actual steepness. Perfectly accurate judgments would fall on the dotted lines. When participants used the palm board to estimate the hills' steepness they were much more accurate than when they gave verbal estimates or adjusted a picture of a hill visually.*

street can have a hill steeper than 9 degrees, by law. People overestimate steepness—not just in their memories but even when they are right in front of the hill. Furthermore, if you hand someone a pair of calipers to be set at the angle of the hill, the person will create an angle very similar to the angle given as a verbal estimate (Proffitt, Bhalla, Gossweiler, & Midgett, 1995).

If you misperceive a slope to be much steeper than it really is, why don't you fall down when you try to climb it? The conscious "what" system generates the perception that results in the overestimation of the steepness of the hill, but the "how" system generates the spatial information used for stepping. Denny Proffitt and his colleagues (1995) tested this hypothesis by having 300 people make judgments about the steepness of nine different hills on the campus of the University of Virginia. Participants gave two estimates of the hills' steepness. They judged the steepness of each hill verbally and by adjusting a little picture to make it as steep as the hill in front of them. By both of these measures, participants overestimated the steepness of the hills, as shown in Figure 2.22. They also made a judgment via the unconscious "how" system by placing their palms flat on a small board mounted on a tripod and adjusting it (without looking at it) so that it was parallel to the hill in front of them. The researchers found that participants' estimates of the hill by the palm board measure were quite accurate and interpreted this result as showing that the "how" system can judge the actual angle of the hill.

BOX 2–2 Functional Imaging Evidence Bearing on the Representation of Space in the Temporal Lobe

We have discussed two conceptions of the separate visual streams: what/where and what/how. Although both propose that the ventral stream in the temporal lobe is the "what" stream, meaning that it is concerned with object identity, they differ in what they propose the "what" stream calculates. Ungerleider and Mishkin (1982) downplayed the role of spatial information in the ventral stream because that was the province of the dorsal stream in the parietal lobe. Goodale and Milner (1992) argued that there is spatial information in both streams, but they are put to different uses. In the ventral stream spatial information provides explicit information about the layout of objects in space, whereas in the dorsal stream spatial information tells us about the objects' positions in service of acting on those objects.

Neuroimaging data from Russell Epstein and Nancy Kanwisher (1998) is relevant to this debate. They report that the ventral stream contains an area that is maximally sensitive to places (that is, to the spatial aspect of local environments). They called this area, which is part of the parahippocampal gyrus (a cortical area on the most ventral aspect of the temporal lobe), the parahippocampal place area (PPA) because it seemed specialized for identifying places.

Epstein and Kanwisher presented slides to participants while their brains were scanned using fMRI. Figure B2.2 shows the percentage change in response of the PPA to different types of stimuli. The PPA is maximally active to slides that depict spatial layouts, in this case outdoor shots that were taken around the university campus where the study was conducted and thus familiar to the participants.

These data are consistent with data from patients with lesions that include this area, who show a deficit called topographic amnesia. Such patients find it hard to navigate in unfamiliar environments (see Epstein et al., 2001). The data from the Epstein and Kanwisher study are especially important in showing that a part of the cortex is devoted to evaluating the spatial layout of the local environment because the PPA is so small that lesions including only this area are quite rare. These data indicate that the ventral stream of visual processing does include the evaluation of spatial information in at least some contexts.

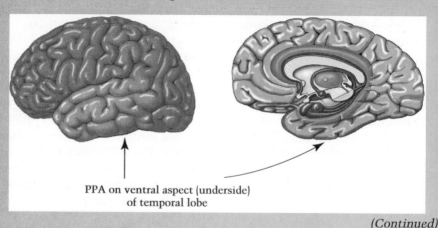

PPA on ventral aspect (underside)
of temporal lobe

(Continued)

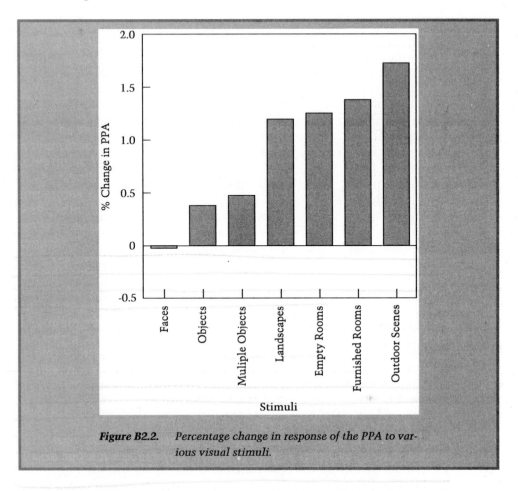

Figure B2.2. *Percentage change in response of the PPA to various visual stimuli.*

Stand-on-One-Foot Questions

10. *What are the two basic ideas about how objects are represented?*
11. *Name two types of evidence indicating that "what" and "how" are represented separately by the visual system.*

Questions That Require Two Feet

12. *Why do you suppose hills look so much steeper than they are? Hint: Consider how much harder it is to climb an 8-degree hill than a 4-degree hill.*
13. *Are there some objects that you almost always see in the same orientation? Do you think that your mental representation of those objects might reflect that select experience?*

KEY TERMS

accommodation
atmospheric perspective
binocular vision
bottom-up processing
computational approach
convergence
correspondence
   problem
critical features
ecological approach
eyeheight
familiar size
feature-matching
   theories
fovea
frames of reference

good continuation
inverse projection
   problem
light source, reflectance,
   and shadow
   indeterminacy
likelihood principle
linear perspective
local contrast
luminance
monocular vision
object-centered
   representation
occlusion
parsing paradox
pictorial cues

random dot stereograms
relative height
retina
retinal disparity
shape and orientation
   indeterminacy
size and distance inde-
   terminacy
stereopsis
template
texture gradient
top-down processing
viewer-centered
   representation
what/how hypothesis
what/where hypothesis

3

Attention

Suppose I ask you to walk the length of a balance beam. You, game stranger that you are, do so. Then I ask you to walk it again but this time to simultaneously sing "Yankee Doodle." You walk and sing. Then I tell you that this is a special balance beam, sections of which can be heated or cooled, and as you walk its length (barefoot) I'd like you to say whether the section you've just stepped on is hot or cold. You'll still be singing, so just interrupt the song when necessary. You perform that task. Then I ask you to do it again, but as you walk along, I'll squirt different scents at you with an atomizer, and as you're walking, singing, and distinguishing hot from cold you should also remember the scents I squirt because you'll have to recite them after you've finished walking the beam.

Clearly, you can walk, sing, feel temperature, or sniff without trouble, but doing all of them simultaneously is hard. You're going to perform more slowly as I add tasks, and you're going to start making errors. Why? The short and obvious answer is that you can't pay attention to all of those tasks at the same time. But what is attention? In an often-quoted passage, William James commented, "Everyone knows what attention is." More than 100 years later, a leading attention researcher replied, "No one knows what attention is" (Pashler, 1998, p. 1). Of course, James meant that everyone has an intuitive sense of what is meant by attention; Pashler meant that we don't have a complete scientific understanding of attention.

Attention can be understood to mean the mechanism for continued cognitive processing. This definition presumes that some preliminary cognitive processing takes place, with or without attention, and that attention affords further processing. For example, we might guess that your cognitive system would identify an object on the wall as a painting even if you were not paying attention to it when you walked into the room. Attention (and the continued cognitive processing it brings about) would be necessary to identify what the painting depicted, whether the artist was known to you, and so on. This definition is applicable not just to perception but to action as well; we speak of paying attention to tasks such as driving, building a model airplane, or walking on a balance beam.

This definition brings to the fore two properties of attention. First, we might guess that attention is **limited**; continued cognitive processing cannot occur for all available stimuli simultaneously. This point brings up the question **In what way is attention limited?** Our definition makes attention seem like mental fuel; you've got only so much fuel to expend, so if you expend it on one cognitive process, there is necessarily less for other processes. This metaphor is intuitively appealing, but the predictions it suggests are difficult to prove. Nevertheless, it is clear that attention is limited in some way.

Second, we know from everyday experience that attention is **selective**; you can expend your mental fuel on one or another cognitive process as you see fit. The very fact that attention is limited means that it must be selective.

What happens to the cognitive processes to which you give little or no attention? The perceptual apparatus is always working, but you are not always aware of all the information it processes. For example, you are probably seated as you read this, but you probably aren't aware of pressure from your chair. The sensation is always present, but you are not aware of it because of the limited nature of attention—you can't focus on both the pressure sensation and reading this text, and you select the text as the focus of attention. But what happens to the unattended sensation of pressure? **What is the fate of sensory stimuli that are not selected to receive attention?** That depends on just how you choose to direct attention. You may direct some attention to other stimuli, as when you're reading a book but still listening to a television to determine the outcome of a vital episode of *Green Acres*. Or you may try to shut out all distractions, as when you're attempting to read your cognitive psychology textbook and ignore your roommate's annoying baby-talk phone conversation with his girlfriend. As we'll see, you have some control over how tight the selection of attention is, but even when you're doing your best to focus on one thing, other material is still processed to some extent.

The final question we will pose concerns selection. Although people can try to select the focus of their attention, they are not always successful. **Why does selection fail?**

IN WHAT WAY IS ATTENTION LIMITED?

> ➤ *Preview* It appears that we have a limited amount of attention to expend on cognitive processing. Psychologists have made predictions about the limits of attention.
>
> - Attention can be distributed between tasks as the person sees fit.
> - Tasks require less attention with practice.
>
> There is evidence that supports these two statements. Two other predictions—that attention can be distributed to more than one task at a time, and that performing multiple tasks does not change how each task is performed—appear not to be correct.

Psychologists have likened attention to mental fuel that makes continued cognitive processing possible. This definition is close to the way researchers thought about attention when they first started considering its limited nature (Bryan & Harter, 1897) and has been central to more recent formulations as well (Kahneman, 1973; Moray, 1967). What can we say about the particular way in which attention is limited? We can make a list of predictions consistent with a limited capacity for attention and with our own experience.

- Attention can be distributed to more than one task at a time; that is, it is possible to perform multiple tasks in parallel.

- The performance of a particular task requires a particular amount of attention that is consistent across situations and does not change depending on other tasks that are being performed.
- When tasks compete, the person can allocate attention to each task in the proportions that he or she sees fit.
- With sufficient practice, a task will come to demand fewer attentional resources.

These four assumptions sound reasonable and fit with our everyday experience, but we cannot be sure that the first two are true. However, there is evidence that the final two are true. Let's look at these assumptions in more detail.

Parallel Performance

It seems obvious that it is possible to perform more than one task in parallel. After all, you frequently do two things at once: talk to a friend while you drive, listen to music while you read, walk and chew gum. A good way to learn about the limited nature of attention is to give the cognitive system too much to do and then observe the consequences. To investigate attention in the laboratory, researchers use a **dual task paradigm** in which the participant must perform two tasks at once.

Here's the key question about parallel performance: How do you know that you're really doing these tasks in parallel and not switching attention rapidly between the two tasks? Couldn't I take a step on the balance beam, then sing a phrase of the song, then take another step, and so on, so smoothly and seamlessly that it seems as if I'm doing the two tasks at the same time?

Researchers have tried to get around this problem by using continuous tasks rather than discrete tasks. A **discrete task** has an identifiable beginning and ending, and there is usually a pause between the end of one trial and the beginning of the next. For example, in a simple response time task a stimulus is presented (a light appears on a computer monitor or a tone sounds) and the participant responds by pressing a button as quickly as possible when the stimulus occurs. Figure 3.1 shows a **response to stimulus interval**, which is the period of time after the participant has responded but before the next stimulus has appeared. During this period the participant waits for the next stimulus to appear and could easily switch attention to some other task. Even if the researcher makes the next stimulus appear immediately after a response, the participant can simply switch attention to the other task at this point, effectively taking a break from this task.

Continuous tasks, in contrast, use a continuous stream of stimuli and often demand a continuous stream of responses. For example, in a pursuit tracking task, a target moves on a computer screen and the participant must chase the target with a cursor controlled by a joystick. Performance is measured as the distance between the cursor and target. The target is always moving, so it would seem that even a momentary lapse of attention would make

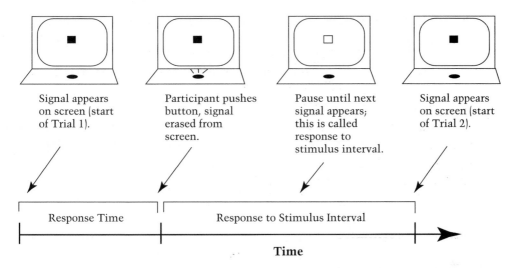

Figure 3.1. *Simple response time task with a visual signal and a button-press response.*

performance suffer. Another continuous task is touch typing. In one experiment a skilled typist could recite nursery rhymes aloud while typing with only a 10% loss of typing speed (Shaffer, 1975). This study was meant to show that typing required very little attention for a highly skilled typist.

The problem with such evidence is that it is probably possible to switch attention between two tasks even if one of them is a continuous task; the participant need not treat it as if it were continuous (Broadbent, 1982; Welford, 1980). For example, experienced typists often report that once they've seen a word, they don't really need to think about the word as they type it, and a number of studies indicate that that is true (Salthouse, 1984). Just because the hands are typing at a steady rate doesn't mean that attentional resources are needed at a steady rate. In the case of typing, it seems likely that attention is needed in bursts; a burst of attention might be needed to read a word and then very little attention would be needed to type the word.

Thus, using dual task paradigms does not seem to guarantee evidence that people can share attentional resources between tasks. No matter how much it looks as if the participant is dividing attention between two tasks, it will remain possible that the participant is rapidly switching attention between the tasks.

Consistent Attention Requirements

If we try to perform more than one task at a time, the two tasks vie for attentional resources. Does one particular task takes up a particular amount of attention—in other words, does it require a certain amount of attentional fuel regardless of the other demands on the attention? Probably not.

Suppose you ask people to perform four tasks in various combinations.

Task A: Generate a mental image of your room.

Task B: Sing "The Star-Spangled Banner."

Task C: Play a video game.

Task D: Remember a list of six words.

You find that participants can generate a mental image of their bedroom (Task A) and simultaneously sing "The Star-Spangled Banner" (Task B) with little apparent cost to the imaging. However, if they are imaging and then start playing the video game (Task C), there is a cost to the imagery task. Therefore, the attentional cost of playing the video game seems to be greater than that of the singing (C > B).

But if you ask participants to remember the list of six words (Task D), you find that adding the video game (Task C) causes little cost to remembering the words and singing (Task B) causes a high cost. Now it appears that the attentional cost of singing is greater than that of playing the video game (B > C). In short, you can't evaluate the attentional demands of a task by pairing it with a secondary task; the attentional demands of a task look different depending on the task you pair it with. We cannot say that a task demands a particular amount of attention independent of other tasks.

MULTIPLE RESOURCE THEORIES.   You can't make a mental image of your room and play a video game simultaneously because you don't have enough attention. So why can you play the game and sing at the same time? One answer would be that there are different types of attention. This is called a **multiple resources** approach to attention (Navon & Gopher, 1979; Norman & Bobrow, 1975). Just as the name implies, the idea is that you have several independent pools of attention, not one general pool. Each works just as we described for the more general attention resource idea, but there are thought to be several types of attention, each specific to particular types of task.

What characterizes these separate attentional pools? In other words, how do they differ? In one of the early articles taking the multiple resources approach, David Navon and Daniel Gopher (1979) cited research indicating a separation based on sensory modality (vision, hearing). They cited an article by Lee Brooks (1968) showing that when participants were trying to recall a sentence, a simultaneous vocal task was much more disruptive than a simultaneous spatial task, but when they were trying to recall the shape of a line diagram, a simultaneous vocal task was less disruptive than a spatial task. Thus there could be separate attentional pools for visuospatial processing and for auditory processing or, more simply put, for vision and for hearing.

Later research, however, did not support that idea. Jon Driver and Charles Spence (1994) showed that there are links between attention in vision and attention in hearing. Participants in their experiment had speakers to their left and right. On each trial a different three-word triplet came out of the left and right speakers and participants were told to repeat the triplet from one speaker.

They were told before each trial which speaker they should attend to. On some trials they also had visual information, with a person speaking the words they were to repeat. The tricky part was that the visual information was presented on a screen either on the same side as the speaker that had the auditory information they were supposed to repeat or on a screen by the other speaker; thus the visual information could be either consistent or inconsistent with the information coming over the auditory channel on the same side (see Figure 3.2).

Driver and Spence's experiment indicated that auditory and visual information are not completely separate. When the visual information was presented on the side consistent with the auditory information, people got about 68% of the words correct; when it was not, they got about 52% correct. Thus auditory and visual attention do seem to be tied together; participants could not allocate visual and auditory attention to different locations in space without cost. Nevertheless, it is true that an auditory task will tend to interfere with another auditory task more than with a visual task. The final word seems

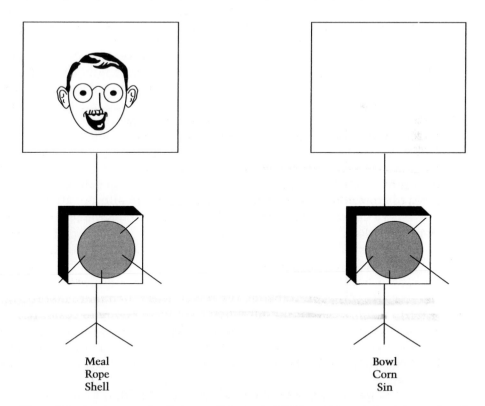

Meal   Bowl
Rope   Corn
Shell   Sin

Figure 3.2. *Basic setup for Driver and Spence's (1994) experiment. Participants heard different groups of three words coming from speakers on their left and right and had to repeat the words from one speaker. A person on the screen mouthed the target words on either the same side as or the opposite side from the auditory information.*

to be that there is some division along modality lines but not completely separate pools of attention.

Chris Wickens (1984, 1992) suggested a different way of splitting up attention in a multiple resource theory with three dimensions of tasks relevant to attention. He asked first, which stage of processing does the task emphasize? For perception the hard part is perceiving the stimulus, whereas for response the hard part is selecting the right reaction. Second, does the task use a verbal or spatial code of processing? Third, what are the modalities of input and output? The input might be visual or auditory; the output might be spoken or manual. Wickens argued that there might be separate attentional resource pools for each combination of these dimensions. In other words, searching for a visual target would be a perceptual task with visual input, and that would call on a particular pool of attentional resources. Different tasks have different properties, so the three task dimensions would require eight separate pools of attention in all.

The idea seems intuitively appealing. Unfortunately, it has proved difficult to specify how different tasks would call on these different hypothetical pools. For a theory to be useful, it must be predictive; in other words, we must be able to analyze two tasks and judge how similar they are in terms of the demands they would place on the different attentional pools. One of the chief criticisms of the multiple resources theory holds that it's not clear how many of these attentional pools are supposed to exist or how they are related to tasks (see Allport, 1989, Luck & Vecera, 2002, for a discussion of some of these issues).

Most researchers believe that it is useful to think of attention as limited, but it has proved frustratingly difficult to be specific about how this happens. It seems that the simple idea of an undifferentiated pool of attentional resources cannot be right, but a satisfactory alternative has not been outlined. Two other properties of attention have been studied in detail, however, and we have a better understanding of them. First, we can allocate attention to different tasks as we see fit, and second, attentional demands appear to shrink as we practice a task.

Allocation of Attention

Psychologists have assumed that when tasks compete for attentional resources, people can allocate more or less attention to a particular task according to their goals. For example, suppose you are driving and simultaneously talking to a friend and suddenly it begins to rain hard, making it difficult to see. You would probably allocate more attention to driving the car and less to the conversation.

The assumption that you can allocate attention in this manner is supported by controlled laboratory studies. George Sperling and Melvin Melchner (1978) showed participants arrays of letters. An inner set of 4 letters was surrounded by an outer set of 16 letters. The arrays flashed by, one at a time, on a computer screen. Each appeared for just 240 ms, and the number of arrays that

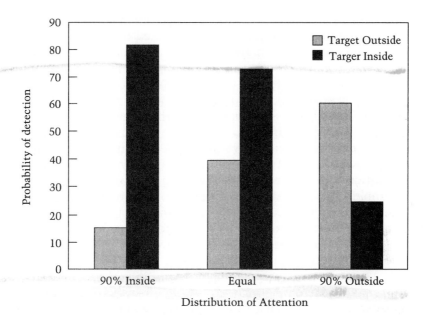

Figure 3.3. *Graph from Sperling and Melchner (1978) showing the probability that a single participant detected the target. The x axis represents the instructions: to direct 90% of attention to the outside or inside stimuli, or to maintain equal attention to both. The black bars show performance when the stimuli actually appeared on the outside, the white when they appeared on the inside. The data show that participants can direct their attention as they are instructed, and that doing so affects performance.*

flashed by on each trial varied. Participants knew that 2 digits would appear in the arrays sometime during the trial, and they were to report the identity and location of the digits. On some trials they were told to allocate 90% of their attention to the inner set of 4 letters; on others they were to allocate 90% of their attention to the outer set of letters; and on others they were to attend to the inner and outer arrays equally. Figure 3.3 shows the probability of correctly detecting a target. The graph shows the data for just one participant, but these data are typical. The important point is that when participants are told to attend mostly to one location, they get most of the targets appearing in that location. Participants can indeed allocate attention as they see fit, and that allocation is reflected in task performance (see also Gopher, Brickner, & Navon, 1982).

Reduction in Attention Demands with Practice: Automaticity

Another strong assumption we make is that the attentional demand of a task goes down as it is practiced. Learning to drive a car may have taxed your attentional resources at first as you were watching for oncoming cars, making sure to stay in the center of your lane, checking the mirrors, watching your speed, monitoring the pressure you applied to the gas pedal, reading the road signs, and so on. With enough practice, however, these tasks became **automatic**, taking few or no attentional resources and happening without intention.

If a task takes few or no attentional resources, obviously it makes little demand on attention, so you should be able to perform several automatic tasks at once. Indeed, an experienced driver thinks nothing of driving while simultaneously eating, talking on a cell phone, and listening to the radio—an accomplished task, if not attractive to watch. In addition, an automatic process that happens without intention occurs whether you want it to or not: if certain conditions are present in the environment, the automatic process occurs. For example, on occasion a passenger in my car will slam his or her foot against the floorboard in a vain effort to stop my car. I always inform such passengers that their foot motion is perfectly understandable; the proper stimulus was present in the environment (danger) to bring about an action (braking) even though the action is futile.

How do we know that automaticity has these two characteristics (it requires little or no attention, and it happens without intention)? First let's consider whether automatic processes really don't require attention.

AUTOMATICITY AND ATTENTION.   In a classic experiment on the training of automaticity, Walter Schneider and Richard Shiffrin (1977) used a visual search task to show the reduced attentional demand of automatic processes. On each trial, participants were given a memory set (for example, the letters *A* and *J*) and were told to search upcoming stimuli for those characters. Participants then saw a series of cards with letters and numbers on them, and they had to report whether a member of the memory set had appeared on one of the cards. The memory set items are called **targets** and the nontarget items on the cards are called **distractors**. Twenty of these cards flipped by on each trial; each card was presented only briefly, on some trials as briefly as 40 ms. On each trial a new memory set and new cards were used (see Figure 3.4).

What does this task have to do with attention? We're discussing automatic processes, and in this case the process is visual search: the participant searches for the target among all the stimuli on the cards. We can use this task to examine automaticity because if the visual search is automatic (takes no attention), the participant ought to be able to carry out visual search on many stimuli simultaneously. Therefore, the number of stimuli on each card shouldn't

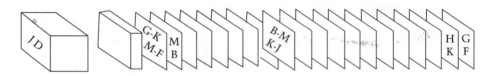

Figure 3.4. *Sample trial from Schneider and Shiffrin's (1977) task, showing cards that flashed in front of participants. The block at the far left represents that memory set.*

matter; if there are four stimuli on each card you'll still be able to do the visual search as effectively as if there is one stimulus on each card.

The first experiment examined two conditions: consistent mapping and varied mapping. In the consistent mapping condition, the target was always a letter and the distractors were always numbers (or vice versa). *Consistent* refers to the fact that a target on one trial could not be a distractor on another trial. In the *varied* mapping condition, the targets and distractors were of the same type, so a target on one trial might be a distractor on another trial.

The results showed that when consistent mapping was used, visual search was automatic. Search was equally fast and accurate whether there was one stimulus on each card or two or four stimuli. It also didn't matter how long each card was presented (40, 80, or 120 ms). Furthermore, in the consistent mapping condition, participants reported experiencing **pop-out**, in which the target seems to jump off the card and is therefore easy to spot. (Pop-out is usually present when a visual search is automatic.) Participants in this task say that they feel as if they hardly need to search under these conditions because they know that the target will pop out of the background.

It was quite a different story in the varied mapping condition, however. Faster presentation rates and more distractors hurt performance, and as you would expect, there was no pop-out in this condition (see Figure 3.5). This experiment shows that visual search can be automatic if you are dealing with letters among numbers or vice versa. But participants already had a great deal of experience with these categories when they started the experiment. Can you start with unfamiliar categories and see automaticity develop during the course of an experiment?

In a second study, Shiffrin and Schneider (1977) attempted to observe this process in the laboratory. They used the same visual search task, but with only letters as targets and distractors. In this experiment, *categorical* meant that the memory set was selected from among the same group of letters on each trial. For example, the memory set might be selected from the letters {GMFP} and the distractors from {CNHD}. For the mixed condition both the memory set and the distractors could be selected from {RVJZBWTX}. Each participant alternated blocks of trials using the categorical and mixed stimuli. The researchers performed 24 one-hour sessions for a total of 9,216 trials (4,608 of each type of mapping).

Automaticity developed only if the target set was selected from the same set of letters on each trial (that is, in the categorical mapping condition). If a letter could be a target on one trial and then a distractor on the next trial, automaticity never developed (see Figure 3.6).

Thus there appears to be good evidence that with practice, tasks become less demanding of attention. The exact mechanism by which this happens is still under debate. Some researchers have suggested that some of the intermediate steps in a complex series of processes are eventually eliminated (Anderson, 1993; Newell & Rosenbloom, 1981) while others suggest that a second process that does not demand attention develops more slowly and finally takes over the task (Willingham, 1998).

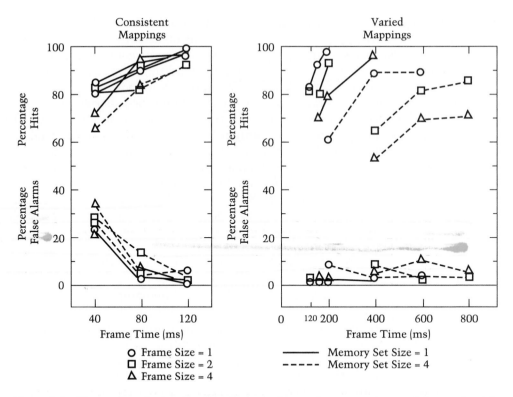

Figure 3.5. *The graph on the left shows performance for consistent mappings, and that on the right shows performance for varied mappings. Hits are successfully finding the target when it is present; false alarms are reporting that the target is present when it is not. Three factors are represented on the graph: how long each card was shown (frame time), size of the memory set, and number of characters on each card (frame size). When the mapping is consistent, none of these factors influences performance; visual search is equally good unless frame time is very short (40 ms). For varied mappings, all three factors influence performance, indicating that this sort of search is not automatic.*

Gordon Logan (1988, 2002) suggested a different account of automaticity: increasing facility with well-practiced tasks may reflect an increasing role of memory. For example, if I asked you how many letters are in the word *quotidian*, you would have to spell it to yourself and count the letters. If I asked you the same question a few minutes later, you wouldn't go through the same process; you'd remember what you had said earlier and say it again. Logan suggested that memory may play just such a role in automaticity. In every task, memory competes with slower processes that actually calculate an answer to the task at hand. With more practice, you have more answers in memory, making it increasingly likely that on any given trial you can use an answer from memory and not need to do the calculation.

AUTOMATICITY AND INTENTION. There is also evidence that automatic processes happen beyond our control, but these data must be interpreted cautiously.

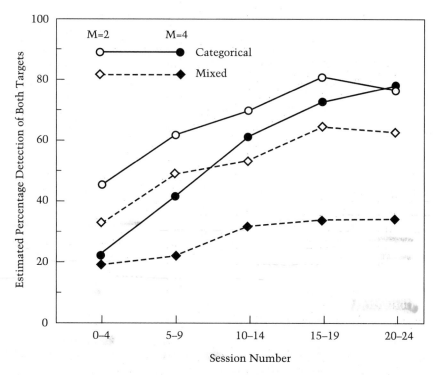

Figure 3.6. *Results from Shiffrin and Schneider's (1977) study. Note that in the early sessions, participants were always more likely to succeed when there were two targets (M = 2) than when there were four (M = 4), and that was equally true in the categorical and mixed conditions. By the end of the training, participants were equally good when M = 2 and M = 4, but only for the categorical condition. In the mixed condition, participants were much better at detecting the target when there were fewer stimuli on each card.*

The evidence in favor of this view comes from a couple of visual search tasks. One is the Stroop (1935) effect, which you have probably seen before. In this task you are asked to name the ink colors of a series of words, but the color names conflict with the words that the ink spells out. For example, if the word *red* is written in blue ink, the appropriate response would be "blue," but the fact that the ink forms the word *red* causes interference. People are slower and less accurate in naming the ink colors than when they read unrelated words such as *rut*. This effect can be taken as evidence that reading is an automatic process. In this case, you actually want *not* to read the word *red*, but reading it seems unavoidable, and because the word *red* conflicts with the correct response, there is interference (see Catena, Fuentes, & Tudela, 2002).

Another task supporting the involuntariness of automatic processes demonstrates the **flanker effect**. In a **flanker task** the participant is asked to respond to a stimulus presented in the center of the screen and to ignore any other stimuli that appear. The participant is shown exactly where the centrally presented stimulus will appear (usually via a crosshair that appears before the target), but some other stimuli appear near the target, flanking it.

The effect of the flankers can be observed when participants are asked to read the target word aloud; in that case, participants begin reading slightly faster if the flankers are semantically related to the target word (that is, if they are related in terms of their meaning). Mark Dallas and Philip Merikle (1976) showed this flanker effect clearly. On each trial participants saw a card with two letter strings: a target word that participants were to read (*table*), and then either a semantically related word (*chair*), an unrelated word (*night*), or a non-word letter string (*lhesl*). A cue appeared 250 ms before the stimuli telling the participant where the target word was going to appear; they other stimulus was to be ignored. Participants were equally fast when the flanker was an unrelated word or a nonword (about 510 ms), but they were faster when the flanker was semantically related to the target (480 ms). The flanker effect is also observed when the task is to name the semantic category of the target word rather than to read it aloud. Categorization judgments also are faster if the flankers are examples of the same semantic category as the target (Shaffer & LaBerge, 1979). These flanker experiments seem to support the hypothesis that reading is obligatory, at least under the conditions in this experiment. If a word appears in a location to which you are attending, you seem to process it for meaning.

That leads us to a final point to consider. What conditions make reading (or any other cognitive process) obligatory? It seems unlikely that the stimulus conditions that elicit the automatic response are very broad. For example, seeing a red traffic light does not always cause you to make a braking motion with your foot. If you're walking when you see the light, you have a different response—namely, you stop walking. It's clear that we must be careful in describing the stimuli in the environment that trigger an automatic response.

Stand-on-One-Foot Questions

1. *Can people divide attention between more than one task? How is this known?*

2. *The dual task paradigm often is used to investigate the limited nature of attention. Describe two consequences of adding a second task that make data from the dual task paradigm difficult to interpret.*

3. *Describe and briefly evaluate the theory that there are multiple pools of attention.*

Questions That Require Two Feet

4. *Some people can read while instrumental music is playing in the background, but if the music has words, they find it distracting. Why might that be?*

5. *I once heard a comic remark that he thought it was funny that people turn the radio off when they are looking for a house number in a strange neighborhood. What theory of attention does this comedian favor?*
6. *Do you think it's safe to talk on a cell phone while driving?*

What Is The Fate Of Sensory Stimuli that Are Not Selected to Receive Attention?

> ➤ *Preview* We attend to only a subset of the stimuli that are out in the world. What happens to the other stimuli? They must be processed and identified at least to some extent; how else would you know when to redirect attention to these other stimuli? In this section we discuss just how much processing is performed on these unattended stimuli. It seems that the physical characteristics of unattended stimuli are identified (color and shape of visual stimuli, loudness and pitch of auditory stimuli), but little information about their meaning is processed. We also look at how selection operates. What does attention focus on? Does it focus on objects or regions of space? And how does selection operate? Does it actually select what to process, or does it filter out extraneous information, leaving only the target? The answer is that it seems to select objects, not space, and it seems to do so by actively drawing attention to the target, not by ignoring the nontarget objects.

You can't attend to everything simultaneously because of the limited nature of attention. Attention must also be selective, and if you select some things to attend to, you will necessarily not be selecting others. What happens to the sensory stimuli that are not selected?

That question may strike you as odd—who cares what happens to unattended stimuli?—but it's actually important. What if you're attending to one stimulus and another stimulus in the environment requires your notice? For example, what if you were sitting in the library reading *Anna Karenina* and someone shouted, "Is that a fire?" That would be a good moment to disengage attention from the novel and direct attention to whatever has made someone shout. If there were absolutely no processing of stimuli that you were ignoring, you wouldn't even know that someone had shouted.

Indeed, you know that attention can be diverted in this way, so there must be some processing of material that you are ignoring. That's why the definition of attention is that it's the mechanism for continued cognitive processing; everything is processed to some extent, and attention affords continued processing. In this section we are asking how much processing occurs in the absence of attention. Most of the work on this topic has concerned the amount of perceptual processing that occurs on stimuli that are not attended.

We have to start our discussion of this problem by outlining an assumption. It's probably a justifiable assumption, but we should be explicit about it anyway. The assumption is that perception follows a processing course like that in Figure 3.7. It is assumed that the physical characteristics of a stimulus are processed first. For visual information these would be shape, color, spatial location, and so on. For auditory information they would be loudness, pitch, spatial location, and so on. After we know the physical characteristics of the stimulus, more processing is necessary to figure out what the object is and therefore its meaning: that shiny red globe is an apple, which means that it is edible, it has seeds, it is a member of the category *fruit*, and so on.

A great deal of sensory information (sights, sounds, smells) bombards us at any given moment, but at the other end of the processing stream only a fraction of that information enters awareness. One hypothesis holds that attention acts as a filter, stopping most of the information before it reaches awareness. The attentional filter stops the processing of most sensory information, allowing continued processing (and eventual entry to awareness) of only the sensory information to which we are attending. We are constantly evaluating information not currently in awareness in order to decide whether other stimuli are worthy of attention.

Theories about how attention acts as a filter fall into two categories: early filter theories and late filter theories. These terms refer to where the filter operates in the processing stream depicted in Figure 3.7. An **early filter** is located early in the processing stream, usually right after the sensory characteristics are processed; thus, according to early filter theories, all stimuli are processed so that their sensory characteristics are determined, and then they hit the filter. Most stimuli are not processed past that point, but the filter allows through whichever stimuli are being attended to.

A **late filter** appears later in the processing stream. All stimuli are processed to determine their physical and semantic characteristics, and only then do the stimuli hit the filter; only the stimuli that are attended to go on to enter awareness. You can see that the key difference between these theories is the location of the filter.

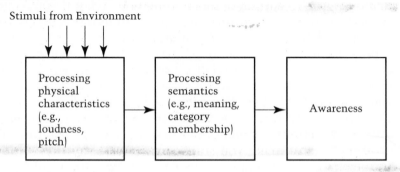

Figure 3.7. *Simple diagram showing the assumed order in which sensory stimuli are processed.*

Early Filter Theories

What is the evidence for the early filter theories? One of the first studies relevant to this question was performed by Colin Cherry (1953) using the **dichotic listening** task. In this task, participants listened to material on headphones. Each earpiece played a different message, and participants were asked to pay attention to just one of the messages. To ensure that participants were attending as instructed, they had to **shadow** the message, meaning that they had to repeat the message aloud. Thus, as they were shadowing what they heard over the right earpiece, another message was playing in the left earpiece. Later, participants were asked to report what they knew about the message from the unattended ear. Participants were terrible at reporting what the unattended message was. In fact, Cherry found that participants didn't even notice if the unattended message switched into another language or if the message was played backwards. Participants did notice if the unattended speech turned into a pure tone or if the gender of the speaker changed.

Cherry concluded that unattended speech is not analyzed to a semantic level; that is, it is not analyzed for meaning. Instead, it is analyzed for physical characteristics such as pitch and loudness. Thus if you're focusing attention on the message in the left ear, you don't know anything about the meaning of what's coming in the right ear. But you know its physical characteristics, so you can tell when it becomes grossly different from speech (like a pure tone) or when the pitch changes (because the gender of the speaker has changed). A dramatic example of the extent to which people don't know the meaning of unattended speech was provided by Moray (1959), who played the same word list for participants in the unattended ear 35 times. On a later recognition test of the words, participants were at chance.

Donald Broadbent (1958) was one of the first to propose a theory incorporating an early attentional filter. Broadbent suggested that information comes into a very brief sensory store (discussed in chapter 4) in which its physical characteristics are ascertained. The filter occurs just after this sensory store, and only a small portion of this information makes it to the next stage, which is primary memory. Primary memory is associated with awareness, and it is where meaning is assigned to stimuli (primary memory is also discussed in chapter 4).

Let's focus on the idea that all stimuli are analyzed for their physical characteristics, but only a limited number (those to which you attend) are also analyzed for their semantic content. Recall that unattended stimuli must be processed in case something important requires your attention. If you are in a crowd and someone shouts "Fire!" the loudness of the unattended message will make you shift your attention to the source of the sound. But presumably if someone merely said "Fire," you wouldn't hear it because the word doesn't stand out from any other of the stimuli coming in to the system.

Late Filter Theories

Broadbent (1958) thought that all incoming stimuli are analyzed in terms of their physical characteristics. If the physical characteristics of a stimulus made it seem worthy of attention, you could switch attention to it, but if it differed only in terms of meaning, you'd never notice because unattended messages aren't processed for meaning. This proposal sounds reasonable, but your own experience might lead you to suggest a difficulty with this theory. Sometimes at a crowded party you might overhear your name being mentioned in another conversation. I've observed the phenomenon not only with my name but with other stimuli that are relevant to me. For example, I'll be at a booth in a restaurant talking with friends and I'll suddenly notice that the people in the next booth are talking about psychology. Just as my name pops into awareness if it is uttered within my hearing, words such as *cognitive* and *psychology* have a similar effect.

In these examples, it is the semantic content, or meaning of the unattended words, that causes attention to be shifted to them, which is not in line with Broadbent's and Cherry's proposal. This effect has been tested in the laboratory using the dichotic listening task. While the participant shadowed a message in one ear, the other earpiece played something in the unattended ear and then added a message with the participant's name. Moray (1959) found that participants sometimes (but not always) noticed their own name on the unattended channel. Only 33% showed the effect, although these data are hard to interpret because Moray didn't test very many people; 4 out of 12 participants tested noticed their name.

Noelle Wood and Nelson Cowan (1995) replicated Moray's experiment and found the same results; 9 out of 26 participants (about 35%) noticed their own name on the unattended channel, and 0 out of 26 noticed someone else's name. Does this result mean that the unattended message was processed semantically (that is, for meaning)? Or does it mean that one-third of the participants didn't really follow the experimenter's instructions? Maybe they did the shadowing task but also switched attention to the other channel every now and then to see what was happening there. This possibility seems likely because when Wood and Cowan told people that they should be ready for new instructions during the task, 80% detected their name. It seems likely that the increase resulted from more participants sampling the channel they were not supposed to attend to, listening for the new instructions.

Other data seem to be consistent with the idea that messages in the unattended ear are processed for meaning, however. Anne Treisman (1960) performed a clever study in which the messages in the attended and unattended ears were switched in midstream. The left ear might have heard "*If you're creaming butter and* piccolos, clarinets, and tubas, seldom play solos." Meanwhile the right ear heard "Many orchestral instruments, such as *sugar, it's a good idea to use a low mixer speed.*" Participants were supposed to shadow the right ear, but their shadowing jumped to the other ear when the semantic sense of the message started coming from the other earpiece. This effect was noted for 15 out of 18 participants. Still, they would shadow the wrong ear only for one or two words, and then they would switch back to the correct ear. Interestingly, none of the participants noticed that they had done so; they all thought they had consistently shadowed the correct ear.

Treisman also varied the sensibility of the passages that participants were shadowing. Some of the passages were easy-to-follow stories, and others were statistical approximations of English; that is, the sentences contained words in proportions similar to spoken English, but the sentences did not mean anything. Treisman found that participants did not switch their shadowing for these passages. She reasoned that the filter does a fairly effective job—participants for the most part remain unaware of the unattended message—but it must be true that the unattended message is processed for meaning to some extent because whether or not a word gets through seems to depend on its contextual appropriateness. If a word that is highly probable (given the semantic context) appears on the unattended channel and an improbable word appears on the attended channel, the filter allows the probable word to get through. Treisman proposed that the filter must be sensitive to context because it allows highly probable or appropriate words to pass on to awareness. She also proposed that certain words (such as one's own name or danger signals like "Fire!") will always be considered contextually relevant and will pass through the filter on to awareness.

These results led some researchers to propose late filter theories, suggesting that the filter occurs late in processing (Deutsch & Deutsch, 1963; Norman, 1968). Specifically, these theorists proposed that all inputs are processed not only for their physical characteristics but also for their semantic meaning. Attention determines what will enter awareness, but the decision about what will enter consciousness can be made on the basis of physical characteristics (such as loudness) or semantic characteristics (meaning).

Late filter theories gained support from studies using **indirect measures** of semantic processing in which researchers infer something about cognition on the basis of how the participant performs a task rather than by asking him or her a question about mental processing. For example, if you wanted to know whether a participant processed material on the unattended channel in a dichotic listening task, a **direct measure** would be simply to ask, "What did you hear on the other channel?" An indirect measure would be to give the participant some other task to do and see whether the way that task is performed is influenced by the material on the unattended channel.

In one of the better-known studies in this vein (Corteen & Wood, 1972) the indirect measure was **galvanic skin response (GSR)**, which detects nervousness. Your palms are always somewhat moist, but the sweat evaporates quickly; when you're nervous, there is more sweat. GSR accurately measures how sweaty your palm is. Two leads are placed on your palm, one to transmit a very mild electric pulse and the other to read electrical activity. Skin is a poor conductor of electricity, but water (including sweat) is a terrific conductor. The more sweat present on your hand, the more current the second lead will pick up. Again, to clarify the distinction between direct and indirect tests, a direct test of nervousness would be to simply ask participants how nervous they felt; GSR is an indirect test.

In Corteen and Wood's study, participants were first exposed to a training session in which they heard some words and occasionally received a mild electric shock. The shock was administered every time one of three city names was mentioned. Soon, participants came to expect the shock when they heard one of the city names, as measured by GSR. They got nervous in anticipation of the shock, and that nervousness was apparent on the GSR measure.

In the second phase of the experiment, participants performed a dichotic listening task, shadowing an irrelevant message coming into their right ear. In the left ear they heard lists of words that included the city names that had been paired with shock, some new city names, and some irrelevant nouns. No shocks were administered during this part of the experiment. Participants could say little or nothing about the material that had been presented to the unattended channel. The GSR told a different story, however. Participants showed the GSR response 38% of the time to the old city names, 23% of the time to new city names, and just 10% of the time to irrelevant nouns. Thus, even if people were unaware of the words on the unattended channel, it seemed that they were unconsciously analyzing these words for meaning.

This influential study was later shown to have problems. First, it was not easy to replicate (Wardlaw & Kroll, 1976). To replicate a study simply means to do it over again to be sure you get the same results. Psychologists consider replication to be quite important because if an effect is real, it should be reproducible. (If you're not familiar with the importance of replication, have a look at the Appendix.)

Second, Michael Dawson and Anne Schell (1982) showed that although the effect might be replicable, it could be caused not by semantic processing of the unattended channel but by shifts of attention during the task. They tried much harder than previous experimenters to measure when participants shifted attention to the channel they were supposed to be ignoring. For example, the experimenters assumed that participants attended to the wrong channel when they made a mistake in shadowing or when they reported having become aware of a word on that channel. When the researchers eliminated all the trials on which participants might have switched attention to the wrong channel, the main effect of interest—heightened GSR to the city names on the unattended channel—was greatly reduced. It didn't disappear completely, but the effect was not as robust as it had looked before.

A different indirect measure was used by Eric Eich (1984), who had participants shadow one ear while word pairs were presented to the unattended ear. Each word pair included homophones (words that can have two meanings but sound the same, such as *fare* and *fair*). If one of these words is spoken in isolation, you can't identify it as *fare* or *fair* because they sound the same. In Eich's experiment, the other word of the pair clarified the meaning of the homophone; for example, a word pair might have been *taxi fare*. Later, participants were asked which words they remembered from the unattended channel, and their memory was very poor. Next they were given an indirect test of their memory for the word pairs: the experimenter said a word aloud, and the participant had to spell it. Some of the words on the spelling test were the homophones that had been on the unattended channel. The measure of interest was whether participants used the spelling consistent with the disambiguating context. In other words, participants might spell *f-a-r-e* more often than *f-a-i-r* because they heard *taxi*, which biases one meaning to the sound *fare*. Eich reported that indeed, participants who heard *taxi* used the spelling *fare* more often than participants who had not, indicating that these unattended words were processed for meaning.

Noelle Wood and her colleagues (Wood, Stadler, & Cowan, 1997) replicated Eich's effect using the homophones, but they were worried about one aspect of the procedure. Participants were shadowing text that was presented at 85 words per minute, whereas a rate of 120–150 words per minute would be more typical of real speech. Perhaps participants were able to switch attention between the two channels because the shadowing they were doing was not demanding. So Wood and colleagues conducted the experiment again, using a faster presentation rate. This time there was no evidence that participants' spelling of the homophones was biased, indicating that the earlier results showing a late filter may have resulted from participants' successfully shifting attention from one channel to another.

The Movable Filter Model

We have seen that it's not clear that all information is analyzed in terms of its semantic content every time. We could account for all the data with an early filter model, such as that proposed by Broadbent, allowing that sometimes the focus of attention will lapse and participants will attend to material that they are supposed to be ignoring. We could even propose that the attentional system is biased to do exactly that. It is prudent to constantly monitor the environment around us, so the attentional system might be biased not to maintain attention to one location as dichotic listening tasks demand.

One possibility is that you can control the filter to be either early or late, depending on your needs, a point made forcefully by Michael Posner and Charles Snyder (1975). You can choose to allocate attention completely to some material, or to allocate attention mostly to the material, while periodically switching attention to other material. Unattended stimuli would always be analyzed for physical characteristics. The filter is not fixed to be early or late: it's movable.

Some data are consistent with that suggestion. William Johnston and Steven Heinz (1978) had participants listen to two word lists spoken simultaneously over headphones. Both lists were presented to both ears. Participants were told to shadow, but some participants were instructed to shadow based on the physical characteristic of the words; they were to shadow the words spoken by a man, so the participant could attend to the pitch of the word to select which one to shadow. Other participants were asked to shadow based on the semantic content of the words; they were to shadow the word that described an occupation, such as *teacher*. While they were doing the shadowing task, all participants also performed a secondary task. They watched a computer screen and pressed a button as quickly as possible when a light appeared on the screen. This secondary task provides an indirect measure of how attention-demanding the shadowing task is. The more attention the shadowing task took, the less attention would be available to watch for the light.

Response times to the light were longer when participants had to shadow based on the semantic content of the words rather than their physical characteristics (482 vs. 433 ms). Furthermore, participants made more errors when they shadowed based on semantic content rather than physical characteristic (20.5% errors vs. 5.3% errors). This experiment indicates that participants are capable of processing words at a semantic level as they perform a secondary task, but there is a higher attentional cost to doing so relative to processing only at a physical level; both shadowing performance and performance on the secondary task are worse.

Thus the available evidence seems to indicate that all stimuli are analyzed at a physical level, but further processing demands some attentional resources. The decision to expend these resources depends on the circumstances. The likelihood that an unattended sound enters awareness depends on allocation of attentional resources, which varies with the situation. It seems that there is a fixed filter—and it seems to be early—but we can allocate our attentional resources so that it's more like having a late filter by frequently sampling other perceptual channels.

The caveat on this reasonable conclusion is that the amount of processing may well be open to training. Stefan Koelsch, Erich Schröger, and Mari Tervaniemi (1999) examined whether processing outside of attention differs in professional musicians compared to nonmusicians if the stimuli are musical. The researchers capitalized on an effect called mismatch negativity, an effect of the brain's electrical activity as measured by event-related potentials (see "Interlude: The Brain" for more details). If the investigator plays a repetitive auditory stimulus and occasionally throws in an "oddball," a negative potential in the brain's frontal lobe is observed. The researchers had professional musicians and nonmusicians listen to a repetitive major chord (composed of three pure tones). Participants were to ignore all the stimuli and read a book they had brought. On 14% of the trials, one of the three tones was marginally diminished in frequency. The professional musicians showed mismatch negativity to the "oddball" chords, even though they were ignoring the stimuli. Indeed, half of them did not notice that the deviant chords had appeared, but they still showed the effect; the nonmusicians did not. Thus training and experience can affect what is processed outside of attention.

What Is Selected?

When we talk about attention being selective, we should pause to ask exactly what is selected. Until the early 1980s, many researchers believed that attention was like a spotlight (Norman, 1968; Posner, Snyder, & Davidson, 1980), a beam of enhanced perceptual processing that could point to locations in space; objects falling within the attentional spotlight were subject to more perceptual processing. Thus attention was thought to select spatial locations. Today it is thought that attention selects objects, not spatial locations.

Two predictions psychologists made using the beam metaphor seem not to be true. First, if attention worked like a beam, then the amount of time required to shift attention from one location to another should be proportional to the distance attention must travel. Second, experiments were conducted that directly compared whether attention was directed to spatial locations or to objects, and objects won. Here's how these two points were made.

If the beam idea were right, it should take a longer time to move the attentional beam a greater distance, but that appears not to be true. Ho-Wan Kwak, Dale Dagenbach, and Howard Egeth (1991; see also Sagi & Julesz, 1985) tested this prediction by asking participants to judge whether two simple stimuli (*T* or *L*) were the same or different. While participants looked at a crosshair fixation point in the center of the screen, two letters appeared on the screen some distance from one another for just 150 ms. Participants were asked to make a "same or different" judgment as quickly as possible. Figure 3.8 shows that the time it took to make the judgment did not vary as the distance between the letters changed. From these data, it seems that attention moves ballistically from one location to another and does not sweep along in space as a beam would.

If attention were a beam, we might expect that when sweeping from one location to another, attention might be captured by an intervening object.

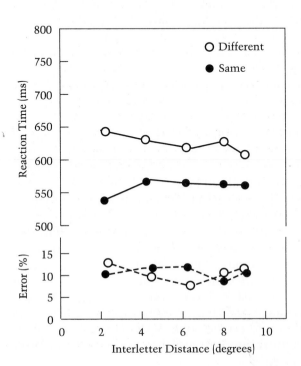

Figure 3.8. *Figure from Kwak et al. (1991) showing that the distance between two stimuli does not affect performance in terms of response times or errors. "Different" and "same" refer to whether the stimuli were the same or different.*

George Sperling and Erich Weichselgartner (1995) showed that that is not the case, again implying that attention jumps from one discrete location to another.

In their procedure, the participant saw a fixation dot at the center of the screen and pressed a button to begin the trial. Digits started appearing at the center of the screen very rapidly (10 per sec). At the same time, letters started appearing to the left of the digits so that they were not adjacent but could be perceived. Letters also appeared at a rate of 10 per sec. The participant was to keep his or her eyes on the digits but to focus attention on the letters. (It's possible to keep your eyes on one thing but to focus attention on another; try it.) When the letter *C* appeared, the participant was to shift attention to the digits and to report the first four digits perceived. It's possible to measure how quickly a participant shifted attention by noting the first digit he or she reported.

The interesting manipulation was that on some trials nonalphanumeric characters (such as #, &, @, or *) appeared between the letters and digits. Did these stimuli slow the shift of attention from the letters to the digits? If it moves as a beam, we might expect these flashing stimuli to slow attention, whereas if attention simply jumps from one location to another, the intervening characters should not matter. The results showed that response times averaged 374 ms without the intervening characters and 383 ms with the intervening characters, a difference that was not statistically significant. Thus, the data are consistent with the idea that attention jumps from one location to another.

Other results directly support the idea that attention selects objects, not space. For example, participants can selectively attend to just one of two objects that overlap in a single spatial location. Ulric Neisser and Robert Becklen (1975) had participants watch a monitor with two different video images superimposed. One video showed two people playing a hand-slapping game, and the other showed three people playing a ball-catching game. Participants were to attend to one video or the other, and they had to indicate when certain key events, such as the ball being thrown, happened in the video they were watching. Thus the task was a bit like a visual version of dichotic listening with shadowing. Neisser and Becklen found that participants knew very little about the unattended video, a result similar to those from dichotic listening studies. Participants find it easy to attend to just one object of two, even if they are in overlapping spatial locations. If attention were directed by spatial location, that should not be possible (or at least it should not be so easy).

Here's another prediction of the object-based account. If attention were directed to space, we would expect that the farther an object is from the location where attention is directed, the less attention it gets. If two object parts are equidistant from the location, they should get equal amounts of attention. For example, if your attention is focused on Judy's face, each of her hands would get the same amount of attention if they are equidistant from her face. Now suppose that Judy has one hand behind her back, Sherry is standing next to her, and Sherry's left hand is the same distance from Judy's face as Judy's right hand is. The spatial theory of attention would predict that Sherry's hand and Judy's hand will get equal amounts of attention because they are equidistant from

Judy's face, the focus of attention. The object view of attention would predict that Judy's hand will get more attention. By looking at Judy's face, you select an object (Judy) for attention, and all the parts of the object therefore get more attention.

BOX 3–1 *Neural Evidence for Selection of Objects by Attention*

Attention enhances perceptual processing, but of what? Does it enhance the processing of a location in space or the processing of an object? Kathleen O'Craven, Paul Downing, and Nancy Kanwisher (1999) collected evidence using fMRI indicating that attention selects objects for processing, not a location in space.

The researchers had participants view stimuli of a semitransparent face superimposed on a house, with one stimulus moving and the other not. Participants were to attend to the house, the face, or the motion. The parts of the brain that respond to each of these stimuli are well established: faces generate activity in the fusiform face area (on the ventral aspect of the temporal lobe), places generate activity in the parahippocampal place area (also on the ventral aspect of the temporal lobe, but not the same as the fusiform face area), and motion generates activity in area MT (in the middle of the temporal lobe).

If attention operates through the enhanced processing of a location in space, all three of the target visual areas should be more active because all three attributes are in the same location. But if attention operates through the selection of an attribute (face, place, or motion), activity should be localized to the brain area that supports perception of that attribute, even though the other attributes overlap in space.

The results showed selective activation of the brain area supporting perception of the attended attribute. In other words, when participants attended to the face, the face area was active but the place and motion areas were not, and so on.

The results for motion were somewhat more complicated, but in a way that provides an excellent test of the object theory of attention. The theory predicts that you select an object for attention, and that should mean that you select the entire object, including all its attributes. That means that if you are told to attend to a face and the face is moving, you can't help but process the motion because motion is an attribute of the face. This prediction was confirmed in the study: if you attend to an object, you process all of its attributes.

This study provides compelling neural evidence supporting the behavioral evidence that attention selects objects, not areas in space, for processing.

Gordon Baylis and Jon Driver (1993) tested this prediction. They showed that it is harder to judge the relative distance of two corners when the corners were parts of different objects than when they were parts of the same object. On each trial, participants saw a picture similar to Figure 3.9. They were asked which vertex was higher, the one on the left or on the right. Some participants were told to examine the white parts of the figure to make these judgments.

Figure 3.9. *Stimuli of the sort used in Baylis and Driver's (1993) experiment.*

For these participants the figure on the left would require comparing parts (the angles) of a single object, but the figure on the right would require comparing parts of two separate objects. Other participants were told to compare the angles of the black parts of the figure; for these participants, the figure on the left required comparing parts of two objects, the figure on the right just one. Thus Baylis and Driver were able to use the same stimulus for each condition; they got participants to interpret the figure as depicting one or two objects by using different instructions. The results showed that participants were reliably slower in making the judgment (by about 30 ms) when the instruction led them to compare the angles of two objects rather than one object. Again, this result is consistent with the idea of attention being focused on objects, not regions of space.

The evidence that attention selects objects, not locations in space, appears compelling. But how exactly does selection operate?

How Does Selection Operate?

The process by which attention selects some objects for further processing has been studied most thoroughly in visual search paradigms in which the participant looks through a large array for one particular character. To get a feel for this type of task, look for the large letter *Q* in the three arrays in Figure 3.10.

You probably found it easy to locate the large *Q* in the first two arrays and more difficult in the third. In the first array, a single feature of the *Q*—the diagonal line that differentiates a *Q* from an *O*—differentiates it from the other letters present. In the second array, again, a single feature—its size—makes the target different from the other letters. In the third array, however, no single feature differentiates the targets and distractors.

These two types of searches are called disjunctive and conjunctive. In a **disjunctive search** the target differs from the distractors on just one feature, as in the two arrays on the left. In a **conjunctive search** more than one feature differentiates the target from the distractors. There are shapes that match the target and sizes that match the target, but there is only one combination (or conjunction) of shape and size that match the target. Visual search experiments have been done with many different features, such as different shapes, sizes, colors, textures, and spatial orientations (see Treisman & Gormican, 1988, for a review).

Figure 3.10. *Stimulus arrays of the sort used by Treisman & Gelade (1980). In each array, the target is a large Q. In the left and center arrays, the target is easy to find because a single dimension differentiates the targets from distractors. In the right array, more than one dimension is necessary to distinguish the target from distractors. The left and center arrays yield automatic searches and pop out; the right array does not.*

When you do this sort of search task, it certainly feels as though the arrays on the left are easier, and laboratory experiments confirm this feeling. The major finding is that disjunctive searches are parallel, whereas conjunctive searches are serial. A **parallel search** is one in which all elements in the array are processed simultaneously. A **serial search** is one in which the elements of the array are evaluated one at a time.

The critical finding from laboratory experiments is this: increasing the number of elements in the array does not affect the reaction time to find the target in the disjunctive search, but it increases the search time in the conjunctive search. The disjunctive search is parallel—all elements are evaluated simultaneously—so increasing the number of items to be evaluated does not raise the total search time. The conjunctive search is serial—elements are checked one by one—so increasing the number of items raises the search time. The participant will locate the target, on average, after checking half of the items in the array. (Note that this key measure of the effect of adding distractors is the same that was used in the Shiffrin and Schneider studies of automaticity.) Indeed, people report the pop-out effect for disjunctive searches. They feel as though they don't even need to search for the target; it attracts their attention, popping out of the array.

The importance of the difference between disjunctive and conjunctive searches was emphasized by Anne Treisman and Garry Gelade (1980). They proposed that the perceptual system is organized as a series of feature maps: a map for color, a map for shapes, a map for textures, a map for distances, and so on. Each map contains information about the locations in the environment of that one feature. The color map shows where different colors are in the environment; the shape map, different shapes; and so on. The contents of these maps are loaded **preattentively**; in other words, attention is not needed to put the information on these maps. Thus if you know that you are searching for a red target, you need only examine the color map because the colors of all the objects in the field are on that map. That's why you can do a parallel search for an object defined by a single feature; each feature is loaded on a map in parallel.

A conjunctive search, however, requires information from two maps. To search for the letter Q, as in Figure 3.10, you look for a diagonal line on the shape map. If there are many of them, you look at the size map for a large letter and find that there are many of those. So you need to compare the contents of both maps. Treisman and Gelade suggest that comparing the contents of maps requires attention. Attention binds features together into objects. (For other points of view on this question see Kubovy, Cohen, & Hollier, 1999.)

Thus when you're searching for a target that is defined by a single feature—for example, scanning a busy street for bright yellow when you want to hail a cab—it seems that you can simply examine the color map, and attention is drawn to the appropriate color. But is attention drawn to the correct color, or does attention filter out all the inappropriate colors?

An experiment by Shui-I Shih and George Sperling (1996) indicates that in a search for a feature such as a color, attention is drawn to the correct stimulus rather than filtering out the others. Participants in their experiment saw arrays of letters flashed on a screen. The target was a single digit that appeared in one array. The interesting part of the experiment was that alternating arrays within a trial varied on a feature; for example, the first array would have large letters, the next would have small letters, the next large, and so on. In a single trial, a participant might see a series of arrays like those in Figure 3.11.

Shih and Sperling asked what would happen if they *told* participants that the target (the digit) would appear in an array with large characters. If visual search operates by filtering out objects with the undesired feature, it should be easier to spot the target; participants would not waste any attention on the arrays with small letters. But telling participants that the target will be among the large characters doesn't help them spot it. Furthermore, misinforming participants by telling them to expect the target among the wrong characters doesn't hurt their performance, either.

In their second experiment, the target differed from the surrounding distractors on one dimension within an array. For example, a small target would appear with large characters. With this change, informing the participants

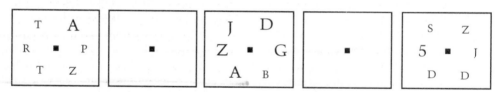

Figure 3.11. *Trial sequence in Shih and Sperling's (1996) task.*

about the critical feature had a big impact on performance. Shih and Sperling interpreted their results as showing that the critical feature can draw attention to a correct stimulus, but it cannot filter out incorrect stimuli. To put it colloquially, when you're searching for a taxi, it's not that you ignore everything that is not yellow and then are left attending to the one yellow thing in the street; rather, your attention is drawn to the yellow thing.

Stand-on-One-Foot Questions

7. *In the final analysis, is the attentional filter early or late?*
8. *What does selective visual attention select?*
9. *Summarize when a visual search is easy and when it's hard.*

Questions That Require Two Feet

10. *In many horror movies, the heroine calmly takes a shower and doesn't notice the scuffling sounds made by the clodhopper shoes of the zombie carrying the axe. How can this be explained as a problem of attention?*
11. *After reading this discussion, can you think of a situation from your own experience indicating that attention is directed to objects, not spatial locations?*

WHY DOES SELECTION FAIL?

In the last section we made it sound as though the selective aspect of attention is wholly under our conscious control and that if selection fails, it is due to a lack of attentional resources. A moment's reflection will tell you that is not so. It would be marvelous if attentional selection were so simple; you would say to yourself, "I'm going to attend to this book chapter for the next hour," and you would do so, instead of finding yourself at the bottom of a page in a reverie about the marvelous spareribs you had last summer when you spilled sauce down your bathing suit. Yes, you can select what you want to attend to, but the selection does not last as long as you'd like. Attention wanders. Furthermore, there are times that you actually can't select what you would like for attention. There are two classes of reasons for such failures. Some are due to properties of attention itself, others to the way attention interacts with other components of cognition.

Properties of Attention that Cause Selection Failures

INHIBITION OF RETURN.   Your attention system appears to have a bias not to go back to something that it has recently examined. This effect was first described by Mike Posner (1978; Posner & Cohen, 1984). The task was quite simple. Two boxes appeared on a computer screen, aligned horizontally, with a crosshair between them. Participants were told to focus on the crosshair while keeping their index fingers poised above two response buttons. When an *X* appeared in one of the boxes, the participant was to push the corresponding response button as quickly as possible. (We'll call the *X* a GO signal because participants were to respond to it.) On some trials, however, one of the boxes would flicker before the *X* appeared; participants were told that the flickering in no way predicted where the X would appear and that they should therefore ignore it. (We'll call the flicker the warning signal.)

The interesting finding concerned the effect of the warning signal (if it was present) when it appeared in the same location as the GO signals. If the delay between the warning and GO was 300 ms or less, participants were faster to respond compared to trials without a warning. If the delay was longer than 300 ms, participants were slower to respond.

Posner and Cohen interpreted this result as follows. Although participants want to ignore the warning, they cannot. It captures attention automatically. At about 300 ms, however, attention disengages and cannot immediately reengage at the box that flickered. Thus if the GO signal appears in the box less than 300 ms after the warning, there is a response time benefit because attention is already localized in the right spot. If the GO signal appears more than 300 ms after the flicker, there is a cost to response time because attention cannot return to the box. That is **inhibition of return**. Further work showed that the effect can be quite long-lasting, perhaps as long as several seconds (Tassinari & Berlucchi, 1995).

Earlier in the chapter we discussed whether attention selects objects or spatial locations, and we concluded that it selects objects. You might therefore wonder whether inhibition of return is based on objects or space. Can attention not return to the box, or to the spatial location of the box? Steve Tipper and his associates (Tipper, Driver, & Weaver, 1991) tested the question in a straightforward way: they had the objects move between the warning and GO signals. A warning signal would appear in association with object *X* at location *X*; then the objects on the screen would move so that object *X* was now at location *Y*. The GO signal could appear either in association with the same object or in the same location (or at a completely new object and location as a control condition). The researchers found that inhibition of return was based on objects, not location—if the objects moved, the inhibition moved too. This result agrees with other literature indicating that attention selects objects, not spatial locations.

Why would the attention system have inhibition of return built into it? Possibly to make search more efficient; if you are investigating a field of objects one by one, it makes sense that there be a bias not to return to an object that has already been inspected (Posner & Cohen, 1984). It may be that as an object becomes the focus of attention, it is "tagged" so that it will not be the focus of attention for some brief time thereafter (Klein, 1988).

IRONIC PROCESS OF MENTAL CONTROL.   Inhibition of return describes a situation in which it is hard to select something that you want to select. There are also times when you cannot help but attend to something that you don't want to attend to. For example, suppose I tell you, "For the next few minutes I'd like for you not to think about a white bear. Think about whatever you like, but try not to think about a white bear." You know what's going to happen: it's going to be very difficult not to think about a white bear. Dan Wegner and his colleagues (Wegner, Schneider, Carter, & White, 1987) performed this procedure in the laboratory. They simply asked participants to "think aloud" for 5 min. If they were warned not to think about a white bear, white bear thoughts intruded approximately seven times during the 5-min period.

Wegner (1994) proposed that there are two processes by which you seek to control the contents of your mental events. The **operating process** seeks mental contents consistent with what you want to think about; for example, if you set as your goal not to think about a white bear, the operating process will search for distractions from that thought. The **monitoring process** searches for mental contents that are inconsistent with what you want to think about. For example, if you're trying not to think about white bears, it searches for mental contents about white bears and related matters. This monitoring process serves as a warning system that you are about to fail in your desired mental control.

A key assumption of the theory is that the operating process demands attentional resources, but the monitoring process does not. Thus, if attentional resources are scarce, perhaps because you're thinking of something else or you're under stress, the operating process can't do its job of searching for the appropriate mental contents. The monitoring process can do its job, however, because it doesn't require attention. Because the operating process isn't generating appropriate thoughts, the monitoring process often finds inappropriate thoughts and brings them to awareness to alert the system that these inappropriate thoughts are present. That process, in effect, generates the unwanted thoughts. Keep in mind that these ironic effects occur only under mental load—for example, if you're tired or distracted; under normal circumstances, mental control works pretty well.

MAINTAINING ATTENTION: VIGILANCE.   **Vigilance** is simply the ability to maintain attention, usually in a search task to detect a target or small set of targets, which might be visual, auditory, and so on. Vigilance is important in many military applications and manufacturing jobs. In a typical vigilance task there are stretches of time in which nothing happens. Driving, for example, is not a vigilance task because the driver is continually making adjustments of speed and direction. Quality control inspection, on the other hand, is a vigilance task; the inspector checks items that are nearly identical but must maintain attention to spot the occasional item that was not produced correctly.

It isn't as easy as you might think to measure performance on a vigilance task. How could you tell whether a sonar operator is doing a good job? Presumably, he or she should not miss reporting a ship when a ship is really out there. But suppose the operator simply called out, "There's a ship!" all the time. He or she wouldn't miss any ships but would constantly cause false alarms. Another person might be very conservative in calling something a ship, so that if he or she said, "There's a ship," you could be sure that there was, but this person would often fail to identify a ship when there really was one out there. Thus different people have different criteria in a task like this.

In fact, the same person could adopt different strategies. I might say to you, "Whatever you do, don't let a ship get by; if anything looks like it could be a ship, call it a ship." Or I might say, "Whatever you do, don't say you see a ship if it's not really a ship." Your absolute sensitivity in detecting ships doesn't change, obviously, but the type of mistakes you make may change, depending on your strategy. It turns out that there is a way to analyze these two factors separately. We can separate **sensitivity**, which is your absolute ability to detect ships, from **bias**, which is a measure of whether you are liberal or conservative in saying that you see a ship. The method of separating sensitivity from bias is called **signal detection theory**. It is described in the Appendix; for now, you

---

Box 3–2 Neural Evidence for Serial Processing of Conjunctive Searches

We have discussed the visual search paradigms as though it is clear that a disjunctive search proceeds in parallel, and a conjunctive search serially. This result is inferred from the fact that disjunctive searches get slower as the number of distractors increases. But isn't it possible that the conjunction search is also parallel but becomes less efficient as the number of distractors increases? Brain imaging data support the parallel processing interpretation.

Maurizio Corbetta and his associates (Corbetta, Shulman, Miezin, & Petersen, 1997) used a variant of Treisman's search task. In disjunctive searches, participants searched for either color (red-orange dot among orange dots) or speed (fast-moving dots among slower-moving dots). In the conjunctive search task the target was a red-orange, fast-moving dot. The researchers varied the number of distractors and got the standard result: disjunctive search incurred no cost for an increasing number of distractors, but conjunctive search was slower as the number of distractors increased.

Participants were performing this task while brain activation was imaged with PET. The most pronounced difference in brain activation between disjunctive and conjunctive search was in the superior parietal lobe, especially in the right hemisphere. This location has been associated with shifts of attention in

(Continued)

other experimental paradigms where it is more obvious that attention must move from location to location for successful performance of the task. Thus the activation of superior parietal lobe in the conjunctive search condition indicates that participants do indeed move attention from location to location when performing a conjunctive search.

Superior parietal cortex

need to know that vigilance is measured in terms of sensitivity, not bias. People's sensitivity in a vigilance task drops after the first half hour or so.

Why does sensitivity decrease? The first thing you would think is, "Well, people get bored," but there are many other possibilities. Alertness might drop when a person does the same thing for a while. Motivation could decline. It could be a process of habituation; if you are exposed to the same stimulus again and again, it loses its force. Think about eating a really spicy dish; the first mouthful tastes like fire, but mouthfuls toward the bottom of the bowl don't have the same power.

Complicating our ability to test these ideas is the fact that sensitivity declines depend on the specific task. In fact, for some tasks sensitivity doesn't drop. Raja Parasuraman and Roy Davies (1977) suggested that sensitivity drops only for successive tasks with high event rates. Successive tasks are those in which there is some standard you are supposed to keep in memory, and then on each trial you must compare the stimulus to the standard. For example, if you have been trained to know what a ship looks like on a radar scope, you must keep that image in memory and compare it to new images that come up on the radar scope. In a simultaneous task, however, you need not keep anything in memory because the stimuli you are to compare are presented simultaneously. The other quality a vigilance task must have to show the drop in sensitivity is a high event rate. That means that stimuli must appear frequently (Parasuraman and Davies said at least 24 stimuli per minute). If either of these conditions is not met—if stimuli are simultaneous or if there is a low event rate—there is no drop in the sensitivity.

Harry Koelega and his colleagues (Koelega, Brinkman, Hendriks, & Verbaten, 1989) suggested that another factor determines whether sensitivity drops: whether the task is sensory or cognitive. They proposed that sensitivity drops for sensory tasks, in which the participant must evaluate brightness, color, or some other perceptual attribute, but is stable or even increases for cognitive tasks. (By cognitive tasks they simply meant identifying stimuli by their meaning, as for letters or numbers.)

To examine this question more carefully, Judi See and her colleagues (See, Howe, Warm, & Dember, 1995) performed a meta-analysis, a statistical technique that allows researchers to combine the results of many studies even if they use different methods. The advantages of doing a meta-analysis are complicated; suffice to say that it provides a better view of what is likely to be true, just as it is better to ask 1,000 people rather than 10 people how they will vote if you're trying to predict the outcome of an election. The meta-analysis by See and colleagues made the story that much more complicated. Whether the task is sensory or cognitive did make a difference. For sensory tasks, sensitivity gets worse for simultaneous tasks and better for successive tasks. For cognitive tasks, it's just the opposite; sensitivity gets better for simultaneous tasks and worse for sensory tasks.

Why is that true? No one seems to have a clear idea. All we know is that vigilance is more complicated than we would like. Other factors may play some role in the sensitivity drop, but we can't predict with confidence whether a new vigilance task will show a sensitivity drop.

Interaction of Attention with Other Components of Cognition

We have discussed three ways in which the design of the attention system causes problems in selection: there is a bias not to return to a recently attended object, attention will perversely select an undesired object when resources are scarce, and the ability to select the same type of stimuli again and again seems to dissipate after about half an hour. In this section we describe a different class of attentional failures that occur not because of how attention operates but because of how it interacts with other parts of the cognitive system.

You'll recall that many of the experiments purporting to show capacity limitations used a dual task methodology; that is, participants were asked to do two things at once. We concluded that there aren't enough attentional resources to fuel both tasks, but it is also possible that performance suffers because of other cognitive processes that contribute to the tasks.

Suppose that a structure in the brain is necessary to perform visual tasks, a sort of screen where the conscious experience of vision happens. You can have only one thing on this screen at a time, so you can't do two visual tasks at the same time (such as play a video game and generate a mental image of your room). This is a **structural explanation** because it posits that interference between two tasks is caused by competition for mental structures, not for attentional resources.

We can make an educated guess as to which structures would be involved in performance limitations. If two tasks require the same perceptual modality—for example, if both are visual tasks—there will be more interference than if they use different modalities. Similarly, if they require the same output modality (such as arm movements), there will be more interference than if they call for different responses (one arm movement and one vocal response). Other work shows that structural limits can be more subtle, however. We review two effects here.

PSYCHOLOGICAL REFRACTORY PERIOD.   Alan Welford (1952) and more recently Hal Pashler (1998) pointed out a less obvious structural explanation for performance limitations. They suggested that there may be a response selection bottleneck. They proposed that three basic processes are necessary for performing any task, even a very simple task such as pushing a button when a light comes on. The three processes are perception (seeing the light), **response selection** (choosing the response of pushing the button), and response production (generating the muscle commands that moves your finger). Welford and Pashler suggested that a person can select only one action at a time; you might be able to perceive two stimuli simultaneously and generate two movements simultaneously, but you can't select two actions simultaneously.

As evidence for the performance bottleneck, Pashler points to the **psychological refractory period**—a period of time after one response is selected during which a second response cannot be selected. For example, suppose that when a light appears on the left side of a computer screen, you are to push a button with your left hand, and when a tone sounds, you are to depress a pedal with your foot. Suppose it takes you about 500 ms to press the foot pedal when you hear the tone. What happens if I flash the light and then sound the tone a mere 50 ms after the light comes on? You will be slower to depress the pedal in this case. The reason is shown schematically

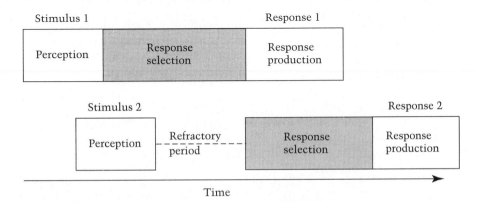

Figure 3.12. *Graphic representation of the refractory period. Time moves from left to right. The response selection for Stimulus 2 cannot begin until the response selection for Stimulus 1 is completed; that is the source of the refractory effect.*

in Figure 3.12. Stimulus 1 is presented and then Stimulus 2 is presented while the first stimulus is still being perceived. Once Stimulus 1 is perceived, response selection for Stimulus 1 is initiated. But when perception of Stimulus 2 is complete, the response for Stimulus 2 is not initiated; it cannot be started until response selection for Stimulus 1 is complete. That is the selection bottleneck.

The effect of the bottleneck is sizable; response time to the tone might be 700 ms instead of 500 ms. According to Figure 3.12, if response selection for Stimulus 1 were completed by the time Stimulus 2 was presented (in other words, Stimulus 2 is moved to the right in the figure), there should be no bottleneck. That prediction is true; as the interval between the first and second stimulus increases, the response time to the second stimulus gets shorter.

The psychological refractory effect is obtained with many different types of stimuli and responses, even if the second response is an eye movement (Pashler, Carrier, & Hoffman, 1993) or a foot movement (Osman & Moore, 1993; see Pashler, 1998, for a review, and Schumacher et al., 2001, for an exception). This result is important because it demonstrates interference even from extremely simple tasks, not just from tasks that demand a lot of attention, and from tasks that do not share obvious structural demands (not just tasks that are both visual, for example). If the tasks were more complex—say, riding a bicycle and working math problems—you would interpret interference between them in terms of attention. Naturally you're slower to work math problems if you're simultaneously riding a bicycle: both tasks demand attention! But in the example just described we are talking about very simple tasks that should take very little attention.

If there is an output bottleneck, you might think, "Heck, maybe we don't need this idea of attentional capacity in the first place. Maybe the problems we see when people try to do two tasks at once are due to output bottleneck problems. The problem is not capacity sharing—it's the crowding of outputs." But that can't be the whole story because capacity seems to be limited even when no output is required; for example, people can't attend to many different types of sensory inputs at once. Nevertheless, the evidence for an output bottleneck raises the possibility that what we thought were effects of limited attention may actually have nothing to do with attention.

ATTENTIONAL BLINK. The psychological refractory period demonstrates that performance may be poor in a dual task paradigm for reasons other than capacity limitations, in this case, because successive responses cannot be selected rapidly. What if successive tasks did not demand responses? Would there still be a decrement in performance?

The **attentional blink** paradigm tests that question and indicates that there is indeed a decrement in performance. The paradigm uses a procedure called **rapid serial visual presentation (RSVP)** in which participants watch a series of stimuli (usually 10–15) that appear briefly one at a time on a computer

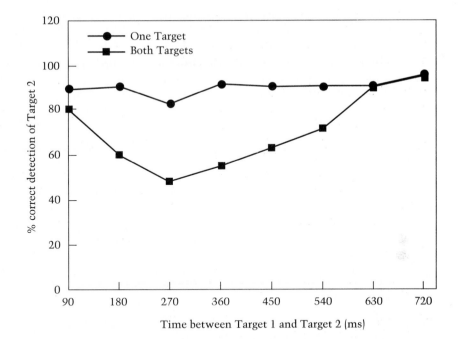

Figure 3.13. *Typical results of the attentional blink experiment. In the one target condition, participants are told to report only the second of two targets, and the time between the first and second targets does not affect performance. In the both targets condition, participants are to report both targets, and performance is poor when the second target appears approximately 100 to 600 ms after the first target. Data based on "Temporary Suppression of Visual Processing in an RSVP Task: An attentional Blink?" by J. E. Raymond, K. L. Shapiro, and K. M. Arnell, 1992,* Journal of Experimental Psychology: Human Perception & Performance, *18, pp. 849–860.*

screen. Participants may be told that most of the stimuli will be digits, for example, but two of them will be letters. After all the stimuli have been presented, participants are to name the two letters.

The attentional blink refers to the fact that observers have trouble identifying the second target if it appears between 100 and 600 ms after the first target, as shown in Figure 3.13. This effect occurs with a variety of stimuli: words (Broadbent & Broadbent, 1987), orientation (Joseph, Chun, & Nakayama, 1997), color (Ross & Jolicoeur, 1999), and dot patterns (Shapiro, Raymond, & Arnell, 1994).

What causes the attentional blink? It cannot be a response selection effect because participants need not hurry their responses; the dependent measure is accuracy, not time. It might seem that the effect is more likely perceptual—perhaps the first stimulus masks the second, for example. But there are data showing that the attentional blink is still robust when the first target is visual and the second target auditory or vice versa (Arnell & Jolicoeur,

1999). This fact argues strongly against the effect being perceptual. Most researchers conclude that the attentional blink, like the psychological refractory period, represents a central bottleneck, but not one of attention. Some researchers believe that there may be some way in which the two effects are related, but just how they are related is still not understood (Arnell & Duncan, 2002; Jolicoeur, 1998; Ruthruff & Pashler, 2001; Wong, 2002).

Stand-on-One-Foot Questions

12. *What properties of attention can cause selection failures?*
13. *Name some sources of apparent attention limitations that are more likely due to other components of the cognitive system.*

Questions That Require Two Feet

14. *Suppose your friend had an ugly breakup with his girlfriend, and he finds he can't stop thinking about her. Try as he might not to think about her, he just can't stop. What would you advise him to do?*
15. *Apply the terminology from signal detection theory to car alarms and comment on their effectiveness.*
16. *Some military radar operators sit in underground bunkers watching radar scopes that monitor whether someone is sending a nuclear missile our way. Comment on the likely effectiveness of those radar operators and suggest ways to make them more effective.*

KEY TERMS

attention
attentional blink
automatic process
bias
conjunctive search
continuous task
dichotic listening
direct measure
discrete task
disjunctive search
distractor
dual task paradigm

early filter
flanker effect
flanker task
galvanic skin response (GSR)
indirect measure
inhibition of return
late filter
limited
monitoring process
multiple resources
operating process

parallel search
pop-out
preattentively
psychological refractory period
rapid serial visual presentation (RSVP)
response selection
response to stimulus interval
selective
sensitivity

serial search   signal detection theory   target
shadow   structural explanation   vigilance

Box 3–3 Automaticity and the Brain

What exactly is happening when a process becomes automatic? Do the controlled processes become more efficient? Or are the processes supporting automaticity altogether different? One way to approach these processes is to examine their neural bases: if the anatomical basis of a process changes as it becomes automatic, that would be consistent with a fundamental change in processing as automaticity develops, but if the anatomical basis remains the same, that would argue for increased efficiency of the same process. It turns out that which pattern you observe depends on the task.

Johan Jansma and his colleagues (Jansma, Ramsey, Slagter, & Kahn, 2001) had participants practice a working memory task (working memory is described in chapter 4, but this experiment is not hard to understand). Participants saw a target set of 5 consonants, then a series of 10 letters one at a time. For each letter the participant had to judge whether or not it was part of the target set. Then a new target set would be presented followed by 10 more test trials, and so on. Participants performed two versions of the task. In one version, the target set always had the same 5 letters, whereas in the other version the target set was different every time. We might expect automaticity could develop when the target set was consistent but not when it varied.

Indeed, participants' response times and accuracy improved a great deal after approximately 800 practice trials with the consistent version of the task; the improvement was not nearly so dramatic for the varied version. The brain regions that were activated for the two versions of the task did *not* differ, however; the dorsolateral prefrontal cortex, the right superior frontal cortex, and the supplementary motor area were involved in each type.

Data for other tasks tell a different story, however. Marcus Jueptner and his colleagues (1997) had participants learn a sequence of eight finger-to-thumb movements. With practice, participants reported that they no longer had to think about the sequence and could do it "on autopilot." In parallel with this developing automaticity, brain activity changed. Early learning was associated with activity in dorsal prefrontal cortex and anterior cingulate cortex, but automatic performance was associated with activity in posterior parietal cortex. When the researchers asked participants to actively think about the movements they were making, the dorsal prefrontal and anterior cingulate cortices were reactivated. This study indicates that for this motor learning task, different brain regions support automatic and controlled performance.

In sum, the brain data indicate that there may be more than one mechanism of automaticity: some tasks may improve in efficiency, whereas others may invoke an altogether different mechanism for automatic performance.

(Continued)

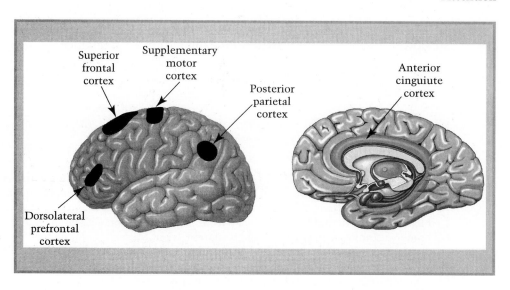

4

Sensory Memory and Primary Memory

WHAT IS SENSORY MEMORY?

WHAT ARE THE CHARACTERISTICS OF PRIMARY MEMORY?

HOW DOES PRIMARY MEMORY WORK?

It is natural to think of memory as a storehouse or repository for facts, rather like a library. In chapter 1, we said that cognitive psychologists conceive of the mind as using representations and processes that manipulate those representations. Thus psychologists interested in memory want to know what these representations look like, how they enter the storehouse in the first place, and how they are retrieved from the storehouse.

In this chapter, we consider what happens to memories before they enter the storehouse of **secondary memory**. This repository is available to the cognitive system but its information is not readily available for use by cognitive processes. First the information must go from secondary to **primary memory**, a hypothetical buffer in which information can be briefly held and manipulated. We have said that processes operate on representations to make cognition happen; primary memory is where processes operate on representations from memory.

For example, if I ask you, "What color is a polar bear?" the answer "White" is in your secondary memory, but this fact is not available to cognitive processes (such as the processes that would enable you to answer my question) until it is retrieved from secondary memory and put into primary memory. Only then is the information available to the processes that construct the sentence to answer my question. Thus primary memory serves as a staging ground for thought. In addition, primary memory serves as a temporary buffer for information. If you and I were in the grocery store and I asked you to get chocolate, bread, and margarine while I shopped for other things, you would maintain these three items in primary memory. You need to retain this information only briefly while you look for the items, so you probably don't enter the details in secondary memory. Thus primary memory both retrieves information from secondary memory and takes in information from the environment, either for temporary maintenance or possibly for entry into secondary memory.

If this description is accurate, we might first want to know how material gets from the environment into primary memory. The process turns out to be complicated. Material perceived in the environment goes through another buffer called **sensory memory** before it ever gets to primary memory. Our first question, therefore, must be **What is sensory memory?** As we'll see, sensory memory has an enormous capacity. A great deal of information can rush into sensory memory simultaneously, but such memory is very short-lived, lasting no more than a second.

Once we have some understanding of sensory memory, we'll be in a better position to consider primary memory. A key question that we would like answered is **What are the characteristics of primary memory?** Researchers became interested in primary memory because it appeared to be fundamentally different from secondary memory. These differences should be reflected in characteristics of primary memory, including how forgetting occurs, how memories are represented, and how much information can be stored at once. Primary memory initially seemed easy to characterize on these dimensions, but it turned out to be more complex than researchers had first appreciated.

Finally, we consider the question **How does primary memory work?** We discuss two conceptions of primary memory: the short-term memory model and the working memory model. The short-term memory model eventually was shown to be incorrect, but it continues to be so important to cognitive psychology that some familiarity with it is necessary. The working memory model has been quite successful in accounting for a great deal of data. We close this chapter with some examples of how working memory contributes to cognitive processing.

WHAT IS SENSORY MEMORY?

> ➤ *Preview* The seeds of the study of sensory memory were planted by the introspectionists. Recall that they were interested in the contents of consciousness, and they were therefore interested in the amount of information that could rush into consciousness simultaneously. They determined that people could perceive four or five complex stimuli (such as letters) in a very brief exposure. Participants in their experiments often reported that they felt as though they had perceived more letters but forgot some of them even as they were reporting the others. It was not until 1960 that psychologist George Sperling showed conclusively that many more stimuli are actually perceived, but only four or five are reported because the remainder are forgotten. Sperling proposed the existence of a memory system that can hold a large number of items, but only for a second or so. In this section we consider the characteristics of sensory memory: how much information it can hold, the type of information it holds, how forgetting occurs, and so on. Later work showed that there is a comparable buffer for the auditory system that holds information for approximately one-fourth of a second.

How much information can you take in simultaneously? In other words, how much can you perceive in an instant? This question has been of interest since psychology's earliest days, and if you think back to chapter 1 and recall the program of the introspectionists, you'll realize it makes sense that they would be interested in this topic. Remember that they were interested almost exclusively in conscious processes. Thus it was important to them to know how much information could get into consciousness at once. They called this measure the **span of apprehension.** Studies of the span of apprehension paved the way for the study of sensory memory because even though researchers were trying to study a purely perceptual process—how much information could be perceived in a very brief exposure—it seemed that memory processes nevertheless were involved in the tasks they used. We begin by briefly reviewing the span of apprehension studies, which will help you understand why the first sensory memory studies were conducted.

Early Span of Apprehension Studies

An early study of the span of apprehension was conducted by Stanley Jevons (1871), a logician. Jevons took a small cup, dipped it into a bowl of black beans, and then tossed the beans onto a black tray, on which there was a small white box. Some of the black beans fell in the white box and some on the black tray. All of this Jevons did while looking elsewhere, so he had no idea how many beans would fall in the white box. He glanced in the box and immediately estimated how many beans were in the box. Then he counted them to see how close he was. He did this 1,027 times, and he found that if there were 3 or 4 beans, his instant estimate was always correct. With 5 beans he was still very good, but not perfect (about 95%). His accuracy dropped as the number of beans increased, so that if there were 15 beans, he was correct a little less than 20% of the time (see Figure 4.1).

So what is Jevons's span of apprehension? You can see that it depends on how you want to define *span*. If you think that his span is the maximum number of beans he could perceive reliably without error, his span is 4 because he began to make mistakes when there were 5 beans or more. That estimate seems a bit conservative, considering he was 95% correct when there were 5. On the other hand, you wouldn't want to say his span is 15 because he was right less than one-fifth of the time when there were that many beans. The usual strategy in these situations is to take the 50% mark, where

Jevons's Estimate	Actual Numbers												
	3	4	5	6	7	8	9	10	11	12	13	14	15
3	23												
4		65											
5			102	7									
6			4	120	17								
7			1	20	113	30	2						
8					25	76	24	6	1				
9					28	76	37	11	1				
10					1	18	46	19	4				
11						2	16	26	17	7	2		
12							2	12	19	11	3	2	
13									3	6	3	2	
14									1	1	4	6	
15										1	2	2	
Totals	23	65	107	147	156	135	122	107	69	45	26	14	11

Figure 4.1. *Results of Jevons's (1871) experiment.*

the participant was right half the time and wrong half the time. In Jevons's case, that put the span of apprehension at 9.

Naturally, Jevons's laboratory conditions could not be everything one would desire for such an experiment. The chief problem was that he had to rely on "a momentary glance" as his exposure to the stimuli, and it's possible that the duration of his momentary glance varied. Perhaps without meaning to, he glanced a little longer when there were a lot of beans in the box, for example. More sophisticated equipment became available by the 1920s that allowed precise timing of the exposure of visual stimuli. One such device is a tachistoscope, which uses a shutter like that of a camera to allow the participant to see the stimulus for a precise amount of time. Today such experiments are conducted on computers. A number of experimenters conducted span of apprehension experiments with better-controlled exposure durations (and substituting black dots on a white card for the beans). Their estimates of the span of apprehension were close to Jevons's; they averaged around 8.4 (Fernberger, 1921; Oberly, 1924; Glanville & Dallenbach, 1929).

These experimenters controlled the duration of stimulus presentation, but there was another problem they could not solve. They were not measuring the span of apprehension directly; instead they were measuring the span of what participants could apprehend *and report*. For example, Douglas Glanville and Karl Dallenbach (1929) reported that some of their participants said that as they were reporting some stimuli, they were forgetting the others. One participant said, "Do not think that the judgment is often made during the exposure except when figures are few in number, or patterns are familiar. Otherwise I have meaning of pattern left from exposure and from that I figure out the number of forms on the card" (p. 220). A popular textbook of the time (Woodworth, 1938) concluded that the span of apprehension must be somewhat higher than measurements showed, but how much higher was not known.

Sperling's Partial Report Procedure

It wasn't until 1960 that a better method of testing the span of apprehension was devised. George Sperling came up with the **partial report procedure** for the experiments in his Ph.D. dissertation. Sperling used arrays of numbers and letters like those in Figure 4.2. Participants saw a display of 4 to 12 items for 50 ms and then had to report as much of it as they could. In a full report, participants reported about 4 items, or 33% of a 12-item array (top row, Figure 4.2). As in earlier experiments, Sperling's participants said that they could see more items but forgot them quickly.

In a partial report, participants saw the display for 50 ms, as before. Then they heard a tone at one of three pitches: high, medium, or low. The pitch of the tone was a cue for which row of the display the participant was to report; participants didn't have to report the whole array, only the cued row. When the partial report procedure was used, participants got, on average, 3 items from the desired row correct (middle row, Figure 4.2). This result doesn't seem so exciting, but keep in mind that participants did not know which row they

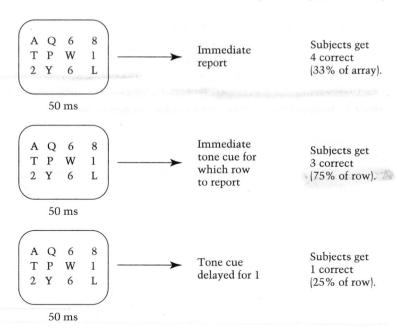

Figure 4.2.   *The design and representative results of Sperling's (1960) experiment. Note that the partial report procedure (center) indicates that much of the array is perceived, but if the cue in the partial report procedure is delayed 1 s (bottom), much of the information from the array is lost.*

would have to report because the tone was random each time. Sperling reasoned that participants must have been equally prepared to report any of the three rows because they couldn't know which row they would have to report. The same logic is used in classroom testing: a professor can't test students on all the material they are supposed to know, so the exam contains a subset of the material, and the professor assumes that students' performance on this subset of the material is a reasonable estimate of their knowledge of all the material. Sperling reasoned that the percentage of the row participants got correct was a good estimate of their knowledge of the entire array. Participants reported an average of 3 items correctly (75% of the row) when the partial report procedure was used, so Sperling inferred that they knew 75% of the full array, or 9 items. Thus full report indicates that the span of apprehension is 4 items, but the partial report procedure indicates that it is 9 items.

If that were true, it would mean that participants perceive much of the array (about 75%), but they lose that information very quickly, either because it decays almost immediately or because interference results from reporting the other items. Sperling tried another experiment in which he showed participants the array and then waited 1 s before presenting the tone that told participants which row to report. Now the partial report advantage was gone: participants averaged only 1 item (25%) out of the desired row, indicating that they could report about 4 items out of the array, as in full report (bottom row, Figure 4.2). Thus, it looked as if the material was lost through decay, not interference from report.

Sperling argued that when the array of stimuli is presented it enters a large-capacity **iconic memory** from which the contents decay rapidly. The participant therefore rushes to report the contents of iconic memory, but by the time he or she has reported 4 letters, the contents have faded. (Sperling actually used the term *sensory memory*, which later came to refer to any of a number of short-term sensory buffers, including a visual buffer, an auditory buffer, and possibly others. The term *iconic memory* came to refer to the visual buffer, and we follow that terminology here.)

Characteristics of Iconic Memory

LARGE CAPACITY.   It's possible that iconic memory maintains most of what the perceptual system encounters. Under some conditions, the capacity of iconic memory can be quite large. For example, Emanuel Averbach and George Sperling (1961) presented their participants with arrays of 18 characters with either a dark field or a light field before and after the letters. The results of this simple manipulation were dramatic. When the prefields and postfields are dark, iconic memory has a bigger capacity and also lasts much longer. The icon—that is, the contents of iconic memory—is still available after a 2-s delay, whereas the icon is gone after 0.5 s with bright prefields and postfields. The bottom line is that the capacity of iconic memory can be large—it holds 17 letters at the briefest delay with the dark fields—but the size and duration depend heavily on the details of experimental situation.

SPONTANEOUS DECAY AND POTENTIAL TO BE ERASED.   We have described the loss of information from iconic memory as being caused by spontaneous decay. Even if the participant does nothing but look at a simple white (or black) field, the contents of iconic memory will degrade. That finding is clear enough from Sperling's original experiments. In the early 1980s researchers realized that although iconic memory does spontaneously decay, the decay begins not when the stimulus disappears but when it first appears.

Vincent Di Lollo (1980) demonstrated this effect in a compelling way. In this experiment participants knew that the basic stimulus was an array of 25 dots. They first saw 12 dots on a field for 10 to 200 ms. After a brief delay (10 ms) they saw another stimulus with 12 dots for 10 ms; thus, they saw a total of 24 dots out of the 25-dot array, and their task was to say which dot was missing. Because they didn't see all 24 dots at the same time, iconic memory must serve as a bridge between the first 12 and the second 12. This task is normally quite easy, as the time to be bridged is just 10 ms, well within the duration of iconic memory. All that varied in the experiment was the duration of the first array. Surprisingly, errors increased when the first stimulus was presented for a longer time, as shown in Figure 4.3.

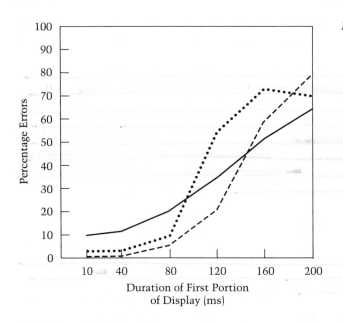

Figure 4.3. *Results from Di Lollo's (1980) experiment showing that iconic memory starts to decay at stimulus onset, not when the stimulus disappears. In this paradigm, iconic memory was needed to bridge between two stimuli; the graph shows that if the first stimulus was present for a longer time before the second appeared, performance was worse. Each line represents data from one participant.*

Researchers had been thinking that iconic memory was some effect of stimulation persisting in the visual system; thus, iconic memory would begin to decay when the stimulus disappeared from the environment. Di Lollo's experiment indicated that iconic memory began to fade when the stimulus first appeared, not when it was extinguished.

In addition to spontaneous decay, there is a second way in which information can be lost from iconic memory. The experimenter can also erase the icon; the technical term is to **mask** the icon, which means to present some random visual stimuli that replace the material currently in iconic memory. In the early 1960s a number of studies showed that the partial report advantage disappears if the stimulus array is followed by a mask, consistent with the idea that the mask erases the contents of iconic memory (see Breitmeyer & Ganz, 1976, and Turvey, 1973, for reviews).

BRIEF DURATION.   As has been emphasized in our description of these experiments, iconic memory can hold a lot of information, but the memory is short-lived, perhaps as short as 500 ms and typically no longer than 1 s, depending on the experimental situation. But even under optimal circumstances, iconic memory lasts only a few seconds, a far cry from other types of memory, which can last your entire lifetime.

REPRESENTATION.   Iconic memory initially was thought to be a rather literal representation of the physical characteristics of the stimuli. In other words, if the stimulus *A* is in iconic memory, there is no information about whether *A* is a number or a letter; iconic memory stores the physical shape of the stimulus but nothing about what it means. Researchers drew this conclusion because only physical characteristics were effective partial report cues. For example, Sperling's initial experiments used the physical location of the stimulus (top, middle, or bottom row) as the cueing characteristic, and that yielded a partial report effect. Other physical characteristics seemed to yield cueing effects as well, such as the size of stimuli when participants were directed to report either large or small stimuli (Von Wright, 1968). But when information about stimulus category was used ("Report only the letters, not the digits") a partial report effect was not found (e.g., see Sperling, 1960). Researchers concluded that iconic memory must not include categorical information, but that view was later challenged, as some experiments showed a partial cuing effect from semantic information. The mixture of results may reflect the fact that semantic information is partly available in iconic memory.

What Is Iconic Memory For?

Ralph Haber (1983) presented a broadly based attack on the very idea of iconic memory, arguing that iconic memory doesn't do anything. We're constantly moving our eyes around, so a new stimulus is constantly replacing the contents of iconic memory.

One idea held that iconic memory helps us keep a stable percept of the world despite the fact that we're always moving our eyes. Haber argued that few data supported that idea, and later work showed he was right: iconic memory does not seem to be useful in maintaining stability when we make eye movements. For example, David Irwin, Steve Yantis, and John Jonides (1983) used Di Lollo's paradigm to examine this question. In their version of the task, participants saw 12 dots from a 5 × 5 matrix of dots, then another 12 dots, and were to report which single dot was missing from the matrix. The first matrix was shown to one side or the other of the center of the screen, and participants were to be looking at the center of the screen when it appeared. They were then to make an eye movement to the place at which the first matrix had appeared, whereupon the second matrix appeared at that location (see Figure 4.4).

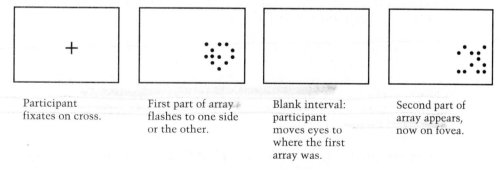

| Participant fixates on cross. | First part of array flashes to one side or the other. | Blank interval: participant moves eyes to where the first array was. | Second part of array appears, now on fovea. |

Figure 4.4.   *Sequence of events in Irwin, Yantis, and Jonides's (1983) study showing that visual integration does not occur across saccades (eye movements). Participants can use iconic memory to integrate the two arrays and spot the missing element, but if an eye movement intervenes between the arrays, they cannot integrate them.*

So the first array of dots appeared to one side or the other when participants were looking at the central fixation mark. Thus, the first array did not hit the fovea. The second array of dots did hit the fovea because participants had made an eye movement to the location of the first array. If iconic memory is useful for integrating information across eye movements, the fact that participants made an eye movement between the two arrays should not affect task performance because iconic memory should preserve the first array during the eye movement.

The results showed that participants were completely at chance in locating the missing dot, indicating that iconic memory is not useful for integrating information across saccades. (Similar results were reported by Rayner & Pollatsek, 1983. For a complete review of this work, see Irwin, 1993.)

If iconic memory is not useful for maintaining the constancy of the world across eye movements, what is it for? Haber suggested that about the only time iconic memory would be useful is if you're trying to read at night during an electrical storm.

Haber pronounced the icon dead (and urged authors to expunge it from textbooks), but researchers thought the announcement premature. Geoff Loftus (1983) argued that the apparent applicability of research to the real world is not an appropriate criterion. Loftus rightly pointed out that experiments under the rigorous control necessary to draw firm scientific conclusions may not bear much surface resemblance to the real world but that control is what makes the conclusions possible. There are no cyclotrons in nature, but they are crucial to our understanding of subatomic particles.

Most researchers agree with Loftus. It is true that we do not currently know what iconic memory does for the cognitive system. Nevertheless, the effects are robust and reproducible and thus provide important clues about how the visual system and primary memory interact; researchers use the idea of iconic memory in accounting for other phenomena (Becker, Pashler, & Anstis, 2000; Wender & Rothkegel, 2000). Therefore, it seems unwise to ignore the work that has helped us understand these effects. Research on iconic memory has slowed in the last 10 years, but researchers are investigating issues such as whether iconic memory is composed of two separate aspects (Cowan, 1995) or not (Massaro & Loftus, 1996).

Echoic Memory

Echoic memory is the auditory version of iconic memory. Again, *sensory memory* is a more general term. Iconic and echoic memory are both forms of sensory memory.

There is good evidence for some storage of sound in the very short term. One source of evidence comes from masking experiments conceptually similar to those we discussed for vision. For example, Dominic Massaro (1970) had participants listen to a tone and identify it as high or low in pitch. The task was made difficult by the presence of a masking tone of random pitch that followed the target tone. If the delay between the target and mask was rather long

(350 ms), participants averaged about 90% correct, but if the mask followed the target without delay, participants averaged just 60% correct.

Presumably, the negative effect of the mask decreases with delay because the auditory system has had more time to get the stimulus into a more stable state (perhaps to transfer it to primary memory). Once the delay between the stimulus and the tone reaches 250 ms, the mask doesn't matter, presumably because 250 ms is how long it takes to get the target safely out of echoic memory and into primary memory. We can tentatively place the duration of echoic memory at 250 ms (Cowan, 1987).

This short duration of echoic memory is consistent with estimates from another task. If echoic memory makes auditory information available for a short time after the stimulus is no longer present, then we should overestimate the duration of very short sounds because they appear to persist after the actual stimulus has stopped. Robert Efron (1970a, 1970b) demonstrated this effect by letting participants control when a light came on and asking them to time the onset of the light with the offset of a sound. By that measure, participants consistently perceived a sound of 30 ms to last about 130 ms; in fact, 130 ms was their estimate for all sounds that lasted between 30 and 130 ms. It appears that the auditory system maintains information in some form briefly (for 250 ms or less), much as the visual system does.

Box 4—1 Tracking Auditory Sensory Memory

Where does sensory memory come from? In one experiment Zhong-lin Lu and colleagues (Lu, Williamson, & Kaufman, 1992) gathered evidence that auditory sensory memory can be viewed as the lifetime of neural activity in primary auditory cortex. In their behavioral task, participants heard a test tone and then some time later (as little as 0.8 s or as much as 8 s) a probe tone. They were to compare the two tones for loudness, pressing one of two buttons to say which tone was louder. Participants performed a total of 6,000 (!) such trials. Human performance on this task is well established. Performance degrades as the delay between the test and the probe increases, and it declines in a consistent way. As the delay increases, people tend to remember the loudness of the test tone as being more average; that is, if the test tone was loud, as time passes participants remember it as quieter, and if the test tone was quiet, as time passes they remember it as being louder. As they forget the test tone, their memory of what it probably sounded like drifts toward the average loudness of tones over the whole experiment.

The experimenters recorded activity in primary auditory cortex using magnetoencephalography (MEG), which is similar to electroencephalography (EEG) in that both techniques record the activity of cortical neurons by placing sensors outside the skull. MEG relies on magnetic properties of neuronal firing, whereas EEG relies on electrical properties. Like EEG, MEG provides mediocre spatial resolution but excellent temporal resolution.

The researchers examined the magnetic fields generated by the test tones and plotted the growth of the fields over time. Using complex curve-fitting techniques,

(Continued)

they estimated the amplitude of the curve, the lifetime of the field, and the time at which the field began to decay. In essence, these measures determine when the neural signal begins to dissipate and how long it takes to dissipate.

The researchers used participants' behavioral data to estimate how long the echoic memory for tone loudness lasted, as shown in Figure B4.2. The experimenters tested four participants; each dot represents data from one participant. Open squares represent trials in which the probe was louder than the test, and closed squares represent trials in which the test was louder than the probe. The important aspect of the graph is the strong linearity of the data. A longer lifetime of activity in the neural trace meant a longer lifetime for the memory of the tone. These data represent evidence that memory of the loudness of sounds over the course of several seconds is supported by transient activity in primary auditory cortex.

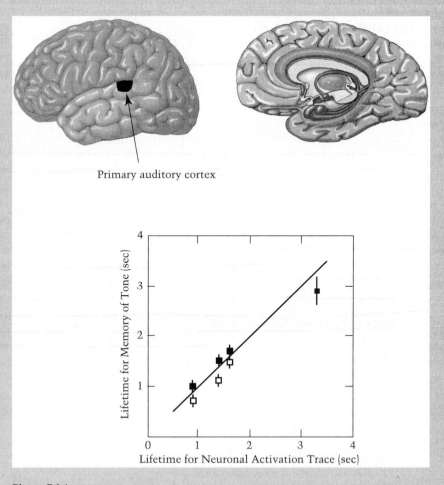

Figure B4.1.

1. *What is the point of the partial report procedure?*
2. *What are the characteristics of sensory memory?*

Questions That Require Two Feet

3. *Haber argued that there seems to be no function for iconic memory. Can you think of a time when you use iconic memory, however briefly? Hint: Think of the movies.*
4. *Most people have noticed that if they stare at something for 30 s or more and then look at something blank (a wall or sheet of paper), they see an afterimage of what they stared at. Is that a demonstration of iconic memory?*

WHAT ARE THE CHARACTERISTICS OF PRIMARY MEMORY?

> ➤ *Preview* It has long been noted that it is possible to hold some information in mind for a brief period of time. For example, if a friend mentions five things he or she needs from the grocery store, you can repeat them back immediately. In the late 1950s researchers began to think that such brief memories might be supported by a separate memory system. Three characteristics of primary memory involve the source of forgetting, the format in which the information is coded, and the amount of information that can be held (the capacity of the system). Both interference and decay appear to contribute to forgetting in primary memory. Primary memory can code material in terms of sound (acoustically), in terms of meaning (semantically), or in terms of visual appearance (visuospatially). In terms of capacity, about 2 s of acoustic material can be coded in primary memory and about four objects can be held in a visuospatial code. The capacity of primary memory for semantic information depends on the content of the information.

Impetus to Study Primary Memory

In this section we characterize primary memory on three dimensions: how material is lost from primary memory, how the system codes material, and how much material it can hold. This work began in the late 1950s when three classic articles were published, energizing psychologists to study primary memory. The concept of a primary memory separate from secondary memory had been around since the late 19th century, but little research had been done on the topic. These articles triggered an avalanche of activity during the 1960s, and primary memory remains a vibrant research topic today. Let's take a moment to consider the exciting research of the 1960s.

Cognitive psychology was born in the late 1950s when researchers began to think the behaviorist approach to psychology wasn't going to work and that descriptions of hypothetical representations and processes in the mind were needed in order to explain human behavior. One of the important thinkers of that time was Donald Broadbent (1958), who likened the human mind to an information processing system, perhaps similar to an electronic information processing system. He is credited as the first psychologist to propose a model that charted the flow of information through the mind, starting with a large-capacity sensory memory (the S system), then going through a filter that deletes most of the information, and finally entering primary memory (the P system). Information in primary memory is associated with consciousness, and this information fades if it is not actively rehearsed. (To **rehearse** material means to practice it in an effort to memorize it.) Furthermore, information can enter primary memory not only from sensory memory but from secondary memory. Broadbent's particular formulation was less important than the fact that at the heart of his information processing model he made a distinction between primary and secondary memory.

A second influential article by George Miller (1956) emphasized two points. First, there seemed to be a fundamental limit or bottleneck in the human information processing system. Miller pointed out that across a number of tasks, the number 7 kept popping up as a limit on human performance. The article was really about this limit to information processing, but it is almost always cited for its inclusion of the primary memory limit of seven items, plus or minus two. Miller's second point was that there had to be a way around this limitation, and he suggested that one way was chunking. A **chunk** is a unit of knowledge that is decomposable into smaller units. Chunking is finding a way to combine several units, such as treating the letters *B, L, U*, and *E* not as four separate letters but as one word. Thus by chunking you can include more information within the limited primary memory system; you can keep only seven letters in primary memory, or you can keep seven words containing many more than seven letters.

These two important papers by Broadbent and Miller convinced researchers that primary memory was important. The third (actually a pair of papers) gave researchers a method by which to study primary memory. Similar findings were published almost at the same time by two different laboratories: John Brown's (1958) in England and Lloyd Peterson and Margaret Jean Peterson's (1959) in the United States. Both Brown and the Petersons were trying to gather evidence that primary memory was fundamentally different from secondary memory. One way to do that is to show that the two hypothetical systems operate differently. Brown and the Petersons sought to show that primary and secondary memory differed in the mechanism by which forgetting occurs. Psychologists were fairly sure that forgetting in secondary memory is caused mostly by interference, meaning that when you forget, the information is still in memory, but you can't get to it because other information in memory is interfering. Brown and the Petersons set out to show that forgetting in primary memory is caused mostly by decay, meaning that the information spontaneously disintegrates.

Brown and the Petersons showed that participants forget even a very small amount of information over a very short delay if they are distracted. The task they used is somewhat similar, so it is called the Brown–Peterson task. The task worked like this. The participant heard a trigram of three consonants such as *TPW* and then a three-digit number like *529*. The participant's task was to immediately start counting backward by threes, beginning with the three-digit number (529, 526, 523, and so on). After some delay (between 0 and 18 s) the experimenter stopped the participant's counting and asked him or her to report what the three consonants were. The point of the backward counting was to prevent the participant from rehearsing the letters.

Three letters are well within the primary memory capacity of most participants, so when the delay was 0 s, participants were nearly 100% correct. But if the participant counted backward for 18 s, recall dropped to around 10% (see Figure 4.5). This result was rather surprising. How could you forget a simple thing like three letters in just 18 s? These results generally were interpreted as showing that information was lost from primary memory by decay. It was already generally believed that secondary memory forgetting was caused

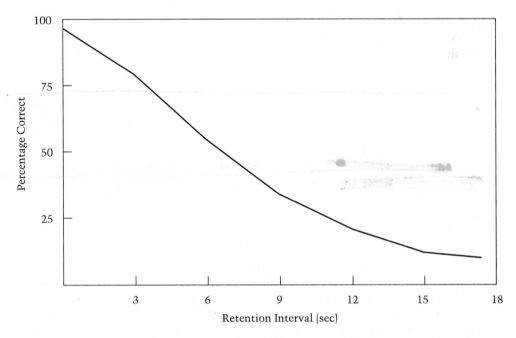

Figure 4.5. *Results from Peterson and Peterson's (1959) study showing forgetting of very little information (three letters) after a brief delay (18 s) if participants are distracted.*

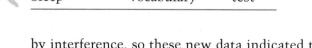

8 a.m.	9 a.m.	10 a.m.
Study Spanish vocabulary	Study French vocabulary	Take French test
Sleep	Study French vocabulary	Take French test

Figure 4.6. *If we compared performance on the French test, the people in the top row would show proactive interference compared to the people in the bottom row.*

by interference, so these new data indicated that the way forgetting occurs is fundamentally different in primary memory. Many researchers therefore set about trying to characterize primary memory.

How Forgetting Occurs

The original experiments by Brown and by Peterson and Peterson were interpreted as showing that forgetting in primary memory occurs through decay. Further work showed that this conclusion was premature because interference also contributes to forgetting in primary memory. There are actually two types of interference: proactive and retroactive. It turns out that both have an effect on primary memory. **Proactive interference** occurs when older learning interferes with new learning. For example, suppose that you're trying to learn some French vocabulary words. Look at the two schedules in Figure 4.6. In both cases you study French vocabulary for an hour and then take a test, but in one case you've just finished studying Spanish. You are likely to remember less French if you've just finished studying Spanish. That is proactive interference: earlier learning interferes with new learning.

In **retroactive interference**, later learning interferes with earlier learning, as shown in Figure 4.7. In this case, studying Spanish comes after the learning we are concerned with (French), so we would say that there is retroactive interference from learning Spanish. (Naturally, there is also proactive interference from the French learning on the Spanish learning in this case.)

Both proactive and retroactive interference are greater if the material studied is more similar. Thus, interference would be worse if you were studying French and Spanish than if you were studying French and geometry.

8 a.m.	9 a.m.	10 a.m.
Study French vocabulary	Study Spanish vocabulary	Take French test
Study French vocabulary	Sleep	Take French test

Figure 4.7. *If we compared performance on the French test, the people in the top row should show retroactive interference compared to the people in the bottom row.*

Because similarity matters for the severity of proactive interference, we might expect that proactive interference could be strong in the Brown–Peterson paradigm. After all, participants have to remember consonant trigrams on each trial, and consonant trigrams are very similar. Geoffrey Keppel and Benton Underwood (1962) examined performance on the Brown–Peterson paradigm and found that even with an 18-s delay, participants average 95% correct on the first trial. On the second trial they average about 70% correct, on the third they are down to 55%, and by the sixth they are down to 40% correct. If forgetting in primary memory were caused primarily by decay, there would be no reason for performance to be so good on the first trial with an 18-s delay.

Judith Reitman (1971) found a clever way to demonstrate that primary memory in the Brown–Peterson paradigm is also susceptible to retroactive interference. She reasoned that retroactive interference increases as the new material becomes more similar to the old material. For example, there would be considerable retroactive interference if you first studied baseball statistics and then studied football statistics, but there would be much less if you first studied baseball statistics and then studied dance steps. Reitman varied what people did during the delay period of the Brown–Peterson paradigm: either they just listened to a humming sound, or they listened to syllables, searching for a target. Because the target material was nouns, if primary memory is susceptible to interference, the second task should interfere more because it's verbal. That's exactly what Reitman found.

What about decay? The fact that there is interference doesn't rule out the possibility that there is also decay, although the problem is difficult to study. If you want to test decay but avoid any possibility of proactive interference, you can test each participant only one time. On the second trial, there could be proactive interference from the first trial. You would therefore need to test hundreds of participants with one trial each to complete an experiment.

That's exactly what Alan Baddeley and Denise Scott (1971) did. They set up a camper in the middle of the University of Sussex campus and offered to donate a small sum of money to charity for each person who took part in their brief experiment. The experimenters gave participants three, five, or seven digits to remember and then distracted them by having them copy dictated letters for 0, 3, 6, 9, 18, or 36 s. Some participants performed just one trial; others performed many trials (the way the experiment is usually conducted), allowing proactive interference. Those data are shown at the left of Figure 4.8. The graph at the right is based on experiments in which each participant performed only one trial, so that there is no opportunity for proactive interference. As you can see, the delay does have some effect, even when participants are tested only once (and therefore proactive interference is impossible). This is shown by the fact that recall drops as the delay increases. Recall drops for the three- and five-digit sequences but not for the seven-digit sequences.

Comparing the rate of decline in performance as the delay increases, we see that proactive interference is a contributor to forgetting in this paradigm—the rate of decrease is greater for the curves on the left—but when there is no

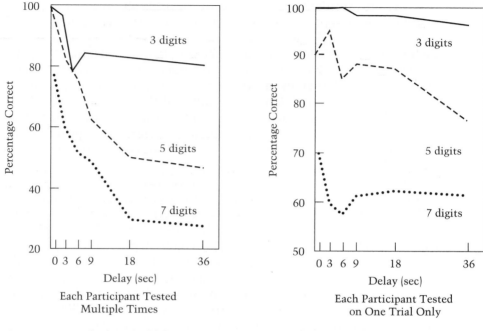

Figure 4.8. *Results from Baddeley and Scott's (1971) investigation of decay in primary memory. The graph on the left shows data from participants who were tested on multiple trials; proactive interference therefore could contribute to forgetting. The data show the usual drop in performance as the delay increases. The graph on the right shows data from participants who were tested on only one trial, so there was no opportunity for proactive interference. Note that as the delay increases, performance drops, indicating that proactive interference is not the only source of forgetting in primary memory.*

opportunity for proactive interference, forgetting still occurs with a delay. This forgetting probably is caused by decay.

Some researchers have suggested that decay may be necessary because without it interference would overwhelm the system (see Anderson, 1989). Here's an example suggested by Erik Altmann and Wayne Gray (2002). Suppose you are driving on a highway and every few seconds you pass a sign posting a new speed limit. After the 100th sign, how could you remember the current speed limit and not confuse it with the previous 99? There should be massive proactive interference. A decay process would mitigate interference because items 1–99 would have been decaying by the time you hit the hundredth. From this functional view of decay, Altmann and Gray predicted that the longer something is in working memory, the more it will decay, and the harder it will be to remember.

In Altmann and Gray's task, a digit appeared on the computer screen and participants categorized it using one of two rules: high/low or even/odd. Only one rule applied on each trial, and the current rule was updated every few trials by a message that appeared briefly on the screen (each message was a speed limit sign, so to say). The important point is that participants had to remember

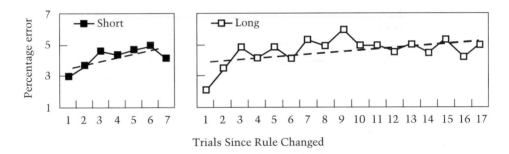

Trials Since Rule Changed

Figure 4.9. *Data from Altmann and Gray's (2002) study of decay in working memory. The data show the percentage of errors participants make in categorizing digits as a function of how many trials have elapsed since the rule changed. The longer the rule has been in working memory, the more errors participants make, indicating decay of the rule from working memory. The dashed least-squares regression lines represent the general trend of the data. Note that the increase is greater (the dotted line is steeper) in the figure at left, for the condition in which the categorization rule is updated more often. Altmann and Gray argue that the decay rate of working memory adjusts to the task; if new material comes in frequently, decay occurs more quickly because the opportunity for proactive interference is greater. Data from "Forgetting to Remember: The Functional Relationship of Decay and Interference," by E. M. Altmann and W. D. Gray, 2002, Psychological Science, 13, Fig. 4, p. 31.*

the current rule in order to categorize digits correctly. The experimenters predicted that as time passed since a rule update, task performance would get worse because it would be harder to remember the current rule (due to decay). Their results are shown in Figure 4.9. Both panels show percentage error as a function of how many trials have passed since the rule was updated. Performance indeed gets worse (errors increase) the longer the rule has been in working memory. Performance also gets worse more quickly (the line is steeper) when the rule is updated more often (left panel). That's because more frequent updates to working memory mean that the decay rate should be faster to counteract the more rapid build-up of interference. Thus, the final word on forgetting in primary memory is that interference and decay both contribute to forgetting.

Representation

It appears that material can be coded in primary memory in at least three ways: visuospatially, acoustically (in terms of sound), and semantically (in terms of meaning). There is also evidence for a working memory component that can store tactile memories—that is, how things feel on the skin—but that work is in its infancy (Harris, Miniussi, Harris, & Diamon, 2002).

The earliest research indicated that everything in primary memory was coded acoustically, and the type of coding was pointed to as a difference between primary and secondary memory: primary memory seemed to use an acoustic code, whereas secondary memory used a semantic code. As we'll see, that conclusion that these codes were unique to each memory system was premature, but the early work did establish that primary memory used an acoustic code at least some of the time. Alan Baddeley (1966) conducted a convincing experiment on this point. To get a feel for how it worked, read the following list aloud, look away from the page, and see whether you can recall the words.

mad, man, mat, cap, cad, can, cat, cap

That probably seemed pretty hard. Now try to do the same thing with a second set of words.

big, long, broad, great, high, tall, large, wide

And finally, try it with a third list of words.

cow, day, bar, few, hot, pen, sup, pit

As you probably noticed, the first list contained words that sounded the same. Baddeley asked participants to remember five words drawn from the lists shown here; 24 five-word lists were compiled from each of these master lists. When the words all sounded the same, participants could produce only 9.6% of the sequences perfectly. When the words were semantically related, as in the second list, they could produce an average of 71.0% of the lists perfectly. When the words were neither acoustically nor semantically related, as in the third list, participants could produce 82.1% of the lists perfectly. Thus there is a huge cost to performance when the words all sound the same, as well as a smaller cost when the words are semantically related. Baddeley concluded from this result that the words had been coded acoustically in primary memory.

The conclusion that an acoustic code was important in primary memory was strengthened by findings showing that if the experimenter presented words visually, as written words, participants would recode them into an acoustic code. Conrad (1964) showed this in an ingenious experiment. He presented a series of letters on a screen at a rate of 1 per 0.75 s. After the six letters appeared, participants were to write them down on an answer sheet, guessing if necessary. One twist was that only a subset of the letters of the alphabet were used: *B, C, P, T, V, F, M, N, S,* and *X.* Conrad was interested in what sorts of errors people made. If they didn't remember *B,* for example, would they just randomly put in one of the other nine letters? No. Participants made systematic errors, based on the sound of the letters. Making such errors is called the **acoustic confusion effect.**

For example, when *M* was presented in the stimulus, if people made an error they were very likely to recall the letter as *N,* which sounds like *M,* rather than recalling *X* or *V,* which look a bit like *M* but don't sound like it. To quantify this point, Conrad had participants read these 10 letters slowly into a tape recorder. Then other participants listened to the tapes, but with white noise (static) overlaid on the tape so that the letters were difficult to understand.

Conrad developed another confusion matrix for listening confusions, similar to the one described earlier for short-term recall confusions. He found that the pattern of confusions was quite similar. If people misheard *M*, they usually mistook it for *N*. The important point of this experiment is that presentation of the stimuli was visual, but the recall confusions were based on sound. Thus it seemed likely that participants spontaneously translated the material from a visual to an acoustic code in primary memory.

Nevertheless, we do not rely only on an acoustic code in primary memory. What do we do with spatial information, for example? Suppose I said to you, "I'd like you to imagine a 4 × 4 matrix of squares because that might help you in this next task. Suppose the upper right-hand cell is the starting square, and in that square, I'd like you to put a 1. In the next square down, put a 2. In the next square to the left, put a 3. In the next square to the left, put a 4." And so on. Then I ask you to reproduce my instructions to you. Almost everyone reports attempting this primary memory task using a spatial code. It's actually more accurate to say people use a visuospatial code, meaning it's both visual and spatial. Information may be spatial but not visual; for example, you could represent spatial information auditorily.

One source of evidence that people code this type of information spatially comes from interference experiments. What would happen if you asked a participant to perform a spatial task at the same time as the matrix task? Alan Baddeley and his colleagues (Baddeley, Grant, Wight, & Thomson, 1975) asked participants to do this primary memory matrix task while performing a pursuit tracking task in which they had to follow a little spot of light with a hand-held stylus. As you might expect, having to do this spatial tracking task played havoc with their primary memory in the matrix task. Performance went from an average of a little over two errors without the tracking task to about nine errors with the tracking task. How do we know that it was the spatial nature of each task that interfered with the other? The experimenters administered a second version of the matrix task that was not spatial, replacing the words *left*, *right*, *up*, and *down* with *good*, *bad*, *slow*, and *quick*. The sentences became a little odd ("In the next square to the *quick*, put a 2"), but that didn't matter because the participants' job was to report back what the instructions were, sensible or not. In this version of the task, participants didn't use a spatial coding scheme, and the tracking task had no effect on their performance; they made an average of about two errors, whether or not they had to do the tracking task at the same time. Again, the point of these experiments is to show that there is a spatial medium in which to maintain information for short periods of time.

We use a third type of code in primary memory: a semantic code that can maintain information about what things mean. A particular task paradigm that has been used frequently to investigate semantic codes in primary memory is called **release from proactive interference**. We noted that proactive interference occurs when information learned earlier interferes with the learning of new information; it is observed in the Brown–Peterson task when performance in remembering the letter trigrams decreases over trials. Release from proactive interference refers to the fact that the proactive interference dissipates if the stimulus materials are changed. For example, Delos Wickens and his associates (Wickens, Dalezman, & Eggemeier, 1976) used the standard Brown–Peterson paradigm, but instead of consonant trigrams, participants were to remember the names of fruits, such as *apple, pear,* and *orange.* After three trials, different groups of participants heard different stimuli. One group (the control group) heard the names of fruits again; another group heard the names of vegetables, another flowers, another meats, and a final group the names of professions. As shown in Figure 4.10, there was considerable difference in the performance on this fourth trial.

Notice that the group that continued to hear the names of fruits performed the worst; they continued on the downward trend caused by proactive interference. The other groups showed varying amounts of release from proactive interference; the most dramatic improvement came from participants whose stimuli were professions, which are arguably the most different from fruits. This experiment constitutes evidence that primary memory codes semantics or meaning; if it did not, the change in semantic content on the fourth trial would make no difference in performance.

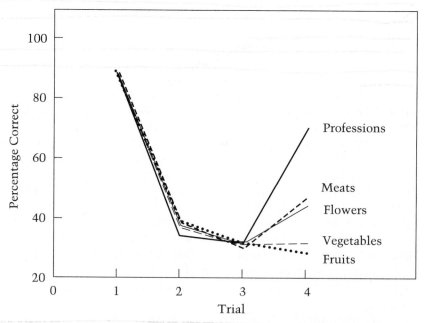

Figure 4.10.   *Results from Wickens et al. (1976). All five groups used the Brown–Peterson paradigm for the first three trials with fruits as stimuli. Notice how performance declined because of proactive interference. On the fourth trial the stimuli changed for four of the groups. Notice that performance increased when the meaning of the stimuli changed. The reduction in proactive interference with the change in stimuli is called release from proactive interference.*

Capacity

How much information can primary memory hold? You may have heard the number 7 mentioned as the capacity of primary memory, and indeed, this was the figure cited by George Miller (1956) in his well-known paper mentioned earlier. Around the turn of the century, researchers began to use the **digit span task** to measure the capacity of primary memory. In this task, the experimenter reads aloud a series of digits at a rate of one digit per second. The participant must repeat back the digits in the correct order. The experimenter increases the number of digits until the participant cannot repeat them back without error. Most adults can reproduce about seven digits. Average digit span often is described as "seven plus or minus two" to reflect the fact that people's performance varies, but most of us can recall between five and nine digits. Thus, an early view was that the capacity of primary memory was about seven. But we've just finished saying that primary memory can hold different codes. Might it not be the case that the capacity depends on the code? That does appear to be true.

The capacity of the acoustic code is actually best described not in terms of the number of items but in terms of time; the capacity is basically as much material as you can say to yourself in about 2 seconds. For the semantic code, the capacity is best described in terms of chunks, and the capacity of the visuospatial code is about four objects.

An important clue to the capacity of the acoustic code comes from the **word length effect**. Participants can remember more short words than long ones in a primary memory task. This effect was demonstrated by Alan Baddeley, Neil Thomson, and Mary Buchanan (1975). They gave participants a simple short-term memory task—listen to country names and repeat them back—and found that participants averaged 83% correct if the names were short (Chad, Cuba) but only 56% if the names were long (Somaliland, Australia). To be certain that it was really the amount of time it takes to say the words and not some other factor that led to the differences, they conducted another experiment in which all words were matched in terms of the number of syllables and the number of phonemes. (A phoneme is the smallest unit of speech sound, such as "buh" or "pa"). For example, the words *coerce* and *wicket* both have two syllables and both have five phonemes, but it takes the average speaker about 0.8 s to say *coerce* and only 0.5 s to say *wicket*. Comparing lists of short-to-say and long-to-say words, the experimenters found that participants got 61.6% of the long words correct and 72.2% of the short words correct.

What is the capacity of primary memory when a semantic code is used? In 1974, Herb Simon published an article on the capacity of primary memory. Simon tested his own primary memory using stimulus materials of different lengths. Simon found that he could remember about 7 one- or two-syllable words but only 6 three-syllable words. He then tested his primary memory capacity using brief phrases with which he was familiar, such as "Milky Way" and "Lincoln's Gettysburg Address." Simon found he could remember

Size of Item	Syllables	Words	Chunks	Syllables per Chunk
1 syllable	7	7	7	1.0
2 syllables	14	7	7	2.0
3 syllables	18	6	6	3.0
2 words	22	9	4	5.5
8 words	26	22	3	8.7

Figure 4.11. *Results from Simon (1974). Simon tested just one participant (himself), but the results are representative. There are two important points to note. First, the capacity of primary memory when measured in syllables or words varies quite a lot, but it varies much less when measured in chunks, indicating that chunks are the right way to measure memory. Second, the amount of information per chunk makes a difference in capacity; as the number of syllables per chunk increases, the number of chunks recalled decreases.*

about 4 of these phrases on average. Finally, he tried some long phrases, such as "Four score and seven years ago" or "To be or not to be, that is the question" and found he could remember 3 long phrases. These data are summarized in Figure 4.11.

What do these results tell us about the capacity of primary memory? Simon could recall fewer three-syllable words than one-syllable words. This result is in line with the word length effect reported by Baddeley et al. (1975). But when words were knit into familiar phrases, Simon could maintain 22 words in primary memory. That seems too many words to keep on his 2-s tape loop, so these phrases must have been represented in terms of their semantic content.

Simon emphasized the importance of chunking in the capacity of primary memory: he could maintain more syllables in primary memory if they were organized into chunks of greater size, held together through the semantic relationships between their parts. This is easy to appreciate in the stimuli that Simon used. The two-word idioms and the eight-word phrases have coherence as chunks because of the semantic relationship of the words, which are recalled from secondary memory. Simon was able to treat "Four score and seven years ago" as an effective chunk because he was familiar with that phrase; it was already in secondary memory. Thus, the capacity of primary memory when using a semantic code depends on the stimuli, specifically, how easily they can be chunked, which depends in part on what is already in secondary memory.

What is the capacity of primary memory when a visuospatial code is used? The answer may well depend on the units in which information is represented. Does primary memory represent visual information in terms of object features (lines, colors, and so on) or in terms of unified objects? For example, the two shapes in Figure 4.12 show the same nine lines, but those on the left form an object.

Steven Luck and Edward Vogel (1997; see also Vogel, Woodman, & Luck, 2001) showed people two arrays, one after the other, with either colored

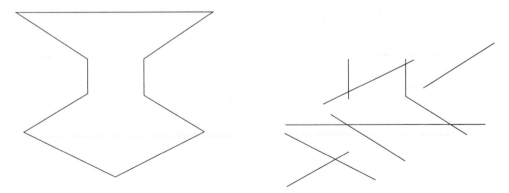

Figure 4.12. *Two figures containing the same nine-line segments. Clearly the figure on the left would be easier to remember because the lines can be chunked on the basis of their spatial relationships.*

squares, black lines at different orientations, or colored lines at different orientations. The type of stimulus was always the same in the first and second arrays. The task was to compare them and say "same" or "different." When the arrays differed, it was only by one feature—that is, one color or one orientation. The important finding was that all three stimulus types—color, orientation, or color and orientation combined—showed the same result: working memory capacity was about four items. Notice that for the condition in which color and orientation were combined, participants were really keeping track of eight features, not four, because each object in the array had both a color and an orientation; adding an extra feature induced no cost to working memory capacity. Thus the capacity of visuospatial working memory is four, and the representation appears to be of objects, not of individual features. Essentially, features can be chunked into objects.

Daeyeol Lee and Marvin Chun (2001) proposed another possible interpretation of Luck and Vogel's experiment. The extra feature was always in the same spatial location as the other feature, so perhaps the representation for working memory was not an object but a spatial location. Participants could hold the contents of four spatial locations in working memory no matter how many objects there might be at those four locations. To test this idea, Lee and Chun used stimuli made up of boxes and lines that could be either separate or overlapping. They kept the number of stimuli constant so that there were always the same number of stimuli for participants to remember, but there were twice as many spatial locations when the stimuli were separate as when they overlapped. The data showed that the number of spatial locations made no difference to working memory capacity; what mattered was the number of objects. Thus visuospatial working memory does indeed code objects.

The capacity of primary memory varies, then, depending on which code is used. When an acoustic code is used, the capacity is limited by time (approximately 2 s). When the code is semantic, the capacity is flexible because meaningful units (chunks) can be used, but the larger the chunk, the smaller the capacity. When the code is visuospatial, the capacity is about four objects.

We have discussed three characteristics of primary memory: how forgetting occurs, the codes that are used, and the capacity. Now we can discuss models of primary memory and speculate on how primary memory is used in cognition.

Stand-on-One-Foot Questions

5. *Before the 1950s, was primary memory known to exist? If not, why not? If so, why was it so little studied?*
6. *What are the three representations in which primary memory may code material?*
7. *Why does forgetting occur in primary memory? Define each of the mechanisms you list.*
8. *Is it accurate to say that the capacity of primary memory is seven plus or minus two items?*

Questions That Require Two Feet

9. *Baddeley and Scott offered evidence that forgetting in primary memory occurs even if researchers exclude the possibility of proactive interference by administering only one trial to each participant. Can you argue that proactive interference may have been at work in their experiment?*
10. *In this section we discussed proactive and retroactive interference using the example of studying French or Spanish. Given that you must study more than one subject, it seems as though there is always going to be proactive or retroactive interference. What is the best way to minimize the effects of interference?*
11. *Languages use different sounds to represent numbers. Would you therefore expect that the digit spans of people who speak different languages would be different? How about the digit span of an individual who speaks two languages?*

HOW DOES PRIMARY MEMORY WORK?

> ➤ *Preview* In this section we discuss two specific models of primary memory and discuss how primary memory contributes to cognition. The modal model of primary memory is an amalgam of many closely related models proposed in the
>
> *(Continued)*

1960s. Though it is now known to be incorrect in its details, it has been influential in psychology. A second model, the working memory model, is currently thought to be accurate in describing primary memory. Researchers have investigated how primary memory contributes to cognition by studying how primary memory affects the recall of long lists of words. Working memory also contributes to general intelligence and reading.

Models of Primary Memory

Baddeley's working memory model (Baddeley, 1986; Baddeley & Hitch, 1974) accounts well for the data we've discussed in this chapter; indeed, these data were collected to test the model. Another model, the short-term memory model, was so important in the late 1960s and early 1970s that every cognitive psychologist must be familiar with it. For that matter, the model was so important that the designations *short-term memory* and *long-term memory* seeped into popular culture. Thus, although some aspects of the short-term memory model are now known to be incorrect, we'll take a quick look at it.

SHORT-TERM MEMORY AND THE MODAL MODEL. From the mid-1960s through the early 1970s psychologists proposed a number of models of human memory that used the sensory, short-term, and long-term systems. The models had so many features in common that Bennet Murdock (1974) pointed out that one could construct a **modal model** of memory simply by listing the properties that these models shared (see Figure 4.13). He named it after a statistical measure, the mode, which is the number that occurs most often in a group of numbers. This was not a criticism of memory theory at the time; Murdock was pointing out that there was general agreement among many researchers on the basic architecture of memory. Some other important models in this vein were proposed by Waugh and Norman (1965) and Atkinson and Shiffrin (1968).

The modal model emphasizes the flow of information through the cognitive system. Information enters from the senses to sensory memory. There may be sensory memory for each of the senses, such as smell and taste, but we know that iconic and echoic memory exist. Some of the information is lost from sensory memory, and some is passed on to short-term memory. Whatever you pay attention to in iconic memory is passed on to sensory memory.

Information in short-term memory decays after approximately 30 s unless it is rehearsed. If it is rehearsed, it can be maintained indefinitely. The amount of processing in short-term memory determines the likelihood that information will enter long-term memory; information that is processed longer in short-term memory is more likely to be encoded (passed on) to long-term memory. Individual models varied in terms of exactly what sort of processing in short-term memory was likely to lead to entry into long-term memory.

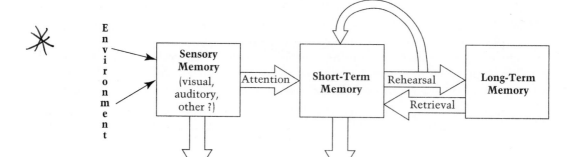

Figure 4.13. *The modal model, showing sensory, short-term, and long-term memories and their interactions. This model has been superseded by newer research.*

Information can also enter short-term memory from long-term memory. Because short-term memory is the site of consciousness, this makes sense. The fact that you like maple syrup on pancakes but prefer lingonberry jam on toast is in long-term memory but not short-term memory. When I ask, "What do you like on pancakes?" you retrieve the answer from long-term memory and it enters short-term memory.

Finally, note that Figure 4.13 shows no arrow indicating forgetting from long-term memory. That's because forgetting from long-term memory was thought to occur via interference, not decay.

The modal model was shown to be incomplete or inaccurate in several respects (see Nairne, 2002, for a recent discussion). For example, the description of rehearsal (the process by which material is transferred from short-term to long-term memory) was incomplete because it proposed that short-term memory used only an acoustic code and long-term memory only a semantic code. The model also proposed that forgetting in short-term memory occurred primarily through decay.

Despite these inaccuracies and deficiencies, the very broad architecture of the modal model—sensory memory feeding into primary memory, which feeds into secondary memory—remains influential today.

Working Memory

The basic architecture of working memory is fairly simple (Baddeley, 1986; Baddeley & Hitch, 1974). It includes a central executive and two slave systems, as shown in Figure 4.14. Note that this figure shows only working memory, not its relationship to sensory or secondary memory. The two storage buffers are called slave systems because they do the central executive's bidding. The **phonological loop** allows the rehearsal of auditory information, and the **visuospatial sketchpad** allows the rehearsal of visual information. The **central executive** is in charge: it resolves conflicts over what cognitive process

Figure 4.14. *The three basic components of working memory. The central executive communicates with the other two components, which do not communicate with one another. The central executive controls the activity of the other two components.*

should happen next; it selects strategies for solving problems; and it coordinates information from multiple sources.

You might notice that there are two differences between working memory and short-term memory. The first is the obvious inclusion of processes in service of cognition, not just briefly maintaining information. Again, that reflects the idea that primary memory is a workspace as well as a short-term storage location. Second, there are separate storage locations for auditory information (the phonological loop) and visual information (the visuospatial sketchpad).

The phonological loop has two components: the **phonological store** and the **articulatory control process**. The phonological store holds about 2 s of auditory information. It is like a short tape loop on which you can copy auditory information. Information can enter the phonological store from the environment; for example, I could say a list of words aloud that I want you to remember. Information can also enter via the articulatory control process, which literally means talking to yourself (articulation). You might use the articulatory control process by repeating a grocery list to yourself. The articulatory control process can also be used to refresh information that is already in the phonological store to keep it from fading.

Evidence for the nature of the phonological loop comes from **articulatory suppression** studies. The articulatory control process that writes material to the phonological loop is supposed to be very similar to speech. Therefore, you shouldn't be able to use it while you're speaking. If you're talking out loud, you can't put anything on your tape loop because the articulatory process is already busy. So suppose an experimenter asked a participant to talk while he or she performed a standard primary memory task. The experimenter wouldn't want the participant to have to think of what to say because that would require attention, so the participant might just say "blahblahblah" aloud while viewing words on a screen to be remembered. How would the participant approach this memory task if the words can't be coded acoustically because the articulatory control process is busy? He or she would have to find some other way to code the words.

If the participant is not coding the words in terms of sound, the acoustic confusion effect should disappear. You'll recall that it's hard to remember a list of words that sound alike (*mad, man, mat*). That effect does indeed disappear if participants say "blahblahblah" while they hear the words: participants remember words that sound alike (*man, mad, mat*) as well as they remember words that don't (*pit, sup, bar*). That's because speaking aloud occupies the articulatory control process, forcing them to code the words in some way other than acoustically, so they are not susceptible to the acoustic confusion effect (Baddeley, Lewis, & Vallar, 1984). You might wonder whether the effect is caused by the attentional requirements of saying "blahblahblah," even though it might seem that saying such a simple syllable repetitively would not demand much attention. The experimenters compared articulatory suppression with finger tapping, another simple task that did not require articulation. With that secondary task, the acoustic confusion effect was still present.

Even though articulation will get material into the phonological store, simply listening to something, even if you are not trying to remember it, guarantees that it will get into the phonological store through **obligatory access**. For example, Herbert Colle and Alan Welsh (1976) looked at participants' memories for strings of letters presented visually with a short delay, tested either in silence or while listening to a tape of a foreign language they did not know. (It was a passage from *A Hunger Artist* by Franz Kafka, in the original German.) Colle and Welsh found that there was significant interference from the speech; errors increased an average of 12%. The interpretation is that speech sounds gain obligatory access to the phonological store, even if you're trying to ignore them, and interfere with memory for target consonant strings. (Some of us discover obligatory access on our own; many a 9-year-old loves to shout random numbers at a friend who is trying to remember a telephone number, then watch the friend sigh and return to the phone book to look up the number again.)

The visuospatial sketchpad is conceived of as a visual analog to the phonological loop. It is a medium in which to keep visual or spatial information active. Earlier in this chapter we discussed evidence that people maintain spatial information in primary memory. (Remember the matrix task with sentences such as "In the next square to the left put a 3.")

Baddeley proposed that spatial information (where things are) and visual information (what they look like) are separable in the visuospatial sketchpad. We noted in chapter 2 that visual and spatial information might be handled separately in perception; it might well be that they are also separate in the visuospatial sketchpad.

Baddeley and Lieberman (1980) came up with a clever way to separate visual and spatial aspects of stimuli. They blindfolded participants and had them sit in a darkened room in front of a swinging pendulum. On the bob of the pendulum was a speaker emitting a tone so the participant could locate the bob. The participant's task was to shine a flashlight on the bob of the pendulum, which had a photocell on it; if light hit the photocell, the tone that the participant heard would change pitch, thus providing feedback that the participant was tracking the pendulum successfully with the flashlight. If that doesn't sound difficult enough, the participant had to do the matrix task described earlier while performing this tracking task. The experimenters found that performance on the matrix task was compromised by this spatial (but not visual) tracking task. Other participants had to perform a visual (but not spatial) task. They compared patches of light and had to judge which was brighter. This task did not affect performance on the matrix task much. Thus, we can say that the visuospatial aspect of primary memory may have dissociable spatial and visual components. As we'll see in chapter 9, a good deal of evidence has been collected showing that visual imagery can be primarily visual (what things look like) or spatial (where things are). There is less evidence on the separability of these two components in primary memory, but the existing evidence is consistent with that separation.

Less work has been directed toward elucidating the central executive that plays the role of cognitive supervisor and scheduler, integrating information from multiple sources and making decisions about strategies to be used on tasks. Baddeley (1996) commented that in some ways this research strategy could be compared to undertaking an analysis of *Hamlet* by focusing on Polonius and ignoring Hamlet. By this he meant that the central executive is the most interesting part of working memory because its responsibilities are so great. Baddeley commented that he chose to study the other components of working memory because they seemed more tractable, but he has turned his attention increasingly toward the central executive in recent years.

Baddeley has suggested that a model of attention proposed by Donald Norman and Tim Shallice (1986) may be a good starting point for considering the operation of the central executive (see Figure 4.15). Their model features two methods to coordinate cognitive activity (specifically, how to decide what action to take next). One method based primarily on secondary memory applies to situations in which an action is automatic. When the right stimuli are in the environment, they can trigger a typical action plan. For example, I don't need to plan to wash my hair when I get in the shower each morning; once I'm standing under the water, I start washing my hair. Of course, at times stimuli in the environment set up conflicting plans of action. Driving is an automatic process for many people, and steering the car so that it stays on the road is one automatic component of driving. The stimulus of the car beginning to edge toward the side of the road automatically triggers the behavior of making a corrective movement of the steering wheel.

For many of us, eating is also largely automatic. Presented with a plate of French fries and ketchup, I can dip and eat fairly automatically. So if I'm driving and a friend in the passenger seat has some fries, why don't I automatically start eating her fries and end up sated but with my car in a ditch? The answer is that there is a process of **contention scheduling**, a set of rules by which the relative importance of two tasks can be compared and one of the tasks selected at the expense of the other. Such comparisons are made automatically and outside of awareness.

The second process of selection is the **supervisory attentional system (SAS)**, which is called on when a task must be planned in advance; the automatic processes appear to be having negative or unexpected consequences; a new, unfamiliar action must be taken; or a strong habit must be suppressed.

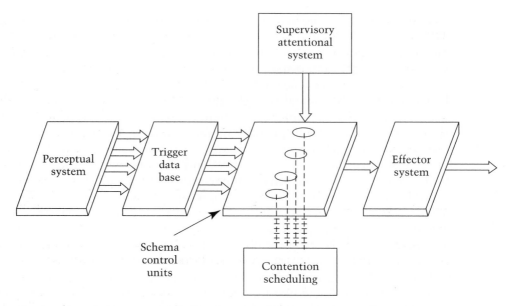

Figure 4.15. *The Norman and Shallice (1986) model of attention.*

The model is complex, but we will describe a few interesting phenomena. Donald Norman (1981) has been especially interested in action slips—engaging in a habitual response when it is inappropriate. You have doubtless had the experience of leaving a friend's house and driving home when you meant to go to the store, or of getting undressed when you meant only to change your pants. In each case, you begin an action program (driving along a specific route, getting undressed) that must be altered midway through its usual course (turn toward the store instead of your house, stop undressing after you've taken off your pants), but this correction entails the action of the SAS. If the SAS is busy with other cognitive problems, the action plan will run on unimpeded, leaving you shirtless as well as pantless.

Experimental evidence supports this relationship between automatic schemata and the SAS. To study this relationship Baddeley (1966) developed the random letter generation task in which participants were asked to produce random letter strings. They were warned that they should not produce letter strings that spelled words (*CAT*) or acronyms (*NCAA, CBS*) and that they should try to mention all letters in the alphabet equally often. Participants had to produce letters at one of four rates: 1 letter every 0.5, 1, 2, or 4 s. The pace was set by a metronome. After the first 20 letters or so the task becomes quite difficult. The interesting finding was that as the pace of production increased, participants produced more nonrandom letter strings. The relationship is quite orderly, with logarithmic increases in letter production speed being related to linear increases in stereotyped responses. Within the Norman and Shallice model we would say that letter retrieval is rather automatic, so that if you say *C* and then *B*, you are more likely to follow with *S* than with another letter. Therefore the SAS must constantly monitor output to ensure that this doesn't happen and to intervene when it is about to. As the pace increases, the SAS can't keep up, and more and more stereotyped responses slip by.

Some recent brain imaging evidence supports the separability of a separate control process (like schema control units) and performance-monitoring process (like the SAS). Angus MacDonald and his colleagues (2000) used a modified version of the Stroop task discussed in chapter 3; it's the task in which the participant must name the color of the ink (such as yellow) that spells a word, and the task is made difficult because the word spells a different color name (such as *red*). In MacDonald's version participants saw an instruction telling them either to name the ink color or to read the word. Then there was a brief delay before the stimulus appeared. The researchers argued that when participants were preparing to name the color, they would recruit control processes that would inhibit the normal bias to simply read the word. They also compared color-naming when the ink color matched the word and when it didn't, arguing that when the two elements did not match, the performance-monitoring process would be especially active. The results showed high levels of activation in the dorsolateral frontal cortex associated with control and in the anterior cingulate cortex for monitoring performance. This evidence does not directly support Norman and Shallice's particular version of control and monitoring, but it is consistent with it and does demonstrate that control and monitoring are separate in the brain.

The working memory model may not seem impressive because it simply brings together or summarizes what we already know about primary memory. The fact is that much of what we know about primary memory derives from the predictions of the working memory model, not the other way around. I presented all of the findings first and the model second because the facts are easier to understand that way.

Primary Memory Contributions to Secondary Memory Tasks

Primary memory has been helpful in accounting for experimental results from the often-used task of remembering a list of words. Most of this work was conducted in the 1960s, before the working memory model was proposed, so I use the more general term *primary memory* in this section, but working memory accounts for the findings equally well.

Suppose I give you a list of 16 words to remember by reading them aloud at a rate of 1 per second, then immediately ask you to recall the words. I can plot the probability of your getting a word correct by its **serial position** (its position in the list—first, second, sixteenth, and so on). Figure 4.16 shows an idealized serial position curve: the proportion of words correctly recalled is plotted on the *y* axis and each word's position in a list on the *x* axis.

The fact that accuracy is high for the last few words in the list is called the **recency effect**. These words are still in primary memory when it is time to recall. The first few words on the list are also remembered better than the

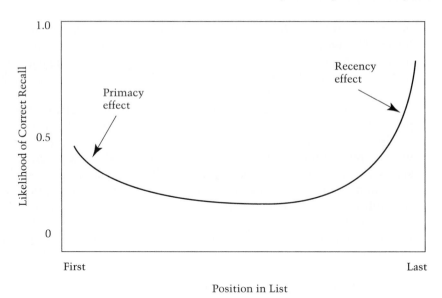

Figure 4.16. *An idealized serial position curve representing recall of a list of items. Stimuli at the beginning of the list usually are remembered well (primacy effect), as are stimuli at the end of the list (recency effect). Memory is worst for items in the middle of the list.*

words in the middle. This **primacy effect** occurs because the first words are more likely to enter secondary memory and you will have more opportunity to rehearse them (see chapter 5). One method of rehearsal is to say each word to yourself. When you hear the first word, you begin to rehearse it ("bottle, bottle, bottle"), and when you hear the second word you start saying both of them ("bottle habit, bottle habit, bottle habit"). If participants are asked to rehearse out loud, this sort of repetition is what they actually do (Rundus & Atkinson, 1970). By the time the sixth word comes in, it can't be rehearsed much because the participant is trying to rehearse all of the words he or she has heard.

If the recency effect is caused by retrieval from primary memory, it should disappear if there is a filled delay after the last word on the list (as in the Brown–Peterson task). Murray Glanzer and Anita Cunitz (1966) conducted such an experiment with lists of 15 words. Some participants recalled immediately after seeing the list, but others had to count backward for either 10 s or 30 s after seeing the list. Figure 4.17 shows that when there was a filled delay after the list, memory for the final words was poor, but memory for the words early in the list was not affected.

In another experiment Glanzer and Cunitz tried to show that the primacy effect can be made more robust. They varied the amount of time between words, which were presented every 1, 2, or 3 s. The idea is that the slower rate should provide more opportunity for rehearsal of the early items, so the primacy effect should be stronger. The recency effect should be unchanged, however,

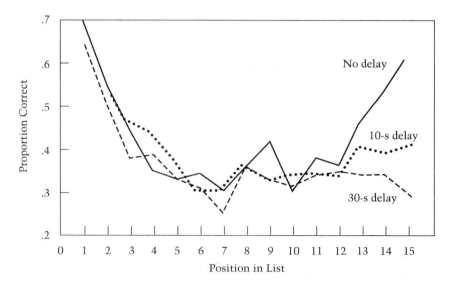

Figure 4.17. *Results of Glanzer and Cunitz's (1966) experiment, showing that asking participants to count for 10 to 30 s after presentation of a list of words affects their ability to recall words at the end but not the beginning of the list. This result supports the idea that the recency effect is supported by primary memory.*

because it relies on primary memory. Their results were broadly consistent with their predictions, although the advantage conferred on the primacy effect was not dramatic.

We initially outlined two important functions of primary memory: maintaining information over a brief period of time and providing a workspace for cognition. The contribution of primary memory to secondary memory tasks falls somewhere between these two functions; it is a contribution to cognition, but it uses primary memory specifically in its brief storage role. In the next section we review data that more obviously show how primary memory serves as a workspace for cognition; these data fit much more closely with working memory as a model of how primary memory operates.

Working Memory as a Workspace

Unlike work examining the relationship of primary and secondary memory, research directed toward the role of working memory in cognition has been more specifically within the scope of the working memory model. We review a few highlights here.

The phonological loop appears to be important in acquiring new vocabulary terms. In a number of studies researchers have looked at the relationship between the size of the phonological loop and the number of words in the vocabulary of children in the early and middle childhood years (for a review, see Baddeley, Gathercole, & Papagno, 1998). The size of the phonological loop is measured by digit span and by asking the children to repeat nonwords such as *loddernaypish*, which presumably can be repeated only if the child successful-ly maintains in the phonological loop the sounds that the experimenter utters. Vocabulary size correlates with digit span and correlates even better with non-word repetition: the correlations are on the order of .35–.60. (That's a big cor-relation—see the Appendix for more information on correlations if you are not familiar with this measure.)

Baddeley and his colleagues argued that the phonological loop is impor-tant for maintaining the sound of the word while more permanent long-term memory representations are being constructed. They argue that the phonolog-ical loop evolved for that function. It is seldom useful to keep 2 s of speech available just so you can repeat it moments later. The real function of the phonological loop, Baddeley and colleagues maintained, is to store the sound of new vocabulary words so that long-term memory representations of the sound can be developed.

Another example of working memory's role in cognition comes from an influential study by Meredyth Daneman and Patricia Carpenter (1980). They devised a task in which the participant must simultaneously manipulate and store information: a sentence such as "The boy asked the bishop for the ball" is followed by a question like "Who asked?" and the participant must answer the question. Then another sentence and question are presented, and so on. After, say, four such questions, the participant must recite the last word of each of the four sentences; thus participants have to keep the last word of each sentence in mind while trying to listen to the new sentences and answer questions about them. The experimenter varies the number of sentences, and the final measure of working memory span is the greatest number of sen-tences in which the participant can answer all the questions and recite the last word of each sentence correctly. This measure of working memory span is an extremely good predictor (correlation = .72) of reading comprehension in college students.

The interpretation of this high correlation is that working memory often is important in comprehending sentences during reading. This fact is especial-ly apparent in sentences such as "The package dropped from the airplane reached the ground safely" (Fodor, 1995). In sentences like this, the grammati-cal structure can fool the reader, who might think that *dropped* is the main verb of the sentence (as it would be in "The package dropped from the airplane safely"). In fact, *dropped* must be interpreted as part of an adjectival phrase; "dropped from the airplane" tells you which package is being discussed. In sentences like this, the grammatical role of some of the words can be misin-terpreted. But if this material is still in working memory, the reader can rein-terpret the early part of the sentence. If it's not in working memory, it must be reread. Thus a good working memory span might help reading comprehension. (This type of sentence is discussed further in chapter 12.)

Another demonstration of the centrality of working memory in all vari-eties of cognition involves older participants in whom working memory is com-promised. Older adults are somewhat impaired on many different reasoning tasks, such as the letter sets task in which the participant is asked to figure out which set of letters doesn't fit with the others in a stimulus like this:

NOPQ DEFL ABCD HIJK UVWX

Older adults also are impaired in other reasoning tasks, such as syllogistic problems in which two premises are presented ("All *As* are *Bs*," "All *Bs* are *Cs*") with a conclusion ("All *As* are *Cs*") and the participant must evaluate the truth of the conclusion (see Salthouse, 1992, for a review).

Age, however, is not as good a predictor of performance on these tasks as working memory. In other words, older participants are bad at these tasks because their working memory capacity has gone down, not simply because they are old. We can tell this is true by comparing old people who happen to have a good working memory with young people who have a poor working memory. Given a reasoning task, who will do well and who will do poorly? Working memory, not age, determines performance (Salthouse, 1993).[1]

Stand-on-One-Foot Questions

12. *Explain the difference between the concepts of primary memory, short-term memory, and working memory.*
13. *Describe the components of the phonological loop and how they operate.*
14. *Name at least two of the three sources of evidence that working memory affects other cognitive processes.*

Questions That Require Two Feet

15. *Service people often thank me after they have done me a favor. For example, I will walk into a department store and ask someone at the perfume counter where the men's shoe department is, and the clerk will answer: "Go to the back of the store, past lingerie. Take the elevator to the fifth floor, walk straight ahead, and turn right at the overcoats; it's right there. Have a nice day, and thank you for shopping with us." What's wrong with adding this last sentence?*
16. *Suppose that a person with brain damage has almost no articulatory loop; the digit span is one or two items instead of the usual seven. How good would you expect the person's long-term memory to be?*

---

[1]Salthouse thinks there is a more fundamental mental process: processing speed, defined as the speed at which cognitive processes operate.

KEY TERMS

acoustic confusion
  effect
articulatory control
  process
articulatory suppression
central executive
chunk
contention scheduling
digit span task
echoic memory
iconic memory

mask
modal model
obligatory access
partial report procedure
phonological loop
phonological store
primacy effect
primary memory
proactive interference
recency effect
rehearse

release from proactive
  interference
retroactive interference
secondary memory
sensory memory
serial position
span of apprehension
supervisory attentional
  system (SAS)
visuospatial sketchpad
word length effect

Box 4–2 Are Counting and Subitizing the Same Thing?

Have another look at Figure 4.1. It's remarkable that Jevons *never* made a mistake with 3 or 4 beans. That result—even though it was derived with just one participant using crude equipment—has held up quite well. People are outstanding in judging the number of objects if there are 4 or less; once there are more than 4, people make errors. This shift in performance from errorless to error-prone is so marked that many researchers have suggested it reflects a shift to a completely different process that is getting the job done (see Trick & Pylyshyn, 1993). Researchers refer to a "subitizing" process for numbers of 4 or less and a "counting" process for larger numbers. Recent brain imaging evidence, however, casts doubt on the idea that these processes are really separate.

  Manuela Piazza and her colleagues (Piazza, Mechelli, Butterworth, & Price, 2002) examined subitizing (1–4 items) and counting (6–9 items) while participants were scanned using PET. The items were simple black dots arranged either randomly or canonically (that is, in a geometric form such as four dots in a square). Participants were to say aloud as quickly as possible the number of dots they saw, and their responses were measured for speed and accuracy. The experimenters used three baseline conditions: participants saw either 1, 6, or 9 dots and were to report the appropriate number as quickly as possible, knowing in advance what they were going to see. This baseline condition thus entails viewing visual stimuli and making a speeded response, but no subitizing or counting. The researchers used three different baselines because the increasing number of dots could lead to increasing activity in visual areas.

  The main result was that counting and subitizing did *not* lead to substantially different patterns of activation. Both tasks led to increased activity (relative to baseline) in occipital and posterior parietal cortex. Activity was higher as the number of dots increased, and it was higher for random as opposed to canonical organization, but the same network of cortical areas was always active.

(Continued)

This study demonstrates an important type of contribution that neuroimaging can make to psychological models. If two tasks are hypothesized to be handled by different cognitive processes, we expect that they will be supported by different parts of the brain. In this case, that prediction turned out not to be true, indicating that counting and subitizing are handled by the same cognitive process. Indeed, some cognitive psychologists (Balakrishnan & Ashby, 1992) had speculated that counting and subitizing might reflect different levels on a continuum of difficulty, and these brain imaging data support their position.

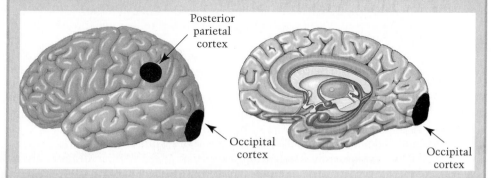

Figure B4.2.

Box 4–3 Brain Components of the Phonological Store

Excellent progress has been made in isolating the components of the phonological loop in the brain, and that work has further solidified the validity of the working memory model. The phonological loop is said to have two components: the phonological store and an articulatory control process that "writes" material onto the phonological store. Eraldo Paulesu and his colleagues (Paulesu, Frith, & Frackowiak, 1993) conducted a PET study to localize the brain areas involved in these hypothetical processes.

Remember that in PET studies the activity associated with one task can be subtracted from the activity associated with a closely related task. In this study, one task consisted of letters being presented on a screen to be remembered. (Note that even though the letters were presented visually, participants have a bias to recode visual stimuli into an auditory code; in other words, people tend to "say" the stimuli to themselves.) In another task, participants were shown letters and asked to judge whether the letters rhymed (Z and C) or did not (Z and K).

The researchers reasoned that the memory task required participants to analyze the letters visually, translate the letters into sounds, rehearse them subvocally, and enter them in the phonological store. The rhyming task (because it requires an analysis of sound) uses these same processes except for entry to the phonological store; that is not required because participants are not

(Continued)

asked to remember the letters, just to make the rhyming judgment. When the activations for the rhyming task were subtracted from those for the memory task, the researchers observed activity primarily in ventrolateral parietal cortex, an area strongly associated with language processing.

In another experiment, the researchers asked participants in both conditions to do a working memory task. In one condition the stimuli were English letters, as before, but in the other condition they were Korean letters. The participants did not speak Korean and could not recode the letters into auditory codes to be rehearsed via the articulatory control process. A subtraction of the activation from the two tasks showed that the English letters led to significantly more activity in Broca's area, an area known to be crucial to the motor planning of speech.

If its components can be isolated in the brain, we would expect to see occasional patients with selective damage to some part of the phonological loop. Giuseppe Vallar and Alan Baddeley (1984) examined one such patient, P.V., who had suffered a stroke that damaged the ventrolateral parietal cortex and was impaired in tasks that would tap the phonological loop, such as remembering a sequence of letters read aloud to her. P.V. could remember only 2 or 3 letters and could reliably repeat back a sentence of just 6 words; normal performance would yield approximately 7 letters and a sentence of approximately 16 words. Despite her poor performance in auditory primary memory tasks, P.V. was able to speak at a normal rate. Thus she seems to have had a selective deficit of the phonological store, but the articulatory control process was largely intact.

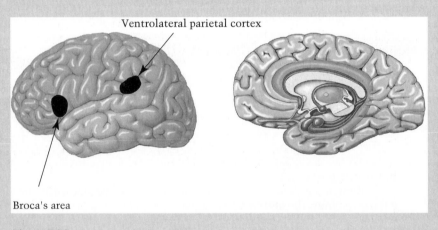

Ventrolateral parietal cortex

Broca's area

Figure B4.3.

Box 4—4 *The Brain Basis of the Central Executive*

In the model of working memory shown in Figure 4.14, the central executive is supposed to support the manipulation of information. So what happens if the researcher adds some requirement for manipulation to a working memory task?

You'll recall from the study by Paulesu and colleagues (1993) that the ventrolateral prefrontal cortex (Broca's area) seems to be critical for the maintenance

(Continued)

of phonological material. A different part of the frontal lobe—the dorsolateral prefrontal cortex—appears to be crucial for its manipulation, an idea first put forward by Michael Petrides (1989).

A study supporting this idea was conducted by Mark D'Esposito and his colleagues (1999). In this fMRI experiment, participants briefly saw a series of five random letters, immediately followed by a cue, either "FORWARD" or "ALPHABETIZE," directing participants to either maintain the list as they saw it or to rearrange the list in alphabetical order. After an 8-s delay, participants saw a number and letter (such as 3 *J*); their job was to say whether the letter was in the position dictated by the number (for example, the third letter is *J*). In the *forward* condition they made this judgment for the list as they saw it, and for the *alphabetize* condition they made this judgment for the list after they had alphabetized it. Thus, both conditions required that participants maintain the information, but only the *alphabetize* condition required them to manipulate it.

As predicted, the *alphabetize* condition led to greater activity in dorsolateral prefrontal cortex, an area that was also somewhat active during the maintenance condition. In other studies, however, that has not been the case (see D'Esposito, Postle, & Rypma, 2000, for a review). Thus while it appears clear that ventolateral prefrontal cortex contributes to maintenance and dorsolateral to manipulation, it is still not clear whether dorsolateral prefrontal cortex contributes to maintenance as well.

Although working memory is complex, it provides an excellent example of cognitive studies working hand in hand with neuroscientific investigations to unravel a difficult problem.

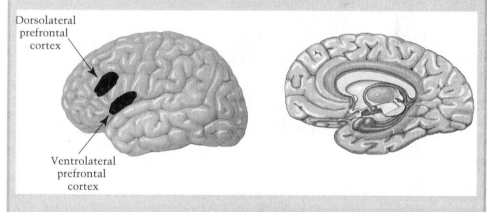

Dorsolateral prefrontal cortex

Ventrolateral prefrontal cortex

Figure B4.4.

5

Memory Encoding

In many ways, life would be simpler if memory were dictated by the intention to remember—in other words, if you remembered the things you wanted to remember and forgot the things you wanted to forget. For example, I want to remember people's names, so why can't I do it? When I'm introduced to someone new, I think to myself, "That's Lisa; remember her name." But if five minutes later we're joined by someone else, I can't introduce Lisa because I've already forgotten her name. "Do you two know each other?" I ask, too embarrassed to take advantage of the opportunity to hear her name again when they introduce themselves.

Similarly, we all have things we'd like to forget. I could live the rest of my life quite happily without the memory of certain moments at junior high dances, but those memories seem branded in my brain, and they pop into consciousness, unbidden, usually at moments when I would pay cash money for them to lie dormant.

In chapter 4 we considered primary memory as a gateway to the storehouse of memory. It's always possible that I wasn't really paying attention when Lisa first said her name—I was thinking that my shirt was wrinkled, or I was wondering whether I had something stuck in my teeth—and I never really had "Lisa" in primary memory. But let's assume for the moment that I did. Why didn't the name get into secondary memory, even though I wanted it to? Apparently information is not guaranteed to go into secondary memory just because you want it to. This fact brings up the question **What determines what we encode in memory?** Researchers have examined a number of different factors, such as whether the material engenders emotion or how often the material is repeated. It turns out that whether something is stored depends on what you do with it; basically, if you think hard about something and use it, the mind figures that you may need to use this material again, and so it is stored. A precise definition of what it means to "think hard about something" turns out to be tricky; we discuss some of the possibilities in this chapter.

This answer leads naturally to a second question: **Why do we encode information as we do?** If *whether* you remember something depends on how you think about it, what determines *how* you think about it? The answer is that how you think about something depends, in large measure, on what you already know about it (your prior knowledge). To take an extreme example, suppose you overhear someone in a restaurant say, "Zut! Qu'est-ce que cet petit singe a laissé dans ma chaussure?"[1] If you don't speak French, you might think, "Oh, someone over there is speaking a foreign language," and you'd probably forget the incident. If you did speak French you would probably be curious to know what was happening at that other table and would think about the incident a lot. Prior knowledge is crucial to how you process new experiences and therefore to the likelihood that you will remember them later.

---

[1]"Hey! What did that little monkey leave in my shoe?"

WHAT DETERMINES WHAT WE ENCODE IN MEMORY?

> ➤ *Preview* Researchers have examined four factors as possible influences on encoding. Whether the material brings an emotional response and whether you relate the material to other things you already know are two factors that have a significant impact on later memory. How often the material is repeated and how much effort you expend thinking about the material do not help memory much, if at all.
>
> The extent to which you relate new material to things you already know is the most important factor in encoding, but getting a clear definition of this factor has been difficult. The relationship between what you think about at encoding and what you think about at retrieval is also important to memory.

Factors that Help Memory: Emotion and Depth

If you tried to think of factors that might influence memory, you might speculate that something will get into secondary memory if it is important to you. "Important to you" might mean emotionally significant. As we'll see in this section, emotion has some influence on memory, but the effect is not huge.

LABORATORY STUDIES OF EMOTION AND MEMORY.   I'm not alone in finding an emotional event particularly memorable. David Rubin and Marc Kozin (1984) asked people to report their clearest memories from childhood. Participants tended to describe birthdays, car accidents, early romantic experiences, and the like, which seems to indicate an important role for emotion in memory. Nevertheless, such evidence is not airtight. When we study real-life events such as humiliation at a dance, we are studying things as they already exist; thus if the dance was an emotional experience that people talked about a lot, we're studying people's memory of an event that was emotional and was discussed a lot. But we don't want to know the effect of an event being emotional and talked about a lot; we just want to know about emotion. The heart of the problem is that we have no control over what people do in this situation. If they want to talk about the dance humiliation, they will.

A number of laboratory studies have sought to examine the effect of emotion on memory by comparing emotional and nonemotional materials. By conducting an experiment in the laboratory, the researcher has much better control over what people think about and how often they think about it than in real-world situations. What the experimenter wants to do is compare people's memory of stimuli that lead to strong emotion with their memory of the same stimuli when they do not lead to strong emotion. Everything should be the same except the emotion so that any difference in the memorability of the stimuli can be attributed to the emotion, not some other characteristics of the stimuli. But how can the same set of materials be emotional for one group of participants and nonemotional for the other?

This problem is very difficult. For example, Alafair Burke, Friderike Heuer, and Daniel Reisberg (1992) used a slide show in which the emotional and unemotional stimuli were not identical but were designed to be similar. They showed participants a brief slide show about a boy visiting his father at work. At the start and end of the slide show, identical slides were used; the slides in the middle differed in the two conditions. In the emotional condition, the father was a surgeon, and participants saw graphic slides of surgery. In the nonemotional condition, the father was an auto mechanic, and participants saw slides of the father working on a car. The surgery slides were better remembered, and the surgery slides surely engendered more emotion than the car slides, but it's possible that the slides differed in other ways (distinctiveness or complexity, for example). The experimenters did their best to match the slides from the two conditions, but it's impossible to know whether the slides differed only in terms of the amount of emotion they engendered.

Larry Cahill and Jim McGaugh (1995) took a clever approach to this problem. All participants saw the same slide show of a boy visiting his father at work in a hospital, but they heard different stories to go with the slides. For the emotional condition, participants were led to believe that graphic slides depicting surgical procedures were real. For the nonemotional condition, Cahill and McGaugh used the same slides but the story said that the boy visited his father just as the hospital personnel was practicing emergency procedures, and people who appeared to be injured were really just actors.

Two weeks later the participants returned, expecting to see another set of slides, but instead they took a test of their memory of the first set of slides. (Participants were first asked whether they had expected a memory test, even though they had been told about it, to ensure that they hadn't been rehearsing the material. All participants said that they hadn't expected the test.) In the first test, participants were asked to recall as much of the story as they could, both the general story line and specific details. Their responses were tape-recorded so that they could be scored later. The scorers judged that a specific slide was remembered if the participant mentioned a piece of information that could be known only from having seen the slide and not from hearing the story or from seeing one of the other slides.

Figure 5.1 shows the results. The first phase (three slides) and third phase (four slides) depicted the arrival and departure from the hospital, respectively. The second phase comprised five slides and showed the graphic surgery slides. As the graph shows, memory is equivalent in the two groups during the first and third phases, which were unemotional for both groups. Memory of the slides is the same during these phases, but it is much better for the emotional group only during the second phase. It looks as if memory is slightly better for the emotional group in the first and third phases as well. Although the average recall is a bit higher, the difference is not statistically significant; it could have occurred by chance and therefore should not be taken to represent an important difference. (The concept of statistical significance is very important in interpreting results from experiments. If you're not familiar with it, see the explanation in the Appendix.)

This study does an excellent job of isolating the effect of emotion from other possible characteristics of stimuli, and it shows quite convincingly that

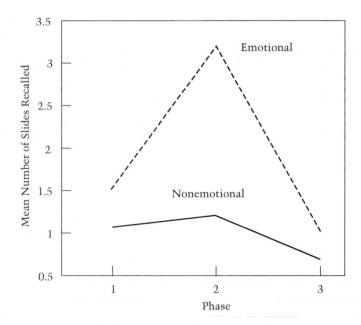

Figure 5.1. *Data from Cahill and McGaugh's (1995) experiment. The slide show participants saw was divided into three phases. All participants saw the same set of slides, but some heard a story about the slides that made the slides during Phase 2 much more emotional. These participants remembered the Phase 2 slides better on a later test.*

Box 5–1 Emotional Processing and Recall of Emotional Information

Larry Cahill and his colleagues (1996) have shown that an emotional experience is more memorable than one that is not emotional. The degree to which participants respond to emotionally changed stimuli predicts how well those stimuli will be remembered later.

The experimenters showed participants two videos, several days apart. Each contained 12 video clips that another group of participants had previously rated as either emotional (such as a violent crime) or unemotional (such as a court proceeding). Participants viewed these while their brains were imaged using positron emission tomography (PET). Three weeks later they returned and were asked to recall all of the film clips.

As predicted, participants recalled more of the emotional film clips than the neutral film clips, replicating previous work in this area. Even more interesting were the results of the PET imaging analysis compared with the behavioral data. The researchers found a strong relationship between the amount of activity in the amygdala as participants watched the emotional film session and the number of clips that they recalled. This relationship does not mean that the amygdala is important for memory per se, however. Amygdala activation observed during the neutral film sessions was unrelated to the number of neutral

(Continued)

films recalled. Indeed, the amygdala is known from other work to be involved in evaluating stimuli for emotional content. The amygdala appears to modulate memory based on its evaluation of the emotional significance of fear-inducing and disgusting events. Other brain areas evaluate the significance of other types of emotional events, and they may modulate memory on the basis of those evaluations.

Other evidence points to interesting sex differences in emotional memory. Turhan Canli and his associates (Canli, Desmond, Zhao, & Gabrieli, 2002) reported that women remembered emotional pictures better than men did, and their brains responded to emotional pictures differently at encoding. Even when the analysis is isolated to pictures that men and women found equally arousing, women showed more left amygdala activation than men, whereas men showed more right amygdala activation. Other evidence (Buchanan, Denburg, Tranel, & Adolphs, 2001) indicates that the left amygdala is more important than the right to the enhancing effect of emotion on memory. Thus it appears that women do remember emotional events better than men, and this result is clear in the brain response to emotion.

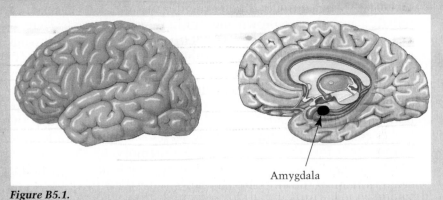

Amygdala

Figure B5.1.

emotion does make things more memorable. We might wonder, however, about the strength of the emotion in this experiment or indeed in any experiment. Seeing slides of surgery is upsetting, to be sure, but events that touch us as individuals are likely to be more upsetting (Eich & Macaulay, 2000). Would the effect of emotion on memory be stronger if we were examining events that affected the participants more than a slide show? We know it's difficult to study memory for events such as birthdays and first dates, but perhaps we're missing something important by ignoring them.

In fact, there is a rich literature on people's memories of highly emotional events that happen outside the laboratory. This literature initially led to the conclusion that this level of emotion had a profound impact on people's memories—so profound that a special memory process might be engaged during moments of great emotion. Later experiments indicated that proposal probably was not true, but the impact of these studies was great, so they are worth reviewing.

FLASHBULB MEMORIES.   If you want to study highly emotional events, you can't do so in the laboratory. It's simply not ethical to make people feel extremes of emotion by telling them that they are the lucky millionth participant to be tested in the laboratory and that at the end of the experiment they will be presented with a Ferrari. It would be ethical if you gave them the Ferrari, I suppose, but the billionaire eccentric enough to support this experiment has not yet stepped forward. Thus if you want to study the effect of high levels of emotion, you must study events that occur naturally in people's lives, and ideally one that is similar in the lives of a large group of people; after all, your birthday and mine might be very different in terms of how memorable they are.

Roger Brown and James Kulik (1977) were the first to conduct such a study. They asked participants to remember where they were when they heard that President John Kennedy had been assassinated. Participants reported surprisingly detailed memories and were confident that they could remember details such as what they were wearing, exactly where they were, who told them, the words that were used, and so on. Brown and Kulik used the term **flashbulb memories** for richly detailed memories encoded when something emotionally intense happens. Flashbulb memories have three special characteristics, according to Brown and Kulik: they are very complete, they are accurate, and they are immune to forgetting. Brown and Kulik suggested that a special memory process is responsible for flashbulb memories. Only in times of great emotional duress, a "NOW PRINT" process can take a memorial "snapshot" of whatever is happening at that moment.

The problem is that it is very difficult to assess whether people's flashbulb memories are accurate. Perhaps people want to think that they remember highly emotional situations, so they set a low criterion for how confident they have to be before they claim to have a memory. Ideally, psychologists would like to compare people's memory of how they heard about Kennedy's assassination right after they heard the news with their memory a year or so later. That way, we could test whether flashbulb memories are accurate and immune to forgetting.

Beginning in the 1980s a number of researchers did that; when an event occurred that they thought would trigger flashbulb memories, they administered surveys to people asking about the circumstances under which they heard the news, and then they contacted people sometime later, asked them the same questions, and compared their memories. Such experiments were conducted for events like the attempted assassination of President Ronald Reagan (Pillemer, 1984), the explosion of the space shuttle *Challenger* (McCloskey, Wible, & Cohen, 1988), the assassination of Swedish Prime Minister Olof Palme (Christianson, 1989), and the death of King Baudouin of Belgium (Finkenauer et al., 1998). (As I write this, no studies have been published on flashbulb memories of the terrorist attacks of September 11, 2001, but some doubtless will be.) As we might expect, the more emotionally involved people say that they were in the event, the more accurate their memory is for the event later. But flashbulb memories can be inaccurate, and as time passes, they become more inaccurate.

Perhaps the most complete study of flashbulb memory forgetting was conducted by Heike Shmolck, Elizabeth Buffalo, and Larry Squire (2000), who studied people's memory for the O. J. Simpson verdict. Three days after the verdict they asked 222 people to write a paragraph describing the circumstances under which they heard the verdict and answering nine specific questions (where were you, when was it, who told you, and so on). They were also asked to rate their interest in the trial and their emotional reaction to the verdict. The researchers tried to contact half of the participants after 15 months and the other half after 32 months to administer the survey again; they couldn't reach everyone, of course, so there were about 30 people in each follow-up group.

What we're really interested in was whether participants' memory was the same 15 or 32 months after the event. The results showed that at 15 months, 50% of the memories were still highly accurate and only 11% contained major distortions. After 32 months, however, only 29% were highly accurate and over 40% contained major distortions. (The detailed method of scoring a memory's accuracy need not concern us here.) Thus it appears that these emotional memories are not immune to forgetting. But what if they weren't really flashbulb memories in the first place? The researchers reported that three days after the verdict over 98% of the participant's reports would be considered flashbulb memories, using standard criteria. Even more interesting, the recollections of most participants at 15 months (78%) and 32 months (80%) would be considered flashbulb memories because the participant could report so many details—but the details were often wrong.

So what's the upshot on emotion and memory? There is good evidence that the emotionality of an event does affect how memorable it is, but there is not good evidence that a special mechanism takes over for flashbulb memories.

DEPTH OF PROCESSING. In the late 1960s the question "What determines what we encode in secondary memory?" was framed in terms of primary memory. In other words, most researchers believed that what mattered most was what happened in primary memory; if material were processed a certain way, or for a certain length of time, in primary memory, then it was encoded to secondary memory.

Fergus Craik and Robert Lockhart (1972) proposed an alternative called the **levels of processing framework**. They suggested that the most important factor determining whether something will be remembered is the **depth of processing**. According to Craik and Lockhart, in a task such as remembering a word, **deep processing** refers to greater degrees of semantic involvement—that is, thinking about what the word means and how its meaning relates to other words. For example, if you answered the question "What do you think of when I say the word *rose?*" you would be engaged in deep processing of the word. My question would force you to think about what the word means and what is associated with the concept *rose* in your memory. You might think that a rose is a flower of romance, that roses are fairly expensive, that they are found in formal gardens, that they have thorns, that they have a nice scent, and so on.

Shallow processing refers to thinking about surface characteristics of the stimulus. For example, if you answered the question "How many syllables are in the word *rose?*" you would be engaged in shallow processing. This question encourages you to think about the physical properties of the word itself. Other questions that would encourage shallow processing would be "How many vowels are there in the word *rose?*" or "Is the word *rose* printed in uppercase or lowercase letters?" We don't categorize processing simply as deep or shallow; there can be degrees of depth of processing as well. At least that is supposed to be true in theory. As we'll see in a moment, specifying slightly deeper or shallower processing has proved difficult, and that's a weakness of the framework.

In an experiment, depth of processing can be manipulated by having the participant answer a question about a word. Table 5.1 lists four levels of processing that are progressively deeper. This table comes from a series of experiments by Craik and Endel Tulving (1975), who sought to gather evidence for the levels of processing framework. As you can see, participants answered questions that led them to think about different properties of the stimulus word, such as what the printed version looks like or what it sounds like.

Depth of processing has a huge effect on people's ability to remember under most testing conditions (but not all, as we'll see later). Craik and Tulving (1975) showed just how strong the effect is, using the levels of processing shown in Table 5.1. Participants were told that the experiment tested perceptual processing, not memory. On each trial of the experiment, participants heard a question such as "Does the word rhyme with *cake?*" Participants saw a word flashed on a tachistoscope for 200 ms and then had to answer the question as quickly as possible by pressing one of two buttons to indicate "yes" or "no." They performed 40 such trials and after a brief rest were presented with a surprise recognition test. The experimenters didn't want participants to actively try to remember the words because then participants would bring their own strategies to the task. Participants' performance on the recognition test is shown in Figure 5.2.

Table 5.1.   *Four Levels of Processing Words*

Level of Processing	Question the Participant Must Answer	Sample Stimulus for Which Participant Answers "Yes"	Sample Stimulus for Which Participant Answers "No"
Structural	Is the word in capital letters?	TABLE	table
Phonemic	Does the word rhyme with *weight?*	Crate	Market
Category	Is the word a type of fish?	Shark	Heaven
Sentence	"He met a ____ in the street."	Friend	Cloud

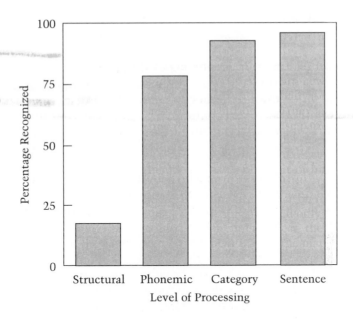

Figure 5.2. *The basic levels of processing effect, showing that words that are processed more deeply are better remembered than words that are processed more shallowly.*

The levels of processing framework holds that deeper processing leads to better memory. At first it might seem that doing the deep processing is just harder. Maybe your memory is better simply because you put more work into it in the first place. But Craik and Tulving (1975) tested that possibility by conducting an experiment in which the shallow processing condition was very difficult. Before each word was presented, the participants saw something like *CVCCVC* (where *C* meant consonant and *V* meant vowel). Then they saw a word like *WITCH* and had to say whether it had the pattern of vowels and consonants specified by the first stimulus. It took participants much longer to perform this shallow processing task than to perform the deep processing sentence task. Nevertheless, shallow-processed words were recognized 57% of the time on a later test and deep-processed words were recognized 82% of the time. So deeper-processed words are not better remembered simply because deep processing takes more effort.

Other researchers touched on notions similar to levels of processing, but focusing more on different types of rehearsal (Cooper & Pantle, 1967; Craik & Watkins, 1973; Woodward, Bjork, & Jongeward, 1973). **Elaborative rehearsal** involves connecting new material to things already in secondary memory and helps establish the new memory. **Maintenance rehearsal** involves repeating material to oneself again and again (today we would say keeping it in the articulatory loop of working memory) but doesn't help the material get into secondary memory.

Craik and Lockhart's (1972) distinction between shallow versus deep processing goes further than the distinction between elaborative rehearsal versus maintenance rehearsal. First, shallow processing may include thinking about the physical characteristics of the stimuli, not just repeating them to oneself over and over again. Second, the levels of processing framework emphasizes that memory is a function of the processing of the material; whether the participant tries to remember the material is unimportant. Although the levels of processing view has these advantages, elaboration does have an effect and cannot be ignored.

DEPTH AND ELABORATION.   The original idea in the levels of processing framework was that deep processing is simply encoding that makes us think about the semantic content of a word. For example, in Craik and Tulving's (1975) experiment discussed earlier, the deepest processing condition was one in which the participant saw a sentence frame ("I met a _____ in the street") followed by a word (*cloud*), with the task of saying whether the word fit the sentence frame. That task was thought to lead to deep processing because the participant had to consider the meaning of the word to answer the question.

But is it true that every task that makes you consider the meaning of a word will lead to equally good memory? Craik and Tulving (1975) examined that question in another experiment by varying the complexity of the sentence frame. In that experiment some sentence frames were simple ("She cooked the _____"), some were medium ("The _____ frightened the children"), and some were complex ("The great bird swooped down and carried off the struggling _____"). Craik and Tulving found that more complex sentence frames led to better memory for the words; indeed, participants remembered twice as many words that fit into the complex sentence frames (about 80% recalled) than words that fit into the simple sentence frames (about 40% recalled).

Nevertheless, we need to be careful about drawing hasty conclusions about elaborative processing. It turns out that elaborative processing does not always add to deep processing to make memory better. Simply adding more information that might connect to things in secondary memory doesn't always work; the elaborations have to be relevant to what you're trying to remember.

Gary Bradshaw and John Anderson (1982) approached this question by reading a sentence about a famous person ("Isaac Newton became emotionally unstable and insecure when he was a child"). Some participants heard more information on the same topic ("Newton became irrationally paranoid when challenged by colleagues; Newton had a nervous breakdown when his mother died"). Other participants heard additional information that was unrelated to the original sentence ("Newton was appointed Warden of the London mint; Newton went to Trinity College in Cambridge"). On a later test, 38% of the people who had only heard the single fact about Newton's childhood remembered it, and 32% of the people who heard the extra, irrelevant facts remembered the fact about his childhood. But 61% of the people who heard the more information related to the fact about his childhood remembered it. This experiment makes a point that is easy to understand but also easy to miss. We can't just say that deep encoding is better if we elaborate on it by providing more information; the information must be relevant.

Factors that Don't Help Memory: Intention to Learn and Repetition

Intention to learn and repetition seem so plausible as memory influences that it is worth going over how we know that they don't influence memory.

INTENTION TO LEARN.   The levels of processing framework proposes that intention to learn—that is, whether or not you're trying to learn—has no impact on memory. Can we really dismiss effort? Certainly, some teachers believe that effort to remember is important; why else would they exhort students, "Remember this!" We need to examine research that has looked directly at the effect of effort to learn on memory.

Research on levels of processing was crucial in showing that memory is not affected by effort to learn. Most of these studies used **incidental memory tests** on words, in which the participants are not expressly told that their memory will be tested later; rather, they are just told to do something to the words (such as answer a question about them). Then later they get a surprise memory test. In an **intentional memory test**, participants are told that their memory will be tested later; the researcher assumes that participants will engage in some processing they believe will be effective for memory.

In depth of processing experiments, researchers used incidental memory tests to see the effect of different types of processing on the words (deep vs. shallow). The experimenters wanted control over the participants' processing and did not mention the upcoming test.

Suppose we wanted to test the effect of the participants' expectation of a later memory test. We could simply tell half the participants that they will later be tested and not tell the other half. Thomas Hyde and James Jenkins (1973) conducted exactly that study. Participants saw a list of 24 words, one at a time, for 3 s each and were to perform one of two tasks for each word: either determine whether the word contained the letter *a* or *q* (shallow task) or rate the "pleasantness" of the word (deep task). If the word invoked pleasant thoughts ("daisy") participants gave it a high rating, and if it invoked unpleasant things ("grave") they gave it a low rating. For both the deep and shallow processing conditions, half of the participants were additionally told that their memory of the words would be tested later (intentional condition); the remaining participants were not told about the upcoming memory test (incidental condition). Whether the test was incidental made no difference in participants' performance on the memory test, as shown in Figure 5.3. Wanting to remember something doesn't help your memory. All that matters to your memory is whether you do the deep or the shallow processing.

At the beginning of the chapter we said that intention to learn is not a guarantee that you'll remember something. That might be true, yet it could

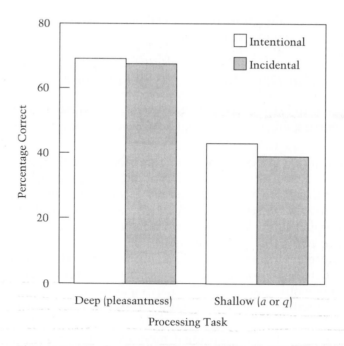

Figure 5.3. *Results from Hyde and Jenkins's (1973) study showing that intention to learn had no impact on learning. The experiment also showed the typical depth of processing effect.*

still be possible that wanting to remember would have some effect. The Hyde and Jenkins (1973) study shows that intention to learn has no effect at all.

Further reflection may make this conclusion more believable. After all, if effort had much impact on memory, studying would be much easier. And your memory (like mine) is probably cluttered with things you didn't intend to put in there—advertising jingles, for example. But the presence of a jingle in my memory raises another question. I don't think I processed it very deeply. Nor was viewing the commercial a particularly emotional experience for me, and we said emotion was the other factor that might influence memory. So if that memory didn't have emotion or depth of processing going for it, what's it doing in my memory? The ready answer is that I know it because I've heard it hundreds of times. Does repetition affect memory?

REPETITION.   Suppose that the likelihood that something makes it into secondary memory depends on how often you see it. Stimuli in the environment that are often repeated should be remembered. But consider this: You think you know what a penny looks like, right? Can you say, with confidence, right now, which way Lincoln faces? Try it. Where is the date written on a penny? Does the phrase "In God We Trust" appear on the front of a penny?

Raymond Nickerson and Marilyn Adams (1979) showed 36 college students the 15 versions of a penny in Figure 5.4. Participants were asked to select

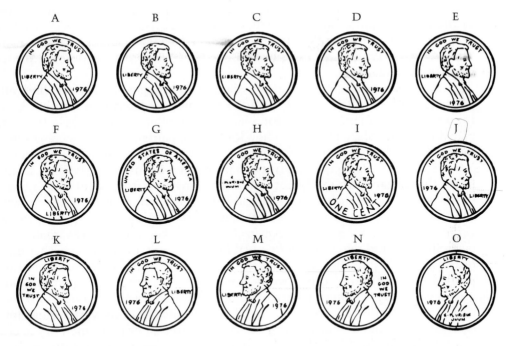

Figure 5.4. *Fifteen penny drawings used in Nickerson and Adams's (1979) recognition memory test.*

which penny was most likely the right one and then to rate the other drawings as (1) "Could easily be right, if my choice proves wrong"; (2) "Might possibly be right, if my choice proves wrong"; or (3) "Definitely not correct." Less than half of the participants (15 of the 36) correctly picked A. Twelve thought it could easily be right, 4 thought it might be, and 5 were sure it was wrong. Pennies E, G, and J were popular choices.

Why was this task so prone to error? Obviously the participants had seen thousands of pennies in their lifetimes. We seldom, if ever, really notice (that is, process deeply) which way Lincoln is facing, what's written on a coin, or any of the other details. When you are looking through your handful of coins in search of a penny, what you're thinking is, "I need the brown one." Pennies are distinguished from other coins by color, not by the way Lincoln is facing. Dimes are the small ones, not the coins with Roosevelt on them; quarters are the big ones; and nickels are the thick ones with smooth edges. You have had thousands of exposures to pennies, but each exposure amounted to little more than "Good, I've got a brown one, so I won't get four brown ones in change."

Nickerson and Adams's experiment gives us an important clue to memory. Sheer repetition of a stimulus in the environment won't necessarily lead to its being encoded in memory because presenting the stimulus does not guarantee that the participant will think about (or even notice) all aspects of the stimulus; participants note the color and size of pennies and little else, so that's the information about pennies that ends up in secondary memory, just as the levels of processing framework predicts. Thus when we speculate that "repetition" is important for memory, it may be that repeated *thought* about the object is crucial to encoding the object into memory, not repeated *exposure* to the object.

But what does it mean to think about something a lot? Fergus Craik and Michael Watkins (1973) conducted an experiment to determine whether keeping a word in primary memory for a longer time made it more likely to be encoded into secondary memory. They told participants that they were going to hear a list of words and to remember the last word that began with a particular letter such as *g*. Participants always had to keep in mind the last word they heard that began with the target letter. The smart strategy would be to listen to the words and silently rehearse the most recent *g*-word until another *g*-word came up, then silently rehearse that one. With the list *radio, giraffe, nurse, game, dog, nutcracker, hotel, squirrel, giant, rake, stapler*, presumably the participant would rehearse *giraffe* until hearing *game*, then rehearse that until hearing *giant*. Note that how long the participant would rehearse a word depended on how many other words intervene until the next *g*-word. Thus *giraffe* would be rehearsed less than *game*. By systematically varying how long participants could rehearse each word, Craik and Watkins varied how long each word remained in primary memory, so if time in primary memory is crucial to encoding, we should see systematic differences in their results.

Participants heard 27 such lists, each with 21 words, and were then asked to recall every *g*-word they had heard in the experiment. This test was unexpected, so naturally participants' recall was poor, but the important thing is that how long a word had been in primary memory—that is, how long it was rehearsed—had no effect on participants' long-term memory of that word.

Clearly, the amount of time a word resides in primary memory, which is the same as how much time you spend thinking about the word, is not the critical determinant in whether the word is encoded. Rather, it is the quality of time in primary memory—quality defined as the depth of processing.

But this result doesn't explain why I can remember an advertising jingle. One possibility is that with more repetitions, it becomes more likely that at least one of the repetitions will be processed deeply. Even if I ignore the advertisement 99 times, perhaps the next time will be the one in which I encode the music deeply and start humming along. (There may also be other effects of repetition that we're not concerned with here, for example, greater liking of the product; see Janiszewski & Meyvis, 2001.)

Interim Summary

We've discussed four factors that researchers have examined closely for their effect on memory: emotion, depth of processing, intention, and repetition. The overall conclusion is that repetition and intention have a minimal effect, if any; emotion has a moderate effect; and depth of processing has a substantial effect. Elaboration can add to deep processing, but the elaboration must be relevant to the material to be remembered.

But you may have sensed a problem. The definition of depth as a greater degree of semantic involvement sounds rather vague. Many researchers, though impressed by the impact depth seemed to have on later memory, were nevertheless concerned by the difficulty of pinning down exactly what *depth* means. In the sections that follow, we'll talk about efforts to define depth more precisely. First we'll talk about elaboration, which also seems to influence memory and yet does not seem to contribute to depth. Next we'll examine criticisms of the theory behind the depth of processing approach, many of them centered on problems in defining depth. Finally we'll see how encoding and retrieval are related and talk about the difficulty of assessing the effect of encoding on memory without simultaneously considering how people retrieve memories.

Problems with the Levels of Processing Theory

Even though deep processing does help us remember, there are problems with the levels of processing theory. First, it's not clear what is meant by the deepness of the levels. How can we tell whether one level is deeper than another? For example, suppose I ask you to make a rhyming judgment on each word that I say. A stimulus example might be, "Rhymes with cake? Lake." (And you say, "Yes.") In another condition of the experiment, other participants have to say whether the voice they hear saying the word is that of a man or a woman. Both of those tasks entail shallow processing, but which task is more shallow? Memory performance for the rhyme participants and the voice participants won't be exactly the same. One group will do at least slightly better, presumably because the task involves slightly deeper processing. But which task leads to deeper processing? Can't I see which group does better and then say, "That's the deeper processing condition"? No, I can't do that. That would be a **circular theory** in which term *A* is used to define term *B*, and then term *B* is used to define term *A*; it would not be valid.

ME: Deep processing leads to better memory.
ALERT CRITIC: How can you tell that people are doing deep processing?
ME: Their memory is better.

The levels of processing framework was never defined in enough detail to specify the depth or shallowness of every processing task.

A second problem was that the levels of processing theory didn't say much about the importance of memory retrieval. It turns out that we can't look at encoding in isolation; we have to consider how it is tested. We turn to that point next.

Match Between Encoding and Retrieval: Transfer Appropriate Processing

Does deeper processing during encoding always lead to better memory? From our discussion so far, it seems as if depth makes it more likely that information gets into secondary memory or makes its representation stronger in some way,

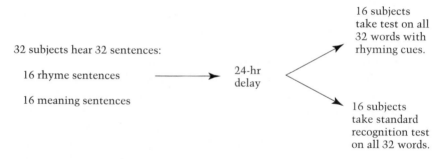

Figure 5.5. *Design of Morris, Bransford, and Franks's (1977) study.*

so you might think the answer is "Yes." Yet this way of discussing memory ignores what might be happening at retrieval.

The mental processes at retrieval must be considered when we're thinking about encoding. Donald Morris, John Bransford, and Jeffrey Franks (1977) performed a simple but ingenious experiment in which they varied not only encoding processes (as in a typical depth experiment) but processes at retrieval (see Figure 5.5). In their experiment participants heard words and were asked to do one of two tasks. Some participants answered a rhyming question, as described earlier ("_____ rhymes with eagle; legal"). The other participants answered a sentence frame question in which they needed to think about what the word meant in order to determine whether it would fit the sentence frame ("I met a _____ in the street; cloud"). The rhyme condition was a standard shallow task, and the sentence frame was a deep task.

Each participant took one of two memory tests. One was a standard recognition test in which participants heard a list of words and had to say which ones they had heard before. As shown in Figure 5.6, Morris and his colleagues got the usual depth of processing effect when participants took this test. Other participants were not given a recognition test but took a cued recall test in which they had to try to remember the words, given a list of cues. A cue is something in the environment (or something you come up with yourself) that serves as a starting point for memory retrieval. In this context, the cue amounts to a hint. Some of these cues rhymed with a word on the original list. For example, if one of the words was *legal*, the word *regal* might have been on the list of cues. These rhyming cues were different from the ones participants heard the first time they saw the words.

As shown in Figure 5.6, when memory was tested with rhyming cues, the usual depth effect reversed: the participants who did the supposedly shallow rhyme task remembered more than those who did the supposedly deep sentence frame task. This result seems obvious once someone tells you about it, but it wasn't at all obvious at the time. Who would have thought you could get the levels of processing effect to reverse by changing the test? Most psychologists were thinking that depth of encoding made the memory representation stronger in some way, which would mean that memory would be better for any type of test.

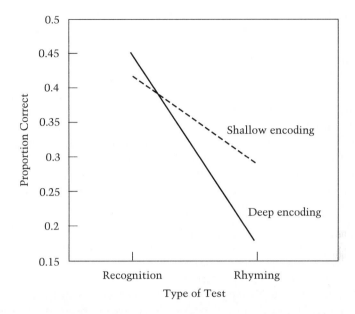

Figure 5.6. *Results of Morris, Bransford, and Franks's (1977) experiment showing that it's not just the depth of processing at encoding that's important; the match between the encoding task and the retrieval test also is important.*

These researchers had an interesting explanation for the reversal of the depth of processing effect. They proposed that memory depends not on the depth of encoding but rather on the extent to which there is a match between the processes engaged at encoding and at retrieval. To illustrate this, suppose you are participating in a memory experiment and you are presented with a word like *bone*. You are going to think about the concept *bone* in some way, and there must be particular processes in the mind that enable you to do that thinking. For example, if you are asked what *bone* makes you think of, there are processes that search your memory to find associated concepts, and perhaps you think of a skeleton. Morris, Bransford, and Franks emphasized the importance of the memory search processes that help you come up with the associated concept *skeleton*. They argued that if those same processes were used at retrieval, you would be very likely to remember the original word *bone*. If other processes were engaged when you were trying to retrieve the word, you would be less likely to remember it. For example, if at retrieval you were encouraged to think of words that sound like *phone*, you would be less likely to remember the word *bone* because you had used different processes at encoding (you used processes that helped you think of the associated concept *skeleton*).

The general hypothesis is that when the same processes are used to think about words at encoding and retrieval, memory will be successful;

when different processes are used at encoding and retrieval, memory will not be successful. This hypothesis is known as **transfer appropriate processing**. According to this hypothesis, one type of encoding, such as deep processing, is not inherently better than another.

The idea of transfer appropriate processing seems to explain the general pattern of results we have discussed. Unfortunately, it has the same problem as the levels of processing idea: circularity. Memory should be better when the same processes are engaged at encoding and at retrieval, but how do we know whether the processes are the same or different? Keep in mind that there is no way to directly observe cognitive processes. We can observe tasks and then make educated guesses about what sorts of cognitive processes would be engaged to perform those tasks. Thus the only way to make a judgment about the similarity of cognitive processes during encoding and retrieval is to make the reasonable guess that similar tasks will employ similar cognitive processes at encoding and retrieval. But there is no way to objectively measure how similar tasks are.

Box 5–2 What is Remembered, and What is Forgotten?

Is it possible to peek at the brain, observe its activity during encoding, and, on the basis of that activity, predict whether the item is likely to be remembered or forgotten? Two research groups have done just that: Jim Brewer and his associates at Stanford and Anthony Wagner and his associates at Harvard (Brewer, Zhou, Desmond, Glover, & Gabrieli, 1998; Wagner et al., 1998). These studies together were conducted in a similar manner, drew similar conclusions, and appeared back to back in the same journal.

Both studies used incidental encoding, meaning participants did not know that their memory would be tested later. Participants lay in a scanner and made judgments about pictures (in Brewer et al.) or words (in Wagner et al.). The researchers used event-related fMRI, which allows quick assessment of brain activity in a narrow time window (as short as several seconds) so they could determine the amount of brain activity immediately after each stimulus was presented. Later, participants in both studies took a recognition test for the material, and each participant's performance on each stimulus was categorized as being remembered well, remembered weakly, or forgotten. The researchers then examined the activity measures of different parts of the brain to see whether activity at encoding differed for items that would later be remembered or forgotten.

Both studies drew similar conclusions. The right dorsolateral prefrontal cortex and bilateral parahippocampal cortex showed more activity for items that would eventually be remembered than for items that would eventually be forgotten. When the stimuli were words (Wagner et al.) the activity was restricted to left parahippocampal cortex, probably because the left hemisphere plays the predominant role in language processing, but when the stimuli were pictures (Brewer et al.) the activity in the parahippocampal cortex was bilateral, perhaps because pictures were coded both visually and in terms of verbal labels.

(Continued)

Previous research had shown that the parahippocampal cortex is active when a new stimulus appears, but it was not known whether this activity reflected encoding processes (which might be strongest for unfamiliar items) or whether the parahippocampal cortex was some sort of "novelty detector" that alerted other areas that a stimulus was unfamiliar and therefore might be worthy of close attention. All of the stimuli in the studies by Wagner and Brewer were equally novel. The differences in activity, which are correlated with participants' eventual memory performance, show that the parahippocampal cortex and the prefrontal cortex are crucial in memory encoding.

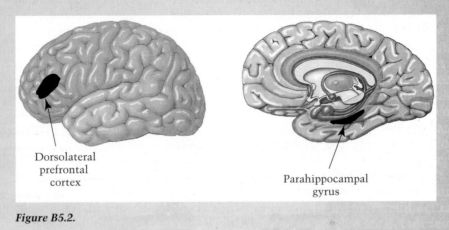

Dorsolateral
prefrontal
cortex

Parahippocampal
gyrus

Figure B5.2.

In some cases it seems a safe bet that two tasks must require fairly different processes; for example, different cognitive processes may be involved in thinking of a word that rhymes with *bone* and thinking of a word related to *bone*. But we don't have an objective way to measure similarity for processes. Still a third task would be judging how many syllables are in the word *bone*. Is that task more similar to thinking about a word that rhymes with *bone* or to thinking of a word related to *bone*? There is no way to tell; if I give the syllable-counting task to all my participants at encoding and then give half of them a standard recognition test and half of them the rhyming cues test, there is no way to predict which group will do better. As with the levels of processing framework, a theory must be able to make predictions for it to be useful.

So does transfer appropriate processing replace the idea of depth? Only in a sense: the transfer appropriate processing idea forces us to realize that there are interactions between encoding and retrieval. The depth of processing framework was predicated on the idea that you could simply make a better memory in the storehouse, one that would be better however it was retrieved. In that sense, transfer appropriate processing is more accurate.

Nevertheless, depth is important because deeper encoding does lead to better recall under most conditions in which memory is usually tested. That's important simply as a practical matter. It tells us that if you want to remember something, deep encoding is the way to go, even if the theory behind the principle isn't completely adequate. It's also important to our attempts to develop theories of memory. Even if the depth idea as articulated is not an adequate theory, deep encoding has a profound impact on memory under most circumstances, and that fact must be explained.

Conclusion

Psychologists do not yet understand what factors determine what people encode in memory, but we have made some progress. Emotion has some effect on memory. Depth of processing has an effect, but it cannot be viewed in isolation. Repetition and effort to learn have little if any effect on memory unless they are coupled with either emotion or depth. That is, repeated deep encoding is better than just a little deep encoding. We have to look at how memory is tested at retrieval and especially at the match between encoding and retrieval processes.

It's interesting to consider the way our memory is set up from a practical point of view. Clearly, not everything the mind experiences is stored equally well in memory; on what basis does the mind store things? The memory system appears to be designed to help us do the same thing (engage the same processes and therefore think about material in the same way) at a later time. That is a conservative and perhaps wise way for the memory system to place its bets; something you have needed to think about before will probably come up again, so memory is set up to make it easy to engage the same cognitive processes a second time.

Stand-on-One-Foot Questions

1. *What factors affect encoding?*
2. *Does repetition affect memory?*
3. *What are the problems with the levels of processing framework?*

Questions That Require Two Feet

4. *Suppose a friend knows that you're taking a cognitive psychology class and asks for your advice on how to study for exams. What would you say? Would your advice be any different to someone who wants to remember people's names at parties?*

5. *Many people say that emotional events are well remembered (as in flashbulb memories), but others say that they don't remember emotional events at all well. (Some people, for example, say that their wedding day was "just a blur.") What explanation might you give for this disparity?*

6. *Why do you think you remember some advertisements well and others not so well?*

WHY DO WE ENCODE INFORMATION AS WE DO?

> ➤ *Preview* We have seen that encoding is determined by how the participant processes the material—that is, what the participant thinks about. But what determines how the participant thinks about the material?
>
> The answer to this question is that participants process material in three ways that depend largely on what they already know about it. Prior knowledge affects encoding by reducing what we have to remember, guiding our interpretation of details, and making unusual things stand out.

Encoding alone does not determine memory—we also have to look at retrieval processes to predict whether something is going to be remembered—but memory does start with encoding. In the experiments described in the previous section, participants usually were told how to process the material at encoding. What do participants do with material when they are not told what to do? That depends on what they already know about it. In a classic demonstration, John Bransford and Marcia Johnson (1972) read the following paragraph to participants.

> The procedure is actually quite simple. First you arrange items into different groups. Of course one pile may be sufficient depending on how much there is to do. If you have to go somewhere else due to lack of facilities that is the next step; otherwise, you are pretty well set. It is important not to overdo things. That is, it is better to do too few things at once than too many. In the short run this may not seem important but complications can easily arise. A mistake can be expensive as well. At first, the whole procedure will seem complicated. Soon, however, it will become just another facet of life. It is difficult to foresee any end to the necessity for this task in the immediate future, but then, one can never tell. After the procedure is completed one arranges the materials into different groups again. Then they can be put into their appropriate places. Eventually they will be used once more and the whole cycle will have to be repeated. However, that is part of life.

The paragraph doesn't make much sense, and not surprisingly, participants remembered very little of it. But some participants were given a title before the paragraph was read and they performed much better. The title is "Washing Clothes." Read the paragraph again now that you know the title and you'll see that it makes much more sense. If you are given the title after reading it, it doesn't help. You have to know the title in advance. Why is the story easier to remember if you know the title?

When you are reading something, things in your memory that are related to it can come into awareness more easily and shape how you think about what you're thinking about. Hence, when you know the title is "Washing Clothes" and you read "First you arrange items into different groups," it readily comes to mind that this vague sentence refers to sorting clothing by color. The prior knowledge (about washing clothes) shapes ongoing processing (reading).

We can point to three ways in which previous knowledge affects encoding. Prior knowledge reduces what you have to remember, guides your interpretation of ambiguous details, and makes unusual things stand out.

Prior Knowledge Reduces What We Must Remember

We defined a chunk as a unit of knowledge with subcomponents that are related to one another, often semantically; because they often occur together, it is possible to think of these subcomponents as a single unit. The term *chunking* refers to the process of creating a chunk. Suppose I ask you to memorize some letters (Bower & Springston, 1970). I read them aloud to you, pausing for 1 s between groups.

FB ICB SNC AAP BS

You'd remember some of the letters, perhaps all, but it would take some effort. Think how much easier it would be if I gave you exactly the same list of letters but I paused in different places.

FBI CBS NCAA PBS

Both lists are organized into chunks by the pauses, but for the second list the chunks derive meaning from prior knowledge. You already know these letters as groups, so the second list essentially has four things in it to remember. Things that are presented as individual items might be encodable as a single, higher-order unit if you have the right background knowledge.

William Chase and Herb Simon (1973) conducted a series of experiments in the early 1970s pointing out the importance of background knowledge in chunking. They tested participants with background knowledge in chess, showing them a chessboard with pieces set up to represent the middle of an ongoing game. Participants viewed the board for just 5 s, and then the board was taken away. After some delay, participants were handed an empty chessboard and the pieces and were asked to replace as many of the pieces as they could. Nonexperts got 8 or 10 of 32 pieces correct, but chess experts got nearly all of them right every time. Why? Chess experts have much more background knowledge. When they look at a chessboard, it looks to them like the second version of the letter task (FBI, CBS, NCAA, PBS). I look at the board and think, "The horsie is over there, and the pointy-headed guy is next to it." The expert glances at the board and thinks, "Queen's gambit declined, 12 moves in, but white has castled early." Knowledge in memory allows the expert to chunk numerous piece positions, representing the whole board in three or four chunks. I, on the other hand, have to remember the board piece by piece because I can't condense multiple-piece positions into one chunk. When it's time to recall, the chess expert can unpack each chunk into its constituents to replace the pieces appropriately. These sorts of expert-knowledge effects have been demonstrated for baseball (Hambrick & Engle, 2002), dance steps (Allard

& Starkes, 1991), bridge hands (Engle & Bukstel, 1978), maps (Gilhooly, Wood, Kinnear & Green, 1988), and music (Meinz & Salthouse, 1998).

How can we be certain that it's really the experts' background knowledge that makes the difference? Maybe the experts are just smarter than other people. Or perhaps they have superior memories, and that's what made them chess experts in the first place. To test this, the experimenters placed the pieces on the board randomly instead of in a way that would simulate an actual game; in this case, the chess experts' advantage disappeared. Their extensive experience with chess was rendered irrelevant when the pieces were placed randomly, so we know it was their prior experience that allowed them to create chunks.

Chase and Simon had another way of testing whether chunking made the difference in this experiment. They reasoned that if participants were really recalling chunks from memory, there would be differences in the times between putting the pieces down. For example, a chunk might be "three pawns in front of the rook." Chase and Simon expected that the participants would put down those three pawns rapidly, and then there would be a pause while the participants recalled the next chunk from memory. Chase and Simon defined a pause of 2 s or longer as indicating that a new chunk was being recalled. In addition, they found that the chunk size (number of pieces put down) for chess experts was bigger than that of novices.

Eyal Reingold and his colleagues (Reingold, Charness, Pomplun, & Stampe, 2001) used a more technical method to verify that chess experts actually perceptually encode positions differently from nonplayers. On each trial participants saw a reduced (3 squares × 3 squares) chess board on a computer. The board appeared with a black king in the upper left or right corner, along with one or two other pieces. The task was to quickly press a button indicating whether or not the king was in check. The experimenters had special equipment that monitored eye movements while participants performed this task. Chess experts were faster and more accurate at this task (although no participants made many errors), which is no great surprise. More remarkable was that the experts made fewer eye movements. On 16% of trials the experts didn't move their eyes at all, compared to 2% for novices. And on trials where they moved their eyes, novices moved them farther and made more movements than experts. These data support the idea that chess experts actually see the board in terms of chunks, in which the relationship of pieces (such as whether the king is in check) can be perceived in a glance. (For a review of chunking work, see Gobet et al., 2001.)

Prior Knowledge Guides the Interpretation of Details

Prior knowledge makes things easier to remember by reducing how much you must remember, and that happens through chunking. Prior knowledge also guides what details you are likely to pick out of a complex story or scene to think about. You are likely to notice the details relating to things you already know about. For example, I am interested in theater; I like going to plays and reading them. I went to see a play called *Voir Dire*, which is about a jury's deliberations, with a friend of mine who is an attorney. At the end of the play, there was a lot of overlap in what we remembered about it, but there were some interesting differences as well. My friend remembered a lot of the legal details—mostly things the playwright had gotten wrong or things she was impressed to see he had gotten right—whereas I remembered moments in the play that I perceived to be turns in dramatic tension and resolution of tension. I'm not an attorney, so I have no background knowledge about legal matters and was oblivious to the happenings in the play that she noticed. Prior knowledge guides what details of an event you attend to and think about and therefore which details end up in secondary memory. How does that work?

Sometimes, the prior knowledge that is applied at encoding is an isolated fact; for example, knowing the abbreviation *FBI* allows you to treat the three letters as a single chunk. At other times, the prior knowledge is best thought of as a set of related facts; the facts come in a packet, so to speak. Such a packet of information is called a **schema**. There have been a number of different definitions of a schema since Sir Frederic Bartlett (1932) first introduced the idea, but the different definitions agree on certain points: a schema is a memory representation containing general information about an object or an event; a schema represents what is generally true of the situation or event; and it represents not a single event but a type of event. Furthermore, the facts within a single schema are related to one another. These two aspects of a schema are especially important: it is general, and it contains information about related facts.

For example, a schema for the concept *dog* would include the information that a dog typically has four legs, is friendly, is furry, and so on. These characteristics are generally true, but each one need not be true. For example, if you met a three-legged dog you would still think of it as a dog. However, if that piece of information is not specified, then you assume that the normal default value of the schema is true and the dog has four legs. A **default value** for a particular piece of information is the value that would normally be true, and thus that you assume is true, unless you are told otherwise. If I tell you I have a dog with three legs, you will change the value of "number of legs" to 3 for the representation of my particular dog. But the default value for "number of legs" in the dog schema would still be 4.

Because bits of information are related, as soon as you think about a dog all of its characteristics become more available in your mind. For example, suppose that I tell you, "I just got a puppy, which probably wasn't a great idea because my landlord has put in new carpets." What does getting a puppy have to do with new carpets? As soon as I say "puppy," the knowledge becomes available that puppies aren't housebroken. When I say "landlord," information in the landlord schema becomes available, including the information that landlords typically are concerned that damage will be done to rented apartments. Understanding this sentence seems effortless, but it turns on having the right information in memory. I don't have to explicitly say, "I'm worried this puppy will pee on the carpet because that's what puppies do, which will ruin the carpets, which will make the landlord angry because the carpets belong to him." The background information stored in schemas allows the listener to make these inferences from the minimal information in the sentence.

Schemas not only help us make inferences but also help us interpret ambiguous details. Returning to the "Washing Clothes" paragraph, we would say that the prior knowledge of the theme of the paragraph (as provided by the title) activates a schema for the steps in washing clothes. This background knowledge guides the interpretation of ambiguous sentences such as "First you arrange items into different groups" and "If you have to go somewhere else due to lack of facilities that is the next step." Without the schema, the sentences would carry little meaning.

Schemas can influence encoding even if none of the details are ambiguous by guiding attention. R. C. Anderson and James Pichert (1978) examined this idea. In their experiment, participants read a story about what two boys did when they stayed home from school. Just before reading it, participants were told to read the story either from the perspective of a criminal thinking about robbing the apartment or from the perspective of a prospective buyer; thus experimenters activated either a "burglar" schema or a "homebuyer" schema. After a 12-min delay, participants were asked to remember everything they could about the story. As expected, the details that participants attended to and remembered were those consistent with the activated schema: they remembered 64% of the items that were consistent with the activated schema and 50% of the items that were consistent with the other schema. For example, participants who took on the perspective of a burglar were more likely to remember objects that were easy to remove from the house rather than things that would be important to a homebuyer, such as a large yard.

Prior Knowledge Makes Unusual Things Stand Out

Prior knowledge leads you to expect that what usually happens in a given situation will happen again. If something unexpected happens, then, it stands out. For example, if you went to a restaurant and the server gave you a menu, that would not stand out. However, if the server didn't give you a menu but instead took you back to the kitchen so that you could view all of the dishes and pick out what appealed to you, that would violate your expectations of what happens in a restaurant (and it would be memorable). That happened to me in a restaurant about 15 years ago, and I still remember it well. (I requested a large fish I noticed in the corner of the kitchen, obviously just caught. The server told me it was inedible, and I didn't ask what it was doing there.)

There has been a lot of research on people's knowledge of what usually happens in common situations. Roger Schank and R. P. Abelson (1977), two computer scientists, proposed that knowledge about common situations such as visiting a restaurant is encoded in a knowledge structure called a **script**, which is a schema for a series of events. For example, you probably have scripts in memory for routine events such as getting up in the morning or visiting a doctor. If asked, you could quickly generate a list as to what each of these events entails.

There is fairly good agreement about the events that are part of such scripts, at least within the culture of American college students. Gordon Bower, John Black, and Terrence Turner (1979) asked 161 students to describe what happens in one of these scenarios.

> Write a list of instructions describing what people generally do when they go to a lecture in a course. We are interested in the common actions of a routine lecture stereotype. Start the list with arriving at the lecture and end it with leaving after the lecture. Include about 20 actions or events and put them in the order in which they would occur.

Bower and his colleagues found quite good agreement among the components that each student listed for these events. Table 5.2 lists the actions associated with the scripts, showing which were listed by most participants, fewer participants, and the fewest participants (the statistical details of how the cutoffs were established need not concern us here).

We're talking in this section about the influence of prior knowledge on memory, and interesting things happen when experimenters give participants a story to remember that is similar to a script. Here's a true story that closely follows a "taking a cab" script.

> I got off a plane in Boston and walked through the terminal to the baggage claim area. I waited a while; then my bags came down the chute, and I took them outside to the cab stand. A cab pulled up and the cabbie put my bags in the trunk. I got in the cab and said, "Take me to 165 Charles Street, please." The cabbie drove about 10 minutes, then handed me a map and in a Boston accent asked me to find Charles Street for him. I found Charles Street on the map and named a major street near it. The cabbie dropped me at my destination and helped me get my bags out of the trunk, and I paid the fare.

The cabbie asking for help in finding the destination is not part of the typical script for this scenario. If I tested your memory for this story a week later, you would probably remember this detail because it violates the script, just as the server taking me back to the kitchen to choose my meal violates the script of going to a restaurant.

As it turns out, the only details that will be remembered are those that are not part of the script and are relevant to the goals of the script. Thus in the "taking a cab" script the cabbie is supposed to know the way to the destination, and the fact that he doesn't makes a material difference in what happens in the script. Another detail that is not part of the script is that the cabbie has a Boston accent. That detail is irrelevant, however, so it is less likely to be remembered. The researchers formulated these hypotheses about scripts and confirmed them; participants had very good memory for things that are inconsistent with the script if they are relevant to the goals of the script, remembering 53% of the script violations, 38% of the regular parts of the script, and 32% of the irrelevant information (Bower et al., 1979).

This phenomenon has been best studied in the case of scripts, but it may well apply to other types of information as well. In fact, Jeffrey Zacks, Barbara Tversky, and Gowri Iyer (2001) have suggested that script-like knowledge

Table 5.2.   Empirical Script Norms at Three Agreement Levels

Going to a Restaurant	Attending a Lecture	Getting Up	Grocery Shopping	Visiting a Doctor
Open door	ENTER ROOM	*Wake up*	ENTER STORE	*Enter office*
Enter	*Look for friends*	Turn off alarm	GET CART	CHECK IN WITH RECEPTIONIST
Give reservation name		Lie in bed	Take out list	SIT DOWN
Wait to be seated	FIND SEAT	Stretch	Look at list	Wait
Go to table	SIT DOWN	GET UP	Go to first aisle	Look at other people
BE SEATED	Settle belongings	Make bed	*Go up and down aisles*	READ MAGAZINE
	TAKE OUT NOTEBOOK			
Order drinks	*Look at other students*	*Go to bathroom*	PICK OUT ITEMS	*Name called*
Put napkins on lap	*Talk*	Use toilet	Compare prices	Follow nurse
LOOK AT MENU	Look at professor	*Take shower*	Put items in cart	*Enter exam room*
Discuss menu	LISTEN TO PROFESSOR	*Wash face*	Get meat	Undress
ORDER MEAL	TAKE NOTES	Shave	Look for items forgotten	*Sit on table*
Talk	CHECK TIME	DRESS	Talk to other shoppers	Talk to nurse
Drink water	Ask questions	Go to kitchen	Go to checkout counters	NURSE TESTS
Eat salad or soup	Change position in seat	Fix breakfast	*Find fastest line*	Wait
Meal arrives	Daydream	EAT BREAKFAST	WAIT IN LINE	Doctor enters
EAT FOOD	Look at other students	BRUSH TEETH	*Put food on belt*	Doctor greets
Finish meal	Take more notes	Read paper	Read magazines	Talk to doctor about problem
Order dessert	*Close notebook*	*Comb hair*	WATCH CASHIER RING UP	Doctor asks questions
Eat dessert	*Gather belongings*	*Get books*	PAY CASHIER	DOCTOR EXAMINES
Ask for bill	Stand up	Look in mirror	*Watch bagger*	Get dressed
Bill arrives	Talk	Get coat	Cart bags out	Get medicine
PAY BILL	LEAVE	LEAVE HOUSE	Load bags into car	Make another appointment
Leave tip				LEAVE OFFICE
Get coats			LEAVE STORE	
LEAVE				

Items in all capital letters were mentioned by the most subjects, items in italics by fewer subjects, and items in lowercase letters by the fewest subjects.

structures are used not only at retrieval but also to interpret ongoing behavior as it happens. They had participants watch videotapes of routine activities such as making a bed and press a button when they thought the behavior reached the boundary of a "natural unit." For example, in making a bed a unit might be "spreading the top sheet" or "putting the pillowcases on." Some participants were asked to find boundaries for the smallest unit that seemed natural, some for the largest. The data indicated that people are biased to perceive event boundaries in a hierarchical fashion and that the parts tend to correspond to functions. The researchers argued that these are characteristics of scripts, indicating that the knowledge structures that participate in memory retrieval also guide the ongoing perception of events.

Stand-on-One-Foot Questions

7. *How does prior knowledge affect encoding?*

Questions That Require Two Feet

8. *Think of an area in which you have expertise. Is your memory for material related to that area superior to that of your friends who do not have that expertise?*
9. *What do you think the schema for the concept* librarian *might look like? How about the schema for the concept* engineer? *Does the fact that you can generate these schemas make you think that you are prejudiced?*
10. *Can you think of a way to chunk the material in this section of the chapter?*
11. *Suppose you had a good deal of prior knowledge about a particular topic. Would that make deep processing easier or more difficult?*
12. *Do you remember the translation of the French sentence at the beginning of the chapter? Why might you be more likely to remember this sentence as opposed to the others in this chapter?*

KEY TERMS

circular theory
default value
deep processing
depth of processing
elaborative rehearsal
flashbulb memories

intentional memory test
incidental memory test
levels of processing
   framework
maintenance rehearsal
script

schema
shallow processing
transfer appropriate
   processing

6

Memory Retrieval

In chapter 5 we discussed why some material ends up in secondary memory and some doesn't. The storehouse metaphor leads naturally to several questions. First, is it guaranteed that we can get information from the storehouse? A moment's reflection will tell you that the answer is "No." We've all had the frustrating experience in which we know that we know something but we can't retrieve it. ("You know, that actress with the funny first name. She was in *Ghost,* and she used to be married to that guy from all the action movies. Not Julia Roberts. Yes, Demi Moore!") This difficulty brings up the question **Why is memory retrieval unreliable?** To put it another way, how come sometimes we can retrieve a memory and other times we can't retrieve the same memory? From what you learned in chapter 5, you won't be surprised that successful retrieval of a memory depends largely on the cues available at the time of retrieval.

But sometimes cues will not help; the memory is simply lost. You know you used to know something, but you've forgotten it. Perhaps you've had this experience in looking over old high school tests: you're looking through a stack of geometry papers with problems worked out in your handwriting, and you think, "I can't believe I ever knew this stuff." In cases like this, it doesn't feel to you that if you were given enough time or better cues you'd eventually be able to retrieve the memory. Rather, it feels as if the memory of how to do those geometry problems is simply gone. Why do some memories become irretrievable? That is, **Why do we forget?** The idea that memories simply fade away with time corresponds to our everyday experience, but it is difficult to prove. It is more certain that new things you learn can interfere with things that you already know, thereby causing forgetting.

WHY IS MEMORY RETRIEVAL UNRELIABLE?

> ➤ *Preview* There are different ways of measuring memory. One measure may indicate that you don't remember something even though another indicates that you do. It thus appears that some measures of memory are more sensitive than others, better able to detect memories that are poorly represented in the storehouse. A crucial factor is the match between encoding and retrieval. Different measures of memory appear more sensitive because they typically provide different cues at retrieval. Just as encoding is affected by prior knowledge, so is retrieval.

It might seem that after information is stored into secondary memory, you should be able to retrieve it whenever you care to. As you know, memory doesn't work this way. Sometimes you try to remember Demi Moore's name and it pops right out of the storehouse, so to say. Other times you can't quite get it, but when someone provides the name you immediately recognize it as correct (and you confidently reject Julia Roberts as incorrect). There are different ways to retrieve memories—or to measure whether a person remembers something—and the way memory is measured has a big impact on whether or not a piece of information appears to be in secondary memory.

Measures of Memory

Before we can talk about the details of retrieval, we need to be more precise about the different ways to measure memory. First we need to define a **cue**, which is some information in the environment that is used as a starting point for retrieval. If I simply say to you, "Remember," the command makes no sense. Are you supposed to be remembering something about pickles, your second-grade teacher, or the structure of barium? A cue for what is to be retrieved from secondary memory might be provided by the experimenter ("Try to remember what I told you an hour ago") or the environment (you see your car and that reminds you to get your oil changed), or you might provide it yourself (you mentally retrace your steps in an effort to remember where you might have left something).

Memory tests differ in the cues that they provide. In a **free recall** test, the experimenter says little more than "Tell me what you remember." For example, in an American history class, a free recall exam question might say, "Summarize in two pages what you have learned about the Civil War." In a **cued recall** test, the experimenter adds some hints, or cues, about the material you're supposed to remember. The cues might be some words that are semantically related; for the history test, the question might include the hint "Think about the coastline" to prompt you to write about the blockade of Southern ports. The cues might also be based on sound; a clumsy clue might be "Don't forget to discuss the battle that rhymes with 'Betty's burg.'" In a **recognition test**, the experimenter provides the targets along with **distractors, foils**, or **lures**, and the participant must pick out the targets from among the distractors. This sort of memory test is used in a multiple choice exam.

In which battle was Stonewall Jackson mortally wounded?

> **a.** Chancellorsville
> **b.** Gettysburg
> **c.** Bull Run
> **d.** Battle of the Bulge

In a **savings in relearning** test, the experimenter asks the participant to learn some material (say, the names and dates of each major Civil War battle) to a particular criterion (until he or she can recite the list perfectly two times in a row). The number of practice trials it takes to reach the criterion is recorded. At retrieval, the experimenter asks the participant to learn the same material to the same criterion a second time. If the participant can reach the criterion in fewer trials, that represents savings in relearning—the participant learns the material faster the second time—which presumably results from some residual memory of the earlier experience.

The type of test used can make it appear that someone either does or does not remember something. For example, people often fail to remember a particular fact on a free recall test but then successfully remember it on a recognition test. Someone might ask you, "What's the name of the battle in which General Custer was killed?" and you say, "I can't think of it now, but I'd know it if I saw it." You're claiming that you could recognize the information even though you can't recall it. It seems that one type of memory test can be easier than another; in this case, recognition may be easier than recall.

In general, free recall is the most difficult memory task, followed by cued recall, then recognition. (Savings in relearning is still easier but is used much less often.) In this case, "easy" or "difficult" refers to the likelihood that you will successfully retrieve the material you encoded.

In truth, it's hard to compare recognition and free recall directly because the difficulty of a recognition task depends on the number of distractors (that is, the other choices on the test) and how similar they are to the target. For example, I may say, "Remember this word" and show you a slide with the word *Boat* written on it. Then an hour later I give you one of four tests, each of which has the target (*Boat*) and one distractor, and you have to choose which stimulus you saw (*a* or *b*). Figure 6.1 lists four possible tests.

In Test 1, you can select *Boat* with confidence only if you remember that the first letter was capitalized at encoding; remembering that you saw the word *boat* isn't enough. In Test 4, remembering the word *boat* is more than enough. All you have to remember is that you saw a word, not a picture, and you'll get the right answer. Clearly, the likelihood that you will correctly recognize an item depends on the other stimuli from which you are choosing. The same logic applies to a cued recall test. Your success on a cued recall test depends on the usefulness of the available cues.

Thus the first conclusion we can draw is that it is very hard to fix memory performance on some absolute scale. Because performance depends on the test, we can't say, "After a delay of 2 minutes, performance on a recognition memory test will be at about 90%." Still, it is generally true that recognition

Test 1	(a) Boat	(b) boat
Test 2	(a) Boat	(b) ship
Test 3	(a) Boat	(b) groundhog
Test 4	(a) Boat	(b)  ♋

Figure 6.1. *Four possible tests of your memory of the stimulus*
Boat *in ascending order of difficulty.*

is easier than cued recall, which is easer than free recall, and this relationship is relevant to the question we are addressing in this section: Why is memory retrieval unreliable?

Sensitivity of Memory Measures

Regarding a memory test as a detection device, we can speak of the **sensitivity** of a test as its ability to detect memories. Free recall is not a very sensitive test. For example, I might ask you, "Who starred in the movie *Ghost?*" If you answered, "I don't know," I might conclude that the information is not in memory, but my conclusion could be wrong. The information might be in memory even if a free recall test is not sensitive enough to pick it up. Suppose I ask, "Who starred in the movie *Ghost?* Was it Demi Moore?" and you confidently answer, "Yes." I am using a recognition test, which we could say is more sensitive than free recall because it detected that you had some information about this movie in secondary memory.

Endel Tulving and Zena Pearlstone (1966) examined the relative sensitivity of recall and cued recall. They tested 948 high school students on lists of 12, 24, or 48 items. The lists consisted of category names followed immediately by examples of the category. For example, part of a list might be *weapons, cannon, bomb; professions, engineer, lawyer.* Participants were told that the words to be remembered would be preceded by a word or phrase that described them, but they didn't need to remember these descriptive labels. Recall occurred after a very brief delay. Some participants received a free recall test and others a cued recall test. For the latter participants, the cues were the descriptive category labels (*weapons, professions*). In addition, all participants made an attempt with a cued recall test.

Two results are important to our present discussion. First, the students' performance was much better with cued recall than free recall. Second, on the repeated cued recall test, the participants whose first test had been free recall suddenly remembered many more words—on average about 50% more.

J. T. Hart (1965, 1967) conducted a study that was in some ways parallel to Tulving and Pearlstone's, but Hart's experiment examined free recall and recognition. Hart asked college students 50 difficult free recall questions of general knowledge, such as "What sea does Pakistan border?" If the participant could not provide the answer, he or she tried to select the correct answer from among four alternatives (Arabian Sea, Caspian Sea, Red Sea, Black Sea). When free recall failed and participants were unable to provide an answer, they were able to recognize the correct answer about 50% of the time. Chance performance would be 25%, so the students were successfully recognizing information that they could not recall.

In this section we are considering why it is sometimes possible to retrieve a memory and other times impossible to retrieve the same memory. We have our first answer: whether a memory is retrievable depends, in part, on the sensitivity of the memory test.

Differences in Cues

Why do different measures of memory have different sensitivities? Psychologists have found it useful to think about different measures of memory in terms of the cues that they provide.

In a free recall test, the instruction is typically "Try to recall the information I showed you earlier." It is understood that you are to recall information from the time and place at which the experimenter had you encode some material. This information about the time and place at which a memory was encoded is usually called the **context**, but in this example you don't have complete information about the context. The experimenter might have said, "Try to recall the information I showed you an hour ago, in this room." Of course, even if the experimenter didn't give you that specific information ("an hour ago, in this room") you might use that information to help you remember the required information. In so doing you are generating your own cues to memory.

In a cued recall test the experimenter provides the context and adds some hints about the material. The hints might be some semantically related words ("One of the words referred to a card game") or a cue based on sound ("One of the words rhymed with smoker").

In a recognition test the experimenter again provides a cue about the context but now also provides the target material along with some other material that was not presented at encoding. The participant's job, therefore, is to determine which of the stimuli go with the encoding context (see Table 6.1).

It seems that free recall, cued recall, and recognition differ in that they provide successively more complete cues. One idea holds that memories may differ

Table 6.1.   *Types of Memory Tests*

Type of Test	Sample Instructions	Reference to Context?	Information About Target	What Must Participant Do?
Free recall	"Please remember the word list."	Yes	None	Generate the target material from the context information.
Cued recall	"Please remember the word list. One of the words was the name of a card game."	Yes	Usually semantic (i.e., related to meaning)	Generate the target from the context information using the cue.
Recognition	"Was the word *poker* on the list you saw before?	Yes	Target itself	Determine whether the stimulus provided matches the context information.

along a simple dimension of how strong they are; the weaker the memory is, the more cues you need to retrieve the memory. The sensitivity of a test is determined by the quality and quantity of cues it provides. We can call this view the **strength view of memory**.

Later experiments showed that there are problems with a strength view of memory. For example, retrieval doesn't work the same way each time. If someone asks you to name the three Rice Crispies characters, you may draw an utter blank on one occasion, whereas another time you might immediately rattle off, "Snap, Crackle, Pop." If the memory is strong, you should retrieve it every time, and if it's weak, you should fail each time; after all, the retrieval cue ("Name the Rice Crispies characters") is the same each time.

Endel Tulving (1967) emphasized this point in a classic experiment. He had people encode a list of 36 common nouns once, then make three successive attempts to recall the list, then encode it again, make three more recall attempts, and so on. Not surprisingly, people recalled more words with each successive encoding. What was more interesting is what happened when they made several recall attempts of the list. Over all recall attempts, participants got an average of 14.21 items correct. On each successive attempt, participants remembered 3.97 words (on average) that they hadn't recalled on the previous attempt, but they also forgot 3.89 words (on average) that they had remembered on the previous attempt. In other words, a participant might report a word on the first test, then fail to recall it on Tests 2 and 3, then recall it again on Test 4, and so on. Tulving pointed out that this pattern of data argued against a simple strength theory of memory; there is no reason for the strength of a memory to wax and wane on successive tests.

Note that this doesn't mean that strength doesn't play some role in memory. The strength with which a cue ("Name the Rice Crispies characters") evokes a target may be one contributing factor. But the variability of memory performance shows that strength is not the whole story.

Encoding and Retrieval Redux

Chapter 5 emphasized that the match between encoding and retrieval is important for memory. What do we know regarding what people think about at encoding and at retrieval? For encoding, what you think about depends on what you already know about the target material. And at retrieval, what you think about is greatly influenced by the cues you are given. A memory can be retrieved or not retrieved because the cues for retrieval differ on the two retrieval attempts.

Indeed, in chapter 5 we saw that changing retrieval cues can have a big impact on memory. Rhyming cues given at retrieval might be good or bad for memory, depending on whether you were thinking about the way the word sounded at encoding. But our discussion of retrieval in this chapter makes it sound as though this effect should be more fine grained: retrieval cues should matter not only at a rough cut (the cues are "about meaning" or "about sound") but even if all the cues concern meaning.

What happens if we change the meaning of retrieval cues? Researchers find that changing the meaning of a word between encoding and retrieval has a sizable effect on memory. Leah Light and Linda Carter-Sobell (1970) had participants read sentences that contained a homophone in a way that biased the meaning toward one definition. For example, participants might have seen this sentence: "The harrassed customer bought strawberry jam at the supermarket." At recall, participants saw an adjective–noun phrase and had to say whether the noun appeared in one of the sentences they saw earlier, ignoring the adjective. Participants saw words from the sentence ("strawberry jam"), a new adjective with a word from the sentence ("raspberry jam"), or a different adjective that changed the meaning of the accompanying noun from the sentence ("traffic jam"). As shown in Figure 6.2, changing the adjective hurts recognition, but changing the adjective so that it changes the meaning of the noun hurts recognition even more.

This effect is not surprising. We would expect to have two separate concepts for *jam* in memory: one for a confection spread on toast and one for traffic tie-ups. At encoding you think of one meaning, and at retrieval the cue biases you to think of the other, so you fail to recall the word. What would happen, though, if you didn't change the meaning of the word but emphasized different aspects or properties of the word?

To determine whether emphasizing a particular property of a concept influenced participants' subsequent memory for it, Richard Barclay and his associates (1974) gave 20 participants target words in the context of a sentence that encouraged them to think of a particular property of the word's referent. For example, a participant might hear "The man lifted the piano" or "The man tuned the piano." At recall, each participant received two nonconsecutive cues that were pertinent to the target words. For *piano*, the cues were "something heavy" and "something with a nice sound." Each participant only heard one sentence with *piano* in it, but each participant heard both cues at recall (on separate testing occasions), so one cue was appropriate and the other inappropriate. Out of 10 words, participants remembered an average of 4.6 that

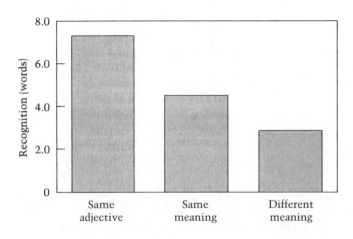

Figure 6.2. *Light and Carter-Sobell's (1970) study showed that biasing the meaning of a noun at recall hurts recognition performance.*

were cued according to the appropriate meaning and just 1.6 that were cued with the inappropriate meaning. Note that in this experiment, it was properties of an object that were changed, not the object itself (as in the *jam* experiment). Nevertheless, there is a sizable effect of changing the cue at retrieval.

Retrieval Cues and Memory Test Sensitivity

This preceding discussion gives us a hint about what is behind the variable sensitivity of different retrieval tests. It's not that more retrieval cues per se are better for retrieval, but that having more cues makes it more likely that one of them will match what you thought about at encoding, leading to successful retrieval. In other words, a recognition test is more likely than a cued recall test to make you process the material the way you did at encoding. If a cued recall test were designed to make participants more likely to think about the material in the same way as they did at encoding, it should be more sensitive than a recognition test.

Endel Tulving and his associate Donald Thomson (1973) set out to show that effect. In this experiment, participants were told that they would see word pairs, and they were to remember the words written in capital letters. An accompanying word written in lowercase letters might help them, but they would be tested on the words in capital letters. Participants saw a list of 24 word pairs such as *glue–CHAIR, ground–COLD, fruit–FLOWER* and then took a recognition test of the capitalized words. Immediately after this task, participants were given the list of cues from the original list: *glue _____, ground _____,* and *fruit _____*. Participants failed to recognize many of the target words on the first test but then successfully produced them on the cued recall test. Tulving and Thomson called this effect **recognition failure of recallable words** to emphasize that the encoding and testing conditions were designed to reverse the usual finding that recognition is superior to recall. This effect has been repeated in many other experiments.

How is it possible for participants to recall *CHAIR* given the cue *glue*, even though moments earlier they had failed to pick out *CHAIR* on a recognition test? There has been a good deal of debate about this phenomenon. (One proposal held that the effect is a statistical oddity and not of any importance; see Hintzman, 1992.) Currently the favored explanation is that the cause of the recognition failure of recallable words effect lies in the lowercase cues, which are selected to be low associates of the target words. The words *chair* and *glue*, for example, are not completely unrelated. You can make a connection between the two words if you think about the joints of a chair, which are often glued. So the presence of the word *glue*, which the experimenter says you are free to ignore, makes you think about the target in an unusual way. If on the recognition test you see *CHAIR* alone and you think about chair in the normal way—as something to sit on—that's not what you thought about at encoding. You thought about something with glued joints, so you say to yourself, "Nah, I didn't see the word *CHAIR* before. Gee, I don't know which of these three words was on the list; I'll just guess." And you might guess wrong. Later on the recall test you see the cue *glue*, and there is some chance you'll say to yourself, "Oh yeah, I thought about glue at encoding—glued joints it was. On a chair. Right, *glue* went with *CHAIR*."

Tulving and Thomson's experiment shows that the match between encoding and retrieval is critical; if you think about the stimulus in different ways at encoding and retrieval, you may not recognize it. We can predict, then, that if participants never really connect the cue and stimulus words (*glue–CHAIR*) semantically, the recall failure effect should disappear, and that seems to be the case (Aerlemalm, 1997; Bryant, 1991).

Retrieval Cues and the Physical Environment

We know that memory is better when the processes engaged in thinking about the material are the same at encoding and retrieval. Can we extend this idea to physical context? Is memory better if the physical context is the same at encoding and retrieval? If you learn some material while you're in a dormitory room, for example, will you remember it when you are tested in a lecture hall? In fact, researchers have demonstrated that there are **context effects** of the physical environment on memory, but they are generally weak.

Duncan Godden and Alan Baddeley (1975) had participants encode and retrieve information while they were either underwater or on dry land. Participants, who were members of a diving club, were outfitted with apparatus that enabled them to hear words read to them underwater and write them on special boards. Then they heard and recalled word lists either underwater, on dry land, or switching between the two conditions at encoding and retrieval. (There was a 4-min delay between encoding and retrieval in all cases so that participants who were switching would have time to make the change.) The results showed that memory was about 40% better in the same context. To be certain that it was the different context and not the disruptive effect of switching that affected memory, Godden and Baddeley conducted a second experiment in which participants encoded and retrieved words on dry land, but during the 4-min delay half of the participants had to jump in the water, swim, and dive down 20 feet before exiting the water and trying to recall the words. This extra, possibly disruptive activity had no effect on memory, indicating that in the first experiment it was the change in context that was affecting memory, not the disruption of switching contexts.

Does physical context affect memory under ordinary conditions as well as underwater? Steven Smith, Arthur Glenberg, and Robert Bjork (1978) had college students study lists of words presented on slides in a windowless room off campus by the experimenter neatly dressed in a tie and jacket. On a second day the students studied another word list that was read aloud, this time in a room on campus with windows, and the experimenter was dressed sloppily. On a third day, they were asked to remember both lists in one or the other context. The experimenters reported that memory was somewhat better if the context matched between encoding and retrieval (59% correct) than if it didn't match (46% correct). All these changes in the environment (room, experimenter, words heard vs. seen) produced a modest effect.

These studies showed that memory is somewhat better when the physical environment is the same during encoding and retrieval. Nevertheless, context effects are usually small or nonexistent; the effect is present for free recall, smaller for cued recall, and absent altogether for recognition (Smith, 1988). It may well be that the effect, when present, is due to the extent to which the participant integrates the target word and the environmental context (for example, the word *powder* might be encoded differently underwater and on dry land). Seen that way, environmental context effects are rather like any other context effects in that they depend on the match between thoughts at encoding and at retrieval.

Identical Cues, Different Memories?

So far all the data point to the importance of a match between encoding and retrieval cues. This explanation emphasizes that different cues are behind the success or failure of retrieval attempts. One of our examples, however, showed that people can either succeed or fail in remembering something given the exact same cue. If the task is to name the Rice Crispies characters, on one day you can do it, and on another you can't. What's going on?

The same cue won't necessarily make you think about the same things each time you hear it. When you hear "Rice Crispies," you might think about the cereal itself, the box it comes in, or a television advertisement for the product. The ad would make you think of the jingle "Snap, Crackle, Pop! Rice Crispies!" and then you can name the characters. Why does the same question make you think about the cereal, the box, or the advertisement at different times?

We might guess that your thoughts in response to a cue depend on what else you've been thinking about recently. How could we test such an idea? Peter Graf, Art Shimamura, and Larry Squire (1985) devised an experiment in which they had people with amnesia due to brain damage and neurologically intact participants listen to a list of 15 words, then rate how much they liked each word. The words were instances of three categories—for example, five types of fruits, five types of furniture, and five types of kitchen utensils (in random order). As you know from your previous reading, having participants rate words for liking is a deep processing task. Next, participants were given category names and were asked to produce eight instances from the category. For example, the experimenter might say "Fruits" and the participant would say "Apple, orange, pear, banana," and so on. Participants named instances for six categories, three of them categories for which they had performed the liking task. In the final phase of the experiment they took a recognition test for the words they had rated for liking.

The key result was that having heard a word during the liking task made it more likely that the participant would produce the same word later when asked to produce words in that category (such as *strawberry* for *fruits*). This finding held even for the patients with amnesia, who did not consciously remember having heard the words and who failed utterly on the final recognition test. Even patients whose memory is completely gone are more likely to

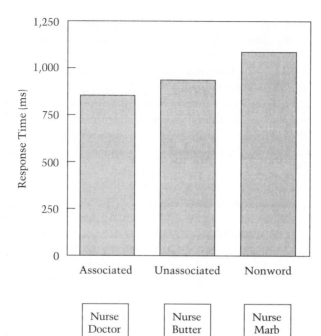

Figure 6.3. *Results of Meyer and Schvaneveldt's (1971) experiment showing that participants are faster to identify a word if they have just read a semantically related word. Response times are time to identify the second word of the pair.*

say *strawberry* when they think of fruits if they heard the word earlier. But this coming-to-mind effect is not supported by regular memory. This effect, called **priming**, generally refers to the facilitation of later processing of a stimulus by prior exposure to it. In the experiment described, exposure to a word made participants likely to think of that word later.

Priming works not only for the same word but for semantic associates. Thus thinking about the word *doctor* can affect how participants process the word *nurse,* as demonstrated by David Meyer and Roger Schvaneveldt (1971). In a simple task, participants saw two letter strings on a computer screen and pressed one button if both strings were words and another button if either string was a nonword. The experimenters were interested in how quickly participants could make this decision. The response time data, graphed in Figure 6.3, show that participants are faster at reading two related words than two unrelated words.

BOX 6–1 The Frontal Lobe and Memory Retrieval

We have seen that different methods of measuring memory retrieval yield different estimates of what a person seems to remember. In other words, using one measure of memory, the person appears to have forgotten some material, but by using a different measure of memory we see that the person remembers the material.

Are there separate brain areas underlying these different methods of retrieval? The answer appears to be "No." Some methods of retrieval rely on extra

(Continued)

processes, but it would be going too far to call these different methods of retrieval truly separate.

Some of the more interesting research on retrieval comes from studies of patients with damage to the frontal lobes. Such patients learn new material, but they have difficulty in retrieval. Usually they perform normally (or are minimally impaired) if their memory is tested via recognition, but they are much more impaired if they are tested with a free recall measure. These patients also have difficulty remembering the temporal order of events (which event came first, which came second, and so on). In addition, they appear to have a particular problem with source memory (remembering not only a bit of information but where or how they learned it).

What all of these deficits have in common is a reliance on memory strategies. In a recognition test, for example, the participant need only evaluate each stimulus the experimenter has provided. In a free recall test, the experimenter provides nothing, and the participant must generate all of the materials.

Felicia Gershberg and Art Shimamura (1995) tested the hypothesis that patients with damage to the frontal lobe have memory difficulties that are attributable to deficient strategies. In one experiment they administered five study–test trials of the same 15-item word list. Normal participants report the words in more or less the same order on each trial; that's a good strategy because recalling a word probably will make you think of the next word that you reported the last time. Gershberg and Shimamura's patients with damage to the frontal lobes did not show ordering effects. In a second experiment, participants heard 15-item lists with three words (such as *car, truck, tractor*) from each of five categories (*vehicles* in this case). Normal participants try to remember all of the vehicles, then all of the fruits, and so on. Patients with damage to the frontal lobes did not use this strategy and simply remembered the words in random order. When all participants were cued with the categories, however, patients with frontal lobe damage were able to improve their recall.

These data indicate that different types of memory measures call on different cognitive processes. Some measures of memory require that the participant adopt strategies, and these lesion studies indicate that the frontal lobe plays an important role in these strategies.

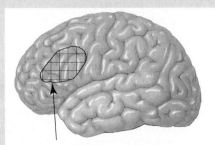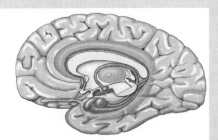

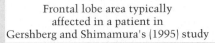
Frontal lobe area typically
affected in a patient in
Gershberg and Shimamura's (1995) study

Figure B6.1.

Theories of how memory is organized that explain priming are discussed in chapter 7. This work on priming shows that recent thoughts about a word or concept make it likely that participants will think about it or semantically related ideas later, but the details of how this process works are understood only for simple situations.

Retrieval and Prior Knowledge

In chapter 5 we saw that prior knowledge (as represented in a script or schema) influences how new material is processed and therefore how it is encoded. For example, if something is happening that can be described by a script ("taking a cab") and a relevant detail is inconsistent with the script (the cabbie gets lost), that inconsistent event will be well remembered. Does prior knowledge also influence retrieval? Yes, but at retrieval it influences memory of the typical events, not the atypical ones.

Suppose that you are trying to remember a story I told you last week about my daughter's birthday party. You have prior knowledge about children's birthday parties that can provide retrieval cues. For example, you probably know that cake and ice cream usually are served at kids' parties, so you might try to remember what sort of cake was served or whether something other than cake was served, such as an enormous chocolate chip cookie. Your expectation that cake was served may be so strong that you may think to yourself, "I really don't remember cake being served, but this was a child's birthday party, so there had to be cake; let me try one more time to remember what kind."

Sir Frederic Bartlett (1932), who first developed the idea of a schema, gave a classic example of its effects on retrieval. He read this Native American folktale called "The War of the Ghosts" to English schoolboys.

> One night two young men from Egulac went down to the river to hunt seals, and while they were there it became foggy and calm. Then they heard war-cries, and they thought: "Maybe this is a war-party." They escaped to the shore, and hid behind a log. Now canoes came up, and they heard the noise of paddles, and saw one canoe coming up to them. There were five men in the canoe, and they said:
>
> "What do you think? We wish to take you along. We are going up the river to make war on the people." One of the young men said: "I have no arrows." "Arrows are in the canoe," they said. "I will not go along. I might be killed. My relatives do not know where I have gone. But you," he said, turning to the other, "may go with them." So one of the young men went, but the other returned home.
>
> And the warriors went on up the river to a town on the other side of Kalama. The people came down to the water, and they began to fight, and many were killed. But presently the young man heard one of the warriors say: "Quick, let us go home: that Indian has been hit." Now he thought: "Oh, they are ghosts." He did not feel sick, but they said he had been shot.
>
> So the canoes went back to Egulac, and the young man went ashore to his house, and made a fire. And he told everybody and said: "Behold I accompanied the ghosts, and we went to fight. Many of our fellows were killed, and many of

those who attacked us were killed. They said I was hit, and I did not feel sick."
He told it all, and then he became quiet. When the sun rose he fell down. Something black came out of his mouth. His face became contorted. The people jumped up and cried. He was dead."

This story has elements that would be unfamiliar to English schoolboys in the 1930s (and probably to most American college students today). It includes unfamiliar cultural elements like canoes, and the story structure itself was different from English stories, which typically have logical links between one event and another; this story introduces new actions without making it clear how they relate to previous actions. Bartlett reported that when his participants tried to recall this story later, their recall was influenced by their schema of what a story is supposed to be like. They added details to put logical connections between events, omitted other details, and changed unfamiliar terms to ones they knew better. Bartlett called attention to one participant who substituted the word *boat* for *canoe* when he recalled the story, and another who reported *fishing* instead of *seal hunting*. The particular results Bartlett reported have not always replicated well (Roediger, Wheeler, & Rajaram, 1993), but the basic effects he reported are very well supported.

Bartlett argued that retrieval is largely a process of **reconstruction**, not simply a matter of pulling information out of the memory storehouse. Rather, Bartlett argued, retrieval is a process whereby we use information from the memory storehouse and information about the world (in the form of schemas) to reconstruct what probably happened.

This idea is supported by data from the study by Bower, Black, and Turner (1979). You'll recall that in chapter 5 we said that events that are inconsistent with the script but relevant to its goal (such as the cabbie getting lost) are well remembered. The experimenters also reported what happens if participants are asked about information that is consistent with the script but was not presented in the original story. For example, participants read a story about going to a restaurant that did not mention the patron paying the bill. A recognition test asked participants to rate their confidence that they had seen seven sentences in the story. The participants gave high ratings to sentences from the script that were actually contained in the story (average = 5.46) but also to actions that were consistent with the script but never mentioned in the story (average = 3.9); these ratings were much higher than the ratings they assigned to events that were not in the story but were unrelated to the script (average = 1.71). (See Table 6.2 for sample sentences.)

Thus it appears that prior knowledge in the form of scripts and schemas influences not only encoding (remember the "Washing Clothes" paragraph from chapter 5) but also retrieval.

But how can we be certain that these effects occur at retrieval? It seems plausible that these schema effects occur at encoding; the participant listening to the story is changing it as it goes to make it fit his or her schema. At recall, the participant remembers the changed story; reconstruction doesn't happen at all.

Table 6.2. **Sample Recognition Test**

Original Story	Recognition Test Sentences	Type of Sentence	Average Recognition Rating
Dan went to a restaurant. The hostess seated him. He scanned the menu. He selected what he wanted, and the server took his order. Dan waited for his food. The waitress brought his food.	Dan waited for his food.	Consistent with the script; in the story	5.46
	Dan paid the bill.	Consistent with the script; not in story	3.91
Dan ate his meal and left the restaurant.	The restaurant was cold.	Irrelevant to script; not in story	1.71

James Dooling and Robert Christiaansen (1977) thought of a clever way to show that reconstruction can happen at recall. They asked participants to read this paragraph.

Carol Harris was a problem child from birth. She was wild, stubborn, and violent. By the time Carol turned eight, she was still unmanageable. Her parents were very concerned about her mental health. There was no good institution for her problem in her state. Her parents finally decided to take some action. They hired a private teacher for Carol.

BOX 6–2 *Functional Imaging Studies of the Frontal Lobe and Memory*

We have discussed the role of the frontal lobe in memory, mentioning the studies by Wagner and colleagues (1998) and Brewer and colleagues (1998) showing that frontal activity at encoding predicted whether a memory would be retrieved later (see chapter 5). We also noted that studies of patients with brain damage have indicated that the frontal lobe is especially important for developing strategies that help memory retrieval.

You may have noticed a paradox: lesion studies indicate that the frontal lobe is important only for strategic processes in memory because patients with frontal lobe damage are largely unimpaired on a recognition test of memory. Yet functional imaging studies give frontal cortex a starring role in memory. Indeed, almost every functional imaging study of memory shows frontal activation. Figure B6.2 shows a summary of such studies, with each circle representing the focus of activation in one study.

Why is there a discrepancy between the lesion studies (which indicate that frontal cortex is not very important) and the imaging studies (which indicate that it is)? In a review of imaging studies, Randy Buckner and his colleagues

(Continued)

(Buckner, Kelley, & Petersen, 1999) addressed this question. They suggested two possibilities. First, patients with damage to the frontal lobes may have more widespread memory deficits than is commonly appreciated, but they may be able to compensate for these deficits. It is possible that people can code the same stimulus in a number of different ways (for example, verbally or pictorially) that rely on different parts of the frontal lobe. Thus a typical patient has damage that leads to poor encoding of one type of stimulus but can recode the stimulus a different way so that it relies only on the part of the frontal lobe that is intact.

A second possibility is that the researchers have been overinterpreting their imaging results. Most often when we observe activity in frontal regions it is at encoding. Buckner and colleagues pointed out that this activation may contribute to memory formation only in a minor way and that this activity represents the cognitive processes that are active at the time of encoding (such as thinking about what the stimulus means) and does not represent activity that is actually forming the memory.

Another review of the data suggests that this second possibility could be correct (Fletcher & Henson, 2001) because three areas of the frontal lobe support three different cognitive functions. The ventrolateral cortex supports the maintenance of information in working memory, the dorsolateral cortex supports the selection and manipulation of information in working memory, and the anterior prefrontal cortex supports the selection of processes or subgoals. These are functions that would likely contribute to some, but not all, memory encoding or retrieval processes.

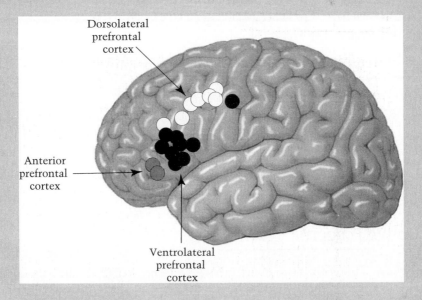

Figure B6.2.

After a 1-week delay, a group of participants were given a recognition test for sentences and had to say whether each sentence was in the story. The critical sentence was "She was deaf, dumb, and blind." Very few participants thought that this sentence had been part of the story. A second group of participants underwent the same testing procedure, except that right before taking the recognition test they were told that Carol Harris was Helen Keller's real name. Many of these participants incorrectly "recognized" the critical sentence as having been in the story. This experiment shows clearly that reconstruction can take place at retrieval. There was no opportunity for the memory error to take place at encoding because participants didn't know that their background knowledge about Helen Keller would be relevant until retrieval.

Stand-on-One-Foot Questions

1. *What four measures of memory are commonly used, and what does it mean to say that they differ in sensitivity?*
2. *Why do different measures of memory differ in sensitivity?*
3. *Which is more important to effective retrieval: the format of the test (recognition, cued recall) or the cues the test provides?*
4. *How does prior knowledge affect retrieval?*

Questions That Require Two Feet

5. *Suppose you asked a friend to tell you what he or she was doing exactly 19 months ago. How much do you think he or she could tell you, and why?*
6. *You probably have had the experience of walking past a friend without recognizing him or her in a place where you don't typically see that person (as when you see a college friend in your hometown during spring break). How can the ideas discussed here explain that phenomenon?*

WHY DO WE FORGET?

> ➤ *Preview* There are two main theories of forgetting: decay and interference. There is little evidence supporting the theory that memories decay, but it is difficult to test. There is quite a bit more evidence for interference. Two sources of interference are response competition and unlearning. The idea that all forgetting is caused by interference seems to favor the theory that all memories are in
>
> *(Continued)*

the storehouse and any failure of retrieval is caused by interference, but there is no good evidence supporting that view. However, if memories are practiced enough, for all practical purposes they will never be forgotten. Repression as a source of forgetting is rare and difficult to prove but probably does happen.

In trying to explain why something that *can* be retrieved sometimes is not, we have emphasized cues, and indeed, changes in cues can make an easily accessible memory appear to be forgotten. Something might happen to make you interpret the cues differently, as in recognition failure of recallable words, or a change in environmental context might do the same. Sometimes, however, a memory seems to be lost not temporarily but permanently: it cannot be retrieved. What happens when information is forgotten?

Figure 6.4 depicts the components of a memory situation. Any instance of memory can be thought of as composed of a cue or cues (either from the environment or generated by the person) and the target material. The cue and the target are linked or associated, and this link may be strong or weak. For example, the cue may be the question "What is your phone number?" which is associated with the target information—the number. Again, cues can be a source of forgetting. Changes to cues (cue bias) might lead to what amounts to a temporary failure to retrieve; if you had the right cues, you could retrieve the memory. But it's also possible that changes in cues could lead to permanent forgetting. For example, you might encode a memory when you are 12 years old and then try to retrieve it at age 40. The cues that would have been effective at age 12 may not work at 40 because the way you interpret them has changed. Indeed, the cues may be thoughts and feelings that are virtually impossible for

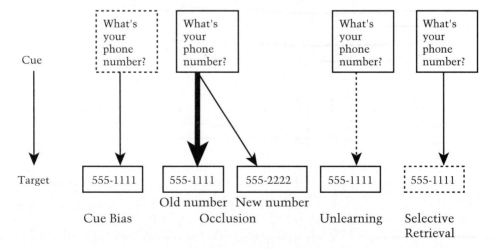

Figure 6.4. *This simple model illustrates different theories of how forgetting could occur. The thick arrow represents a more robust association; dotted lines indicate some degradation.*

you to have now. Without those cues, the memory cannot be recovered. Thus in some situations the cues associated with a memory cannot be recovered, and so the memory cannot be retrieved.

Three theories of forgetting incorporate changes to the links between cues and associated target memories. In occlusion, there is a stronger link from the cue to some undesired memory than to the target, and the cue therefore always calls up the undesired memory. In unlearning, a link is thought to weaken when the cue is practiced with another target memory. In decay, the link is thought to spontaneously weaken over time.

Occlusion

Occlusion makes it seem as if the memory is hidden or covered by another memory. The cue may be associated with the target just as strongly as it ever was, but it may also be associated with other memories more strongly, and every time the cue is presented, another memory intrudes. For example, if you move to a new city, whenever you are asked what your phone number is, your old phone number may consistently intrude, making it difficult to remember the new number.

An easily appreciated example of occlusion is the **tip-of-the-tongue phenomenon** (Brown & McNeill, 1966). This aptly named effect occurs when you are certain you know a concept but cannot think of the proper term for it. For example, someone might ask you the term for "a nautical device using the angle of the sun and horizon to find your position." An incorrect term, *compass*, might come to mind, and even though you know it's incorrect, it might keep coming to mind, seeming to block out the correct term, *sextant* (see Burke, MacKay, Worthley, & Wade, 1991).

Although occlusion is a plausible source of some forgetting, it is probably not the major contributor. Most of the time when we forget, there is not another memory occluding the target. Even when we are in the tip-of-the-tongue state, there is usually not a persistent intruder memory. Other factors must play a part in forgetting.

Unlearning

Unlearning—the weakening of the association between a cue and a target due to new learning—is usually thought to occur because a cue is practiced with a new target. For example, when I move to a new city, the association between the cue "What is your phone number?" and the target memory "555-2222" not only gets stronger, but the association between that cue and my old number "555-1111" gets weaker. Notice that a theory of forgetting would not *have* to posit that it gets weaker. We could say that this old association just stays the same, but eventually the association to the new phone number is strong enough to "drown out" the old association.

Arthur Melton and Jean Irwin (1940) first proposed unlearning. In their experiment, participants learned a list of 18 nonsense syllables such as *vez*.

Participants practiced the list five times. On each practice run, they saw a word presented for 2 s and were asked to spell the word that they thought would appear next.

Thirty minutes later participants were retested on the list. Melton and Irwin varied what different participants did during the 30-min wait; some read magazines, and others had to learn a second list of nonsense syllables. The experimenters varied how much participants studied the second list (either 5, 10, 20, or 40 repetitions). The critical measure came when everyone was retested on the first list. The experimenters were interested in whether **intrusions** occurred when people were retested on the first list. That happened when a response from the second list was produced instead of one from the first list. (More generally, an intrusion produces an answer that would be right in another context.) If the old targets were still in memory, participants would show intrusions, and the more they studied the second list, the more intrusions there would be. This is true up to a point, but as shown in Figure 6.5, as the second list is studied more, the number of intrusions begins to drop. Melton and Irwin proposed that studying the second list caused unlearning of the first list.

Unlearning may well account for some types of forgetting, but it is not clear that it is a significant contributor to forgetting most of the time. If the chief problem in forgetting were the degradation of the associative bond between the cue and response, then *any* task that relies on that bond should be impaired. The paradigms that arguably lead to unlearning—including the one used by Melton and Irwin—lead to poor recall performance, but recognition

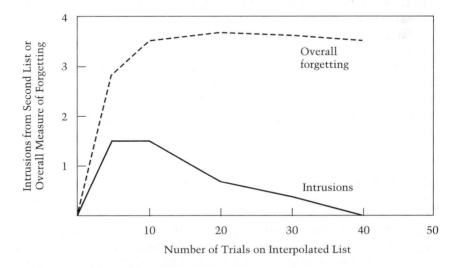

Figure 6.5. *Graph from Melton and Irwin's (1940) experiment showing that more practice on a second list does not produce more intrusions from the second list, when you later try to recall the first list. Initially there is a rise, but then the number of intrusions falls. Nevertheless, forgetting increases. The measure of intrusions and forgetting is a complex percentage estimate designed to make these two measures comparable on one graph.*

performance is relatively unaffected. Yet recognition should rely on the associative bond between cue and target just as much as recall does.

Decay

The **decay** theory of forgetting proposes that the link between a cue and a target memory spontaneously decays over time. If you rehearse the memory again it will be "refreshed," but all links are breaking down, so refreshing the association doesn't prevent decay: it simply revives the link. Most people would find this idea reasonable because the passage of time seems to be culprit in forgetting.

A simple version of decay theory was proposed by Edward Thorndike (1911), the great turn-of-the-century learning theorist. His law of disuse proposed that if a memory is not used, it decays. This idea, however, predicts that older memories should always be more decayed than newer memories and therefore more difficult to retrieve. Yet we know that some older memories remain strong, whereas newer memories are lost. I can't recall what I had for breakfast a few days ago, but I still remember the name of my first-grade teacher.

We could combine decay theory with some version of a strength theory and say that all memories decay at a constant rate, but some start out with more strength than others. Older memories that started out with more strength, such as my first-grade teacher's name, could be easier to retrieve than recent memories that started out with less strength. Until the 1930s, most psychologists thought that something like this was behind forgetting. In the last section we went over problems with a strength theory, but people didn't spot these problems until the 1960s. The case against decay was made by John McGeogh in 1932. He pointed out that it seems natural to blame time as the great causative agent in forgetting. We forget as time passes, and we therefore think of the passage of time as causing the forgetting. McGeogh pointed out that time itself is not an explanation; instead, some process *happening in time* causes forgetting. He suggested the analogy of metal rusting. Metal rusts not because of time but because of oxidation, a process that happens in time. For decay to be an explanation, we must specify what the process of decay is.

There is a more serious problem with a decay theory: it is difficult to test. Decay is supposed to occur spontaneously—as time goes on, the representation degrades, irrespective of what the cognitive system is doing. Thus, the ideal experiment would be to have people learn something, then do nothing for a period of time, and then test their memory for decay. That experiment cannot be conducted. People can't think about absolutely nothing; there is a constant stream of thought, and any thoughts that occur after encoding can interfere with memory. If we look for decay and observe forgetting, it is always possible that we are really observing the effect of interference. For decay to provide a testable account of forgetting, researchers will probably need to propose more specific theories of exactly how decay operates, as has been done for decay in working memory (see chapter 4; see Altmann & Gray, 2002).

Changes to Target Memories

Mike Anderson (in press; Anderson & Levy, 2002) has demonstrated convincingly that one source of forgetting is changes to the target memories themselves. At first this fact seems surprising, even counterproductive. If a memory must be forgotten, wouldn't it be better if the links were lost rather than the target memory itself? What if you need the target memory in some other context? Anderson points out, however, that dampening the target memory makes sense in some situations. We discuss two situations in which it has been shown that memory representations are dampened.

INHIBITION.   Cues are usually associated not with just one target memory but with many memories, most of which you don't want to retrieve along with a specific target. If one memory completely dominates retrieval, we say that occlusion has occurred. Most of the time, however, occlusion does not occur; you successfully retrieve the target even though other memories are also associated with the available cues. **Inhibition** could suppress the unwanted, competing memories to keep them from being retrieved instead of the target memory. Any given cue might lead to the activation of several candidate memories, so inhibition dampens the undesired memories and allows the desired memory to be retrieved.

If this process of inhibition occurs, it should make suppressed memories more difficult to retrieve. In other words, retrieving a memory will actually dampen related memories that the cue also activates but that are not retrieved. This phenomenon of **retrieval-induced forgetting** was demonstrated by Mike Anderson and his colleagues (Anderson, Bjork, & Bjork, 1994). Participants studied word pairs that were a category and an instance of the category (*fruit–banana, fruit–orange*). After the study phase, they practiced retrieving half of the items in cued recall (*fruit–or_____*) and didn't practice the other half. Some categories (*drink*) were not practiced at all, and these items served as a baseline of comparison. The final phase was a cued recall test for all items. Sample results for the final test are shown in panel A of Figure 6.6.

When subjects had practiced retrieving a pair such as *fruit–orange*, they improved on that pair compared to unpracticed items like *drink–Scotch*. That's no surprise—practice improves memory. More important, an unpracticed item like *fruit–banana* was *worse* at final recall by virtue of being in the same category as the practiced item (*fruit–orange*). That's retrieval-induced forgetting.

But various theories could explain this effect. For example, retrieving *fruit–orange* could make the *fruit–banana* link weaker; this unlearning account seems consistent with this experiment. The selective retrieval account can make a unique prediction, however. Since it is supposed to be the target memory (*banana*) that is inhibited, the particular cue should not matter. In other words, practicing *fruit–orange* should inhibit *banana* whether *banana* is cued by *fruit* or by something else.

Anderson and Bobbie Spellman (1995) tested that prediction. They used a paradigm similar to that of Anderson and colleagues (1994) but with the added

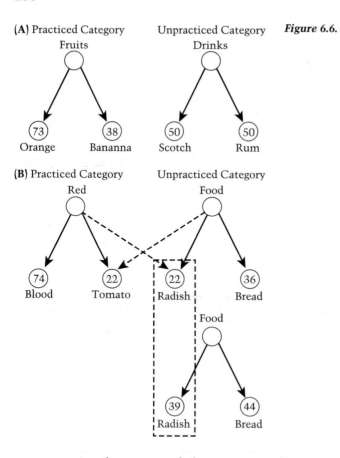

Figure 6.6. *The numbers indicate the percentage of participants recalling the stimulus. Panel A shows that practicing fruits–orange leads to poorer performance on an unpracticed item (fruits–banana) compared to items from a category that wasn't practiced (drink–Scotch). Panel B shows that this poorer performance is due to inhibition of the item, not the link to it. Practicing* red–blood *inhibits* radish *(another red thing) even if memory for* radish *is probed using the cue* food. *Because a different cue to* radish *still leads to poor performance, we know the inhibition is not in the association of the cue* red *to* radish. *The inhibition is observed even when a different cue (food) is used; hence, the inhibition must be in* radish *itself. The bottom part of the figure shows the control condition—performance on* food–radish *when* red–blood *is not practiced. From "Inhibitory Processes and the Control of Memory Retrieval," by B. J. Levy and M. C. Anderson, 2002,* Trends in Cognitive Sciences, 6, *p. 300.*

twist that some of the instances fit more than one category. As shown in panel B of Figure 6.6, *tomato* and *radish* fit two of the studied categories: *red* and *food.* Practicing retrieval of *red–blood* will impair an unstudied pair in the same category, like *red–tomato.* According to the inhibition hypothesis, practicing retrieval of *red–blood* should also impair the unstudied pair *food–radish.* Why? Bear in mind what practicing retrieval of *red–blood* does: it inhibits the representation of all red things, dampening the incorrect red things to help you retrieve *blood. Radish* is a red thing, so the representation of *radish* is inhibited, even though *radish* was studied as part of the *food* category. As shown in the figure, that inhibition of *food–radish* takes place: people are less likely to recall *food–radish* if they have studied *red–blood.* The control condition is shown at the bottom of the figure—that's memory for *food–radish* when people didn't practice *red–blood.*

The key point in this rather complicated pair of experiments is that at least one source of forgetting is shown to be the inhibition of the target memory representation itself, not the degradation of the associative links between the cue and the target memory.

CONTROLLED RETRIEVAL.   Other evidence supports a different mechanism by which a memory representation may be inhibited: it occurs when the person actively tries not to think about something, which we might call **controlled re-trieval** (Anderson & Green, 2001). In other words, if a particular cue leads to a memory that you would rather not think about, trying to suppress that memory can actually work.

In this experiment, participants first studied word pairs such as *flag–sword* and *ordeal–roach*. In the next phase they were given the first word of one of the pairs, and for most of these cues they were to say aloud the word that went with it. For some cues, however, they were told *not* to say or even to think about the associate but to try to suppress it. In the final phase, their memory for all of the words was tested, as shown in Figure 6.7. Participants' memory for the suppressed words was impaired, and the more times they suppressed a word, the worse their memory for it was. Further, their memory was impaired whether they were tested with the original cue (*ordeal*) or a new cue (*insect–r____*). The fact that the memory for *roach* is impaired even with a different cue indicates that what is inhibited is not the association between a cue and the target memory but the target memory itself.

SUMMARY.   We've talked about three ways in which memory can be forgotten. (1) Cues may be ineffective because they are interpreted differently than they were at encoding. (2) The associative links between memories may be lost due to decay or unlearning, or a link may be ineffective because the cue also leads to another memory via a stronger associative link. (3) The representation of the memory itself may be dampened, either by the process of inhibition or by the person actively stopping retrieval.

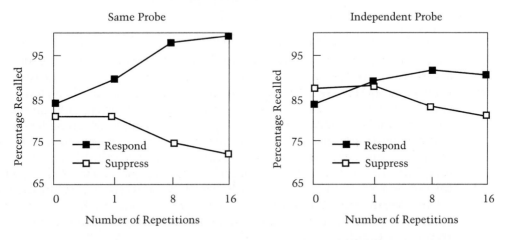

Figure 6.7. *Anderson & Green (2001) showed the effects of controlled retrieval, or trying to forget. If participants try not to think about a memory when given a cue, they find it more difficult to later retrieve that memory when given the cue. The more times the memory is suppressed, the harder it is to later retrieve (left panel). The right panel shows that it's hard to access the memory even if the cue is different from the one used during the suppression trials. This cue independence indicates that the memory itself is inhibited, not the association between the cue and the memory. From "Suppressing Unwanted Memories by Executive Control," by M. C. Anderson and C. Green, 2001,* Nature, 410, *Fig. 1, p. 366.*

Which of these is the most important factor in forgetting? In a practical sense, cues are clearly the most important. If you don't have the right cues, there is no chance that you'll retrieve a memory. Also, most memories have multiple cues associated with them, so if you lose an associative link, or if the memory is somewhat inhibited, more and better cues might still enable you to retrieve the memory. There is a great deal of evidence regarding the importance of cues. There is also evidence that inhibition of memory representations contributes to forgetting. There is less evidence that the loss of associative links makes a significant contribution to forgetting.

Repression

Repression is the active forgetting of an episode for the sake of self-protection: remembering it would be too painful. The term implies some active form of dampening the memory, but this dampening process happens outside of awareness. It is that you try not to think about the memory.

We're treating repression separately from other types of forgetting because the focus in this area of research has not been on how forgetting and remembering work, but rather on whether or not repression happens at all. It is difficult to gather scientific evidence about repression, and the study of repression is itself charged with emotion (for example, see Yeager, 2002).

If you're studying repression, you need to ask three questions.

1. Did the event this person remembers actually happen?
2. Did this person fail to remember the event from the time it happened until much later? (That is, was the memory really repressed?)
3. Did the forgetting result from repression, not some other process?

To consider the first question, look at a case report from Jonathan Schooler (1994). A 30-year-old man's memory was jogged by seeing a movie about sexual abuse. Several hours after seeing the movie, the man was lying in bed and suddenly remembered being abused by his parish priest on a camping trip when he was 11 years old. How could you verify whether the man was abused? Child molesting is usually a crime that has no witnesses, and it is typically quite difficult to find corroborating evidence. In this case the man confronted the priest, who confessed, but that sort of verification is rare. The legal implications and the emotional consequences of abuse to the psyche of the victim are important, but for the moment we're focusing on whether the mind is capable of repressing memories. And to know that, we must know that the memory is genuine.

The second question asks whether the person really had forgotten the memory of the abuse during the time he or she said it was forgotten. Strangely, people can forget that they have remembered. Jonathan Schooler, Miriam Bendiksen, and Zara Ambadar (1997) described a case in which a person's memory of a traumatic event was ambiguous. W.B., a 40-year-old woman, recounted recovering a memory of having been raped at knifepoint when she was 16. W.B. described the memory recovery as having been triggered by an encounter with a male co-worker at a party. She commented on his advances toward a young woman, and he defended himself by saying, "She isn't exactly a virgin" (p. 268). W.B. was so upset that she left the party. That night she had nightmares and awoke knowing that she had been raped. Her reaction was very emotional, and she felt shocked. This certainly sounds as though that memory had been repressed. However, in a subsequent interview, W.B. said that she hadn't necessarily forgotten the incident completely; she likened the experience to one's first day of school: "You know that the event occurred, but you don't think about it, or even remember how it was, but you know it was there" (pp. 268–269). On the other hand, W.B. also firmly said that there were times when, had she been asked directly whether she had ever been raped, she would have answered, "No." Her ex-husband reported that several times during their marriage, W.B. had mentioned that she had been raped, but her statements had always been completely without emotion. W.B. had no recollection of having told her ex-husband. This case report, then, shows that even if a person says that he or she has completely forgotten an event for some period of time, that report cannot simply be taken at face value.

The third criterion to be sure that repression has occurred is that the forgetting must not be due to some other process. In this chapter we've been discussing many sources of retrieval failure. Isn't it possible that the memory was not actively repressed, but rather that the appropriate cues were not in the environment until the time or memory recovery?

Given these three stringent criteria, is there evidence for a process of repression? A panel appointed by the Royal College of Psychiatrists in Britain concluded that "there is a vast literature [on repression] but little acceptable research" (Brandon, Boakes, Glaser, & Green, 1998, p. 296). That said, there are several case reports and systematic studies indicating that repression does occur. For example, Jonathan Schooler (2001) reported seven cases, each of which had been carefully researched to comply with the criteria listed above.

If repression exists, just how common is it? Linda Williams (1995) interviewed 129 women who, 17 years earlier, had been admitted to a hospital emergency room because of sexual abuse. All of them were age 13 or younger at the time, and in all cases the abuse had been documented in hospital medical records. Thus in this case there can be no doubt that abuse occurred. The women underwent a 3-hr interview that covered many topics, including questions designed to elicit any history of sexual abuse. The interviewers knew nothing of the sexual history of the women they were interviewing. The survey showed that 75 of the women recalled the event. It is difficult to be sure of the reason for the inability to recall the event in the other 54 women; it may simply be because people often cannot remember details of their childhood well or because they may be resistant to reporting the event. Thus Williams focused her analysis on the 75 participants who could remember the event.

Twelve of these 75 women reported that there had been a time in the past when they did not remember the event (that is, it had been repressed). Indeed, 7 of these 12 believed that their memory of the incident was still incomplete and had not been entirely recovered. The women with recovered memories were on average 3 years younger at the line of the incident than the women who had always remembered the incident.

Is it possible that because of the vagaries of childhood memories, some of these women forgot the abuse but then later remembered it? This may be possible for some of the participants—about half were under age 6 at the time of the abuse—but it seems unlikely to be true for all the participants. Other data (Epstein & Bottoms, 2002) indicate that at least some of forgetting of childhood sexual abuse may be due to other mechanisms, such as trying not to think about the memory.

It is also possible that some of the women failed to report the abuse during the interviews. This conjecture is based on the results of a study by Donna Femina and her colleagues (Femina, Yeager, & Lewis, 1990). As in the Williams study, there was independent confirmation of abuse for all of the participants. The researchers reported that a similar percentage (38%) of participants failed to report the event during interviews, indicating that they may have forgotten it through repression. Unlike Williams, however, Femina and colleagues performed a second interview with 8 participants. During the second interview, participants were told of their abuse, and all 8 admitted that they remembered the incident but had not reported it during the first interview, usually because of embarrassment.

Little evidence supports the idea that repression can occur, probably because of two factors. First, repression is rare; most studies show that memory for traumatic events is vivid in both children and adults (Leopold & Dillon, 1963; Pynoos & Nader, 1989), although memories may not be wholly accurate. Second, it is inevitably difficult to find airtight evidence because it is impossible to conduct formal experiments on repression. We can investigate life events only after they occur, and life events are not designed to satisfy critics' demands for neatness.

Like other memory researchers (such as Schacter, 1996) as well as a panel of experts appointed by the American Psychological Association to study the issue (Alpert et al., 1996), I believe repression occurs, although the relevant studies have flaws, and it is always difficult to draw broad conclusions based on case studies of individuals.

The Permanence of Memory

From the previous sections you might conclude that forgetting is caused mostly by a lack of good cues. Perhaps everything is recorded in your mind, like a library of videotapes, and if you can't remember something it's not because the tape is lost but because you can't find it due to poor cues. This idea is written up in newspaper and magazine articles from time to time, usually reported as though it is fact. Most memory researchers, however, would disagree.

This idea is impossible to disprove, however, because the basic proposition is that all memories are retrievable if you can get the right cues. If you can't remember something, you can always say, "Well, I just don't have the right cues yet." Even after testing with a million different cues, you can maintain that the next cue might be the right one, and you will remember. Although I can't state flatly that this proposal must be wrong, I think it's unlikely to be true.

The reasons were laid out in an article by Geoff Loftus and Elizabeth Loftus (1980), pointing out that three factors support the idea that all memories lie somewhere in the memory vault: spontaneous recovery, memory under hypnosis, and an interesting study by neurologist Wilder Penfield. As we'll see, there are problems with each of these sources of evidence.

SPONTANEOUS RECOVERY.   **Spontaneous recovery** is the sudden uncovering of a long-lost memory. Often there is an identifiable cue that clearly leads to recovery of the memory. For example, people who revisit a house they lived in during childhood may report that the sight of a room brings back vivid memories. It's as though the cue (seeing the house again) is one end of a very fine chain, and if you pull it gently you find there are charms (memories) attached to the chain.

Even if we accept the fact that the recovered memories are accurate, the fact that some memories can be spontaneously recovered does not mean that all memories are recorded. It means that some memories that you haven't retrieved in a long time can be retrieved given the right cues.

MEMORY AND HYPNOSIS.   We sometimes hear or read about amazing feats of memory performed under hypnosis (bricklayers accurately reporting descriptions of bricks they laid in walkways years ago, and so on). In a word, bunk.

It is easy enough to test whether hypnosis helps memory. In one study, David Dinges and his colleagues (1992) showed participants 40 drawings of common objects. Participants immediately tried to remember as many as they could. One week later they attempted to recall the drawings, half of the participants under hypnosis and half not. The experimenters asked the participants to try to recall the whole list five times; they wanted to give an effect of hypnosis every opportunity to become manifest. They also examined participants who were very susceptible to hypnosis and participants who were not to see whether that factor made a difference. Hypnosis did nothing to improve the accuracy of memory. Many such experiments have been conducted (Lytle & Lundy, 1988; Register & Kihlstrom, 1987; for a review, see Erdelyi, 1994).

PENFIELD'S EXPERIMENTS.   As part of the preparation for brain surgery, Wilder Penfield (1959) directly stimulated patients' brains. A local anesthetic was administered in the scalp and part of the skull was removed. Penfield then used a stylus that generated a very mild electrical current to stimulate different places in the patient's brain. The patient was awake during this procedure but felt no pain. (The brain has no pain receptors.)

When Penfield stimulated some parts of the brain, a patient might say that a memory had been triggered. For example, one patient said, "Oh, a familiar memory—in an office somewhere. I could see the desks. I was there and someone was calling to me—a man leaning on a desk with a pencil in his hand" (p. 45). Another patient reported hearing her small son playing in the yard outside her kitchen window, as well as the typical neighborhood sounds. If these are indeed memories, the fact that they can be produced via direct stimulation of the brain certainly fits the idea that everything is recorded in the brain but often cannot be accessed. Perhaps the normal route to recalling memory has been bypassed—Penfield with his stylus reached in and physically jiggled loose a memory that otherwise would have been unrecoverable.

Such results sound compelling, but there are a lot of problems in interpreting them. First, something like this happened in only a small fraction (fewer than 10%) of Penfield's patients, even among those who were stimulated in the part of the brain in which memories are thought to be stored (the temporal lobe). Second, those who did report it often said that the experience was not especially like a memory. For example, the woman who heard her son playing in the yard was asked 10 days later whether this experience was a memory. She said, "Oh, no. It seemed more real than that" (p. 51). Thus it's possible that Penfield's stimulation created pictures in the person's consciousness based on things in their memories but did not evoke an actual memory. In much the same way, dreams are constructed out of things that happened to you, but they are not exact replays of events. It seems likely that the memories of Penfield's patients were **constructions**: memories that feel like bona fide memories to the person experiencing them but are actually combinations of a real memory and other information, such as what the person believes probably happened.

PERMASTORE.   Is forgetting inevitable? We all have certain bits of information that we know so well, it is difficult to believe we could ever forget it. In J. D. Salinger's book *The Catcher in the Rye* Holden Caufield helps a little girl adjust her skate and gets a rush of nostalgia from the feel of the skate key. He comments, "You could put a skate key in my hand in about fifty years in pitch black, and I'd still know what it is."

Some evidence shows that Holden was right. Enough practice makes memory immune to forgetting. Harry Bahrick did a series of studies on the permanence of memory (see Bahrick, 2000, for a review). In one study, Bahrick (1984) rounded up 733 people who had studied Spanish in high school between 1 and 50 years earlier and gave them vocabulary tests, comprehension tests, and so on (see Figure 6.8). Bahrick looked at how much Spanish the participants had retained, estimating how much they had initially learned by how many courses they had taken, their grades, and so on. He also measured how much practice these people had had with Spanish since they last took a Spanish class (whether they had visited a Spanish-speaking country, how often they estimated they were exposed to Spanish in the media, whether they had studied another Romance language, and so on).

As you can appreciate, this was a stupendously complex study to conduct, but it paid off with a very interesting result. First, as you would expect, people forget their Spanish. The forgetting is rapid for the first 3–6 years, but then it more or less plateaus, and there is little additional forgetting until

Vocabulary Recognition
1. romper
   a. to roam   b. to break   c. to look   d. to roar   e. to search
2. mandar
   a. to make   b. to mend   c. to yell   d. to command   e. to arrange

Grammar Recall: Write the correct form of the verb given in the blank provided.
1. El _____ (estudiar). He studies Spanish
2. Yo _____ la menor (ser). I am the youngest.

Idiom recall: Write the English meaning of the Spanish idiom.
1. hace mal tiempo _____
2. en vez de _____

Figure 6.8. Sample questions from Bahrick (1984).

about 30 years have passed. Then there is a second, more gradual drop-off until about 50 years (the last time point measured). This pattern, shown in Figure 6.9, was observed for almost all the measures of Spanish that Bahrick used.

There are two results to note here. First, for some of these participants, this knowledge of Spanish was retrievable 50 years after it was last encoded or rehearsed even if it had not been practiced at all during the intervening time. For all practical purposes, we might say that this information was not going to be forgotten. Bahrick referred to such memories as being in **permastore**, a hypothetical state of memory from which information is not lost.

Knowledge of Spanish did not end up in permastore for everyone; what seemed to make the difference was extended practice. The longer participants had studied Spanish, the more Spanish they had in permastore. Studying Spanish for at least several years seemed to ensure that some of it would end up in permastore.

Whether permastore is really a form of memory, separate from secondary memory, is not known. Bahrick argues that it is separate because he notes that most of the memories have a life span of 3–6 years—after that they are forgotten—and others have a life span of 50 years or more, but no memories have a life span of 10 years or 20 years. There is no forgetting between 6 and 50 years, which indicates a transition to a different state of memory. Other researchers, such as Ulric Neisser (1984), think that "permastore" is just a description of secondary memories that are so well represented that they will not be forgotten. There has been little work on permastore compared to other types of memory, probably because it is so difficult to conduct studies of the sort Bahrick has done.

Stand-on-One-Foot Questions

7. *Name the two main theories of forgetting, and evaluate the likelihood that each is correct.*

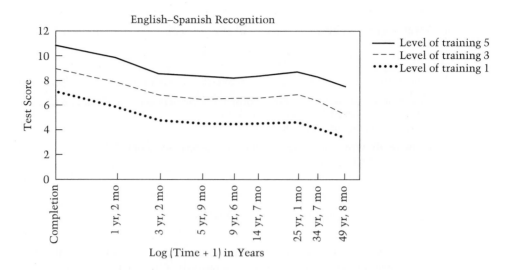

Figure 6.9. *The effect of training level on the retention of recognition vocabulary from Bahrick (1984).*

8. *Is all learning permanent, with failures of retrieval caused only by interference?*
9. *Can memory of traumatic events in childhood be repressed?*

Questions That Require Two Feet

10. *Given what you know about forgetting, how would you advise someone to schedule his or her time studying in school?*
11. *In chapter 3 we discussed iconic processes of control, and the theme there was that it is very difficult not to think about something (like a white bear). In this chapter, Anderson's work on controlled retrieval indicates that not thinking about a memory can make you forget it. What is going on?*

KEY TERMS

construction   context effects   cue
context   controlled retrieval   cued recall

decay
distractors, foils, lures
free recall
inhibition
intrusions
occlusion
permastore
priming

recognition failure of
  recallable words
recognition test
reconstruction
repression
retrieval-induced
  forgetting
savings in relearning

sensitivity
spontaneous recovery
strength view of
  memory
tip-of-the-tongue
  phenomenon
unlearning

7

Memory Storage

What Is in the Storehouse?

The Classical View of Categorization
The Probabilistic View of Categorization
Summary

How Is Memory Organized?

Addressing Systems
Content-Addressable Storage
Hierarchical Theory
Spreading Activation Theories
Spreading Activation Models: An Example
Evidence of Activation
Criticisms of Spreading Activation
Distributed Representation (Parallel Distributed Processing)
Criticisms of Parallel Distributed Processing Models

What Else Is in Memory?

What Are Separate Memory Systems?
Procedural and Declarative Memory
Cognitive Differences Among Memory Systems

In the last two chapters we've covered how memories get into the storehouse and how they are retrieved. This final chapter on memory discusses the storehouse itself. The first question we might consider is **What is in the storehouse?** Suppose I show you a coffee cup and ask you to name it. You say, "It's a cup." I ask you how you know that and you say (after giving me a fishy look), "Well, it has a handle, it's the right size, and you could put coffee in it, so it's a cup." Then I show you a tea bowl from a Chinese restaurant and I ask you to name that. Again you say, "It's a cup." This cup has no handle and it's much smaller, yet it's a cup. Similarly, if I showed you a cup with a small hole in it (so that it couldn't hold liquid), it would still be a cup. Different-looking objects are all identified as cups. So the provisional answer to the question "What is in the storehouse?" must be, "The storehouse contains memory representations that allow us to identify objects with different properties as nevertheless belonging to the same class." As we'll see, this property of memory representations is very useful, but we still don't know exactly how these representations work.

Our second question concerns organization within the memory storehouse. In chapter 6 we skipped over a daunting aspect of retrieval: finding the right bit of information among the millions of things you know. If you had 10,000 comic books and you wanted to be able to find any one of them quickly, what would you do? You'd organize them, of course: chronologically, or by main character (Superman, Green Lantern), or by plot (superhero loses powers, world is held hostage by nuclear threat). The organization of memory is crucial to solving such retrieval problems. You have a good organization system that allows you to access material quickly. Our next question, then, is **How is memory organized?** As we'll see, memory is organized around meaning.

Our last question is one that psychologists did not pose in a serious way until recently: **What else is in memory?** We normally think of declarative memory, the type associated with conscious recollection; procedural memory, on the other hand, is not associated with awareness. How can you remember and not be aware of it? Procedural memory is expressed as you show greater facilitation in performing skills. In this chapter we discuss how procedural memory works and how it differs from declarative memory.

WHAT IS IN THE STOREHOUSE?

> ➤ *Preview* A key component of memory is the ability to generalize. Initially, researchers assumed that people assigned objects to categories by using a list of properties that an object must have to be a member of the category. But some objects are more typical of a category than others; for example, an apple is a typical fruit, but a raisin is not. If categorization were achieved with a list of properties, we wouldn't get typicality effects. And as we'll see, the typicality of an object affects not just how we categorize but also how we reason about and speak about
> *(Continued)*

that object. We'll also discuss the models that were proposed to account for these new data—prototype and exemplar models—that were based on the idea that people categorize objects not with rules but by judging their similarity to other objects of the same category. More recently, researchers have found problems with these models and have suggested that we sometimes use similarity, but at other times we actually may use rules, as was originally thought.

When you see an apple, how do you know it has seeds inside? You've never seen this apple before, but you know about the seeds because you generalize from other apples to this apple; in other words, you put this object in the category *apple*. You can identify the class or category to which an object belongs, even if you've never seen that particular example of the object before. A **category** is a group of objects that have something in common (for example, *dog* is a category). An **exemplar** is an instance of a category (a particular dog is an exemplar of the category *dog*). Your experience allows you to **generalize**, to apply information gathered from one exemplar to a different exemplar of the same category. In other words, things you know from your experience with dogs (it eats, it breathes, it could bite you but probably won't, it smells when wet) can be applied to any dog.

The importance of the ability to generalize is hard to overestimate. The first sentence of Ed Smith and Doug Medin's (1981) book about categorization is, "Without concepts, mental life would be chaotic." It would be chaotic because you would approach any object you had not interacted with as though it were completely novel. "Hey, look at this furry thing. Hmm. Four legs. Wagging tail. I wonder whether it has lungs? I wonder whether it can fly?" Concepts, then, are the mental representations that allow us to generalize.

THE CLASSICAL VIEW OF CATEGORIZATION

According to the **classical view of categorization**, first articulated by Aristotle, a **concept** is a list of necessary and sufficient conditions for membership in a category. In other words, a concept is the mental representation of *dog* or any other class of objects. A concept does not refer to one particular example of the object; it represents all the objects that can be included in that category. Every object must have all attributes on the list, and having those attributes is sufficient to be an example of the concept. For example, the concept *grandmother* is composed of two conditions: female and parent of a parent. Those two conditions are necessary to be identified as a grandmother—you must have both of them to be a grandmother—and they are sufficient, meaning it does not matter what sort of other characteristics you have or do not have, you're still a grandmother if you have those two.

The earliest research on concepts took the classical view. For example, Clark Hull (1920) displayed Chinese ideographs one at a time and asked participants to categorize them (see Figure 7.1). Each category had a single feature in common; for example, the ideographs in one category always had a large feature that looked like a check mark, but otherwise all the members of the category looked quite different. Hull didn't tell the participants anything about the stimuli, but he gave corrective feedback as participants tried to categorize them. Participants improved with practice, and Hull interpreted his results as showing that participants came to associate the key feature of the category with the appropriate category name.

In another classic study, Jerome Bruner and his colleagues (Bruner, Goodnow, & Austin, 1956) set out to show that participants learn categories not by association but by hypothesis testing, actively constructing hypotheses about what rule might describe category membership and testing the rule. The experimenters used cards with four features: number of figures on the card, shape of the figures, color of the figures, and number of borders around the edge of the card. The experimenter might give a participant a card with three black circles and two borders, and the participant had to select another instance of the category from among all the possible cards laid out on a table. The participant's job was to figure out what made a card an example of the category.

The researchers found that participants used different strategies to figure out category membership. **Focus gambling** is the strategy of generating a narrow hypothesis about the necessary and sufficient properties that define a

Figure 7.1. *Chinese ideographs used in Hull's (1920) study of classification.*

category. For example, the participant might choose a card with three white circles and three borders. If the experimenter said that this card was an example of the category, the participant would know that the two features that changed (color and number of borders) were irrelevant. If the experimenter said that this card was not a positive instance, the participant would not gain as much information.

In another strategy, **successive scanning**, the participant formulated a hypothesis and made selections based on that hypothesis until it was disconfirmed, at which point the participant would generate a new hypothesis. For example, the participant might begin by choosing a card with black circles.

I've said that these experiments are examples of the classical view of categories. How so? The experimenters assumed that category membership should be set up as a list of necessary and sufficient conditions: a particular feature of an ideograph, a feature or two of the cards. In each case, as long as it included the critical features, the rest of the stimulus was irrelevant. In the real world, however, many categories don't work that way.

The classical view does work well for certain real-world concepts, such as kinship terms (*grandmother, sister*) and formally defined categories (legal concepts such as *murderer*, mathematical ideas such as *rectangle*). But there are many concepts for which a list of necessary and sufficient conditions would be difficult to generate. This objection to the classical view was raised by philosopher Ludwig Wittgenstein (1953) in regard to the concept *game*. What makes something a game? Does it have to be a contest? No; children's games such as ring around the rosie are not competitive. Does a game have to be fun? For example, is a professional tennis player in the Wimbledon finals having fun? If not, is she still playing a game? And some things are fun (perhaps reading a textbook) that are not games. Wittgenstein concluded that we can't come up with a list of necessary and sufficient properties to define the concept *game*. However, this may mean only that we are not good at making lists of properties; the mind could still use such lists as the mental representation for concepts. The fact that you can't describe something doesn't mean that your mind doesn't use it. I certainly can't describe for you all the rules of English grammar, but my mind nevertheless uses these rules when I construct sentences. There are other reasons to think that the classical view of concepts is wrong, however, and we turn to those reasons now.

TYPICALITY EFFECTS. How do we judge **typicality**—that is, how do we decide whether something is a typical representative of its class? For example, not all birds are equally "birdy." Some birds are really good examples of a bird (a real bird's bird), whereas others are pretty crummy birds. In the following list, how would you rate each bird from 1 (terrific example of a bird) to 7 (not a good example of a bird)?

wren
chicken
robin
ostrich
eagle

Eleanor Rosch (1973) gave participants lists such as this and asked them to rate the items as typical members of their class (see Table 7.1). The first thing you might note about this task is that it doesn't seem stupid. One response you could give when asked to perform this task is to say, "These are all birds. What are you talking about, 'birdy birds, nonbirdy birds'—they're all birds. Except the bat." The fact is, when Rosch said "birdy birds," or "fruity fruits," or "furniturey furniture," people knew what she was talking about. Not only do people think some birds are birdier than others, but they agree on which ones are the birdy ones, as shown in Table 7.1. You can see that people tend to agree on their ratings of natural objects (such as birds) and manufactured objects (such as vehicles). This result means that we need to look again at the way people categorize. If the classical view of categorization were true—if an object could be labeled on the basis of a list of necessary and sufficient conditions—there would be no gradations of membership in the concept; a penguin and a robin would be seen as equally good examples of the concept *bird*.

Ed Smith, Ed Shoben, and Lance Rips (1974) showed that people are more efficient in categorizing typical than atypical examples. On each trial,

Table 7.1. Some Results of Rosch's (1973) Typicality Ratings

Category	Member	Rating
Fruit	Apple	1.3
	Plum	2.3
	Pineapple	2.3
	Strawberry	2.3
	Fig	4.7
	Olive	6.2
Sport	Football	1.2
	Hockey	1.8
	Wrestling	3.0
	Archery	3.9
	Gymnastics	2.6
	Weight-lifting	4.7
Bird	Robin	1.1
	Eagle	1.2
	Wren	1.4
	Chicken	3.8
	Ostrich	3.3
	Bat	5.8
Vehicle	Car	1.0
	Boat	2.7
	Scooter	2.5
	Tricycle	3.5
	Horse	5.9
	Skis	5.7

participants saw a word on a computer screen and had to decide as quickly as possible ("Yes" or "No") whether the word was an example of a category. Some were typical instances (*robin*), some were medium typicality (*cardinal*), and some were low typicality (*goose*). As expected, response times were faster for more typical examples.

This effect of typicality on categorization is also observed when participants are asked to freely generate examples of a category (Battig & Montague, 1969). The central finding is that the most frequently generated exemplars are the ones that are rated as most typical of the category. This finding holds true not only for adults but for children as young as 5 (Nelson, 1974; Rosner & Hayes, 1977). Some examples appear in Table 7.2.

Typicality also makes a difference in how people use concepts in reasoning. Lance Rips (1975) asked people to make some inferences using either typical or atypical examples of a category as a reference point (see also Osherson, Smith, Wilkie, López, & Shafir, 1990). For example, they were asked to imagine a small island on which there were only eight species of animals: sparrows, robins, eagles, hawks, ducks, geese, ostriches, and bats. Then they were told that one of the species had a contagious disease, and they were asked to estimate the probability that other animals on the island had the disease. Some participants were told that sparrows had the disease, others were told that

Table 7.2.   Frequencies With Which Items Were Listed as Category Exemplars

Fruit		Beverage	
Response	Total (First)	Response	Total (First)
Apple	429 (263)	Milk	366 (89)
Orange	390 (78)	Coke	327 (202)
Pear	326 (29)	Water	295 (16)
Banana	283 (20)	Orange juice	226 (11)
Peach	249 (17)	Coffee	225 (5)
Grape	247 (8)	Tea	217 (11)
Cherry	183 (1)	Pepsi	151 (21)
Plum	167 (4)	Lemonade	119 (3)
Grapefruit	154	7-Up	105 (2)
Lemon	134 (4)	Grape juice	103 (5)
Tangerine	110	Soda	89 (40)
Apricot	102	Root beer	74 (3)
Pineapple	98	Ginger ale	73 (5)
Lime	69	Fruit juice	51 (3)
Tomato	63 (6)	Juice	48 (2)
Strawberry	58	Punch	45 (1)
Watermelon	47	Tomato juice	44
Prune	44	Kool-Aid	40
Cantaloupe	31	Milkshake	28

ducks had the disease, and so on. The results showed that if a more typical bird (the robin or sparrow) had the disease, it was judged that other birds probably had the disease. If an atypical species such as the ostrich was described as having the disease, it was judged less likely that other species did. The interpretation was that participants know that typical instances of a category share many properties with other members of the category. When confronted with a new feature (the disease) whose distribution is not known, participants assume that it is distributed the way other features are; if a typical instance has the feature, it's likely that the other instances of the category have the feature. If an atypical member of the category has the feature, there is less reason to assume that other members of the category will have it because atypical category members have many features that others do not.

This finding does *not* hold, however, for people who have expertise in the category (López, Atran, Coley, Medin, & Smith, 1997; Proffitt, Coley, & Medin, 2000). Experts use other strategies that employ their deeper knowledge. In addition, recent work indicates that there may be some cultural specificity to this result—Itzá Maya are reported to use more causal reasoning and to rely less on typicality than other groups (Bailenson, Shum, Atran, Medin, & Coley, 2002).

CATEGORY HIERARCHIES. Another interesting aspect of categorization is that categories are nested within one another. For example, a wren is a bird, but it is also an animal. The category *bird* is nested in the category *animal*, which in turn is nested in the category *living things*. For that matter, you could also consider *wren* as a category because there are different types of wrens such as house wrens and marsh wrens. Thus, an object can be thought of as being a member of a number of different categories. What does this mean for cognition?

Eleanor Rosch and her colleagues (1976) outlined three types of category structure (see Table 7.3). **Basic level categories** are the most inclusive (the broadest), but members still share most of their features. For example, the category *bird* has members that for the most part share the attributes "winged," "lays eggs," "sings," and so on. **Superordinate level categories** are one level

Table 7.3.   Examples of Nested Category Structures

Superordinate Level	Basic Level	Subordinate Level	
Musical instrument	Guitar	Folk guitar	Classical guitar
	Piano	Grand piano	Upright piano
Fruit	Peach	Freestone peach	Cling peach
	Grapes	Concord grapes	Green seedless grapes
Tree	Maple	Silver maple	Sugar maple
	Birch	River birch	White birch
	Oak	White oak	Red oak

more abstract than that. For example, the members of the category *animal* do not all share features: some are winged, some are not; some have tails, some do not; some are warm-blooded, some are not. **Subordinate level categories** are less abstract than basic level categories. For example, the members of the category *wren* are all very similar; only a few features differentiate a house wren from a marsh wren. But members outside the category *wren* also share many features with members of the category. That is, there are objects outside the category *wren* that share many features with wrens; they are winged, egg-laying, and so on.

In a series of experiments, Rosch and her colleagues showed that basic level categories are the broadest categories possible that have three characteristics: they have many attributes in common, people interact with them in similar ways, and they have similar shapes. Thus, all pianos (basic level) share many attributes: they produce music, they have many keys, they are made of wood, and so on. People also interact with every piano in a similar way (by moving their fingers and hands while seated), and pianos of the same type have similar shapes. These three characteristics are not true of all musical instruments, which have different attributes, call for different movements, and have different shapes. These three characteristics are true of more specific categories such as *grand piano*, but that is not the broadest category possible that still retains these characteristics.

Rosch and her colleagues argued that the basic level category is psychologically privileged; it's the type of category we use most in thinking. For example, in one experiment participants heard an object name and 500 ms later saw a slide depicting an object. They were to press one button if the slide showed the object named and another button if it did not. The experimenters varied whether the object name that preceded the slide was superordinate (*fruit*), basic (*apple*), or subordinate (*Granny Smith apple*). Half the slides depicted the named object and half did not. Participants were faster when the object name was at the basic level.

In another experiment, the researchers showed participants color photographs of objects and asked them to name the objects. Participants used the basic level category to name objects more than 99% of the time. (In a follow-up experiment, the experimenters used a recognition test to be sure that participants actually knew the superordinate and subordinate categories for these objects; they did.)

The definition of basic level categories seems to depend on how much participants know about the objects in a category. A basic level category is defined as the broadest category in which most of the objects share most of their features. So if you knew a lot about dogs, wouldn't that mean that you knew many ways in which a German shepherd differed from a beagle and therefore that you didn't think of them as being part of the same basic level category *dog*? Rather, *beagle* would be a basic level category, and different types of beagles (*standard beagle, miniature beagle*) would be the subordinate categories.

James Tanaka and Marjorie Taylor (1991) examined this issue and found support for the idea that expertise plays a role in what is defined as basic. First, they asked dog experts and bird experts to list features of categories: superordinate (*animal, furniture*), basic (*dog, chair*), and subordinate (*beagle, easy chair*). The critical measure was the number of new features participants listed as a category became more specific. Typically, participants list a few features for superordinate categories (animals breathe, they have skin), many more characteristics for basic level categories (dogs have four legs, they have sharp teeth, they have paws, they are carnivores), and fewer distinguishing features for subordinate categories (beagles have curved ears). Tanaka and Taylor found exactly that pattern when participants were outside their area of expertise. But experts could think of a larger number of distinguishing characteristics for subordinate categories than for the basic category. In other words, dog experts know the features all dogs share, as a nonexpert does, but they also know many features of individual breeds. Each breed has so many unique features that a breed acts as a basic level category for an expert. In other studies, the experimenters showed that experts tend to use subordinate categories when naming pictures.

In a more thorough study, Kathy Johnson and Carolyn Mervis (1997) examined the effects of expertise on categorization in bird watchers. They tested novices, intermediate level experts, and advanced experts on five tasks: generating attributes of exemplars, naming exemplars, identifying silhouettes, verifying category membership, and visually identifying birds after being primed by bird songs. The results of this extensive study are summarized in Table 7.4. Each cell shows the preferred level of category use: basic (*bird*), subordinate (*wren*), or sub-subordinate (*marsh wren*). Novices always use the basic level, intermediate experts use the basic and subordinate levels, and advanced experts use the basic, subordinate, and sub-subordinate levels. The basic level never loses its privileged status on two of the tasks.

The Probabilistic View of Categorization

We have seen that typicality makes a difference when we use concepts: typical examples of concepts are categorized more quickly, they are easily brought to mind as examples of the category, and we use them differently in making inferences. The level of categories also is important; the basic level appears to hold some different status than other levels of categorization. These facts are

Table 7.4.   *Effects of Expertise on Categorization*

Measure	Advanced Experts	Intermediate Experts	Novices
Attributes	Subordinate = basic	Subordinate = basic	Basic
Object naming	Sub-subordinate	Subordinate	Basic
Silhouette identification	Sub-subordinate	Subordinate	Basic
Category verification	Sub-subordinate = subordinate = basic	Subordinate = basic	Basic
Auditory recognition	Sub-subordinate	No effect	Basic

important and must be accounted for in a theory of categorization. Therefore, the classical view of categorization cannot be complete. Researchers have determined that categories are not represented as lists of necessary and sufficient features as the classical model maintains, but the work done so far does not tell us how categories are represented.

In the **probabilistic view of categorization**, category membership is proposed to be a matter of probability. The mind's representation of a concept is not set up to make a black-and-white judgment about category membership. Rather, an object is seen as more or less likely to be a member of a category. A central assumption of this view is that there is no feature or group of features that is essential for category membership. Rather, each member of the category will have some but not all of the features. For example, a given bird might have the features "sings" and "eats insects" but not the feature "lives in trees." There are two versions of the probabilistic view: prototype theories and exemplar theories.

PROTOTYPES.   A crucial experiment in developing the prototype view was conducted by Mike Posner and Steve Keele (1968). Rather than using categories that their participants already knew, such as birds or furniture, they created two categories from scratch. The categories were patterns of dots; each feature was one dot located in a particular position. Posner and Keele created the categories by taking random dot patterns and calling them "A," "B," and "C" (see Figure 7.2).

Those patterns were defined as the **prototypes** that had all of the features characteristic of those categories. To create an example for category A,

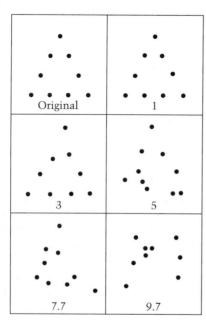

Figure 7.2.   Random dot categories of the type used by Posner and Keele (1968). The numbers refer to the distance (in arbitrary units) that each dot was moved to change the original figure.

the experimenters took the prototype for dot pattern A and moved each dot a bit in a random direction. To create another example for category A, they used the same prototype and again moved the dots randomly to get a different pattern. They created four examples of each category and mixed the examples in random order, then asked participants to categorize them. Participants just guessed initially, but they got feedback as they went as to whether their categorization judgments were right or wrong, so after a while they learned to categorize correctly. They had to keep studying the list until they could categorize all 12 items correctly two times in row.

The interesting phase of the experiment came next. Participants were given a recognition test of three types of stimuli: old stimuli, which they had seen in the first phase of the experiment; new stimuli, which were novel examples of the category; and the prototypes from which the examples had been generated. They were to select the familiar member of the category from among four choices, so chance performance would be 25%. Participants got 86.0% of the old items correct and 67.4% of the new items; they remembered the items they had seen before quite well and could also recognize new members of the category. Most interesting, they got 85.1% correct on the prototypes. Participants selected the prototype, which they had never seen before, as accurately as the training items.

Most researchers interpreted these data as showing that the memory representation supporting categorization is an amalgamation of the examples of the category. As you see many examples of category A, you abstract the critical features of category A, and the memory representation you put in the storehouse has the characteristic features of the examples of category A. It's as though you average all the examples of category A that you see. Thus, during the training session, where you are given feedback about which stimuli are As, Bs, and Cs, what you end up storing is basically the prototype of A (and, of course, separate representations for the prototypes of B and C).

To say whether a new stimulus is an A, B, or C, you compare it with your stored representation of each prototype and judge which one it is more similar to. If the new stimulus is one of the prototypes, it will match what is in your memory; because you have been taking the average of all the different examples, which were derived through small random changes to the prototypes, the averages and the prototypes are identical. In a second experiment Posner and Keele (1970) showed that the prototype is still very well recognized after a 1-week delay.

These data seem to demonstrate that people abstract the central features of examples and store the prototype. How else could we account for Posner and Keele's results and their participants' recognition of prototypes that they had never seen? But we should ask whether people store only the prototype. After all, I can categorize a new cat when I see it, but I also recognize specific cats, such as the orange one who has commandeered a corner of my yard for his restroom. Have I stored a representation of the prototypical cat, and alongside representations of all the cats I can identify as individuals? It is possible that prototypes are not involved after all.

EXEMPLAR MODELS.   In 1978, Doug Medin and Marguerite Schaffer showed that prototypes are not necessary to understand categorization or typicality effects. Posner and Keele's (1970) results indicate that abstraction takes place, and according to the prototype model in Figure 7.3, the abstraction takes place at encoding. But why would it have to take place at encoding? Suppose that you store every experience you have with an example of a category—for example, every experience you have with a dog—and then abstract a prototype only when you need it (see Figure 7.4). Thus, the same process of abstraction could take place, but at retrieval, and only if the prototype is needed.

Furthermore, typicality effects would work out perfectly in such a model. You would judge typicality by comparing the similarity of an object to all the exemplars in memory. If you see a sparrow sitting in a tree and compare it with all the birds in memory, the similarity is very high; therefore, you would think this sparrow is a very "birdy" bird. A flightless, 6-foot-tall ostrich is not very similar to birds in memory, so you wouldn't think it was such a good example of a bird. The **exemplar model** maintains that all exemplars are stored in memory, and categorization judgments are made by judging the similarity of the new exemplar to all the old exemplars of a category.

In both the exemplar and prototype models, similarity is the key factor in categorization. Yet the models are very different in terms of what they propose is stored in memory. The exemplar model holds that multiple exemplars of a category are stored in memory, and the prototype model holds that only the prototype is stored.

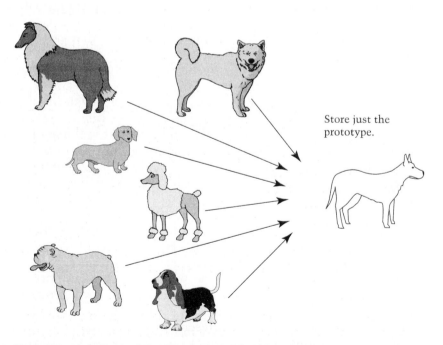

Store just the prototype.

Figure 7.3.   *Schematic of the prototype model. Although many exemplars are seen, only the prototype is stored. The prototype is updated continually to incorporate more experience with new exemplars.*

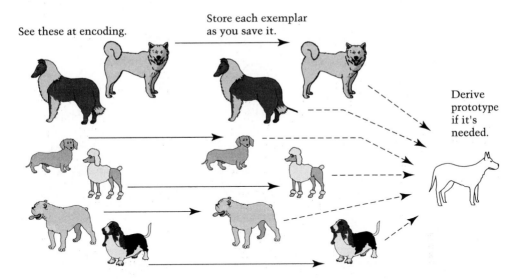

Figure 7.4. *Schematic of the exemplar model. As each exemplar is seen, it is encoded into memory. A prototype is abstracted only when it is needed, for example, when a new exemplar must be categorized.*

When comparing exemplar models to prototype models, researchers specify the model of categorization in enough detail to run a computer simulation of human performance using the model. These models make specific predictions about how fast people learn categories, how fast they forget them, what transfer to new exemplars should look like, and so on. We can compare the success of exemplar and prototype models by comparing their predictions with actual human performance. If the prototype model predicts that participants will get 65% correct after 100 training trials and the exemplar model predicts it will be 72%, and humans get 71%, then obviously the exemplar model is doing a better job of predicting the data. Research that relies on comparing the performance of specific models with human data is called mathematical psychology. In these contests, exemplar models have consistently come out ahead of prototype models (for a very thorough and readable overview, see Estes, 1994; see also Smith & Mimda, 2000).

During the late 1980s, however, more and more evidence accumulated indicating that there is more to categorization than similarity. These findings pose a problem for both exemplar and prototype models because they both are rooted solely in similarity. We turn now to these findings.

PROBLEMS WITH SIMILARITY MODELS. If similarity is judged by the number of features two objects share, how do we determine the appropriate features to compare? We can almost always select features to make any two objects look similar or dissimilar. For example, if I want an elephant and a plum to be considered similar, I could draw attention to these shared features: both cannot perceive infrared light, both cannot jump 6 feet, both are not found on the

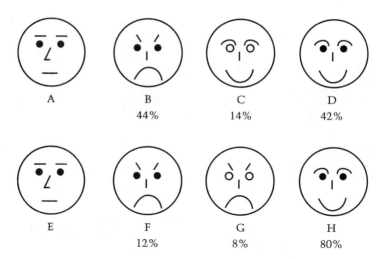

Figure 7.5. *Stimuli used in Tversky's (1977) experiment. The top row is one set of stimuli that participants saw, and the bottom row is a second set. Also shown are the percentages of participants who picked a face as being the most similar to the leftmost face in the row. Thus, the top row and the bottom row call for the same comparison but in the context of different exemplars; the context affects similarity judgments.*

moon, both are less than 128 years old, and so on. On the other hand, if I want an elephant and a plum to appear dissimilar, I could point out that they differ on many features: they are different weights, different sizes, different colors, and so on. The features I select determine how similar they will seem.

Other researchers have pointed out that the similarity of two objects appears to depend on the context in which they appear. Amos Tversky (1977) showed participants schematic drawings of faces similar to those in Figure 7.5.

Some participants were asked to make rate the similarity of face A to faces B–D. Others rated the similarity of face E to faces F–H. The figure shows the percentage of participants who thought that face was most similar to their "standard" (either A or E). Note that the standard faces are identical and some of the faces to be rated are identical—yet the similarity ratings are quite different for identical faces! What varies, of course, is the *context* in which these identical faces were rated.

> **Box 7–1 Brain Differences Between Rule Application and Similarity Judgments in Categorization**
>
> A key function of being able to categorize objects is generalization: if you can put a novel object in a category, you know that it is similar to other members of the category you have encountered. The question is how you determine whether something is a member of a category. One view is that there are criteria or rules (such as "People with the flu have a fever") the new object must
>
> *(Continued)*

meet. The alternative view is that we evaluate the similarity of the new object to other members of the category without applying a set of rigid rules.

In this chapter we discussed a task in which participants could be induced to categorize according to either rules or similarity depending on their instructions (Allen & Brooks, 1991). Ed Smith and his colleagues (Smith, Patalano, & Jonides, 1998) administered a similar task with the purpose of categorizing alien creatures. Some participants were given five characteristics, and if an alien had any three, it was from Venus; otherwise it was from Saturn. Other participants were not given any rules but were asked to memorize the correct categorizations for 10 animals. During the test phase, participants categorized novel animals, and brain activation was imaged with positron emission tomography.

As shown in Figure B7.1, activations in the rule condition are associated with particular brain areas: secondary visual areas, superior parietal lobe, premotor cortex, and dorsolateral frontal cortex. This pattern of activation is readily interpretable. Participants must scan for visual features (activating the secondary visual areas) to compare the features with the rule held in working memory (in the premotor and dorsolateral prefrontal areas). Moving attention relies on superior parietal cortex. The memory condition, in contrast, activates the occipital cortex and right cerebellum. The visual cortical activation may reflect the recovery of visual memories that were used in the memory condition, although based on other studies, some temporal lobe activation would have been expected in that context. The cerebellar activation is difficult to interpret. This study provides converging evidence that participants can recruit different cognitive processes to solve categorization problems, and these different processes are supported by different neural structures.

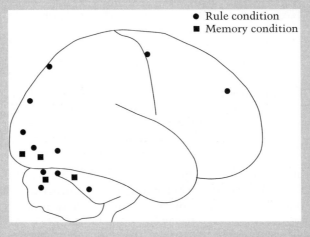

Figure B7.1.

Are we using similarity to make decisions about categorization, then, or are we using a different mechanism? A number of researchers have argued that categorization can proceed not only via similarity but via rules; in other words, in some cases there are necessary and sufficient properties that define categories (as in the classical view).

In a seminal study on this topic, Lance Rips (1989) had participants make categorization judgments with very little information about the object (just one feature). He also restricted the choices to two categories; one of the categories was inflexible as to the described feature and the other was not. For example, one item was "The object is 3 inches in diameter. Is the object a pizza or a quarter?" Most participants (63%) said it was a pizza, even though a separate group of participants had more often (70%) judged that a quarter was more similar to a 3-inch object than a pizza is. Rips argued that people are sensitive to necessary, inflexible features. A quarter must be a particular size; that feature cannot change.

This finding does not mean that rule-based categorization is always used. As pointed out before, rule-based categorization cannot readily account for typicality effects. Instead, it might be the case that either rule-based or similarity-based categorization can be used. A study supporting that view was conducted by Scott Allen and Lee Brooks (1991). In their experiment, participants saw new creatures and were asked to categorize them as "diggers" or "builders." Some participants were encouraged to learn the categories by memorizing exemplars and their category. Others were given a rule by which to categorize. Builders have two of the following three characteristics: long legs, an angular body, and spots.

After both groups of participants learned the categories, the experimenters showed them some new exemplars. Some of the new exemplars were actually builders, but they looked very much like diggers that participants had seen during training. Participants in the memory group called them diggers 86% of the time, indicating that they were comparing the new items with remembered items from training. But those in the rule group called them diggers just 45% of the time, indicating that they were most often relying on the rule. It appears that people can use either rules or similarity in categorization.

Allen and Brooks used task instructions to induce participants to categorize using either similarity or rules. People don't normally have instructions, though. So what makes us choose one strategy or another? Ed Smith and Steven Sloman (1994) argued that rules might be invoked primarily when there are no features that are characteristic of any category. For example, in Rips's (1989) study, the only feature given is diameter: the object is 3 inches across. That size is not characteristic of either category, so Smith and Sloman suggested that people use characteristic information when it is available, and that makes them categorize via similarity. In their study, they gave participants descriptions of objects just as Rips had done, but for some participants they added a feature that is characteristic of one category. For example, some participants were told, "The object is 3 inches in diameter. Is it a pizza or a quarter?" Others were told, "The object is 3 inches in diameter and it is silver colored. Is it a pizza or a quarter?" Note that this description contains a necessary feature (size) indicating that the object should be a pizza, but it also contains a feature that is highly characteristic of a quarter. Most participants (67%) picked *pizza* when given only the necessary feature (size), but when given both the necessary and characteristic features (size and color) most (58%) picked *quarter*. (See also Hampton, 1995.) Studies like this one will help psychologists unravel when people tend to use similarity and when they use rules.

Summary

The classical view of categorization was that categories were defined by a set of necessary and sufficient rules. In the 1970s, it became clear that category structure is not all-or-none, as the classical view would predict, but rather is graded; some exemplars of a category are considered more typical, or better examples of the category, than others. This finding and others led to probability models in which categorization is viewed as a matter of probability, not all-or-none decisions. Two types of probability models were developed: prototype models (in which exemplars are abstracted into a prototype that is stored) and exemplar models (in which all the exemplars are stored). In the late 1980s new results indicated that similarity could not account for all categorization. It seemed that rules are used to categorize at least some of the time. The latest work in this area has been directed toward determining when similarity is used and when rules are used.

Stand-on-One-Foot Questions

1. *Describe the classical view of categorization. What data indicated that it could not provide a complete account of categorization?*
2. *List the effects of typicality on cognition.*
3. *What are the two main types of categorization theories that rely on similarity, and what is the key difference between them?*
4. *What is the final word on the difference between the rule-based view of categorization and the similarity view?*

Questions That Require Two Feet

5. *What is the logical problem with a model that proposes that each new exemplar is stored in memory and categorization decisions are made based on its similarity to groups of exemplars already in memory?*
6. *You may have noticed that newspapers (especially the more sensationalist tabloids) often run headlines that report on a grandma doing something atypical of grandmas: "Grandmother Swims English Channel," "Grandma Guns Down Intruder." Given what you have learned about categorization, comment on why newspapers do this.*

HOW IS MEMORY ORGANIZED?

> ➤ *Preview* Organization allow us to retrieve the right memory from the store-house. Our memory system does not merely allow us to find the desired memory quickly. If what is desired is not in memory, the system provides something close in meaning, or it provides material that may help us guess about the desired information. One early theory of memory organization, the hierarchical model, suggested that concepts were placed in a taxonomic hierarchy (*animal* above *bird, bird* above *canary*). Later models used an idea called spreading activation, whereby thinking about one concept would bring semantically related concepts to mind; for example, thinking about the concept *doctor* makes it a little more likely that you'll think of the related concept *patient*. A variant of the spreading activation model uses distributed representation, meaning that one concept is represented by many units of the model; in fact, many concepts are in those units simultaneously, and which concept is represented at any moment depends on the state of the entire model.

We each have an amazing amount of material stored away in memory (although it doesn't always feel that way). Most college students have a reading vocabulary of perhaps 60,000 words. Add to that all of your memories about what things are, how things work, memory for faces, voices (Mom), music ("My baby takes the morning train …"), and so on. The mind is faced with the formidable problem of finding useful information quickly among these riches, and our ability to find memories efficiently is truly amazing. For example, people can identify popular songs (say, "Macarena") when presented with a snippet as short as 200 ms (Schellenberg, Iverson, & McKinnon, 1999). We are unsure about how categorization operates; can we nonetheless say something about how memory is organized? We can, but let's start by explaining a bit about memory systems in general so you will have a better idea of what the human memory system might be doing. You will also understand why cognitive psychologists have posed the questions we will consider.

Addressing Systems

Let's begin with an information storage system that we understand: a library. How do you find the right book in a library? Books are ordered according to the Library of Congress system so that we can look for them according to their subject matter. To find a particular book, you need its unique number, which you find in the catalog—a master list with the specific numbers of all the library's volumes. The system used in a library is called an **addressing system** because each entity in the storehouse has a unique address, which is critical for finding what you want. If the number 798.30 is erased from the book or from the master list, or if the book is accidentally shelved as 898.30, no one will be able to retrieve it, or at least not quickly.

Your computer uses an addressing system to find information on its hard drive (the computer's storehouse). When you create a new computer file and store it on the hard drive, its location goes into a master list called a disk directory.

The human mind, however, does not use an addressing system; our memory behaves in ways inconsistent with such a system. If your mind used an addressing system, the kinds of memory errors you made would be unpredictable. For example, suppose someone asked you, "Is there a good coffee shop around here?" If your master memory list contained the name of a good coffee shop at memory address 78342, but your memory system made an error in one digit and looked up memory location 88342, anything could be at that address and you might answer the question by saying, "Ratatouille." Your memory system doesn't work that way, however. If you make a memory error, it tends to be a near miss: an answer that is wrong but is at least related to the right answer, such as thinking that Julia Roberts starred in *Ghost*. Usually such errors are related in terms of meaning. For example, I might ask you, "What was Buffalo Bill's last name?" You might answer "Hickok," which is wrong (it was Cody) but close because it was the last name of another well-known Bill from the Old West.

Content-Addressable Storage

In **content-addressable storage,** a system that seems to work more like human memory, the content of the memory is itself the storage address. You find a memory's location in the storehouse based on the actual content of the memory.

This system would produce near misses; if you search memory for the name of a well-known Bill from the Old West (Buffalo Bill) and you have a similar concept in memory (Wild Bill), Wild Bill Hickok pops out of memory. Content-addressable storage systems are very fast, so the time it takes to retrieve a memory from the storehouse does not increase as you add more information. Our memory systems also seem to work that way; as we learn more things, it doesn't take longer to retrieve facts about the old things.

Unfortunately, the feature of this system that makes the speed possible also poses a problem. The point of the system is that you access memories based on their content. But how does a memory "know" when it is being called upon? You could set up a memory system in which each memory compares its content with whatever is being asked for. For the system to work, every memory must have the capability of knowing what you're asking for and evaluating whether its content is a good enough match. Making each memory "smart" in this way requires a big commitment in processing resources, whether the system is computer memory built on this principle or a speculative model of how the brain works.

The human memory system has a capability even beyond that of a simple content-addressable system, however, which is best illustrated by example. Suppose I ask you this question: "Does Tobey McGuire have a large intestine?"

You would answer "Yes" to this question, but why would you do so? It's likely that you've never encoded that fact, so it can't be in memory. On what basis do you give a confident "Yes"?

Your "Yes" is not based on a fact in memory about Tobey McGuire; it is based on an inference. When you try to retrieve information that has not been encoded directly, your memory system often pulls up related information that allows you to make an inference to answer the question, as follows:

> FROM MEMORY: Humans have a large intestine.
>
> FROM MEMORY: Tobey McGuire is a human.
>
> INFERENCE: Therefore, Tobey McGuire has a large intestine.

The requested information is not in memory, but you do have in memory other information that can help you answer the question, and that information is retrieved. How does the memory system "know" the right information to produce when what is requested is not in the system?

I mentioned at the start of this section that the discussion of memory systems and their capabilities was relevant here because it was one such capability that motivated cognitive psychologists in their study of the organization of memory. This is the question that motivated the initial work on the organization of secondary memory: What is the organization that allows not just the simple retrieval of facts but also the retrieval of relevant facts that we would not expect to necessarily be declaratively stored?

Hierarchical Theory

The **hierarchical theory**, one of the first models to address this question, came from Allan Collins and Ross Quillian (1969, 1972). It proposed a clever solution. In their model (and in many of the models that followed) memory is composed of two basic elements: nodes and links.

Nodes represent concepts such as *red, candy, bird, president,* and so on. Nodes have levels of **activation**, meaning that they have some level of energy, or excitement. In practical terms, nodes become active when the concept they represent is present in the environment. Thus, the concept *bird* might become active through my seeing a picture of a bird, seeing a real bird, or hearing or reading the word *bird*, and so on.

Links represent relationships between concepts, such as "has this property" or "is an example of." As shown in Figure 7.6, links in a hierarchical memory structure connect nodes and can provide property descriptions of concepts. Thus the idea that a living thing must breathe is represented in the model through a concept (*living thing*), a property (*breathe*), and a link (*must*).

An important characteristic of the model is **property inheritance**. Moving down the hierarchy from *animal* to *bird* to *chicken*, we see that concepts inherit properties from the concepts above them in the hierarchy. Hence, an animal is a type of living thing, so it inherits the properties of living things. For

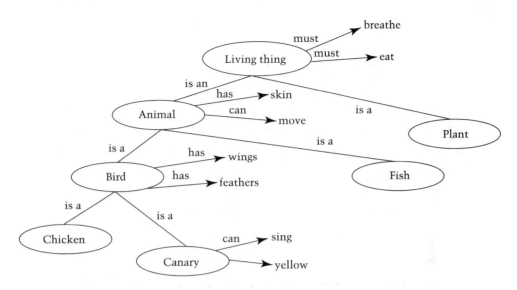

Figure 7.6. *An example of a hierarchical network described by Collins and Quillian represent-ing* animal, canary, *and* chicken, *among other concepts. There are also links such as "is a" and "has."*

example, chickens inherit the properties *must breathe* and *must eat* from the concept *animal* (but see Sloman, 1998).

You'll remember that we asked earlier what happens when an inference is needed to answer a question. The inheritance of properties can be important in such situations. If I were to ask you, "Does a canary breathe?" the model predicts that you would first go to the node representing the concept *canary*. You would examine the properties associated with *canary* and discover that breathing or not breathing is not part of the representation of what a canary does, so you would move up one level in the hierarchy to the concept *bird* to see whether breathing or not breathing is stored with being a bird. You'd dis-cover it is not, and you'd continue to the concept *animal* and finally to *living thing*, where you would finally find the relevant information.

Suppose we make the simple assumption that moving up the hierarchy takes time. We would predict that each of these successive sentences would take a longer time to verify. Collins and Quillian (1969) tested exactly that pre-diction by showing one sentence at a time on a computer screen and asking participants to decide whether the sentence was true or false. Half of the time the sentence was false ("A canary is a plant"), but the experimenters were in-terested in how long it took participants to verify the sentences when they were true. Response times came out in the order that the model predicted. (The numbers in parentheses are the response times to verify the sentences.)

A canary is a canary. (1,000 ms)
A canary is a bird. (1,160 ms)
A canary is an animal. (1,240 ms)

The effect worked just as well for properties.

> A canary can sing. (1,305 ms)
> A canary has wings. (1,395 ms)
> A canary has skin. (1,480 ms)

Thus, the findings seemed to support the model for the tricky ability we discussed in regard to McGuire's intestine. Unfortunately, it soon became apparent that the model didn't always make the right predictions. One problem was that the hierarchy sometimes didn't seem to hold. For example, people were faster to verify the sentence "A chicken is an animal" than to verify "A chicken is a bird."

Another problem of this model grows out of a property that initially seemed to be a strength. Looking at Figure 7.6 you'll notice that the property *has wings* is stored only once, with *bird*; it makes sense to store this property along with all the other common properties of birds. The principle of **cognitive economy** refers to designing a cognitive system in a way that conserves resources. Yet this principle does not appear to be true in the brain, at least not the way Collins and Quillian implemented it. Carol Conrad (1972) gave participants a list of words and asked them to write down what each word made them think of. She found that participants often wrote information that was one or two levels higher in the hierarchy. For example, if you give people the word *robin, canary,* or *bluebird* they are very likely to write the verb *flies* as one of the properties, even though *flies* goes with the higher-level concept *bird*. The property *flies* also seems to be stored along with *robin, canary,* and *bluebird*.

Spreading Activation Theories

Allan Collins and Elizabeth Loftus (1975) proposed a **spreading activation model** to address the shortcomings of the earlier model. This is another network model, again consisting of nodes and links, but now the links represent associations between semantically related concepts. Memory is thus conceived as a vast web of linked concepts called a **semantic network**. Collins and Loftus used links that had properties such as *is a* and *has a*. Later models that built on their work did not (see McClelland, 1981), and our discussion is based on these. In a semantic network, as in a hierarchical network, nodes can become active, and you can think of this activity as the node having energy. Nodes become active through stimulation from the environment. Thus, the concept *President* might become active through my seeing a picture of the president or through hearing or reading the word *President*.

Figure 7.7 shows three nodes in a memory network. (I'm taking a break from canaries and chickens.) Time moves from left to right in the figure, so at left we see a node without activation; then the word *President* comes in from the environment (because someone said it, for example), and at right we see the same node, now activated, with the activation represented by the

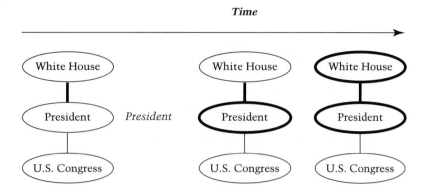

Figure 7.7. *When the word* President *is perceived in the environment (left), the corresponding concept becomes active in memory (center), and activation spreads to related concepts (right). The amount of activation depends on the weight of the link between concepts.*

thicker border on the node. Active nodes send some of their activity to other linked nodes, which can also become active. Activated nodes send a high proportion of their activation to closely related concepts. Hence, *President* might send a lot of activation to *White House* but less to *Congress*. This principle is shown in the right part of the figure.

A formal definition has been proposed for the six properties of a semantic network (Rumelhart, Hinton, & McClelland, 1986).

1. *A set of units*. Each unit represents a concept.
2. *A state of activation*. Each unit has its own state of activation, an amount of "energy" at a given moment.
3. *An output function*. Units pass activation to one another. The amount of activation a unit passes to its neighbors depends on its output function, which relates the current activation state of the unit to the amount of activation it sends down its links. The output activation function may simply be to multiply the activation by 1 (sending the same amount of activation down the links as the unit itself has) or 0.5 (sending half the activation). Other models use a threshold function, so that the unit must meet an activation threshold before it can influence its neighbors.
4. *A pattern of connectivity*. Units are connected to one another by links of different strengths. The extent to which you know that birds fly, for example, depends on the strength or weight of the link between *bird* and *flies*.
5. *An activation rule*. A unit follows a rule to integrate the activation sent to it by other units via links. If I say to you, "caramel color, carbonated, cold," these words are closely associated with the concept *cola*. Suppose

that these three concepts (*caramel color, carbonated, cold*), which were activated when I said the words, send activation of 0.85, 0.48, and 0.15 to the concept *cola*. What will the activation of *cola* now be? Should we add the three, yielding 1.48? Should we find the mean, yielding 0.49? Should we allow only activations higher than 0.25 to enter our calculations and take the mean of those, yielding 0.67? The activation rule determines how the inputs should be combined.

6. *Learning rules to change weights.* A semantic network cannot be static. The knowledge of the network is in weights, so there must be a mechanism to change the weights if the model is to learn. Suppose you didn't know that horses love candy peppermints. The link between *horse* and *peppermint* would be 0. Now that you've read that fact one time, what should the weight of that link be? There must be a rule by which the weights change. (Horses do like peppermint, by the way.)

Spreading Activation Models: An Example

We've gone over the properties of spreading activation models. For a better sense of their strengths, let's have a look at one example developed in some detail (McClelland, 1981). Table 7.5 lists information about 27 men. All the information in this list can be represented in a semantic network. A subset of the list is shown in Figure 7.8; the units in the center of the network that do not represent any concept are important for passing activation between nodes.

This sort of model has a number of useful characteristics. First, it obviously allows for the retrieval of properties. If you say "Lance," that word is

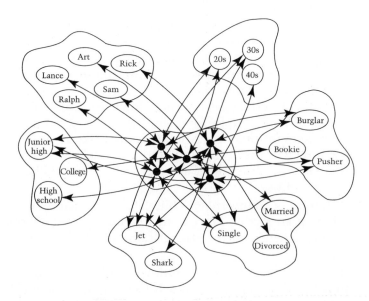

Figure 7.8. *Some of the information from Table 7.5 presented in a network.*

Table 7.5.   **The Jets and the Sharks**

Name	Gang	Age	Education	Marital Status	Occupation
Art	Jets	40s	Junior high	Single	Pusher
Al	Jets	30s	Junior high	Married	Burglar
Sam	Jets	20s	College	Single	Bookie
Clyde	Jets	40s	Junior high	Single	Bookie
Mike	Jets	30s	Junior high	Single	Bookie
Jim	Jets	20s	Junior high	Divorced	Burglar
Greg	Jets	20s	High school	Married	Pusher
John	Jets	20s	Junior high	Married	Burglar
Doug	Jets	30s	High school	Single	Bookie
Lance	Jets	20s	Junior high	Married	Burglar
George	Jets	20s	Junior high	Divorced	Burglar
Pete	Jets	20s	High school	Single	Bookie
Fred	Jets	20s	High school	Single	Pusher
Gene	Jets	20s	College	Single	Pusher
Ralph	Jets	30s	Junior high	Single	Pusher
Phil	Sharks	30s	College	Married	Pusher
Ike	Sharks	30s	Junior high	Single	Bookie
Nick	Sharks	30s	High school	Single	Pusher
Don	Sharks	30s	College	Married	Burglar
Ned	Sharks	30s	College	Married	Bookie
Karl	Sharks	40s	High school	Married	Bookie
Ken	Sharks	20s	High school	Single	Burglar
Earl	Sharks	40s	High school	Married	Burglar
Rick	Sharks	30s	High school	Divorced	Burglar
Ol	Sharks	30s	College	Married	Pusher
Neal	Sharks	30s	High school	Single	Bookie
Dave	Sharks	30s	High school	Divorced	Pusher

perceived and the *Lance* node becomes active. That node passes activity to other nodes and it will lead to activity of the nodes *Jets, 20s, junior high, married*, and *burglar*.

Second, the model allows content-addressable storage. Recall that this is a system whereby memories are accessed not by an address but by their content. For example, if we activated the nodes *Jets* and *40s*, the activation would spread and *Art* and *Clyde* would become active. If we activated *Jets* and *30s*, then the four Jets in their 30s would become active: *Al, Mike, Doug*, and *Ralph*.

Third, it is easy to see how typicality grows naturally out of the model. A concept such as *robin* will have strong links to many concepts that are in turn strongly linked to bird (*small, sits in trees, lays eggs*). An atypical bird such as an ostrich has many links to concepts that are weakly linked to bird (*large, runs fast, can't fly*). If I say "bird," all the nodes that have strong links to that concept will become active. Thus it is easy for me to describe the typical bird. Similarly, in the model in Figure 7.8, if I say "Jet," the features of the prototypical Jet become active, even if no one Jet has all of the typical qualities.

Fourth, the model naturally creates **default values** that a variable or an attribute takes in the absence of any other information. For example, how does a bird get around? In the absence of any other information, we can assume that it flies; this is the default state. Default values are assigned for concepts as a natural part of the spreading activation. If you have reason to think that the object you're dealing with is a bird, then the connection between *bird* and *flies* will lead to activation in the concept *flies* unless you are specifically told that this bird does not fly.

Fifth, spreading activation models are resistant to faulty input. Suppose I tell you, "I went to a pretty good restaurant last night. I can't remember the name, but it was a fast-food place, and they had something called a Big Mac, and the restaurant had green arches out front." You would say to me, "You mean McDonald's, but the arches are gold." Notice that you've retrieved the right memory even though I've given you faulty information. It's easy to imagine that you could check the memory system for a description of my restaurant and find nothing; indeed, you've never heard of a restaurant matching the description I gave. But your memory system is resistant to faulty input and can come up with the right memory. Spreading activation models have this property. The concepts *fast food* and *Big Mac* are so strongly linked to *McDonald's* that the node is activated, despite the fact that *green arches* might inhibit its activation a bit. Once *McDonald's* is activated, that in turn activates *golden arches*, which makes me surmise that you have made an error in your description.

Evidence of Activation

There is evidence consistent with the idea that concepts in memory become active and that when the activity surpasses a threshold they enter awareness. Many paradigms demonstrate an effect called **repetition priming**. The participant reads a list of words and sometime later (usually an hour) performs a second task. Some of the words used in the second task are in the original list, but the participant is not told that. Table 7.6 lists the type of tasks that researchers have used to measure priming.

In each task described in Table 7.6, participants show some bias caused by the processing of the words on the original list. These repetition priming effects often are interpreted as showing that nodes representing concepts become active when participants first read the words on the list, and for the second task an hour later, they are still somewhat active, making these concepts easier to access. Repetition priming effects indicate that activation of nodes lasts an hour or more and that this activation is measurable.

Another effect, **semantic priming**, indicates that activation passes between nodes. We discussed this effect in chapter 6: participants were faster to

Table 7.6.   ***Tasks Used to Measure Priming***

Task	Description	Priming Measure	Reference
Fragment completion	Participants must complete word fragments to form words. Each fragment has just one possible completion.	Number of fragments successfully completed that were on the original list versus fragments completed that were not.	Tulving, Schacter, & Stark (1982)
Stem completion	Participants must complete word stems to form a word. Each fragment has at least 10 possible completions.	Number of stems completed to make a word on the original list versus stems completed to make words not on the list.	Warrington & Weiskrantz (1968)
Category exemplar generation	Participants must name category members.	Somewhat unusual category members appear on the original list. Priming is measured by how many of these unusual members participants mention.	Graf, Shimamura, & Squire (1985)
Lexical decision	Participants see a letter string appear and must respond with a button press as quickly as possible to indicate whether the letter string forms a word.	Priming is reflected by shorter response times to words that were on the list compared to words that were not.	Just & Carpenter (1980)

confirm that two letter strings were words when they were related (*doctor–nurse*) than when they were not (*radio–nurse*) (Meyer & Schvaneveldt, 1971). A straightforward interpretation is that when participants saw the word *doctor*, the node representing the concept became active and immediately passed activation to all semantically related concepts, including *nurse*. When participants read the word *nurse*, the concept representing it was already somewhat active and it was easier for them to identify the word.

Criticisms of Spreading Activation

The spreading activation idea is quite popular in cognitive psychology, and the use of spreading activation is widespread in models of memory (see Anderson, 1976, 1983; McClelland & Rumelhart, 1981; McNamara, 1992). Nevertheless, the concept of spreading activation is often somewhat vague; researchers are not always specific about exactly how to determine the location and strength of links. Instead, if one item primes another, we assume that they must be linked—but that means the theory is circular and therefore not valid.

A second problem concerns just how far activation spreads. Activation appears to spread not just one but at least two and possibly three links away. For example, it has been demonstrated that the word *lion* primes the word *stripes*. Presumably, *lion* primes *tiger*, which primes *stripes*. Priming that goes through another word in this fashion is called **mediated priming** (McNamara & Healy, 1988). Some evidence indicates that mediated priming can extend through two mediators, not just one. But Roger Ratcliff and Gail McKoon (1994) pointed out a problem. Suppose that each word spreads its activation to 20 other words; when I say *lion*, then, 20 concepts (one of them *tiger*) are activated. If each of these 20 concepts activates 20 more, which in turn activate 20 more (as three-step priming indicates would happen), then $20 \times 20 \times 20 = 8,000$ concepts are activated by the utterance of just one word. Because most adults have a vocabulary of about 64,000 words, hearing a single word would activate one-eighth of all the words you know. The idea of spreading activation becomes pointless if most concepts would be active most of the time in ordinary conversation. (See Ratcliff & McKoon, 1988, for an alternative account of priming that does not include spreading activation; see McNamara, 1992, 1994, for a spirited defense of spreading activation.)

Distributed Representation (Parallel Distributed Processing)

In contrast to the spreading activation model, in which each node represents a single concept with **local representation**, another class of models uses **distributed representation**, meaning that a concept is represented across multiple nodes. Suppose, for example, that I have four nodes. In a local representation, each node represents a concept: *vanilla, chocolate, strawberry*, and *coffee*. If the *vanilla* node has an activation of 1, then I'm thinking about vanilla, and so on for the other nodes. That would be the one-node, one-concept scheme described earlier. In a distributed representation you must look at all four nodes simultaneously, and meaning is based on what all four nodes are doing, as shown in Figure 7.9. You can't look at one node and know whether the concept *vanilla* is active. You have to look at all four nodes simultaneously. One advantage of a distributed representation is obvious: you can get more concepts into the same number of nodes with a distributed representation.

Many distributed network models, called **parallel distributed processing (PDP)** models, have a structure that looks something like Figure 7.10, with a series of input nodes, some number of "hidden" nodes, and a series of output nodes. In a simple taste network, for example, the input nodes would get their input from the senses of taste and smell. For example, vanilla ice cream might input the values +1 0 0 +1 −1 +1 0 0 into the eight input nodes. These inputs activate the hidden nodes, which in turn activate the output nodes. The output nodes represent the concepts *vanilla, chocolate, strawberry*, and so on.

This model has all the advantages of the model using local representations and some new ones. For one, the model exhibits another very useful property of memory called **graceful degradation**, which means that if part of

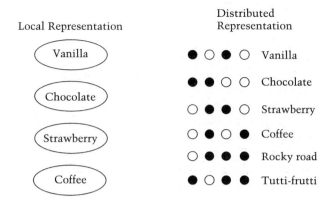

Figure 7.9. *Examples of local representations (each node represents one concept) and distributed representations (each concept is represented across multiple nodes).*

the system is damaged or malfunctions, it doesn't shut down. Performance gets worse, but the system is still somewhat functional. For example, if one or two of the nodes were removed from the model in Figure 7.10, the rest of the model would still work—not perfectly, because the pattern of activation would be disrupted—because each node gets inputs from many other nodes. If just a few nodes are lost, each node still gets most of its usual input. Graceful degradation seems to be a property of the human memory system as well. The amount of damage to cognitive function is roughly proportional to the amount of damage to the part of the brain that supports it. Minimal damage causes minimal cognitive loss. This feature is very different from a computer's memory, where minimal damage can be catastrophic.

Another strength of these models is that they can actually learn in a convincing way. In many models using local representation, knowledge (for

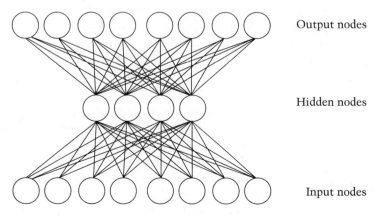

Figure 7.10. *A parallel distributed processing network showing nodes and links.*

example, that birds have wings) is put into the model by the experimenter. Distributed representation models typically assume that the learner is given feedback about correctness. At the start of training, the model is assumed to know nothing; all the strengths or weights of the links are set to values near zero. Then the researcher inputs values corresponding to vanilla ice cream (for example) into the model. The activation works through the model, and the output nodes might take the values 0 0 0 +1 0 0 −1 0, which is not close to the correct identification of the concept *vanilla*. The model gets feedback (that the correct output was +1 0 0 +1 −1 +1 0 0), and the weights are changed slightly to bring the model slightly closer to producing the correct output, given that input. The rule for how the weights are changed depends on the difference between the input and the output. It may seem like cheating to you that the model is told what the correct answer is, but when you think about it, that's how things work in real life. Someone gives you ice cream and tells you, "This is vanilla." On successive trials the model would get the inputs for *chocolate*, *strawberry*, and all the other flavors, with feedback and weight changes on each trial. Thus, the strength of the model is that it seeks not just to show us how memories are represented after they are learned but also how memories are acquired.

An important strength of this learning process is that it automatically finds both prototypes and exceptions to prototypes. Suppose we include training of three flavors: vanilla, French vanilla, and vanilla bean. As you can see from Table 7.7, the input patterns of these three flavors are quite similar, and so is the output pattern. It should be harder for the model to learn to distinguish these three input–output patterns than three that are quite different; and indeed, that task is harder for the models, just as it would be harder for you. Now suppose that you have trained the model so that it knows these three flavors, and then you present the last flavor, "bland," which is basically ice cream with no flavoring at all. What should a memory model do with this novel flavor? You might think, "If you've never tasted it before, there is nothing in memory about this flavor, so you don't know what it is." But that wouldn't happen. You would say, "It's not vanilla, but it sort of tastes like vanilla." That is **generalization**, a key property of human memory: you are responding to a new stimulus in the way you would respond to an old stimulus that is similar. Generalization is a natural outgrowth of this sort of model.

Table 7.7.   ***Training with Input and Output Patterns***

Flavor	Input Pattern	Output Pattern
Vanilla	+1 0 0 +1 −1 +1 0 0	+1 0 0 +1 −1 +1 0 0
French vanilla	0 0 0 +1 −1 +1 0 0	+1 −1 0 +1 −1 +1 0 −1
Vanilla bean	−1 0 0 +1 −1 +1 0 0	+1 0 −1 +1 −1 +1 0 0
Bland	+1 −1 0 +1 −1 +1 0 0	+1 0 0 +1 −1 +1 −1 0

Box 7–2 How Are Concepts Organized in the Brain?

Does the organization of the brain tell us anything about how concepts are organized in the mind? There are two sources of conflicting evidence on this point.

First, let's consider lesion evidence. Over the years, a number of cases have been reported of patients who have suffered strokes resulting in deficits that are specific to one narrow category of stimuli. For example, some patients have difficulty naming living things (*lion, tiger, ant*) but not other objects (*book, truck, cake*). Other patients have still more specific deficits. For example, patient E.W. could name 100% of fruits and vegetables and 92% of manufactured objects (*furniture, tools*) but only 34% of pictured animals (Caramazza & Shelton, 1998). E.W. also had difficulty distinguishing between real and unreal animals (made by combining body parts of different animals), and she had difficulty in affirming property statements about animals (such as "A horse has four legs"). Her performance with objects other than animals was normal. One interpretation of these data is that the organization of knowledge in the brain follows the categories we use in describing the world. Just as we categorize things in the world as fruits or tools, our conceptual knowledge about these objects is organized in these categories in the brain. Thus a patient might have a stroke that affects only a small part of the brain, and it happens to knock out knowledge about a specific category of objects.

Neuroimaging evidence does not support this contention, however. Concepts in the brain are not organized by their category. Rather, different aspects of an object are located in different parts of the brain: what the object looks like is stored in one part of the brain and what it is for is in another part, for example. In one study, Alex Martin and his colleagues (1995) showed participants an object such as a wagon and asked them to think about either its color (*red*) or an action appropriate to the object (*pull*). They found different areas of activation: color in the ventral temporal lobe and action in a more superior part of the temporal lobe. In each case, the stored attribute of objects was just anterior to the location that is believed to support the visual processing of the attribute. The researchers suggested that concepts are represented as a conglomeration of semantic primitives such as form, color, characteristic motions, and ways of manipulating an object. Each concept has different attributes represented in different locations of the cortex.

But are objects localized in cortex within a modality? For example, is the visual representation of faces localized? Different researchers have presented evidence favoring different representations. On the one hand, there is some evidence for rather specific cortical representations for visual identification of certain classes of objects, such as faces, places, and parts of the human body (Downing, Jian, Shuman, and Kanwisher, 2001; O'Craven & Kanwisher, 2001). Such data seem to support a local visual representation.

Other imaging data tells a different story, however. A group of researchers at the National Institutes of Health (Haxby, Gobbini, Furey, Ishai, Schouten, & Pietrini, 2001; Ishai, Ungerledier, Martin, & Haxby, 2000; Martin, Ungerleider, & Haxby, 2000) have reported that while a particular category of objects (such as faces, or cats, or houses) may yield maximal activity in one area of cortex, that

(Continued)

doesn't mean that this area alone supports the identification of the object. Other cortical areas also show a particular pattern of response associated with that category of objects. These data indicate that the cortical representations supporting visual identification of different types of objects are not localized but widespread and overlapping.

Which view is correct? Are concepts organized by their category, as the lesion data suggest, or are they distributed throughout the cortex as a collection of attributes, as the functional imaging data suggest? Further, within a modality, are the visual properties of objects localized or distributed? The data do not clearly support any one theory over the other at this point. My money, however, is on the more distributed theory of the National Institutes of Health group. The more localized theories may be brought into line with the localized theory if we imagine that what is localized is not "living things" or "faces" but a particular feature that everything in this category shares. Such a theory that successfully accounts for the data has not been proposed, however.

Criticisms of Parallel Distributed Processing Models

PDP models seem to be racking up all of the points. Nevertheless, there are problems with these models. Many of them suffer from catastrophic interference: if the model learns one set of associations (Set A) and then learns a different set (Set B), Set B will overwrite Set A, which will be lost (McCloskey & Cohen, 1989). Set A and Set B can both be learned if the two sets are interleaved in training; the problem is observed only if the sets are trained sequentially. This is not a characteristic of human memory, however. Researchers have come up with several suggestions to try to address the problem (French & Chater, 2002; Hamker, 2001; Lewandowsky & Li, 1995; Sloman & Rumelhart, 1992).

A second problem involving the ability of PDP models to learn rules came to the fore when Steve Pinker and Alan Prince (1988) criticized a well-known model developed by David Rumelhart and Jay McClelland (1987) that sought to account for how children learn the past-tense of the English language. As you may know, children go through a period in which they add -ed to words inappropriately. For example, a child might say, "Yesterday Mom and I goed to the park." Interestingly, children initially produce the correct past tense (went), then make overregularization errors (goed), and then go back to the correct past tense (went). Many researchers have proposed that this pattern results from the child acquiring a rule about producing the past tense. Initially, the child doesn't know the rule but memorizes the word went and applies it in the right situation. Then the child learns the rule "To make the past tense, add -ed to the infinitive of the verb." That rule should be applied only to regular verbs, but the child applies it to irregular verbs such as go. Later, the child learns that there are exceptions to the rule and memorizes these exceptions.

Rumelhart and McClelland's model produced the same pattern of output as the child does, only without any representation of a specific rule. They argued that a representation of a rule was not necessary. Pinker and Prince, in a detailed analysis of the model and of children's language learning, argued that there were many subtle aspects of children's language that the model did not account for and that these aspects required some rule-based representation. The details are beyond the scope of this chapter, but many researchers were convinced that an adequate model of children's language learning probably needs to include some representation of rules, and implementing rules in PDP models appears difficult.

So what is the final word on the organization of memory? Right now it appears that memory might be organized in some manner consistent with spreading activation, but that hypothesis has not been immune to criticism. As to whether the representation is local or distributed, that point is also not settled, but there is increasing evidence from neuroscience favoring the distributed model (see Box 7.2).

Stand-on-One-Foot Questions

7. Name two formidable problems that any large memory storage device, including human memory, must solve.

8. Name some of the advantages and disadvantages of the spreading activation model that uses a local representation.

9. What is the difference between spreading activation models that use local representation and those that use distributed representation?

Questions That Require Two Feet

10. Can you see how the spreading activation model might be related to early associationist ideas discussed in chapter 1? If not, can you see how it might be applied to the flow of consciousness?

11. Given what you know about the brain, do you think a local representation or a distributed representation is more realistic?

12. One way of measuring what concepts are connected in a spreading activation model is simply to name a word and ask people to say the next word that comes to mind. For example, what do you think of when you hear salt? Presumably, when you hear the word, it passes its activation to linked concepts. You pick the most active word as your response. Try another one. What is the first word you think of when you hear pepper? For salt the first word many people pick is pepper, but few people who hear pepper list salt as the first associate. (Although you may have because I

had just reminded you of the association between them.) Why should salt *activate* pepper *but* pepper *not activate* salt? *What does this result imply for spreading activation models?*

What Else Is in Memory?

> ➤ *Preview* Most researchers believe that there are many forms of memory and that the type of memory we discussed in chapters 5 and 6 is just one form. That view was motivated by data from amnesic patients showing that although this form of memory is impaired, many other types of memory are still intact. Initially, proposals for two forms of memory were considered, but as researchers became more inquisitive about possible forms of learning and as the underlying anatomy of memory became clearer, it was determined that there are at least five forms of memory that have different anatomical bases.

Have we covered everything that is in the storehouse? Until about 30 years ago the answer might have been a guarded "Yes." Memory research was conducted using mostly verbal materials in a laboratory setting and often tested memory for these materials over short intervals. Since that time, several important distinctions have been proposed that broadened our definition of memory. A number of researchers have suggested that there are several types of memory—the storehouse contains fundamentally different types of representations.

What Are Separate Memory Systems?

The rest of this chapter often refers to separate memory systems, an idea that has received a great deal of attention in the last 20 years. Why is this question interesting or important? Recall that in chapter 1 we said that cognitive psychologists were interested in mental representations and the processes that operate on them. When researchers propose that there are separate memory systems, they are proposing that there is more than one type of memory representation. We can draw an analogy to your computer: a word processing program such as WordPerfect uses a particular format to store data. The WordPerfect program is a set of processes that can work with this representation to read and modify the data in the file. In addition to this set of processes and representations, is there a second set that serves memory? To go back to our software analogy, if you have Excel on your hard drive, it uses a different format for its files. The Excel program is a different set of processes, and it uses a different type of representation. Similarly, the question of whether there are separate memory systems is at the very heart of cognitive psychology; it is concerned with processes and representations, and we want to know how many different types there are.

Procedural and Declarative Memory

We said that **declarative memory** is conscious and seems to fit the storehouse metaphor, and **procedural memory** is unconscious and does not call to mind representations entering a storehouse but rather changes to the processes that use representations. What is the origin of the procedural versus declarative distinction?

The story begins with patient H.M., who was mentioned in chapter 1. H.M. is the man who had much of his medial temporal lobe removed to relieve intractable epilepsy, leaving him with profound anterograde amnesia characterized by difficulty in storing new memories. H.M. is likely the most thoroughly tested anterograde amnesic patient. By 1965 his memory had been tested using just about every type of material you could think of: words, nonwords, rhythms, songs, faces, and so on (Corkin, 1984). In 1968 Suzanne Corkin (1968) administered a motor skill learning task to H.M. In this task, called the pursuit rotor, a target the size of a nickel rotates on a circular platter. The participant holds a stylus, similar to a pen, and tries to keep its tip on the moving target. Initially, people do badly at this, keeping the stylus in contact with the target for perhaps 5 s out of a 25-s trial, but they quickly improve. Corkin reported that H.M. improved as well: he learned the skill. (Interestingly, H.M. did not remember any details of the testing situation when asked about it later. He was shown the testing apparatus but did not recognize it and could not say what it was for.) This finding is evidence for **anatomic dissociation**, meaning that different tasks are supported by different parts of the brain. In this case, we can conclude that the medial temporal lobe (which is damaged in H.M.) is important for remembering the testing situation but not for motor skill learning. We can call it a partial dissociation because these data don't tell us which part of the brain is important for motor skills. We just know it's not the medial temporal lobe. We could interpret this evidence in terms of multiple memory systems; perhaps motor skill learning uses different processes and representations than the type of memory that supports recognizing the testing apparatus and knowing that you've done the task before. The medial temporal lobe, which is damaged in H.M., might support this sort of recognition, but motor skill learning is supported by another part of the brain, so it is not compromised in H.M.

This finding and interpretation did not rock the memory world at the time; no one thought that learning to ride a bicycle was the same thing as memorizing the Pledge of Allegiance. Psychologists thought that memory and motor skills were entirely different. *Memory* meant what is measured by recognition or free recall tests. The distinction between memory and motor skills didn't seem controversial or all that interesting.

WHAT MEMORY PROCESS IS ABSENT IN AMNESICS? The simple distinction between memory and motor skills got complicated because of a new finding with amnesic patients. Elizabeth Warrington and Larry Weiskrantz (1968) developed a clever task, using 10 words such as *porch* photographed through filters that showed three successively more incomplete versions of the word; it was as though participants were trying to read the words through heavy fog.

In this task, the participant is shown the least complete version of the word and asked to identify it. Successively more complete versions are shown until the participant can read the word. The list is repeated in the same manner, and the experimenter records whether the participant is able to read less complete versions of the words with practice. Participants do indeed improve, and amnesic patients also show significant improvement, although not quite as fast. When participants were shown other incomplete words that they had not seen before, they were not especially good at them; therefore, they must have been learning something about the specific words used in training, not a general skill in reading incomplete words. Amnesic patients who normally would not be able to remember a word list at all show good retention of the word list when tested via this method.

Most researchers did not interpret this finding in terms of multiple memory systems, although it is possible to do so; the finding is comparable to the case with the pursuit rotor, a new task that amnesic patients learn normally. This new finding from Warrington and Weiskrantz was a bit more dramatic because the same word list appears to be either remembered or not remembered by amnesic patients, depending on how they are tested. Warrington and Weiskrantz interpreted their result in terms of a missing process in amnesia. If multiple cognitive processes are necessary for normal memory performance, but because of their brain damage amnesic patients are missing one of those processes, they will be impaired on most memory tasks. Occasionally, we might come across a task to which this process doesn't contribute. Amnesic patients should learn such a task normally because the process they lost is not needed.

Warrington and Weiskrantz's results indicated that amnesic patients had a problem with the process of retrieval. There was nothing special about the conditions under which the words were encoded, but the experimenters changed the retrieval process. They didn't ask the participants to remember anything but simply asked them to try to read the degraded words. There was a fundamental difficulty with this idea, however. Amnesic patients could still retrieve material from before the onset of their amnesia. If the damaged process were retrieval, why was the memory problem limited to material they had encoded since the onset of brain damage?

Other studies in the 1970s investigated other hypotheses about what this missing process might be. Some researchers suggested that encoding might be faulty in amnesic patients. Perhaps these patients consistently encode material only at a shallow level instead of at a deep level, as nonamnesic participants do (Cermak & Butters, 1972). But the idea that encoding was the faulty process in amnesia was largely discounted when several studies failed to show much effect on amnesic patients' memory when they were forced to encode material deeply. Imagine three conditions in an experiment: participants may be told to encode shallowly, to encode deeply, or simply to learn the material. In the first two conditions, they are not told about an upcoming test. Normal participants, when told about an upcoming memory test, will spontaneously encode material deeply, so their performance will be the same as it is when they are forced to encode deeply. However, amnesic patients spontaneously encode shallowly when told to learn material, so if they are simply told to learn, their performance looks the same as when they encoded shallowly.

Andrew Mayes and his colleagues (Mayes, Mendell, & Neary, 1980) examined this prediction by asking amnesic patients to examine photographs of faces. In the shallow encoding condition they judged whether the person had straight or curly hair; in the deep condition they judged whether the person appeared friendly or unfriendly; and in the learning condition they were simply told to study the faces for a later memory test. The data were not consistent with an encoding deficit. Amnesic patients' memory was worse in all conditions, but they showed the same advantage of deeper encoding (and disadvantage of shallow encoding) that the controls did. Thus amnesic patients do not have a special problem with encoding.

Perhaps, then, the problem lies in forgetting. Perhaps amnesic patients show poor memory because they forget material very quickly. It's difficult to evaluate how quickly amnesic patients forget, however, because they don't remember very much in the first place. Felicia Huppert and Malcolm Piercy (1978) varied the amount of time that amnesics and controls saw the stimulus materials in an effort to equate their performance. They showed 120 colored pictures to amnesic patients and controls. Controls saw them for 1 s each, and amnesics for either 4 or 8 s. These times were selected so that everyone would have a recognition accuracy of about 75% after 10 min. Participants were also tested 24 hr later and a week later, and the results showed that amnesic patients did not show faster forgetting; they forgot at the same rate at which controls did.

IDENTIFYING THE MISSING MEMORY PROCESS.   While researchers were trying to figure out which memory process was missing in amnesic patients, their job was becoming more difficult. Other experimenters were discovering new memory tasks that amnesic patients learned normally, despite their memory impairment. For example, Warrington and Weiskrantz (1979) reported that amnesic patients showed normal acquisition of a classically conditioned response. In this experiment, a tone was paired with a puff of air to the eye. With practice, participants learned this association and blinked when the tone sounded. Amnesic patients learned as quickly as normal participants. In another experiment, participants learned to read mirror-reversed words (Cohen & Squire, 1980). The actual time it took participants to read the words aloud was measured, and amnesic patients, like controls, improved with practice. As the number of tasks that amnesic patients could learn normally grew, it became harder to think of a single process that would both account for deficit in amnesia and account for all the tasks that amnesics were able to learn normally. (For a recent review of memory disorders, see Kopelman, 2002.)

In the late 1970s and early 1980s a number of researchers proposed that there must be multiple systems of human memory (Cohen & Squire, 1980;

O'Keefe & Nadel, 1978). The system that supported performance on standard recognition and recall tests was severely compromised in amnesia. The other system supported performance on tasks such as motor skills, classical conditioning, and perceptual skills (such as mirror reading). These tasks were intact in amnesia because this other memory system was not damaged.

Box 7–3 Separation of Implicit and Explicit Learning

The initial impetus for multiple memory system proposals came from studies of amnesic patients, who were grossly impaired on tests of declarative memory but intact on tests of motor skill learning, priming, emotional conditioning, and classical conditioning. If each of these five memory systems is separate, we should expect to see patients who have a single memory system selectively knocked out (with the other four systems remaining intact, of course).

Finding such patients has been difficult, partly because when these different systems were first proposed, no one knew which part of the brain supported them. When educated guesses could be made, it wasn't always easy to find a patient who happened to have damage to just that part of the brain and no other (brain imaging wasn't in common use yet).

One of the better sources of evidence in this vein came from patient M.S., reported by John Gabrieli and his associates (1995). M.S. had a large portion of his occipital lobe removed to treat intractable epilepsy. An MRI image of M.S. appears in Figure B7.3; the lighter gray is cerebrospinal fluid that has filled the cavity left by the surgery.

The researchers tested M.S., two patients with amnesia, and control participants on declarative memory and a priming measure. Participants were presented with 24 words, one at a time for 2 s, and were asked to read each aloud. They went through this list twice. A short time later the priming measure was administered using the 24 studied words and 24 new words. Participants saw a blank screen, a word presented very briefly, and then a row of xs as a mask for 250 ms. The word was initially presented for 16.7 ms, and the presentations continued, with the duration increasing by 16.7 ms increments until the participant could identify the word. In this paradigm, priming occurs if participants can identify the studied words at faster presentation times than the new words. The declarative memory test was administered after the priming measure and was a straightforward recognition test; participants saw the 24 studied words and 24 new words and had to say whether each had been on the studied list.

The results showed that, as expected, the amnesic patients were grossly impaired on the declarative measure but showed normal levels of priming. Patient M.S. showed just the opposite pattern of results: he showed normal performance on the recognition test, but he showed no priming whatsoever.

This sort of result is important in determining that declarative and procedural memory systems are truly separate. Suppose that all we had was the data from amnesic patients—damage to the medial temporal lobe impairs declarative but not procedural memory. We could argue that memory is distributed across many areas of the brain but procedural memory tasks are just easier. Thus brain damage will always knock out the hard test (declarative) and leave intact the

(Continued)

easy test (procedural). The results of Gabrieli and associates show that such an account is not correct: declarative memory and priming are supported by distinct brain systems.

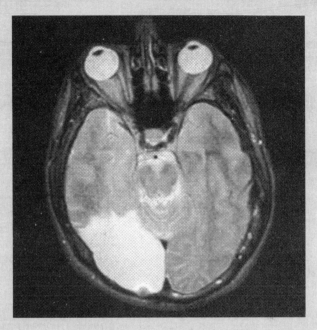

Figure B7.3. *From "Double Dissociation Between Memory Systems Underlying Explicit and Implicit Memory in the Human Brain," by J. D. E. Gabrieli et al., 1995,* Psychological Science, *6, Fig. 1, p. 78.*

Researchers tried to characterize these different memory systems. An early and important distinction was between procedural and declarative memory (Cohen & Squire, 1980). Procedural memory is memory for skills and is often called "knowing how" memory. For example, if you know how to ride a bicycle, that ability is supported by procedural memory. Declarative memory supports memory for facts and events and is often called "knowing that" memory, such as knowing that George Washington was the first U.S. President.

These hypothetical memory systems are closely identified with the implicit versus explicit distinction, which is a distinction of tasks (Graf & Schacter, 1985). Explicit tasks are those that directly query memory ("Who was the first President?"), and usually they are supported by the declarative memory system. Implicit tasks do not directly query memory ("Ride this bicycle"); rather, memory is inferred from the participant's performance. Implicit tasks usually are supported by procedural memory.

Proposals for multiple memory systems grew out of attempts to account for the memory performance of amnesic patients. Researchers tried to maintain a single-system framework but couldn't see a way to do it, so they concluded that there must be more than one memory system.

The 1980s saw two developments in memory theory. First, researchers continued to study patients with brain damage and started to fractionate memory still further in multiple subsystems. Second, they began to look for evidence of multiple memory systems in neurologically intact people.

FURTHER FRACTIONATION OF MEMORY.   The data from amnesic patients made it appear that declarative memory was supported by the hippocampus and other structures near the center of the brain (for a review, see Squire, 1992). But what brain structures supported procedural memory? Researchers soon discovered that different procedural tasks (classical conditioning, repetition priming, motor skill learning) were supported by different parts of the brain. There has been some disagreement over exactly how many memory systems there might be, but there is general agreement about the list provided in Table 7.8 (for a review, see Gabrieli, 1998; Willingham, 1997).

As shown in Table 7.8, there is evidence for at least five memory systems. As discussed earlier, the declarative system supports conscious memory of facts and events. We've also discussed priming, which makes representations of concepts more available for use either because they have been used recently (repetition priming) or because a semantically related concept has been used recently (semantic priming). Motor skill learning, the improved accuracy of movements as a consequence of practice, is discussed in more detail in chapter 9. Classical conditioning, as mentioned in chapter 1,

Table 7.8.   *Memory Systems*

System	Function	Neural Substrate	Reference or Review
Declarative	Conscious memory of facts and events	Hippocampus and other structures	Squire (1992)
Priming	Brief activation of existing representation	Occipital, temporal, and frontal cortex	Schacter, Chiu, & Ochsner (1993)
Motor skill learning	Acquires new motor skills	Striatum, motor cortical areas	Willingham (1998)
Classical conditioning	Learns relationships between perceptual stimuli and motor responses	Cerebellum	Thompson (1986)
Emotional conditioning	Learns relationships between perceptual stimuli and emotional responses	Amygdala	Maren & Fanselow (1996)

involves an unconditioned stimulus such as food that elicits an unconditioned response like salivation; it is paired with a conditioned stimulus (such as a bell) until the conditioned stimulus elicits a conditioned response (salivation). **Emotional conditioning** is a classical conditioning situation in which one of the unconditioned responses is an emotion. Fear is the emotion that has been studied most frequently. For example, a participant might be shown different color slides, and each time the slide depicts a snake, the participant is given a mild electric shock. In time, pictures of snakes will come to elicit fear.

The multiple memory systems hypothesis is rooted in anatomy on the assumption that these memory systems are different because they are localized in different parts of the brain. Basing memory systems on anatomy seems to make sense, but we would like to see cognitive differences among memory systems as well. If declarative memory and motor skill learning are really different, this difference should be visible in behavior, not just anatomy. For example, perhaps the rate of learning is different, or perhaps one type of learning is more flexible than the other. However, differences in behavior between the putative memory systems have been difficult to observe.

Cognitive Differences Among Memory Systems

How do the hypothetical memory systems differ? The most reliable difference has been in terms of awareness; this distinction separates declarative memory from all other memory systems. Declarative memory is always associated with awareness, meaning that you always are aware that you are learning something, and you are aware of what you are learning. If you learn that hydrogen has an atomic weight of 1, for example, you are aware of having learned something, and you are aware of what you have learned. Other types of learning are not necessarily associated with awareness. For example, in a priming task you might see the word stem *sta* _____ and complete it to spell *stamp* in part because you saw that word an hour ago, but you need not be aware of this priming effect for it to influence your behavior.

Again, the point is that we would like to see some difference between declarative and procedural memory, not just in terms of the brain structures that support them but in terms of how the systems seem to operate in normal participants. The fact that awareness seems to be necessary for declarative but not procedural memory is some evidence that they differ.

Unfortunately, it has been difficult to find convincing evidence of other differences. Much of the focus has concerned potential differences between declarative memory and other memory systems. For example, it was suggested that declarative learning is fast and can even occur on a single trial, whereas other types of learning such as motor skills are slow and require multiple trials (Sherry & Schacter, 1987). Such a distinction is hard to evaluate, however, because it is not clear how to equate the two tasks. If we want to compare the speed of learning a word list to the speed of learning how to ride a bicycle, how long should the word list be to make it a task of equivalent difficulty? And how much practice riding the bicycle is equivalent to, say, one reading of the word list? Such problems in comparing what may be inherently different types of memory make it difficult to evaluate claims about behavioral differences.

EPISODIC AND SEMANTIC MEMORY.   There is another distinction that is important to know about (Tulving, 1972), although its status is not quite as clear as that of the systems described in Table 7.8. **Episodic memory** is associated with a particular time and place (that is, you know when and where you acquired the material). Episodic memories are associated with a "this happened to me" feeling; there is a personal quality to the act of remembering. If I asked you, "When was the last time you bought a pair of shoes?" you would recall an episodic memory. You would have time and place information associated with this memory ("I last bought shoes at the mall, a week ago."). Part of the memory would also be the feeling that you did this thing. Such memories can be contrasted with **semantic memory**. Suppose I asked you, "Is a loafer a type of shoe?" You would answer, "Yes," but there is no time or place information associated with that memory, nor is there an "it happened to me" feeling. Semantic memory sometimes is called knowledge of the world. All of your knowledge of what things are, what they look like, how they work, and so on is part of semantic memory.

Tulving (1972, 1983, 2002) argued that semantic and episodic memory differ in a number of important ways. Episodic memories are more prone to forgetting, they are more likely to contain sensory information, they are organized by time, and they take longer to remember. Semantic memories are less prone to forgetting, they contain more conceptual than sensory information, they are organized by meaning rather than time, and they are recalled more quickly.

There is some evidence supporting the semantic versus episodic distinction, most of it from neuroscience. First, there have been reports of patients who have a selective loss of episodic but not semantic memory. If episodic and semantic memory are separate systems, they might well be localized in different parts of the brain, so we would expect to see the occasional patient who happens to have had selective damage to one system or the other. Such patients are rare, but some have been identified (see Wheeler & McMillan, 2001). For example, Endel Tulving and his colleagues (Hayman, Macdonald, & Tulving, 1993; Tulving, Schacter, McLachlan, & Moscovitch, 1988) reported on a man, K.C., who suffered extensive damage to the left hemisphere and some damage to the right as a consequence of a motorcycle accident at age 30. K.C. shows intact intellectual functioning. His ability to use language, working memory, and problem-solving skills are all intact. K.C.'s semantic memory seems to be intact. His vocabulary appears to be of normal size, and he can provide accurate descriptions of scripts (see chapter 5) such as going to a restaurant or changing a flat tire. He can also remember technical terms associated with his job. What K.C. seems to have lost is his episodic memory. He does not remember events from his life that should be quite vivid: for example, he does not remember the events surrounding a train derailment in which

240,000 people (including K.C.) had to evacuate their homes for a week, any of the circumstances of the death of his brother by drowning, or a bar fight in which his shoulder was broken.

In another remarkable report, Farena Vargha-Khadem and her associates (1997; Vargha-Khadem, Gadian, & Mishkin, 2002) described three patients who suffered severe hippocampal damage early in life (between birth and 9 years). All three patients have very poor memory for personal episodes in their lives, yet all three have fairly normal semantic memories: they have attended mainstream schools and acquired factual knowledge about the world that is about the same as (or perhaps slightly less than) what would be expected of others their age.

What of neuroimaging? In the mid-1990s it seemed that a fairly clear distinction could be drawn: semantic retrieval was consistently associated with activity in the left frontal cortex, whereas episodic retrieval was more often associated with right frontal activity (see Buckner & Petersen, 1996). More recent data, however, have shown that that distinction is not as reliable as was first thought (Cabeza & Nyberg, 2000; Mayes & Montaldi, 2001). Most direct comparisons of episodic and semantic memory have shown some differences of activation, but they are not consistent across studies.

A difficulty with the interpretation of all of these studies is that episodic and semantic memories are different in more ways than the distinction proposes. Episodic memories typically are encoded and rehearsed much less often than semantic memories. I might encode an episodic memory only once (the time I went to McDonald's and they let me try on one of the McDonald's caps) and then rehearse the memory a few times over the course of a few years when I tell the story. But how many times have I rehearsed the semantic knowledge that a quarter is 25 cents? This difference in rehearsal makes it difficult to interpret neurological studies as straightforward evidence supporting the episodic versus semantic distinction.

There is also a problem in distinguishing just what is episodic and what is semantic. If you tell me a new fact that I didn't know (the three main Hindu gods are Brahma, Vishnu, and Shiva), that is an episodic memory: I will know when and where I acquired that memory. Suppose someone else tells me that fact tomorrow. I now have two episodic memories of this fact. If different people keep telling me that fact, at some point it will turn into a semantic memory. But at what point does it stop being an episodic memory and start being a semantic memory? The line is not clear.

Here's another problem. Suppose that, 5 years from now, the three main gods of Hinduism are firmly in semantic memory. Someone comes up to me and starts lecturing me in a patronizing way about Hinduism. The next day I have an episodic memory of being lectured to, but embedded in that episodic memory is a semantic memory: I was annoyed that this person thought I didn't know the three main Hindu gods (which are in semantic memory). Thus most, if not all, episodic memories must have semantic memories in them. We need semantic memory to make sense of the world, so it seems that semantic and episodic memory must be closely linked, at the very least.

Because of conceptual problems such as these, some memory researchers (Glenberg, 1997; Johnson & Hasher, 1987; McKoon, Ratcliff, & Dell, 1986; Richardson-Klavehn & Bjork, 1988; Toth & Hunt, 1999; Weldon, 1999) have argued that episodic and semantic memory are not separate memory systems (but see also Schacter & Tulving, 1994). They interpret the different anatomic bases as reflecting a few different processes at work or perhaps the difference in the amount of practice the memories have received. They suggest that the distinction may be most useful for its heuristic value. In other words, the distinction helps our thinking about memory and may help us generate interesting experiments, whether or not it turns out to be psychologically important. Indeed, you may note that this book uses the episodic versus semantic distinction in its organization. Chapters 5 and 6 on encoding and retrieval were concerned primarily with episodic memory, and this chapter is concerned primarily with semantic memory.

CURRENT STATUS OF MEMORY SYSTEMS.   Research in the last 20 years has shown that our previous definitions of memory were too narrow because they were restricted to conscious, declarative forms of memory. Most memory theorists believe that many cognitive systems are capable of learning. For example, your visual system learns with experience, and that learning can support performance on priming tasks. Similarly, the motor control system that allows you to move around in the world changes with experience, and those changes support motor skill learning. So you have a system that is devoted to memory—that's the declarative system, with the storehouse—but you also have other systems that are dedicated primarily to another function such as vision or movement, and these systems also have the capability to learn. The motor system can learn motor skills, the visual system can learn perceptual skills, and so on. In these forms of memory nothing is stored per se, but there are changes to the actual processes; the motor system or the visual system is changed. Declarative memory seems to fit the storehouse idea, with memory being supported by the creation and storage of new representations.

Stand-on-One-Foot Questions

13. *What key feature would make potential memory systems separate?*
14. *What is the origin of the multiple memory systems idea?*
15. *What is the current count of memory systems?*

Questions That Require Two Feet

16. *How likely does it seem to you that separate memory systems interact in some fashion?*

17. Can you think of a time when two of your memory systems may have conflicted?

KEY TERMS

activation
addressing system
anatomic dissociation
basic level category
category
classical view of
   categorization
cognitive economy
concepts
content-addressable
   storage
declarative memory
default values
distributed
   representation
emotional conditioning

episodic memory
exemplar model
exemplar
focus gambling
generalization
generalize
graceful degradation
hierarchical theory
links
local representation
mediated priming
nodes
parallel distributed
   processing (PDP)
probabilistic view of
   categorization

procedural memory
property inheritance
prototypes
repetition priming
semantic memory
semantic network
semantic priming
spreading activation
   model
subordinate level
   category
successive scanning
superordinate level
   category
typicality

8

Motor Control

The end product of thought is usually behavior, and behavior entails some movement: you shift your eyes to look at something, you reach to move a pawn in a chess game, you dance closer to an attractive stranger. **Motor control** refers to our ability to plan and execute movements.

Among the various cognitive functions, motor control is rather like visual perception in that it is difficult to appreciate the difficulty and complexity of the function precisely because humans are so good at it. Attempts to get machines to make coordinated movements have been, in many instances, impressive, but they still have a distance to go until they equal biological systems.

One recent development is the "robot rat" (Talwar et al., 2002). A human using a computer keyboard can get a living rat to move forward, and to turn right or left, via operant conditioning. How does it work? Electrodes implanted in the rat's brain can stimulate two centers: one electrode stimulates neurons that would be activated if something touched the rat's whiskers, and the other stimulates a reward center that makes the rat feel good. The whisker neurons provide cues for which direction the rat should move; if the rat then makes the right movement, it is rewarded by stimulation of the reward center. The electrodes and the other equipment needed to operate them are mounted on a little backpack so the rat is free moving, and the equipment can include a small camera so that the researcher can see where the rat is going. The researchers suggested that the robot rat could be useful on rough terrain where robots have trouble moving (as in rubble left after an earthquake). This comparison of the robot rat and the mechanical robot is notable: biological systems (humans or rats) can figure out ways of moving in environments that are difficult to negotiate and that we've never seen before. Why are biological systems better than robotic systems?

To answer that question, we have to understand some requirements for *all* moving things, whether animal or robot. For a movement system to be effective, it must have flexibility so that any given movement can be made many different ways, even something simple liking flipping on a light switch. Flexibility is important because there are times when the environment will constrain your options (an obstacle in front of the switch might force an awkward reach instead of the more typical reach) and times when your body does the same (if you're carrying groceries you might flip the switch with your elbow). All these possibilities bring up a question: **How do we select a movement?** The obvious answer might be "Pick the simplest," but as we'll see, there are several ways to define simplicity. It may be that the motor system combines several different principles to select the appropriate movement.

The question makes it sound as though we select one movement at a time, although that is not the case. Rather, we must assemble sequences of multiple movements. One advantage that computers have over the rat (and us) is raw processing speed. It takes at least 100 ms for us to process visual feedback—somewhat less for proprioceptive feedback (the feeling of having moved). That means that we can't execute a single movement, observe its effect on the environment, make another movement, observe *its* effect, and so on. For even moderately fast movements, that would take too long. **How are**

movements sequenced? We will review evidence that movements are sequenced in hierarchical programs.

When considering the robot rat (or any motor system) it is easy to focus on the motoric aspects of the rat's behavior and to forget about its reliance on the perceptual system. But the ability to move through obstacle-filled terrain depends on knowing where the obstacles are. Further, it isn't enough to know where the obstacles are at the start of the movement; we want to update that perceptual information as the movement is ongoing. Imagine yourself at the end of a long, obstacle-free hallway. Assuming you are sighted, would you be comfortable walking its length blindfolded? Why not? People are used to sampling perceptual information as movements are ongoing, perhaps to update the movement plan in midstream. **How is perceptual information integrated into ongoing movements?**

A motor system also needs to incorporate learning. We usually think of motor skill learning in terms of identifiable skills that people practice, such as playing soccer or violin, but all of us have a vast repertoire of motor skills that we take for granted. If your movements never improved in speed or accuracy no matter how much you practiced, how long would it take you to tie your shoes? How safe would highways be if everyone drove as though it were their first time behind the wheel? Our final question in this chapter is **How are motor skills learned?** We will discuss three basic principles of motor skill, as well as two theoretical approaches that researchers have employed.

HOW DO WE SELECT A MOVEMENT?

> ➤ *Preview* Even the simplest reaching movement can be made in an infinite number of ways. How do we select one way to move from among these infinite choices? Three classes of theories address this problem. Efficiency theories propose that we select the most efficient movement. The problem then becomes to find the right definition of efficiency. Synergy theories suggest that the problem is minimized because many parts of the body are designed to work together in systematic ways, so there are not as many choices as it first appears. The mass spring theory proposes that the pathway of the movement does not need to be planned.

In this chapter when we speak of motor control, we're talking about the physical process of getting a movement accomplished, not *why* we want to make the movement. In other words, our topic concerns accomplishing a goal, not choosing one.

Because of its flexibility, the motor system can accomplish a given goal under different circumstances. For example, to pick up the coffee cup on my desk, I might have to reach around my computer speaker, grasp the cup handle at an awkward angle, and delicately pull the cup toward me in a curved trajectory to avoid hitting a swing-arm lamp. If my wrist were in a cast and I couldn't bend it, which I would normally do when making a reaching movement, the other parts of my arm would compensate for the constraint of my wrist being immobile, and the reaching movement would still occur smoothly.

Flexibility like this is rooted in a basic property of the motor system: any movement can be made in an infinite number of ways. Thus when one way is made difficult or impossible by obstacles in the environment or bodily limitations, we can still find another way to make the movement. Yet flexibility presents a problem to the psychologist interested in accounting for motor behavior. If there are an infinite number of options for performing even the simplest movement, how do we ever decide which way to make a move? This **degrees of freedom problem** can be appreciated through a simple demonstration. Grasp an object, preferably one that is immobile, but don't try to move it. Your hand is now in a new position, and to get your hand to that new position, you had to move your arm. Keeping your hand immobile on the object, move your arm. You're able to move it, right? There was more than one way in which your arm could end up as you grasped the object; you can tell that's true because if there was only one single position in which your arm could end up, you would not have been able to move it. So why did your mind choose the final arm position it did instead of one of the other possible positions?

The endpoint of the movement is the position of your arm when your hand is at the goal position (grasping the cup). The path of movement that your hand takes on the way to the endpoint is called the **trajectory**, and it opens an infinite number of pathways to the object. An **effector** is a part of the body that you use to make or effect the environment, such as your hand or foot. What if you reach with your other hand, or try to grasp the cup in your teeth, or rake it toward you along the table with your forearm? All of these possibilities must be eliminated so that a reaching movement using one endpoint, one trajectory, and one effector can be made.

Now that we have a feel for the degrees of freedom problem, we can move on to the three classes of theories that address its solutions: efficiency theories, which favor the most efficient movement possible; synergy theories, which minimize the degrees of freedom problem; and the mass spring model, which argues that trajectories are naturally "calculated" because of the way the body is designed.

Efficiency Theories

Efficiency theories claim that all of the possible movements toward a goal are evaluated for their efficiency, and the most efficient movement is executed. For example, moving your hand in a straight line to the cup is more efficient than moving it in a serpentine pattern.

The problem is that there are a number of measures of efficiency that sound quite reasonable. Take the idea of moving the effector the shortest distance possible. Do we mean the shortest distance in Cartesian space? But movements could instead be planned in terms of **joint space**, a representation for planning movements that uses joint angles. You can think of getting your hand to a desired location by setting your joints at particular angles. The most efficient movement might not be the one that makes your hand travel the shortest distance in Cartesian space, but the one that makes you move your joints the shortest distance. These definitions of efficiency lead to different movements.

When we consider how joint angles are derived, we realize that they are set by muscle contractions that create torques on the joints. Perhaps, therefore, efficiency should be defined as the movement that calls for the minimum joint torque (Uno, Kawato, & Suzuki, 1989). One potential problem with this solution is that nothing in the nervous system is set up to detect torque change. Muscle torque should be directly related to the tension exerted on muscles, however, so another potential solution would be to minimize muscle stiffness (Hasan, 1986).

Another definition of efficiency takes advantage not just of the spatial characteristics of movement but of the typical profile of movement speed. Your hand picks up speed slowly, reaches maximum speed in the middle of the movement, and then decreases speed slowly. If the hand increased or decreased speed very rapidly, we would say that the movement was jerky. We can define **jerk** (in a reaching movement) as the rate of acceleration of the wrist. Tamar Flash and Neville Hogan (1985) proposed that the degrees of freedom problem is solved by selecting the movement that minimizes jerk.

Which of these definitions of efficiency is the correct one to solve the degrees of freedom problem—distance traveled in Cartesian space, distance traveled in joint space, joint torque, joint stiffness, or effector jerk? The usual strategy to compare these hypotheses is to make precise measurements (such as the speed at different points during the reach, or the shape of the trajectory) and then compare models based on these different principles to see which one most accurately predicts how people move. Most of the models are fairly good at predicting the main features of movement; the tests are rather technical. (For examples of this sort of work, see Gomi & Kawato, 1996; Todorov & Jordan, 1998.)

Synergy Theories

Some researchers have emphasized that although any movement can be performed in many different ways, some possibilities are eliminated because muscles are designed to work together; they do not need to be independently controlled all the time. There are more than 600 muscles in the human body. Each of them can take two states—contracted or relaxed—so in theory there are 2^{600} possible states for the system as a whole. We can immediately cut that number in half because there is a strong bias in the system for opposing muscles to take opposite states. Muscles are organized in pairs on opposite sides of a joint; when one contracts, the opposite muscle relaxes to allow the bone to move at the joint. (Muscles can only pull—they can't push.)

Figure 8.1. *Example of a synergy. In Task 1, start with both your elbow and your wrist extended (your knuckles are as close to your forearm as possible). Then simultaneously flex your elbow and flex your wrist. In Task 2, start with your elbow extended but your wrist flexed. Now flex your elbow, but extend your wrist. This movement is much harder, indicating that there is a synergy for your elbow and wrist to be flexed or extended together, not in opposition.*

But coordinated organization goes beyond pairs of muscles. Joints are also biased to work together. To see this, extend your elbow so that your arm is straight, and extend your wrist so that the back of your hand is as close to your forearm as you can get it, as shown in "Task 1, Start" in Figure 8.1. Now flex your wrist and your elbow at the same time so that you end up as shown in "Task 1, Finish." That should be fairly easy. Now start again, with your elbow extended, but this time with your wrist already flexed, as shown in "Task 2, Start." This time *extend* your wrist while you flex your elbow, so that you end up as shown in "Task 2, Finish." Task 2 should be much more difficult than Task 1. Typically, the wrist and elbow either flex or extend together, so it is difficult to flex your elbow and extend your wrist at the same time. Such biases for joints or muscle groups to work together in a particular way are called **synergies**.

To derive formal evidence for synergies, Marco Santello, Martha Flanders, and John Soechting (1998) asked participants to pretend that they were grasping 57 common objects (such as a bucket, a screwdriver, and a doorknob) while wearing a glove with 15 embedded sensors that provided data about the positions of their fingers. The experimenters measured the joint angles of the fingers and the angles between adjacent fingers. The average hand postures for six objects are shown in Figure 8.2. The data were analyzed with a complex set of statistical procedures called discriminant analysis, which basically tells how different the hand postures are for various items. The analysis showed that certain joint angles were frequently correlated; for example, the angles of the second joint of the ring finger and the second joint of the pinky were usually very similar. Looking at the postures overall, the experimenters determined that two basic postures account for most of the difference among all of the grasps that participants made. The experimenters concluded that there may be just a few synergies that regulate the basic shape of the hand, along with a mechanism that makes finer adjustments for different objects.

Evidence for synergies can be found not only in grasping but in reaching. Some movements could make you unsteady on your feet; for example, when you use an elevator, your center of gravity changes when you reach toward the controls because your arm has mass, and the pressure you exert pushing a floor button also pushes your body backwards. Yet reaching, or pressing, or pulling something doesn't ordinarily make you unsteady because you make **anticipatory postural adjustments**, muscle contractions that correct for the change in your center of gravity. The particular type of anticipatory postural adjustment—in the back, the legs, the abdomen, and so on—is designed to counteract whatever is making you unstable (Nashner, Woollacott, & Tuman, 1979), but it is thought that there is a relatively small repertoire of such movements (Massion, 1984) and that they constitute part of a synergy with other movements. In other words, when you decide to push an elevator button, the anticipatory postural adjustments are made automatically to ensure that you remain upright and stable (but see Benvenuti, Stanhope, Thomas, Panzer, & Hallet, 1997 for an argument that anticipatory postural adjustments are planned).

The Mass Spring Model

The degrees of freedom problem is made more manageable if trajectories are not calculated at all. How is that possible? The **mass spring model** capitalizes on a biomechanical property of the way our muscles and limbs are designed: they can be likened to springs. As a simple analogy, consider a café door that swings in either direction. It is mounted on hinges with springs so that when

Circular ashtray　　　　　　Frying pan

Zipper　　　　　　Computer mouse

Light bulb　　　　　　Beer mug

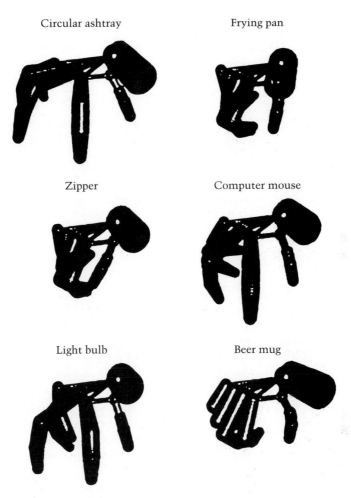

Figure 8.2. *Reproduction of average hand postures produced by one subject for six different objects. To make it easier to compare postures, the hand has been rotated so that the palm is always downward. From "Postural Hand Synergies for Tool Use," by M. Santello, M. Flanders, and J. F. Soechting, 1998,* Journal of Neuroscience, 18, *Fig. 2, p. 10107.*

you push and release the door, the springs push it back toward the jamb, the door's inertia takes it past the jamb, the spring brings it back to the center, and it continues to swing in smaller arcs until finally coming to rest in the center of the door jamb. Why does the door come to a rest in the middle of the door jamb? Obviously because the springs are of equal tension. You don't need to know the path the door is going to take to know where it will stop. If one spring were too tight, the door would end up not in the middle of the jamb but more to

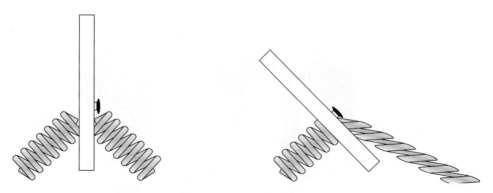

Figure 8.3.   *The café door analogy of muscles and joints. If a door can move freely in a door jamb and is set with springs on each side, the door will always return to the center of the jamb if the springs are of equal tension. If the springs are not of equal tension, as shown in the right side of the figure, then the door will not return to the center of the jamb.*

one side, as shown in Figure 8.3. Your muscles and joints can be likened to the café door. Joints move when muscles contract, pulling the bone. You can move the position of a joint by changing the tension of the muscles attached to it.

If you changed the tension of the springs on the door, you wouldn't need to know the path that the door would take to get to its endpoint. Similarly, perhaps if you change the tension of your muscles, you won't know the path your hand will take. All you really care about is its endpoint. You could just set the opposing muscle tensions so that your hand will end up in the right stopping place; you don't need to plan the trajectory, so there is a huge reduction in the complexity of the degrees of freedom problem.

To test this hypothesis, Andres Polit and Emilio Bizzi (1978) had a monkey sit in a chair facing a line of lights, as shown in Figure 8.4. The monkey's forearm was strapped to a hinged rod so that it could sweep in an arc parallel to the floor, and the monkey's view of its arm was blocked by a collar. The task was to swing the forearm to point at a light when it came on. When successful, the monkey was rewarded with a sip of fruit juice. A motor at the hinge allowed the rod to be moved by the experimenter, who would displace the rod to the right or left in mid-movement. The monkey was very good at recovering from the displacement and pointing the rod at the light. This result is not all that surprising. The arm wasn't visible, but the monkey could feel that its arm had been displaced because special receptors in the joints, skin, and muscles detect where the parts of the body are. This sensation of body location is called **proprioception**.

Now comes the interesting result. Pollit and Bizzi cut the dorsal roots of the spinal cord, which meant that the monkey received no proprioceptive information from its arm to its brain; the arm felt completely numb. But the monkey still made accurate pointing movements, even when the experimenters disturbed the location of the arm in mid-movement. How is that possible? The monkey could not see or feel its arm. Wouldn't the monkey have to know that its arm had been displaced so that it could correct for the displacement?

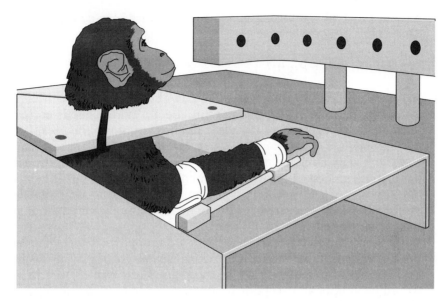

Figure 8.4. *A monkey in position to respond in Polit and Bizzi's (1978) experiment. From "Characteristics of Motor Programs Underlying Arm Movements in Monkeys," in A. Polit and E. Bizzi, 1979,* Journal of Neurophysiology, *42, Fig. 1, p. 184.*

This puzzling result is explained in terms of the mass-spring theory. Just as a café door ends up in the middle of the door jamb even if you knock it out of place, the monkey's limb ends up pointing to the light even when it is knocked out of place. Just as the café door's final location is fixed by the tension of the springs and it doesn't need to "know" that it has been displaced to end up there, the final position of the monkey's arm is determined when the monkey sets the tension of opposing muscles, and it does not need to know that the arm has been displaced. (For another theory emphasizing the endpoints of movements but using a different approach, see Feldman, 1986; Flash & Gurevich, 1999.)

Some recent evidence provides provocative neurophysiological evidence favoring the mass spring model. Michael Graziano and his colleagues (2002) electrically stimulated the primary and secondary motor cortices of monkeys while their arms were unconstrained. Stimulation studies done in the past had almost always used brief (50 ms) pulses of stimulation; this study stimulated for 500 ms. The researchers argued that this value is closer to the length of time accompanying normal reaching and grasping. They found that the stimulation evoked complex movements across many joints—for example, when one brain site was stimulated the monkey opened its mouth, put its hand in a grip position, and brought the hand to the mouth. Most remarkable, this complex movement was executed *no matter what the starting position of the limbs.* In other words, the stimulation predicted the endpoints of the movement, not the particulars of how the movement would be executed. This result provides nice physiological support for the mass spring model and other models emphasizing the endpoints of movements.

Which Model Is Right?

Three types of movement theories have been proposed—efficiency theories, synergy theories, and the mass spring theory. Which one is correct? It is more difficult than you might first think to compare these theories. For example, is the representation of movements in Cartesian space or joint space? Here are some relevant data. First, you need to know that the relationship between hand movements and joint movements is complex. In order to move your hand in a straight line, your joint angles undergo a complex set of changes. Simple joint angle changes lead to hand movements that are not straight. This relationship is illustrated in Figure 8.5.

We might assume that the brain would opt for simple changes. Hence, if the brain plans movements in Cartesian space, you'd assume a simple, straight movement in Cartesian space. If the brain plans movements in joint space, it would be simple and straight in joint space, but the hand movement that we observe would be curved. When people to point to targets, they move their hands in relatively straight lines (Morasso, 1981), evidence favoring a theory that movements are planned in Cartesian space.

But John Soechting and his colleagues (1986) reported work indicating that drawing movements are planned in terms of joint angles, not in Cartesian space. Their participants drew circles and ellipses on different planes (for example, on

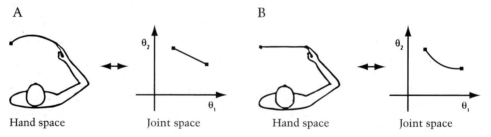

Figure 8.5. *The relationship between movements in joint space (shown on the graph) and resulting movements of the hand in Cartesian space (shown by the person). In A, the joint angles θ_1 and θ_2 change at the same rate, leading to a simple movement in joint space—but this simple movement in joint space leads to a complex, curved movement of the hand in Cartesian space. In B, the hand makes a simple, straight movement in Cartesian space, but the graph shows that the necessary movement in joint space to make that happen is complex. From* **Human Motor Control**, *by D. A. Rosenbaum, 1991, San Diego, CA: Academic Press, Fig. 6.11, p. 219. They adapted this figure from "Characterization of Joint-Interpolate Arm Movements," Generation and Modulation of Action Patterns, H. Heuer and C. Fromm, Eds., by J. M. Hollerbach and C. G. Atkeson, 1986, Berlin: Springer-Verlag.*

a table or a chalkboard). The data showed that there was consistency in the joint angles participants used when drawing in these different positions, even though the muscle forces changed when they had to draw on different surfaces. That consistency makes it seem that the movement was planned in terms of joint angles.

It is of course possible that all of these theories may be partially right. Different types of planning may be possible under different circumstances. The correct model may need to incorporate several of the principles discussed above. One candidate was proposed by David Rosenbaum and his colleagues (Rosenbaum, Engelbrecht, Bushe, & Loukopoulos, 1993; Rosenbaum, Loukopoulos, Meulenbroek, Vaughan et al., 1995; Rosenbaum, Meulenbroek, Vaughan, & Jansen, 2001). The model assumes that people have a large database of postures (body positions) stored in memory. A posture is calculated that will serve as a good endpoint for a movement. For example, if you want to touch a thumbtack, you need to calculate the posture of your body when you're touching the thumbtack. When a spatial target for movement is identified, each posture makes a "bid" as to how appropriate it is to reach the target. If a posture would be very effective to get the body to the desired position, it makes a high bid; if it would only bring the body close to the target, it makes a somewhat lower bid; and so on. The postures are evaluated with regard to how accurate the reach would be if that posture were assumed, and with regard to how much energy would be consumed in assuming that posture. For example, a posture that requires bending at the waist consumes more energy than one that only requires bending the elbow. The weight of each posture is based on both its bid and the energy it would take to assume that posture. The final posture that a person uses to move is a combination of all of the postures that have bid, and postures with higher weights contribute more to the final position. Once this target posture has been selected, the movement is executed by allowing the joint angles to change from their current state to those of the target posture.

This theory has been described in considerable detail, and a working computer simulation has been developed for reaching. The model produces an impressive array of effects that humans show in reaching, including how we deal with the sudden introduction of losing joint motility (as with a cast), how movements change when we are required to move very quickly, the manner in which reaching movements can vary from trial to trial, the types of reaching errors people typically make, and so on.

You can see that this theory combines elements from different approaches described above. Like the mass spring theory, it proposes that only the endpoint of the movement is selected, and the trajectory develops naturally as the joint angles go from the current posture to the target posture. Like the efficiency theories, it assumes that the movement is selected by using a criterion (in this case, two: accuracy and energy cost) to select among candidate movements. Models such as this one that combine several strategies for solving the degrees of freedom problem may prove the most effective.

Stand-on-One-Foot Questions

    1. *What are the three main approaches to solving the degrees of freedom problem?*

    2. *Which criteria of efficiency have been proposed for efficiency theories?*

    3. *Is it possible to move against a synergy?*

Questions Requiring Two Feet

    4. *What is the heart of the degrees of freedom problem, and is it always a problem?*

    5. *The mass spring theory proposes that trajectories aren't planned. Wouldn't that pose a problem when there is an obstacle between your hand and the thing you want to reach? How do you avoid bumping into the obstacle if you don't plan the trajectory?*

HOW ARE MOVEMENTS SEQUENCED?

> ➤ *Preview* The first theory of movement sequencing proposed that movements are chained together, with proprioception providing the link between successive movements. In the late 1950s that idea was replaced by the motor program idea, which argues for a representation of movement sequences that can be executed without perceptual feedback. The latest evidence supports the program idea, although in a form modified from the original proposal. Some evidence shows that programs have movements organized in hierarchies.

The previous section discussed simple movements such as reaching, but often our movements are more complex. You don't simply reach for a cup of coffee: you reach for it, grasp it, bring it to your mouth, tip the cup, swallow the coffee, replace the cup, and release the handle. These parts of the movement must be executed in the correct sequence or you'll end up with coffee in your lap. Movements are planned several components at a time. How are complex sequences of motor behavior generated?

Response Chaining

An old idea, going back to William James (1890), is that the different movements in a sequence might be likened to links in a chain. Proprioceptive feedback about limb position from special receptors in the joints, skin, and muscles provides the bond between the links. That is the heart of the **response**

$$M_1 \rightarrow P_1 \rightarrow M_2 \rightarrow P_2 \rightarrow M_3 \rightarrow P_3 \rightarrow M_4 \rightarrow P_4 \ldots$$

Figure 8.6. *Representation of a response chain. M stands for a movement, P for a proprioceptive feeling resulting from having made a movement. The subscript stands for the number in the response chain. Note that a movement naturally leads to a proprioceptive feeling of having done the movement. The response chaining theory proposes that a particular proprioceptive feeling is associated with the next movement in the sequence.*

chaining theory. A simple model of such a chain is represented in Figure 8.6, in which *M* stands for a movement, *P* stands for the proprioceptive feeling of having executed a movement, and the subscripts refer to particular movements in the sequence. The first movement leads to the proprioceptive feeling of having made the first movement. That feeling is the cue to initiate the second movement, which generates the proprioceptive feeling of having made the second movement, and so on.

In a classic paper on the complexity of behavior sequences, Karl Lashley (1951) argued against this theory. One of his arguments concerned timing. It takes time for proprioceptive feedback to get from the fingers (or wherever the movement occurs) to the brain so that it can serve as a signal that the next movement should be executed. Such an arrangement seems to preclude a rapid series of movements. Lashley argued that skilled pianists and typists produce fast bursts of key presses in which the time between keystrokes is so short (it can be considerably less than 100 ms) that there simply isn't time for the proprioceptive feedback to reach the brain from the muscles of the fingers.

In the 1960s, other studies showed that proprioception was not necessary to the performance of motor sequences. Edward Taub (1976; Taub & Berman, 1968; Taub, Perrella, & Barro, 1973) cut the dorsal roots of the spinal cord that would normally provide proprioceptive feedback from monkeys limbs. Ordinarily the monkey would not use the numb limb, but if forced to do so (for example, if the other arm was bound) the monkey could learn to use it effectively for climbing, eating, and so on. Humans too can execute sequences of movements without proprioceptive feedback (Forget & Lamarre, 1987; Nougier et al., 1996).

Motor Program Theories

Steven Keele (1981; Keele & Posner, 1968) offered an alternative to the response chain. He proposed that complex motor control may be directed by a **motor program**, which can be likened to a computer program in that it has a list of motor commands to be executed in order. The motor program has had slightly different definitions at different times, but the key concept has three features.

1. A program contains a full set of commands for movement.

2. These commands can be executed without the need for perceptual feedback.

3. The commands are abstract, meaning that they can be applied to more than one set of muscles.

The concept is general enough that a number of different theories could be described as motor program theories. Still, the three principles listed above are specific enough to be tested, and the evidence generally supports these principles.

The idea that a motor program contains a list of commands is supported by data showing that the time it takes to initiate a series of movements depends on the number of movements in the series. Franklin Henry and Donald Rogers (1960) were the first to describe this effect. In some cases they had participants hold down a telegraph key, then release it. In other cases participants were to release the telegraph key, then grab a tennis ball. In other cases, a third movement was tacked on; participants knew in advance what the required movement sequence was, and a tone indicated when they should start the sequence. Henry and Rogers observed that the time to release the telegraph key increased with the complexity of the movement sequence. Similar effects have been observed in other motor tasks, such as typing (Sternberg et al., 1978) and speech (Klapp, Anderson, & Berrian, 1973). Why should the number of movement components to be made *later* affect how quickly a person makes the first movement? It appears that we don't plan a movement, execute it, plan the next movement, execute it, and so on. Rather, we plan a sequence of movements all at once.

The second feature of the motor program is that perceptual feedback is not needed for its execution. As described above, experiments by Taub and his colleagues showed convincingly that monkeys can still produce a number of actions (walking, climbing, reaching) even if they lack proprioception. Studies of humans show that they are less accurate than monkeys when deprived of proprioception, but they are nevertheless able to make movements. Although the gross features of motor programs are probably executable without perceptual feedback, feedback seems to be quite important for ongoing movements. In a later section of this chapter, we'll discuss how perceptual feedback is used, but for the moment, suffice it to say that it's probably true that motor programs can be executed without feedback. It's also true that programs seem to use feedback to fine-tune the movements.

The third feature of the motor program is that it can be applied to different muscle groups. Suppose I asked you to write a phrase with your dominant hand, and then to write the same phrase with your nondominant hand or with a pen attached to your foot. Your writing would be sloppier when you wrote in these unfamiliar ways, but the handwriting would still look like yours, not someone else's. Figure 8.7 gives a demonstration of this phenomenon, first

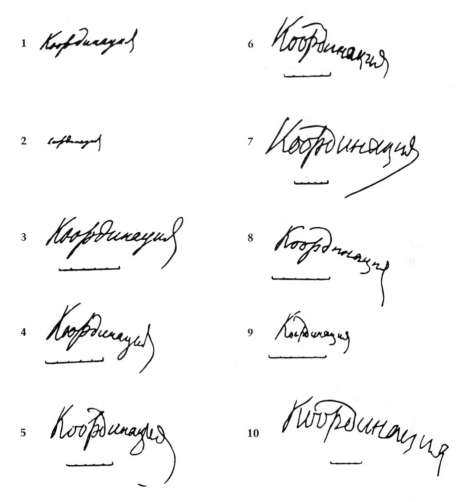

Figure 8.7. *You can try this experiment yourself. This example in Russian shows handwriting produced when a pen is held by different effectors. In each case the signature retains the same overall shape. The signature was written with the pen held normally (1, 2), with the hand moving as a unit (3), with the pen attached near the wrist (4), with the pen attached near the elbow (5), with the pen attached to the shoulder (6), with the pen attached to the right shoe (7), with the pen held in the teeth (8), with the pen held by the left hand (9), and with the pen attached to the left shoe (10). The size of the writing has been scaled to fit the figure; the scale for each trial shows centimeters. From "Motor Programs: Concepts and Issues," by S. W. Keele, A. Cohen, and R. Ivry, 1990, in* Attention and Performance 13: Motor Representation and Control, *M. Jeannerod, Ed., Hillsdale, NJ: Erlbaum, p. 89. They got the figure from Bernstein, N. A. (1947). [On the formation of movement]. Published in Russian by State Medical Literature Publisher (Medgiz).*

shown by Bernstein (1947, reprinted in Keele, Cohen, & Ivry, 1990; see also Castiello & Stelmach, 1993; Wing, 2000). Two things are clear from the figure. The overall shape of the writing is roughly similar, but the writing does differ in legibility. Indeed, more detailed analysis shows that there are important differences in the timing and fluency of the strokes (Wright, 1990). These differences are understandable, given the likely differences in the coordination of the limbs, which are used for quite different tasks day to day.

We have discussed three sources of data consistent with an abstract motor program. Programs contain sets of commands for motor movements; these commands can be executed without perceptual feedback; and these commands can be applied to different effectors. The data we have reviewed tell us that the program idea seems to be at least partly right; programs can be executed without perceptual feedback and can be applied to different effectors, although the resulting movements are not as skilled under these circumstances.

Hierarchical Control in Motor Programs

There is compelling evidence that motor sequences are organized hierarchically. A hierarchy is simply a tree diagram (see Figure 8.8). The circles in the diagram are called nodes, and the lines connecting the nodes are called links, just as in the network memory models described in chapter 7.

In most hierarchical sequencing schemes, **movement nodes** are proposed to control the muscles that make movement possible. The nodes above them in the tree are **control nodes** that tell the movement nodes what to do. Thus in Figure 8.8, node 4 would make the right finger flex, then the left index finger.

David Rosenbaum, Sandra Kenny, and Marcia Derr (1983) tested this idea by having participants practice some sequences of key presses such as *IiIiMmMm*, where *I* and *i* refer to the index fingers of the right and left hands,

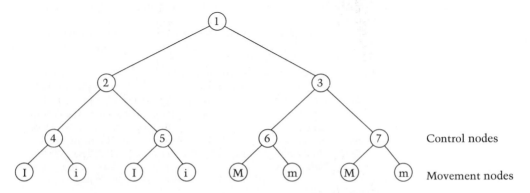

Figure 8.8. *Hypothetical hierarchy that could control movement. The movement nodes control muscles that move fingers. I = index finger right hand; i = index finger left hand; M = middle finger right hand, m = middle finger left hand. The control nodes tell the movement nodes what to do.*

respectively, and *M* and *m* refer to the middle fingers of the right and left hands. Participants were asked to produce these responses as quickly as possible. The experimenters were mainly interested in the time between key presses. They started with the simple assumption that nodes on the tree must be traversed to execute a response. For example, the first two key presses (*Ii*) have just one node between them (node 4). But the next key press (*I*) requires traversing three nodes (4, 2, and 5). Making the further assumption that it takes time to traverse nodes, the experimenters could make predictions about the time between key presses. The researchers found that the number of nodes traversed in the hierarchy was an extremely good predictor of the time between key presses, as shown in Figure 8.9.

Other evidence supports the idea of levels of a hierarchy, with lower levels controlling motor output and higher levels supporting more abstract representations of desired output. Donald MacKay and Robert Bowman (1969) tested this idea in a clever way with English/German bilingual participants in a speech production task. Participants practiced 12 repetitions of a sentence they would not be familiar with, such as "I have rearranged this bed fourteen times in one morning." Participants said the sentence twelve times, and they got faster with practice, as shown in Table 8.1. After a short break, participants switched languages and had to say another sentence as quickly as possible. This new sentence was either an unrelated transfer sentence or a translation of the sentence they had just practiced. Participants were faster in saying the transfer sentence if it was a translation of the training sentence. (Ignore the data on scrambled sentences for the moment.)

MacKay and Bowman interpreted the results as revealing at least two levels of control of speech production. The bottom level controls the articulators (tongue, lips) that pronounce the words. A higher, more abstract level controls the words that are to be said. (There may well be intermediate levels that control syllables, but we will not discuss them here.) The representation is abstract

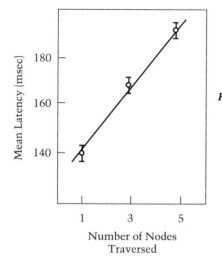

Figure 8.9. *Results from Rosenbaum, Kenny, and Derr (1983) supporting the hypothesis that movements are planned hierarchically in a key pressing task. The graph shows that the time between key presses depends on the number of nodes that must be traversed for the next key press (assuming that they are organized in a hierarchy). From "Hierarchical Control of Rapid Movement Sequences," by D. A. Rosenbaum, S. B. Kenny, and M. A. Derr, 1983, Journal of Experimental Psychology: Human Perception and Performance, 9, Fig. 3, p. 93.*

Table 8.1.   *Results from MacKay and Bowman's (1969) study showing good transfer in speaking time (in s) between languages for practiced sentences*

Material	First Four Training	Last Four Training	Transfer—New	Transfer— Translation
Normal sentences	2.33	2.03	2.44	2.30
Scrambled sentences	2.90	2.38	2.79	2.83

in that it doesn't necessarily represent a specific word but may represent a concept associated with a word.

Participants improved in saying "I have rearranged this bed fourteen times in one morning" during training (from 2.33 to 2.03 s). The experimenters argued that all of the improvement came from the more abstract level, in sequencing abstract representations of words into a sentence. They argued that there was little room for improvement in the lower level because we have so much practice in using our articulators that they already move as effectively as they can. When asked to switch into the other language, the participants were still able to use that abstract representation; they could employ a different set of rules to translate these abstract representations into commands to the articulators.

If the words were not organized into sentences but were instead scrambled ("Fourteen have times morning I one in this rearranged bed"), no transfer was observed. Participants practiced the same scrambled sentence, but there was no transfer into the other language, presumably because the random words could not easily be organized into a hierarchical structure.

This study provides further evidence that programs can be abstract and not only transfer from one effector to another (as handwriting transfers from one hand to another) but can be implemented into the same effectors (the vocal apparatus) in different ways.

There appears to be good evidence for motor programs that are abstract in that they can be applied to different effectors. There is also evidence that more complex programs take increasing time to generate. Further, it appears that motor programs are represented as multilevel hierarchies, with the lower levels controlling muscle movement and the higher levels representing more abstract aspects of the desired movement.

Stand-on-One-Foot Summary Questions

    6. *What are the arguments against the response chaining hypothesis?*

    7. *What are the key features of a motor program?*

    8. *What evidence is there that motor programs are organized hierarchically?*

> 9. *Initially it was thought that motor programs don't need feedback. Now we see that that was an overstatement. What negative consequences could you see for programs not using perceptual feedback?*
>
> 10. *One of the advantages of a hierarchical representation of a motor program is generalization, the ability to apply old knowledge to a new situation. Can you see why a hierarchical representation is especially well suited to generalization (and chaining theories were not)?*

How Is Perceptual Information Integrated into Ongoing Movements?

People sometimes think of perceptual and motor functions as separate, but that is not really accurate. Perception obviously influences motor activity. We gather perceptual information before making an action, as when we judge the distance of an object to determine whether we can reach it, and during an action, as when we use visual feedback in driving a car. In less obvious ways, movement also aids perception. Moving our bodies allows our sense organs to be transported to different places, and moving our eyes and head allows us to maintain a stable image of a moving object on the retina. In this section, we will focus on how perceptual information informs the motor system.

Vision

In chapter 2, we discussed the evidence that there are two visual systems, the "what" system and the "how" system. The "what" system is responsible for object recognition and for determining object location, and the "how" system is responsible for determining how objects can be manipulated by the motor system. In this section, we'll discuss data that reveal how visual information is used by the motor system. Most of these data were collected before the what/how distinction was proposed, so they were not interpreted within that framework. Still, today we would guess that the effects discussed in this section are relevant to the "how" system.

One question of long-standing interest to researchers is the frequency with which visual information is needed. Is a reaching movement completely planned before it is initiated so that it doesn't need any visual feedback along the way, or is it only partially planned so that ongoing visual feedback is required in order to complete the movement accurately?

In one experiment Howard Zelaznik and his colleagues (1983) measured the accuracy of participants moving a stylus to a target. The researchers varied whether lights were on or off during the movement and how quickly the movement was to be made. If there is no opportunity to collect perceptual feedback during a movement, it makes no difference whether the lights are on or off. How slow does a movement have to be before having the lights on makes a difference? Figure 8.10 shows that the speed of the movement is irrelevant to accuracy when the lights are off because no perceptual feedback is available. For the fastest movements, having the lights on doesn't help (compared to the no-lights control group), but when movements take 150 ms or longer, perceptual feedback makes them more accurate.

The researchers also tried the experiment another way. They let the participant start the movement but then turned off the lights. At what point in the movement is it irrelevant if the reachers turn out the lights? How close to the target does the participant have to be before turning out the lights has no effect on the movement? The answer using this method was quite close to the other estimate; if the movement was 135 ms (or less) from completion, perceptual feedback didn't matter. (See also Carlton, 1981a, 1981b; Elliott & Allard, 1985; Spijkers & Lochner, 1994.)

The question of how visual feedback is used has also been examined by asking participants to intercept a moving target, typically by catching a ball. In these experiments, visual information is sometimes available and sometimes

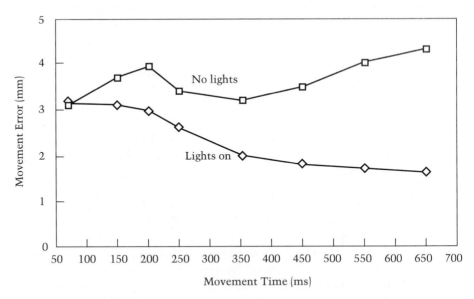

Figure 8.10. *Graph showing the results of Zelaznik et al. (1983). Participants who have vision available while making a simple movement can make use of it even when the movement is as fast as 150 ms, and the advantage of having vision available increases as the movement may be made more slowly. There is no advantage for vision at the fastest movement time, which is 70 ms. Adapted from "Rapid Visual Feedback Processing in Single-Aiming Movements," by H. N. Zelaznik, B. Hawkins, and L. Kisselburgh, 1983,* Journal of Motor Behavior, 15, *Fig. 2, p. 229.*

unavailable and is meant to mimic real-life situations such as driving through fog or attempting to catch a baseball that is "lost in the lights." The basic finding from such studies is that constant visual information is not needed; periodic visual information can be substituted with little cost to performance (see Elliott, Calvert, Jaeger, & Jones, 1990; Elliott, Zuberec, & Milgram, 1994; Lyons, Fontaine, & Elliott, 1997; and van der Kamp, Savelsbergh, & Smeets, 1997, for this and related work).

For example, Digby Elliott and his colleagues (1994) asked participants to catch tennis balls shot from a ball machine at a distance of 8 to 12 meters. The participants wore liquid-crystal spectacles that could either be transparent or opaque, controlled moment to moment by a computer. The ball traveled about 10 meters per second, so the total time that the ball could be visible was about 800–1,200 ms. Across four experiments using a variety of conditions, the experimenters found that catching was reasonably successful so long as participants were able to see the ball for a 20-ms snapshot that came at least every 80 ms. When vision was occluded for longer than 80 ms, performance deteriorated rapidly. This variable—the frequency with which participants could see a visual snapshot—seemed to be the most important in predicting performance. The experimenters also manipulated how long the snapshot was and the percentage of time that participants could see the ball. Neither of these factors influenced performance very much. The results of one of their experiments appears in Figure 8.11. Performance was good in all cases, considering that participants were seeing just 10–30% of the ball's trajectory, but seemed to be worst when the "off" time was longer than 80 ms; the "on" time did not matter much. This pattern of results may mean that the visual system is able to integrate successive views of a stimulus, but if the time between views is too long, the integration process is unsuccessful.

It is clear, then, that visual information is used to refine ongoing movements and thus to improve accuracy, but vision is not sampled continuously. The visual system updates the ongoing motor plan periodically, as evidenced by the fact that vision can be interrupted with little cost to motor performance.

Proprioception

Although proprioception is very important to many aspects of motor behavior, it has been studied less than other types of perceptual information, partly because it is rather difficult to manipulate. Unlike the case for vision or hearing, in which the experimenter can create stimuli for the participant, proprioceptive inputs are difficult to control.

Proprioception is driven by receptors in the muscles and skin and perhaps the joints. There are two types of receptors in the muscles: **muscle spindles** in the fleshy part of the muscles are most active when the muscle is stretched, and **golgi tendon organs** located where muscles and tendons are joined are most active when the muscle contracts. **Cutaneous receptors** are located in and under the skin, and some of these (often called mechanoreceptors) respond when the skin is displaced by pressure. Pressure is often caused by motor

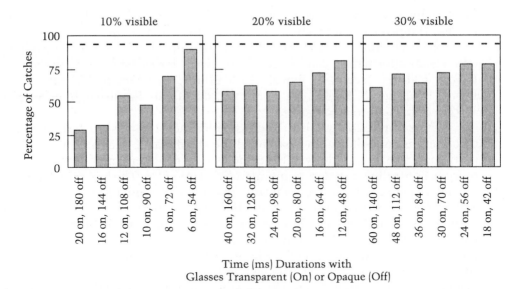

Figure 8.11. *Results from Eliott et al.'s (1994) experiment on the use of visual information in catching. Each graph shows the percentage of catches on the y axis. The dotted line shows performance when participants have full vision. Each graph shows performance with a different percentage of time when the ball is visible. The x axis shows the amount of time the glasses were transparent (on) and opaque (off). The glasses alternated on and off during each trial. Notice that there is not a big difference between seeing the ball 10, 20, or 30% of the time. There is also not a big effect of how long the glasses were transparent. What really matters is how long they were opaque, that is, the frequency with which participants could get a glimpse (however brief) of the ball. Adapted from "The Effects of Periodic Visual Occlusion on Ball Catching," by D. Elliott, S. Zuberec, and P. Milgram, 1994,* Journal of Motor Behavior, 26, *Fig. 8, p. 120.*

movements, as when one picks up an object. To appreciate the importance of cutaneous receptors, imagine picking up a glass and being unable to tell how much pressure your grip was exerting. It would be hard to know whether you were about to crush the glass or it was going to slip through your fingers. Joint receptors are a type of neuron located in joints. It was initially thought that many of these receptors fired preferentially when a joint was set to a particular angle (Skoglund, 1956), but later experiments cast doubt on this interpretation; it appears that joint receptors may fire mostly in response to extreme joint angles (Clark & Burgess, 1975).

Some important information has come from neurological patients who experience a selective loss of proprioception. One such patient, known by his first name, Ian, has been described by Cole (1995; see also Cole & Paillard, 1995 for a description of another patient with a similar problem). Ian is unusual because he has lost proprioception from the neck down. It is not rare to lose feeling in one arm or leg, but it is quite rare to lose feeling throughout the body. Ian's problem appears to have been caused by a virus that led his body's defense system to attack the nerve cells that carry proprioceptive information.

By observing the difficulties Ian has, we can deduce some of the likely functions of proprioception in motor control.

Most striking is the extent to which the loss of proprioception devastated Ian's ability to move. After Ian lost proprioception, he had no control over his body. Trying to move was, in fact, dangerous as his limbs flailed uncontrollably. Nor could Ian maintain a posture. For example, if a nurse tried to seat him in a chair, he would lean sideways and flop to the floor in a disorganized heap.

Ian eventually relearned how to move by replacing his reliance on proprioception with a reliance on vision. This relearning process was far from easy, however. It took one year of practice before Ian could stand. In time, he learned to walk, but his movements would not be mistaken for those of a healthy person. His walking is also easily disrupted. If someone accidentally bumps into him, he will likely fall. To this day, walking requires all of his attention; there seems to have been no development of automaticity despite years of practice.

There are some types of movements for which vision is not a suitable replacement for proprioception, notably, grip strength and fine motor movements. For example, Ian must maintain full concentration when holding an egg because it is hard for him to modulate his grip strength. If he gets distracted, he will likely crush it. Fine motor movements refer to movements (usually of the fingers) that require multiple small adjustments, for example, buttoning buttons or writing with a pen. Vision can't replace proprioception for these small movements because the effectors (your fingers) block your view.

When proprioception from the mouth is lost, visual information cannot substitute. A patient described by Jonathan Cole and Jacques Pailliard (1995) was initially unable to speak and had so much difficulty swallowing that for several months she could eat only pureed foods. She eventually discovered strategies to deal with the problem, but they require ongoing attentional resources. I have observed a similar problem firsthand. My father lost proprioceptive sense in one side of his tongue after an operation, so it is hard for him to keep track of his tongue when he is eating. Dad is usually able to be mindful of the problem, but about once a month he forgets and bites down hard on his tongue; unfortunately, his pain receptors work just fine.

Formal studies verify the anecdotes from such case reports. For example, Jerome Sanes and his colleagues (1985) tested seven patients who had lost proprioception (the term for loss of proprioception is *deafferentation*). These deafferented patients had typically lost feeling in their hands or feet, varying in how far toward the trunk the loss went. The experimenters tested the patients' ability to maintain a position of the wrist and to maintain wrist position when force was applied. These tasks were performed either with or without vision of the wrist.

Patients were able to perform the tasks with vision, but without vision they could not maintain posture normally. Figure 8.12 shows the performance of the patients and one control participant when they were asked to maintain the position of the wrist joint. When visual feedback was removed, the wrists of the patients rapidly drifted in random directions.

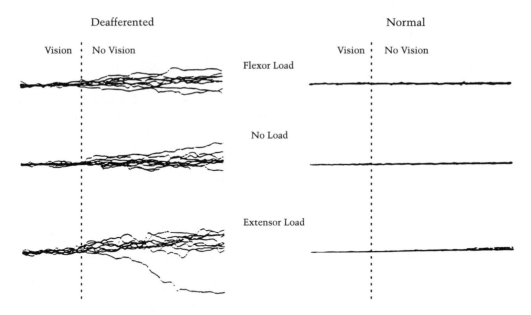

Figure 8.12. *Tracings showing the position of the hand in a deafferented patient (left) and a normal control participant (right). Each line represents hand position on one trial. In the top and bottom tracing there was a load (meaning pressure in one direction or the other); the middle tracing shows no load. Notice that for the control participant, hand position is steady. For the patient, hand position is fairly steady at the left part of each tracing when vision is available. Once vision is not available, the patient cannot maintain a steady hand position, with or without a load. From "Motor Control in Humans with Large-Fiber Sensory Neuropathy," by J. N. Sanes, K.-H. Mauritz, M. C. Dalakas, and E. V. Evarts, 1985,* Human Neurobiology, 4, *Fig. 1, p. 105.*

The patients showed similar deficits in making movements. With visual feedback, their movements were quite accurate. Without the feedback, their movements had abnormal trajectories and endpoints. (See also Cole & Paillard, 1995; Fleury et al., 1995; Ghez, Gordon, Ghilardi, & Sainburg, 1995.)

Exactly what is it that proprioception contributes to movement? It is likely that proprioception plays more than one role, but at least one function may be to contribute to **egocentric spatial representation**, in which we locate objects in relation to our own bodies. There is no set of absolute coordinates by which we can locate objects (a point made in chapter 2). We can locate objects in space only relative to other objects. Consider Figure 8.13, and imagine that it represents a label on a picture on a wall. You could say that the label is in the upper right corner of the wall. You could also say that the label is in the lower left corner of the picture. Which is correct? Obviously, both descriptions are correct, and neither is more correct than the other. This example makes it clear that if we want to locate an object in space, we must locate it relative to another object—the picture or the wall, in the example.

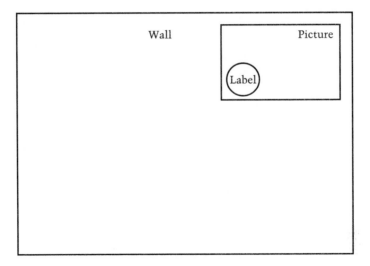

Figure 8.13.   *Illustration of the arbitrariness of the descriptions of locations in space. The label could be described as on the lower left corner of the picture or in the upper right corner of the wall. Either the picture or the wall can serve as the reference frame.*

In contrast to an egocentric representation, an **allocentric spatial representation** is one in which objects are located relative to other objects. An example of each type of representation is shown in Figure 8.14. In the left part of the figure, the white square is located relative to the table; the table has an imaginary grid to show that the square could be located in terms of x and y coordinates defined relative to the table. The right part of the figure shows an egocentric spatial representation of the square, with a location coded relative to the observer's shoulder. The direction of the object is coded by the angle that the arrow subtends relative to the shoulder, and the distance is coded by the length of the arrow.

You need to locate objects relative to part of your body in order to make a movement; in other words, you need to know where an object is relative to *you*, not relative to a table. If you want to know whether you can reach an object, you need to know how far it is from your shoulder. And if you decide that you can reach the object, you need to know where the object is relative to your hand. A great deal of evidence shows that egocentric representations are used to support movement. Such representations can be centered on different parts of the body, including the head (Bard, Fleury, & Paillard, 1990; Roll, Bard, & Paillard, 1986), the shoulder (Caminiti, Johnson, & Urbano, 1991; Graziano, Yap, & Gross, 1994), and the trunk (Yardley, 1990).

So what does egocentric space have to do with proprioception? If the locations of objects are to be coded relative to your body, you need to know where

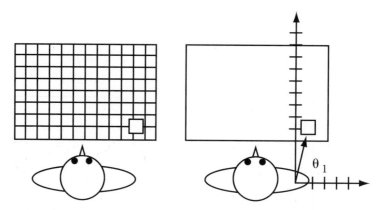

Figure 8.14. *Different ways of representing information in space. At left, the white square is located relative to the surface of the table. Hence the table is shown as having a grid, like graph paper, and the square can be localized relative to the grid marks in an allocentric representation. At right, the square is located relative to the observer's shoulder. The length of the arrow shows how far it is from the shoulder, and the angle of the arrow relative to an axis defined by both shoulders shows the direction of the object. This is an egocentric representation. From "The Neural Basis of Motor Skill Learning," by D. B. Willingham, 1999,* Current Directions in Psychological Science, 8, *Fig. 1, p. 179.*

your body parts are. For neurologically intact participants, that knowledge is acquired through proprioception. What happens if proprioceptive input is unavailable, as it was for Ian? Ian has no egocentric space, so if he tries to initiate a reaching movement, the muscles can flex, but the target is not specified and his hand flails.

Jean Blouin and his colleagues (1993) confirmed this conjecture by having participants point toward targets made with light-emitting diodes (LEDs). The participants had LEDs attached to their index fingers. Some movements were made when the participants could see a highly structured visual background (a crowded experimental room) behind the target; the experimenters argued that participants would likely code the target in allocentric space. Other movements were made with the lights off, so the structured background was not visible; participants would likely code the targets in egocentric space in this condition.

Whether or not the background was visible did not influence pointing accuracy for normal participants. A deafferented patient, however, showed much better pointing accuracy when the background was visible, as shown in Figure 8.15. Control participants can use either an egocentric or allocentric reference frame to point. The deafferented patient could work with the allocentric frame, but the lack of proprioception means he could not use an egocentric frame to locate the objects relative to his body. Other studies using

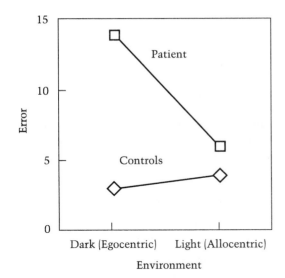

Figure 8.15. *Results from Blouin et al. (1993) showing that the pointing accuracy of a deafferented patient is affected by whether egocentric or allocentric coordinates are used to locate a target, whereas the accuracy of control participants is not. Adapted from "Reference Systems for Coding Spatial Information in Normal Subjects and a Deafferented Patient," by J. Blouin, C. Bard, N. Teasdale, J. Paillard, M. Fleury, R. Forget, and Y. Lamarre, 1993, Experimental Brain Research, 93, Fig. 2B.*

more complex measurement techniques with neurologically intact participants agree with these data (see Carrozzo, Stratta, McIntyre, Lacquaniti, 2002; McIntyre, Stratta, & Lacquaniti, 1998).

Both proprioception and vision, then, are important for motor control (for sighted people). Visual information appears to be sampled fairly frequently—perhaps as often as every 150 ms—and is used to update and refine the ongoing movement. Proprioceptive information appears to be crucial for normal movement. In order to move effectively, we must know where our effectors are, and proprioception seems to be the chief source of that information. Visual information can substitute for proprioception, but at a relatively high cost of attention; even if the substitution is practiced, it never gets easier.

Stand-on-One-Foot Questions

11. *How would you summarize the ways vision is used in ongoing motor movements?*

12. *What are the two frames of reference that were discussed, and how do they relate to proprioception?*

Questions Requiring Two Feet

13. *Have you ever had a loss of proprioception?*

14. *What happens to egocentric representations as you move around?*

How Are Motor Skills Learned?

Motor control refers to planning and executing movements. **Motor skill learning** refers to increasing accuracy of those movements with practice. Acts can become more accurate spatially or temporally. Spatial accuracy means moving the effectors to the correct positions in space, as when a diver positions his body correctly for a twist. Temporal accuracy means moving the effectors at the right time and with the right speed, as when a batter learns to time his swing for a change-up pitch.

Three Properties of Motor Skill Learning

Three seemingly obvious properties of motor skill are more subtle than they seem at first. Other properties of skill learning are not at all obvious. Theories of motor skill learning attempt to tie all these properties together.

Perhaps the prototypical example of motor skill acquisition is learning to ride a bicycle. If you endured this rite of childhood you can well appreciate three properties of motor skill learning. First, motor skills generalize. Once you have learned to ride a bicycle, you can ride any bicycle, not just the one on which you trained. The properties of the bicycle may be different—the wheel size, the gear ratios—but your skill will transfer to the new machine. You can also ride in new environments, not just the one you trained in. Second, retention of motor skills is quite good. The expression "Once you learn how to ride a bicycle, you never forget" has been tested and proved true by more than one creaky forty-something who hasn't been on a bicycle in over twenty years. Third, motor skills become automatic. Early in training motor skills demand attention, but with practice attention demands drop significantly. Let's look at each of these principles more closely.

GENERALIZATION.   Earlier in this chapter we noted that although people are trained to write on a horizontal surface using small movements of the dominant hand, writing skill generalizes readily, if imperfectly, to other muscle groups (such the entire arm), to other effectors (such as the nondominant hand), and with spatial transformations (as when you write on a vertical surface such as a blackboard). Similarly, once you have learned to throw a baseball, the skill will transfer to new situations: you can throw different distances, you can throw a tennis ball or softball, and so on.

Although it is true that many skills are generalizable, there are surprising exceptions to this rule. Daniel Lordahl and James Archer (1958) used a laboratory device called the pursuit rotor (described in chapter 7). In this task, the participant must try to keep the tip of a stylus in contact with a target on a rotating platter. The dependent measure is the amount of time during a trial the stylus is on the target. Participants practiced with the platter turning at either 40, 60, or 80 rotations per minute (rpm). At transfer to the 60 rpm version, participants who had trained at 40 or at 80 rpm performed much worse than those who had trained at 60 rpm (for whom transfer involved no change, obviously). The 40 rpm group scores were 14% those of the 60 rpm group, and the 80 rpm group scores were 31% of the 60 rpm group.

Why was transfer so poor? A long-held idea is that transfer will be good to the extent that the new task is similar to the old task (Thorndike & Woodworth, 1901; see also Holding, 1976). But in the experiment just described, adjusting the speed of the platter doesn't seem like a big change; aren't the tasks still very similar?

It may be that transfer depends not just on overall similarity, but on the representation used in the skill. If the experimenters change something that is irrelevant to the skill, good transfer will be observed; if they change something that is part of the representation of the skill, transfer will be poor (Willingham, 1997; 1998). The pursuit rotor data may indicate that timing is a crucial part of what is learned in this skill, so when the timing is changed, performance suffers. Presumably, the experimenters could change other aspects of the task that are not part of the representation, such as the size of the target, with little impact on the skill.

LONG-TERM RETENTION.   Remarkable retention has been reported for some motor skills. For example, Edwin Fleishman and James Parker (1962) trained participants on a complex control task meant to simulate an attack run in an airplane guided by radar. Participants saw a randomly drifting target on an oscilloscope and were to maintain contact with it by manipulating stick and rudder controls. Training took place in 17 sessions across 6 weeks, each session comprising 21 one-minute trials. Performance during training is shown in the left side of Figure 8.16. Participants were retested after delays of 9, 12, or 24 months. As shown in the right side of the figure, retention of this skill was complete.

In other experiments retention is not complete but is still impressive. Eva Neumann and Robert Ammons (1957) used a quite different skill involving 16 switches arranged in two concentric circles of 8 switches. Participants were to turn a switch in the inner circle and then turn the correct switch in the outer circle; a buzzer sounded if the choice was correct. Participants were trained for 63 trials, with 8 attempts in each. Participants were retested between 1 minute and 1 year later. Figure 8.17 shows that there is forgetting of this perceptual–motor skill; participants seem to have forgotten everything after a year. Yet they improve somewhat faster in the retraining session, so we can see that some memory was preserved. Although the researchers called this a perceptual–motor skill, the task doesn't seem very perceptual or very motoric. We might suspect that most of what participants learned was the mapping between the inner and outer circles of switches. It may be that this skill was especially susceptible to forgetting because it had a heavy declarative memory component.

These data are impressive, especially when we consider the more or less perfect retention of a skill after 2 years with no intervening practice in Fleishman and Parker's study. Nevertheless, we must note a conceptual problem.

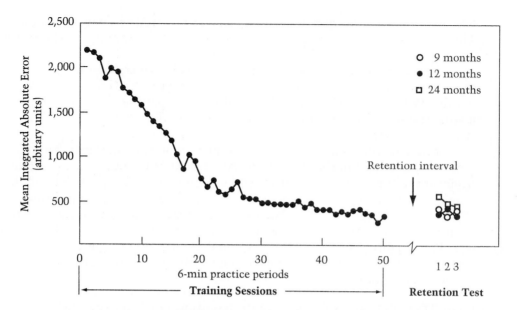

Figure 8.16. *Results from Fleishman and Parker (1962). Retention is nearly perfect on this task, despite no practice for 2 years. From* Motor Control and Learning: A Behavioral Emphasis, *by R. A. Schmidt and T. D. Lee, 1999, Champaign, IL: Human Kinetics Press, Fig. 14.3, p. 392. Adapted from "Factors in the Retention and Relearning of Complex Psychomotor Performance and Related Skills," by E. A. Fleishman and J. F. Parker, 1962,* Journal of Experimental Psychology, 64.

We expect that memory will improve if we practice more; perhaps a skill is retained well if it is practiced a lot. The problem is that there is no way to compare the amount of practice across skills, or to compare practice of motor skill with verbal memory. Practice in skill experiments is usually defined by the number of trials, but the definition of a trial is arbitrary.

AUTOMATICITY.   Perhaps the most notable feature of motor skill learning is the development of automaticity. As the skill is practiced, the attentional demands of the task are reduced, as is the feeling to the participant that the movements must be consciously directed. For example, when you learned to drive, you likely attended to and consciously directed how hard to press the accelerator and how far to turn the steering wheel. With practice, these components of driving became automatic; you didn't need to attend to them. Unlike the two previous principles, this obvious principle actually seems to hold up rather well under laboratory scrutiny. You may recall from chapter 3 that for automaticity to develop, the conditions of training remain consistent. So long as that condition is met, it does seem that automaticity is a consistent feature of well-trained skills (see Wulf & Prinz, 2001).

There is, nevertheless, a feature to motor skill learning that you might not expect. For some skills, awareness seems to be optional from the start of

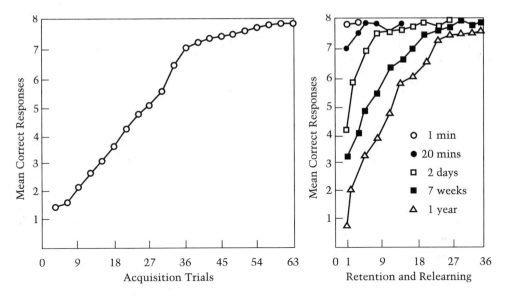

Figure 8.17. *Results from Neumann and Ammons (1957). Retention is cut in half 2 days after training and has apparently disappeared after 1 year. But note that the skill is relearned much more quickly in the second training session. From R. A. Schmidt and T. D. Lee, 1999, Fig. 14.4, p. 393. Adapted from "Acquisition and Long-Term Retention of a Simple Serial Perceptual–Motor Skill," by E. Neumann and R. B. Ammons, 1957, Journal of Experimental Psychology, 53.*

training. In chapter 5 we drew a distinction between procedural and declarative memory. Procedural memory is "knowing how" memory—that is, it can guide actions—and we do not have access to its contents. Some motor skills can be acquired wholly procedurally, meaning that the participant learns but is never aware of having learned anything.

An example is a serial response time task in which the participant sits before a computer screen marked with four locations (Nissen & Bullemer, 1987). A stimulus appears in one of the four locations, and the participant must respond by pushing one of four buttons as quickly as possible. The stimulus disappears, and a new stimulus appears almost immediately. Unbeknownst to the participant, the stimuli actually appear in a repeating sequence. Because the sequence is fairly long (12 stimuli in most studies) the participant may think that the stimuli are appearing randomly.

The dependent measure in this task is response time to the stimuli. The consistent finding is that response time gets faster with more training on the sequence. An important result is that toward the end of the experiment the stimuli appear randomly, and response times slow. This slowing indicates that participants are not getting faster simply because they are becoming more motivated or gaining skill at button pushing. Rather, we know that the speed increase is due to sequence learning because when the sequence is no longer present, the response times slow.

Although the response time data show clearly that participants learn the sequence, they have no declarative knowledge of the sequence. If you ask them to produce the sequence, they cannot do it. Indeed, if you simply ask them whether or not they think the stimuli were sequenced, they have no idea. Many experiments using the serial response time task have been conducted (see Stadler & Frensch, 1998) showing fairly consistent results.

Other motor skill tasks have been devised that are learned outside of awareness as the serial response time task is (see Willingham, 1998 for a discussion). For other motor skills you may be aware of learning them, but you may be unaware of the critical knowledge that supports learning. For example, do you really have conscious access to the knowledge that allows you to ride a bicycle? Could you describe in detail to a novice rider how you do it? It may be that you know that you can ride a bicycle (because you have seen yourself doing it) but you cannot access the representations that allow you to do it.

Two Approaches to Motor Skill Learning

Two approaches to motor skill learning, each typified by a particular theory, emphasize different phenomena. This type of learning is so complex and multifaceted that it is difficult for a single theory to capture all of its aspects.

GENERALIZED MOTOR PROGRAM.   One approach capitalizes on the idea of a motor program, which is a representation of a set of commands to make a movement, as discussed earlier in the chapter. A **generalized motor program** can produce a whole class of movements. In this type of theory, motor skill learning is a matter of acquiring generalized motor programs. Richard Schmidt (1975) introduced this idea with his schema theory.

By a class of movements, we mean similar movements that might have different endpoints or results with small changes to the program. An example would be a throwing motion: throwing a baseball 20 yards or throwing a basketball 5 yards are acts that require different patterns of muscle activation, but they obviously have much in common. The generalized motor program produces these different movements when different value for program parameters are used.

Suppose I tell you that I have a catapult and I offer to let you play around with it. You take it out to a field, and you begin hurling baseballs with it. The catapult arm is marked from 1 to 10, signifying how far back the arm is pulled. You find that with the catapult arm set to position 1, the baseball goes 10 yards. If you set the arm to position 3, the baseball goes 30 yards; position 8, 80 yards. Now suppose you want to hurl a baseball 50 yards—what's your best guess as to where to place the arm? Position 5, obviously.

The relationship can be described by the function *distance = 10 × arm position*. Since distance is the outcome you're interested in, and arm position is available for you to control, you can produce any desired distance by plugging in the appropriate arm position, once you know the relationship.

Motor skill learning might work in an analogous way, but instead of varying the arm position of a catapult, you vary the muscle force you apply in a throwing motion. You could learn the relationship between muscle force and the distance a ball goes. Naturally, throwing depends on more than just muscle force; it depends on the trajectory your arm takes, how you move your back as well as your arm, and so on. Those complications do not change how the theory could work in principle, but the final program will be more complicated.

The generalized motor program, then, can be thought of as a function that relates some input parameters to a pattern of movements that will produce a desired outcome. A great advantage of the schema theory is that it can account for the generalizability of motor behavior. The schema theory posits that practice leads not just to improvement in a particular skill but also to the development of a generalized motor program. Just as we can learn the relationship between the arm position and the distance a catapult will throw a ball, we can learn how various input parameters of the human body will change the distance a thrown ball will go.

One of the key predictions of schema theory is that your ability to generalize what you've learned should be better if you've had training in a broader variety of situations. To see why, imagine that two groups of people are using identical catapults that have 100 possible arm settings. Each group throws a ball 20 times. One group practices with targets 30 and 35 feet away (see the left panel of Figure 8.18). From the results of that group you can relate distance and arm position with the formula

$$\text{Distance} = \text{Arm position} + 7 \text{ feet}$$

Thus if the next day I asked one of these participants to produce a distance of 50, they would guess that the proper arm position would be 43.

Now suppose another group practices throwing at targets 30 and 90 feet away (see the right panel of Figure 8.18). The relationship between arm position and distance is not what we thought it was. Based only on the observations of arm positions around 30, it looked like the relationship between arm position and distance is more or less linear. When you have observations across a wider range of arm positions, it is clear that the relationship is not linear. It is in fact best described by this equation:

$$\text{Distance} = -0.01 \, (\text{arm position})^3 + 0.924 \, (\text{arm position})^2 - 24.9 \, (\text{arm position}) + 233.7$$

If you've tested only arm positions near 30, you end up with the first formula and you predict that to achieve a distance of 50 you should set the arm position to 43. If you've tested arm positions near 25 and arm positions near 90, you will use the second formula and will predict that to achieve a distance of 50 you should set the arm position to 30 or 31, not to 43. The underlying properties of the systems are identical, but you see the properties of the system much better with training across a broader range of the parameters.

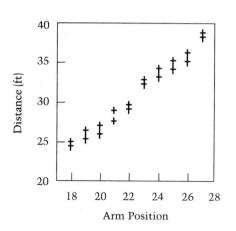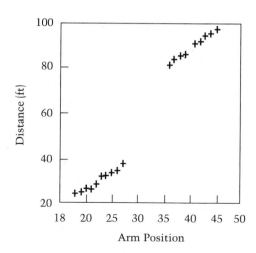

Figure 8.18. *Two hypothetical data sets. On the left, a group uses a catapult to shoot a ball at two targets, 30 and 35 feet away. On the right, a group shoots at targets 30 and 90 feet away. The graph on the left makes it look like the relationship between arm position and distance is a straight line—it's only when you see data from a larger variety of arm positions that you know that that is not true. More variability in the parameter that you set (arm position) makes it more likely that you will end up with an accurate idea of the relationship between the parameter that you set (arm position) and the outcome (distance).*

It is not clear whether the data support this prediction of Schmidt's theory, despite the fact that dozens of studies have addressed the issue (see Newell, 1991, and Shapiro & Schmidt, 1982, for reviews). Some researchers (such as Newell, 1991) claim that the data do not support the theory, whereas others (Schmidt & Bjork, 1992) argue that they do.

MULTIPLE PROCESSES.   When we try to locate the anatomical basis of motor skills, we quickly discover that a great many brain regions contribute to motor skill learning. Recently, researchers have suggested that this multiplicity of areas indicates that motor skill learning may well involve several closely interlinked systems (see Willingham, 1998; Hikosaka, Nakamura, Sakai, & Nakahara, 2002). There is no single process that learns all types of skill; rather, there are several systems that each learn a different aspect of skill.

I suggest that motor skill learning closely follows motor control processes: motor skill is simply the adjustment of motor control processes to work more effectively in particular environments (Willingham, 1998, 1999). The motor control processes that get adjusted are the focus of this chapter: how we decide how to move, how we sequence movements, and how perception contributes to movement (Rosenbaum, 2002). The hypothetical skill-learning processes based on these motor control processes are shown in Table 8.2.

Strategic learning occurs when we select more effective environmental goals. For example, a bowler facing a difficult split may decide to try to make

Table 8.2. ***Processes Proposed to Support Motor Skill in Willingham's (1998) Model***

Process	Function in Motor Control	Mechanism of Improvement in Motor Skill Acquisition	Tennis Example
Strategic	Selects goal of movement in environmental coordinates	Select more effective environmental goals	Hit a lob when opponent rushes the net
Perceptual–motor integration	Selects spatial target or targets for movement that will fulfill environmental goal; represented in egocentric space	Learning a new relationship between environmental and egocentric space because of a change in vision or proprioception, or an incompatible stimulus–response mapping	Use a racquet instead of the hand to hit a ball
Sequencing	Orders spatial targets in the correct sequence	Learning a repeating sequence when the same movement is made repeatedly	Stereotyping the movements for a tennis serve
Dynamic	Translates egocentric spatial targets and a pattern of muscle firing	Learning a new relationship between egocentric targets and the pattern of muscle firing necessary to move the effector to the spatial target	Learning fine coordination with the nonpreferred hand

Adapted from *Current Directions in Psychological Science, 8,* by D. B. Willingham, 1999, "The Neural Basis of Motor Skill Learning," Table 1, p. 179.

the 10 pin hit the 7 pin. This type of learning is called strategic because it corresponds to the everyday use of the term *strategy*. Perceptual–motor integration learning occurs when a person improves in selecting appropriate spatial targets to achieve an environmental goal. For example, a tennis player who wants to hit a ball with the head of a racquet must calculate where to move his or her hand so that the head of the racquet hits the ball. Selecting the appropriate target for where the hand should move so that the racquet head hits the ball requires perceptual–motor integration learning. Sequencing learning occurs when a particular sequence of movements is learned. For example, a tennis serve requires a particular set of movements, and indeed, the goal of learning a serve is to stereotype the movement, to produce the movement in the same way each time. Dynamic learning occurs when the pattern of muscle activation does a better job of moving the body to the desired point in space. This type of learning is rarely observed in the laboratory because the translation from spatial goal to muscle activation is so highly practiced that there is not much opportunity to improve. Each of these four processes is proposed to rely on a different set of neural structures (see Willingham, 1998, for details).

The theory also proposes that these processes can operate in either a conscious or an unconscious mode. Most skills are typically executed in the unconscious mode, in which the participant is aware of only the goal and not the particular spatial targets for movement that have been selected and sequenced. For example, when you pick up a water glass (a highly practiced movement) you are aware of wanting the glass moved, not the particular trajectory your hand takes. In the conscious mode the strategic process that typically selects the goal also usurps control of the other processes, selecting the spatial targets and sequencing them; thus when reaching for the water glass you *can* be aware of and control the particular trajectory if you want to.

The conscious mode is typically engaged when executing a difficult movement or when accuracy is very important. If your tennis coach said, "Don't let your head come up until after your follow-through on your backhand," you would consciously sequence those two movements. Other times, you might be thinking about your opponent's court position as you hit your backhand; in that case, you would be engaging the unconscious mode when you hit the backhand (that is, unconscious processes would select and sequence spatial targets for the backhand).

This model was designed to account for a number of phenomena, including the brain basis of motor skills, how different types of skills are represented, and how motor skills differ from one another. In addition, the model emphasizes that learning can be either conscious or unconscious, and that either type of learning can occur at any time during training. Thus, some types of motor skill learning may remain entirely unconscious, and indeed this is known to be true (Willingham, Nissen & Bullemer, 1989). It also emphasizes that skills that are typically learned unconsciously can also be learned consciously.

One of the notable themes to emerge from the study of motor control and motor skills—and indeed, it is a recurring theme in cognitive psychology—is the extent to which our introspection provides a useful guide to cognitive processes. For each cognitive process discussed, we have found that introspection is either deceptive or incomplete or, quite often, that it misses most of the interesting questions.

Stand-on-One-Foot Questions

> 15. *For which of the three obvious properties—generalization, long-term retention, and automaticity—can we say that the property applies without qualification across skills?*

16. Why should skills that have been practiced under more variable conditions be easier to generalize than skills that were practiced under less variable conditions, according to Schmidt's schema theory?

17. Explain the difference between learning and performance in motor skill.

Questions Requiring Two Feet

18. If a generalized motor program is behind skilled motor behavior, what parameters of movement do you think would likely be a part of the program?

19. One of the features of the Willingham (1998) model of skill learning is that conscious processes can contribute to skill not just early in training but at any point. For what practical feature of motor skill training is this important?

20. We said that some motor skills can be learned outside of awareness (that is, you're never aware of learning them), but it is not clear whether or not these skills require attention. If a skill could be learned outside of attention but required attention, what might that mean?

KEY TERMS

allocentric spatial
  representation
anticipatory postural
  adjustments
control nodes
cutaneous receptors
degrees of freedom
  problem
effector
efficiency theories

egocentric spatial
  representation
generalized motor
  program
golgi tendon organs
jerk
joint space
mass spring model
motor control
motor program

motor skill learning
movement nodes
muscle spindles
proprioception
response chaining
  theory
synergy
trajectory

Box 8–1 Further Evidence for Movements Specified as Endpoints

The evidence described in the text is consistent with the idea that movements are specified in terms of the movement's endpoint, rather than specified as a direction. But where in the nervous system is this endpoint represented? There is evidence from Georgopolous that the motor cortex does represent movements in

(Continued)

terms of direction. Other work by Bizzi indicates that there are indeed representations of movement in terms of endpoints, and localizes these representations in the spinal cord.

Bizzi and his colleagues (1991) performed a revealing experiment on the spinal cord of a frog. Projections from the brain stimulate interneurons in the spinal cord, which in turn stimulate motoneurons that directly stimulate muscles, causing them to contract. The experimenters surgically disconnected a frog's spinal cord from its brain stem so that they could stimulate the interneurons in isolation from brain input. They recorded the resulting muscle forces on the frog's ankle (see panel A in Figure B8.1). They stimulated the same set of interneurons a number of times with the frog's leg in different starting positions, and the pattern of forces created by the stimulation changed (see panel B in Figure B8.1). The arrows represent the forces resulting from stimulation: the direction of each arrow represents the direction of the muscle force of the leg, and the length of each arrow represents the amount of force. As you can see, if you stimulate the same set of interneurons, the resulting forces are designed to move the leg to a particular location in space (represented by the filled circle), whatever the starting position of the leg. This pattern of stimulation results is obtained only with spinal cord interneurons. When motoneurons are stimulated, the resulting forces always lead to forces in the same direction and of the same amount, regardless of the leg's starting position (see panel C of Figure B8.1).

There is evidence, then, for different representations of movement in different parts of the nervous system. Cortical areas appear to represent movements in terms of the direction and distance that the movement is to take. Spinal cord interneurons, however, appear to translate that direction/distance information into a representation of the endpoint of the movement. The interneurons activate the correct pattern of motoneurons, which in turn activate the correct pattern of muscles to move the limb to the desired location.

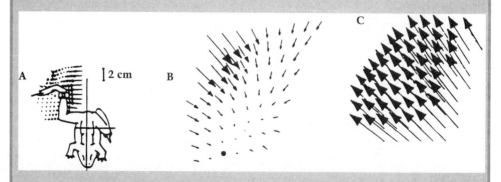

Figure B8.1.

Adapted from "Computations Underlying the Execution of Movement," by Bizzi et al., 1991, Science, 253, Fig. 2, p.289.

Box 8–2 *Is There a Location for Motor Planning?*

Most of the brain areas that are devoted to motor behavior seem to be more important to the planning of actions than to their execution. For example, most lesions to the motor system do not leave patients unable to move; rather, movements become clumsy or poorly planned in some way, but they can still be executed. The exception is the primary motor area, which, if lesioned, leaves the patient unable to move. Of course, that result does not mean that the primary motor cortex is not involved in planning. It means that the primary motor cortex is definitely involved in the execution of movements.

Researchers have tried to examine which brain areas are involved in motor planning (and not execution) by asking people to plan a movement but not execute it—in other words, to engage in motor imagery. Early results showed a great deal of activity in the supplementary motor area and no activity in the primary motor cortex. Not surprisingly, the somatosensory cortex was active only when participants actually moved; we wouldn't expect peripheral feedback if people don't move. Thus it seemed that movements were planned in the supplementary motor area (just anterior to primary motor cortex) and executed by the primary motor cortex.

Work in the mid-1990s indicated that the primary motor cortex might actually be active during motor planning, but these studies did not account for the possibility that participants might be making small movements when they were supposed to merely imagine making them. A study by Martin Lotze and his colleagues (1999) addressed this problem. They had participants engage in a 60- to 90-min training period during which they imagined making a fist and opening their hand in time to a metronome. The participants were to work on making the imagery as vivid as possible, but the experimenters also recorded

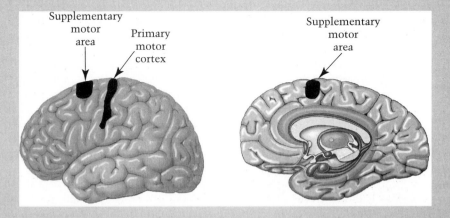

Figure B8.2.

(Continued)

electromyographic activity to make sure that the participants were not making any muscle movements.

After this training period, participants were scanned with fMRI while they either imagined the movements or actually executed the movements. The results showed considerable activity in secondary motor cortex during motor imagery. There was activity in primary motor cortex, but less in the imagery condition than in the execution condition.

Can we interpret this activity as reflecting a motor program? That interpretation is probably going too far, but it does seem fair to say that the supplementary motor area is a key cortical region for the planning of motor acts, and that may include the retrieval of a motor program. Greater specification of exactly what the supplementary motor area does will have to await future studies.

Box 8–3 What Happens When Vision and Proprioception Conflict?

We have discussed the use of vision and proprioception in guiding movement. What happens if those two sources of information conflict, that is, if vision and proprioception suggest different locations in space for objects? A conflict between sources of spatial information would probably be very confusing. How could that situation arise? Proprioception can change naturally if the body changes rapidly—for example, during a growth spurt in adolescence—or if the body is maimed. It is possible to examine such situations experimentally by asking a participant to wear wedge prism spectacles that shift the visual world to the right (or left). Wearing the spectacles greatly disturbs motor behavior. Imagine, for example, throwing a ball at a target. Vision may indicate that the target is directly in front of you, but you would have to make a throwing movement 30 degrees to your left to hit the target. This throwing movement would feel wrong—proprioception (arm is moving to left) would disagree with vision (target is straight ahead).

People wearing prism spectacles are indeed quite impaired in throwing objects at targets, but they greatly improve after about 30 trials. Tom Thach and his colleagues (1996) had participants throw clay balls at a target, and they observed this pattern; participants initially made errors by throwing to the left of the target but rapidly adapted. When participants removed the glasses, they again made errors, this time to the right of the target. This continued compensation for the spectacles (although participants no longer wore them) is called an aftereffect; it dissipates after another 30 trials. These effects are shown in Figure B8.3.

The aftereffect occurs because proprioception has changed. It feels to the participant as though he or she is throwing directly ahead of the body, even though the arm moves to the right. These results show that the nervous system can adjust to changes in perceptual input. The system is biased to assume that vision and proprioception should agree, and if they disagree, proprioception is changed to bring it in line with vision.

(Continued)

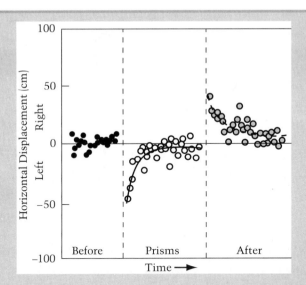

Figure B8.3. *From "Throwing While Looking Through Prisms. I. Focal Olivocerebellar Lesions Impair Adaptation," by T. A. Martin, J. G. Keating, H. P. Goodkin, A. J. Baston, and W. C. Thach, 1996, Brain, 119, Fig. 1B, p. 1185.*

What part of the brain is responsible for this learning function? The cerebellum has been implicated. The researchers also tested patients with lesions to the cerebellum or lesions to brainstem structures that provide input to or receive output from the cerebellum. These patients typically did not improve their throwing accuracy when the prism spectacles were worn, nor did they show the aftereffect when the spectacles were removed. Other work with monkeys (Baizer et al., 1999) indicates that the caudal portion of the cerebellum is critical to this function. This area of the cerebellum receives visual input from the cortex and thus is consistent with the idea that part of the cerebellum is important in the modification of different sources of sensory input if they disagree.

9

Visual Imagery

WHAT PURPOSE DOES VISUAL IMAGERY SERVE?

Imagery in Early Psychology
Imagery Reenters Psychology
Imagery and Perception

ARE VISUAL IMAGES SUPPORTED BY A SEPARATE REPRESENTATION SYSTEM?

Propositional versus Analog Representation
The Metaphor Is Misleading
Demand Characteristics and Tacit Knowledge
The Brain and the End of the Imagery Debate

HOW DOES VISUAL IMAGERY WORK?

Image Generation
Image Inspection
Image Transformation

If you want to, you can imagine Jackie Chan walking on the moon. In fact, you can put a ponytail on Jackie and make him stand on this head and plow through the lunar surface like a motorboat, with his ponytail acting as a propeller. What use is a cognitive ability that allows such nonsense?

The first question we take up in the study of mental imagery is **What purpose does visual imagery serve?** This may seem like an odd place to start, but the function of a mental process is actually crucial to the way we study it. Once we know what the function of a process is, we know something about what the process must do; knowing its job helps us divine the mechanisms the process might use. Our study of perception is informed by our belief that perception tells about the physical features and locations of objects. The function of mental imagery has been the subject of some debate, as we'll discuss in this chapter. At this point, the fairly settled view is that imagery serves a memory function (making the visual properties of objects available under some conditions) and a problem-solving function (allowing us to try out changes in the positions of objects or our bodies by moving them in our mind's eye before we move them physically).

These two functions both imply that mental images are pictorial representations; images are a way of representing information in the mind that is different from verbal representations. If you want to communicate to me the idea "The hat rack is in the parking lot," you could say those words to me, or you could show me a picture of a hat rack in a parking lot. We can propose that similar representations are used in the mind—representations that are verbal and representations that are pictorial—although as we'll see, we don't think either in words or in pictures, exactly.

The proposal that mental images are a different sort of representation from verbal representations upset some researchers. Bear in mind what cognitive psychology is all about: we're trying to discern the processes and representations that the mind uses to support thinking. If we all agree that there are verbal representations and then someone proposes that there are also mental images, that rather significant addition requires not only a new set of representations (images) but a whole new set of processes that can operate on those representations. There's no reason to think the processes that manipulate verbal representations can be applied to images, just as you wouldn't expect a computer's word processing program to be able to use files designed to perform statistics.

It might seem obvious that we do, in fact, use mental images, even if proving they exist is complicated. If we pose the following questions to participants, they almost always report using visual imagery to answer them.

What shape are a German shepherd's ears?
Which is a darker green, a Christmas tree or a frozen pea?
In which hand does the Statue of Liberty hold her torch?
How many windows are there in your house or apartment?

It's obvious that people believe that they use mental imagery, but it is not obvious that mental images actually serve a function. Remember, we first started thinking about a separate mental representation system because of the functions images serve. If we could get verbal representations to serve those same functions, would we still think that visual images might be necessary? **Are visual images supported by a separate mental representation system?** The answer is "Yes," but it was rather difficult to prove. In fact, the existence of such a system was not proved to the complete satisfaction of most psychologists until about 1980. We'll go over why it was so complicated to settle this question. Once that question was resolved, researchers started to take more seriously the next question: **How does visual imagery work?** What does the representation of a visual image look like, and how does it operate? We will discuss how visual images are generated, inspected, and transformed.

WHAT PURPOSE DOES VISUAL IMAGERY SERVE?

> ► *Preview* This section follows the history of visual imagery in experimental psychology to learn how people have studied imagery, why they studied it, and how they determined its functions. In the late 19th century visual imagery was at the center of experimental psychology. Psychologists using introspectionist methods believed that visual images were a direct window to thought. After behaviorism swept introspectionism aside in the 1920s, visual imagery went largely unstudied. In the 1960s visual imagery reentered experimental psychology, mostly through Alan Paivio's ingenious demonstrations of the importance of visual imagery to memory. This work showed that visual imagery makes available for later inspection the visual properties of objects. In the early 1970s, researchers began to examine ways in which mental images could be transformed (for example, rotated or expanded). This work made salient another function of imagery: it allows us to try out changes mentally before going to the trouble of executing them in the real world.

Visual images have been of interest to researchers since the beginnings of experimental psychology in the late 19th century, and philosophers were intrigued for centuries before that, at least back to Plato. The same is true of memory, perception, and other cognitive processes, but there has been general agreement about the functions those other processes serve in cognition. Visual perception determines the locations and some characteristics of objects in the world. Memory makes available the properties of objects that are not currently present but that you have experienced before in the same or similar objects. So what is visual imagery for? If I say, "Image a cat," and you do so, what function could that serve? Perhaps because it is not immediately obvious, the answer to this question has changed over the history of experimental psychology. The history of visual imagery research has been contentious, partly because the view of imagery's function has changed. Our views of imagery's function developed, in part, as a reaction to the past, so to get to the bottom of this issue we must go back to the start of experimental psychology.

Imagery in Early Psychology

Recall from chapter 1 that experimental psychology began with an approach called introspectionism. To account for the contents of consciousness, the introspectionists sought to describe a small set of irreducible elements that could be combined to create more complex mental states, especially mental images. No sharp distinction was drawn between generating a mental image and seeing an object (Wundt, 1894). Imagery was considered tantamount to thought: psychologists believed they could understand thought by understanding images.

This point of view suffered a blow in what came to be called the imageless thought controversy: is it possible to have thoughts that are not accompanied by images? This controversy was primed by a series of experiments by Sir Francis Galton (1883), who reported on fairly extensive individual differences in participants' reports of the vividness of their mental images. Some people claimed to be good at imagery, but a few (about 10%) said they really didn't have mental imagery. For example, one respondent said, "My powers are zero. To my consciousness there is almost no association of memory with objective visual impression" (Galton, 1907/1973, pp. 63–64).

These results spell trouble for the introspectionist program. If imagery is more or less synonymous with thought, how are these people who claim not to have images thinking? These data were not taken as conclusive evidence that thought can proceed in the absence of images—after all, most people did report having images—but new results came in that seemed more troubling because they indicated that for certain types of tasks, no one reported using images. For example, Marbe (1901) reported that when participants were asked to hold one weight in each hand, they could readily say which was heavier, but they reported doing so without any images. Another problem raised was that some concepts (for example, the abstract definition of a triangle) did not lend themselves to imagery.

Defenders of introspectionism (notably Titchener, who was one of Wundt's students) argued that participants who think they don't have images as they perform a task simply haven't followed their own thought processes very carefully, probably because the experimenter didn't tell them to do so. And they further argued that one can have an image of an abstract idea such as a triangle (Titchener, 1909).

The imageless thought controversy was swept clean in 1913 when John Watson proposed that psychology should shift to a behaviorist point of view. Watson wasn't interested in arguing about whether some types of thoughts were imageless. He claimed that studying the mind was going to be fruitless and that researchers should focus on behavior. Thus the study of visual imagery went from being the star to being eliminated from the field.

Imagery was largely ignored by psychologists in the United States for about 50 years, until the early 1960s. The main reason for that neglect was that it was deemed impossible to study imagery objectively. By definition, images are accessible only to the person doing the imagery, so the experimenter has no choice but to take the participant's word for whatever he or she claims to be seeing. That's no way to build a science. Woodworth and Schlossberg summed up the attitude toward the study of imagery in their very popular textbook, written in 1954.

> An outstanding characteristic of modern experimental psychology is its emphasis on objective experiments. As we have just seen, this reliance on objectivity misses some aspects of the act of recalling. One such aspect is the presence of images, but imagery is such a fluid thing that it is very difficult to study. (pp. 720–721)

In other words, imagery is interesting—what a pity we can't study it.

Imagery Reenters Psychology

Alan Paivio published an influential book on imagery and memory in 1971. By that time, many psychologists had become sympathetic to the idea of describing mental processes; they didn't believe that psychology should focus solely on behavior. Nevertheless, they thought that imagery was off limits as a research topic because it was subjective and inferential.

The opening chapter of Paivio's book refuted the argument that imagery was impossible to study. When participants describe a memory (for example, a word list the experimenter read to them), they describe it in words. Researchers are willing to accept the participant's verbal description of their memory as bearing a close relationship to what the participant actually remembers. Researchers believe that participants can talk about their thoughts, yet the words participants utter are not an exact reproduction but a model of their verbal thoughts. Paivio pointed out that it is just as possible to produce a verbal description of a mental image; there is no reason psychologists should be willing to make the jump from spoken words to a mental construct such as "verbal representation" and not make the jump from spoken words to a mental construct such as "visual image representation." Paivio also pointed out that images do have a functional role. He noted that imageless thought is a theoretical problem only if we want to argue that all thought is based on images. Paivio didn't want to make that claim; rather, he claimed that *some* thoughts were based on images. The fact that some thoughts might be imageless was not a threat to Paivio's position.

So what functional role do images play? Paivio discussed a role for imagery in a paired associate task. In this task, the experimenter presents a pair of words to the participant (*fork–tape*) and later the participant must produce the word *tape* if given the word *fork*. Most of Paivio's experiments used verbal materials and required verbal recall. How, then, could he show that imagery played a role in memory when he used only verbal materials? Paivio used two strategies: he varied the characteristics of the stimuli, and he varied the instructions to the participant.

The characteristic that Paivio usually varied was the concreteness or abstractness of the stimulus word. **Concrete words** like *potato* refer to a physical object. **Abstract words** like *intellect* do not refer to a physical object. Paivio (1963) reasoned that people could use imagery for concrete words but not for abstract ones. In a direct test of this hypothesis, Paivio (1965) administered a paired associate test, varying the concreteness or abstractness of the word pairs. There are four possible combinations of concrete and abstract words in a paired associate test: concrete–concrete, concrete–abstract, abstract–concrete, and abstract–abstract. Memory is best when both words are concrete and worst when both are abstract. Paivio interpreted this result as showing the effectiveness of imagery in memory.

To examine the reported use of imagery as a learning strategy, Paivio and Dennis Foth (1970) used a list of 30 word pairs. On each trial the participant was instructed to rehearse a word pair either via an image (including drawing the image to ensure that the participant had created one) or via verbal mediation (including writing the phrase created to link the two words). Each participant performed some verbal rehearsal and some imagery rehearsal. Paivio and Foth also varied the types of word pairs: some were abstract (*democracy–intellect*) and some were concrete (*tree–pencil*). Participants had better recall for abstract stimuli when they used verbal encoding, and they performed better with concrete stimuli when they used imagery.

To account for these data, Paivio proposed a **dual coding hypothesis** stating that there are two ways to represent concepts: through a mental image or through a verbal representation. Concrete concepts such as *fork* can be represented via a verbal representation that would be used in understanding and producing language and in certain types of thinking. Concrete concepts can also be represented as visual images. Abstract concepts, in contrast, have only one representation. For example, a concept such as *democracy* would have only a verbal representation, not a visual one (see Figure 9.1). What sort of image, after all, could represent *democracy*? Someone voting? Someone reading a noncensored newspaper? Those images are neither compelling nor specific. There might also be concepts for which there is a visual image but a verbal description is harder to generate. For example, someone who knows the odd shape of a crankshaft might have a hard time describing it, although he or she can image it.

Verbal and imagery representations operate in parallel, and if both are working, it is more likely that memory will be successful; if one representation can't be retrieved when you try to recall the memory, you might be able to retrieve the other one. Concrete words are easier to remember than abstract words because they are more likely to activate a representation in the imagery system. Abstract words are likely to activate only a verbal representation. Thus, concrete words are better remembered because there are two representations, and if one fails, the other representation might still be available.

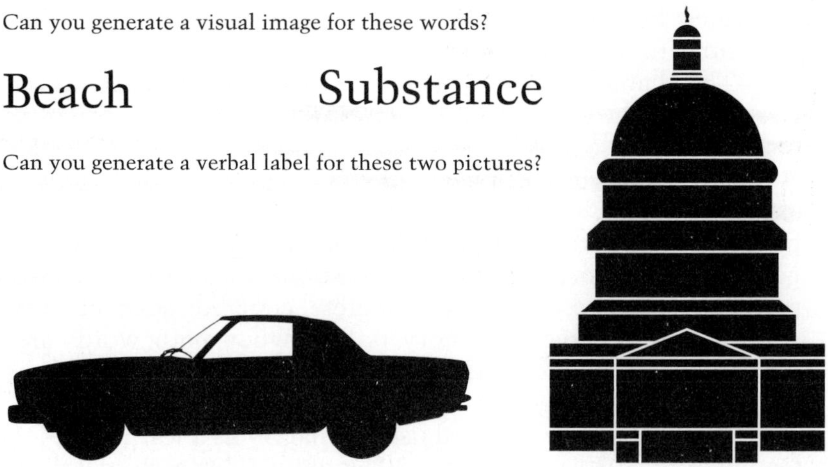

Can you generate a visual image for these words?

Beach   Substance

Can you generate a verbal label for these two pictures?

Figure 9.1.   *It's easy to generate an image of* beach, *a concrete word, but hard to generate an image of* substance. *Most people would agree that the picture on the left should be named* car, *but there would be less agreement about the picture on the right. It could be called* democracy, *or it could be* capitol *or* dome. *If the picture on the right is a bad representation of* democracy, *what would be a better one?*

Paivio offered a specific interpretation of his dual coding theory, depicted in Figure 9.2. According to Paivio (1986), both verbal and nonverbal stimuli enter the sensory systems. Verbal stimuli tend to activate representations in the verbal system. Paivio called these representations **logogens**, a term borrowed from Morton (1969). The representations in the nonverbal system that support images are called **imagens**. Notice that imagens can be embedded within one another. For example, you might be able to generate an image of your family standing together, within which is an image of your brother; you could image your brother separately if you wanted to, and within that image you could image just his face if you wanted to. Logogens do not have this quality of one being embedded in the other. Paivio also proposed that imagens and logogens have connections; for example, the logogen for *poodle* has a connection to the corresponding imagen. Note too (as represented in Figure 9.2) that some logogens don't have a connection to imagens. These would be abstract concepts such as *villainy* and *woe*. There are also imagens that do not have connections to logogens; these would be familiar concepts for which you have no verbal representation, such as the crease below the nose and above the lip, which most people can image but cannot name (it's called the philtrum).

Paivio's theory describes in considerably more detail exactly how logogens and imagens relate and why memory is better when images are used, but that story would take us too far afield into memory (see Paivio, 1986, 1991, and Sadoski & Paivio, 2001, for reviews). The key point is that Paivio showed

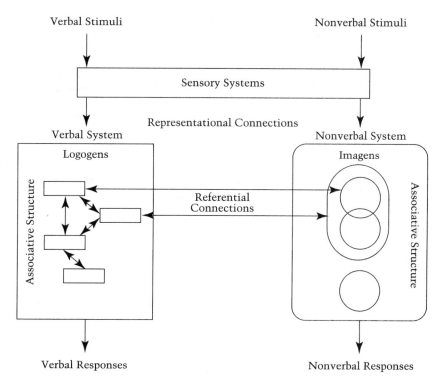

Figure 9.2. *Diagram of Paivio's dual coding theory.*

that imagery affects memory. He probably did more than any other person to bring visual imagery back within the purview of experimental psychology. This work does not address directly how imagery is thought to work or how images are generated or transformed; rather, it examines how imagery affects memory.

Imagery and Perception

Imagery seems to be most obviously related to perception. Although Paivio took note of this fact, his experiments were not directly addressed to the possible relationship of imagery and perception. However, other researchers examined this relationship. In one of the better known examples, Lee Brooks (1968) used a dual task method to examine codes in primary memory. In the verbal task, participants were given a sentence such as "A bird in the hand is not in the bush" and were required to identify each word as either a noun or not a noun. Hence a correct response would be "No, yes, no, no, yes, no, no, no, no, yes." In the imagery task, participants were asked to image a block letter (such as *F*), and beginning in the lower left-hand corner, to mentally travel around the letter clockwise, responding "Yes" when a corner was at the top or bottom of the letter and "No" for other corners. Thus the first task is largely verbal, and the second task is spatial. Brooks also had participants use either a verbal or a spatial mode of response. In the verbal mode, they were simply to say "Yes" or "No" aloud. For the spatial mode, participants had a piece of paper in front of them with rows of irregularly placed Ys and Ns, and they were to point to a letter to signify "Yes" or "No."

For the sentence task (which is verbal) participants were better off responding by pointing, whereas for the letter task (which is spatial) they were better off responding verbally. This pattern of results indicates that there might be separate verbal and spatial forms of representation; you can use verbal and spatial representations simultaneously and they don't interfere, but if you try to use two different verbal representations simultaneously or two different spatial representations simultaneously, they interfere. These results can also be taken as indirect support for a relationship between perception and imagery because the letter task requires the use of imagery and is interfered with by a task that requires the use of perception (pointing).

Box 9–1 The Overlap of Imagery and Perceptual Processes

Many researchers believe that imagery and perception overlap. Behavioral experiments were conducted to test this hypothesis (for example, through interference paradigms). One study has examined in a very direct way the overlap in the anatomic structures that support imagery and those that support perception.

Stephen Kosslyn and his associates (Kosslyn, Thompson, & Alpert, 1997) predicted that there should be considerable overlap between perception and imagery in terms of higher-level processes, although low-level visual areas might not participate in imagery. Their research strategy was therefore quite simple: they administered a perceptual task and an imagery task that call on high-level processes while participants were in a PET scanner and noted how many brain areas overlap between the two tasks. Furthermore, they sought to make the perceptual and imagery tasks fairly different so that any observed anatomic overlap would be all the more convincing.

The perceptual task was object naming. In one version of the task, participants saw drawings of objects such as a guitar or a fence and were to name the object. Brain activity for this task obviously would involve not only perceptual processes to identify the object but also retrieval of the name. A second task was to name objects viewed from an unusual ("noncanonical") position. Participants might have seen the guitar tilted from the edge and the picket fence from above; such objects are difficult to identify and thus require further visual processing to name. The researchers subtracted the activation from the first task (naming pictures) from the activation from the second task (naming noncanonical pictures) to yield activation specific to high-level perceptual processes.

(Continued)

For the imagery task, participants saw a lowercase letter (such as *f*) which they knew was a signal to generate an image of a block capital letter (*F*). Participants then saw a grid with an *X* in one square and were to say whether the letter they were imaging would cover the *X*. In the baseline condition for this task, they simply responded when they saw the *X*, without having to generate an image.

When the activations for the imagery and perceptual tasks were compared, there was a good deal of overlap. A total of 21 areas were activated: 14 were active in both the perceptual and the imagery task, 2 were active in perception but not imagery, and 5 were active in imagery but not perception. The areas that both tasks activated, shown in Figure B9.1, are focused in the secondary visual cortex, with 2 activation sites in the parietal lobe and 1 in dorsolateral prefrontal cortex. This study supports the conclusions from behavioral studies: there is considerable but not complete overlap between the system that supports perception and the system that supports imagery.

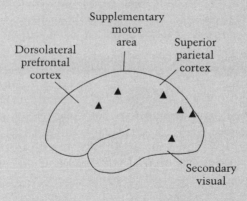

Figure B9.1.

A second result truly rocked the psychological world. Roger Shepard and Jacqueline Metzler (1971) sought to examine the process by which images are transformed. They showed participants shapes like the ones in Figure 9.3. Participants were asked to evaluate whether the two pictures were of the same object but at different angles or whether the objects were different. Half of the objects depicted were different; they were mirror reflections of one another. The other half showed figures that were the same, but one picture was rotated in space relative to the other. The amount of rotation was varied, and the figures could be rotated in the picture plane or in depth. Participants were

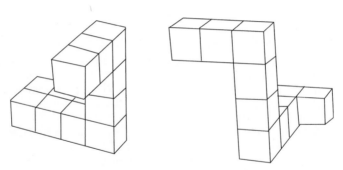

Figure 9.3. *Figures similar to those used by Shepard and Met-zler (1971).*

to pull a lever to indicate their decision (same or different). Eight participants each performed 1,600 trials over the course of 8 to 10 hour-long sessions.

The interesting trials were those on which the objects were the same. Two findings stood out. First, the amount of time it took participants to make their decision was an orderly function of the degree of rotation between the two pictures, as shown in Figure 9.4. Second, response time was the same whether the rotation was in the picture plane or in depth.

Researchers got very excited about these results for several reasons. First, the experiment opened an entirely new area of research. Until that point, most researchers had treated images as static; if you imaged a tree, for example, the tree just sat there. When Shepard and Metzler studied how images are transformed, they highlighted an important function of mental imagery: it allows us to try something out mentally before we try it out physically. Will the sofa fit in the alcove? Can I reach the top shelf with this feather duster? Will this magazine cover the stain on the coffee table? These are questions we might try to answer using visual imagery. This point may not seem important to you—didn't everyone know it was possible to do things like that with imagery? But as Michael Kubovy (1983) put it, "Often, formulating something that we all know but have not been able to put into words is a major step in its own right" (p. 662).

A second reason psychologists were enthusiastic about Shepard and Metzler's results is that their data were so orderly. The graph shows a remarkably systematic relationship between the angle of rotation between the two figures and the amount of time it took people to declare that the figures were the same. The line in Figure 9.4 is the best fit: a straight line drawn so that all of the circles are as close as possible to the line. In this case, the circles are extremely close to the line. Furthermore, these circles represent averages from all of the participants tested. The little lines above and below the circles (called error bars) are a measure of how far most of the data are from the arithmetic mean (the average). If the mean is 3, half the values could be about 1 and half about 5, with none close to 3. In this case, the very small error bars show that most of the values were quite close to the mean.

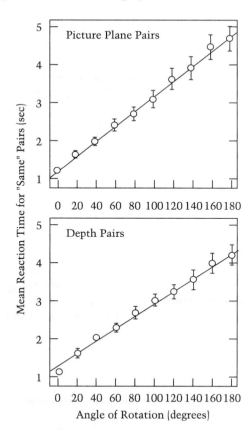

Figure 9.4. *Results from Shepard and Metzler (1971). The graphs show the time it takes participants to respond "same." Note that the mean values form an almost perfect straight line. The lines above and below each circle are a measure of variability; the lines are very small, which means that most of the individual values are quite close to the mean. Also note that the slope of the line going through the points is the same for the picture plane pairs and the depth pairs. That indicates that the speed with which mental rotation can be performed is about the same in the picture plane and in depth.*

Psychologists usually do experiments dealing with types of behavior determined by many factors. For example, I might vary how many times participants rehearse a word list, and then a day later test their memory for the list. How many words will the participants remember? The answer depends in part on how many times the list was rehearsed a day earlier, but it also depends on a lot of other things, such as whether the participants paid attention the day before, whether they pay attention during the test, what they have done in the past few hours, and so on. People sometimes use the term *multiply determined* to describe behavior, which simply means that many factors contribute to behavior. That means that the data will be somewhat sloppy; my manipulation of how many times participants rehearse the word list definitely will affect their memory, but so will a lot of other things that are beyond my control. The remarkable thing about Shepard and Metzler's data is that they are not sloppy: they follow a perfect linear trend. This orderliness indicates that the task they used is not multiply determined. The task appears to depend on one process that is affected by angle of rotation.

So what might the single process be? That's the third thing that got researchers excited about the result. An obvious candidate is mental rotation of the image. All eight participants in this experiment reported performing this task by mentally rotating one of the objects to see whether it could be matched to the other object, implying that there is a representation to be rotated. Roger Shepard and Susan Chipman (1970) proposed that images are a **second-order isomorphism** to pictures, which means that the parts of images and the parts of pictures have the same functional relationship to one another. A mental image is not a picture in the head; indeed, that wouldn't make any sense—who would be looking at such a picture? But an image has some similarity to a picture because the parts of each have the same functional relationship to one another.

These data and similar experiments by Shepard and his colleagues (see Shepard & Cooper, 1986, for a review) helped convince researchers that it is possible (and important) to study another aspect of imagery: the functions afforded by the transformation of images. Furthermore, this work made real the possibility that there may be a representation system (imagery) that is qualitatively different from the verbal representation system.

We started this section by raising the question "What is mental imagery for?" Let me summarize the progression of the answers. The introspectionists thought that imagery was a window into all thought processes and therefore put imagery at the center of their psychology. The behaviorists pointed out that imagery was unobservable because it was completely private to the observer, and they thought it was not relevant to the concerns of psychology because psychology was the science of behavior, not of thought. The field lay dormant for about 50 years until Paivio pointed out that mental imagery is indeed important because it affects memory and speculated that imagery may be supported by a separate representation system. Shepard and others offered a way of studying mental transformations in imagery (the unobservable events that behaviorists exorcised) and offered compelling (but not conclusive) circumstantial evidence that imagery might be supported by a separate representational system.

We will return to the work of Shepard and his colleagues later in the chapter when we discuss imagery transformations. Shepard raised the possibility that images constituted a separate representation system, but he did not make it a priority to prove that this was the case. As it turns out, some scientists were far from convinced that this work demonstrated that visual images were important to human cognition. In the next section, we discuss a decade of research that did not address how imagery operates but rather was concerned with demonstrating that mental imagery is important to human cognition in the first place.

Stand-on-One-Foot Questions

1. *What was the imageless thought controversy, and why was it important?*
2. *In the early 1960s cognitive psychologists were still ignoring visual imagery and seemed unwilling to accept as data participants' reports about*

what they experienced during imagery tasks. What did Paivio say about that unwillingness?

3. *What were the two key results from Shepard and Metzler's (1971) study, and why were they so important?*

Questions That Require Two Feet

4. *Do you see a problem with asking people to rate their imagery abilities, as Galton did?*

5. *We've discussed in detail the fact that imagery helps memory. Do you think it would help memory still more if the images were bizarre? What is your reason for your answer?*

6. *Given what we've discussed about the apparent overlap of perception and imagery, can you see any situations in which it might be downright dangerous to listen to a sporting event on the radio?*

ARE VISUAL IMAGES SUPPORTED BY A SEPARATE REPRESENTATION SYSTEM?

> ➤ *Preview* Some researchers argued that visual images did not have to be supported by a separate representation system and that the data from imagery experiments could be accounted for by verbal representations. They also argued that although the sensation of seeing visual images in the mind's eye might be real, that does not imply that there is a separate representation that helps cognition. In addition, they proposed that many of the results of imagery experiments could be explained by the participants' knowing what was expected of them and being willing or eager to produce the expected results. Imagery researchers met these criticisms and convinced cognitive psychologists that there is indeed a separate representation for visual images.

How could there be a question about whether or not visual imagery exists, when it seems so clear to most of us that we have and use visual images? This section will summarize a decade of active research (roughly 1972–1982) on exactly this point. The conclusion turned out the way you might have guessed, but it is instructive to go through the argument because it shows that firm conclusions about the mind are won only through systematic research.

Propositional versus Analog Representation

Many of the arguments against the use of visual imagery in psychological theory were put forward by Zenon Pylyshyn (1973; 1981), who offered four key reasons psychologists should be cautious in proposing a new representational system.

THE PROBLEM.   A key argument against a separate set of images to represent visual imagery is that images simply aren't needed to account for human behavior; instead, verbal representations are sufficient to take care of everything. The verbal representation in question is the **proposition**, usually defined as the most basic unit of meaning that has a truth value (that is, the proposition is either true or false). Propositions have a particular syntax: they take the form *relation(argument)*. A relational term can be a verb, an adjective, or a conjunction, and the arguments are nouns. For example, the proposition *red(car)* represents the idea that a particular car is red. The proposition *kicked(giraffe, lion)* represents the idea that the giraffe kicked the lion.

Images, on the other hand, often are defined as **analog**, meaning that they have some of the important qualities of pictures but are not themselves pictures. As noted earlier, Shepard and Chipman (1970) proposed that one of these qualities is that the parts of images have the same functional relation to one another that parts of pictures have.

Stephen Kosslyn (1980) outlined five key properties that differentiate propositions from images.

1. **A proposition is relational.** That is, it describes a relation between an object and a quality or between two objects. An image does not describe a particular relation. For example, an image of a ball and a box could just as easily describe "The box is under the ball" or "The ball is on the box."

2. **A proposition has a syntax.** There is a right way and a wrong way to form a proposition. An image has no syntax.

3. **A proposition has a truth value.** *On(ball, box)* either truly reflects the state of the world or it doesn't. This is not so for an image. Ludwig Wittgenstein (1953) pointed out that an image of a man walking up a hill could equally well be interpreted as an image of a man sliding down a hill backwards. The image does not make an unambiguous statement about the world.

4. **A proposition is abstract.** The proposition makes a statement about *some* ball and *some* box but says nothing about the relative sizes of the ball and box, their dimensions, their color, and so on. An image is necessarily specific on these points.

5. **An image occurs in a spatial medium.** That means images preserve geometric qualities of real objects in space. A proposition, however, does not.

We can see that there are differences between images and propositions. Yet some researchers said that a second type of representation is not needed—we can account for everything the mind does by using propositions.

Here's an example. One strategy to demonstrate that images are used by the mind is to show that people's behavior during imagery tasks reflects the spatial properties of images. For example, Stephen Kosslyn (1973) had participants

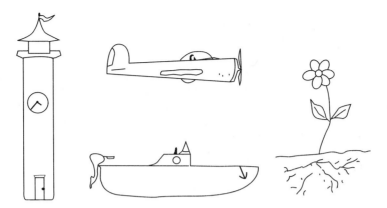

Figure 9.5. *Sample pictures from Kosslyn's (1973) experiment. Participants were asked to memorize these pictures so that they could image them later.*

memorize pictures of objects. (Sample drawings are shown in Figure 9.5.) In the second phase of the experiment, participants were asked to verify parts of the object: the experimenter would say, "Focus on the speedboat. Is there a propeller?" and the participant should respond "Yes." (On half the trials a part would be named that was not part of the image—for example, "Is there a mast?") Half the participants were asked to focus on the left or top of the image when they generated it and half on the bottom or right. Participants focusing on the left were quick to verify parts on the left (the propeller), slower to verify parts near the center (a porthole), and still slower to verify objects near the right (an anchor). Kosslyn interpreted these results as showing that participants had to scan across the image to locate the requested part and thereby verify it.

Kosslyn (1980) described a phone call he received from computer scientist Danny Bobrow shortly after this experiment was published. Bobrow pointed out that another, purely verbal representation would yield the same result Kosslyn reported (see Figure 9.6). It consists of nodes that represent object parts (such as the propeller and porthole) and links that represent relations (*behind, attached to*). If it takes more time to traverse a greater number of links in the representation, the same pattern of results that Kosslyn reported in the imagery condition would still be seen. For example, starting with your attention focused on the propeller, you must traverse three links to get to the porthole but four links to get to the anchor. The point is that an experiment that appears to support the use of visual images may not *compel* an account involving images if we can account for the data using only propositions.

But wait a minute. Don't psychologists care that people *feel* like they are using visual images? How can you be using propositions to scan images when it so clearly feels like you're scanning something like a picture?

Pylyshyn did not argue against the internal sensation of generating and manipulating visual images. The argument is about what those sensations mean. The fact that you have a sensation of a visual image doesn't mean that

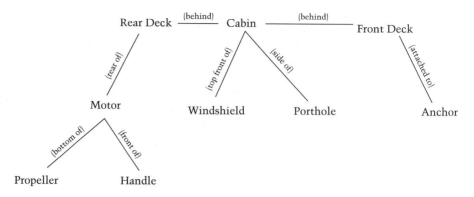

Figure 9.6. *Hypothetical propositional representation of the motorboat in Kosslyn's (1973) experiment.*

there is a representation supporting the visual image. The sensations may be an **epiphenomenon**, a perfectly real phenomenon that is not related to the function of the system but is a byproduct of the processes that are doing the actual work. Here's an example. I used to have an old Honda station wagon. Every time I went over 65 miles per hour, the car shook. If I slowed down to 60, there was no shaking. If I sped up to 70, the car started shaking. From this it seems I can conclude that shaking made the car go fast. This conclusion is obviously ridiculous, but the logic is exactly the same as in the imagery case.

In the case of the car, you notice that every time you accomplish a particular type of task (going fast) you get a sensation (shaking), so you assume that the sensation causes the task to be accomplished (shaking makes the car go fast). In the case of imagery you notice that every time you accomplish a particular type of task (mental rotation) you get a sensation (it feels as if you're seeing pictures in your head), so you assume that the sensation causes the task to be accomplished (pictures in the head are solving the imagery task). The sensation of the images could be an epiphenomenon. Like the shaking of the car, the sensation of mental imagery may be perfectly real, yet it might not be involved in the processes that are getting the work done.

The main barb to this criticism is that the burden of proof should be on those who want to claim that imagery is supported by a separate system of representations. That's because a theory with just one type of representation (propositions) is more **parsimonious** than a theory with two representations (propositions and images); it is the simplest theory possible that still accounts for all the data. The idea that parsimony is important in scientific theory, often called **Occam's razor**, was proposed by William of Occam, a 14th-century philosopher. He suggested that when two scientific theories account for the facts equally well, the simpler theory is preferred. A propositional theory was a simpler one because it used only one form of representation.

THE RESPONSE. No one disputed that people use propositional (verbal) representations. The question was whether it was necessary to add to the cognitive system another set of representations plus all of the processes to manipulate those representations.

Imagery researchers did not try to prove that a propositional representation could not possibly account for the data. Instead they collected data that made it increasingly difficult to make a propositional representation plausible. The results of this research program showed that certain tasks had properties that were very easy to account for with visual images but clumsy to account for using only propositions. I'll provide two examples (for more detail, see Kosslyn, 1980) involving scanning and screen detail.

Recall that in the scanning experiment with the motorboat there was an alternative explanation. It could be that the propositional representation was used and that it took more time to traverse a greater number of links in the representation. In a follow-up experiment, Kosslyn, Thomas Ball, and Brian Reiser (1978) used new stimulus materials to be sure that it was the distance between scanned objects that was important, not the number of parts or objects scanned. In other words, it should still take a long time to scan a long distance, even if the distance is filled with white space. Participants were asked to memorize a map depicting a fictional island, with landmarks such as a well and a hut.

After they memorized the map, participants were asked to image it and to scan between pairs of landmarks. Participants were to focus attention on the first location and press a button when they "arrived" at the second location. They were to press another button if the second location was not on the map. (On some occasions the second location was not depicted on the map, although it was a plausible location, such as "beach.") The time it took for participants to "arrive" at the second location was again a linear function of distance scanned, even though there were no object parts intervening between the beginning and end points of the scan. These results confirmed that it is indeed distance that determines scanning time.

Another property of imagery concerns the amount of detail or "grain" participants report. If images are represented in a spatial medium, then physical features are not represented in an image if the image is made very small; if you image a tiny elephant, you may not be able to see its toenails in your mind's eye. Kosslyn (1975, 1976) tested this prediction. He asked participants to imagine a rabbit with a fly next to it (see Figure 9.7). Once they said they had the image in mind, he asked them a question about a rabbit: "Does a rabbit have a pink nose?" Another set of participants got exactly the same tasks, except that they were asked to imagine the rabbit next to an elephant.

Participants were faster to answer whether a rabbit has a pink nose when the rabbit was imaged next to a fly than when it was imaged next to an elephant. As you would expect, this task was performed with many different animals. In fact, to be sure it was the size and not the particular animals that led to the results, Kosslyn had participants image enormous flies and tiny elephants. Participants' introspective reports were in line with the predictions. When asked to report a physical detail of an animal that they had imaged in a very small size, participants reported zooming in on the animal to increase its size so that they could inspect the image for the desired detail.

≈ 2,250 ms to answer "Does
a rabbit have a pink nose?"

≈ 2,050 ms to answer "Does
a rabbit have a pink nose?"

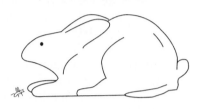

Figure 9.7. *Sample illustration of what participants were supposed to image in Kosslyn's (1975, 1976) experiments. In one case, they imaged a rabbit next to an elephant, and in another they imaged a rabbit next to a fly. Participants were slower to verify that a rabbit has a pink nose in the former than in the latter, presumably because they had to enlarge the image of the rabbit to see its nose.*

The approach of imagery researchers was to turn the parsimony argument back against those who thought that propositions alone could account for all the data. Imagery theorists kept producing experimental findings that were easy to account for if images exist. To keep a single system of representations (just propositions) would have required an increasingly complex set of processes to act on that simple set of representations. It was theoretically still possible to get along with nothing but propositions, but such a theory would have many many processes, some of which were obviously tossed in to account for the latest imagery results. Meanwhile the imagery account was simple. Thus, by the early 1980s it was the imagery theory that was more parsimonious than the propositional theory.

The Metaphor Is Misleading

THE PROBLEM. Pylyshyn argued that it was not clear what was meant by a visual image. How detailed was an image? If you imaged a tiger, could you count the stripes on its tail? If not, why not? He pointed out that the concept of a mental image had not been developed in enough detail to allow predictions about how imagery operated and what would happen in different types of imagery tasks.

Pylyshyn also argued that the idea of mental imagery often was used as a metaphor ("looking at a picture in the mind's eye") and that this metaphor is dangerously misleading. Who exactly is looking at a mental image? If there are pictures in the head, there must be a viewer who can see the pictures. This approach conjures up images of a **homunculus**, a small person sitting at the center of the brain, pulling levers and spinning dials (and looking at visual image screens) to make thought happen. A homunculus is a fatal feature to have in a model because it simply moves the problem of cognition one step farther into the mind. We would still want to know how the mind of the homunculus worked. Pylyshyn claimed that arguing for images was the same as arguing for a homunculus to sit in the mind and appreciate the visual images.

THE RESPONSE.   Pylyshyn's criticisms forced imagery theorists to be more specific about what they thought imaginal representation contained and how it worked. Most researchers held to some version of a **picture theory of imagery**, meaning not that there are literally pictures in the head but rather that seeing an object leads to a certain pattern of activation in the brain associated with the experience of seeing. A representation is stored in memory that is capable of restoring that pattern of activation, at least in part, and that is the experience of visual imagery (Bower, 1972; Hebb, 1968; Neisser, 1967, 1972). The problem is that this theory's origin is vague. Most people say that when they image a tiger, they cannot count the stripes. Why not? You might argue that images are less detailed than perception is. But if you image a die, you can count the spots. What's the difference? Kosslyn (Kosslyn & Schwartz, 1977; Kosslyn, 1980) provided one of the earlier and more notable theories of imagery that was quite specific about the representation and how it operated; it was specific enough to later be embodied in a computer simulation of imagery (Kosslyn, Flynn, Amsterdam, & Wang, 1990; Kosslyn, 1994).

Demand Characteristics and Tacit Knowledge

THE PROBLEM.   Pylyshyn (1981) pointed out that participants could hardly fail to guess what was supposed to happen in most imagery experiments. For example, rotating images a greater distance should take a longer time because rotating real objects a greater distance takes a longer time. **Tacit knowledge** is participants' knowledge of how objects in the real world behave. According to one argument, participants use tacit knowledge to simulate real-world movement and thereby produce results in imagery experiments that match real-world phenomena (for example, scanning longer distances takes a longer time, and rotating images a greater distance takes a longer time). By another account, participants know what results the experimenter expects, and the participant tries to produce the expected data, in an effort either to be nice or to appear "normal" (that is, like everyone else). **Demand characteristics** are signals to the participant about the desired, appropriate, or expected behavior in an experiment. Do experimenters subtly communicate to participants what they should do? Do participants have tacit knowledge about how imagery works?

THE RESPONSE.   Pierre Jolicoeur and Stephen Kosslyn (1985) told the people testing the participants that they should expect not a linear relation between time and distance scanned but a U-shaped function. Despite these instructions to the experimenters, the participants produced data showing the linear relation between distance and scanning time. Thus it doesn't seem that experimenters subtly communicate to participants what they should do. (Or if they do, participants ignore them.)

Other data indicated that participants don't know what the "expected" results are in an imagery experiment. Michel Denis and Mayvonne Carfantan (1985) administered a questionnaire about imagery to 148 undergraduates taking their first course in psychology. Each of the 15 questions described a basic paradigm in the study of visual imagery and asked the participant to select the correct outcome from among several alternatives. For example, one question read:

If it takes a given time to imagine a 60° rotation for one object . . .

  a. It takes longer to imagine a 120° rotation.
  b. It takes less time to imagine a 120° rotation.
  c. It takes the same time to imagine a 120° rotation.
  d. Can't answer.

Very few students could predict the basic result at issue in imagery experiments (that it takes a longer time to scan longer distances). Only about 15% correctly said that it takes longer to rotate the object 120°. Most (41%) thought it takes the same amount of time. Thus it appears that participants don't have much tacit knowledge to go on if they want to produce the "correct" results in imagery experiments.

The Brain and the End of the Imagery Debate

By the early 1980s, most cognitive psychologists had made up their minds that the evidence in favor of a representational system of mental images was compelling. In the late 1980s and early 1990s a new tool became available that convinced any final holdouts. Imaging of the brain using positron emission tomography (PET) and functional magnetic resonance imaging (fMRI) allows indirect measurement of how active different parts of the brain are. The predictions for imagery are quite clear. If imagery is a separate representation that has a lot in common with perception, then when participants perform imagery tasks, the part of the brain that usually handles visual tasks will be most active; that's an area toward the back of the brain called primary visual cortex. If instead propositions do the work behind these imagery tasks, then the language centers of the brain should be most active during imagery tasks because propositions are linguistic. The results of neuroimaging studies supported the imagery theorists' predictions.

In one study Denis Le Bihan and his colleagues (1993) used fMRI. Participants were shown a pattern and then either waited for the next pattern or imagined the pattern they had just seen until the next pattern appeared. Imagery led to significant activation of primary visual cortex. Furthermore, the whole brain is not active when participants perform the task; rather, the activation is specific to visual areas. A number of other investigators reported activation of primary or secondary visual cortex during imagery tasks (Charlot et al., 1992; Chen et al., 1998; Fletcher et al., 1995; Sabbah et al., 1995; Mellet,

Tzourio, Denis, & Mazoyer, 1995). The important conclusion from the imaging work is that the activations observed are in the same brain areas known to support visual perception rather than areas known to support language (as the propositional theory of imagery would predict).

Stand-on-One-Foot Questions

7. List the key criticisms of the idea that visual images are supported by a separate representation system.
8. What are the key differences between images and propositions?
9. How did imagery theorists respond to the criticisms of propositional theorists?

Questions That Require Two Feet

10. We discussed how a propositional representation could yield the same results as an imagery representation for visual scanning (that is, scanning longer distances takes a longer time). How could a propositional representation account for participants reporting that they have to zoom in to see a small detail on an image?
11. Psychologists seemed to completely discount participants' introspections about how they perform imagery tasks; that is, even though participants are quite sure that they are creating images, their feelings that they are doing so seem to count not at all as evidence for whether images exist. Why do you think cognitive psychologists distrust participants' introspections?

HOW DOES VISUAL IMAGERY WORK?

> ➤ *Preview* Images are generated sequentially from parts: first one part is generated, then another part, and so on. Evidence from neuropsychology shows that there are separate processes for the visual and spatial aspects of imagery. The number of objects that can be actively maintained in imagery appears to be limited but can be increased via chunking. Images may be inspected, apparently through processes similar to inspection processes in perception. Images of objects transforming exhibit many properties that physical objects show when they move; for example, an image of a rotating object has inertia.

We began our discussion by trying to determine the function of imagery. Some researchers suggested that imagery has a memory function (Paivio, 1971) and helps us solve problems by imagining the outcome of moving things without actually moving them (Shepard & Cooper, 1986), whereas others suggested that imagery may have no function and may be an epiphenomenon (Pylyshyn, 1973, 1981). Over a decade, work proceeded to show that imagery is not an epiphenomenon but is supported by a separate representation system.

Having established that imagery is not an epiphenomenon, we can return to the question "How does imagery work?" There are two components to this question. First, we might ask where images come from: how are they generated and maintained? Second, we might ask how they are used: how are images inspected and transformed (that is, rotated or expanded)?

Image Generation

Images are generated one part at a time. This finding is a bit surprising because it does not match our introspection; it feels to us as though images pop into mind all of a piece.

Kosslyn and his associates (Kosslyn, Cave, Provost, & von Gierke, 1988) examined the issue of image generation by parts using a modification of a task first described by Podgorny and Shepard (1978). They first showed participants block capital letters such as the one in Figure 9.8. Participants were to familiarize themselves with these letters so that they could image them. Later participants were shown the lowercase version of the letter and then a blank grid like the one in Figure 9.8, and they were told to image the uppercase block letter on the grid. After a brief delay, Xs appeared in two of the cells, and participants were to say whether the imaged letter would cover both Xs. An important aspect of the experiment's design is that the delay between the lowercase cue and appearance of the Xs was only 500 ms. Previous estimates of the time it takes to generate images were on the order of at least 1.5 s, so participants should still have been generating the image when the Xs appeared.

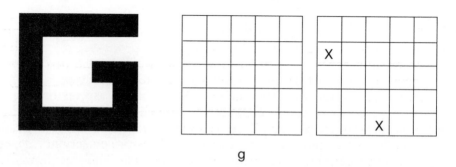

g

Figure 9.8.   *Sample block letter to be imaged (left) and the cue to image it (center) in Kosslyn et al.'s (1988) experiment. Participants were to verify whether the two Xs (right) would be covered by the block capital.*

The results showed that images with more parts take longer to generate than images with fewer parts. In this case, multiple-part images are letters that take multiple strokes to write, such as *G*, and images with fewer parts are letters that take fewer strokes to write, such as *L*. The number of strokes necessary to complete the letter varied from two to five. The response time was about 900 ms for a two-stroke letter such as *L* and about 1,200 ms for a five-stroke letter such as *G*. This extra time must be used to generate the image because in a separate condition in which the block capital was present (and therefore imagery was unnecessary), the number of segments in the letter didn't affect judgment time.

A second feature of this experiment was that the experimenters systematically varied the locations of the *X*s. On some trials the *X*s appeared in locations that they thought would be imaged first, and on other trials the *X*s appeared in locations that they thought would be imaged last. They assumed that participants image block capitals by strokes, in the same way that they write them. Thus the block capital *G* would be imaged beginning with the topmost horizontal bar, then the vertical bar on the left, then the bottom horizontal bar, and so on. (The experimenters verified this order by watching a separate group of participants as they drew block capital letters.)

The results showed that response times were shorter for *X*s on line segments that participants tend to generate first, and response times increased for *X*s on segments that would be imaged later. Because the delay between the cue to image the letter and the *X*s was so short, participants' speed in responding to the *X*s depended on where the *X*s appeared. If the *X*s appeared in the top horizontal bar, participants could respond quickly, but if the *X*s appeared in the small horizontal "tail" of the *G*, they were not so quick to respond. A straightforward interpretation is that when the *X*s appeared, the participants were in the middle of generating the image. If the *X*s were in the part of the image that the participant had already generated (the top horizontal bar), then the participant could respond quickly (about 850 ms), but if the *X*s were in a part that the participant had yet to image, the participant had to continue generating the image to see whether the *X*s would be covered, so the time to respond was longer (about 1,400 ms).

VISUAL VERSUS SPATIAL ASPECTS OF IMAGE GENERATION.   Think back to our discussion of perception in chapter 2, and you can see that this result in imagery is broadly consistent with the idea that imagery and perception overlap a good deal. (Indeed, the overlap of imagery and perceptual processes has been a theme throughout the imagery literature; see Craver-Lemley & Reeves, 1992; Finke, 1980; Finke & Shepard, 1986; O'Craven & Kanwisher, 2000; Podgorny & Shepard, 1978.) It appears that images are generated in parts, which necessarily means that the parts must be put together in the correct spatial configuration; in other words, the parts of the object imaged might be separate from their spatial configuration. We discussed the neuroanatomic separation of object identity and spatial location in visual perception, referring to the "what" stream and the "where" stream (Ungerleider & Mishkin,

1982). Therefore, it seems possible that anatomically separate processes support the generation of image parts and the configuration of the parts into the correct spatial locations.

Supporting evidence can be gleaned from patients with brain damage. If a patient has selective brain damage to the "what" stream or the "where" stream, we would expect selective deficits in imagery, either in generating the parts or in manipulating the spatial aspect of an image. More generally, researchers have drawn a distinction between visual imagery and spatial imagery. It's a bit confusing because the term *visual imagery* is often used to describe any sort of imagery task in the visual modality. In this context, **visual imagery** refers to imagery tasks that emphasize what things look like, and **spatial imagery** tasks require knowledge of where objects or parts of objects are located in space. Table 9.1 lists some visual imagery and spatial imagery tasks. The question is whether there is any reason to believe that visual and spatial imagery are anatomically separable.

Martha Farah and her associates (Farah, Hammond, Levine, & Calvanio, 1988) provided evidence supporting the anatomic separation of visual and spatial imagery, matching the "what" and "where" perceptual brain areas. They reported the case of patient L.H., who had damage to the temporal lobe, which is part of the ventral or "what" processing stream. This damage caused a perceptual deficit in L.H. called **agnosia**: he had trouble identifying objects

Table 9.1.   *Visual Imagery and Spatial Imagery*

Visual Imagery	Description	Spatial Imagery	Description
Animal tails	Judge whether an animal has a long tail proportional to its body size.	Letter rotation	Participant must say whether a rotated letter is mirror reversed.
Colors	Name the color of a common object that has a characteristic color (such as a football).	Mental scanning	Participant judges whether an arrow, if continued, would hit one of two distant dots.
Size comparison	Compare sizes of two objects that are close in size (such as a cigarette pack and a Popsicle).	Letter corners	Classify corners of a block letter as to whether each is at the top or bottom or the middle of the letter.
State shapes	Participant hears 3 state names and must say which 2 states are the most similar in shape.	State locations	Participant hears 3 state names and must say which 2 states are the closest on the U.S. map.

through vision, but the difficulty was not caused by a low-level visual problem. L.H. could see lines and curves accurately, but he could not put those parts together to recognize an object. Someone with agnosia might be able to describe an object as having five short tubes attached to a larger pocket but not recognize that the object is a glove. L.H. had minimal problems visually locating objects; if you put a glove on a large desk, for example, he could easily find it even though he couldn't identify it. L.H. had problems with imagery tasks that mirrored his perceptual deficits. He was grossly impaired in the visual imagery tasks described in Table 9.1, but he performed the spatial memory tasks normally.

In a somewhat less detailed test of another patient, David Levine, Joshua Warach, and Martha Farah (1985) described a patient who had damage to the "where" processing stream. In terms of perception, this patient had difficulty with spatial aspects of vision such as localizing objects in space but had no problem identifying objects on the basis of their appearance. This patient could also describe the appearance of objects from memory using visual imagery but could not describe from memory the locations of landmarks and objects that should have been familiar to him.

Functional imaging results seem to support the data from patients with brain damage. Bessie Alivisatos and Michael Petrides (1997) used PET to image 10 participants while they performed a mirror rotation task. Participants saw a rotated letter and had to say whether it would be mirror reversed when upright. Strong activation of the parietal cortex (dorsal stream) was associated with the mental rotation.

In another study, Emmanuel Mellet and his colleagues (Mellet, Tzourio, Denis, & Mazoyer, 1998) used a strongly visual task while imaging with PET. Participants heard concrete nouns and were to generate an image of each word's referent. This task led to little activation in the parietal lobe but significant activation in the temporal lobe.

We have seen that there is good evidence that visual images are generated from memory representations used to identify objects. Furthermore, anatomically separate processes appear to underlie the visual aspect of this task (recruiting the mental representation of what the object looks like) and the spatial aspect (spatially arranging and possibly transforming the parts). The anatomical separation implies that there could well be differences in the storage of visual and spatial aspects of images, but these details are not yet known.

IMAGE MAINTENANCE. We've been talking about the processes involved in generating an image. Bear in mind that once an image is generated, it does not remain in memory unless it is actively maintained, and that requires attention. You can easily demonstrate this fact yourself. If you create a visual image (say, a cat running with a ball in its mouth), the image disappears if you divert attention from it. An image fades very quickly and needs constant refreshing, perhaps because imagery shares processes with vision, and vision requires fast fading so that our view of the world doesn't get confused as we move our eyes (Kosslyn, 1995).

Images are limited, then, because they must be refreshed continually. They are also limited in the amount of information they can contain. Again, you can appreciate this fact intuitively simply by imaging an object and adding objects to your image; you'll quickly find it difficult to keep all the objects in mind. Nancy Kerr (1987; see also Attneave & Curlee, 1983; Cornoldi, Cortesi, & Preti, 1991) studied the capacity limitations of visual imagery. She showed participants a matrix with one square designated as the start of a pathway. The picture of the matrix was removed and the participant heard seven direction instructions (*left, right, up, down,* and so on) for the pathway. The matrix was shown again and the participant was to show the current location within it. The matrices varied in size, and some were two-dimensional and some three-dimensional. As shown in Table 9.2, dimensionality had a big impact on performance. Performance was much better on a $3 \times 3 \times 4$ matrix than a 6×6 matrix, even though the matrices had the same number of squares.

One interpretation of this result is that participants chunk spatial dimensions; it is easier to maintain an image of four 3×3 arrays than to maintain a single 6×6 array. Kerr tested this possibility in another experiment by presenting participants with an 8×8 array but instructing them to consider it as composed of four 4×4 arrays. To aid in this chunking, she added heavy lines to the 8×8 matrix so that the 4×4 arrays were apparent. As shown in Table 9.3, performance was almost the same on this 8×8 array as it was on a $4 \times 4 \times 4$ array and better than it was on an 8×8 array without instructions to chunk.

Image Inspection

What does it meant to inspect a visual image? Again, it sounds like we're talking about a person (make it a very small person) who inspects a screen in the brain. I keep emphasizing that that's not what is meant because it is so easy to misunderstand the claim. Inspecting the image means interpreting the representation that is on the visual buffer. It requires a small person no more than perception does.

Several sources of evidence help us understand **image inspection**, which we can define as processes we engage to better know the visual characteristics of an image. We engage similar processes in visual perception. When you're looking at a painting, for example, you scan the painting, looking at different

Table 9.2.   Results of Kerr's (1987) Imagery Capacity Experiment

Matrix Size	Number of Squares	% Correct
3×3	9	99
$2 \times 2 \times 2$	8	99
6×6	36	57
$3 \times 3 \times 4$	36	79

Table 9.3.   *Effects of Chunking in Kerr's (1987) Experiment*

Matrix Size	Number of Squares	% Correct
8 × 8 without chunking	64	30
8 × 8 with chunking	64	53
4 × 4 × 4	64	59

parts of it, and perhaps moving closer to an area to get a good look at it. It is thought that the inspection of images recruits some of the same processes that are used in inspecting the world in perception. Several sources of evidence indicate that this is true; visual perception and imagery interfere with each other if you attempt to inspect different objects, and the two processes complement each other when you inspect a single object.

You'll recall that in Alan Baddeley's working memory model, the visuospatial sketchpad was thought to be similar to, if not synonymous with, visual imagery. In chapter 4 we discussed a relevant experiment performed by Baddeley and his colleagues (Baddeley, Grant, Wight, & Thomson, 1975). They asked participants to remember a series of sentences such as "In the next square down, put a 1. In the next square to the left, put a 2." Some participants were told that it might help them to remember the sentences if they imaged a 4 × 4 matrix and considered the upper right square as the starting square. Other participants heard sentences that made it very difficult to use an imagery strategy; the directional terms *up, down, right,* and *left* were replaced with the nonsense words *good, bad, quick,* and *slow,* making odd sentences such as "In the next square bad, put a 2."

While participants were listening to (and trying to remember) these sentences, some also had to perform a demanding tracking task, keeping a handheld stylus on a moving target. The results showed that memory for the sentences was greatly affected by the tracking task. Participants made about three errors on the sentences when they were not performing the tracking task, but they made about nine errors with the tracking task. Furthermore, the tracking task did not interfere with sentence tasks that did not encourage the use of imagery; performance for these sentences was about three errors with or without tracking. That indicates that the high error rates with tracking occurred not simply because a secondary task was performed but because participants were trying to use imagery for one task (sentences) at the same time as they were trying to use perception for a different task (tracking). The interpretation of this result is that imagery and perception share resources.

Baddeley and his colleagues showed that imagery and perception interfere when we try to do different things with them. Martha Farah (1985) showed that imagery can facilitate perception if both processes are doing the same thing. Participants were asked to watch a video monitor on which a box appeared for 850 ms, the box disappeared for 100 ms, and then another box appeared for 850 ms in the same location. One of the two boxes contained a faint letter (either an *H* or a *T,* but participants didn't know which beforehand). Participants had to say which of the two boxes contained the faint letter. In addition, participants were to perform this task while they imaged either an *H* or a *T*. On some trials the letter they imaged matched the faint letter on the screen, but on others it didn't. When the imaged and perceived letters matched, participants averaged 85.3% correct, but when they did not match, participants averaged 76.8%. In a second experiment, Farah showed that the facilitation works only if the participant images the letter in the same place where it appears on the screen. This finding shows that the effect is not caused just by thinking about the letter. Activating a memory representation of the matching letter is not enough; the image and the perception share some truly visual property.

Even more striking are demonstrations by Ronald Finke and his associates (see Finke, 1996, for a review) that participants can use imagery to combine simple parts and then see unexpected wholes on the visual image. For example, Finke and his colleagues Steven Pinker and Martha Farah (1989) showed that participants can manipulate mental images of simple figures and recognize the resulting patterns as something different from what they started with. Here are the instructions participants heard. The first item was for practice. (The answers appear at the end of the chapter.)

Practice

Imagine the letter *Q*. Put the letter *O* next to it on the left. Remove the diagonal line. Now rotate the figure 90 degrees to the left. The pattern is the number 8.

Test Items

1. Imagine the number 7. Make the diagonal line vertical. Move the horizontal line down to the middle of the vertical line. Now rotate the figure 90 degrees to the left. What is it?
2. Imagine the letter *B*. Rotate it 90 degrees to the left. Put a triangle directly below it having the same width and pointing down. Remove the horizontal line. What is it?
3. Imagine the letter *Y*. Put a small circle at the bottom of it. Add a horizontal line halfway up. Now rotate the figure 180 degrees. What is it?
4. Imagine the letter *K*. Place a square next to it on the left side. Put a circle inside of the square. Now rotate the figure 90 degrees to the left. What is it?
5. Imagine a plus sign. Add a vertical line on the left side. Rotate the figure 90 degrees to the right. Now remove all lines to the left of the vertical line. What is it?
6. Imagine the letter *D*. Rotate it 90 degrees to the right. Put the number *4* above it. Now remove the horizontal segment of the *4* to the right of the vertical line. What is it?

The transformations were successfully carried out 58.1% of the time (so that the final image looked the way the experimenters intended). When the transformations were executed correctly, participants could identify the object that the new resulting pattern depicted 59.7% of the time. Thus this task is not trivially easy, but it is quite possible to mentally manipulate images, inspect the results, and in so doing discover a new emergent pattern.

Another aspect of image inspection is the ability to inspect different parts of an image in isolation from other parts. We have already discussed this ability earlier, when we talked about Kosslyn's (1975) results showing that participants can zoom in on parts of an image when necessary to inspect a specific subpart. For example, a participant might focus on a rabbit's nose to determine whether it is pink and even rescale the size of the image if necessary to make this determination (see also Bundesen & Larsen, 1975, for more on size rescaling).

It seems that we would need to shift attention to various locations of the visual image to inspect different parts of it. There is evidence that this attentional process has much in common with those that support visual perception. These data come from patients with brain damage. Edoardo Bisiach and Claudio Luzzatti (1978) tested several patients with **hemispatial neglect** who ignore half of the visual world (almost always the patient's left side). This is a deficit of attention, not perception. Visual perception is normal if attention can somehow be focused on the neglected side of the world, but under most circumstances it cannot. The patient behaves as if that side of the world does not exist. If you show the patient a painting and ask for a description, the left side will be ignored. If you ask the patient to split a candy bar down the middle, the cut will be made about three-fourths of the way to the right: the left half is ignored, so the patient divides the half that he or she sees.

Remarkably, this deficit of attention extends to visual imagery. Bisiach and Luzzatti asked the patients to imagine taking a walk around Milan, their hometown. At one point, patients were asked to "walk" into the Piazza del Duomo, a well-known square in Milan, and describe what they saw; they described landmarks on the right side of the piazza. Patients were asked to continue their mental walk and again enter the Piazza del Duomo and describe what they saw, but this time from the opposite end of the square. Patients again described only objects on the right side, but because they entered from the other side, they were now describing the objects they had previously ignored. These patients can image the whole square, but because of their attention deficit, either they image just half of it at a time, or they image the whole thing but cannot direct attention to the left side of the image. In either case, the important point is that the perceptual deficit extends to imagery. The implication is that attention is directed to inspect both the parts of an image and perceptual scenes in the same way.

Another interesting finding about image inspection concerns the relation of eye movements during perception of a moderately complex pattern and visual imagery of the pattern (see Stark & Ellis, 1981, for a review). Stephan Brandt and Lawrence Stark (1997; see also Laeng & Teodorescu, 2002) showed participants irregular checkerboard-type matrices and recorded participants' eye movements when they inspected pictures of the matrices and when they later imaged the matrices and inspected the images. The researchers found that saccades (eye movements) and fixation times (how long the eye stayed in a particular spot) were closely correlated in the perception and the imagery conditions. Figure 9.9 shows one of the matrices, with the locations of eye fixations when the checkerboard was viewed and when it was imaged. Each number refers to a place where the eyes fixated.

Why would participants move their eyes when they inspect a visual image? The eyes aren't seeing anything helpful, so why move them? Eye movements are closely linked to shifts of attention; we normally move our eyes when we shift attention. Scanning a visual image means shifting your attention to a different part of the image, so it is likely that eye movements are generated and executed simply because eye movements are so typically a part of a shift of attention.

Image Transformation

We mentioned earlier that image transformation is used to examine the consequences of a physical action before we go to the trouble of taking the physical action. Will your car fit in that tight parking space? Is this brick the right size to prop up the sofa with the missing leg?

In the course of this chapter we have described some of the ways in which images can be transformed. A list of the transformations we have described (and some that we haven't) appears in Table 9.4. Most of the work examining the transformation of visual images has asked participants to rotate the images. An important result of this work is the conclusion that mental image

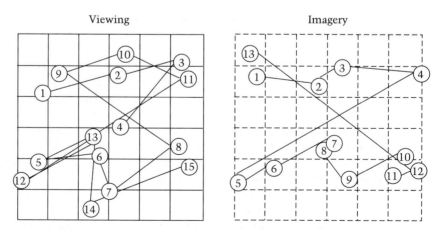

Figure 9.9. *Checkerboard-type matrix used in Brandt and Stark's (1997) eye movement experiment.*

transformation faithfully reflects the physical properties of objects. Mental images in motion obey the same laws of motion that real objects do. How do we know that?

Objects in the world rotate all of a piece; that is, you don't see one part rotating, then the next part rotating, and so on. Thus, the complexity of the object (how many parts it has) doesn't affect the ease with which we can perceive the object rotating. The same should be true of imagery. Lynn Cooper (1975) tested this hypothesis, using made-up objects with different numbers of angles to represent different levels of object complexity. Participants first underwent training to learn the objects; they learned which orientation was to be considered standard and which was mirror reversed. In sessions 2–6 participants were asked to judge whether the standard or mirror-reversed figure was presented, but the figures were rotated either 0, 60, 120, or 180 degrees from the training orientation. In each session participants performed 128 trials. The critical question was whether the time it took for participants to make the rotation varied with the complexity of the object, and the answer is that it did not, as shown in Figure 9.10.

The crucial information in Figure 9.10 is the slope of the lines, which show the best fit for the response times to evaluate each figure at each rotation. We can evaluate how hard it is to mentally rotate the object by measuring the slope of the line. If it's harder to rotate an object a greater distance, response times for 180 degrees will be much higher than for 120 degrees, which will be much higher than 60 degrees, and the slope will be quite steep. As you can see, the slopes are about the same for all of the figures; thus more complex figures are not more difficult to mentally rotate. It's as easy to image

Table 9.4.   *Image Transformations*

Transformation	Description	Citation
Rotation	Rotate the image about an axis.	Shepard & Metzler (1971)
Expansion and contraction	Expand (or shrink) an image in size.	Bundesen & Larsen (1975)
Sequenced transformation	Apply more than one spatial manipulation in a sequence.	Sekuler & Nash (1972)
Folding parts to make a whole	Move parts of an object that have limitations on how they can move to make a whole with a different shape (for example, fold paper to make a box).	Shepard & Feng (1972)
Transforming color	Change the color of an object.	Watkins & Schiano (1982)

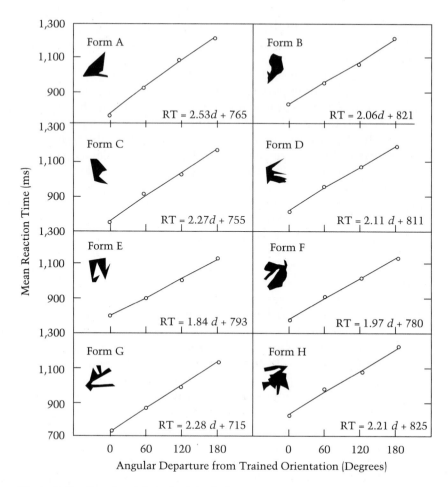

Figure 9.10. *Results of Cooper's (1975) object rotation experiment.*

a complex object rotating as a simple one, just as it's equally easy to perceive the rotation of a complex object or a simple object.

A second source of evidence that mental transformations mirror the real world is that imaging rotations takes longer if the rotation would be difficult in the real world. Parsons (1987a, 1987b) showed participants drawings of hands and asked them to judge whether each one was a right or left hand. The data showed that, as with other stimuli, greater rotation took a longer time. More interesting was that it took longer to make the judgment if the rotational movement would be uncomfortable to make because of a biomechanical constraint—that is, because of the way the joint is constructed. (Parsons had participants rate the comfort of different hand positions.)

Participants saw the right hand, palm down, as the "standard" hand, and the hand was rotated through various angles. Parsons recorded the time it took respondents to judge whether the hand shown was a right or left hand. Participants were much slower to identify a hand with the thumb pointing down than one with the thumb pointing up, even though both positions were 90-degree rotations from the "standard" hand. This result indicates that participants performed this task by imagining their own hands making the required transformation and that when they would be slow to assume a particular position (as with the right thumb pointing down) they were slow to mentally image taking that position (see also Cooper & Shepard, 1975). Again, this result is consistent with the idea that mental imagery mirrors what happens in perception.

More evidence that mental images mirror perception comes from experiments showing that rotating images have momentum. There is no reason an image of a rotating object shouldn't be able to stop on a dime, except that a real object doesn't do that. But how do we know that when participants imagine a rotating object, they actually imagine it rotating just a bit beyond the stopping place they might intend because of momentum? Jennifer Freyd and Ronald Finke (1984) tested this possibility by showing participants three pictures of a rectangle in successive positions of rotation, telling them to remember the third picture (the target). The experimenters then showed the participants a test picture, which they were to compare with the target picture. Presumably they would compare the test picture (which was visible) with an image of the target. The experimenters reasoned that if rotating images have momentum, participants would likely remember the target picture as continuing the rotation slightly and should say that the test picture was the same as the target if the test actually continued the rotation slightly. That's exactly what the results showed. If the test stimulus continued the rotation, participants made errors about 45% of the time. If the test stimulus was rotated slightly the wrong way, they made errors only 5% of the time. Freyd and Finke interpreted these results as showing that the rotation continues to a small extent, so there is momentum in the rotation of a visual image, just as there is in the rotation of a real object (see also Freyd, 1987; Munger, Solberg, & Horrocks, 1999).

Box 9–2 Direct Evidence for Smooth Rotation

There has been some controversy over whether image rotation occurs smoothly—with the object occupying all intermediate positions between the starting and ending position—or by flipping through a series of snapshots, each some distance closer to the endpoint. Behavioral and neuroscientific data indicate that the image does occupy all of the intermediate positions.

Apostolos Georgopoulos and his colleagues (1989) trained a rhesus monkey to perform mental rotation. The monkey sat in a chair in front of a table with eight lights arranged in a circle. There was also a jointed arm with a handle. At the start of each trial the monkey was to move the handle to the center of the circle of lights. Then one of the lights illuminated and the monkey moved the handle to the light to get a reward. In another condition, the monkey moved the handle not to the illuminated light but to the light that was 90 degrees counterclockwise

(Continued)

from the illuminated light. While the monkey was performing this task, the researchers were recording from individual neurons in primary motor cortex.

The analysis of these data is complicated. How is a direction for movement represented? (Suppose we call movement directly away from the body 90 degrees.) It is not the case that a movement of 90 degrees is represented by a small pool of cells that fire when you want to move that way, and these neurons do not fire otherwise. Rather, each cell has a preferred direction of movement, and when you move in that direction it fires a lot; when you move in other directions it still fires, but less intensely. Thus for every movement, all cells in primary motor cortex fire, but an individual cell fires in proportion to the similarity of its preferred direction of movement to the desired direction of movement of the arm. It's as if each cell is a bidder at an auction; when some other part of the system determines that the arm should move 90 degrees, all of the cells start bidding, and the cell that likes to move 90 degrees bids the highest (fires the most). The bids can be summarized and the average bid ends up being the direction that the arm moves.

Georgopoulos and his colleagues tested what happens when they trained the monkey not to point directly to the illuminated light but instead to another light 90 degrees counterclockwise from it. The summary of neural activity, calculated every 10 ms between the appearance of the light and the time when the monkey made the movement, showed that initially the neurons fired in the direction toward the light but then changed in a way consistent with a counterclockwise sweep until the selected direction was the required 90 degrees counterclockwise. The researchers could see the pattern of neural activity change in time, rotating from the location of the light to the required location, as shown in Figure B9.2.

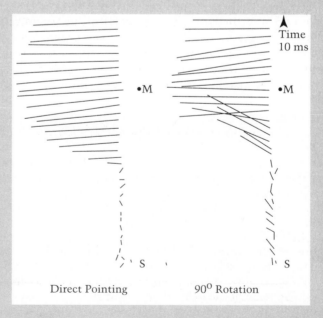

Direct Pointing   90° Rotation

Figure B9.2.

(Continued)

It should be noted that these recordings were taken in the primary motor cortex; thus the spatial rotation is unlikely to be taking place in these cells. Rather, the rotation occurs elsewhere (likely parietal cortex), but instead of completing the rotation and then feeding the final direction for movement to motor cortex, the cortical area that performs the rotation continually feeds the current best guess about the direction of movement to the motor cortex. By eavesdropping on the motor cortex, we have another source of solid evidence that mental rotation occurs via smooth rotation, including all the positions between the starting and stopping points of the rotation

We have seen that mental images show many of the same properties of actual physical objects. Mental images, like real objects, rotate holistically, occupy intermediate positions as they rotate, are subject to biomechanical constraints, and have momentum. Why do images behave like real objects when they do not need to? One possible explanation lies in a distinction first made explicit by Michael Kubovy (1983). Kubovy pointed out that when researchers talk about image transformation, they often speak as though there is a representation that rotates. Nothing in the data we've discussed necessitates this interpretation, however. Instead, it could be that people image the object rotating. We don't form an image of an *R* and then rotate the representation of *R*. Rather, we form an image of a rotating *R*. This subtle distinction may help explain why mental images move in ways that are consistent with real objects. It seems odd that they do so because we don't expect that mental entities (such as representations) should necessarily move in the same ways that physical entities do. But this oddity is explained if we instead assume that the mental entity is not being moved at all; rather, the mental entity represents the movement of a physical entity. In that case, it makes sense that mental images move as physical objects do because they represent the physical world.

Stand-on-One-Foot Questions

12. Name the key processes involved in using visual imagery.
13. Describe the difference between visual imagery and spatial imagery, and describe the anatomic locations of each.
14. How do we know that images are generated by parts, not all at once?

Questions That Require Two Feet

15. What evidence have we discussed in this chapter that is relevant to Baddeley's working memory theory?

16. *Many of the functions of imagery described in this chapter are closely tied to imagery itself. We've talked about using transformations to imagine the outcome of moving physical objects, and we've talked about the memory function of imagery. Can you think of another cognitive process that imagery might help?*

17. *Evaluate the truth of this broad characterization: "Visual imagery is just perception running backwards."*

KEY TERMS

abstract words
agnosia
analog
concrete words
demand characteristics
dual coding hypothesis
epiphenomenon
hemispatial neglect

homunculus
image inspection
imageless thought
    controversy
imagens
logogens
Occam's razor
parsimonious

picture theory of
    imagery
proposition
second-order
    isomorphism
spatial imagery
tacit knowledge
visual imagery

Answers to imagery questions on p. 356

1. the letter T
2. a heart
3. a stick figure person
4. a television
5. the letter *F*
6. a sailboat

10

Decision Making and Deductive Reasoning

You probably don't even notice the number of decisions you make each day. Take the bus or walk? Say "hello" to the acquaintance or pretend not to see her? Paper or plastic? Similarly, you probably do not notice the frequency with which you reason deductively. I may say to you, "If we buy the milk up the street, we'll save a nickel." If you then go up the street and buy the milk, you obviously expect to save a nickel. This expectation is based on deductive reasoning, although you probably wouldn't notice that you had engaged in reasoning at all. In this chapter we examine how we make decisions and how we reason.

We consider these two topics in the same chapter because for both types of problems, we can derive answers that are objectively correct. As we'll see later in the chapter, we could argue about whether these "objectively correct" answers are necessarily the ones psychologists should pay attention to, but to a first degree of approximation, problems that involve decision making and deductive reasoning have clear answers. Other questions do not have such clear answers, and we consider those in chapter 11. The first question we take up in this chapter is **Do people consistently make optimal decisions?** That is, if there is an objectively correct answer, is that the one people choose? As we'll see, the answer often is "No."

That fact doesn't mean that people never make optimal decisions, but it does indicate that we do not use rules designed for optimality. One reason is that it would often be time-consuming and difficult to derive optimal answers to moderately complex questions. We need shortcuts to help us derive good (but not necessarily optimal) solutions. **What shortcuts do people use to make decisions?** As we'll see, the most influential answer to this question is that people use what we might call reasoning shortcuts, procedures that allow us to arrive at an answer quickly and with little effort and that usually produce a correct answer.

In decision making, a choice must be made from among two or more outcomes. In most reasoning problems, we are presented with an argument and asked what conclusion can be made, or we are asked to evaluate the validity of a conclusion that is supplied. For example, I might ask what conclusions (if any) could be drawn from these two premises.

On Thursdays I eat melon.

Today is not Thursday.

As mentioned earlier, deductive reasoning is similar to decision making in that we can identify objectively correct answers. Deductive reasoning is different, however, in that the problems often are less complex, at least in principle. We might therefore entertain the possibility that people are optimal problem solvers in this domain (that is, they reason in accordance with the rules of formal logic). **Do people reason logically?** Alas, the answer is "No," as you probably already guessed. If people use shortcuts in decision making, we might guess that they use shortcuts in reasoning problems as well. To some extent that's true, but some models of reasoning that don't use such shortcuts seem to do a better job of accounting for people's behavior.

Do People Consistently Make Optimal Decisions?

> ➤ *Preview* Decision making generally entails selecting from two (or occasionally more) options. We can define criteria by which some choices are better than others. One criterion is rationality, which means that choices are internally consistent: decisions are made in the same way each time. In normative models of decision making, a second criterion dictates which choice is best. For example, a possible criterion would be to maximize financial gain. Evidence shows, however, that people's choices are neither rational (they are not consistent) nor normative (they do not conform to any criterion such as maximizing financial reward). Yet people don't necessarily make irrational, poor choices; instead, whatever mechanisms guide decisions are not tuned to make optimal decisions consistently but are guided by some other principle.

In a way, **decision making** can be said to encompass all of human behavior. As you read this book, you are making a decision not to find a pair of scissors and cut it into very small pieces, you are making a decision not to hunker on the floor and chatter like a squirrel, and so on. When researchers say that they study decision making, however, they usually mean a situation in which someone must select one path from two or more explicit courses of action.

Normative or Rational Models

Most of us would like to think of ourselves as sensible, and part of being sensible is making effective choices. There are two ways in which our choices can be effective or ineffective. First, our choices may or may not be **rational**, meaning internally consistent. For example, we might expect choices to show **transitivity**: if some relationship holds between the first and second of three elements and also between the second and third elements, then it ought to hold between the first and third. For example, if I prefer apple pie to Bavarian cream pie and Bavarian cream to chocolate cake, then I should prefer apple pie to chocolate cake. Rational choices must also be consistent; I can't say that I like classical music better than funk and I also like funk better than classical. Notice that the requirement of rationality has no bearing on the particular choices a person makes. The theory doesn't prescribe that I should like apple pie better than Bavarian cream. Rationality simply means that there is consistency across the choices made.

Other theories, however, are prescriptive, meaning that some choices are considered better than others and usually that one choice is optimal from among the possibilities. These are called **normative theories**. What makes a choice the optimal one varies with the particular theory. In **expected value** theory the optimal choice is the one that offers the largest financial payoff, taking into account the probability of the payoff. For example, suppose you were offered the following choices.

A. 0.5 chance of winning $50

B. 0.25 chance of winning $110

The expected value of each choice is easy to calculate: it's the probability of winning multiplied by the value of the prize. Thus the expected value of the first choice is $0.50 \times \$50 = \$25$. The expected value of the second choice is $0.25 \times \$110 = \$27.50$. Hence, if expected value guides our decisions, we will always select the second choice.

In the next section we discuss in more detail how people's choices violate normative and rational models. People often make choices that are not optimal if expected value is the guide. Anyone who buys a lottery ticket or gambles in a casino is not making choices guided by expected value. Every bet in a casino favors the house, not the player (see Table 10.1); hence, expected value dictates that casino guests should make the choice of not wagering.

Setting casino games aside, it is easy to think of instances where expected value would not guide your choices. For example, suppose that it's late in the afternoon, you skipped lunch, and you're broke. I offer you these choices.

A. 0.85 chance of winning $8

B. 0.25 chance of winning $28

Expected value dictates that you should take Choice B. The expected value of Choice A is $6.80 and for Choice B it's $7. But we've said that you're hungry, and you're broke. You may well think to yourself, "I'm quite likely to get the $8, but I'm not very likely to get the $28. Although it would be nice to have the extra $20, I really want to make sure I get some money so that I can go get something to eat." This is an example of maximizing **expected utility**. Utility is the personal value we attach to outcomes rather than to their absolute monetary

Table 10.1.   *Average Return for Casino Games*

Game	Bet	Average Return (%)
Roulette	Single number	94.7
Roulette	Red or black	97.2
Blackjack	Varies	~99
Craps	Pass or don't pass	98.6
Slot machine	Nickel	84.8
Slot machine	Quarter	89.8
Baccarat	Banker	98.6
Baccarat	Player	98.2

Average return indicates the percentage of your money you can expect to recoup over an infinitely long session of betting. Odds are from Reber (1999). Roulette odds depend on the wheel, which varies by locale; odds shown are for most U.S. casinos. Odds of blackjack and baccarat depend in part on the skillfulness of choices made by the player and on the rules, which vary slightly by locale. The return of slot machines also varies.

value. In this case, the extra $20 does not have sufficient utility to justify the risk of not getting the $8. Similarly, I might offer you 1 sandwich for $1 or 100 sandwiches for $50. In terms of expected value, you're better off with 100 sandwiches. But what will you do with 100 sandwiches?

Here's another example of a choice that is probably guided by expected utility, not expected value.

A. 1 chance of winning $1

B. 0.00000014 chance of winning $3 million

This problem represents the typical odds of winning the state lottery in Virginia. You can either be certain of keeping your dollar (by not playing in the first place), or you can sacrifice your dollar to try to win $3 million at odds of about 1 in 7 million. The expected value clearly favors keeping your dollar. From the utility perspective, however, the expected utility of losing $1 dollar is low, and expected utility of $3 million is quite high.

Although the concept of utility (first introduced by von Neumann and Morgenstern, 1944) helps in understanding people's choices, people do not always behave as expected utility theory would predict.

Demonstrations of Human Irrationality

We can point to at least two principles that should be observed if decisions are made rationally: description invariance and procedure invariance. **Description invariance** means that people will consistently make the same choice irrespective of how the problem is described to them as long as the basic structure of the choices is the same. **Procedure invariance** means that people will consistently make the same choice irrespective of how their preference for that choice is measured. You might ask them to choose among several alternatives, make a series of pairwise comparisons, or assign a monetary value to each choice; it shouldn't matter. Experiments have repeatedly shown, however, that neither procedure invariance nor description invariance holds.

Here are two problems that were presented to participants in a study by Amos Tversky and Danny Kahneman (1986). They gave each problem to about 125 participants. The numbers in parentheses indicate the percentage of participants selecting each choice.

Suppose I give you $300, but you must also select one of these two options:

A. 1 chance of gaining $100 (72%)

B. 0.5 chance of gaining $200 and a 0.5 chance of gaining nothing (28%)

Suppose I give you $500, but you must also select one of these two options:

A. 1 chance of losing $100 (36%)

B. 0.5 chance of losing nothing and a 0.5 chance of losing $200 (64%)

Notice that these two problems are formally similar to one another; the monetary outcomes (factoring in the $300 or $500 you start with) are the same, so the expected utilities should be the same, but the dominant choice nevertheless reverses. Why? The **problem frame**—the way the problem is described—has changed. The first gives you a choice between gains; the second offers a choice between losses. Although the formal outcome of the two problems is the same, the description (or frame) affects the choice that people make. Thus description invariance is violated in this problem.

Here's another problem showing framing effects. Participants are told that a disease is expected to kill 600 people and they must choose between two programs to fight the disease. As before, the percentage of people selecting a choice is shown in parentheses, and as in the monetary example, people are conservative when selecting between potential gains, but they take risks when they select among potential losses.

A. 200 people will be saved. (72%)

B. There's a 1/3 chance that 600 people will be saved and a 2/3 chance that no people will be saved. (28%)

A. 400 people will die. (22%)

B. There is a 1/3 chance that no one will die and a 2/3 chance that 600 people will die. (78%)

There is evidence that physicians make different recommendations for treatments such as the use of chemotherapy against cancer when presented with death rates than when presented with survival rates. In general, people's assessment of risks differs depending on whether the outcome is described in terms of its costs or its benefits. People are averse to taking risks if the outcome is described positively but more willing to take risks if the outcomes are negative.

Another aspect of framing, **psychic budgets** (Thaler, 1980), concerns how we mentally categorize money that we have spent or are contemplating spending. For example, you may not buy yourself a coat that you like because you consider it too expensive. You are putting it in the mental category "luxury" and are unwilling to allocate that sum to a luxury. Suppose your spouse suggests buying that coat as a present for you. Now the same coat at the same price is in a different mental category—"gift"—and it doesn't seem to be such a bad deal anymore, even though if you and your spouse share a checking account, the cost to you is the same.

Tversky and Kahneman (1981) offered a compelling example of this sort of psychic budgeting. They presented scenarios like these to participants.

> Suppose you and a friend are going to the theater. When you get to the theater you realize that somewhere on your way you've lost the tickets, which cost a total of $100. You have more than $100 cash with you. Tickets are still available at the box office. Would you buy tickets to replace those that you've lost?

> Suppose that you and a friend are going to the theater. When you get to the theater you realize that somewhere on your way you've lost $100 cash. The tickets cost $100, and you can get a full refund. Would you cash in the tickets to offset the loss?

Both scenarios involve the loss of $100 and a decision about whether to see the show. Only 46% of participants said that they would buy a second set of tickets, but almost all the participants would still see the play if they had lost cash. People make different decisions because the first scenario leads them to put the $100 loss in the "ticket budget," so buying more tickets makes it seem as though the show is costing $200. The second problem leads people to put the loss in the "bad luck budget," so to speak, so it seems irrelevant to whether they see the show.

There are several related effects. One is that the cost or gain of some part of an item is considered relative to the cost of the entire item. For example, suppose that you were buying a car for $15,000 and someone told you that you could buy an identical car for $14,975 at a dealership across town. Most people would not consider it worth the trouble to go across town to the other dealership. On the other hand, suppose you were buying a briefcase for $75 and someone told you that you could get the same briefcase for $50 across town. You might well think it was worth pursuing that deal. In each case the cost (traveling across town) and the benefit (saving $25) is the same, but the benefit is evaluated relative to the total amount spent in the purchase, not in absolute terms. Car dealers are notorious for exploiting this irregularity of human reasoning, convincing consumers to buy stereo systems, rust proofing, and other options that they would consider poor choices in other situations by pointing out that the option costs only a few hundred dollars, which is nothing considering that the customer is already spending $15,000.

Another related effect involves the **sunk cost**, an investment that is irretrievably spent and therefore should not affect present decision making. The investment need not be of money; it could be time, emotion, and so on. Sunk costs almost always refer to an investment that, in retrospect, was spent unwisely. For example, have you ever sat through a movie you weren't enjoying because you wanted to "get your money's worth"? When you think about it, you really can't get your money's worth. The movie stinks, and nothing will make it worth $8. The $8 is gone—it's a sunk cost. Whether you stay (and suffer through a bad movie) or leave (and do something more pleasurable) does not change the fact that your $8 is gone. Interestingly, animals are insensitive to sunk costs (Arkes & Ayton, 1999); this could be considered an instance in which animals make better choices than people.

A related concept is **loss aversion**: the unpleasantness of a loss is larger than the pleasure of a similar gain. People may be more motivated to make risky choices because of loss aversion. In a classic study on this phenomenon, Kahneman, Jack Knetsch, and Richard Thaler (1990) showed all the participants in their study a coffee mug, telling half of the participants that the mug was theirs to keep. All participants were told to assign a value to the mug and were also told that the real market value of the mug would be revealed at the end of the experiment. If the price an individual participant assigned to the mug was higher than the market value, the participant got the mug (for example, someone who assigned a value of $10 to a mug with a market value of $8 could keep the mug). If the assigned price was lower, the participant got the cash. The interesting finding was that people who were initially told they could keep the mug assigned much higher prices to the mug ($7.12) than people who were merely shown the mug ($3.12). This effect is caused by the way people view the transaction. The people who were shown the mug figured they were going to get a mug or some cash. The people who were told that they owned the mug viewed the transaction as their having to give up their mug (a loss) to get some cash. Because of loss aversion, people don't want to give up "their" mugs, and they demand a high price ($7.12) for doing so.

People's decisions also change when other choices are added, sometimes in unexpected ways. For example, consider this problem, described by Eldar Shafir and Amos Tversky (1995; see also Huber, Payne, & Puto, 1982; Tversky & Simonson, 1993).

Participants were allowed to select one of two prizes:

A. An elegant Cross pen (36%)
B. $6 (64%)

Participants were allowed to select one of three prizes:

A. An elegant Cross pen (46%)
B. $6 (52%)
C. An inferior pen (2%)

The addition of the inferior pen rendered the Cross pen more attractive; the percentage of people selecting it increased. The addition of the nonpreferred pen should not influence how one compares $6 with the Cross pen, but it does.

You'll recall that we initially said that we might test people's decisions for two types of rationality: description invariance (making the same choice irrespective of the problem description) and procedure invariance (making the same choice irrespective of the procedure by which preference is measured). The previous examples show violations of description invariance: people make different choices depending on how the problem is described. What about procedure invariance? Does the way that a preference is measured affect the choice? Research has repeatedly shown that people's choices change depending on how the choice is elicited. For example, suppose you give people a choice between these two outcomes.

A. 8/9 chance to win $4
B. 1/9 chance to win $40

When asked to choose directly, most people (71%) prefer Choice A. Now suppose we elicit choice another way: "What is the minimum price at which you would sell your right to this choice? You know that you have an 8/9 chance to win $4, but I am ready to give you cash so that I now have an 8/9 chance to get the $4. What is the minimum amount of money I would have to give you for you to sell your right to play this game to me? And what price would you assign to Choice B?" When asked to assign prices, 67% of participants assign a higher monetary value to Choice B than to Choice A (Tversky, Slovic, & Kahneman, 1990).

Another example comes from a study by Tversky, Shmuel Sattath, and Paul Slovic (1988). They asked participants to select between two programs that were designed to reduce casualties caused by traffic accidents. Program X cost $55 million, and 500 casualties would be expected in the next year. Program Y cost $12 million, and 570 casualties would be expected next year. When comparing them directly, most participants selected the more expensive program that saves more lives. In another version of the problem, participants were told only the number of casualties, and they were asked to assign a price differential that would make the two programs equivalent choices. Nearly all participants assigned a price difference indicating that $43 million is too much extra to pay to save 70 lives. Again, people's decisions vary depending on how these decisions are elicited.

Thus far, we have shown that people don't make their decisions based on the principles of expected value or expected utility, and indeed that their choices vary depending on how the problem is described or how their preference is elicited. But how optimal is optimal selection? Optimizing means picking the best solution out of all those available. Thus, to optimize, we must either evaluate all possible options or develop a formula that will provide the best solution, even if we don't evaluate all options. Either one of those may require a lot of calculation, especially for moderately complex problems. If you are choosing a car, for example, are you going to test-drive every model on the market? Are you going to thoroughly research the safety of each car and bargain with multiple dealers for the best price on every model before making a selection? Wouldn't those steps be necessary if you are to optimize? Getting the optimal solution may not be optimal in terms of the cost to you of computing it.

Herb Simon (1957) suggested that instead of optimizing, people satisfice. **Satisficing** means selecting the first choice that is above some threshold (in other words, that is satisfactory). One option would be to start generating all possible solutions and select the first satisfactory solution. Even better would be to start by generating solutions that are likely to be satisfactory. We can't generate all of the possibilities, so we need a shortcut that will generate a few that are likely to be satisfactory. We want to know what sorts of shortcuts could generate likely solutions.

Stand-on-One-Foot Questions

1. *What is the difference between normative and rational models?*
2. *What is the difference between expected value and expected utility, and how are they similar?*
3. *How do we know that people do not make rational choices?*

Questions That Require Two Feet

4. *Can utility theory explain why people gamble in casinos?*

5. *Suppose I offered you a bet: if you win, you get a nickel, but if you lose, you die. Presumably I would have to give you pretty steep odds in your favor before you would accept such a bet. In fact, you might even say that you would not accept such a bet no matter what the odds were. Try rephrasing the question so that more people would accept the bet. Hint: Think of a situation in which people don't necessarily realize that they may be risking their lives.*

What Shortcuts Do People Use to Make Decisions?

> ➤ **Preview** Instead of making detailed calculations to select choices, people appear to use heuristics—simple rules that require little calculation and usually yield an acceptable solution. However, heuristics can lead to nonoptimal choices. We discuss three heuristics in this section: representativeness (an event is judged to be probable if it has properties that are representative of a process or category), availability (an event is judged to be probable if one can think of many examples of the event), and anchoring and adjustment (the judged probability of an event is influenced by an initial estimate of its probability). In addition, we examine the sorts of information people systematically ignore even though it would be informative in making decisions. We'll also examine another approach to choice, spearheaded by psychologist Gerd Gigerenzer, who suggests that humans are evolutionarily prepared to think about frequencies (how often something occurs) rather than probabilities (the likelihood that something will occur).

Most psychologists think that people use **heuristics** as shortcuts when they make decisions. These are simple cognitive rules that are easy to apply because they don't require much calculation. Heuristics usually yield acceptable choices but may lead to disadvantageous or inconsistent decisions. A heuristic can be contrasted with an **algorithm**, a formula that produces consistent outcomes and may, if selected correctly, produce optimal outcomes. Algorithms can be complex and difficult to compute. Expected value, for example, is an algorithm; if you calculate the expected value of two choices, you will always end up making the same decision, no matter how the problem is described or how preferences are elicited. We've just shown that people don't use expected value or expected utility. It has been proposed that they use heuristics instead of these algorithms.

Representativeness

Representativeness is a heuristic used when people are asked to judge the probability that something belongs to a category. We are likely to place something in a category if it has features strongly associated with that category. For example, consider these two descriptions from a study by Tversky and Kahneman (1983).

Linda is 31 years old, single, outspoken, and very bright. She majored in philosophy. As a student, she was deeply concerned with issues of discrimination and social justice and also participated in antinuclear demonstrations.

Which of these is more likely?

A. Linda is a bank teller.
B. Linda is a bank teller and is active in the feminist movement.

People incorrectly think that the second statement is more likely to be true than the first. There is some probability that Linda is a bank teller, and if she's a bank teller, she may or may not be a feminist as well. The odds of a conjunction of probabilities (two simultaneous probabilities) can never be higher than one of the constituent probabilities. But people erroneously select the second statement because the description of Linda evokes that of a stereotypical feminist. The representativeness heuristic dictates that an individual (Linda) with features (deeply concerned with social justice) strongly associated with the category (feminist) is likely to be a member of the category.

Representativeness also can be based on the feature that is strongly associated with a process. For example, suppose I toss five pennies two times; designating H as heads and T as tails, on the first toss I obtain HHHHH, and on the second I obtain HHTHT. Which outcome is more likely? The answer is that both outcomes are equally likely. The second toss seems more random, however, because there is no pattern apparent in the toss. For that reason, the second toss is representative of randomness, and because you know that randomness is the process that produces patterns of coin tosses, you judge it to be more likely than the first toss.

Availability

To use the **availability** heuristic to judge the probability of events, you simply try to call examples of the event to mind, and if many examples can be called to mind easily, you judge an event to be more probable. Tversky and Kahneman (1973), for example, asked 152 participants whether there are more words in English that have r as the first letter or r as the third letter. The answer is that there are more with r as the third letter of the word, but 69% incorrectly judged that it's the first. Tversky and Kahneman argued that it is easy to think of words with r as the first letter but quite difficult to think of words with r as the third letter; your mind is not organized in a way that lets you access words according to their third letter.

Here's another problem (Tversky & Kahneman, 1973) in which participants may use availability to make a judgment.

Ten people are to form committees.
How many different committees of x members can they form?

They showed 118 people this problem, with x equal to some number between 2 and 8. As shown in Figure 10.1, as x increased, participants' estimates of the number of committees decreased systematically, although the true value increases and then decreases. The experimenters argued that people use the availability heuristic to answer this question. It is easier to mentally generate two-person committees than six-person committees, so people assume there must be more of them.

Availability may also be the mechanism behind **illusory correlation**, which refers to the fact that people sometimes are inaccurate in judging correlations as they occur in the real world. (Correlation means the degree to which two things are related; see the Appendix if you are not familiar with this concept.) In particular, people often assume that events are correlated if they had a prior belief that the events go together or if the two events are natural associates. For example, I may think to myself, "Anyone who is an actor must be a real egomaniac. How else could a person have the nerve to perform in front of

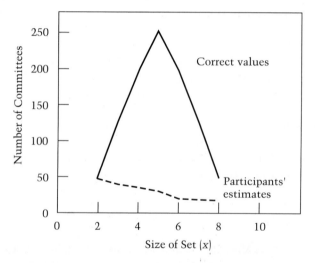

Figure 10.1. *People's estimates of the numbers of committees that can be created from a group of 10 people. The experimenters varied the size of the committees. Note that the graph for the correct values is in an inverted U shape; that's because you can create the same number of committees from two values of x that add up to 10. In other words, every time you create a two-person committee, you have also created a de facto eight-person committee (the people you excluded in creating the two-person committee). Participants' estimates systematically decrease as x increases because it is more difficult to generate committees as x increases (i.e., they are less available).*

large groups of people?" I have the hypothesis that actors will tend to act in an egotistical way. Note that I can observe four possible types of behaviors: people can act egotistically or not, and the person I'm observing may be an actor or not. It is more noticeable when people act in ways that confirm my expectations, so it is more memorable when an actor behaves in an egotistical way. Furthermore, if someone behaves ambiguously—the behavior might be egotistical, or it might not—I am more likely to interpret it as egotistical if the person is an actor. Meanwhile, the other three types of events (the ones that are not consistent with my hypothesis) are not noticed as much and not remembered as well. Hence, when I ask myself, "Is it true that actors are egomaniacs?" I can think of many instances in which I have observed egotistical behavior, and because many instances are available, I judge that the general statement must be true.

Anchoring and Adjustment

The **anchoring and adjustment** heuristic is used to estimate probabilities. We start with an initial probability value (the anchor) by doing a partial computation of the problem or using a probability estimate suggested by some statement in the problem, then adjust this estimate upward or downward on the basis of other information in the problem. For example, Tversky and Kahneman gave participants 5 s to estimate the answer to this problem: $1 \times 2 \times 3 \times 4 \times 5 \times 6 \times 7 \times 8$. The correct answer is 40,320, but the median estimate was 512. When the order of the factors was reversed to $8 \times 7 \times 6 \times 5 \times 4 \times 3 \times 2 \times 1$, the median estimate was much higher: 2,250. The experimenters hypothesized that participants start this problem by multiplying a few of the first numbers (anchoring) and then adjusting this initial estimate upward. The order of the factors matters because it affects the size of the anchor. Both estimates are too low because adjustments usually are insufficient in any problem in which anchoring and adjustment is applied.

Anchoring and adjustment has been shown to influence many judgments, including preference judgments (Carlson, 1990), judgments of answers to factual questions (Tversky & Kahneman, 1974), estimates of probabilities of events such as nuclear war (Plous, 1989), and estimates of preferences of one's spouse (Davis, Hoch, & Ragsdale, 1986). In one study, anchoring and adjustment was also shown to be important in some legal settings. Gretchen Chapman and Brian Bornstein (1996) had participants read a one-page description of a personal injury suit in which a woman sued a health maintenance organization, arguing that the birth control pills prescribed for her had caused her ovarian cancer. The experimenters varied the amount of compensation the woman sought: $100, $20,000, $5 million, or $1 billion. Participants awarded greater compensation as the amount of requested compensation increased. The researchers argued that participants used the requested amount of compensation as an anchor and then adjusted their award depending on their assessment of the facts of the case.

Information We Ignore

Researchers have argued that there are certain types of information that we systematically ignore when we make decisions. Thus, these are not heuristics that are invoked, but these effects nevertheless have important consequences for decision making.

IGNORING SAMPLE SIZE.   **Sample size** is the number of things in a group that you are evaluating. For example, suppose you want to know how tall the average student at your college or university is. It's unlikely that you will measure the height of each student; instead, you'll pick a group of students to measure. How big a group should it be? It turns out that whether the sample is large or small has an impact on what you're likely to find in your measurement. When a sample is large, its average value is closer to the average value of the entire group. In other words, suppose that there are 4,000 people at your school, and their average height is 67 inches. If I randomly select 100 people of the 4,000 (sample size = 100) I am more likely to find that the average height of those 100 is close to 67 inches than if my sample size is 10 people.

Sample size is important in calculating such probabilities, but people do not seem to be naturally sensitive to this information. Tversky and Kahneman (1974) gave participants this problem.

> A certain town is served by two hospitals. In the larger hospital about 45 babies are born each day, and in the small hospital about 15 babies are born each day. About 50% of all babies are boys. However, the exact percentage varies from day to day. Sometimes it may be higher than 50%, sometimes lower.
>
> For a period of 1 year, each hospital recorded the days on which more than 60 percent of the babies born were boys. Which hospital do you think recorded more such days?
>
> **A.** The larger hospital (22%)
>
> **B.** The small hospital (22%)
>
> **C.** About the same (that is, within 5% of each other) (56%)

The correct answer is B. A large sample is much less likely to deviate from 50% than a small one, but people seem not to appreciate that fact. Kahneman and Tversky argue that people solve this problem by using the representativeness heuristic: whether a particular birth is a boy or girl is random at each hospital, and because the process producing the gender is random, it seems that there is an equal chance of deviation from randomness.

IGNORING THE BASE RATE.   A classic problem is used to demonstrate this principle.

> In a certain city there are two cab companies, the Blue and the Green. In this city the Blue company owns 85% of the cabs and the Green owns 15%. A cab is involved in a hit-and-run accident. An eyewitness says she

thinks it was a green cab. The eyewitness vision is tested and it is determined that under the lighting conditions at the time of the accident, she can correctly identify the color of the cab 80% of the time. What are the odds that the hit-and-run cab was green?

Many participants think that there is an 80% chance that it was green, but in fact there is only a 40% chance that it was a green cab. Why? Think of it this way. If I told you that 80% of the cabs were blue cabs and that there wasn't an eyewitness, what would you say the chances are that it was a blue cab? Assuming the drivers of the two companies are equally safe or reckless, you'd say 80%, right? In the problem described above, you still have that information (80% are blue), but now you have additional information based on the eyewitness. The eyewitness account does not invalidate the information about the percentage of cabs; that information should still be taken into account. This information is the **base rate**—the frequency of an event (such as the number of blue cabs) among a larger pool of events (the total number of cabs).

If this seems difficult to understand, consider another example. Suppose you and I are walking along the Champs-Elysées in Paris one Sunday afternoon and I suddenly say, "Wow! I just saw a penguin in that café. Did you see it? It popped out for second and then ran back in. At least, I think it was a penguin. I'm 80% sure." What would you say the odds are that I actually saw a penguin? Even if vision tests showed that I'm 80% accurate in identifying penguins under those conditions, you'd say chances are very small that I actually saw one because with the extremely rare exception of a zoo escapee or perhaps the shooting of a television commercial, there are no penguins in Paris cafés. The base rate is extremely low.

People use base rate information unless they also get additional information, and then they usually ignore the base rate. Notice that the base rate should be ignored if the additional information you get is infallible. If the penguin is walking around the street and I have time to inspect it, watch it walk, and so on, then the chances of my successfully identifying penguins goes from 80% to 100%. If the additional information is 100% accurate, the base rate becomes irrelevant.

A practical and very important example of the importance of base rate information in medical decision making was illustrated by David Eddy (1982). The diagnostic tests physicians use usually are imperfect. Eddy's example concerned the use of mammography to detect breast cancer. Suppose 10,000 women are given a mammogram and if a woman has cancer, the probability is 0.92 that the test result will be positive. If she does not have cancer, the probability is 0.88 that the results will be negative. Eddy asked, "If a woman's test result comes back positive, what are the odds that she does indeed have cancer?" The answer is not 0.92; again, it depends on the base rate.

In Table 10.2, the base rate is set at 1 woman out of 100 having cancer. A total of 100 women out of 10,000 have cancer, and of those 100 women, 90 have a positive test (0.9 probability). Of the 9,900 women without cancer, 8,700 have a negative test (0.88 probability). So a total of 1,290 women have a

Table 10.2.   *Hypothetical Mammogram Outcome for 10,000 Women*

	Women with Cancer	Women without Cancer	Total
Women with positive test	90	1,200	1,290
Women with negative test	10	8,700	8,710
Total	100	9,900	10,000

positive test, but only 90 of those have cancer. With a positive test, the odds of having cancer is about 0.07. Most of the women who show a positive mammogram don't have cancer—the test is a false positive.

How is this possible? The overall low rate of cancer given a positive test comes about because of the low base rate. We assumed a low base rate of 1% because we said that these 10,000 women were selected randomly. Depending on their age, all women are encouraged to get mammograms, so a low base rate among these women may not be unreasonable. The situation would be quite different for a group of women who were getting a mammogram because they had some other symptom indicative of cancer, such as a lump in the breast. Then we would expect the base rate of the presence of cancer to be quite a bit higher.

Probabilities versus Frequencies

Some researchers, notably Gerd Gigerenzer and Ulrich Hoffrage, claim that much of the work we've discussed in this section has a serious flaw. They have made an evolutionary argument that our minds are designed to keep track of frequencies, not probabilities. They cite work from animal researchers (see Gallistel, 1990) indicating that foraging animals keep track of frequencies (for example, for information about food sources) in their environment and argue that people have a hard time reasoning and making decisions when problems are presented in terms of probabilities because our minds are not set up to deal with probabilities.

The implication is that people should perform much better on choice problems presented in terms of frequencies instead of probabilities. Over the last 10 years, Gigerenzer and Hoffrage have tested this hypothesis in several different paradigms. In one study (Gigerenzer & Hoffrage, 1995) they presented participants with 15 problems that had been used in the past to study base rate neglect. Participants either saw the standard probability version or saw the problem in a frequency format (p. 688).

Probability Format

The probability that a woman at age forty will get a positive mammography in routine screening is 10.3%. The probability of breast cancer and a positive mammography is 0.8% for a woman at age forty who participates in routine screening. A woman in this age group had a positive mammography in a routine screening. What is the probability that she actually has breast cancer?

_____%.

Frequency Format

103 out of every 1,000 women at age forty get a positive mammography in routine screening, and 8 out of every 1,000 women at age forty who participate in routine screening have breast cancer and a positive mammography. Here is a new representative sample of women at age forty who got a positive mammography in routine screening. How many of these women do you expect to actually have breast cancer?

_____ out of _____ .

Sixty participants each solved 15 problems, including this mammography problem and the cab problem described earlier. They saw each problem in either the frequency or the probability format. Participants averaged 48% correct with the frequency description and 22% correct with the probability description (see also Cosmides & Tooby, 1996; Gigerenzer, Hell, & Blank, 1988).

In another study, Hoffrage and his colleagues (Hoffrage, Lindsey, Hertwig, & Gigerenzer, 2000) asked 96 advanced medical students to solve problems that involved using these sorts of probabilities (like the breast cancer problem) in medical diagnosis. Each participant saw two problems in the frequency format and two in the probability format. Figure 10.2 shows that the students performed much better with frequencies than with probabilities. It has also been shown that AIDS counselors do not understand how to interpret a positive HIV test result (Gigerenzer, Hoffrage, & Ebert, 1998) and that judges and advanced law students do not know how to interpret DNA test results (Hoffrage, Lindsey, Hertwig, & Gigerenzer, 2000).

Why is base rate neglect apparently greater for probability than for frequency information? Gigerenzer and Hoffrage argue that because our minds evolved in preliterate societies where information would be remembered in terms of frequencies, we are not designed to think about probabilities. By analogy, numbers can be represented as Roman numerals, but we wouldn't want to do long division that way because the representation is inappropriate for the process. Similarly, it is possible to solve these sorts of problems using probabilities, but since

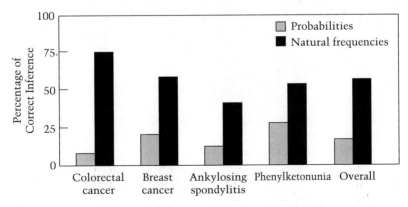

Figure 10.2. *Advanced medical students were much better at solving diagnosis problems presented in frequencies rather than as probabilities. From Hoffrage et al., 2000,* Science, 290, *p. 2261 (Fig. 1).*

we usually represent this information in frequencies, we're not very good at dealing with probabilities.

Other researchers take issue with Gigerenzer's statement that "the mind is a frequentist." They don't take issue with the data—people perform much better with data presented in some formats than others—but they do take issue with the conclusion that it's frequencies that make the difference. They claim that the frequency version of the problem does not simply change probabilities and frequencies but that it changes the *type* of probabilities presented. Other critics claim that important information implicit in the probability version is made explicit in the frequency version; deemed especially important is that some groups are really subsets of other groups, for example, that some people who test positive don't have the disease (Evans, Handley, Perham, Over, & Thompson, 2000; Fiedler, Brinkmann, Betsch, & Wild, 2000; Girotto & Gonzalez, 2001; Johnson-Laird, Legrenzi, Girotto, Legrenzi, & Caverni, 1999; Lewis & Keren 1999; Macchi, 2000; Mellers & McGraw, 1999). You will not be shocked to learn that Hoffrage and Gigerenzer disagree with these critics (Gigerenzer, 2001; Gigerenzer & Hoffrage, 1999; Hoffrage, Gigerenzer, Krauss, & Martignon, 2002). This debate is still far from settled. It is obvious that presentation format makes a substantial difference in performance, but the reasons are not yet clear.

Social Factors

Some researchers have pointed out that the researchers of decision making have been so concerned with statistical optimality that they have ignored other factors that contribute to decision making. People make choices based on social contracts, opportunities to cheat, implications for future choices, and so on (Cosmides & Tooby, 1994, 1996; Gigerenzer & Hoffrage, 1995; Gigerenzer, Hoffrage, & Kleinboelting, 1991; Gigerenzer & Hug, 1992). Gerd Gigerenzer (1992) cited the following story (which he credited to psychologist Brendan Maher).

> A small town in Wales has a village idiot. He once was offered the choice between a pound and a shilling, and he took the shilling. People came from everywhere to witness this phenomenon. They repeatedly offered him a choice between a pound and a shilling. He always took the shilling. (p. 108)

Many choices occur in a social context, which should not be ignored. In the case of the village idiot, the choice is irrational by any metric, but it's the social context that guarantees the opportunity for future choices and thus makes his choice beneficial.

Early research on choice conceived of the mind as a statistician, calculating the probabilities of different rewards that might accrue from different choices. Philip Tetlock (1991, 1992, 2002) pointed out that other metaphors for choice may be more appropriate. The mind may not simply act as a statistician that calculates probabilities. It may also be a theologian protecting values and principles that are sacred, as in choosing human life over any monetary value. It may sometimes act as a politician mediating between conflicting concerns; for example, you may know that your mother has certain expectations regarding your behavior, whereas your friends have other expectations. It may sometimes act as an attorney prosecuting others who are deemed to have violated social contracts.

Goods and services that are normally exchanged have been the stuff of the problems we have examined so far. What happens if you include sacred values in choice problems? Tetlock maintains that pitting a secular value against a sacred value is taboo—for example, putting a dollar value on a life. When sacred values are pitted against one another, Tetlock says that choice is regarded as tragic, as when one must choose between death and dishonor.

Tetlock and his colleagues (Tetlock, Kristerl, Elson, Green, & Lerner, 2000) examined decisions like this by having participants read a story about a doctor who either must choose which of two sick boys' lives to save, or must choose whether to save a sick boy (at a cost of $1 million) or to use $1 million for other hospital needs (including salaries for desired doctors). The researchers found that participants shun and direct anger toward the doctor who makes the taboo trade-offs. Furthermore, the researchers observed an interesting effect concerning the length of time participants believed the doctor took to make his decision. If the doctor thought about the taboo trade-off (life versus money) for a long time, the doctor's reputation was damaged, even if he or she ultimately selected life over money. In contrast, if the doctor thought about the tragic trade-off (life versus life) for a long time, he or she was regarded as wise.

Social influences on decision making are doubtless a significant factor, yet they have been little studied, perhaps because early work in the field grew out of economics; it seems likely that social influences will see more investigation in the future.

Box 10–1 Decision Making and Emotion: The Somatic Marker Hypothesis

You may have noticed that emotion has played no role whatever in our discussion of decision making thus far. That doesn't seem right because many of the decisions we make have emotional consequences. If I see an attractive woman at a restaurant, for example, I must decide whether to speak to her. No matter what my decision, there are emotional consequences: if I speak to her she'll either be friendly or not (with obvious consequences to my emotions), and if I don't speak to her, I will likely feel regret.

Anthony Damasio, Dan Tranel, and their associates (for example, Tranel, Bechara, & Damasio, 2000) highlighted emotional consequences in their somatic marker theory of decision making. A starting point of the theory was the observation of patients with damage to the medial ventral frontal cortex. These patients perform normally on standard neuropsychological tests of memory,

(Continued)

language, intelligence, and so on. Nevertheless, they show marked personality changes: they don't respond normally to punishing consequences, they have an overly optimistic view of themselves and their capabilities, and they often show inappropriate emotional reactions. Furthermore, they seem incapable of making long-range plans in their own best interests. They make poor decisions in selecting friends, planning their careers, and so forth.

Damasio and Tranel suggested that these prefrontal cortical areas are important for learning associations between higher-order stimuli and the emotional consequences that follow. In a typical person, when the higher-order stimuli are present, the ventromedial prefrontal cortex reactivates the somatic response that the stimulus has engendered in the past, including emotional responses generated by the autonomic nervous system: a racing heart, sweaty palms, a peaceful feeling, or whatever. For example, when I see the attractive woman in the restaurant, the ventromedial prefrontal cortex makes available all the emotional states that might result from various courses of action in this situation, such as nervousness in speaking to her or happiness if she seems to like me. Damasio and Tranel argued that these emotional reactions, as well as more logical, cognitive processes, help to limit the possible field of choices of actions.

Thus patients with ventromedial frontal damage make poor decisions because they have lost the ability to make associations between complex stimuli and their consequences. In one study, Tranel tested the responsiveness to emotional stimuli of patients with ventromedial prefrontal cortical lesions. These patients were shown pictures with emotionally charged subjects, such as nude people or mutilations, while their skin conductance was measured. Skin conductance is a measure of how sweaty the palms are and therefore provides an indirect measure of emotion. Although the patients showed a normal skin conductance response to a loud noise, they showed no response to the emotionally charged pictures. Patients with damage to other cortical areas showed a normal response.

In a different task that entailed choice (Bechara, Damasio, Damasio, & Anderson, 1994) patients were to choose a card from one of four decks, A–D. They began the task with $2,000 in play money. They received $100 for selecting from decks A or B and $50 for selecting from decks C or D. Each card carried a financial penalty that varied from card to card and was subtracted from the $100 or $50. Unknown to the participants, the penalties on the A and B deck were on average greater than the penalties in the C and D deck. In the long run, it was advantageous to select only from the C and D deck. As shown in Figure B10.1, patients with ventromedial frontal damage continued to select primarily from the A and B decks, although patients with brain damage in other regions and normal control participants learned to select primarily from the C and D decks.

Recall that these patients are intellectually intact. This study forcefully makes the point that emotion plays a role in decision making. Decisions can have positive or negative consequences, and we learn from them, in part, because of their emotional content. Patients who do not show normal emotional responses do not make advantageous choices, at least for some tasks.

(Continued)

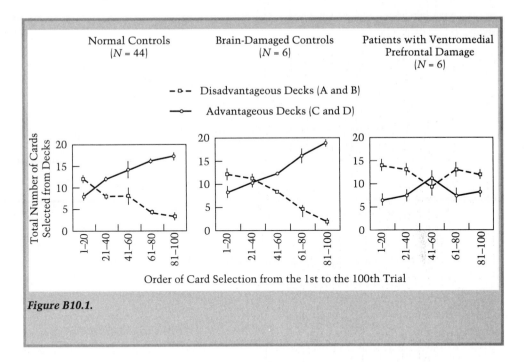

Normal Controls
(N = 44)

Brain-Damaged Controls
(N = 6)

Patients with Ventromedial
Prefrontal Damage
(N = 6)

– ◦ – Disadvantageous Decks (A and B)

— ◦ — Advantageous Decks (C and D)

Total Number of Cards Selected from Decks

Order of Card Selection from the 1st to the 100th Trial

Figure B10.1.

Summary

There are two main points in the preceding sections. First, people do not behave rationally when they make choices. This irrationality takes two forms: our choices don't show procedure invariance (making the same choice no matter how preference is measured) or description invariance (making the same choice no matter how the choice is described).

   Second, people do not always make optimal choices of the type dictated by expected value or expected utility theory. Note that the claim is not that people *never* make an optimal choice. Rather, we're assuming that there is some set of mechanisms that guides people's choices, and if the mechanisms were built to optimize, people would select optimally every time. Because they don't select optimally every time, we assume that a mechanism built on a different principle guides choice. So what is it? The argument presented here is that people use different heuristics, or rules, that are easy to use and that provide rapid answers that are usually effective.

   It's important to emphasize that heuristics usually provide good answers. In the examples we've gone over, heuristics are made to look maladaptive or even foolish. These problems were set up to pit heuristics against expected utility or probability calculations, so the answers based on heuristics are not optimal, but that doesn't mean that heuristics don't lead to good answers most of the time.

Stand-on-One-Foot Questions

6. What are the three heuristics that people use to estimate probabilities, and how do they work?
7. What type of information do people typically ignore when making choices?
8. What is the core of Gigerenzer's argument about why the problems posed to participants in typical choice experiments are unfair and make people look more foolish than they really are?

Questions That Require Two Feet

9. Explain what this sentence means: "You should have no faith in lie detector tests because people who evaluate lie detector tests ignore the base rate of liars."
10. You may have noticed that projects often seem to take longer than you expected when you planned them. Can you apply the anchoring and adjustment heuristic to guess why your estimate is often wrong?

DO PEOPLE REASON LOGICALLY?

> ► **Preview** We have seen that people don't always make optimal choices. What happens with a problem that is more obviously amenable to logical processes? Two important conclusions about deductive logic, as it applies to conditional statements and syllogisms, are that people do not use deductive logic to solve these problems and that the content of the problem has a big impact on people's success in solving it. People can best evaluate conditional statements that are thought of as permissions ("If you want to do *A*, you must do *B* first to be allowed to do *A*") or precautions ("If you want to do *A*, do *B* first as a precaution"). Broadly speaking, the same conclusions apply to our ability to evaluate syllogisms—people are not logical, and the content of the syllogism matters—but it is harder to say what allows people to solve syllogisms successfully.

Decision making is not the only type of problem with which humans are faced. Indeed, another class of problems also arguably has a single answer. These problems can be analyzed using formal logic, and we start with the same question that began our discussion of decision making: Do people use these formal processes to answer such questions? It is not an exaggeration to say that our ability to reason supports much of what we think makes our lives as humans pleasant and interesting; even the simplest actions we perform often are the end product of reasoning processes (for a broader discussion of the role of reasoning in life, see Calne, 1999). We engage these processes dozens of times each day, usually without even noticing that we are doing so. Suppose you're sitting in your room and you know that you have a class at 11:00. You check the clock and see that it is 10:50. You leave your room to go to class. We could say that that simple act has this structure.

> If it's almost 11:00, I should leave for class.
> It's almost 11:00.
> Therefore, I should leave for class.

This example probably seems so simple as to be uninformative, and in fact people are quite good at reasoning in this sort of situation. As we will see, however, there are many other situations in which people do not reason quite so well.

Formal Logic

We noted that there are optimal or correct answers to many choice problems. That is also true of **deductive reasoning**, in which answers can be derived by formal logic. As was true with choice behavior, people do not always select this objectively correct answer; in fact, there are certain types of problems that people consistently get wrong, and they tend to make the same types of mistakes. These errors indicate that formal logic processes do not drive people's behavior. The mechanisms that do drive reasoning are under debate, and we discuss several proposals.

In a deductive reasoning task, we can apply formal logical processes and derive an objectively correct solution. These problems begin with some number of **premises**, statements of fact that are assumed to be true. Given these premises, deductive reasoning allows us to make further statements of fact—**conclusions**—that must also be true.

Premise	If an election is contentious, many people will turn out to vote.
Premise	This election is contentious.
Conclusion	Many people will turn out to vote.

Because of the structure of the two premises, the conclusion must be true. What's important in deductive reasoning is the form of the argument. We don't use deductive reasoning to ascertain the truth of the conclusion in the real world; we use it to determine whether the conclusion necessarily follows from the premises. For example, consider the following:

Premise	If snow is black, it makes a good hiding place for coal.
Premise	Snow is black.
Conclusion	Snow makes a good hiding place for coal.

In this case the second premise is false; nevertheless, the argument is deductively valid, meaning that the conclusion must be true if the premises are true. It may seem silly to get excited about (or even mildly interested in) deductive reasoning if it can lead to ridiculous conclusions like this one, but the point is to let you know what kind of conclusions can be drawn soundly, given the evidence of what you already know. Ascertaining the accuracy of what you already know (such as whether snow is black) is up to you.

Inductive reasoning shows that a conclusion is more likely (or less likely) to be true. It does not allow us to say that the conclusion must be true, as deductive reasoning does.

Premise	If I cook cabbage, then the house smells funny.
Premise	The house smells funny.
Conclusion	I cooked cabbage.

This conclusion is not deductively necessary. There could be other reasons the house smells funny: I may have cooked brussels sprouts, I may be cat-sitting for a friend, and so on. Although the conclusion is not deductively necessary, we could still inductively conclude that it is more likely that I cooked cabbage than if the premises were not true. If my house didn't smell funny, it would certainly be less likely that I had cooked cabbage. Thus deduction allows conclusions to be made with certainty, whereas induction allows the assessment of the probability of a conclusion being true to be changed.

How do we know when a deductive argument is valid? Deductive arguments have been studied extensively in two formats: conditional statements and syllogisms. **Conditional statements** actually have three statements. The first is a premise of the form "If P, then Q." P is a condition and Q is a consequence; if condition P is met, then consequence Q follows. The second premise makes a statement about whether P or Q is true or not true. The third premise is a conclusion about P or Q. If you follow the four classic logical forms shown in Figure 10.3, you will understand why some of the conclusions are valid and some are not. The first one (*modus ponens*) is rather obvious: If I ate too much dessert, then I must be uncomfortably full. The next example (affirming the consequent) states that I am uncomfortably full, but it doesn't necessarily follow that I must have eaten too much dessert; I might have eaten too much dinner, for example. In logical problems, the word *if* does not mean "if and only if." "If P then Q" means that P causes Q, but it does not preclude other things from causing Q. Similarly, in the third example (denying the antecedent), I didn't eat too much dessert, but it doesn't necessarily follow that I am not uncomfortably full; I might be full for other reasons. In the final example (*modus tollens*), we are told that I am not uncomfortably full; it must be true, therefore, that I did not eat too much dessert.

The other logical form that has been studied in some detail is the **syllogism**, which, like a conditional statement, has three parts: two premises followed by a conclusion. Conditionals include an "if–then" statement, whereas for syllogisms, all three statements are statements of fact. This is an example of a syllogism.

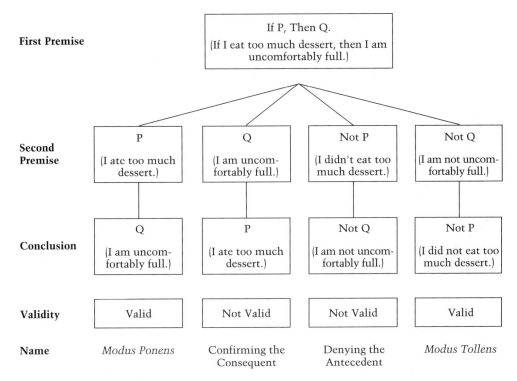

Figure 10.3. *The four common conditional statement forms. The first premise states a condition (if P, then Q), and the second premise asserts that either P or Q is not true. Although an infinite number of invalid conclusions might be drawn from the premises, the four conclusions shown here are important enough to be considered in detail in the psychological literature.*

Box 10–2 Are Inductive and Deductive Reasoning Supported by Different Brain Structures?

We have noted that deductive reasoning is susceptible to the application of logical rules and allows us to draw a firm conclusion about the truth of a conclusion. Inductive reasoning allows us to say that a conclusion is likely (or unlikely) to be true but does not allow us to state that a conclusion must be true or false. Do people use qualitatively different cognitive processes for these two types of reasoning? One way to address that question is to examine the processes in functional imaging and see whether they appear to have distinct neural bases. This approach has been taken by two research groups.

Vinod Goel and his colleagues (Goel, Gold, Kapur, & Houle, 1997) presented participants with three sentences on each trial.

All Capricorns pass their exams.	Lithium is a poison.
No Aries pass their exams.	Poisons cause vomiting in monkeys.
No Aries are Capricorns.	Lithium will cause vomiting in humans.

(Continued)

The examples show a deductive statement set (left) and an inductive statement set (right). Participants saw one statement set and were asked to judge whether the conclusion was necessarily true or false (deductive judgment) or probably true or false (inductive judgment). In the control condition they identified the number of sentences in which people were the subject, thus ensuring that participants processed the meaning of the sentences, but they didn't need to engage reasoning processes. The researchers compared the activations for inductive and deductive conditions with the control. Deductive and inductive reasoning led to different patterns of activations. Deductive reasoning was associated with activation primarily in the left inferior frontal gyrus, whereas inductive reasoning was associated with activity in broader areas of the left frontal lobe but showed much greater activity than deductive reasoning in the superior frontal gyrus.

Another study using similar techniques only partly replicated these results. Dan Osherson and his colleagues (1998) also presented sets of three sentences and asked participants to judge the truth of the final statement, its likelihood, or whether the final statement contained elements not mentioned in the first two statements (control). Despite the similarity of the method, these researchers reported very different sets of activations. Deductive and inductive reasoning both were associated with activity in the supplementary motor area, bilateral cerebellum, right caudate, and left thalamus. The probability task alone was associated with activity in the cingulate gyrus and the right midfrontal gyrus, whereas the deductive reasoning task was associated with secondary visual cortical activity.

The difference in results between these two studies is disquieting. It may be a result of the differences in the control tasks they used, but it may also be a result of the very complex nature of inductive and deductive reasoning tasks. The complexity of the tasks may make it difficult to develop suitable control tasks, and also makes it more likely that participants adopt different strategies. We must wait for more data to clarify some of the discrepancies between studies before we can draw firm conclusions about differences in brain activation between inductive and deductive reasoning.

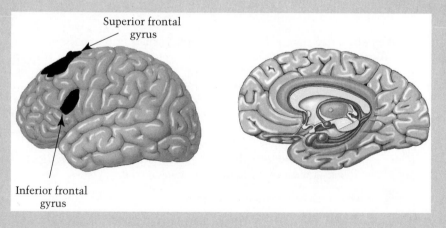

Figure B10.2.

All computers are annoyances.

A Macintosh is a computer.

Therefore, a Macintosh is an annoyance.

The easiest way to evaluate the truth of a syllogism is use a Venn diagram, as shown in Figure 10.4. It's also important to try to falsify the syllogism. Many syllogisms can be true under some circumstances, but we're interested in logical imperatives: if the first two premises are true, can we conclude that the third statement must be true?

Naturally, you don't need to phrase syllogisms using just letters, as in the figure. For example, consider this problem.

Some cigarettes are made from tobacco products.

Some tobacco products are unhealthful.

Therefore, some cigarettes are unhealthful.

This syllogism sounds like it might be true, but in fact it is false. It has the same logical structure as the second syllogism in Figure 10.4, which is also false. (The "∴" symbol means *therefore*.)

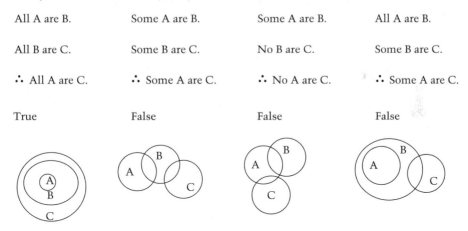

All A are B.	Some A are B.	Some A are B.	All A are B.
All B are C.	Some B are C.	No B are C.	Some B are C.
∴ All A are C.	∴ Some A are C.	∴ No A are C.	∴ Some A are C.
True	False	False	False

The syllogism must be true under all conditions to be considered true. Thus, a syllogism that we call "false" may be true under certain conditions. Such a syllogism is still considered false.

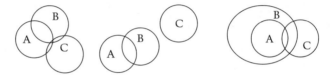

Figure 10.4. *Four sample syllogisms, one true and three false. Note that for a syllogism to be true, it must always be true. The second line of illustrations shows that many syllogisms may be true under some circumstances, but because they are not always true, they are considered false.*

As with conditional statements, the point of syllogisms is to discover how statements can be combined so that a logically valid conclusion must follow. Researchers investigating syllogistic reasoning typically ask participants to evaluate a syllogism to see whether any conclusions can be drawn from the two premises, and if so, what they are.

Human Success and Failure in Reasoning: Conditional Statements

It was long assumed that humans are rational, behaving according to the rules of logic. If a correct deduction can be made, humans will make it, was the thinking. This point of view originated with the ancient Greek philosophers, particularly Aristotle, and continued into the 20th century. Jean Piaget, the famous developmental psychologist, argued that the final stage of cognitive development is characterized by the use of logic. You should keep in mind that people need not be aware of the rules of logic for those rules to guide their behavior; I may speak grammatically, but that does not mean that I can consciously produce the rules of grammar, any more than I can give a precise description of the physics of bicycle riding, although my movements may conform to those physical laws when I ride one.

THE WASON CARD PROBLEM.   In the late 1960s Peter Wason (1968, 1969) devised a compelling demonstration that humans do not always reason well. He posed this problem.

> The figure shows four cards. Each card has a letter on one side and a digit on the other side. You are to verify whether the following rule is true: If there is a vowel on one side, there is an even number on the other side. You should verify this rule by turning over the minimum number of cards.

Before you continue reading, think over the problem in Figure 10.5. Which cards would you turn over, and why?

Most college students (and, more generally, most people) do not answer this problem correctly. The correct answer is that you should turn over the A

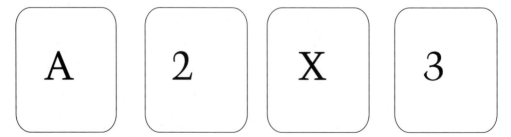

Figure 10.5.   *The Wason card selection problem embodies a conditional logic problem. The first premise is the rule "If there is a vowel, there is an even number" ("If P, then Q"). Each card is equivalent to a second premise; from left to right they are P, Q, Not P, and Not Q. By selecting cards to turn over, the participant is deciding which of these second premises can lead to a valid conclusion.*

card and the 3 card. Most people realize that you must turn over the A card. The tricky one is that 3 card. This problem has the same form as the "If P, then Q" problems discussed earlier. The cards from left to right give you the following information: P, Q, Not P, and Not Q. Only P and Not Q allow valid deductions. To put it another way, for the card with the A you can see that because there's a vowel on one side, there must be an even number on the other. For the card with the 2, it doesn't matter whether there is a vowel or a consonant on the other side. The X card can also have anything on the other side, but the 3 card cannot have a vowel on the other side; if it does, it disproves the rule. Across a wide variety of studies, about 15% of college students answer this problem correctly, although the percentage varies a bit from study to study (for some recent examples, see Ahn & Graham, 1999; Gebauer & Laming, 1997; Oberauer, Wilhelm, & Diaz, 1999). Even students who have just finished a one-semester course in logic don't do much better (Cheng, Holyoak, Nisbett, & Oliver, 1986). These studies indicate that people do not have a sort of all-purpose system into which they can deposit problems and produce the logical answer. Does that mean that we never act logically?

CONCRETENESS OR FAMILIARITY?   Consider this version of the Wason card task administered by Richard Griggs and James Cox (1982), shown in Figure 10.6.

> The cards in front of you have information about four people sitting at a table. On one side of a card is a person's age and on the other side of the card is what the person is drinking. Here is a rule: If a person is drinking beer, then the person must be over 19 years of age. Select the card or cards that you definitely need to turn over to determine whether they are violating the rule.

Participants averaged 72% correct (they turned over the Beer and 17 cards), even though none got the problem correct when they did the abstract version that uses letters and numbers. Why are participants so good at this version and so poor at the abstract? There are two obvious differences between the letters/number and coke/beer versions. They differ in terms of how abstract or concrete the materials are, and how familiar they are.

Other researchers noted the possibility that participants failed when the stimuli were abstract (letters and numbers) but did better when the stimuli were concrete (objects). Ken Manktelow and John St. B. T. Evans (1979) had participants test rules about what sorts of food and drink go together, such as "If I eat haddock, then I drink gin" or "If I eat macaroni, then I don't drink champagne." The researchers also administered an abstract version of the task

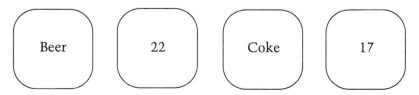

Figure 10.6.   *This problem is analogous to the one using vowels and digits in Figure 10.5, but people find it much easier. Why?*

to each participant. Across five experiments, performance on both the concrete and abstract versions was poor (about 25%). Other researchers using different concrete versions of the problem also observed poor performance (Griggs, 1984; Reich & Ruth, 1982; Valentine, 1985; Yachanin, 1986).

Another possibility is that the beer/coke version of the problem is familiar. Participants don't really need to do much reasoning; they have seen this rule enforced, and so can simply rely on their memory. (Indeed, Griggs and Cox had asked participants whether they were familiar with this rule, and not surprisingly, almost all of them said that they were.) **Case-based reasoning theories** hold that we reason about problems by remembering similar problems and how they were solved (see Kolodner, 1992, 1994; see Leake, 1998, for a review). Such theories typically have been implemented in artificial intelligence programs, which are able to recognize problems that are similar to known problems.

The familiarity explanation doesn't seem to be complete, however, because unfamiliar versions have been used with participants who solve the problem at high rates. For example, Leda Cosmides (1989) told a story about a foreign culture in which married men had a tattoo on their chests and cassava root was an aphrodisiac. When told to check the rule "If a man eats cassava root, then he must have a tattoo on his chest," participants' performance was very high. Thus familiarity with a rule is not necessary to good performance.

PRAGMATIC REASONING SCHEMAS.   Patricia Cheng and Keith Holyoak (1985) suggested that abstract mental structures help us reason. **Pragmatic reasoning schemas** are generalized sets of rules that are defined in relation to goals. They are called *pragmatic* because they lead to inferences that are practical in solving problems. Logical rules, in contrast, can lead to valid inferences that may not be of much help. For example, the rule "If I have a headache, I should take an aspirin" leads to the valid inference "If I need not take an aspirin, then I don't have a headache." This deduction is logically sound but not very practical.

Cheng and Holyoak suggested that people have abstract reasoning schemas for experiences such as permissions, obligations, and causations. The permission schema (which is most relevant to the problems we've been looking at) describes a situation in which a precondition must be satisfied before some action can be taken, such as "If you want to drink beer, then you must be at least 21 years old." The schema for permissions is composed of four if–then rules.

Rule 1	If the action is to be taken, then the precondition must be satisfied.
Rule 2	If the action is not to be taken, then the precondition need not be satisfied.
Rule 3	If the precondition is satisfied, then the action may be taken.
Rule 4	If the precondition is not satisfied, then the action must not be taken.

Once the schema is active, these rules serve as a guide to what sort of evidence (if any) is needed to evaluate whether the permission rules are being followed. If you know that people are not taking the action (not drinking beer) then they need not satisfy the precondition (be over 21) from Rule 2; if they are taking the action, they had better have fulfilled the condition, from Rule 4.

How does the schema become active, or applied to the problem? The problem itself may be described directly as one involving permission (by use of the word *permitted* or *allowed*) or by describing the problem in terms of Rule 1. For example, if I said, "To use this exercise machine, you must put on a safety harness," that would activate the permission schema because I have described an action and a precondition for that action. Prior knowledge (or cases, if you like) may be also important in activating the schema; for example, hearing a description of drinking and age or paying tuition and attending classes would be enough to activate the permission schema to most American college students.

Cheng and Holyoak (1985) demonstrated the importance of the permission schema by varying whether they gave participants a rationale for the rule they were to evaluate in a card selection problem. They gave participants the standard abstract card selection task but phrased it in terms of permission; they said that to take action A, one had to have fulfilled precondition P. The cards said, "Has taken action A," "Has fulfilled precondition P," and so on. They found that 61% of college students they tested answered correctly, whereas only 19% got the right answer when the problem was not framed in terms of permission. Thus, even though the materials were abstract and unfamiliar, participants were much more successful when the permission schema was activated.

THE EVOLUTIONARY PERSPECTIVE.   Leda Cosmides and John Tooby (1992, 2000) and Gerd Gigerenzer and his colleagues (Gigerenzer & Hug, 1992; Gigerenzer & Todd, 1999) appealed to evolutionary concerns in reasoning (as they did in choice behavior, as described earlier). They argued that humans evolved as social animals, meaning that we live in communities and have social ties that we rely on to help us survive. A social network requires that individuals either help or punish other members of the community, depending on their behavior. Cosmides and Tooby argued that this rule is so important that our cognitive systems have evolved to make the rule easy to understand. They argue that we are especially good at detecting cheaters—people who are violating a social contract, such as underage people drinking alcohol.

An interesting prediction of the evolutionary perspective is that the definition of *cheater* varies depending not on the logical structure of the problem but on the observer's social perspective. Gerd Gigerenzer and Klaus Hug (1992) provided a compelling example of this effect. They used the rule "If an employee works on the weekend, then that person gets a day off during the week." For half of the participants, the story surrounding the rule encouraged the participant to take the role of the employer; the other half took the perspective of the worker (see Figure 10.7).

Participants who took the employer's perspective tended to select Q and Not P: they are trying to catch cheaters (people who take a day off during the

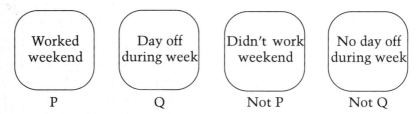

Worked weekend	Day off during week	Didn't work weekend	No day off during week
P	Q	Not P	Not Q

Figure 10.7. *The cards people select in this version of the problem depend on the perspective they are instructed to take—as an employer or a worker.*

week without working on the weekend). Participants who took the employee's perspective tended to select Not P and Not Q. These participants also seem to be trying to catch cheaters, but in this case they are trying to be sure that the *employers* are not cheating. They seek to ensure that if a fellow employee worked during the weekend, he or she got a day off during the week. (See Cheng & Holyoak, 1995 for the pragmatic reasoning schema account of these perspective effects.)

Cheng and Holyoak (1989) pointed out that participants sometimes are effective in solving reasoning problems that do not have the social exchange structure the evolutionary perspective posits. Participants seem to reason effectively with precaution rules as well. For example, using the rule "If you clean up spilt blood, you must wear rubber gloves," Ken Manktelow and David Over (1990) found that participants were quite successful in solving the card problem. Other researchers have confirmed that participants perform well with permission scenarios, even when they are unfamiliar. For example Cosmides and Tooby (1992) had participants verify the rule "If you go outside at night, you must have a volcanic rock tied around your ankle." Participants performed better when the rule was presented in the context of a precaution in a society that believed that the rocks protected people from night-stalking evil spirits than when they believed people went outside at night to take out the garbage (80% versus 44%).

So if permission rules are as easy for people as catching cheaters, how does that fact fit in with the evolutionary story? Evolutionary psychologists have proposed that two separate modules may have evolved (Cosmides & Tooby, 2000): one for catching cheaters and one for dealing with precautions. Critics have charged that this proposal is post hoc (Johnson-Laird, 1999), meaning that the new module was proposed only after it became clear that the old module could not accommodate the findings. If we simply created new modules whenever necessary, the theory could account for anything, but it would account for choices only after the outcome was known and could predict nothing; it would be useless as a theory.

So in the end, what do we know about how people reason in this paradigm? We know that people are not logic machines who can plug any problem into logic algorithms, with the correct answer popping out. The content of the problem matters. We also know that familiarity with the content (that is, the problem is about something you know) is neither necessary nor sufficient for successful reasoning. It's not necessary because we know that people can reason well about unfamiliar things (such as cassava roots and tattoos), and we know it's not sufficient because in some situations people reason poorly about domains they probably are somewhat familiar with (for example, foods and drinks that go together).

Human Success and Failure in Reasoning: Syllogisms

We would like to understand the critical features of a problem that help people reason well. So far we have discussed evolutionary theories and pragmatic reasoning schemas as hypotheses about the key features of reasoning. Later we will discuss more general theories of reasoning that encompass conditional statements as well as other sorts of problems. But first we turn to another type of logic problem: syllogisms.

The first thing to know about our ability to reason with syllogisms is that we're not very good at it. In one study that used many of the possible forms, participants got 52% correct (Dickstein, 1978; see also Johnson-Laird, 1999, and Evans, Handley, Harper, & Johnson-Laird, 1999). Chance performance was 20% because participants were shown five possible conclusions and were asked to select one. Why do people find syllogisms so difficult? It is not the case that people simply cannot deduce the correct implications and then make a guess. Errors on syllogisms are quite systematic (see Dickstein, 1975), which indicates that people aren't guessing; rather, there is some principle guiding their choice of conclusions, but that principle leads to incorrect conclusions. Researchers have proposed several candidates for this faulty process. Note at the outset that all of the hypotheses we're about to discuss may account for the performance of people on some problems, but none of them is a complete account.

One type of mistake people make is **conversion error** (Dickstein, 1975, 1976; Revlis, 1975) in which the participant reverses terms that should not be reversed. Some terms, such as *no* and *some*, can be reversed. If I say, "No dogs are plumbers," I can also say, "No plumbers are dogs." Similarly, if I assert, "Some knives are weapons," I can assert, "Some weapons are knives." The terms *all* and *some ... not* are not convertible, however. If I assert, "All canaries are birds," that does not justify asserting, "All birds are canaries." And stating, "Some mammals are not whales" does not justify saying, "Some whales are not mammals." The conversion error occurs when participants believe that they can safely convert a statement that they should not convert. For example, the syllogism "Some Cs are Bs; all As are Bs" does not have a valid conclusion. But if the person reading it converted the second premise, then he or she could conclude that some Cs are As, and indeed, that conclusion is a typical error that people make, possibly indicating that they convert the second premise (Evans, Newstead, & Byrne, 1993). Although conversion probably leads to some errors, it cannot be a complete account because some participants are aware that some of the quantifiers cannot be converted (Newstead & Griggs, 1983) and because participants make errors where conversion is not a potential problem.

Another problem is **conversational implicature**. This daunting term refers to the fact that syllogisms are a logical form and thus use the language of logicians, which is not always the same as everyday language, although it is easily confused. For example, when the term *some* is used in a syllogism, it really means "at least one, and possibly all." It is perfectly appropriate to say "Some triangles have three sides," even though all triangles have three sides. In normal usage, people say "some" to mean "more than one, but not all." Thus, when people read "some" in a syllogism they probably think of the term in its conversational sense instead of its logical sense (Begg & Harris, 1982). Although these interpretations occur, analyses of the types of errors people make indicate that conversational implicature accounts for some but not many syllogistic reasoning errors.

Another source of the systematic errors people show in syllogistic reasoning is the **atmosphere** created when the two premises of a syllogism are both either positive or negative or when the quantifiers (such as *all* or *none*) of the premises are the same (Woodworth & Sells, 1935). For example, consider these syllogisms.

No *A*s are *B*s.	Some *A*s are *B*s.
No *B*s are *C*s.	Some *B*s are *C*s.
No *A*s are *C*s.	Some *A*s are *C*s.

Both conclusions seem appropriate because they are consistent with the atmosphere created by the premises, either because they are all negative (example on left) or because they all use the same quantifier (example on right). Yet neither syllogism is true. (See the Venn diagrams in Figure 10.4.)

Atmosphere accounts for about 50% of the erroneous responses in a multiple-choice format (Dickstein, 1978) and nearly that many in an open-ended test where the participant must supply the conclusion (Johnson-Laird & Bara, 1984). Nevertheless, it is not a complete explanation of syllogistic reasoning because it explains how participants approach only a subset of syllogisms.

People may also be influenced by **prior beliefs**. Syllogisms are supposed to be a purely logical exercise in which we evaluate the conclusion only in light of its relationship to the premises. In other words, the premises "All *A*s are *B*s" or "All dogs are cats" should contribute to our evaluation of a syllogism in the same way. In fact, however, people are more likely to reject a syllogism as false if the conclusion is known to be false. John St. B. T. Evans and his colleagues (Evans, Barston, & Pollard, 1983; see also Newstead, Pollard, & Evans, 1992) compared two syllogisms of the same form.

No cigarettes are inexpensive.	No addictive things are inexpensive.
Some addictive things are inexpensive.	Some cigarettes are inexpensive.
Some addictive things are not cigarettes.	Some cigarettes are not addictive.

Both syllogisms are valid, but 81% evaluated the one on the left as valid, whereas only 63% evaluated the one on the right as valid.

In another example, Jane Oakhill, Phillip Johnson-Laird, and Alan Garnham (1989; Oakhill & Johnson-Laird, 1985) presented participants with one of these two syllogisms.

All of the Frenchmen in the room are wine drinkers.
Some of the wine drinkers in the room are gourmets.
Some of the Frenchmen in the room are gourmets.

All of the Frenchmen in the room are wine drinkers.
Some of the wine drinkers in the room are Italians.
Some of the Frenchmen in the room are Italians.

Note that both have same form ("Italians" has replaced "gourmets" in the second syllogism). No valid conclusion can be drawn from the first two premises, but the majority of participants incorrectly accepted the conclusion in the first syllogism, whereas almost none did in the second syllogism (see also Cherubini, Garnham, & Oakhill, 1998; Klauer, Musch, & Naumer, 2000).

These four factors—conversion errors, conversational implicature, atmosphere, and prior beliefs—can affect performance on syllogistic reasoning tasks, but it should be emphasized that these effects do not overwhelm whatever other mechanisms might be at work; many participants get the problem right. Even more important is that each effect applies to only selected problems, and thus their explanatory power is limited. We cannot consider the naming of these effects to be a model of reasoning. We turn next to a discussion of more complete models of reasoning that have been proposed.

General Models of Reasoning

There are three families of deductive reasoning models: syntactic models, semantic models, and probability models. **Syntactic models** propose that we apply rules to the premises we are given in an effort to prove that a conclusion is true (or in an effort to find a conclusion that can be proved true). This process may sound like trying to solve a proof in high school geometry class; that is not a bad analogy, although the process may well be unconscious, at least in part. **Semantic models** are based on the idea that an argument is deductively true if the conclusion is true under all conditions in which the premises are true. **Probability models** take a third approach. Some researchers (such as Oaksford & Chater, 2001) have argued that when presented with what experimenters think of as reasoning problems, participants actually treat them as probability problems.

BRAINE'S NATURAL LOGIC THEORY. Martin Braine (Braine, 1990; Braine & O'Brien, 1998) offered a syntactic model of reasoning. He suggested that humans do reason according to a set of rules, although clearly not the set of rules described by logicians. Rather, he postulated a set of simple inference schemas he called primary skills. Humans probably are born with a genetic predisposition to learn these simple reasoning schemas (for a discussion of the development of logical concepts in children, see Falmagne, 1990). They can be supplemented by reasoning strategies that people learn through experience. Here are some sample postulates.

> There is a cat. There is an apple. Therefore, there is a cat and an apple.
> There is a chicken and a horse. Therefore, there is a chicken.

As you can see, the inferences seem childishly simple, but that's the point. These are inferences that Braine argues humans are hard-wired to understand.

How are these inferential schemas used? Braine offered a universal reasoning program, a method of applying these inference schemas to derive conclusions from syllogistic reasoning problems. The program consists of two steps, one direct and one indirect. The direct step is a variant of the **British Museum algorithm**, which can be used to derive conclusions from a list of premises. The algorithm works like this.

1. Begin with a list of premises.
2. Apply the rules to the premises.
3. If new conclusions are derived from this application, add the conclusions to the list of premises.
4. If the conclusion to be proved is in the premise list, stop. Otherwise apply the list of rules again, adding new conclusions to the premise list.
5. Continue until the conclusion is proved or until no new conclusions are added to the premise list.

The British Museum algorithm is so named as a play on the idea that given an infinite amount of time, a chimp at a typewriter could eventually produce all the books in the British Museum. In other words, the algorithm is extremely simple, but it is also fairly stupid in the way it searches for a conclusion.

In Braine's theory, if the direct method does not work, a second, indirect method is invoked. The indirect method invokes new inference schemas that are qualitatively different from those used in direct reasoning. For example, one schema proposes a starting point for reasoning that is outside of the premises of the problem. Another schema introduces **suppositions** that are supposed to be true and then evaluates the consequences of their being true. If the consequence of a supposition's being true is that one of the premises would have to be false, then you can conclude that the supposition was incorrect. Here is an example.

1. If he brought a cake, we'll have dessert.
2. We're not having dessert.
3. He did bring the cake. (a supposition)
4. We're having dessert. (*modus ponens* applied to 1 and 3)

There is a contradiction between a premise ("We're not having dessert") and a conclusion ("We're having dessert") that was derived from a supposition. Therefore, the supposition must be wrong.

5. Therefore, he did not bring the cake.

Braine proposed that the indirect method of deduction is more difficult to use than the direct method because it is not certain that a person will find the line of reasoning that will lead to a successful solution to the problem. He suggested that heuristics influence the choice of inference schemas in indirect reasoning. Braine's model has had some success in accounting for the pattern of data produced by participants. As his theory predicts, if you give participants simple problems that require application of only one of the inference schemas, then almost no one errs, even children (Braine & Rumain, 1983). Here is an example of such a problem.

There is a firefighter or a police officer. There is not a firefighter.
Conclude: There is a police officer.

Furthermore, there is evidence that participants' accuracy decreases on problems as the number of inference schemas necessary to solve the problem increases (Braine, Reiser, & Rumain, 1984). Many logical problems simply are too complicated for the system to handle, even when the indirect method is used. Braine and his colleagues did not propose that humans simply shut down when faced with these problems. Rather, they proposed that their model accounts only for certain types of (fairly simple) reasoning problems, and that when other problems are posed, people recruit other reasoning methods.

JOHNSON-LAIRD'S MENTAL MODELS THEORY.   Philip Johnson-Laird and his associates (Johnson-Laird, 1999; Johnson-Laird & Byrne, 1991) proposed a very different approach to reasoning, saying that the meaning, or semantics, of a problem is crucial to its solution. Braine's model treats the premises of a conclusion as logical statements; it is assumed that the premises we read or hear are translated directly into some format that can be plugged into the inference schemas that combine to allow inferences to be made. In the **mental models theory**, the meaning of the premises remains in a meaning-based format. The premises are used to construct a mental model of the situation that represents a possible configuration of the world; for example, the premise on the left of Figure 10.8 might give rise to the mental images on the right. (Mental models

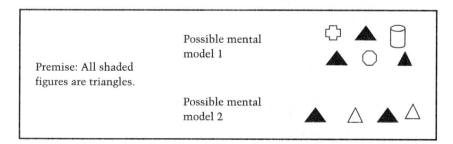

Figure 10.8.   *Mental models for the premise "All shaded figures are triangles." The mental models are presented as visual images for simplicity; true mental models are meaning-based structures that might be used to generate mental images but are not images themselves.*

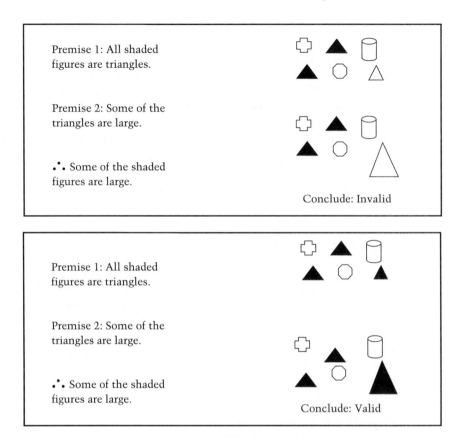

Figure 10.9. *This example shows how your mental model might change as new premises are stated and how you would use the mental model to evaluate the validity of a conclusion. Look at the top example. The first mental model is one of several possible models based on this premise. The mental model is changed when the second premise is stated. The conclusion, "Some of the shaded figures are large," is inconsistent with the mental model, so you would conclude that the syllogism is invalid. In the second example, you start with a different mental model of Premise 1. With this mental model, you end up accepting the validity of the conclusion.*

are not the same as mental images. For the sake of simplicity, we won't represent the mental models themselves.)

Mental models don't just represent the world; they can also be used for deduction because we can combine mental models. The fact that more than one mental model can represent a premise (as in Figure 10.8) has important implications for the way the theory works. Figure 10.9 shows two mental models that might be drawn from a pair of premises. In the top example, the conclusion is valid. In the bottom example, the conclusion is invalid. This invalid conclusion is traceable to the image based on the mental model for the first premise. The person may have committed a conversion error, believing that because all shaded figures are triangles it is also true that all triangles are shaded figures.

How can we avoid such errors? We must generate multiple mental models representing all possible situations, given the stated premises. Thus, we may have to keep several mental models in working memory simultaneously, corresponding to these multiple possibilities. A conclusion is possible if it is represented in one of the models; it is impossible if it is represented in none of the models; and it is necessary if it is represented in all of the models.

It sounds as if the theory predicts that success in reasoning depends strongly on the size of working memory. If you have a bigger working memory, you'll be able to maintain more mental models simultaneously and will therefore be able to keep track of more possible ways in which premises can be interpreted. That prediction seems to be supported by the data; as syllogisms offer more possible interpretations, participants have a harder time evaluating their truth (Johnson-Laird, Byrne, & Schaeken, 1992).

John St. B. T. Evans and his colleagues (Evans, Handley, Harper, & Johnson-Laird, 1999) presented participants with 256 syllogisms, in each case asking them to evaluate the conclusion as necessary, possible, or impossible. The mental models theory was quite successful in predicting participants' responses. Of 36 problems whose conclusions are necessary, 18 could be solved with a single mental model and 18 required multiple models, according to a previous analysis by Johnson-Laird and Bara (1984). Evans and his colleagues found that 81% of the single-model problems were evaluated correctly, but just 59% of the multiple-model problems were.

Limitations of working memory seem only to predict that people will fail on problems that are difficult, but the types of errors that people make are systematic, beyond this failing. Johnson-Laird proposes that many errors arise from the **principle of truth**, which states that people tend to construct mental models representing only what is true and not what is false. One reason they do so is to reduce the load on working memory. For example, for the premise "There is a mailbox or a pair of glasses" they would construct three mental models representing (1) the mailbox, (2) the glasses, and (3) both mailbox and glasses. They would *not* represent what is missing: that is, in the case where they represent only the mailbox, they would not represent that fact that the glasses are not present.

Most of the time, failing to explicitly represent all possibilities leaves the reasoner unable to draw a conclusion. Sometimes, however, it leads systematically to an incorrect conclusion. Consider this problem regarding a hand of cards.

> If there is a king in the hand then there is an ace in the hand, or else if there is a queen in the hand then there is an ace in the hand.
> There is a king in the hand.
> What, if anything, follows?

Most people believe that "There is an ace in the hand" is a valid conclusion, but that is a fallacy. You may be relieved to know that this fallacy is so powerful

Figure 10.10. *Mental models people construct from the statements "If
there is a king in the hand, then there is an ace in the
hand, or else if there is a queen in the hand, then there
is an ace in the hand." This model fails to capture a key
aspect of the statement: there are two conditionals in
the statement, only one of which is true.*

that when Johnson-Laird first started working with this problem, he thought the
computer had made an error when it reported the conclusion as false. Why do
people make this error? Johnson-Laird and Fabien Savary (1999) argue that it is
because they fail to construct mental models that include what is not true. Given
the premises, people construct the two mental models in Figure 10.10. The problem states that one of two conditional statements is true: either (if there is a king
there is an ace) or else (if there is a queen there is an ace). Each model describes
one of the two conditionals. The second premise (there is a king) seems to pick
out which of the two hands is true: It's the one with the king in it, and that hand
has an ace in it, so it seems valid to conclude that there is an ace in the hand.

But you have to keep in mind that the conditional statements are disjunctive: they include the term *else*, meaning that either one is true *or* the
other is true. Thus, either (if there is a king there is an ace) or (if there is a
queen there is an ace). If it is true that (if there is a king there is an ace) then it
is *not* true that (if there is a queen there is an ace). You don't know which of
the two conditionals is true.

Suppose it is true that (if there is a king there is an ace). In that case it is
not true that (if there is a queen there is an ace). If it is not true that (if there is
a queen there is an ace), then knowing that there is a queen means that there
is not an ace. Now suppose the other conditional is true. If it is true that (if
there is a queen there is an ace), then knowing that there is a queen in the
hand does indeed lead to the conclusion that there is an ace. Hence, you have
to know which of the two conditionals is true before you can draw any conclusions about the problem.

In Johnson-Laird and Savary's (1999) Experiment 1, none of the participants got the problem correct. Performance improved to 25% when the experimenters changed the phrasing to make it more explicit to participants that

only one of the two conditional statements could be true. (For more on similar problems, see Johnson-Laird, Legrenzi, Girroto, & Legrenzi, 2000.)

The mental models theory successfully accounts for participants' responses and even predicts fallacies that people will evaluate as true. Furthermore, it can be applied not only to syllogisms (as we have discussed) but to reasoning problems such as Wason's card selection task. Nevertheless, the theory has its critics, as you would expect, and some of them are champions of other theories. A recent development has been an altogether different approach emphasizing statistical selection of choices.

OAKSFORD AND CHATER'S INFORMATION GAIN MODEL.   Probability models of reasoning, including Oaksford and Chater's model, hold that people seldom engage in deductive reasoning in the everyday world. Rather, they make judgments based on probabilities. For example, when you hear "Rover is a dog" you assume that Rover has fur not by deduction ("Dogs have fur; Rover is a dog; therefore, Rover has fur") but because you know there is a high probability that dogs have fur. Thus when participants apparently "fail" on logical reasoning tasks in the laboratory, it's because they treat them as probability tasks—the same way they treat everyday reasoning tasks.

Box 10–3 Mental Models, Spatial Reasoning, and Brain Imaging

Johnson-Laird's mental models theory can be applied to different forms of reasoning, as described in the text. Some of the problems used are classic syllogistic forms like the one on the left. Others are relational problems like the two shown at center and on the right.

Some officers are generals.	Officers are next to generals.	Officers are heavier than generals.
No privates are generals.	Privates are behind generals.	Generals are heavier than privates.
Some officers are not privates.	Privates are behind officers.	Privates are lighter than officers.

Introspection might indicate that you would use a spatial representation to evaluate the second set of statements because the descriptors are spatial. You could also use a spatial representation to evaluate the set on the right. Vinod Goel and his colleagues (Goel, Gold, Kapur, & Houle, 1998) asked participants to evaluate these three types of stimuli—syllogisms, spatial relational, and nonspatial relational—to examine whether parts of the brain known to be involved in spatial reasoning are activated differentially.

The results showed that there was considerable overlap in the activations associated with each condition. In all three conditions, the most active areas were the left inferior frontal gyrus, the left middle frontal gyrus, and the left cingulate gyrus. Other areas showed activity particular to individual tasks in various parts of the left temporal lobe.

(Continued)

There are two important points in this study. The first is that the overlap in the activations for the different reasoning tasks is fairly impressive. It is not complete, but the most active areas are the same for all three problem types. Even though one of the problems is explicitly spatial, one is not, and the third is at least amenable to a spatial representation. The other noteworthy feature of the activations is that none of them are in areas typically associated with spatial reasoning such as the right hemisphere parietal areas.

The predominance of left hemisphere activations indicates that reasoning may be largely language based, even when the contents of the reasoning problem are inherently spatial. Still, it would be wise to delay final judgment until there has been further work on this topic

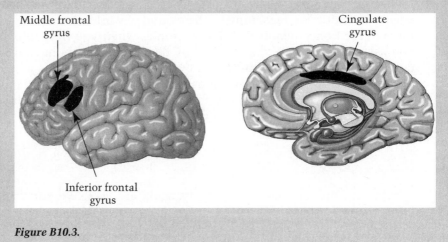

Figure B10.3.

One implication of this view is that people use probabilities to assess the likelihood that they will find useful information. Consider the version of the Wason card problem in Figure 10.11. Are you really going to snatch the cup from the 4-year-old and inspect it to ensure that she's not drinking beer? Kris Kirby (1994) reported that 65% of participants said they would check the 4-year-old, compared to 86% who said they would check the 19-year-old (the drinking age was 21 when this experiment was conducted). The base rate of 4-year-olds drinking beer is extremely low. Nick Chater and Mike Oaksford (1994; Oaksford & Chater, 1996, 1998) point out that most researchers act as

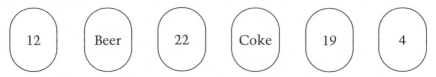

Figure 10.11. *Version of the Wason card problem used by Kirby (1994). People are more likely to check the 19-year-old than the 4-year-old, indicating that people are sensitive to the likelihood that they will find useful information.*

though the potential relationships of P and Q are equally probable in the world; that is, that given P (drinking beer) there is an equal likelihood of Q (22 years old) or Not Q (4 years old). In this problem, that is clearly not the case, and participants are sensitive to the difference.

These researchers argue that prior probabilities should be accounted for in analyzing where to seek more information, and they believe that people do so. For example, suppose you were evaluating the statement "If it is a raven, then it is black," which is the sort of conditional statement found in the Wason card task. It would be ridiculously inefficient to try to check all nonblack objects in order to see if they are ravens. But if you were evaluating the statement "If a person at the party ate the old tripe, he or she will be sick," it would make sense to look for people who attended the party and ate tripe but are not sick; you can perform such a search with a small group (Over & Evans, 1994). You seek information where you are likely to find something that will help you make a decision.

Oaksford and Chater used a statistical method that they claimed could evaluate the amount of information likely to be obtained when each card was turned over. They assumed that people turn over cards in the Wason task that are most likely to reduce uncertainty in the problem. Their model has received a great deal of attention. Many researchers believe that Oaksford and Chater are on the right track in emphasizing that people's main motivation in reasoning tasks may be to seek out information that will be maximally informative, not necessarily information that will lead to answers that are correct according to formal logic. Still, their model has detractors; some investigators claim that it cannot account for some data (see Almor & Sloman, 1996) and others complain that Oaksford and Chater did not measure information correctly (Laming, 1996).

Other researchers agree that probability is involved in decision making, but they add that people may place a value on particular types of evidence in some situations (see Evans & Over, 1996). For example, if you believe that ravens are not black, you might be biased to seek out evidence to confirm your belief; hence you *would* look for nonblack things to see if they were ravens. It is also possible to place costs and benefits on particular outcomes. For example, in Kirby's (1994) experiment, he asked people to imagine that the boss didn't like it if underage people were needlessly carded because it offended customers (bias not to check the ages of young people) or to imagine that the business was about to lose its liquor license (bias to check for underage drinkers). Kirby showed that the presumed costs and benefits of turning over cards (that is, checking the age of drinkers) made a difference in people's decisions.

Chater and Oaksford have developed a model using the same principles that accounts for syllogistic reasoning (Chater & Oaksford, 1999; for a summary of their work, see Oaksford & Chater, 2001).

Summary

We've reviewed two types of reasoning problems. Conditional reasoning problems ("If P, then Q") can be difficult or easy depending on the materials used; we examined several theories accounting for these effects, including the evolutionary perspective and pragmatic reasoning schemas. Syllogisms have four features that affect performance, but none of the current theories is a complete theory of reasoning.

We also examined three general theories of reasoning: Braine's natural logic theory, which emphasizes simple inference schemas and a syntax by which they can be combined; Johnson-Laird's mental models theory, which emphasizes the semantic content of the premises; and Chater and Oaksford's probability model, which emphasizes that people may have nonlogical reasons that motivate their choices in a reasoning problem.

Stand-on-One-Foot Questions

11. *What is the difference between deductive and inductive reasoning?*

12. *Is it true that familiarity is the critical feature that determines whether people will successfully evaluate a conditional statement such as the one embodied in the Wason card selection task?*

13. *What is the difference between the syntactic and semantic models of reasoning?*

Questions That Require Two Feet

14. *Case-based reasoning seems to have been given little attention. How often do you think you engage in case-based reasoning?*

15. *We saw before that conditional statements may be hard or easy to evaluate, and we saw in this section that syllogisms may be hard or easy to evaluate. Do you see any similarities between what makes each type of problem hard or easy?*

16. *The probability models seem to argue that people don't actually reason in reasoning problems but rather try to maximize the amount of information they can obtain. Assuming that this result is true, can we say that people don't reason?*

KEY TERMS

algorithm	base rate	conclusion
anchoring and adjustment	British Museum algorithm	conditional statements conversational
atmosphere	case-based reasoning	implicature
availability	theories	conversion error

decision making
deductive reasoning
description invariance
expected utility
expected value
heuristics
illusory correlation
inductive reasoning
loss aversion
mental models theory

normative theories
pragmatic reasoning
   schemas
premise
principle of truth
prior beliefs
probability models
problem frame
procedure invariance
psychic budgets

rational
representativeness
sample size
satisficing
semantic models
sunk cost
supposition
syllogism
syntactic models
transitivity

11

Problem Solving

How Do People Solve Novel Problems?

Problem Spaces
Selecting Operators

How Do People Apply Experience to New Problems?

Background Knowledge
Analogy
Functional Fixedness

What Makes People Good at Solving Problems?

How Do Experts Differ from Novices?
How Do People Become Experts?
What Makes Nonexperts Good at Solving Problems?

In chapter 10, we discussed decision making and reasoning for closed-ended problems, meaning that there was a limited number of possible answers or that a subset of the possible answers was provided, with the person left to choose between them. A **problem** can be defined very generally as any situation in which a person has a goal that is not yet accomplished. That general definition encompasses what we called decision making in chapter 10. When psychologists talk about problem solving, however, they mean open-ended problems in which the person knows the goal, but nothing in the problem describes how to accomplish the goal.

According to this definition of a problem—you have a goal and you have not accomplished the goal—you are faced with dozens of problems every day. You want a pizza and you don't have one; that's a problem. You want to be outside but you're in a classroom; that's a problem. These problems are uninteresting because you have faced them (and solved them) countless times before. Your response to these problems is so automatic that you don't even think there is a problem to be solved. When you think of a problem you more likely think of something like one of those little puzzles made out of two twisted nails that you are supposed to disentangle.

Problems like getting outside and untwisting nails are at opposite ends of a continuum, namely, a continuum of relevant experience. The "getting outside" problem can be solved based on past experience. The twisted nails problem usually cannot. In the nails problem, you don't have much in memory that will help you, so you must recruit processes that will give you some guidance as to how to try to solve the problem, even though you don't have relevant experience. We could imagine that all problems will vary in the extent to which previous experience guides us.

Indeed, the ends of this continuum illustrate two main themes of research on problem solving: memory (that is, prior experience) is important, and general problem-solving routines also come into play. Many problems are not at the extremes I've just described; they are neither completely familiar (so you can't solve a problem by remembering how it was solved last time) nor completely unfamiliar (so past experience is no guide). Rather, most problems are solved through using a combination of memories of similar problems that might be applicable to the current problem and general-purpose problem-solving strategies.

To study general problem-solving routines, psychologists have used problems with which most people are unfamiliar to prevent participants from relying on their memories of similar problems. Our first question is **How do people solve novel problems?** As we'll see, people engage general-purpose strategies to deal with problems they have never seen before.

Again, it is not always the case that people have either complete knowledge or absolutely no knowledge of a problem. Often, they have some knowledge that might be applicable to a problem. **How do people apply experience to new problems?** You would think that some experience would be better than no experience, but that's not always true. Although experience with similar problems can help, it is often difficult to recognize that past experience is relevant.

Furthermore, prior knowledge can put you in a mental rut; you might approach new problems in the same way you approached old problems, even if that approach is not appropriate.

Finally, we'll consider the question **What makes people good at solving problems?** As you might guess from the foregoing discussion, there are two main sources of skill in problem solving. You might be good at using the general-purpose processes; or you might have many problem solutions in secondary memory that will apply to other problems.

HOW DO PEOPLE SOLVE NOVEL PROBLEMS?

> ➤ *Preview* When people have experience with a problem, they can proceed as they did the last time they faced it. Without relevant experience, people fall back on general strategies. Working forward means to look for ways to get closer to the goal, but it is often ineffective. Working backward means to begin at the goal and try to mentally work back to the beginning of the problem. Means–ends analysis combines working forward and backward on problems, dictating when it is effective to set subgoals that should be completed before the main goal should be tackled.

The heart of problem solving is change. When you are presented with a situation that is not satisfactory, you want to change it in some way in order to meet a goal. There are usually so many ways to make changes that it is unclear how to proceed.

Problem Spaces

Before we get to the particulars of how people solve unfamiliar problems, we need to discuss how psychologists think about and describe problems. Allan Newell and Herb Simon (1972) emphasized the usefulness of thinking in terms of a **problem space** that includes all possible configurations a problem can take. For example, consider the classic puzzle called the Tower of Hanoi depicted in Figure 11.1. The puzzle includes a board with three pegs and three

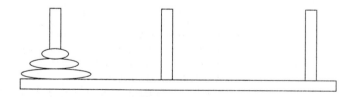

Figure 11.1.   *The Tower of Hanoi puzzle.*

rings of decreasing size. The goal is to move all the rings from the left peg to the right peg. There are three rules describing how you can move the rings.

1. You can move only one ring at a time.
2. You can move only the top ring on a peg.
3. You cannot put a larger ring on top of a smaller ring.

The Tower of Hanoi is used as an example several times in this chapter. You'll get more out of these examples if you work through the problem yourself using coins of different sizes—a quarter, a nickel, and a penny—as described in Figure 11.2.

The problem space for the Tower of Hanoi puzzle can be thought of as all possible configurations of the puzzle board (see Figure 11.3). Each position is called a state of the problem space. More generally, a **problem state** is a particular configuration of the elements of the problem. Notice that links between the different states indicate the possible paths through the problem space. You can't simply jump from one state in the problem space to another; you must move from state to state by way of the links. What determines how the states are linked? The links represent **operators**, processes that can be applied to the problem to change its configuration (to change where you are in the problem space). For example, an operator in the Tower of Hanoi problem is to move a disk.

Typically, certain conditions must be met before you are allowed to apply an operator. In the Tower of Hanoi there are three conditions: you start with all the rings on the left peg, your goal is to move all the rings to the right peg, and you move through the space by applying operators.

Selecting Operators

The key to problem solving is selecting the operators that will move you efficiently through the problem space to the goal. Obviously, if you simply move through the problem space randomly, you might accidentally end up at

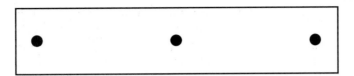

Figure 11.2.   *Use this figure to work the Tower of Hanoi puzzle shown in Figure 11.1. Put three coins of decreasing size (a quarter, a nickel, and a penny) on the leftmost dot and try to move the coins to the rightmost dot, following these rules: you can move only one coin at a time, you can move only the top coin on a stack, and you can't put a larger coin on top of a smaller coin. If this is puzzle seems too easy, use four coins.*

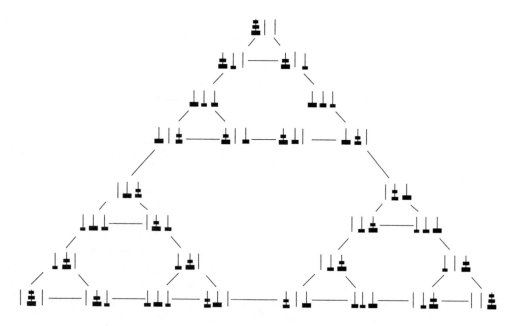

Figure 11.3. *Problem space for the Tower of Hanoi puzzle. It's easist to understand the figure by starting at the top and following the choices. You always have the option of moving backward in the space by returning to the position you just occupied.*

the goal, but you'd like to be certain that you will reach the goal. Furthermore, it would be desirable to reach the goal directly rather than via a circuitous route. How do you select operators to ensure a reasonably direct route to the goal?

You could imagine doing a **brute force search**, examining every possible answer until you find the correct one. For example, suppose you were working a crossword puzzle and saw the letters _alt with the clue "seasoning." You could sequentially substitute each letter of the alphabet (*aalt, balt, calt*) in the blank space until you get to *s* and solve *salt*. The advantage of a brute force search is that it's very simple to apply, but the disadvantage is that it doesn't restrict the part of the problem space through which you must search; you have to try all the possibilities. As the number of possibilities increases modestly, the number of combinations increases rapidly because of a phenomenon called **combinatorial explosion**. For example, suppose the clue was _al_. You could still do a brute force search by putting *a* in the first blank space and trying the letters of the alphabet in the second blank space (*aala, aalb, aalc,* and so on.) If that doesn't work, you can try the next letter of the alphabet in the first space and the others in sequence in the second blank space (*bala, balb, balc*). Notice that although we've doubled the number of blank letters, the number of states in the problem space that we must explore has more than doubled. In fact, if there are 26 possible letters to fill in the blanks and 2 blanks to be filled, there are 26^2 possible combinations of letters in the blanks for a total of 676. If we add one more blank, the possibilities increase to 26^3 or 17,576. Thus, it's clear that a brute force search is often impractical.

What strategy do we use instead if a brute force approach is not helpful? It appears that people use heuristics to guide their search for operators that will move them through the problem space. A **heuristic** in problem solving means the same thing that it did in reasoning and decision making: it's a simple rule that can be applied to a complex problem. Heuristics require minimal computation and often yield an acceptable answer but do not guarantee one.

One problem-solving heuristic is **hill climbing**, which means that you look for an operator that will take you to a state in the problem space that appears to be closer to the goal than where you are now. Imagine the goal of the problem state as the top of a hill. Each step you take is a change in the problem space; to decide where to step, you evaluate whether the step you are contemplating would take you closer to the top of the hill. The hill-climbing heuristic is certainly more effective than brute force—you are at least evaluating moves before you try them—but it is still applicable only to a limited number of problems. Many problems require that you move backward in the problem space to reach your goal. Take the *hill climbing* name literally for a moment and suppose that your goal is to reach the highest point in an area. You take a few steps, the choice of each step guided by whether taking that step leads you upward, and find yourself at the top of a hill. But nearby you see a hill that is still higher than the one you're on. Given your present position, you can't use the hill-climbing strategy to get to the top of this highest hill because you would have to go downhill, away from the goal, in order to ultimately reach the goal.

Animals sometimes get caught in a similar bind. Maybe you have seen a dog on a leash straining to reach something that it could easily reach if it went around an obstacle so that the leash would no longer be caught. Although we might snicker about the mental superiority of our species, the fact is that humans are not indifferent to moving backward in a problem space. We can do it, obviously, or else many problems would be insoluble, but we are more likely to make errors if we must move backward, and we are slower to make these moves than hill-climbing moves. This phenomenon was demonstrated by John Thomas (1974; see also Greeno, 1974), who examined participants solving the familiar Hobbits and Orcs problem. In this version the participant is told that there are three Hobbits and three Orcs on one side of a river. They all want to cross the river, but their boat can hold only one or two creatures. Orcs must never outnumber Hobbits on either side of the river—otherwise the Orcs will devour the Hobbits. How can all the creatures get across the river safely? The problem space for the Hobbits and Orcs problem is depicted in Figure 11.4. The asterisk marks the state from which participants are slow to move and from which they often make errors. At that point, moving forward in the problem space (that is, toward the goal) requires the participant to make a move that seems to be away from the goal, taking some creatures away from the goal side

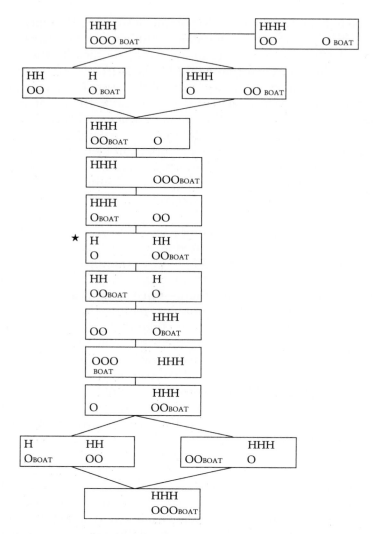

Figure 11.4. *Problem space for the Hobbit and Orcs problem. The space is fairly linear (there are few branches) because the boat greatly restricts what you can do at any point. The key is that at one point in the problem (marked by the asterisk) you have to move some creatures away from the goal shore back to the starting shore. People are slow to make that move, indicating that they are influenced by the hill-climbing heuristic.*

of the river. Although humans can move away from a goal, we are reluctant to do so.

Another heuristic for moving through a problem space is **working backward**. As the name suggests, in this heuristic one begins at the goal state of the problem space and tries to work back to the starting state. This heuristic is useful when the goal state is known but the initial state is not. For example, consider the double-money problem, posed by Wayne Wickelgren (1974).

> Three people play a game in which one person loses and two people win each game. The one who loses must double the amount of money that each of the other two players has at that time. The three players agree to play three games. At the end of the three games, each player has lost one game, and each player has $8. What was the original stake of each player?

We could try to solve this problem by selecting some initial state for the stakes of the three players and working forward, evaluating the outcome, and if the correct answer is not obtained, trying to adjust the initial state. However, it is much easier to work backward. If all three players end with $8, after the last game the loser had doubled the money of the two winners; hence before the last game the winners must have each had $4, and the loser must have had $16. Because we know that each player won exactly once, it is easy to trace back the stakes, as shown in Table 11.1. (In each game the asterisk indicates the loser.)

As you can see, the problem is easy to solve if we work backward from the goal state to the initial state. Wickelgren argued that problems are well suited to this heuristic if the goal state is known but there are many possible initial states. If there are many possible initial states, there may not be an intelligent heuristic by which one could select an initial state (and then see whether it leads to the goal state). Working forward on problems like this has been likened to finding a needle in a haystack, but working backward on such problems is more like the needle working its way out of the haystack (Newell, Shaw, & Simon, 1962).

Here's another example in which working backward is useful; see whether you can solve it.

> Fifteen pennies are placed on a table in front of two players. Each player is allowed to remove at least 1 penny but not more than 5 pennies at his or her turn. The players alternate turns, each removing from 1 to 5 pennies, until one player takes the last penny on the table and thereby wins all 15 pennies. Is there a method of play that will guarantee victory? If so, what is it?

How can you solve this problem by working backward? If you leave 6 pennies, your opponent will have to leave you with 1 to 5, so you can take all of them and win the game. How can you ensure that you leave 6? If you are able to leave 12, no matter how many your opponent takes on his or her turn, you'll be able to take some number that will leave 6. Thus, if you go first in this game, you should take 3, leaving 12. This game provides a nice example

Table 11.1.   **The Double-Money Problem**

Game	Player 1	Player 2	Player 3
Ending stake	8	8	8
Stake before game 3	16*	4	4
Stake before game 2	8	14*	2
Stake before game 1	4	7	13*

*Loser of a game.

of the working backward strategy because the initial state (15 pennies) is specified.

There is some evidence that people use the working backward heuristic in solving problems. Robert Rist (1989) asked 10 undergraduates taking their first computer programming course to write brief programs. (He also asked them to describe their problem-solving strategies as they worked, a technique we'll discuss shortly.) Rist examined the computer code that participants wrote and found that when they were using unfamiliar concepts, participants often worked backward. They started by considering the answer they wanted the program to produce. For example, in writing a program to calculate the average daily rainfall over 30 days, participants often began by writing the code for the final step in the program, finding the average, and then tried to figure out how to get the total rainfall.

Hill climbing and working backward have their applications, but as we have seen, the range of problems to which they can be applied is limited because most problems require moving both backward and forward. Indeed, Rist found that once participants had a bit of experience with a programming concept, they typically worked both backward and forward in the course of writing a program, even if it was possible to solve the problem only by working backward.

By far the most thoroughly tested and probably the most broadly applicable heuristic is **means–ends analysis**, which uses a combination of forward- and backward-moving strategies.

1. Compare the current state with the goal state. If there is no difference between them, the problem is solved.
2. If there is a difference between the current state and the goal state, set as a goal to solve that difference. If there is more than one difference, set as a goal to solve the largest difference.
3. Select an operator that will solve the difference identified in Step 2.
4. If the operator can be applied, apply it. If it cannot, set as a new goal to reach a state that would allow the application of the operator.
5. Return to Step 1 with the new goal set in Step 4.

Take as an example the simple act of taking a cat to the vet. Means–ends analysis would solve that problem this way.

Step 1. What is the difference between my current state (at home) and my goal state (at the vet with my cat)? The difference is one of distance.

Step 2. Set goal to reduce distance.

Step 3. What operator reduces distance? A car reduces distance.

Step 4. A condition of using a car is that it not have an uncaged cat in it.

Step 5. Set as a subgoal to make the car suitable to carry cats.

Step 1. What is the difference between my current state (no cat carrier) and my goal state (have a cat carrier)? The difference is one of distance (at pet store).

Step 2. Set goal to reduce distance.

Step 3. What operator reduces distance? A car reduces distance.

You get the idea. Being able to set a new goal is the key advantage of means–ends analysis. More accurately, the new goal is a subgoal in service of the larger goal of being able to apply the operator of using the car to take the cat to the vet. Setting subgoals is important to allow you to move away from the goal when necessary (unlike the hill-climbing heuristic) in service of achieving another goal that will bring you closer to the goal state. If there is a potentially useful operator that can't be applied, the means–ends analysis heuristic tries to make it applicable. The hill-climbing heuristic abandons an operator that can't be applied immediately and seeks another method (for example, if you can't take the cat in your car without a pet carrier, you could walk to the vet with the cat in your arms).

Even if problems can be described in ways that sound consistent with means–ends analysis, do people actually use means–ends analysis when they solve problems? Alan Newell and Herb Simon (1972) developed a computer program that solved problems by using means–ends analysis. The program was designed to be general in its applicability to a broad range of problems and so was called the **General Problem Solver**.

Newell, Simon, and their colleagues have used three methods to test whether the General Problem Solver provides an accurate description of how humans solve problems: verbal protocols, problem behavior graphs, and aggregate statistics from larger groups of participants. In a **verbal protocol**, the experimenter asks the participant to solve a problem while talking out loud, continuously describing his or her thoughts about solving the problem. The experimenter prompts participants to speak if they fall silent for more than a second or two. The assumption is that the participant has conscious access to at least some of the mental processes that support solving the problem. Although this assumption is controversial (Nisbett & Wilson, 1977), Anders Ericsson and Herb Simon (1993) made an effective case that such data are useful, and indeed, they have proposed a model of how and when information becomes available for verbal report. Newell and Simon (1972) examined the verbal protocols of several participants who worked abstract logic problems and found an impressive degree of correspondence between the steps they reported taking as they solved the problem and the steps that the General Problem Solver took. The important finding was not so much the detailed match between participant and model but the finding that the general character of their approach was similar: both humans and the model sought to reduce differences between their current state and the goal, and both created subgoals when an operator could not be applied that would reduce a difference.

A **problem behavior graph** is a representation of the problem space through which participants moved as they solved (or attempted to solve) a problem. Newell and Simon's problem behavior graphs consisted of rectangles, representing the cognitive state of the participant at a given moment (that is, how far he or she had gotten in the problem), and lines connecting the states, representing changes in states. Often a change in state came about as the participant applied an operator. At other times the participant might abandon a line of reasoning and jump to a different part of the problem or try a new strategy. When Newell and Simon categorized each transition between states in their problem behavior graphs, they found that about 82% of the state transitions were consistent with those expected from the application of means–ends analysis. The other 18% were activities such as reviewing what had been done or trying to avoid paths through the problem space that the participant thought would be difficult.

Both of these methods entailed detailed analysis of decision making by just a few participants. In a third method Newell and Simon examined the data for a larger group (64 participants) who were asked to solve similar logic problems. The researchers made the same categorization judgments of the steps taken to solve the problem, but in this case they used written steps rather than verbal protocols. Again, they found evidence that was broadly consistent with means–ends analysis.

These three sources of evidence were collected using the same type of problem: logical proofs. Similar methods have been applied using many other problems. Some of the problems that the General Problem Solver has solved successfully are listed in Table 11.2 (Ernst & Newell, 1969).

So far we have discussed a specific type of problem in which the problem solver has no experience that seems relevant. Although such problems arise periodically in real life, it is probably more typical that you have some experience in memory that seems to apply to some aspect of the problem.

Stand-on-One-Foot Questions

1. *Why are heuristics needed for problem solving?*
2. *Name three heuristics for unfamiliar problems.*
3. *Summarize how means–ends analysis works.*

Questions That Require Two Feet

4. *We said that the hill-climbing heuristic would not be successful in getting you to the top of the largest hill in an area if you happened to first scale a smaller hill. Could means–ends analysis get you to the top of the largest hill in the area? How would it do so?*
5. *Which has a bigger problem space, chess or checkers? Why? How could you shrink the problem space of either game?*
6. *Which of the methods we've discussed so far do you think the average person would use in trying to open a safe? Which method might a professional safecracker use?*

Table 11.2. ***Problems Solved by the General Problem Solver***

Problem	Description
Hobbits and Orcs	As described earlier.
Tower of Hanoi	As described earlier, the General Problem Solver was given the four-disk version.
Proving theorems from first-order predicate calculus	Logical theorems are to be proved, given a limited number of axioms and ways that the axioms can be combined
Father and sons task	A father and his two sons want to cross a river using a boat that can hold only 200 lb. The father weighs 200 lb and each son weighs 100 lb.
Three coins puzzle	There are 3 coins. The first and third coins show heads; the middle coin shows tails. A move consists of turning over 2 of the 3 coins. Make all 3 coins show the same side (heads or tails) in exactly three moves.
Parsing sentences	Finding parts of speech (such as noun phrases) in sentences.
Water jug task	Given a 5-gallon jug and an 8-gallon jug, how can precisely 2 gallons be put in the 5-gallon jug? The jugs are empty, but there is a tap for water and a drain for excess. (Other problems use different-sized jugs and demand different amounts of water.)
Letter series completion	Partial sequences are provided, with the goal to continue the sequence (for example, *B C B D B E B _ _*).

HOW DO PEOPLE APPLY EXPERIENCE TO NEW PROBLEMS?

➤ ***Preview*** Problem-solving strategies change if we have relevant background knowledge. Background knowledge may help us classify problems and see their underlying structure. It may also help because sufficient knowledge means that some of the operators may be automatized, leaving attention free for unfamiliar aspects of the problem. Drawing an analogy to a different problem that shares the same underlying structure may help, though people are not very skilled in drawing analogies. Background knowledge can actually hurt performance if people try to apply old knowledge to a new problem when it isn't applicable. Even when people make this mistake, the problem sometimes yields to repeated attempts to solve it. Researchers have begun to investigate how people are able to avoid mental traps and go on to solve problems.

For problems that are completely unfamiliar to the solver, we don't have to worry about how prior knowledge might affect attempts at a solution. Now we're ready to consider what happens when the solver has some relevant background knowledge. We can assume that some knowledge must be better than no knowledge for solving problems. As we'll see, that is generally true, but in some situations background knowledge hurts problem-solving efforts, and psychologists have been especially interested in exploring those situations.

Background Knowledge

Although we'll discuss how prior knowledge can negatively affect problem solving, bear in mind that most of the time background knowledge is helpful. The ways in which background knowledge helps are pretty straightforward in the context of the General Problem Solver. First, if you have background knowledge of the domain, you are better able to classify the problem and therefore to understand the problem's critical components. Recall from chapter 4 our discussion of chess masters in William Chase and Herb Simon's (1973) study. They showed that chess masters are able to remember the positions of chess pieces very accurately by chunking pieces into meaningful configurations. They don't perceive 32 chess pieces; they perceive a much smaller number of chunks, each composed of several pieces. The perception of the board in chunks relies on prior experience: if the pieces are arranged randomly, chess masters perceive (and remember) the board no differently than novices.

How does the perception of the board in chunks help problem solving? It greatly reduces the search space of problem solving. By perceiving configurations of pieces, the master can instantly perceive that the black queen is in jeopardy or that white is dominating the center of the board. These patterns are recognized from memory, and they provide a clear guide for how to focus problem-solving strategies to formulate the next move. Thus we can generally state that domain knowledge allows better perception of the most important part of the problem that should be addressed and thereby restricts the search to the key part of the problem space.

The second way that domain knowledge can help problem solving is by automatizing some of the problem-solving steps so that they do not demand attention. One of the first (and most important) steps to automatize is what operators are available and how they move in the problem space. For example, if you are just learning how to play chess, you must think hard about how the knight and the rook move, as well as the oddity that the pawns move ahead one space but can move two spaces from their starting position, can take other pieces on the diagonal, and can take pieces in passing ("en passant") from their starting position. Until you have thoroughly learned the rules for piece movement, it is difficult to form much strategy.

Here's an example of a problem in which the rules are fairly complex; we might imagine that the problem will be difficult to solve without gaining greater familiarity with the rules.

> In the inns of certain Himalayan villages is practiced a refined tea ceremony. The ceremony involves a host and exactly two guests, neither more nor less. When

his guests have arrived and seated themselves at his table, the host performs three services for them. These services are listed in the order of the nobility the Himalayans attribute to them: stoking the fire, fanning the flames, and pouring the tea. During the ceremony, any of those present may ask another, "Honored Sir, may I perform this onerous task for you?" However, a person may request of another only the least noble of the tasks which the other is performing. Furthermore, if a person is performing any tasks, then he may not request a task that is nobler than the least noble task he is already performing. Custom requires that by the time the tea ceremony is over, all the tasks will have been transferred from the host to the most senior of the guests. How can this be accomplished?

You probably had to read this problem several times just to understand what the rules are. It's hard to even consider how to get to the goal because the operators are so complicated that they consume all of my working memory capacity.

Contemplating moves through a problem space requires working memory; it becomes difficult to maintain the goal and the operators in working memory if the operators are not automatized so that they take little or no working memory capacity. Recall the example of taking the cat to the vet. The solution to this problem relied heavily on background knowledge, especially on knowledge of how subgoals could be achieved. When confronted with a problem of distance, we know immediately that an automobile is an effective operator to reduce distance; we don't have to cast about for a solution. If we did not know that a good solution is to use a car, that subgoal might require a considerable search that would occupy working memory, which might mean that other components of the problem would be lost from working memory.

You would think that having some knowledge about a problem is bound to be better than having no knowledge, and in some cases familiarity does

---

Box 11–1 Using Background Knowledge: The Role of the Frontal Lobe

Problem solving is hard to localize in the brain, probably because it requires the contribution of multiple cortical and subcortical structures. Nevertheless, patients with lesions restricted to the frontal lobes seem to have particular difficulty in solving problems, apparently because of an impaired ability to develop strategies. This problem was mentioned in the context of memory in chapter 6. Patients with frontal lobe lesions are also impaired in divergent thinking, that is, in coming up with different ideas instead of always thinking along the same paths.

Tim Shallice and Margaret Evans (1978) asked participants questions with answers that were very unlikely to be in memory. Instead, participants would need to devise a strategy by which a reasonable answer could be derived, based on information that was in memory. Here are some sample questions.

How fast do racehorses gallop?
What is the best-paid job or occupation in Britain today?
What is the length of the average man's spine?
How tall is the tallest building in London?
How many camels are there in Holland?

(Continued)

It is not expected that anyone will be able to answer these questions accurately; the expectation is that patients with frontal lobe lesions, because they cannot devise a strategy to come up with a reasonable answer, will produce truly bizarre answers. Therefore, patients' answers were evaluated for how near or far they were from the answers of normal participants. Patients with damage to the frontal lobe were much more likely to produce bizarre answers than patients with more posterior lesions. For example, one patient said that the tallest building in London was between 18,000 and 20,000 feet, that the best-paid occupation was long-distance truck driver, and that the length of the average man's spine was between 4 and 5 feet.

Another task, the Wisconsin Card Sorting Task, tests the participant's ability to respond flexibly. The patient is given a deck of cards bearing symbols. Each card has three features, including the number of symbols (one to four), the symbol type (diamond, star, plus sign, circle), and the symbol color (red, green, yellow, blue). The participant is asked to sort the cards into piles but is not told what feature to use in sorting; corrective feedback is provided by the experimenter, so participants usually catch on to the rule fairly quickly. The trick is that once the participant understands the rule and sorts 10 cards correctly, the experimenter changes the rule. Normal participants (and patients with nonfrontal brain lesions) quickly understand that the rule must have changed, and they set about figuring out the new rule. However, patients with frontal damage keep sorting according to the old rule. They have great difficulty breaking free of the behavior in which they are currently engaged. This tendency is called perseveration.

You can see how these problems would affect successful completion of many different types of problems. Effective problem solving requires the ability to develop a strategy and often requires divergent thinking; we must break free of old ways of doing things and try something new. If the old way of doing things were effective, there would be no problem!

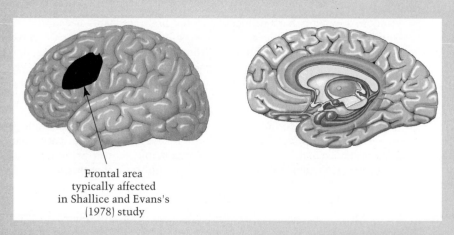

Frontal area
typically affected
in Shallice and Evans's
(1978) study

Figure B11.1.

help. We think about how the various parts of a problem relate to one another and draw an analogy between those relationships and the relationships in another familiar problem that we know how to solve. For example, if you are familiar with calculating probabilities in gambling games and are confronted with a probability question in a statistics class, you may see the similarity of the statistics question to gambling questions you are familiar with and successfully solve the statistics question.

Another type of familiarity with part of a problem is not so helpful, however. Instead of being familiar with the relationships between parts of a problem, you may be familiar with the isolated components of a problem. In those situations, people often have a hard time thinking of objects outside of their normal use. For example, a rubber dog bone is a toy—that's its attribute—and it won't seem to be something that could be used as a pencil eraser in a pinch. In this case, familiarity with the object hurts problem-solving performance.

Analogy

Were you able to solve the problem involving the Himalayan tea ceremony? Did you notice that an analogy could be drawn between this problem and the Tower of Hanoi problem that you saw (and perhaps solved) earlier in this chapter? Figure 11.5 should make this analogy concrete. What can we say about the effect of prior knowledge on problem solving? Here's a situation in which you thought about a problem quite recently, and you were given a new problem that is directly analogous to it, yet you didn't use your knowledge of this prior problem to solve this one. How is that possible?

The first thing you should know is that this finding is common. The classic studies on analogy were conducted by Mary Gick and Keith Holyoak (1980, 1983). They used a problem originally devised by Karl Duncker (1945) called the radiation problem that reads as follows:

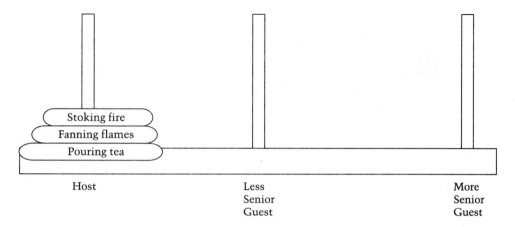

Figure 11.5. *The tea ceremony problem is analogous to the Tower of Hanoi problem. Did you see the analogy.*

Suppose you are a doctor faced with a patient who has a malignant tumor in his stomach. It is impossible to operate on the patient, but unless the tumor is destroyed the patient will die. There is a kind of ray that can be used to destroy the tumor. If the rays reach the tumor all at once at a sufficiently high intensity, the tumor will be destroyed. Unfortunately, at this intensity the healthy tissue that the rays pass through on the way to the tumor will also be destroyed. At lower intensities the rays are harmless to healthy tissue, but they will not affect the tumor either. What type of procedure might be used to destroy the tumor with the rays without destroying the healthy tissue?

Most people find this problem extremely difficult, and even if they work on it for a long time, only about 10% of participants solve it. The answer is that you could use several of the rays at low intensity and point them in such a way that they all meet at the tumor. Thus, only the tumor would be exposed to a high intensity of the rays, and surrounding tissue would not be damaged. (This principle is actually used in cancer treatment.) Again, this is a difficult problem, but suppose that when you took up the radiation problem, you had just finished reading the following story.

A dictator ruled a small country from a fortress. The fortress was situated in the middle of the country and many roads radiated outward from it, like spokes on a wheel. A great general vowed to capture the fortress and free the country of the dictator. The general knew that if his entire army could attack the fortress at once it could be captured. But a spy reported that the dictator had planted mines on each of the roads. The mines were set so that small bodies of men could pass over them safely, since the dictator needed to be able to move troops and workers about; however, any large force would detonate the mines. Not only would this blow up the road, but the dictator would destroy many villages in retaliation. A full-scale direct attack on the fortress therefore seemed impossible.

The general, however, was undaunted. He divided his army up into small groups and dispatched each group to the head of a different road. When all was ready he gave the signal, and each group charged down a different road. All of the small groups passed safely over the mines, and the army then attacked the fortress in full strength. In this way the general was able to capture the fortress.

Gick and Holyoak found that if participants were told that the fortress story that they had just read might help them solve the radiation problem, 100% came up with the correct solution. However, if the experimenters did not tell them to use the fortress story, only 35% of the participants solved the radiation problem. Furthermore, that estimate of 35% spontaneously using the analogous story might be high because some of these participants may have suspected that there was supposed to be some connection between the two stories, even though they were not told about it. Therefore, Gick and Holyoak conducted another study in which the dictator story was just one of three stories participants read before the description of the radiation problem. In that experiment, only 20% got the problem correct; thus when the connection between the radiation problem and the fortress problem was made less obvious, even fewer participants drew the analogy. Indeed, if the two stories are separated by a delay or presented in different contexts, almost none of the participants use the analogy (Spencer & Weisberg, 1986).

Do people need to be told to use an analogy? That doesn't seem right—surely we spontaneously use analogy sometimes. A critical predictor of whether people will use an analogous problem that they've seen before is **surface similarity**, that is, whether the problems use the same elements (such as tumors and rays). **Structural similarity** refers to whether the content of the problem that allows you to solve it is the same. For example, the radiation and fortress problems are structurally similar because the solution to both entails dispersing strength and focusing it only at the point to be attacked. People seem to be more sensitive to surface similarity when considering analogy. For example, Mark Keane (1987) found that 88% of his participants used analogy to solve a problem even if they had read the analogous story several days before, as long as the analogous story was extremely similar—in this case another surgery story. When the story was changed so that it still entailed rays being focused on a target, but now the target was intercontinental missiles, the use of the analogy dropped to 58%.

In another experiment emphasizing the importance of surface similarity, Miriam Bassok (1990) trained participants in some algebraic problem-solving procedures using word problems as examples. She tested whether participants could transfer the procedures from one training domain (physics) to another (finance). In an earlier experiment, Bassok and Holyoak (1989) reported poor transfer of problem-solving procedures learned in physics to any nonphysics domain. In her 1990 study, Bassok found that transfer across domains was good as long as the new problems used variables similar to those used during training (for example, if participants were trained on a procedure using the speed of an object and later encountered a problem using typing rate). In such cases, transfer of the learned procedure was spontaneous. If the new problem used a different type of quantity, such as interest accruing in a bank, transfer was not spontaneous, although with a hint that they should do so, participants could map the learned procedure onto the new problem. Thus this study indicated that surface similarity might be important for spontaneously thinking about using an analogy, but people were still capable of using an analogous problem with no more than a general hint to do so.

From these studies we might conclude that surface similarity of problems is the key to whether participants will think of using an analogy. Studies directly examining this issue support that interpretation, although structural similarity seems to have some effect as well. In one study Richard Catrambone (2002) systematically varied the structural and surface similarity of stories. For example, in one story a hunter shoots an arrow at a hawk but misses because the arrow does not have feathers on it and so will not fly straight; later the hawk gives some feathers to the hunter, who promises not to shoot at hawks anymore. In another story, an aggressive country attacks a neighboring country with missiles that miss because they have a poor guidance system. The neighbor sells the aggressive country supercomputers; in thanks, the aggressive country promises not to attack its neighbor. These two stories clearly share a structural similarity, but they have minimal overlap in surface features. Now consider this story, with less structural similarity and greater surface similarity: an eagle offers some of her tail feathers to a sportsman and tries to exact a promise from him not to hunt her. The eagle is later shot by the sportsman, using arrows that carry the eagle's tail feathers.

Catrambone (2002) had participants read 15 stories; only 3 were stories the experimenter was researching and the other 12 were filler, but the participants didn't know that. A week later participants returned and read 15 new stories. They were asked to say which, if any, of the stories reminded them of ones they had read the previous week. The stories varied as to whether they overlapped with the target stories on surface features, structural features, or both. The results showed that surface features always served as reminders; for example, reading about a hawk would remind participants about a story involving an eagle. As the surface features got a little more abstract—for example, something shooting something else—the stories needed to have structural similarity for the reminder to work. Although results have varied across different experiments and methods, most have supported the greater importance of surface features over structural features (Chen, 1995; Gentner, Ratterman, & Forbus, 1993; Ross, 1987, 1989), although structural features do seem to play a role as well (Holyoak & Koh, 1987; Clement, Mawby, & Giles, 1994).

Thus far we have talked about analogy in terms of people's success in considering whether to use an analogous problem, and we're assuming (rightly, it seems) that if a participant considers using it, he or she will be successful in doing so. Sometimes, however, you have already thought of using an analogy but still have problems mapping a sample problem to the problem to be solved. For example, for students studying physics, chemistry, or statistics, having a formula to work from is not enough; they need to see sample problems to fully understand how to use the formula. Brian Ross (1987; see also Novick & Holyoak, 1991; Ross, 1989; and Chen, 1995) studied people's success in using sample problems to help them solve novel problems. In all cases, the formulas to solve the problems were available. The upshot of Ross's study was that people are strongly influenced by the surface similarity of sample problems. If the objects play different roles in the problems, people often are confused. Here's how the study worked. Participants learned mathematical principles—for example, how to calculate the probability of an occurrence over repeated trials—and read an example of the principle's application. Then they were asked to work another problem. In one version of the new problem, the objects could be mapped to the example problem in an obvious way; in the other version, the objects played a different role in the new problem. One problem set was as follows:

> **Study Problem**. The Brite-Lite Company makes all kinds of light bulbs. The red ones are hard to make. Of these bulbs, 5/7 work and 2/7 don't work. John has a new job in which he tests each red bulb by screwing it into a socket and seeing if it lights. What is the probability that the first red bulb to fail to light is the third one he tries?

Objects Correspond Test. The Brite-Lite Company makes all kinds of light bulbs. On 5/8 of their bulbs their name is legible while on 3/8 it is illegible. John's job is to inspect bulbs to see if the name is illegible. What is the probability that the first bulb with an illegible name is the fourth one he tries?

Objects Don't Correspond Test. The Brite-Lite Company makes all kinds of light bulbs. On 3/8 of their bulbs their name is legible while on 5/8 it is illegible. John's job is to inspect bulbs to see if the name is illegible. What is the probability that the first bulb with a legible name is the fourth one he tries?

When mapping the entities in the study problem and the test problem is easy (objects correspond), 74% of participants get the test problem correct. When the mapping is difficult (objects don't correspond), only 37% solve the problem.

We can see that at least two processes are needed to make effective use of an analogy. It must occur to the person that an analogous problem may be helpful, and as we've seen, starting with the Gick and Holyoak study, it often does not occur to people that they can draw an analogy even if they have recently seen an analogous problem. The second process is drawing a mapping or correspondence between the elements of the two problems. In the Gick and Holyoak problem, this mapping did not seem difficult; once people were reminded to use the fortress story, they were very successful in solving the radiation problem. In other problems, however, the mapping can be difficult, as Ross demonstrated in his study.

Can we make it easier for people to draw analogies? Some researchers have suggested that with continued exposure, participants develop an abstract schema for a particular type of problem (Holyoak & Thagard, 1989; Ross & Kennedy, 1990). Recall from chapter 5 that a schema is a memory representation that captures the general features of an object or event. In this case, a schema would contain the deep structure of the problem and a solution strategy that would be applicable across a variety of problems with this structure. As we discuss later in this chapter, it is certainly true that experts can readily describe the underlying structure of problems that have different surface structures. It therefore seems logical to infer that when we practice a particular type of problem, such as calculating conservation of energy in physics, we are building a schema that can be applied to a variety of problems in that domain.

There does seem to be evidence that practice with a class of problems promotes development of a schema that is general enough to handle problems of that class. Laura Novick and Keith Holyoak (1991) gave participants problems that illustrated the use of algebraic procedures. Participants then tried to apply these principles to novel problems. The experimenters assessed whether applying the analogous problems to the new problems created a schema; they measured schema quality by asking participants to describe which parts of the solution procedures were common to the two problems. The participants with higher-quality schemas tended to show more transfer from the analogous problem. Other experiments supporting the idea of schema induction have shown that repeated solution of analogous problems makes participants better able to make inferences consistent with the schema (Donnelly & McDaniel, 1993; Robins & Mayer, 1993).

A key theme in this section on analogy is that mapping is important—specifically, the relational mapping between the parts of one entity and another entity. For example, if you're drawing an analogy between the solar system and an atom, then the relationships of the parts of the solar system should be similar to the relationships of the parts of the atom. The attributes of the objects are not so important in mapping the analogy. It doesn't matter that the sun is hot; what matters is how the sun relates to the planets (they orbit around it, just as electrons orbit the nucleus of an atom).

We might ask what happens if you don't have a ready analogy. What happens if you don't focus on the relationships between the parts of the problem and instead focus on the attributes? For example, if you aren't thinking about the planets revolving around the sun, will you focus on the sun's heat? Focusing on the common attributes of objects can cause difficulties in problem solving when these attributes are not the ones that are critical for solving the problem.

Functional Fixedness

We'll start this section with a sample problem adapted from a classic experiment by Karl Duncker (1945).

> In an empty room are a candle, some matches, and a box of tacks. The goal is to have the lit candle about 5 feet off the ground. You've tried melting some of the wax on the bottom of the candle and sticking it to the wall, but that wasn't effective. How can you get the lit candle to be 5 feet off the ground without your having to hold it there?

Could you solve the problem? The solution is to dump the tacks out of the box and tack the box to the wall, where it can serve as a platform to support the candle.

Here's another simple problem. Dan and Abe played six games of chess. Dan won four and Abe won four. There were no ties. How is that possible? The answer to that problem is that they were not playing against one another. Both of these are examples of **insight problems** in which it feels to the solver that the solution (assuming that it is solved) comes all at once, in a moment of illumination. It has long been assumed that insight problems differ from other problems in that they do not yield to an analytic approach; for example, the Hobbits and Orcs problem described earlier usually is solved step by step, through an analysis of the requirements and constraints of the problem. The candle problem requires just one thing: understanding that the box can serve as a platform. The lack of analytic procedure and the flashing "Aha!" feeling to the solution go hand in hand. People usually report feeling stumped by an insight problem, as though they've hit a brick wall. Then they get an idea, seemingly out of nowhere, and the problem is solved.

The subjective impression I've just described may ring true to you, but do we really know that it's true? Do people feel as though they can't solve the problem and then suddenly find that they have solved it? In a word, yes. Janet Metcalfe and David Wiebe (1987; see also Metcalfe, 1986a, 1986b) examined this question by administering insight questions or algebra problems to their participants. Sample problems are shown in Table 11.3. Participants were given 4 min to solve each problem. Every 15 s, they were to rate from 1 to 7 how close they thought they were to a solution (how "warm" they were getting). The pattern of warmth ratings differed between the algebra and insight problems. For the algebra ratings, at the time of solution everyone gave a rating of 7, which makes sense because they had just solved the problem. Fifteen seconds before that, many of the ratings were still at 6 or 7; participants knew that they were getting warm. Moving backward in time, the warmth ratings for the algebra problems became more crowded toward the bottom of the scale. The ratings for the insight problems reflected a different pattern. Although participants were confident at the time of solution, just 15 s before then they did not feel very "warm" at all. Indeed, the pattern of ratings was the same at every time interval until solution. Thus there is good evidence that insight is a sudden solution, not incremental, and that people don't know that it's coming.

The other types of solutions we've talked about have all been quite incremental. Means–ends analysis is a systematic working through a problem space. Applying an analogy also seems incremental: we must find the appropriate analogy, then map the new problem to the old one, then work through

Table 11.3. *Insight and Algebra Problems Used in Metcalfe and Wiebe's (1987) Study of Insight*

Sample Insight Problems	Sample Algebra Problems
A prisoner was trying to escape from a tower. He found in his cell a rope that was half long enough to permit him to reach the ground safely. He divided the rope in half and tied the two parts together and escaped. How could he have done this?	Factor: $x^2 - 6x + 9$
A landscape gardener is given instructions to plant four special trees so that each one is exactly the same distance from each of the others. How is this possible?	$(3x^2 + 2x + 10)(3x)$
Describe how to cut a hole in a 3×5 in. card that is big enough for you to put your head through.	Solve for x: $1/5x + 10 - 25$

the old solution, and so on. How are insight problems solved, given that these incremental solutions don't seem appropriate?

We can characterize insight problems as involving an impasse; something in the description of the problem doesn't fit, and we are tempted to say, "This problem can't be solved." When we hear that two people played six games of chess and each won four, at first it seems that information can't be right. If we accept that insight problems entail an impasse, we can ask two questions: what causes the impasse, and how is the impasse resolved?

WHAT CAUSES THE IMPASSE IN AN INSIGHT PROBLEM? Many insight problems reach an impasse because of the way in which a concept is used. For example, in the candle problem, the box is presented as something that can hold tacks, not as a piece of cardboard with a flat surface that could serve as a platform. In the tree-planting problem, people typically do not think of planting a tree on top of a hill, but nothing in the problem precludes that solution, just as nothing precludes finding an alternative use for a box.

Thus it seems that one cause of an impasse may be that people's interpretation of concepts is biased, based on their prior experience: boxes serve the function of holding things, trees are planted in flat gardens, and so on. This phenomenon of **functional fixedness**, as the name implies, means that people tend to fixate on an object serving its typical function and fail to think of an alternative use, even though it would be helpful in the problem.

If the key object were presented so that it is not so obviously typical, would problem solving be facilitated? That strategy does seem to work. People more often solve the candle problem if the box is depicted as empty, with the tacks next to it (Adamson, 1952). In another example of this effect, Martin Scheerer (1963) presented a problem in which part of the solution required that participants tie two sticks together. People readily noticed and used a piece of string depicted as hanging from a nail in the wall, but if the piece of string was holding up a picture, it seldom occurred to them that they could use it.

Another prediction of this interpretation of functional fixedness based on prior experience is that children should be less likely to show it because their prior knowledge is less extensive. That prediction has been verified. Tim German and Margaret Defeyter (2000) used a variant of the candle problem and showed that when 6- or 7-year-olds were first shown the normal function of a box (container) they were slower to think of a novel use for it (platform). Five-year-olds, however, were just as fast to think of the novel use, even when prompted to think of the typical use first via the demonstration.

At other times an impasse is reached not because an object needs to be used in an atypical fashion but because the description of the problem encourages people to represent it in a way that makes its solution very difficult. In the tree-planting problem, for example, people think of a garden as a flat (or perhaps sloped) lawn, which leads them to represent the problem as "Place four points equidistant on a plane," an impossible task. Nothing in the problem says that the four points must be in a plane, but most people's concepts of gardens lead them to represent it that way.

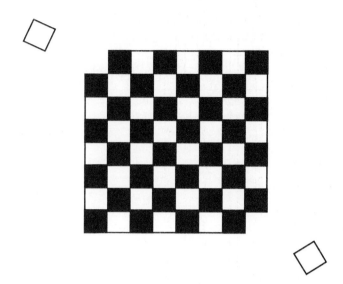

Figure 11.6. *This checkerboard has been mutilated by removing two squares. Sixty-two squares remain. If you had 31 dominoes, each of which could cover two squares, could you cover the remaining 62 squares? If so, show how it can be done; if not, prove that it cannot be done.*

A classic problem that is difficult because of its representation is the mutilated checkerboard problem (see Figure 11.6). Most people who try this problem start out by mentally covering the checkerboard with dominoes. This is not an effective strategy, although it is the one the phrasing of the problem encourages. In one computer simulation, it took 758,148 domino placements for the program to conclude that the task couldn't be done (cited in Kaplan & Simon, 1990). It is much more effective to use a fact that the problem description does not make reference to: both of the removed squares are white. That means that of the remaining squares, 30 are white and 32 are black. Because each domino must cover 1 white square and 1 black square, it is impossible to cover the mutilated board with the dominoes.

In the cases described so far, people tend to think too narrowly about the functions of the objects in the problem. We can reach an impasse not only because we typically use an object in a particular way but also because we are used to using a particular procedure to solve a problem. The classic case in which participants become fixed in a problem solving-procedure is Luchins's water jar problem (Luchins, 1942). To measure a particular amount of water, the participant is provided with three measuring jars, a water tap, and a drain to pour off excess water. For Problem 1 in Table 11.4, the required amount (20 ounces) could be obtained by filling jug A (29 ounces) and then pouring off enough to fill jug B (3 ounces) three times.

All the problems in Table 11.4 except 1 and 9 can be solved by filling jug B, then subtracting A, then subtracting C twice (desired amount = B − A − 2C).

Table 11.4.   Luchins's (1942) Water Jug Problem (capacity in ounces)

Problem	Jug A Capacity	Jug B Capacity	Jug C Capacity	Required Amount
1	29	3		20
2	21	127	33	40
3	14	163	25	99
4	18	43	10	5
5	9	42	6	21
6	20	59	4	31
7	23	49	3	20
8	15	39	3	18
9	28	76	3	25
10	18	48	4	22
11	14	36	8	6

Problems 7 through 11 can also be solved in a simpler way, involving only A and C (either adding or subtracting). The interesting finding is that participants who have solved Problems 2 through 6 continue to use the formula B − A − 2C for these later problems, even though it is unnecessarily complex. Not surprisingly, if you start participants immediately on Problem 7, they solve it the simpler way. Furthermore, Problem 9, which can't be solved with B − A − 2C, proves difficult for participants who have been using that formula for the other problems, even though a much simpler solution is correct. **Set effects** like this occur when a particular problem-solving procedure is applied because of past experience even if it is not appropriate to the current problem.

Oddly enough, the literature on set effects and functional fixedness makes it sound as though knowledge can impair problem solving. If you knew nothing about what boxes usually are for, wouldn't you be more likely to use that piece of cardboard as a platform and solve the candle problem? The idea that knowledge or expertise is behind set effects was examined in an experiment by Jennifer Wiley (1998). She administered the Remote Association Test (RAT), in which participants read three words and must find another word related to all three. For example, for *blue, knife,* and *cottage,* an answer would be *cheese,* forming *blue cheese, cheese knife,* and *cottage cheese.*

Wiley used two types of stimulus sets. In some, the first word was consistent with a baseball term (baseball-consistent stimuli), such as *plate, broken,* and *rest,* which could be solved by *home* (*home plate, broken home,* and *rest home*). In other sets, the third word was changed so that the baseball interpretation would no longer lead to a correct solution: an example would be *plate, broken,* and *shot,* which could be solved by *glass* (*plate glass, broken glass,* and *shot glass*). These stimuli were called baseball-misleading. A third set of neutral stimuli had nothing to do with baseball.

Wiley tested participants who either had a great deal of baseball expertise or very little. The prediction is that people with more baseball knowledge should be poorer at generating solutions on the baseball-misleading items because *plate* will make them think of *home plate* (a baseball term) and the second term (*broken*) fits *home* as well, but that last item does not. These participants will have difficulty generating other solutions, it is predicted, because their baseball expertise causes them to generate *home* for *plate*.

High-knowledge and low-knowledge participants performed comparably except on the baseball-misleading questions. The low-knowledge participants were able to ignore any initial baseball-related responses they may have generated, but participants who knew a lot about baseball were not able to do so and often gave incorrect baseball-related responses. In a second experiment Wiley showed that even a warning failed to keep high-knowledge participants from getting stuck in inappropriate baseball answers.

Bear in mind that in most cases, being an expert helps you solve problems, as we discuss later in the chapter. In this case, being an expert was detrimental only because the task was designed to make expertise ineffective. The interesting point of this study, I think, is that it is a more transparent version of how set effects usually work. Set effects and functional fixedness occur because we are all experts, so to speak, in mundane things such as what a box is for; a box is for holding things, such as tacks. It is difficult not to apply this expertise when we see the box full of tacks, just as it is difficult for the baseball players not to apply their expertise to the baseball-misleading questions on the RAT in Wiley's experiment.

How Is the Impasse Resolved?   We've gone on at some length about how an impasse is created in these problems, but some people solve them, so we must consider how the impasse is resolved. Why does it finally occur to some participants to dump the tacks out and use the box as a platform? And why did that idea occur after several minutes of thinking, and not after a few seconds of thinking?

The insight problems we've been discussing were first proposed by Gestalt psychologists, who are best known for their work in perception. A key point they made was that perception of a figure often is determined by the relationship between its components. (You may recall that in chapter 2 we discussed the Gestalt principle of good continuation in our discussion of vision.) The Gestaltists emphasized that the same figure may be perceived in more than one way. For example, in the well-known Necker cube illusion, perception of the cube's structure flips between two stable organizations (see Figure 11.7). Gestalt psychologists suggested that a similar process called **restructuring** was at work in insight problems (see Kohler, 1929), making participants perceive a whole that had not been seen before. The relationship of the elements of the problem change, just as the relationships of the lines making up the cube change; the lines themselves do not alter, but your interpretation of how they relate to one another changes. In problem solving, suddenly the box is not related to the tacks as a container; it is thought of as something

Figure 11.7. *A Necker cube. The perceptual organization of the cube is unstable, so it flips between two interpretations. Simply staring at the figure for several seconds usually will make your perception of the figure change.*

that the tacks can stick on the wall. The processes that support this restructuring were thought to be unconscious.

An interesting finding indicated that the restructuring actually is not so sudden; the feeling of insight might be sudden, but it is preceded by a more gradual cognitive process. Kenneth Bowers and his colleagues (Bowers, Regehr, Balthazard, & Parker, 1990) gave participants a variant of the RAT in which participants saw two sets of words, such as the following:

Playing	Still
Credit	Pages
Report	Music

For one set, a single unnamed word could make noun phrases of each presented word. In this case, it's the first set, and the word is *card*, yielding *playing card, credit card*, and *report card*. The words in the other set were selected randomly, and there was no single word to unify them. Every 8 s the participants made a judgment about which was the coherent triad of words. They had to make this judgment even if they hadn't found a solution; they were to simply make a guess based on any hunch that they had, and they were asked to rate their confidence about their judgment. The findings showed that when participants thought they were merely guessing about which was the coherent triad, they did indeed perform at chance. When they started having some confidence in their judgments (even though they still had not solved the triad), they were correct about 60% of the time. In other words, when people had a hunch or an intuition about which was the coherent triad, their intuitions were better than chance predictors.

This study indicates that people have meaningful intuitions before they solve a problem, even though the eventual solution of the problem might feel like a sudden insight. Can it be shown that something like restructuring is happening to support these intuitions? Francis Durso and his colleagues (Durso, Rea, & Dayton, 1994) found a way to measure restructuring in a rather open-ended problem, and they too found that the change came slowly and started before participants were aware of it. They gave participants this puzzle: "A man walks into a bar and asks for a glass of water. The bartender points a shotgun at the man. The man says 'thank you' and walks out." Participants were asked to figure out what piece of information was missing that would make the story sensible. Participants were allowed to ask the experimenter yes–no questions to help them get to the answer. Half of the participants could not solve the puzzle and half solved it. (The solution is that the man wanted the water because he had the hiccups, but the bartender cured him by scaring him with the shotgun.)

The experimenters asked participants to rate the relatedness of pairs of words in the puzzle. Some were relevant to the puzzle (*man, bartender*), some were relevant to the solution (*surprise, remedy*), and some were objects that might be in a bar (*TV, pretzels*). Participants rated 91 combinations of 14 words, and the experimenters used the relatedness ratings to construct graphs of relatedness through a technique called pathfinder scaling. Graphs for people who could and could not solve the puzzle are shown in Figure 11.8. The bold box shows the concept that is the focal point of the graph (that is, the concept with the shortest distance to other concepts). As you can see, the central concept for solvers was "relieved," whereas for nonsolvers it was "bartender." The people who couldn't solve the puzzle focused on the bartender pulling out the shotgun; those who could solve it focused on what drew the story together, namely, the relieving effect of the shotgun.

In a second experiment, the researchers took these same measures as a second group of participants were attempting to solve the puzzle. From Experiment 1 they derived three categories of word pairs, based on the relatedness judgments: related words were connected in all pathfinder graphs, and unrelated words were not connected in any of the pathfinder graphs. Insight words were connected in the pathfinder graphs for people who solved the problem but not the graphs for people who didn't solve the problem. The experimenters collected ratings of related, unrelated, and insight word pairs (plus some filler word pairs) as participants worked on the problem. The average similarity of word pairs stayed the same for related and unrelated words, but it increased for the insight word pairs. Even more interesting, these words started to seem related before the participant had solved the puzzle! Thus, restructuring was taking place before the participant successfully solved the problem.

So far we have seen that impasses are broken as people restructure a problem and that restructuring takes place slowly and outside awareness. Can we take this discussion one step further and speculate on what causes the restructuring? Gunter Knoblich and his colleagues (Knoblich, Ohlsson, Haider, & Rhemius, 1999) suggested a framework for thinking about how impasses are broken in insight problems. They agreed that impasses occur because there is a constraint in the way in which the problem solver uses a concept (for example, a box must be used as a container). They suggested that one way to solve insight problems is to relax these constraints; in other words, you begin to entertain the notion that a box need not be used as a container. They proposed that repeated failure on a problem automatically leads to relaxation of constraints. The participant first relaxes constraints that are narrow in scope and if that doesn't lead to a solution moves on to broader constraints.

Knoblich and his colleagues suggested a second response to repeated failure to solve a problem, arguing that people tend to perceive the world in familiar chunks. Recall from chapter 4 that a chunk is a unit of knowledge that can be decomposed into smaller units. If a problem cannot be solved, Knoblich argued, people automatically decompose these chunks and regroup the components into new configurations.

To test these predictions, Knoblich and his associates asked participants to solve matchstick problems showing Roman numerals that describe an

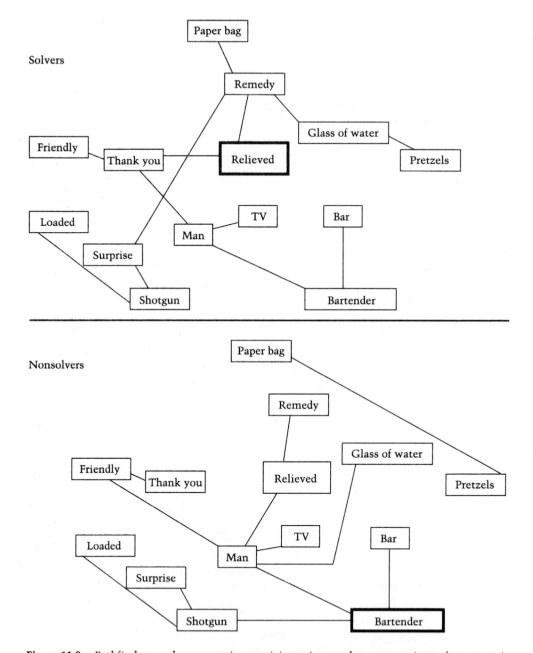

Figure 11.8. *Pathfinder graph representing participants' mental representations of concepts in the bartender–shotgun problem used by Durso et al. (1994). Compare the differences in the representation of those who solved the puzzle and those who did not. The boldface box is the representation with the shortest distance to other concepts.*

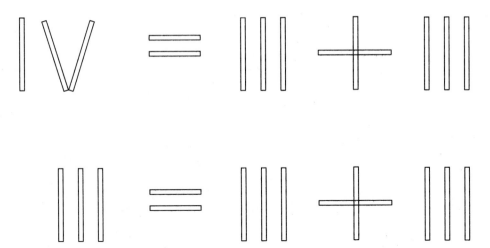

Figure 11.9. *Two matchstick arithmetic problems. The goal is to move a single matchstick to make the expression valid.*

arithmetic relation (see Figure 11.9). The goal is to make the relation true by moving, rotating, or sliding a single matchstick. A slanted stick cannot be interpreted as vertical, nor vertical as slanted. A stick cannot be discarded. You can transform the first problem into the equation VI = III + III. That one is pretty straightforward. The second problem is more difficult. You can change the plus sign to an equal sign, leaving III = III = III.

The authors argued that to solve matchstick arithmetic problems, people must relax constraints they learned in school about math. Examples of such constraints are that tautological statements such as x = x are not useful and that making a change to one side of an equation requires a corresponding change to the other side of the equation. Furthermore, the solution to the problem entails decomposing numerals or arithmetic symbols (chunks); for example, you must be able to see that you can remove one matchstick from VII and get VI.

The authors tested how quickly participants could solve matchstick arithmetic problems, varying which type of constraint needed to be relaxed or which chunk needed to be decomposed. They argued that composite numerals such as VI are easy to decompose because they contain meaningful chunks (V and I), whereas noncomposite numerals would be harder to decompose (such as changing V to an X). They also offered a hierarchy of the difficulty of relaxing constraints, for example, that it is easier to change a number (IV to VI) than to make an equation into a tautology (III = III = III).

The results were broadly consistent with the authors' predictions. If the solution required relaxing a broader constraint or decomposing noncomposite numerals, participants took longer to solve a problem and were more often unable to solve it. The account Knoblich and his associates give of insight problems is appealing because of its applicability to a wide range of problems. Functional fixedness proposes that an impasse occurs because the problem solution requires that an object be mampulated in an unusual way, but the unusual use cannot be generated because the typical use is retrieved from memory time and again. The functional fixedness idea cannot account for the difficulty of matchstick arithmetic problems, and certainly not for differences in their difficulty. Although little research has been directed toward the ideas of constraint relaxation and chunk decomposition, the approach appears promising (see also Sternberg & Davidson, 1995, for a number of different views of insight).

PRIOR KNOWLEDGE IN OTHER SYSTEMS.   We seemed to have dropped our discussion of problem spaces and the General Problem Solver. Is this approach incompatible with insight problems, or indeed with problems in which the participant has some knowledge relevant to the problem but has not solved this particular problem before? Proponents of these models have applied them successfully, but usually in situations in which the person has a great deal of relevant prior knowledge—in other words, when he or she is an expert in a particular domain. We discuss those studies in the next section.

Regarding insight, Craig Kaplan and Herb Simon (1990) examined the mutilated checkerboard problem, which we discussed earlier. This problem does not seem well suited to the metaphor of a search space. Think for a moment about how you would describe the problem in terms of a search space.

The typical participant might set up a search space in which the states were the checkerboard covered by various numbers of dominoes. The available operators are the placing and removing of an individual domino, and those operators move you around the space. As we discussed earlier, that search space is so vast that it is almost impossible to explore all of it, so it is almost impossible to be sure that there is not a way to cover all the squares. What's needed is to get out of that search space.

Kaplan and Simon suggested that just as we think of a space of different problem states, we can think of a metaspace of different problem representations. Each representation has its own space of problem states. In the mutilated checkerboard, the phrasing of the problem or the participants' background knowledge might bias solvers to represent the problem in a particular way when they first hear it. If the search through that space is unproductive, they might start searching for another representation.

James MacGregor and his colleagues (MacGregor, Ormerod, & Chronicle, 2001; Ormerod, MacGregor, & Chronicle, 2002) have adapted a means–ends analysis approach in another way. Rather than searching for new problem spaces, the model suggests that people monitor their ongoing process and seek to relax constraints on the solution steps they had been selecting, in a manner similar to that suggested by Knoblich and colleagues (1999).

In this section we have examined what happens when a problem solver has some knowledge that is relevant to a problem, but not extensive knowledge. We have emphasized situations in which partial knowledge is detrimental to problem solving. Again, such situations are rare; psychologists engineer problems to have this characteristic because they help us understand how people solve problems, just as psychologists interested in visual perception design visual illusions.

Stand-on-One-Foot Questions

7. Name the two ways in which background knowledge can aid problem solving.
8. What seems to be the main reason people are not better at using analogies to solve problems?
9. How are set effects and functional fixedness similar?

Questions That Require Two Feet

10. You may have heard this advice when you couldn't solve a problem: "Stop thinking about it and come back to it later." Given what you know about how impasses are broken in insight problems, do you think the advice might be sound?
11. Do any of the phenomena we've discussed in this section seem to bear on creativity? Can you think of any ways you could encourage creative behavior in yourself or others?

WHAT MAKES PEOPLE GOOD AT SOLVING PROBLEMS?

> ➤ *Preview* The most important difference between expert problem solvers and novices seems to be that experts have much more knowledge about the domain. Surprisingly, they differ less in terms of the processes they use to select operators. Their expertise is a function of applying those operators to a better part of the problem space. There is no great secret to how people acquire expertise; a great deal of practice is crucial. Although certain talents (such as intelligence as measured by intelligence tests) appear to be largely innate, how such innate talents contribute to expertise is not yet clear. One factor that seems to predict success in solving problems is working memory capacity (over which one has little control), but other strategies may be open to practice.

In the preceding sections we focused on the difficulties of problem solving. What do people do when they lack experience that is relevant to a problem, and how can prior experience lead people astray? In this section we turn our attention to successful problem solving. By characterizing the differences between expert problem solvers and novices, we hope to better understand why experts are so successful in solving problems. By extrapolating the findings about experts to novices, we may be able to learn how novices can improve their problem solving.

How Do Experts Differ from Novices?

By definition, an expert is someone who is very good at solving problems in a particular domain, such as chess, physics, or baking. Some of the earliest and most influential work on expertise examined chess masters. Chess is an excellent domain in which to study expertise because it has a large number of possible moves (in contrast to, say, tic-tac-toe) allowing high levels of expertise, but at the same time the game is bounded, so comparing performance among players is straightforward (it is not easy to compare the expertise of two bakers). In fact, chess masters are an ideal group to study because their expertise is verified through tournaments that have a standard scoring system by which players can be compared.

On the basis of our previous discussion of problem solving, we might expect two differences between experts and novices: experts might have more knowledge about the domain, and they might be better at selecting operators to move through the problem space. There is excellent evidence for the first proposal (more knowledge) but mixed evidence for the second (better operators).

William Chase and Herb Simon (1973), following up on classic experiments by Adrianus De Groot (1946/1978), reported that chess masters have extensive knowledge of game positions, as we discussed in chapter 5. Chess masters can remember nearly perfectly all of the positions of the pieces after just a brief exposure to the board. However, masters perform about as well as novices if the chess pieces are not in a midgame position but are arranged randomly. The importance of the midgame position indicates that masters rely on their stored memory of previous games in performing this working memory task. Novices and masters both remember the same number of chunks of information from the chess board, but for a novice, a single piece is a chunk of information, whereas for a master a group of chess pieces is a chunk. For example, a master might perceive a rook, king, and three pawns in the corner of the board as a chunk: this is the standard position of these pieces after a player has castled. It is estimated that chess masters may have as many as 50,000 chess patterns stored in secondary memory (Gobet & Simon, 1998; Simon & Gilmartin, 1973). That experts have a large number of patterns stored in secondary memory has been verified in other domains such as bridge, electronic circuit design, and computer programming.

Experts not only have more information stored in secondary memory than novices do, but they also organize the information differently. For example, Micheline Chi and her colleagues (Chi, Feltovich, & Glaser, 1981) asked participants to sort physics problems depicted on cards. Physics novices tended to sort cards on the basis of surface features of the problem, such as the objects used; for example, all the problems that concerned inclined planes might be grouped together. Physics experts classified problems according to the physical law applied; for example, all problems concerning conservation of motion might be classified together. These results have been extended to other domains, such as computer programming, and to objects such as rice bowls and pictures of dinosaurs (Bedard & Chi, 1992).

Experts' secondary memory is more extensively interconnected than that of novices, and it is interconnected in ways that are consistent with their expertise. For example, a study by Frank Hassebrock and his colleagues (1993) examined the memory of participants at three levels of expertise (novice, trainee, and expert) for information about a medical case. Participants were asked to make a diagnosis and then recall the information presented in the case. Initially, all participants remembered about the same amount. One week later, however, those with more medical expertise remembered less of the case overall.

A more fine-grained analysis of the recall data showed that participants with more expertise remembered a greater proportion of the information that was critical in making a diagnosis. Furthermore, their memory recall was structured similarly to their diagnosis; they remembered information in the same order in which they used it to make the diagnosis. This study shows that new memories within participants' domains of expertise are influenced by the organization of existing memories in that domain (see Figure 11.10).

There is very good evidence that experts have more domain-relevant information stored in memory and that they store this information differently than novices. How about the processes (operators) that move us through a problem space? Do experts engage different problem-solving strategies than novices? Early research indicated that they do (Larkin, McDermott, Simon, & Simon, 1980; Simon & Simon, 1978). For example, in one study (Larkin et al.,

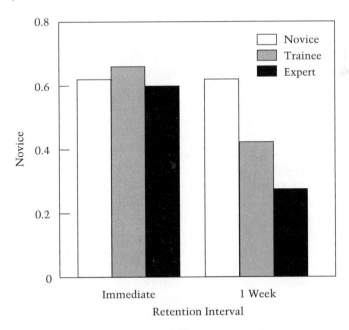

Figure 11.10. *Data from Hassebrock et al.'s (1993) study showing that experts remember fewer of the details from a medical case than novices do after a 1-week delay. More detailed analysis showed that the experts remembered the details that were important for diagnosis and little else.*

1980) participants were asked to talk aloud about their strategies as they solved physics problems. It appeared that novices most often worked backward: they identified the variable requested in the problem and then tried to think of a formula that would yield that variable. Next they considered what variables in the formula were unknown and tried to generate other formulas that could give them those values. Experts, however, seemed to examine the problem and then solve it starting at the beginning of that chain of inference as though they could look ahead and see the entire solution path.

More recent evidence has questioned this distinction in processing between novices and experts (Zajchowski & Martin, 1993, cited in Clarke & Lamberts, 1997). In one study (Priest & Lindsay, 1992), the experimenters sought to test a larger group of participants than had been tested in the typical experiment, and they also sought to use some measure other than verbal protocols to assess whether people were working forward or backward. Therefore, they asked 79 participants to write out all the equations and formulas they used as they solved problems. One measure of reasoning is the order in which formulas appeared in the solution. The results showed that there was no difference between experts and novices in terms of how they worked the problems; both groups used primarily forward reasoning.

Not only is there apparently little difference in the procedures that experts and novices apply to problems, but it has also been suggested that these processes are not very important in expertise. Indeed, in his original studies of chess expertise, De Groot claimed that top-level masters and expert players search the problem space equally deeply; however, the best players are able to restrict their search to branches of the tree that are much more productive (that is, that lead to better moves). In another study, Fernand Gobet (1994, cited in Gobet & Simon, 1996) found that masters do search the problem space more deeply than amateur players. Thus, it may be that early in training some of the acquisition of chess expertise results from improved or deeper search but that this source of improvement is quickly exhausted, and further improvement results from increasing the memory database of chess positions.

The relative unimportance of search processes in very high level chess is supported by a study by Fernand Gobet and Herb Simon (1996). They examined the play (via nine published matches) of the then highest-ranked chess player, Gary Kasparov, under two conditions: when he played a single opponent in a tournament and when he played four to eight opponents simultaneously in exhibitions. In the exhibition games Kasparov was limited to an average of 3 min for each round (with one move against each of his four to eight opponents). However, his opponents had an average of 3 min to make each *move* in the round. That is, the other players in simultaneous matches had full tournament time to make their moves, whereas Kasparov had one fourth to one eighth of tournament time to make his moves.

As mentioned earlier, the skill of all chess players is ranked on a common scale, so it is easy to compare Kasparov's performance when he had full tournament time for each move with his performance when his time was severely restricted. That analysis showed that Kasparov's play suffered surprisingly little from the time restriction. The authors argued that the fact that Kasparov's play did not deteriorate indicates that looking ahead is much less important than the processes of recognition memory that allowed him to identify cues to weaknesses in his opponent's position.

How Do People Become Experts?

We have seen that experts differ from novices chiefly in their amount of knowledge about the domain, but we haven't discussed how to become an expert. The evidence points to two factors that you probably can name: you need to practice a great deal, and to reach great heights of proficiency you probably need some inherent talent as well. Although this chapter is about problem solving, much of the interesting work on expertise comes from other domains (such as athletics and music), so this section cites that literature as well. As far as we know, generalizations can be made from the development of expertise in those domains to the development of expertise in problem solving.

The importance of deliberate practice has been emphasized by Anders Ericsson (Ericsson, Krampe, & Tesch-Roemer, 1993). Ericsson defines **practice** as having the following characteristics.

- The subject must be motivated.
- The task must be at the appropriate level, neither too easy so that the person can perform it effortlessly nor too difficult so that the person cannot perform it.
- There must be immediate corrective feedback. (For example, high-level chess players study games published in newspapers, try to anticipate the next move of each player, and then check to see whether they have anticipated correctly.)
- It involves the repetition of the same or similar tasks.

These characteristics distinguish practice from play (in which the purpose is to derive pleasure) or performance (in which the purpose is to give pleasure to others).

It takes not only practice but extensive practice to become an expert. A number of authors have referred to a **ten-year rule**: about a decade of intense practice is needed to reach the upper levels of expertise. Herb Simon and William Chase (1973) noted that the ten-year rule seemed to apply to chess expertise, and it also seems to apply to a number of other domains, including musical composition (Hayes, 1981), musical performance (Sosniak, 1985), mathematics (Gustin, 1985), tennis (Monsaas, 1985), long-distance running (Wallingford, 1975), livestock evaluation (Phelps & Shanteau, 1978), radiographic diagnosis (Lesgold, 1984), and medical diagnosis (Patel & Groen, 1991).

All these studies examined people who had already achieved expertise in their respective fields and then determined how long they had been practicing; the figure was always 10 years or more. Another approach to determining the importance of practice is to examine people who are trying to become experts and see whether those who are practicing more now seem to be making better progress toward expertise. That was the approach taken by Ericsson and his colleagues (1993). The experimenters studied violinists at a music academy. Some were studying to be music teachers, so although they were competent players, they had no aspirations to become professionals. From other students who hoped for professional careers, the professors at the academy nominated a group of 10 violin students who were most likely to succeed as soloists. Ten other violin students were selected who, although very good, were not quite at that level. The experimenters then had the three groups of participants (future music teachers, good violinists, and best violinists) keep diaries of their practice schedules (and other activities) and estimate the number of hours they had practiced at different ages (see Figure 11.11).

As you can see in Figure 11.11, the best violists practiced more than the good violinists, who (not surprisingly) practiced more than the aspiring music teachers. Keep in mind that these are self-reported data, meaning that participants told the experimenters how much they practiced, so these numbers may reflect the amount of practice they aspired to rather than actually executed. Still, the results are noteworthy, especially given that one could propose that the best violinists would be the ones with the most innate talent and they would not need to practice as much as the other groups.

Thus far, we've emphasized practice, practice, practice. What about talent? Doesn't the raw material with which we start have some impact on success? Interestingly, some researchers argue that talent has little to do with success and it's practice that really matters. Some aspects of performance are clearly attributable to practice. As we've discussed, chess masters can remember chess positions so well not because they have superior working memory capacity but because they have studied chess positions. But what about perfect

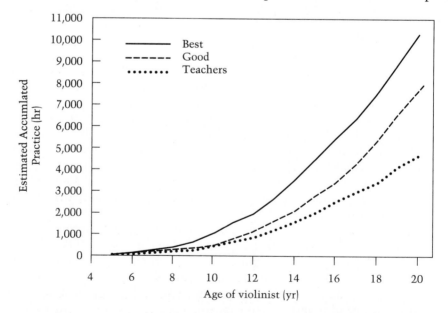

Figure 11.11.   *Graph from Ericsson et al. (1996) showing the cumulative amount of practice by two groups of aspiring musical performers (expert violinists and good violinists) and those who planned to teach music.*

pitch (the ability to name tones accurately), which professional musicians are more likely to have? Isn't perfect pitch something you're born with? Ericsson (1996) suggested that perfect pitch can be acquired at an early age (Takeuchi & Hulse, 1993) and indeed suggests that other apparently innate factors such as strength and speed are the product of training.

That's probably taking the influence of practice too far. Returning to problem solving for a moment, there is a great deal of evidence that certain types of talent are at least in part innate (that is, you are born with them). The best known of these is intelligence, at least as measured by standard intelligence tests. How can you tell whether people are smart because they were born smart or because they have done things that made them smart? Tom Bouchard and Matt McGue (1981) examined identical twins who were raised apart. Because they are identical twins, they have the same genetic inheritance, but because they were raised apart (usually because they were adopted by different families), their life experiences could be quite different. McGue and Bouchard reported that the intelligence test scores of identical twins reared apart were more similar than the scores of fraternal twins (who don't have identical genes) reared apart. A similar technique was recently applied to examine whether perfect pitch is innate or learned, and it appears that the genetic component is much greater than the environmental component (Drayna, Manichaikul, de Lange, Snieder, & Spector, 2001).

Another way to answer the question "Which comes first, talent or practice?" is to look at the histories of people who have achieved prominence in their fields. After interviewing experts from a variety of fields, Benjamin Bloom (1985) proposed that there is some consistency in the development of children who later become eminent. In the first stage, the child becomes exposed to the domain under playful conditions. The child shows interest and promise relative to other children. In the second stage, the parents arrange for instruction with a teacher or coach who works well with children. The importance of practice and a regular schedule of practice is emphasized. During this stage, the parents show a great deal of enthusiasm and support for the activity, providing a series of teachers of increasing expertise and increasing the financial commitment (which can be great). In the third stage, usually in the mid-teens, a decision is made to commit to the activity full time and to seek out the very best teaching and training conditions, which often means that the child must leave home. Nearly all students who eventually achieve greatness have a teacher at this stage who has reached the top level of the field. In the fourth and final stage, the student has absorbed most or all of what the teachers can offer and begins to make innovations in the domain.

From these data, it appears that talent and practice interact. In the second and third stages, the parents clearly set up an environment that is optimal for the practice and development of the skill. But the very first stage is characterized by the student showing talent and promise. Parents often report that the skill seems to "come out of nowhere." Indeed, it is possible that the children who practice the most (including the violin players in the 1993 study by Ericsson and colleagues) are those who have the most talent. As Ellen Winner (2000) points out, most children must be cajoled into practicing violin or working math problems; gifted children must be torn away from these activities.

It seems a safe bet that both talent and practice are crucial to high levels of success. We mostly have data on people who have been identified as gifted, and we have verified that these people were talented and worked hard (see also Lubinski, Webb, Morelock, & Benbow, 2001). What we don't have is much data on other groups of people, such as those who were talented but didn't work hard or those who were not talented but worked very hard. These data are needed to sort out the relative contributions of talent and practice.

What Makes Nonexperts Good at Solving Problems?

In this section we are discussing what makes people good at solving problems, but thus far we have focused on experts. Suppose you don't want to be an expert—you're not willing to commit the next 10 years to practice—but you'd like to improve your problem-solving skills. What makes people more effective problem solvers? We'll discuss three factors. First, having a large working memory capacity seems to help problem solving, but of course you can't increase your working memory capacity. Two other strategies that may improve problem solving are setting subgoals and comparing problems.

WORKING MEMORY CAPACITY. Working memory seems to make an important contribution to problem solving. A prominent role for working memory in problem solving is sensible in light of the framework discussed early in this chapter: using operators to move through a problem space. You must keep several things in working memory simultaneously in order to use means–ends analysis, for example, the current subgoal, the operator you are trying to apply, and the conditions of that operator. Perhaps more important, you must shuttle information between working memory and secondary memory; as a subgoal is achieved, you must retrieve the next goal, search secondary memory for appropriate operators, and so on.

Kenneth Kotovsky and his colleagues (Kotovsky, Hayes, & Simon, 1985; Kotovsky & Simon, 1990) argued for the importance of working memory in problem solving. They administered different **isomorphs** of the Tower of Hanoi problem to participants. These are problems with a different cover story but with a problem space that is the same size and has the same number of branches and the same minimum solution path. Here is one such isomorph.

> Three five-handed extraterrestrial monsters were holding three crystal globes. Because of the quantum mechanical peculiarities of their neighborhood, both monsters and globes come in exactly three sizes with no others permitted: small, medium, and large. The small monster was holding the medium-sized globe; the medium-sized monster was holding the large globe; and the large monster was holding the small globe. Because this situation offended their keenly developed sense of symmetry, they proceeded to shrink and expand the globes so that each monster would have a globe proportionate to its own size. Monster etiquette complicated the solution of the problem because it requires the following:
>
> > Only one globe may be changed at a time.
> > If two globes have the same size, only the globe held by the larger monster may be changed.

A globe may not be changed to the same size as the globe of the larger monster.

By what sequence of changes could the monsters have solved this problem?

You can see that this problem is like the Tower of Hanoi problem discussed earlier. People found this version of the problem extremely difficult, however. Why? Kotovsky and his colleagues argued that the problem is one of working memory. The rules are complicated. There is no physical realization of the problem (such as a board with pegs), so participants have to remember where they are in the problem space (in this case, which monster is holding which globe). Just thinking about the rules and imagining the monsters uses up most people's working memory capacity, so they have nothing left over to work the problem.

Box 11–2 Functional Imaging of Problem Solving and Working Memory

Is it possible to obtain functional images of complex problem solving? It may seem like an extremely difficult exercise because even moderately difficult problems are likely to lead to widespread brain activation. Nevertheless, several studies have successfully localized at least some of the processes associated with problem solving.

In one such study Kalina Christoff and her colleagues (2001) had participants solve variants of problems from Raven's progressive matrices test (1976), which measures intelligence and predicts performance on a wide variety of reasoning tasks. In their version of the test, participants were shown a pattern of eight stimuli and had to select a stimulus (from four choices) that completed the pattern.

Figure B11.2 shows three versions of the task that Christoff used. These problems vary on relational integration, which refers to considering multiple relations simultaneously. Problem A is 0-relational, meaning that no dimensional variation needs to be considered to solve it. Problem B is 1-relational, meaning that a single dimension needs to be considered; participants need to recognize that the rows contain the same figure. Problem C is 2-relational, meaning that two dimensions must be considered simultaneously to solve the problem; rows determine the internal part of the figure, and columns determine the external part of the figure.

Christoff and colleagues had participants solve these three types of problems while they were imaged with fMRI. The results showed that the left rostrolateral prefrontal cortex was preferentially active when 2-relational problems were compared to 1-relational problems. This activation was due to the relational nature of the problem, not to the fact that these problems take longer to solve, because the activation was still present when the analysis was restricted to trials that were matched for response time. Interestingly, the rostrolateral prefrontal cortex was not active when the 1-relational problem was compared to the 0-relational problem. The researchers interpreted these results as showing that the rostrolateral prefrontal cortex is active only when the participant must compare more than one relation simultaneously; in other words, this cortical area seems to support relational integration.

Children cannot solve 2-relational problems until approximately age 5, and nonhuman primates never learn to solve these problems. Thus, relational integration may well be an important component of high-level problem solving.

(Continued)

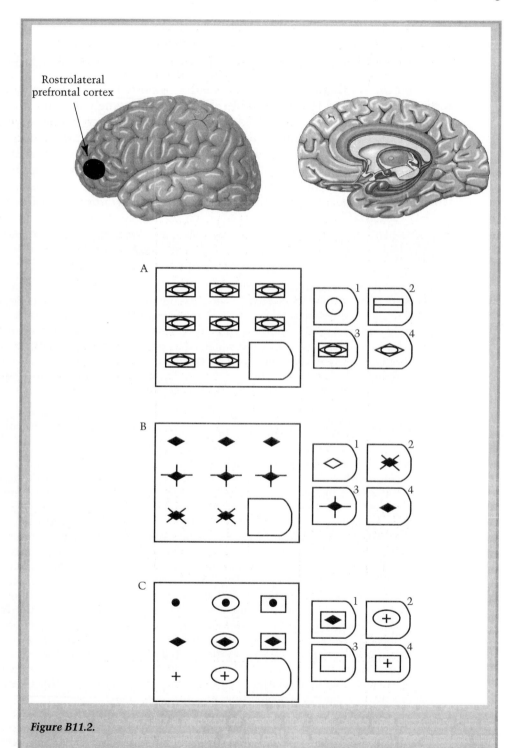

Figure B11.2.

Other work has shown that people are less successful in solving syllogisms if the premises are given orally rather than in writing, presumably because maintaining the premises in working memory reduces the capacity to manipulate them to evaluate the syllogism (Gilhooly, Logie, Wetherick, & Wynn, 1993). A somewhat similar approach was taken in a study by Pierre Barrouillet (1996), who examined working memory contributions to transitive inference by varying the amount of irrelevant information that appeared between key statements that could be used to make inferences. He reported that increasing the number of irrelevant statements increased erroneous inferences, presumably because of the difficulty of maintaining the statements for a longer time in working memory.

Other studies have examined the role of working memory and problem solving by using **dual task paradigms** in which participants perform a task either by itself or simultaneously with a second task. The second task is designed to occupy working memory, so if the first task does not require working memory, it should be performed equally well either alone or with the second task.

Louise Phillips and her colleagues (Phillips, Wynn, Gilhooly, Della Sala, & Logie, 1999) examined the Tower of London task using a dual task paradigm (see Figure 11.12). The Tower of London is similar to the Tower of Hanoi and was named after its better-known cousin (Shallice, 1982). In the Tower of London, colored disks (or beads) must be moved one at a time from an initial state to a goal state that is depicted on a card. Participants typically perform several versions of the task with different initial and goal states. The minimum number of moves required varies from 3 to 11. This task has typically been taken as a measure of problem solving, especially the ability to plan in problem solving, because participants are supposed to plan the whole solution before making the first move (Lezak, 1995; Owen, 1997; Shallice, 1982).

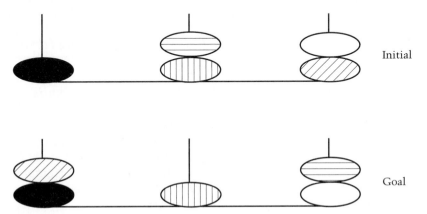

Initial

Goal

Figure 11.12.   *The Tower of London problem is composed of three pegs with some number of colored disks (here distinguished by patterns). The participant is shown the puzzle with the disks in a particular configuration, is shown a goal state on a card, and must move the disks so that the puzzle matches the card. The disks must be moved one at a time, and the participant is asked to plan the entire sequence mentally before beginning to move the disks.*

In the secondary task, participants were asked to say digits aloud in time to a metronome beat. The digits were to be random, with no discernible order (for example, 123, 654, or 246 would be obviously ordered and thus forbidden). This task is fairly difficult, and simultaneously performing it was detrimental to performance on the Tower of London. Participants performing only the Tower of London task made an average of approximately 5 excess moves, whereas participants also performing the secondary task made nearly twice that many. The authors concluded that this task relies heavily on working memory, and similar conclusions have been drawn about other problem-solving tasks through the use of dual task paradigms (Howe, Rabinowitz, & Powell, 1998; Logie, Gilhooly, & Wynn, 1994).

Another method that has been used to examine the relationship between working memory and problem solving is statistical association. In an article provocatively titled "Reasoning Ability Is (Little More Than) Working-Memory Capacity?" Patrick Kyllonen and Raymond Christal (1990) reported that people who have a large working memory capacity also score well on tests of reasoning, whereas those with small working memory capacity score poorly. They reported four studies, each with 400 or more people tested. Reasoning ability was tested with a total of 15 tests across the four experiments. Sample problems are shown in Table 11.5.

The authors found a consistently high correlation (around .8 or .9 across experiments) between their measures of working memory and measures of reasoning ability. This strong relationship is consistent with the idea that effective reasoning and problem solving depend on working memory capacity (see also Carpenter, Just, & Shell, 1990; Engle, Tuholski, Laughlin, & Conway, 1999; Reber & Kotovsky, 1997).

Thus far, our discussion of how nonexperts can be better problem solvers has focused on working memory, so the advice really boils down to this: "If you want to be a good problem solver, have a good working memory." But

Table 11.5.   *Sample Questions from Kyllonen and Christal's (1990) Study*

Test Name	Sample Question
Arithmetic reasoning	Pat put in a total of 16.5 hours on a job during 5 days of the past week. How long is Pat's average workday?
Number sets	Select the set that doesn't fit: 234 567 357 678
Necessary arithmetic operations	Chairs priced at $40 each are being sold in lots of four at 85% of the original price. How much would four chairs cost?
Nonsense syllogisms	All trees are fish. All fish are horses. Therefore, all trees are horses. True or false?
Three-term series	Dick is better than Pete; John is worse than Pete. Who's best: Dick, John, or Pete?

working memory capacity does not feel as if it is under our control. You can increase the amount of information you can keep in working memory by studying a particular domain; for example, you can increase your working memory capacity for chess positions by learning a lot about chess. But that is tantamount to committing yourself to becoming an expert. Is there no simpler way to improve problem-solving skills? Two methods have been pursued: setting subgoals and comparing problems.

SETTING SUBGOALS. Richard Catrambone (1994, 1995, 1996, 1998; Catrambone & Holyoak, 1990) has investigated the effect of encouraging people to set subgoals. Catrambone noted that people tend to memorize a series of steps that depend on the surface features of the problem (Chi et al., 1981; Larkin et al., 1980; Ross, 1987, 1989). Therefore, if the surface features of the problem change, the memorized solution is of no use because the solution steps were tied to the surface features (Reed, Ackinclose, & Voss, 1990). Catrambone suggested that people should be taught to form subgoals because problems within a domain are likely to share a subgoal even if the steps to achieve it vary. For example, in physics problems of the sort used by Chi and colleagues (1981), people should be taught the subgoal of first determining which of the physical laws is applicable to the problem; that subgoal will always be useful, although achieving it will vary from problem to problem.

Unfortunately, trying to teach people subgoals explicitly is not very effective. For one thing, people like to see examples, not just abstract solution procedures, when they are trying to solve problems (Cheng, Holyoak, Nisbett, & Oliver, 1986; LeFevre & Dixon, 1986). And attempts to teach people subgoals directly have not worked well (see Reed & Bolstad, 1991). Catrambone (1996) tried a different method. He showed participants example problems and applied labels to groups of steps, with the idea that people would chunk these steps together into a subgoal. Here is one problem.

> A judge noticed that some of the 219 lawyers at City Hall owned more than one briefcase. She counted the number of briefcases each lawyer owned and found that 180 of the lawyers owned exactly one briefcase, 17 owned two briefcases, 13 owned three briefcases, and 9 owned four briefcases. Use the Poisson distribution to determine the probability of a randomly chosen lawyer at City Hall owning exactly two briefcases.

Catrambone had participants study the solution. In one condition, one of the steps was labeled "Total number of briefcases owned," thereby highlighting that an interim step was to calculate the total number of objects. At transfer, all participants saw a different problem.

> Over the course of the summer, a group of five children used to walk along the beach each day collecting seashells. We know that on Day 1 Joe found four shells, on Day 2 Sue found two shells, on Day 3 Mary found five shells, on Day 4 Roger found three shells, and on Day 5 Bill found six shells. Use the Poisson distribution to determine the probability of a randomly chosen child finding three shells on a particular day.

This is similar to the briefcase problem, but it requires finding a total frequency in a different way. Finding the total is actually simpler in the transfer problem, but participants might not know how to solve it if they didn't understand that part of the solution procedure is to find the total number of objects. Catrambone (1995, 1996) found that participants who had seen the subgoal as part of the solution procedure during training were about twice as likely to solve this new problem.

COMPARING PROBLEMS.   Gick and Holyoak (1983) proposed that transfer to new problems occurs if there is an abstract schema for the problem and its solution—that is, for the deep structure of the problem. For example, the schema for the radiation problem would include the idea of the dispersal of force and its regathering at the critical point. Gick and Holyoak suggested that participants could be made to induce the deep structure of problems by having them compare problems that have different surface structures but share deep structure. They conducted a study that supported the idea, but a more complete set of studies was presented by Richard Catrambone and Holyoak (1989).

Catrambone and Holyoak had half of their participants read two stories with same deep structure (the fortress problem and another problem in which firefighters encircled a fire and threw buckets of water on it). The other half heard one of these stories and a control story with a different deep structure. Next, half of the participants in each group were asked to compare the stories, and half were not. Finally, all participants were given the radiation problem we discussed earlier. As you might expect, reading one analogous story did little to help solve the problem—about 15% of these participants solved it. The group that read two analogous stories and did *not* compare them fared little better—about 25% solved it. But 47% of the participants who read two stories and compared them solved the radiation problem. The interpretation is that the process of comparison induced participants to extract the deep structure of the problem, which they spontaneously applied to the new problem.

However, further experiments by Catrambone and Holyoak showed that it is not always that easy to get participants to spontaneously apply previous problem solutions. Participants seem to draw the analogy only if something in the environment indicates that they should do so: either the experimenter hints at it, or the transfer problem contains some surface elements in common with the training problems, or there is no delay between training and transfer so that the participant infers that the two must be related somehow.

What these experiments seem to highlight is the difficulty of the problem; when we learn a new solution to a problem, we tend to represent the problem in the concrete terms in which it was presented, and when a new problem comes along, we search memory for problems that are similar in surface structure, not deep structure. Hence, comparison, with all its limitations, seems to do a good job of helping transfer, considering the difficulty of obtaining transfer in the first place. What we're trying to do is find a shortcut to the usual route to success in problem solving: "Practice, practice, practice."

Stand-on-One-Foot Questions

12. *How do experts differ from novices?*
13. *What is the definition of practice?*
14. *Other than practice, what makes someone good at solving problems?*

Questions That Require Two Feet

15. *Does practice guarantee expertise?*
16. *Do you think working memory capacity is an important limitation in insight problems?*
17. *Considering everything you've read in this chapter, what is the best advice you would give to, say, a high school student studying geometry who wants to know the best way to learn to solve problems in that domain?*

KEY TERMS

brute force search	isomorph	restructuring
combinatorial explosion	means–ends analysis	set effect
dual task paradigm	operator	structural similarity
functional fixedness	practice	surface similarity
General Problem Solver	problem	ten-year rule
heuristic	problem behavior graph	verbal protocol
hill climbing	problem space	working backward
insight problems	problem state	

12

Language

Dixon was alive again. Consciousness was upon him before he could get out of the way; not for him the slow gracious wandering from the halls of sleep, but a summary, forcible ejection. He lay sprawled, too wicked to move, spewed up like a broken spider crab on the tarry shingle of the morning. The light did him harm, but not as much as looking at things did; he resolved, having done it once, never to move his eyeballs again. A dusty thudding in his head made the scene before him beat like a pulse. His mouth had been used as a latrine by some small creature of the night, and then as its mausoleum. During the night, too, he'd somehow been on a cross-country run and then been expertly beaten up by secret police. He felt bad.

—Kingsley Amis, *Lucky Jim*

In this chapter, we discuss in some detail why we should be amazed by our ability to understand this paragraph from *Lucky Jim*, and we try to unravel some of the processes that make the feat possible.

First, note what your experience is when you read a paragraph or listen to someone speak. You feel that you read or hear words, not individual letters or sounds. Of course it must be the case that you do read individual letters—how else could you differentiate *dead* and *bead*?—but you must do so with such speed that the process is not open to awareness. As we'll see, the process of differentiating individual speech sounds is even more difficult than identifying letters during reading.

Identifying letters to form words seems difficult enough, but the problem is still more complicated. For example, did you stumble over the word *light* in the paragraph? Presumably you did not pause to wonder whether it referred to brightness, or lack of weight, or a joyous mood. It seems difficult enough to find the right word in memory amid the clutter of the approximately 60,000 words we know; what do you do when the word you need to find in memory has more than one meaning?

We can also note that even if the mind successfully retrieved the meanings of all of the words, there is still great ambiguity in a simple string of words. Take the simplest sentence of the paragraph, "He felt bad." Interpreting those three words depends critically on word order, the importance of which becomes obvious if we change the word order. "He bad felt" might mean he is likened to a piece of felt cloth of poor quality. "Felt he bad" gives the same sense of someone enduring negative sensations, but it has an interrogative note and sounds as though it were uttered by Yoda. And how do you know that "He felt bad" was not an imprecation of the manner in which Dixon feels things? Sure, he feels, but he's not very good at it. The longer sentences in the paragraph are all the more open to confusion. Word order is not the proper way to think about this factor, of course; what we're really talking about is grammar, and we'll discuss in this chapter how strings of words are interpreted to signify meanings.

Finally, we might consider the larger context of the paragraph. Even if you understand an individual sentence, the meaning of that sentence often is lost if it is not put in the context of the surrounding sentences. Does Amis really want you to know that Dixon has a bad taste in his mouth and that it hurts to move his eyes? Yes, but the author wants you to know those things as a way of communicating that Dixon is awaking with a historic hangover. Amis's purpose probably was achieved—you likely made this inference—although a hangover is never mentioned. How did you know it? There must be some process by which successive sentences are put together into broader ideas and themes, and indeed this process is so successful that you can draw new inferences from these ideas.

Our goals in this chapter are straightforward. **What makes language processing difficult?** Our analysis of the Amis paragraph gives you a sense of the kinds of problems the mind faces in trying to decode language. Language appears to be full of ambiguities—words have multiple meanings, sentences can be interpreted in more than one way—so why is it that other people's speech and the text we read rarely seem ambiguous? In the second part of the chapter we ask **How are ambiguities resolved?** As we'll see, a key idea is the use of multiple sources of information at the same time. A word may be ambiguous in isolation, but if we recruit other sources of information—such as the sentence the word is in or the conversational context—that usually helps resolve ambiguity.

In the final part of this chapter we consider language in the broader context of other types of cognition: **How are language and thought related?** In particular, we take up two questions that have been of intense interest to psychologists and the public. First, can animals be taught the rudiments of language? We've all seen popular television programs in which great apes appear to be communicating with humans via sign language. Just how effective are the apes at communicating? Second, we look exclusively at humans to consider whether the particular words and grammar of our language influence the way we think. It sometimes appears that we think by talking to ourselves; does that mean that the selection of words available to us ultimately proscribes certain types of thought? As we'll see, the answers to both questions in this section have less glamour than we might hope. Apes may have some rudimentary linguistic ability, but their skills have been exaggerated in the popular press; and the particular language you speak probably does have some effect on how you think.

WHAT MAKES LANGUAGE PROCESSING DIFFICULT?

> ➤ *Preview* The task of defining language is difficult, but a definition is crucial to let us know what we are trying to account for. There are ambiguities at every level of language: sentences, words, and even the sounds that compose individual words can be ambiguous. The structure of our language, or grammar, shows us just how complex language is and lets psychologists know exactly what they are trying to explain.

Before we approach the upper reaches of linguistic usage, we will follow the example of grade schools and begin at the beginning, with the definition of language.

What Is Language?

We've begun several previous chapters by defining terms: attention, working memory, and so on. **Language** proves more difficult to define. Nevertheless, the following properties usually are deemed critical in its definition (Clark & Clark, 1977).

- **Communicative:** Languages permit communication between individuals.
- **Arbitrary:** The relationship between the elements in the language and their meaning is arbitrary. There is no special reason the word *chair* must have the referent that it does. It would be perfectly acceptable for the utterance *table* to have the referent that *chair* now does. The word *big* doesn't have to be in some sense "bigger" than the word *minuscule*. Arbitrariness is a key feature of symbols. A set of sounds stands for a particular meaning, but which sounds stand for which meaning is arbitrary.
- **Structured:** Language is structured, meaning that the pattern of symbols is not arbitrary. It makes a difference whether you say, "The boy ran from the angry dog," "The dog ran from the angry boy," or "Boy the from dog ran the angry."
- **Generative:** The basic units of language (words) can be used to build a limitless number of meanings.
- **Dynamic:** Language is not static. It is changing constantly as new words are added and as the rules of grammar (slowly and subtly) change.

These characteristics are important because they give us information about what we are trying to account for when we try to understand how people use language. For example, consider generativity. You may recall from chapter 1 that this property was behind one of the important criticisms Noam Chomsky leveled at B. F. Skinner's behavioristic account of language. Skinner argued that the principles of operant and classical conditioning could account for how children learn language. Chomsky argued that they could not because language is generative; behaviorist principles can account for whether someone is more likely to repeat an action taken before, but a distinctive property of language is that we almost never say the same thing twice. In essence Chomsky was saying that Skinner's theory was bound to miss the mark because Skinner failed to appreciate what language is. That is why psychologists are eager to define language; it's a mistake we don't want to make again.

Language is almost always considered at multiple levels of analysis. The lowest level is an analysis of the sounds that make up words. (Throughout the chapter we refer to spoken language, with the understanding that similar analyses would apply to languages that use gesture, such as American Sign Language.) The next level is the words themselves. One level higher, words are combined into sentences, and at the highest level, sentences are combined into a story or text. Each level of analysis brings different problems.

PHONEMES.   Individual speech sounds, called **phonemes**, roughly correspond to letters of the alphabet. Some letters must do double duty: for example, *a* is pronounced differently in *baby* and *back*, and *th* is pronounced differently in *thin* and *then*; these are different phonemes. In all, there are about 46 phonemes in English—the exact count varies among experts—and something like 200 phonemes worldwide. Table 12.1 shows a standard taxonomy of phonemes found in English. The 46 English phonemes are combined in various ways to produce all of the approximately 600,000 words in the English language.

Why is the perception of phonemes difficult? After all, there are only 46 sounds to be perceived and categorized in English. In visual perception, you might have to identify anything out in the world, but if someone utters the word *boot*, you simply perceive the three phonemes that compose that word (*b, u, t*), string them together, and thereby hear the word. Even though people can perceive phonemes quite rapidly in accelerated speech—perhaps as many as 50 phonemes per second (Foulke & Sticht, 1969)—the problem doesn't seem like it should be that tough because there are only 46 possible things to hear.

The first difficulty is that individual speakers produce phonemes quite differently. Differences between speakers from different regions of the United States can be quite large. For example, New Englanders are famous for dropping *r* except at the beginning of a word ("Pahk the cah in Hahvahd Yahd" means "Park the car in Harvard Yard"). Variation in phoneme pronunciation

Table 12.1.   Standard Taxonomy of Phonemes in English

Consonants				Vowels		Diphthongs	
p	pill	O	thigh	i	beet	ay	bite
b	bill	ŏ	thy	l	bit	æw	about
m	mill	š	shallow	e	bait	ɔy	boy
t	till	ž	measure	ɛ	bet		
ḍ	dill	č	chip	æ	bat		
n	nil	ǰ	gyp	u	boot		
k	kill	l	lip	ʊ	put		
g	gill	r	rip	ʌ	but		
n	sing	y	yet	o	boat		
f	fill	w	wet	ɔ	bought		
v	vat	ʍ	whet	a	pot		
s	sip	h	hat	ə	sofa		
z	zip			i	marry		

Source: Clark & Clark (1977).

becomes still more extreme among nonnative speakers of English, who may have learned a different set of phonemes than the 46 used in English. When infants babble, they use all the 200 phonemes found worldwide, but by the age of 1 year, the sounds they produce are already whittled down to the phonemes of their native tongue (Blake & de Boysson-Bardies, 1992; Brown, 1958). For example, the two phonemes *r* and *l* are similar in many respects, but they differ in the position of the tongue when they are pronounced. In Japanese, the sounds *r* and *l* are interchangeable, so adult Japanese speakers do not differentiate them. Therefore, it is not trivial for a Japanese speaker learning English as an adult to produce *l*s and *r*s reliably.

Despite substantial variations in how speakers produce phonemes, listeners are able to understand their speech; you have doubtless heard English spoken by native speakers of Russian, Chinese, Arabic, and so on. Nevertheless, it is true that native speakers of English make more errors in perceiving speech generated by nonnative speakers of English, and the extent to which they make errors depends on the strength of the speaker's accent (Schmid & Yeni-Komshian, 1999).

Another difficulty of phoneme perception is that phoneme production varies not only between speakers but for an individual speaker. If you had a stockpile of phonemes that you could string together like beads to form words, a phoneme would sound the same regardless of the word in which it appeared, but individual phonemes are affected by the surrounding phonemes. For example, if you say the word *tulip* slowly, you'll notice that you round your lips before the *t* sound. Why? Because your lips need to be rounded to properly say the upcoming *u* sound. Rounding your lips early doesn't affect the *t* sound, so you may as well round them early. This phenomenon of making one movement in a way that anticipates future movements or is influenced by a past movement is called coarticulation. When you say the word *tulip*, you don't simply utter each phoneme in the order it appears. Because of these anticipatory movements, phoneme production is somewhat sloppy, irregular, and variable from word to word. Why is it, then, that we don't hear other people's pronunciation as sounding sloppy and irregular? We take up the answer in the next section, but first we consider still more confusing problems as we discuss the perception of words.

WORDS. When you hear someone speaking, your perception is that the person utters discrete words: it seems that there are small pauses between words, small bits of dead air. That turns out not to be true. When people speak, they produce a continuous stream of phonemes. To convince yourself that this is true, recall the last time you heard someone speak a language you do not understand. It is impossible to tell where the breaks are between words. For this reason, researchers sometimes call speech a **speech stream** to emphasize its continuous nature.

The segmentation of phonemes into words is subject to error. A rich source of such errors is misheard song lyrics. Most of us have had the humiliating experience of mentioning an interesting song lyric to a friend, only to discover we had been mishearing the lyric all along. Some examples appear in Table 12.2. How are we able to segment phonemes into words? Why do we seldom mishear spoken words but make more errors when words are sung? Even if you hear the word correctly, many words have multiple meanings. If I say "I really like hot dogs," do I mean that I like frankfurters or that I like athletes who show off? How do you access the correct meaning?

SENTENCES.   Suppose that all of the problems we've discussed so far have been resolved, and perceiving words (and their constituent phonemes) is effortless. Can we therefore understand all sentences? Unfortunately, the problems are just beginning.

It seems clear enough that the order in which the words are perceived is a crucial determinant of the meaning of the sentence; drawing words from a sack would yield meaningless word strings, not sentences ("Wish John he jumped had higher"). Even small changes in word order can dramatically change the meaning of sentences. Compare "John wished he had jumped higher" to "He wished John had jumped higher." The reversal of two words completely changes the meaning.

Word order is the heart of syntax, which we'll discuss later. The problem of ambiguity in sentences goes deeper, however. Consider the sentence "Time flies like an arrow." The meaning seems unambiguous, yet there are at least five grammatically correct interpretations. Note that in interpretations 2–5, *flies* refers to a type of insect.

Table 12.2.   **Examples of Misheard Song Lyrics**

Misheard Lyric	Actual Lyric	Song and Artist
Let go your heart, let go your hat and fail it now bad alone.	Let go your heart, let go your head and feel it now Babylon.	David Gray, "Babylon"
Changes come around real soon make us swimmin' in debt.	Changes come around real soon make us women and men.	John Mellencamp, "Jack and Diane"
Hollandaise! Salivate!	Holiday! Celebrate!	Madonna, "Holiday"
I wanna shave with you in the sink.	I wanna bathe with you in the sea.	Savage Garden, "Truly, Madly, Deeply"
Please smell my feet before you leave.	Closer than my peeps you are to me.	Shaggy, "Angel"
And the four-eyed girl can make me cry.	And the four right chords can make me cry.	Third Eye Blind, "Semi-Charmed Life"
I don't know where my toe [or hole, or phone] is.	I don't know where my home is.	Nelly Furtado, "I'm Like a Bird"

From www.amiright.com.

1. Time moves quickly, as an arrow does.
2. Assess the pace of flies as you would assess the pace of an arrow.
3. Assess the pace of flies in the same way that an arrow would assess the pace of flies.
4. A particular variety of flies (time flies) adores arrows.
5. Assess the pace of flies, but only those that resemble an arrow.

Despite the fact that there are five possible interpretations of the sentence, few people perceive the ambiguity, and most perceive the intended meaning (interpretation 1).

What is the process by which the mind assesses word order so that we appreciate the difference between "Hit John with the big bat" and "John hit with the big bat" and we choose one among many interpretations of an ambiguous sentence such as "Time flies like an arrow"?

TEXTS. When psychologists refer to a **text** they typically mean a group of related sentences forming a paragraph or a group of related paragraphs. One of the most notable (and most frequently studied) phenomena of text comprehension is that people make inferences when they read a text. For example, consider this rather mundane text.

> I went to the store to buy a CD but I didn't see anything I liked. Next I went to the mall to buy a shirt, but I didn't have much cash. Then I bought some lunch, and on the way home I ran into a friend. We talked on the corner for a while, and then I went home.

Did I bring anything home? Your answer probably is "no," but the paragraph never states explicitly whether I did. I could have bought a CD as a gift for a friend even if I didn't care for the music. I could have purchased the shirt with a credit card (or shoplifted it). I might have brought my lunch home with me; the paragraph never said where I ate the lunch. These objections seem silly, but their very silliness drives home an important point: most people reading this text probably would make the same inferences you made. Nevertheless, the reason we make these inferences is far from obvious. What is it about a text that leads you to make an inference? You probably didn't infer that I wept when I found I didn't have the money for the shirt. Why not? That's not stated in the text, but neither is the fact that I came home without the shirt, and you probably were happy to make that inference. What inferences are important enough that our cognitive system makes them (often outside of awareness), and what aspects of a text lead us to make inferences?

Grammar

Thus far, this section has contained a great many questions and almost no answers. Answers to these questions begin with a discussion of **grammar**. This term does not refer to diagramming sentences as you did in school; it means a set of rules that describe the permissible sentences that can be constructed in a language. We begin with grammar because it tells us what people do when they produce and perceive sentences.

If our goal is to describe the set of rules that allows the production of grammatical sentences, we must define what makes a sentence grammatical. We can't use the rules found in a grammar book. We're trying to find out what rules are in people's minds as they produce and perceive sentences, and those need not correspond to the rules of "accepted" grammar that appear in books. One option might be to follow some people around and note what they say; from what they say we can divine the rules they used to generate these sentences. That's not a bad idea, but what people say is not a clear window into the rules that produce sentences. Sentences often have stops and starts and "ums" because people lose their train of thought, forget a word and start the sentence over again, and so on. Thus a friend might say, "Have you gone to that new… uh… not the taco place, but it's the one with the, you know, where John used to work, but across the street from there?" You probably wouldn't protest if you heard this sentence in casual conversation, but both you and the person who produced it would agree that it is not grammatical. (The next time you're in a group of people, take note of how often sentences are ungrammatical.)

For these reasons, Noam Chomsky (1957, 1965) argued persuasively that a distinction should be made between competence and performance. **Competence** is people's knowledge of grammar; **performance** is the way people actually talk. Competence is our pristine, pure knowledge of how we think sentences should be produced. Performance is the way we actually produce them once this knowledge has passed through the vagaries of an imperfect memory, the social pressures of conversation, and the other factors that influence sentence production. How, then, can you know what people's competence is when you can't judge competence from performance? Chomsky suggested having people read a sentence and asking them whether it seems grammatical. Participants typically show good agreement when this method is used. For example, which of following sentences appear grammatical to you?

The dog ate the bone.
Dog ate.
The dog ate.
Ate bone the dog.
The bone ate the dog.
By the dog the bone was.
The dog the bone was eaten.
The bone was eaten by the dog.
The dog ate the bone?

Now we have a method by which to analyze grammar. So what are the rules by which sentences are generated? Early attempts to describe these rules by behaviorist psychologists treated sentences as chains of associated words we'll call **word-chain grammars**, which propose that grammatical sentences are constructed word by word, with the speaker selecting the next word based on the associations of the rest of the words in the sentence. If you have the start of a sentence such as "The boy took his baseball bat and hit the _____" you might well guess on the basis of past associations that the next word is likely to be *ball*. The problem with word-chain grammars is that someone could end that sentence with the word *window, umpire,* or *squid,* and these sentences would still be grammatical. How can we explain the grammaticality of these weird sentences using the concept of associations?

Chomsky (1965) developed the famous sentence "Colorless green ideas sleep furiously" to demonstrate that a sentence composed of words that are very unlikely to follow one another can still be grammatical. This sentence, although odd, certainly passes our test of sounding grammatical, yet how often have we heard something green also described as colorless? How often have ideas been said to sleep? Probably never, yet we effortlessly understand the sentence.

One step that might seem to bring us closer to a correct grammar is to specify only what the next part of speech will be instead of trying to specify the next word. We're still dealing with word-chain grammars, so the next part of speech would be based on associations of the parts of speech of the words that have already appeared in the sentence. For example, we could specify that a noun will have to fill the space in the sentence about the baseball bat. Some researchers did develop such grammars, but they were ineffective. There are two problems with grammars that treat language as parts-of-speech chains. First, there are still too many possible combinations. For example, the sentence "The boy took his baseball bat and hit the _____" could be completed by a noun (*ball*), but the next word could also be an adjective (*smelly ball*). Nevertheless, the fact that we could make a lot of choices in creating sentences does not seem an insurmountable problem. It points to a more complicated device to generate the proper chain of words but does not indicate that developing a grammar is impossible.

Chomsky pointed out a second problem that is fatal to word-chain grammars: languages have dependencies in them that can span many words and can be embedded within one another. Uttering a particular word commits the speaker to uttering another word (or type of word) later in the sentence. For example, once you utter a singular (or plural) subject of a sentence, the verb must agree in number, wherever the verb later appears in the sentence ("The little *dogs,* whose master was the nastiest, most foul-mouthed monster who had ever simultaneously threatened me with litigation and tried to romance me, *were* nevertheless quite loving to me"). Despite all the intervening words (and there is no telling how many or few intervening words there will be), the speaker must be sure that the subject and verb agree in number. There are other word dependencies in English. For example, you use the word *either,* then you will probably use the word *or* later.

Dependencies can be combined and embedded within one another. For example, you can start with "Either Dan or Bobbie will go" and then embed another clause, forming "Either Dan or Bobbie will go, or Karen and Jon will go." The options for embedding are endless, and each way in which these dependencies might be embedded requires a different mechanism within a word-chaining device. We could generate an infinite number of such embedded sentences, but an infinitely complex word-chain generator is not an option.

The solution is to abandon linear chains and switch to a grammar that represents sentences as hierarchies. In particular, psychologists have turned to **phrase structure grammars** in which each node of the hierarchy is a phrase (see Figure 12.1).

The advantage of phrase structure grammar is that it specifies a limited number of sentence parts and a limited number of ways in which these sentence parts can be combined. Nevertheless, the system offers great flexibility in creating sentences. Here is a partial list of sentence parts.

Sentence = noun phrase + verb phrase
Verb phrase = verb + noun phrase
Noun phrase = noun
Noun phrase = adjective + noun
Noun phrase = article + noun
Verb = auxiliary + verb

Note one way in which we have greatly simplified our grammar: *noun phrase* has been defined just once, but it appears within other phrases. Thus a noun

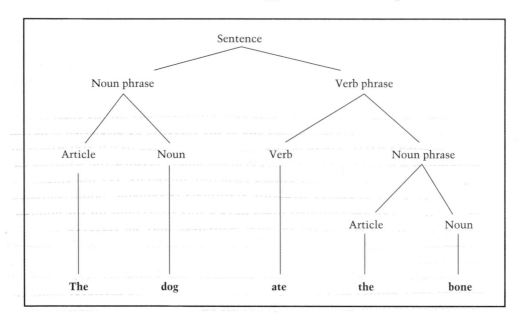

Figure 12.1. A sample phrase structure.

phrase is part of a sentence, and it is also part of a verb phrase (as shown in Figure 12.1). A word-chaining grammar would have needed to duplicate the machinery of generating noun phrases for the two different functions they serve. In a phrase structure grammar, phrases are treated as interchangeable parts, and phrases can be joined into the hierarchies representing sentences as needed.

Phrase structures can handily account for the embedding problem that arises when forms such as *either... or* are used. We can define phrases like this.

Sentence = noun phrase + verb phrase
Sentence = *either* sentence *or* sentence
Sentence = sentence *and* sentence
Sentence = *if* sentence *then* sentence

This definition allows **recursion**. In this case recursion is a symbol that has the same symbol embedded within it as part of the definition; for example, "sentence" may be part of the definition of another "sentence."

Thus by defining a limited number of phrases and a limited number of ways in which they can be combined, but allowing these parts to be interchangeable and to be embedded within one another, we end up with a very powerful grammar.

An important feature of the grammar is that it can account for some of the ambiguities of language. As you know, there are occasions in which the meaning of a sentence is unclear. Steve Pinker (1994) provided this example from a television guide.

Tonight's program discusses stress, exercise, nutrition, and sex with Celtic forward Scott Wedman, Dr. Ruth Westheimer, and Dick Cavett.

Two possible phrase structure trees are consistent with this sentence; the difference between them is shown in Figure 12.2. The hierarchy on the left is consistent with the interpretation that there are many topics to be discussed with Dick Cavett, one of them being sex. The hierarchy on the right is consistent with the interpretation that one of the topics to be discussed is having sex with Dick Cavett. There is nothing in the sentence to tell you which interpretation is correct—the sentence is ambiguous—because the sentence can be parsed into more than one phrase structure hierarchy. Let me emphasize that this property of phrase structure grammars is valuable. Some sentences are ambiguous, so our grammar must have a way to account for the ambiguity. (Naturally, the ambiguity of such sentences may be resolved by background knowledge such as the likelihood of various topics being discussed on television.)

As helpful as phrase structure grammars are, Chomsky (1957) pointed out that they cannot give a complete account of how we interpret language. He provided the now-classic example of the sentence "Visiting relatives can be a nuisance." This sentence is ambiguous; it can be interpreted as "Going to

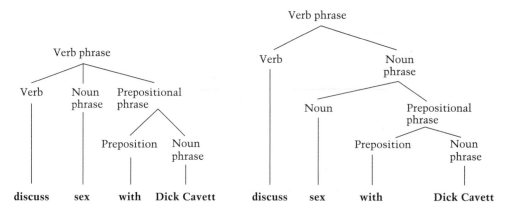

Figure 12.2. *Two possible phrase structures corresponding to the same sentence, illustrating one source of ambiguity in sentences.*

visit one's relatives can be a nuisance" or "Relatives who are visiting can be a nuisance." Despite this ambiguity of meaning, the phrase structure for both interpretations is the same. Why, then, is the sentence ambiguous?

Chomsky argued that ambiguous sentences such as these constitute evidence for two different levels of representation. One is **deep structure**, which refers to the representation of a sentence constructed according to a basic set of phrase structure rules. We can take the deep structure of a sentence, apply transformations to it, and obtain a different phrase structure hierarchy called the **surface structure**, which yields the order in which words will be uttered. The idea, then, is that we might start with the deep structure "Dan hit the ball" but then apply a transformation to the deep structure that yields different surface structures: "Dan hit the ball" or "The ball was hit by Dan."

A single deep structure can be transformed in different ways, leading to different surface structures. Similarly, transformations of different deep structures can lead to the same surface structure. That is the account provided for sentences that have only one phrase structure but are nevertheless ambiguous. Thus we might start with the deep structure corresponding to "Relatives visiting someone can be a nuisance" or the deep structure "To visit relatives can be a nuisance." Although the deep structures are different, when the proper transformations are applied to each, they yield an identical surface structure.

The distinction between surface and deep structures has changed over the years, particularly in terms of the transformations that change deep structures into surface structures (see Gernsbacher, 1994, for different alternatives). Nevertheless, the differentiation of surface and deep structure is still useful.

We have identified a number of ambiguities in language that make the cognitive system's job formidable. There are ambiguities at every level of analysis: in phonemes, in words, in sentences, and in groups of sentences or texts. At the same time, the analysis of language provided by linguists offers a helpful starting point. It suggests a way in which the language comprehension system might be organized. In the next section we discuss how these ambiguities are resolved.

Stand-on-One-Foot Questions

1. What is language?
2. Why is the perception of phonemes difficult?
3. What's the difference between competence and performance?
4. What is wrong with word-chain grammars?

Questions That Require Two Feet

5. I've argued here that structure is important in language, but it seems that sometimes structure is not so important. For example, if a child said to you, "You, me, cookie, go now, hurry," you would know what the child meant even though this is not a grammatical utterance. How is that possible?

6. Can you guess why song lyrics, in particular, are easily misheard? Hint: Look at the actual lyrics in Table 11.2 and imagine a friend saying them to you during a conversation.

7. If the relationship between sound and meaning is arbitrary (as definitions of language claim), where do words come from? Are they random?

HOW ARE AMBIGUITIES RESOLVED?

> ➤ **Preview** We have discussed ambiguities in language at four levels of analysis. Our cognitive system uses various strategies to resolve these ambiguities. Ambiguous phonemes are identified through the use of higher-level context and through mechanisms that are somewhat forgiving of slight mispronunciations. Words can be read in either of two ways: through a process that directly matches spelling to the word in memory or through a process that translates the spelling into a sound pattern, which is then matched to the word's sound in memory. Sentences also are disambiguated through higher-level contextual information, and a similar mechanism may be at work that helps to make inferences in longer texts.

Our ability to resolve ambiguities allows the effective perception of language.

Phonemes

We said that the perception of phonemes is difficult because there is so much variability in how they are produced, both across different speakers (because of accents, for example) and even by the same speaker because of coarticulation. However, other factors help listeners makes sense of this noisy input. First, the surrounding context helps to disambiguate phonemes that are pronounced sloppily. Richard Warren (1970) showed that listeners can not only adjust for phonemes that are poorly pronounced but can adjust when phonemes are missing altogether. In one experiment, participants heard this sentence: "The state governors met with their respective leg*slatures convening in the capital city." Participants heard this sentence on tape, with a cough spliced into the sentence where you see the * replacing the phoneme corresponding to the letter *i*. Remarkably, not only did everyone understand the sentence, but almost none of the participants perceived that any part of the sentence was missing. In another experiment (Warren & Warren, 1970; see also Warren & Sherman, 1974), participants heard several sentences.

> It was found that the *eel was on the axle.
> It was found that the *eel was on the shoe.
> It was found that the *eel was on the orange.
> It was found that the *eel was on the table.

Once again, the * indicates the location in which a phoneme was replaced by a cough spliced into the tape. Participants heard different phonemes depending on the context. In the first sentence they heard *wheel*, in the second they heard *heel*, in the third *peel*, and in the fourth *meal*. People were not consciously contemplating what sound was missing and then making a guess as to what they should have heard; they believed that they heard the complete word. This demonstration is all the more remarkable because the information that clarified the missing phoneme occurred four words later. This phenomenon is called the **phoneme restoration effect**: a missing phoneme is restored by the context and is never consciously identified as missing (see Samuel, 1996 for a review). If you think about your own experience, it seems believable that participants didn't notice that one phoneme was replaced by a cough; someone might cough while you are sitting in a lecture hall listening to a speaker, and it doesn't disrupt your perception of the talk.

A second source of disambiguating information comes from vision. You may have noticed that if you are listening to someone whose speech is difficult to understand (because of a thick accent, for example, or because he or she speaks softly), you find yourself watching the person's mouth carefully as he or she talks. When I was in college I had an English professor who was very shy, and his lecturing style was to look toward the floor and mumble. Although the class was small and the auditorium was large, we all sat in the front row and stared at his mouth, straining to get all possible information to help us catch his words.

The use of vision in the perception of speech is at the root of the **McGurk effect**, named for one of its discoverers (MacDonald & McGurk, 1978; McGurk & MacDonald, 1976). To demonstrate this effect, researchers show a videotape of someone pronouncing "pa pa pa" repeatedly. However, the soundtrack has been dubbed with someone pronouncing "na na na" repeatedly. Participants perceive the person on the videotape to be saying "ma ma ma." (Other sets of phonemes yield similar effects.) Participants fuse the two differing sources of information into a sound that best fits that auditory and visual pattern. The effect holds even when the visual information is degraded (MacDonald, Andersen, & Bachmann, 2000) and even when participants try to ignore the visual information (Kerzel & Beckering, 2000).

Still another factor that aids in our perception of phonemes is **categorical perception**, which refers to the fact that we do not perceive slight differences in phonemes; phonemes can vary along certain dimensions with no cost in their perceivability. The phonemes *p* and *b* are produced in a similar way; the lips are initially closed and then opened, releasing air. When *b* is pronounced the vocal cords vibrate simultaneously with the expulsion of air, whereas when *p* is pronounced there is a short delay between the expulsion of air and when the vocal cords begin to vibrate. That delay (called voice onset time) is the only difference between *b* and *p*, so listeners must be alert for the length of the voice onset time. We would imagine that when voice onset time is very short the phoneme will sound like *p*, when it is long it will sound like *b*, and when it is of medium length it will sound like something between *p* and *b*. That's not what happens, however. The utterances are categorized as *b* or *p*; we never hear something as a mushy, between-*p*-and-*b* sound.

Alvin Liberman and his associates (Liberman, Harris, Hoffman, & Griffith, 1957) conducted the landmark study on this phenomenon. They programmed a computer to synthesize speech and could therefore precisely separate in time the sound simulating the rush of air from the sound simulating voicing. They varied voice onset time between −150 ms (voicing starting before the rush of air) and +150 ms. Their results were systematic. Up to a value of about 10 ms participants agreed the sound was *b*, and above a value of 40 ms participants agreed it was *p*. If the voice onset time was between 10 and 40 ms, people might hear the sound as *b* or *p* (the likelihood varied between people), but the interesting finding was that if it sounded like *b* with a 20-ms voice onset time, that *b* sounded perfectly well formed, just as good as a *b* with a −10 ms voice onset time. The point is that the auditory system seems to place each speech stimulus into a category, and once the stimulus is categorized, it becomes a perfectly good example of the category. The advantage for speech perception is obvious. It doesn't matter if a phoneme is produced somewhat sloppily as long as it is closer to the target phoneme than to another phoneme.

We've listed three ways in which the auditory system can disambiguate phonemes. What have researchers said about how these sources of information are put together? Can we be more specific about the mechanism by which phonemes are perceived?

Liberman and his colleagues (Liberman, Cooper, & Shankweiler, 1967; Liberman & Mattingly, 1985) proposed a **motor theory of speech perception**. The core of this theory is that speech perception shares processes with speech production or relies on knowledge about how speech is produced. For example, the phonemes at the start of the word *put* and at the end of word *top* are produced differently because of the phonemic context—that is, because of coarticulation—but they don't sound different to the listener. Liberman would argue that the speaker does not intend for these sounds to be different, and the listener knows that. The speech perception processes are closely tied to speech production mechanisms, making it easy to infer what the speaker wanted to produce and thereby undoing the effects of coarticulation. The speech perception processes can account for coarticulatory effects and therefore perceive what the speaker intended to produce (well-formed *p*s) rather than the sloppy phonemes that were actually produced.

Some recent evidence provides interesting support for the motor theory of speech perception. This experiment used transcranial magnetic stimulation, a technique that applies a brief magnetic pulse through the skull to stimulate the brain in a localized area. Stimulating the part of the motor cortex that controls the right index finger, for example, makes the person move that finger. A mild magnetic pulse might not elicit a finger movement unless the person was thinking of moving his or her finger anyway; in that case, the pulse might push the movement over the threshold, so to say.

Luciano Fadiga and his associates (2002) took advantage of this property to test the motor theory of speech perception. They stimulated the area of the motor cortex that controls the tongue, using a weak pulse, and at the same time had participants listen to phonemes over headphones. The weak magnetic stimulation caused tongue movements only if participants were listening to a phoneme that called for a lot of tongue movement when pronounced; when they listened to other phonemes, stimulation did not produce any tongue movement. This experiment provides fairly direct evidence that a brain area known to be involved in the production of speech is influenced by (and possibly participates in) speech perception.

This motor theory holds that speech perception is the product of a specialized module designed to perceive phonemes and "clean up" the sloppy ones. However, other evidence calls that interpretation into doubt. First, categorical perception occurs not only for speech but for nonspeech sounds such as chirps and bleats (Pastore, Li, & Layer, 1990). Furthermore, categorical perception occurs not only in humans but also in other animals, including chinchillas, quail, and chimpanzees (Kuhl, 1989; Moody, Stebbins, & May, 1990), and crickets show categorical perception of pure tones (Wyttenback, May, & Hoy, 1996). Thus categorical perception may not be an adaptation that is specific to human linguistic abilities but rather may be an accidental property of the way our (and other species') auditory system is designed. (If you're wondering, it's not hard to test the perception of *b* versus *p* in a nonhuman animal. Simply teach it via operant conditioning that it should press a button upon hearing a *b* to get a reward and that pressing the button when a *p* is heard earns no reward. Then start playing speech sounds with varied voice onset times and see when the animal presses the button. My first week in graduate school, I met a woman who had kept a chinchilla from one of these studies. I was impressed.)

Other researchers have developed phoneme perception theories that do not invoke special mechanisms of perception (Marslen-Wilson & Warren, 1994; Marslen-Wilson, 1987; Massaro, 1989; Massaro & Oden, 1995; McClelland & Elman, 1986).

Words

We have said that there are mechanisms that help our perceptual system make sense of poorly pronounced phonemes: the context of a sentence helps us infer what missing phoneme would be appropriate, and categorical perception lets us hear a phoneme correctly as long as it's close to the intended phoneme. Does that mean that recognizing words is a snap? No.

Most researchers believe that people recognize words through a matching process in which a spoken word is compared with a mental dictionary called a **lexicon** that contains representations of all of the words they know—not the meaning but the pronunciation, spelling, and part of speech for each word. The lexical entry has a pointer to another place where the meaning is stored. A sample lexical entry is as follows:

> Pronunciation: blæk
> Spelling: black
> Part of speech: adjective
> Meaning pointer: → (This directs the system to another location where the meaning is stored.)

When someone is speaking and pronounces a string of phonemes, the phoneme string is compared with the pronunciations of the words in the lexicon. If the phoneme string matches an entry, the word has been identified, and the cognitive system has access to the other properties of the word, including the spelling, part of speech, and meaning. Of course, the matching process must be incredibly rapid to keep up with naturally occurring speech. Psycholinguists have sought to better understand this matching process by examining the conditions under which it fails. How resistant is the system to poor input (that is, mispronounced words)?

The straightforward way to address this question is to let people listen to words—some correctly pronounced and some mispronounced—and see which ones get access to the lexicon. If a word is mispronounced but still gets access to the lexicon, then clearly the mispronunciation was not important to the matching process. But how do you know whether the cognitive system has gained access to the lexicon? Researchers have capitalized on the idea that entry to the lexicon gains access to all components of the lexicon; if you hear blæk, then the other information in the lexical entry becomes active, such as the spelling *black*. Researchers can therefore measure access to the lexicon via **cross-modal priming**. In this experimental paradigm the participant listens to spoken words and periodically sees a word appear on a computer screen. The participant is to make a **lexical decision** about whether it is a real word (*black*) or a nonword (*blarb*). The idea is that if the word on the screen is the same as the word that was heard, it is primed. **Priming** changes a word to a more active state, resulting in easier processing. For example, a participant might hear, "The man considered retiling his kitchen using black and white checkerboard tiles." Just after the word *black* is uttered, the word *black* appears on the screen. Suppose another participant also sees *black* on the screen, but the sentence doesn't contain the word *black* and instead mentions rough and smooth tiles. The person who hears the word *black* should be faster in deciding that the printed word *black* is a real word. Hearing the word provides access to all the information in the lexicon, and because the spelling is readily available, the person is a bit faster in deciding that the letter string is a real word; that's priming. (This case is called cross-modality priming because the first word is auditory and the second is visual, so the word is presented in two modalities.)

Researchers would use the method by comparing lexical decision times to the letter string *black* when participants hear *black* properly pronounced and mispronounced (perhaps as *blab*). Do participants still gain access to the lexicon (as measured by priming) when the word is mispronounced? More specifically, what kinds of mispronunciation block access to the lexicon, and what kinds don't affect the matching process?

Surprisingly, initial research indicated that the lexicon was fairly picky about how words are pronounced. William Marslen-Wilson and his associates (Marslen-Wilson, Moss, & van Halen, 1996; Marslen-Wilson & Zwitserlood, 1989) used a slightly different version of cross-modal priming in which the prime and the target word are related in meaning instead of identical (the participant might hear *honey* and see *bee*). They found no cross-modal priming at all when the primed word was changed (*noney* instead of *honey*), and access to the lexicon was blocked even when the changed phoneme was quite similar to the correct phoneme (*task* changed to *dask*) or when the changed phoneme was the final sound in the word, not the initial sound (*apricot* changed to *apricod*).

How could the lexical system be so choosy about pronunciation, given that the input to the system is so frequently degraded, either by ambient noise, because the speaker has an accent or is eating something, or by some other factor? A further experiment by Garth Gaskell and Marslen-Wilson (1996; see also Gaskell & Marslen-Wilson, 1998) clarified the conditions under which degraded input blocks access to the lexicon. They looked more carefully at the kinds of mispronunciations used in the experiment. Some mispronunciations occur naturally because of the positions of the articulators (the tongue and lips) as different phonemes are pronounced; in other words, some mispronunciations can occur easily because of coarticulation. Other mispronunciations would be unlikely to occur. For example, in saying *pine bench* a natural mispronunciation would be *pime bench* because the position of the articulators is similar for *m* and *b* (note that you close your lips to pronounce them). So if you position the articulators for the *b* a bit early, you might say *pime* instead of *pine.* An unnatural mispronunciation would be to say *pime cupboard* because the place of articulation is quite different for *m* and *c*.

The experimenters used four types of stimuli, shown in Table 12.3, representing conditions in which there was a mispronunciation (or not) and varying whether the mispronunciation was a natural one. When the changed phoneme was a natural one, participants still were able to access the lexicon. When the change was unnatural, however, they didn't get lexical access, even though the change was a small one.

What does this result indicate about lexical access? In the previous section we pointed out that there is variability in how phonemes are produced, which means there is variability in how words are pronounced. How does the language system deal with that variability? The traditional approach was to treat the variability as noise, or static. There is an ideal way to pronounce a word, according to this view, and any deviation from that ideal simply means that the word is poorly pronounced and therefore less likely to be identified. The Gaskell and Marslen-Wilson results indicate that this view is unlikely to be correct because not all mispronunciations are treated equally; they are not all treated as noise.

Another approach would be to have the stored version of the word account for the variation in pronunciations. For example, instead of having the required sound pattern be the entire word, the required sound pattern could consist of a smaller set of the key features of the word. Variations in pronunciation that still had the key features would be tolerated, but if the key features were disturbed or absent, the word would not be recognized (Lahiri & Marslen-Wilson, 1991).

Still another approach would be to assume that there is a single, fully specified version of the word, but there are also inferential processes that make guesses about what some phonemes probably should have been. One such model is the TRACE connectionist network model of James McClelland and Jeffrey Elman (1986), of a type we introduced in chapter 7. The model has nodes that may become active; they are connected by links that can pass activation to other nodes or inhibit the activity of other nodes. As shown in Figure 12.3, there are three layers of nodes. The bottom layer represents acoustic features that are the building blocks of phonemes. The next layer represents phonemes. A particular pattern of active acoustic features is connected to an individual phoneme, so if all those features are active, the node for the

Table 12.3.   *Stimuli Used in Gaskell and Marslen-Wilson's (1996) Experiment*

Sentence Type	Changed	Unchanged
Natural change	Pime bench	Pine bench
Unnatural change	Pime cupboard	Pine cupboard

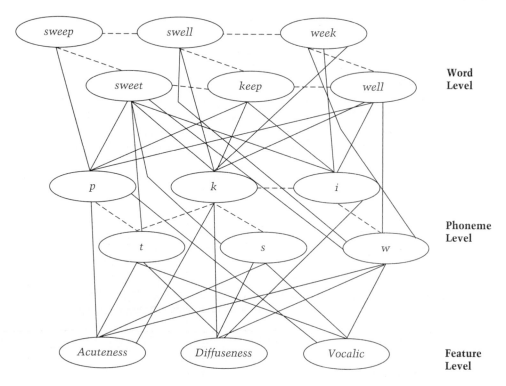

Figure 12.3. *A simplified version of McClelland and Elman's (1986) TRACE model. The lines indicate links between nodes; to keep the figure simple, only some of the links are shown. The solid lines are excitatory connections, and the dotted lines are inhibitory. Note that the links within a level are inhibitory (again, not all links are shown) because more than one word is not pronounced; if the word is more likely to be* sweep, *then it is less likely to be* sweet, *and* sweet *should be inhibited. The links between levels are excitatory, and they are bidirectional. If the phonemes s, w, and i are active, that will activate the words that are consistent with those phonemes (such as* sweet *and* sweep*); the word activations will activate phonemes that are consistent with those words (p and t).*

phoneme becomes quite active; if one or two features are missing, the phoneme is active, but less so. The third layer of nodes represents words. A particular pattern of phoneme nodes is connected to an individual word node, so if the right phonemes are active they pass their activation to the word node, making the word active. An important feature of the model is that there are connections not only from the lower-level layers going up but also going in the other direction. Suppose you heard the phonemes *swi* (corresponding to the letters *swee*). The activation of those phonemes would propagate activation upward to the word level, activating words that start with that sound, such as *sweet* and *sweep*. The activation of those words would in turn propagate activity downward in the model, leading to activity of the phonemes *t* and *p*. Thus, the TRACE model includes processes that could compensate for poorly pronounced or missing phonemes.

All findings we have discussed thus far have concerned the comprehension of spoken words. What about reading written words? The popular **dual route models of reading** contend that there are two mechanisms for reading (Baron & Strawson, 1976; Behrmann & Bub, 1992; Coltheart, Curtis, Atkins, & Haller, 1993; Coltheart & Rastle, 1994; Forster & Chambers, 1973; Paap & Noel, 1991; for an approach to reading that is not dual route, see Seidenberg & McClelland, 1989). One route uses a direct lexicon lookup procedure based on the word's spelling; this route simply matches the written word to the spelling entries in the lexicon. The second route uses a translation procedure that converts the written letters to a sound and then matches the sound to the auditory entry in the lexicon; after the written input has been converted to sound, recognizing the written word is similar to recognizing a spoken word.

Box 12–1 *Functional Imaging of Single-Word Processing*

Our discussion in the text has focused on lexical access in reading. Much work using functional imaging has focused on the different contributions of brain structures to processes strictly within auditory processing.

In some of the seminal studies using positron emission tomography, Steve Petersen and his colleagues (1988) sought to examine processes related to word perception and production. Recall that effective use of brain imaging requires control conditions that are tightly matched to the experimental condition. Here are the three conditions Petersen used.

Control Task	Experimental Task	Critical Component
View fixation cross	Hear or see words	Automatic word-level processing
Hear or see words	Repeat words	Motor programming of articulation
Repeat words	Generate verbs associated with words	Semantic association

Thus participants performed four tasks: looking at a fixation cross, passively hearing (or seeing) words, repeating words that they saw or heard, or generating an appropriate verb to go with a word they saw or heard (for example, viewing a picture of a cake and saying *eat*). The tasks were set up so that the researchers could subtract the activations from the control task from the experimental task to yield activations associated with one critical component of single-word processing.

Figure B12.1 shows the activations resulting from the subtractions. As you can see, presentation of the words leads to automatic processing in the appropriate sensory areas: primary visual cortex for visual presentation and primary auditory cortex (or more broadly, activity around the Sylvian fissure) for auditory presentation. The activity associated specifically with programming the articulators to repeat a word is isolated in motor areas: primary motor, premotor, and supplementary motor cortices and cerebellum. When participants must access the meaning of words, activation is observed in left frontal cortex (working

(Continued)

memory), anterior cingulate (attention), and right cerebellum (the function of which is not understood). In this original study Petersen and his colleagues did not observe activation in temporal lobe, which is where most researchers thought word meanings are stored, but subsequent studies observed activation of the temporal lobe when the lexicon is accessed.

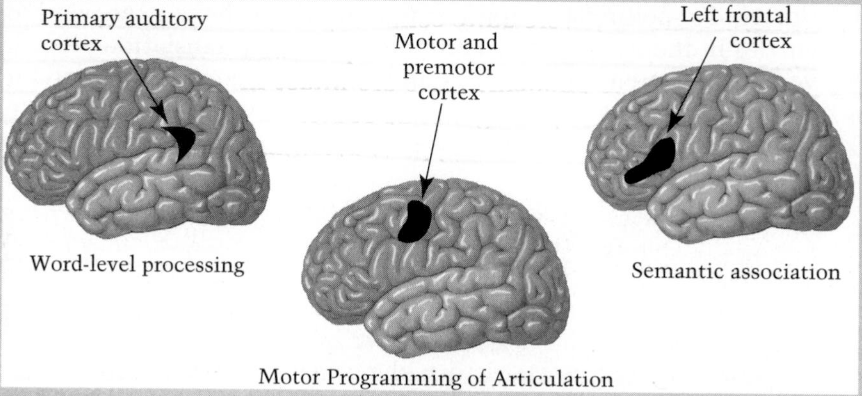

Figure B12.1.

    This dual route model neatly accounts for several findings that are otherwise difficult to accommodate. When you see words like *slint* or *papperine*, you can read them aloud, if you so desire. How? These aren't real words, so you have no lexical entry for them. This ability seems to require postulating that readers know a set of rules that convert letters and groups of letters into phonemes—call them letter-to-phoneme rules. This set of rules cannot completely account for reading, however, because readers also successfully read so-called exception words such as *colonel* and *pint* whose pronunciation is not in line with the letter-to-phoneme rules. The dual route model proposes that these words are not handled by the letter-to-phoneme translation processes. If they were, you would pronounce *colonel* as *kahlownell* and *pint* would rhyme with *hint*. Instead, you use the spelling of these words to establish that they are in the lexicon. The spelling also lets you gain access to the lexical entry for the word and then its pronunciation.

    Thus the dual route model can easily account for our ability to read nonwords such as *slint*, which uses the letter-to-phoneme route; irregular words like *pint*, which uses the spelling-lookup route; and regular words like *cake*, which might use either route. But do we really need two routes? Can we find more compelling evidence that these routes are truly separate?

    One form of evidence comes from different types of dyslexia. You are probably aware that dyslexia is a problem in reading. **Acquired dyslexia** is a reading problem in an adult that is caused by brain damage (as from a stroke or removal of a brain tumor) in people who were normal readers before the injury. There are two types of acquired dyslexia. In **surface dyslexia** the reading of nonwords (and regular words) is preserved, but the patient has difficulty reading irregular words. Hence, the patient could read *nurse* or *glebe* but might read *glove* as rhyming with *cove* and *flood* as rhyming with *mood* (Marshall & Newcombe, 1973). An extreme case of this disorder, patient K.T. (McCarthy & Warrington, 1986), could read irregular words correctly only about 47% of the time, even if they were quite common, but could read regular words accurately 100% of the time. The clear interpretation within the dual route model is that the letter-to-phoneme rules are intact in this patient, but there is selective damage to the spelling-lookup route.

An altogether different type of dyslexia is observed in other patients who have selective difficulty in reading nonwords. They can correctly read irregular words like *yacht* and regular words such as *cup*, but they cannot read nonwords. This pattern of reading abilities is called **phonological dyslexia** (Beauvois & Derouesne, 1979). One extremely impaired patient could read regular words correctly with 90% accuracy even when they were long (like *satirical*) but could not read even simple nonwords such as *nust* aloud. Even more incredibly, the patient could name individual letters successfully, but he could not say which sound they made, although he could repeat the sound if it were given to him (Funnell, 1983).

We have been discussing acquired dyslexia, which strikes an accomplished reader as a result of brain damage. A second type of dyslexia, **developmental dyslexia**, is abnormal development of reading processes in children. A number of reading researchers have argued that developmental dyslexia takes one of two patterns, corresponding closely to the surface or phonological dyslexia seen in acquired dyslexia (Harris & Coltheart, 1986; Marshall, 1984).

The dual route model also accounts for some patterns of data in normal adult readers. For example, suppose I gave you a lexical decision task in which you must say whether a letter string forms a word; for example, you might see *wolt* or *beep*. Now suppose you saw the word *koat* or *phocks*. Both have pronunciations that match real words (*coat* and *fox*), but they are not words. What should the dual route model predict? Response times to these nonwords should be slower than to nonwords whose pronunciation does not match real words because the two routes will conflict as to the correct answer. The letters-to-phonemes route identifies the sound pattern as matching a word in the lexicon, whereas the spelling-lookup route does not identify a word in the lexicon with this spelling. This expected pattern of response times has been verified (Rubenstein, Lewis, & Rubenstein, 1971).

The dual route model also predicts that normal readers, when reading aloud, should be slower with exception words such as *yacht* than regular words such as *round*. Exception words lead to two conflicting readings of *yacht*: the correct pronunciation derived from the lexicon (which was accessed via the spelling-lookup route) and an incorrect pronunciation derived from the letter-to-phoneme rules that would sound something like *yatcht*, rhyming with *patched*. There is no conflict for regular words such as *round*, however, because both routes produce the same sound. The data are more or less consistent with the prediction (Paap & Noel, 1991; Seidenberg, Waters, Barnes, & Tanenhaus, 1984; Taraban & McClelland, 1987), but the effect seems small or nonexistent when researchers examine irregular words that are very common in the language and that participants therefore are likely to have a great deal of experience reading.

Sentences

Although we just finished discussing the processing of words, we must immediately reconsider how the lexicon is accessed in the context of sentences because once we have words grouped in a sentence, we can ask whether access to the lexicon is biased by the context of the sentence. To take a classic example (Swinney, 1979), consider these two sentences, each containing the word *bugs*.

> The room was filthy, and there were *bugs* in the corner, according to my friend.
>
> The embassy was not secure, and there were *bugs* in the corner, according to my friend.

Had you read each sentence in isolation, you probably would have been aware of only one meaning of the word *bugs*. We can ask whether our introspection matches what our cognitive system is actually doing. Does the beginning of the sentence bias access to the lexicon, so that the meaning of *bugs* that is appropriate to the context is accessed and the other meaning is not accessed?

Early research indicated that both meanings are accessed but that the meaning inappropriate to the context is suppressed rapidly. More recent research indicates that that conclusion is not wholly right, but I'll describe that first study because it is important to understand the method. David Swinney (1979) presented participants with sentences such as the *bugs* sentences auditorily. As they listened, they also had to perform a lexical decision task about words that periodically appeared on a computer screen. The critical word appeared on the screen right after participants heard the word *bug*. The lexical decision was to be made for the word *spy*, *ant*, or *sew*. *Sew* is related to neither meaning of *bug*, so you wouldn't expect people to respond especially quickly to it, but *spy* and *ant* are related to the separate meanings of the word *bugs*; if one meaning of *bugs* has been accessed in the lexicon, you would expect that the participant could verify a related word quickly. So if you present *bugs* in the dirty room sentence, you expect people to respond quickly to *ant*; do they also respond quickly to *spy*? If they do, both meanings of *bugs* are probably accessed from the lexicon, even though the sentence clearly indicates that only one meaning is appropriate.

Swinney reported that both word meanings are accessed; there was an advantage in recognizing the word *ant* or the word *spy*, and the advantage was there for either sentence. But when Swinney changed the experiment by probing for lexical access not immediately after *bugs* but four words later, he observed facilitation only for the context-appropriate meaning; if participants heard the dirty room sentence and saw *spy* on the screen at the end of the sentence, they showed no priming when they identified *spy* as a word. Swinney concluded that both meanings of a word are accessed but that the context of the sentence usually makes one meaning of the word clearly inappropriate, and that inappropriate meaning is suppressed quickly.

However, further work indicated that a strong biasing context could affect access to the lexicon, resulting in only the appropriate meaning being retrieved. Greg Simpson and Merilee Kreuger (1991; see also Tabossi & Zardon, 1993) had participants read sentences aloud in which the last word was a homophone. The sentences biased the homophone toward either the dominant (that is, more common) or subordinate (less common) meaning or did not bias the interpretation, as follows:

Dominant: This has been a cold and rainy spring.
Subordinate: This is a broken and rusty old spring.
Ambiguous: This really is not a very good spring.

Participants were asked to read each sentence aloud. As they read the last word, another appeared on the screen and they were to read it aloud as quickly as possible. The final word could be related to the dominant meaning (the season), the subordinate meaning (a coil), or an unrelated word (such as *cow*). The assumption was that it would be easier to read a word if a semantically related word had been activated recently. The unrelated word therefore provides a baseline for how quickly each participant can read words. If the biasing context doesn't affect lexical access, then people should be faster at reading words related to either the dominant or subordinate meaning because both meanings are activated, no matter how the sentence biases your interpretation. The results showed that the context did matter.

When the biasing context matched the final word, participants were faster in reading it (compared to their time in reading the completely unrelated word). If the biasing context did not match the final word, there was no advantage in reading time and therefore presumably no lexical access for that meaning of the word. The delay between the end of the sentence (when the lexicon would be accessed for the homophone) and the presentation of the word had no effect on the pattern of results (see Figure 12.4).

The reasons for the difference between these results and Swinney's are not entirely clear. One possibility is that the experiments differed in the strength of the biasing context. It may be that the context must be strong enough to restrict lexical access. Another possibility is that the results depend on the task. Swinney's task is really two tasks: participants must always be watching the screen as they listen to the sentences, so they must divide attention. The division of attention may water down the biasing effect of the context. In any event, it does appear that lexical access can be affected by context, at least under some conditions.

Suppose that the perception of phonemes and words has proceeded apace, and we are attempting to understand how these words combine to form a sentence. As we mentioned earlier, it is obviously not sufficient to simply perceive

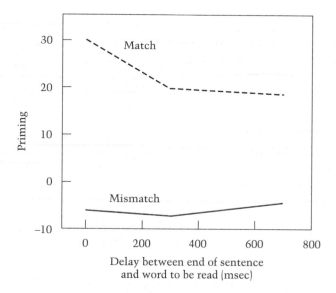

Figure 12.4. *Results of the experiment by Simpson and Krueger (1991). When the biasing context matched the final word, priming was observed, but no priming was observed when it did not. Priming is shown as a difference score; it's the degree to which people could read the last word faster than a control word. Note that the delay between the end of the sentence and the occurrence of the to-be-read word had no impact on the amount of priming. These results indicate that lexical access is biased by context.*

words; the sentence "I'd rather die than swim" has very different meaning from "I'd rather swim than die," and the difference between those sentences clearly is not a difference of words but of the arrangement of words. We said earlier that sentences are represented in terms of phrase structures. Thus much of the debate centers on how listeners take the word-by-word input of speech and build the appropriate hierarchical phrase structure representation for each sentence. For example, consider this sentence: "The horse raced past the barn fell."

Even after rereading it, you still may not understand what the sentence means. Here's a rephrasing that makes it clearer: "The horse that was raced past the barn is the one that fell." Even if you understood the meaning without the rephrasing, you probably felt jarred when you came to the word *fell*. A sentence like this is a **garden path sentence**, one in which your cognitive system builds a phrase structure, but later it becomes clear that something must be wrong with the phrase structure as built. The cognitive system is led down the garden path, so to say, by a pattern of words that indicates one structure but actually requires another structure. Let us call the psychological mechanism that derives phrase structures from sentences the sentence parser. The sentence parser assumes that *raced* is the main verb of the sentence. This assumption need not be true; why, then, doesn't the sentence parser wait until all of the evidence is in? For whatever reason, the parser takes gambles. Most of the time the gambles are good ones, and sentence processing proceeds smoothly. Occasionally it makes a mistake and needs to tear apart the phrase structure representation it had been building and start over again.

Box 12–2 Syntactic Processing

What part of the brain is important for parsing grammar? Lesion studies going back to the classic work of Broca in the late 19th century implicate an area in the lateral inferior frontal lobe, just anterior to the primary motor strip, called Broca's area in honor of his contribution. The classic Broca's aphasic patient who has damage restricted to this area shows grammar-related deficits in production and comprehension of speech. When speaking, a patient with Broca's aphasia shows what is called telegraphic speech, omitting articles and function words, often omitting tense, and in general showing sparse use of grammar. Here is an example from Gardner (1977).

INTERVIEWER: What was your work before you entered the hospital?
PATIENT: I'm a sig ... no ... man ... uh, well, ... again.
INTERVIEWER: You were a signal man?
PATIENT: ... right.
INTERVIEWER: Were you in the Coast Guard?
PATIENT: No, er, yes, yes, ... ship ... Massachu ... chusetts ... Coastguard ... years [holds up hand to indicate 19].
INTERVIEWER: You were in the Coast Guard for nineteen years?
PATIENT: Oh ... boy ... right ... right
INTERVIEWER: Why are you in the hospital?
PATIENT: [patient points to paralyzed arm] Arm no good [points to mouth] Speech ... can't say ... talk, you see.
INTERVIEWER: What happened to make you lose your speech?
PATIENT: Head, fall, Jesus Christ, me no good, str, str ... oh Jesus ... stroke.

This patient knows what he wants to say but has problems generating the sentences to say it. Patients with Broca's aphasia also have difficulty understanding complex syntactic structures, and they rely on context and meaning to help them understand even simple syntax. For example, a Broca's aphasic patient would be able to understand "The boy hit the ball" because the meanings of *boy*, *hit*, and *ball* constrain who hit what. If the sentence were "The boy hit the girl" the patient might make errors because either the boy or the girl might do the hitting. Once embedded clauses are added ("The boy that the girl saw hit the dog"), a patient with Broca's aphasia would make many errors.

Functional imaging data support the importance of Broca's area. For example, in one study David Caplan and his associates (Caplan, Alpert, & Waters,

(Continued)

1998) had participants read sentences that varied only in their syntactic structure. Some sentences had a center-embedded relative clause ("The juice that
the child spilled stained the rug"). Control sentences conveyed the same
meaning, but with right-branching relative clauses ("The child spilled the
juice that stained the rug"). Participants were to read the sentences for meaning; some meanings were plausible and some were not, and participants made
a plausibility judgment about each sentence. Behavioral studies have shown
that sentences with center-embedded clauses are more difficult to process (they
take longer to read). The researchers subtracted the activation associated with
the simpler sentences from the activation associated with the syntactically
more complex sentences and found a strong activation restricted to part of
Broca's area as well as activation in the cingulate gyrus (probably caused by increased attentional demands of the more complex sentences). Work is continuing to further elucidate the various subprocesses that must contribute to a
complex function such as syntax comprehension.

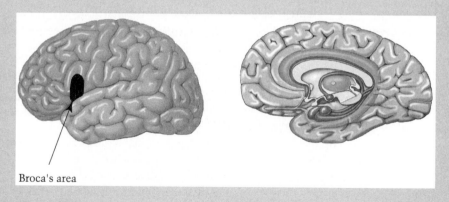

Broca's area

Figure B12.2.

This simple example points the way to some of the important dimensions on which models of sentence processing differ. First, we might ask what
cues the sentence parser uses to derive an interpretation. Second, we might
ask when the parser commits to an interpretation. Clearly it had committed
itself to a particular interpretation of the ongoing sentence before it reached
the last word (*fell*). Does it have to assign a place to each word coming in?
Does it have a buffer of three or four words so that it can suspend judgment on
a particular word until it gets more information? Third, we might ask whether
the parser is influenced by surrounding context. Suppose you saw this pair of
sentences.

ANNA: Did the horse standing by the pond fall, or was it the one that
Rebecca raced past the barn?
WARREN: The horse raced past the barn fell.

Or perhaps the parser is sensitive to the semantics of the words that it is parsing. For example, suppose the sentence had been, "The horse led past the barn fell." *Led* typically is not an active verb for horses. Horses are led; they don't lead others. Would that make any difference at all in how people interpret the sentence, perhaps making them less likely to traipse down the garden path? Let's look at some of the cues the parser uses to build phrase structures.

Key words provide an important cue to the correct phrase structure organization. For example, the word *a* indicates that a noun phrase follows; *who*, *which*, and *that* indicate a relative clause. One source of support for their importance comes from studies in which the key words are omitted. Jerry Fodor and Merrill Garrett (1967) presented participants with one of two variants of a sentence; one had the key words and the other did not.

The car that the man whom the dog bit drove crashed.

The car the man the dog bit drove crashed.

Both sentences contain relative clauses, but in the second sentence the relative pronouns have been removed. Participants were to listen to one of these sentences and paraphrase it to show that they understood it; they were faster and more accurate in paraphrasing the sentences that contained the relative pronouns. Presumably the relative pronouns are cues that there is a relative clause in the sentence (see also Hakes & Cairns, 1970; Hakes & Foss, 1970).

Another cue the parser uses is word order; more specifically, the parser assumes that sentences will be active. People are faster in determining the meaning of a sentence in the active voice ("Bill hit Mary") than in the passive voice ("Mary was hit by Bill") (Slobin, 1966).

There are many sentences in which word order and key words are not enough to go on, however. When a new word is perceived, it's not clear how it should be parsed. Lyn Frazier (1978, cited in McKoon & Ratcliff, 1998) proposed a rule that the parser might use in such cases: the **principle of minimal attachment.** The idea is that the parser is biased to add new words and phrases to a node that already exists on the hierarchy rather than creating a new node. In a classic study examining this proposal, Keith Rayner and his associates (Rayner, Carlson, & Frazier, 1983) showed participants two similar sentences that differed in their phrase structures.

The spy saw the cop with binoculars but the cop didn't see him.

The spy saw the cop with a revolver but the cop didn't see him.

The relevant part of the phrase structure for each sentence is shown in Figure 12.5. Note that in the sentence on the left, *binoculars* is part of the verb phrase started by *saw*, whereas in the sentence on the right, *revolver* requires that a new node be generated to represent the noun phrase. Rayner and his associates recorded participants' eye movements while they read these (and similar) sentences and found that reading times were longer when minimal attachment was violated, and the increased time resulted from locations of the violation;

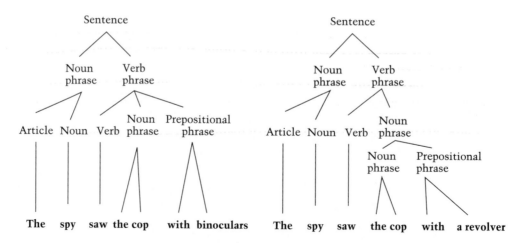

Figure 12.5. *Phrase structures for the key parts of the sentences in the experiment by Rayner et al. (1983). Note that the hierarchical structure is more complex for the phrase on the right.*

participants' eyes dwelled on those locations longer (see Frazier & Clifton, 1996 for a review of supportive evidence).

Other researchers have suggested that other syntactic cues help guide parsing. Some have suggested that the most important cue is recency, meaning that people try to attach a new word to the words most recently encountered (Phillips & Gibson, 1997). This prediction often overlaps with the principle of minimal attachment, but not always. Still other researchers emphasize the role of working memory in parsing. There is much evidence that the size of working memory is correlated with how quickly and accurately a person can parse complex sentences (King & Just, 1991) and with how many interpretations of an ambiguous sentence he or she can maintain simultaneously (Gibson, 1998; MacDonald, Just, & Carpenter, 1992; Miyake, Carpenter, & Just, 1994).

Until the mid-1990s, most researchers thought that the types of cues we've been discussing—key words, minimal attachment, word order, working memory—accounted for how sentences were parsed. Note that all these cues are syntactic cues; the semantics or meaning of the sentence plays no role in parsing it. This conclusion was based on studies that used a variant of the "spy with binoculars" study. Fernanda Ferreira & Charles Clifton (1986) used sentences like these.

The defendant examined by the lawyer shocked the jury.

The evidence examined by the lawyer shocked the jury.

In the first sentence, *examined* could be the main verb, and the fact that it is a participle is clear only once the word *by* has been read. In the second sentence, *examined* couldn't be the main verb because the evidence could not examine something; *examined* must be a participle. Nevertheless, researchers observe the same garden path eye movements seen in the "spy with binoculars" study. The conclusion was that semantic content does not help constrain the way a sentence is parsed (see also Mitchell, Corley, & Garnham, 1992; Rayner, Garrod, & Perfetti, 1992).

Research in the early 1990s called that conclusion into doubt (Altmann, Garnham, & Dennis, 1992; Altmann, Garnham, & Henstra, 1994; Britt, 1994; Britt, Perfetti, Garrod, & Rayner, 1992). For example, Gerry Altmann and Mark Steedman (1988) provided participants with a strong semantic context to bias the interpretation of the key phrase.

> **Noun phrase context**: A burglar broke into a bank carrying some dynamite. He planned to blow open a safe. Once inside he saw that there was a safe which had a new lock and a safe which had an old lock.
>
> **Verb phrase context**: A burglar broke into a bank carrying some dynamite. He planned to blow open a safe. Once inside he saw that there was a safe which had a new lock and a strongbox which had an old lock.
>
> **Noun phrase target**: The burglar blew open the safe with the new lock and made off with the loot.
>
> **Verb phrase target**: The burglar blew open the safe with the dynamite and made off with the loot.

The experimenters generated stimulus materials that could bias a reader toward either a noun phrase interpretation or a verb phrase interpretation. Then the target sentence could contain a noun phrase or a verb phrase (as in the "spy with binoculars" study).

Normally we would expect strong garden path effects for the target sentence when the "old lock" version was presented, and indeed a prior experiment with a neutral context showed that such effects were obtained. In this experiment, however, the effects were moderated by the biasing context: people read the critical phrase more quickly when the context had biased them to expect it.

Although this work indicated that semantics did influence parsing, other researchers demonstrate different results. Some studies (such as Boland & Boehm-Jernigan, 1998; MacDonald, Pearlmutter, & Seidenberg, 1994; Trueswell, Tanenhaus, & Garnsey, 1994) indicated that the parsing system is sensitive to frequency information. In other words, if a verb is most often used in one syntactic context, the parser assumes that context is being used until other evidence disconfirms that assumption. For example, *examined* may be used more often as a main verb than as a past participle.

So what, finally, can we say about parsing? We've discussed a number of candidates that might guide parsing, including syntactic factors (key words, minimal attachment, recency), frequency, and semantics (that is, meaning). Which of these possibilities are correct? As you might guess, recent models suggest that multiple sources of information are integrated (see Boland & Blodgett, 2001; Gibson & Pearlmutter, 1998; McRae, Spivey-Knowlton & Tanenhaus, 1998), although they vary a good deal in how they combine the information and in the time course for doing so.

Texts

A text is a group of connected sentences forming a paragraph or paragraphs. We started our discussion of sentences by noting that a sentence is much more than a group of words. Likewise, a text is more than a group of sentences. We will discuss two key aspects of text comprehension: making inferences about texts and seeking coherence within texts.

Much of what we understand to be true in a text is never explicitly stated but rather is inferred. Here's an example.

Billy walked slowly to the front of the room. The teacher waited for him.

How old is Billy? Is he a student? Why is he walking slowly? In a text that is just two sentences long, you probably infer that Billy is young and that he's walking slowly because he's reluctant to face the teacher, and in turn you've inferred that he's reluctant to face the teacher because he's done something wrong. You know these facts although they are never stated because you apply background knowledge to your understanding of the text.

People exert effort to make texts coherent. We do not passively record the meanings of the sentences given; we tie them together so that they make sense. Sometimes we struggle to integrate sentences so that they make sense together. Imagine your reaction if I presented this text.

Billy walked slowly to the front of the room. The teacher waited for him. The crowd roared as the Americans won the gold.

The final sentence seems out of place, as though it belongs in some other story. Our response to a sentence that doesn't make sense is to search long-term memory for information that might make the text sensible. Suppose that earlier in the story you had been told that Billy's father is on the Olympic hockey team and that Billy had been caught listening to the game on a contraband radio, despite his teacher's stern warning not to do so. If you search long-term memory and find that information, the final sentence becomes comprehensible.

When do we make inferences? When do we recruit background knowledge to help us make sense of a text? To address these questions we need first to consider how texts are represented. Most researchers (see Fletcher & Chrysler, 1990; Glenberg & Langston, 1992; Schmalhofer & Glavanov, 1986) agree that there are three levels of representation in text processing, as first suggested by Teun van Dijk and Walter Kintsch (1983): a surface code, a textbase, and a situation model. The **surface code** represents the exact wording and syntax of the sentences. The **textbase** represents the ideas of the text in a format called propositions, but it does not preserve the particular wording and syntax. If you make inferences as you read the text, those inferences are stored in the textbase as well. The **situation model** refers to still deeper knowledge, corresponding to an integration of the knowledge provided by the text and prior knowledge (Zwaan & Radvansky, 1998). Figure 12.6 shows the textbase and situation model representations corresponding to a text.

Textbase:

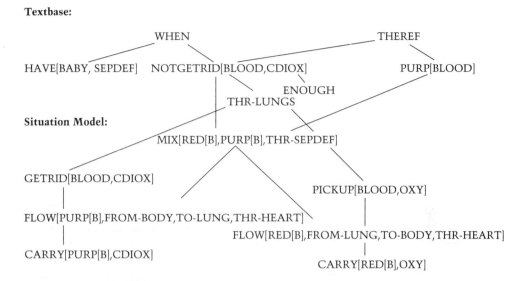

Figure 12.6. *Contraint satisfaction network.*

We have already discussed the components of the surface code—wording and syntax—but the components of the textbase and situation model take a different form. The basic unit of textbases and situation models is the **proposition**, which we have defined as the most basic unit of meaning that has a truth value. We discussed propositions in the context of visual imagery, when we compared visual images with verbal representations (propositions). Propositions have the syntax *relation(argument)*. A relational term can be a verb, an adjective, or a conjunction, and the arguments are nouns. For example, the proposition *red(car)* represents the idea that a particular car is red. The proposition *gave(boy, girl, ball)* represents the idea that the boy gave the ball to the girl.

How do we know that the surface code, textbase, and situation model are separate in the mind? A commonly used technique is to have participants read a text and then take a recognition test for different types of sentences. For example, participants might read this text (adapted from Reder, 1982, who used only a subset of the probe questions described here).

> The heir to a large hamburger chain was in trouble. He had married a lovely young woman who had seemed to love him. Now he worried that she had been after his money after all. He sensed that she was not attracted to him. Perhaps he consumed too much beer and french fries. No, he couldn't give up the fries. Not only were they delicious, he got them for free.

Later, participants could be asked whether the following sentences were part of the story.

He had married a lovely young woman who had seemed to love him. (verbatim sentence)

The heir had the feeling that the woman did not find him good-looking. (paraphrase)

The heir got his french fries from his family's hamburger chain. (plausible inference based on the situation model)

The heir was careful to eat only healthful food. (false statement)

Participants are to say whether the sentences presented appeared in the story. We can estimate the contributions of different representations to performance on the recognition test. For example, to the extent that people are accurate in rejecting paraphrases and accepting verbatim sentences, they must be using a memory of the surface code. If they accept paraphrases but reject inferences, that is a measure of their reliance on the textbase representation, and if they accept inferences but reject false statements, that indicates a reliance on the situation model.

Most studies show that participants' reliance on different representations changes over time. If they are tested soon after reading the text, participants rely on the surface code (that is, they remember what they have read almost word for word). However, if there is a delay, participants come to rely more on the textbase (they remember the meaning of what they read, but they are not very accurate in remembering the exact words used to convey the information), as shown in Figure 12.7.

Factors besides time contribute to the detail of the surface code, the textbase, and the situational model. Rolf Zwaan (1994) examined whether the genre of the writing influences how people read text. He provided a short text for participants to read and told them that it was either a passage from a novel or a clipping from a newspaper story.

Participants' memory for the text varied depending on the genre they thought the text was from. If they thought they were reading a newspaper story, participants didn't remember specific words and phrases used in the story (the surface code) and instead remembered the broadest outline of the story (situation model). The reverse was true if they believed they were reading part of a novel. This finding is sensible: when you read a novel you expect the style to be important, whereas for a newspaper story you're concerned mostly with the facts. Other work indicates that people remember different aspects of a text depending on the perspective they are encouraged to take (Baillet & Keenan, 1986; Lee-Sammons & Whitney, 1991) or their goals in reading it (Aaronson & Ferres, 1986; Noordman, Vonk, & Kempff, 1992).

These differences in memory that appear with changes in time or perspective of the reader are taken as evidence that the surface code, textbase, and situation model are separate. How and when are the textbase and situation model constructed? According to the most influential models of reading (Just

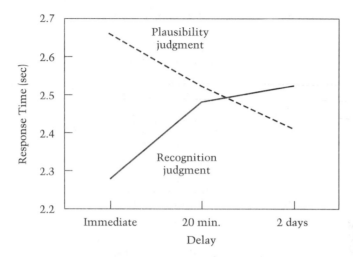

Figure 12.7. *Data from Reder (1982). The data show response times to make recognition judgments (this sentence appeared in the story) and plausibility judgments (this sentence describes something plausible, given the story). Shown here are data from plausible sentences. Note that plausible judgments initially are slower, but the pattern reverses as time passes, indicating that participants initially rely on the surface code to make judgments but later rely on the textbase.*

& Carpenter, 1992; Kintsch, 1988), the textbase and situation models are built in parallel as people comprehend the surface code. If that's true, that means that people make inferences as they read. Again, remember that these inferences are automatically generated, not consciously considered and weighed.

There has been debate about the type of inferences people draw. Most researchers agree that inferences are drawn when information is missing from the text. If the text says, "Jennifer drove the nail," no information is provided about what she used to drive it. Our background knowledge about nails would lead to the inference that Jennifer used a hammer. In Kintsch's (1988) model, the inference is made this way. A word or set of words from the text would enter working memory and then activate related concepts in long-term memory. This activation would cycle between working memory and long-term memory several times in such a way that concepts with strong activations become more active and those with weak activations become less active. After this process, concepts from long-term memory that are strongly related to concepts in the text become strongly activated; that is, reading about someone driving a nail results in the concept *hammer* becoming active because it is so closely related to *nail* and *drive*.

The number of inferences that could be generated from even a brief, simple text is almost unlimited. One can make inferences about the characters' motivations, why they did what they did, things they might have done that were not in the text, things they didn't do, and so on. The cognitive resources to generate inferences are assumed to be limited, so a limited number of inferences must be drawn. What sorts of inferences might be drawn?

Most theorists agree that inferences are drawn to enhance the coherence of a text. Thus an inference becomes necessary when some incoherence is noted. The disagreement between researchers arises over what sorts of representations readers (or listeners) seek to make coherent. For example, suppose you saw this sentence: "The collie rushed at Jimmy, who cowered because he was afraid of the big dog." In this case, there is little doubt that a reader would use the knowledge in memory that a collie is a type of dog and that in this sentence *collie* and *dog* refer to the same entity. Gail McKoon and Roger Ratcliff (1992) hypothesized that the only inferences people make are ones that are necessary to maintain coherence within a sentence or across two sentences. They tested this hypothesis with two short paragraphs. The first paragraph introduced a goal (e.g., killing the president) and a subordinate goal (using a rifle). The second paragraph took one of three forms. In the control condition, the goal and the subordinate goal were achieved. In the try-again condition the subordinate goal could not be met, so the character tried to meet the goal a second time. In the substitution condition the subordinate goal could not be met, but the character abandoned it, substituting a new subordinate goal.

Introduction paragraph:	The crowd's cheers alerted the onlookers to the president's arrival. The assassin wanted to kill the president. He reached for his high-powered rifle. He lifted the gun to his shoulder to peer through its scope.
Control condition:	The assassin hit the president with the first shot from his rifle. Then he started to run toward the west. The searing sun blinded his eyes.
Try-again condition:	The scope fell off as he lifted the rifle. He lay prone to draw a sight without the scope. The searing sun blinded his eyes.
Substitution condition:	The scope fell off as he lifted the rifle. So he reached for his hand grenades. The searing sun blinded his eyes.

Participants read the stories one sentence at a time. After the last sentence a word appeared on the screen, and they were to say whether that word had appeared in the story. One test word was *kill*, which was relevant to the goal set up in the first paragraph. If people make inferences as they read to make a text globally coherent, then they would need to access the general goal of killing the president in the substitution condition; the participant should be puzzled as to why the character is reaching for the hand grenades, but the participant will recall from long-term memory that the goal is to kill the president, and the hand grenade sentence will make sense. Because they have just accessed this memory, it should be easy for these participants to verify that *kill* was in the text. In the control condition, the character has a new goal (escape), so participants should be slower to verify that *kill* was in the sentence.

McKoon and Ratcliff made a different prediction, however. They maintained that readers do not make inferences to maintain global coherence. Rather, they argued that readers make inferences only to make sentences coherent, so they predicted that there should be no difference between the three conditions in time to verify that *kill* was in the text. The data showed that McKoon and Ratcliff's prediction was verified.

The data included verification times for the word *rifle*. These times were faster overall, which is not surprising given that participants read this word more recently. Verification times were fastest in the try-again condition, the only condition in which the subordinate goal of using the rifle was maintained until the end of the story. This result shows that the word verification method McKoon and Ratcliff used is sensitive enough to detect participants' inferences. The important conclusion is from the verification times for *kill*, which indicate that participants may not seek global coherence as they read.

McKoon and Ratcliff claimed that the methods other researchers have used to test whether readers draw inferences are inaccurate because these methods really test whether people draw inferences during the test, not while the person is reading. For example, I might have you read a short story about someone visiting a restaurant and then later ask you, "Did you read that the person ate his or her food?" If you say, "Yes, the story said that," how can I know whether you inferred that fact when you read the story or when I ask the question the next day?

Other researchers posit that there are higher-level memory representations that cause people to draw inferences across much broader segments of text than a sentence or two; these researchers argue that as we read, we build a textbase or situation model, and if these representations are self-contradictory or are missing pieces that are easily filled by knowledge in long-term memory, then inferences will be made (Albrecht & O'Brien, 1993; Graesser, Singer, & Trabasso, 1994; Hess, Foss, & Carroll, 1995; Singer, Graesser, & Trabasso, 1994).

In one experiment, Edward O'Brien and Jason Albrecht (1992) measured reading times as participants read a paragraph. A sentence in the paragraph was made to be either consistent or inconsistent with an earlier sentence. Here is an example of the sort of paragraph they used.

> As Kim stood (inside/outside) the health club she felt a little sluggish. [Workouts always made her feel better. Today she was particularly looking forward to the exercise class because it had been a long, hard day at work. Her boss had just been fired and she had to fill in for him on top of her own work.] *She decided to go outside and stretch her legs a little.* She was getting anxious to start and was glad when she saw the instructor go in the door of the club. Kim really liked her instructor. Her enthusiasm and energy were contagious.

In the first sentence, half of the participants read that Kim was inside the club and half that she was outside. The critical sentence is in italics, and you can see that this sentence describes her as going outside. This sentence makes sense if Kim was described in the first sentence as being inside, but not if she was described as being outside. The experimenters also manipulated how far apart this potentially conflicting information was in the story. In the sample paragraph there are three sentences between the two conflicting sentences. Those three intervening sentences were omitted for some participants. Thus there were two independent variables in this experiment: whether the initial information conflicted with the crucial sentence and whether this initial information appeared one sentence before the crucial sentence or three sentences before the crucial sentence. Figure 12.8 shows reading times for the crucial sentence. Participants are always faster in reading the crucial sentence when it is consistent with the information presented earlier. It is presumed that reading times are longer because participants are struggling to make sense of the conflicting information. It is also important that the advantage for the consistent version is maintained even when three sentences separate the initial and the test sentence.

McKoon and Ratcliff's theory would also predict slower reading times in the close condition because the information in the test sentence conflicts with information presented just one sentence earlier. Their theory would not predict the observed difference in the distant condition, however. O'Brien and Albrecht

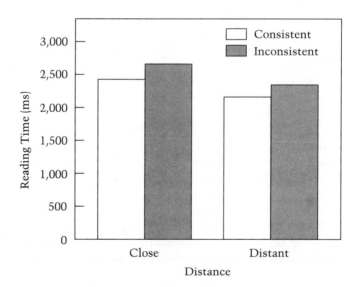

Figure 12.8.   *Results from O'Brien and Albrecht's (1992) study indicating that participants compare information in new sentences with information from prior sentences. Participants were slower to read a sentence that was inconsistent with an old sentence, even if the conflicting sentence was distant from the one they were reading.*

argued that participants maintain a situation model as they read, and ne[w] [infor]mation is integrated in the model as it comes in. If the reader has been tol[d] Kim is outside and later is told that she *goes* outside (implying that she is no[t] [al]ready outside), the inconsistency is detected and is reflected in a slower readin[g] time as the participant tries to make sense of the conflicting information.

We've discussed two studies that examine when readers make inferences, and these studies conflict. Indeed, the most recent research indicates that the answer to the question "What sort of inferences are made?" is not going to be a simple one. It is possible that the longevity of inferences may vary: some inferences are made and discarded, whereas others are maintained (see Millis & Just, 1994). It is also likely that making inferences depends on working memory, so there may be substantial individual differences in the number of inferences made, depending on the reader's working memory capacity (Whitney, Ritchie, & Clark, 1991; for a review of the literature on inferences, see Graesser, Millis, and Zwaan, 1997).

Stand-on-One-Foot Questions

8. What factors help in the perception of phonemes?
9. What are the two routes to the lexicon in reading, according to dual route theories?
10. What are garden path sentences, and why are they important?
11. What causes people to draw inferences from texts?

Questions That Require Two Feet

12. Given what you know about lexical access, describe what happens when someone tells a pun.
13. What do you think would happen to a text if the writer ensured that you did not have to draw any inferences? Would the text seem especially well written and clear?
14. Suppose you and I are planning a hike. I look out the window, where I see it is pouring rain. I turn to you and say "This is ideal weather." What does this example tell you about sentence processing?

HOW ARE LANGUAGE AND THOUGHT RELATED?

➤ **Preview** To examine the relationship of language and thought, we focus on two particular issues. First, the question of whether nonhuman primates can acquire

(Continued)

st because their ability (or inability) provides important in-
cognitive abilities of apes. As we'll see, the linguistic abili-
ed; using linguistic symbols and acquiring grammar is not
they excel. Second, we examine the relationship between
. Languages differ in the concepts they make explicit; some
nct words and phrases to express a particular concept,
e same concept in another language might be considerably
more clumsy. Does that mean that thought about the concept is more efficient in
the first language? To date, the answer is that the advantage is small, but it does
seem to exist.

To this point we have focused on language as an independent system. We have
treated language as though it were disconnected from the other topics in this
book: memory, problem solving, reasoning, and so on. In one way—a trivial
way—we know that language influences thought because different words lead
to different thoughts. We can also safely draw the trivial conclusion that different thoughts lead us to utter different words. The deeper question is
whether there is a more intimate relationship between language and thought.
For example, are certain types of thought dependent on having the words to
express them? Can we use linguistic abilities as a measure of people's abilities
to think in particular ways?

Ape Language

As you no doubt know, several human researchers have undertaken to teach
language to nonhuman primates (chimps, gorillas, bonobos). Why did they do
so? The obvious answer—that it would be cool to talk to apes—is accurate, but
it is not sufficient motivation. Most researchers are interested in these language projects because they tell us something interesting about the cognitive
capabilities of nonhuman primates. In this chapter we've discussed some of
the complexities of the grammatical structure of language. Are nonhuman primates able to master these complexities?

Notice that this goal is very different from the goal of being able to communicate with a chimp. If you simply want to be able to know what a chimp
wants to do (perhaps you want it to be able to make requests) and you want to
be able to give it commands, that is a different undertaking from teaching the
chimp language. To keep the distinction clear in our minds, we can return to
the definition of language that we discussed earlier in the chapter, and we can
contrast that with simple communication. We said that language is communicative, arbitrary, structured, generative, and dynamic (again, recognizing
that the exact criteria are not universally recognized). Most animal communication systems have only the first of these properties. In the wild, chimps use
a series of grunts and howls to communicate specific meanings—danger from

a snake, for example—but these communicative signals are not arbitrary. They are fixed in their meaning and seem to be part of the animal's genetic inheritance. The same is true of the communication systems of honeybees (which communicate about food sources), birds (whose song often signals ownership of territory), and other nonhuman animals.

Some researchers of ape language have commented that as some humans discover greater and greater linguistic abilities in primates, other humans scurry off to redefine language, effectively raising the bar to ensure that we are the only species that can *really* use language (see the exchange between Kako, 1999, and Shanker, Savage-Rumbaugh, & Taylor, 1999). Having read this far in the chapter, you can appreciate that the insistence on the use of grammar is not an arbitrary requirement but is essential to a definition of language.

So just how well can nonhuman primates learn a language? Not all that well. Early attempts to teach language to primates were doomed to fail because the researchers tried to teach chimps vocal speech. The chimp's vocal tract and articulators are unsuited to form the sounds properly. Asking chimps to produce vocal speech is like asking humans to flap their arms and fly; our arms aren't suited to make us airborne, and the chimp vocal tract is not suited to allow the clear pronunciation needed for vocal speech.

In the 1960s several projects were initiated to solve that problem. Beatrice and Allen Gardner (Gardner & Gardner, 1967a, 1967b, 1975; Gardner, Gardner, & Van Cantfort, 1989) raised a chimp, Washoe, in the manner of a human infant, with exposure to toys, play areas, and activities. More importantly, the Gardners spoke American Sign Language (ASL) to Washoe and used only ASL in her presence. Furthermore, the Gardners actively taught ASL to Washoe. They molded her hands into the correct shape for signs and rewarded her for signing correctly. This process of actively teaching the language to the chimp and actively teaching it how to articulate the words of the language was adopted by other researchers. Herb Terrace and his associates (Terrace, Petitto, Sanders, & Bever, 1979) also used ASL to train a chimp that they named Nim Chimpsky (a play on the name of linguist Noam Chomsky). Still another researcher who sought to use ASL is Francine Patterson (1978, 1981), who taught a gorilla, Koko. Koko may be the best-known nonhuman "speaker" because she seems to have been the most widely covered in popular press. There were even references to Koko in two different episodes of the TV show *Seinfeld*. (If that's not making it I don't know what is.)

David Premack (1971, 1976a, 1976b) took quite a different approach. He trained a chimp, Sarah, to communicate by placing metal-backed chips on a magnetic board. The chips symbolized nouns (*chocolate, dish, Sarah*), verbs (*is, give, insert*), concepts (*same, if–then*), and adjectives (*red, yellow*). The chips were arbitrary in their appearance; for example, the chip corresponding to the concept *chocolate* did not look like a piece of chocolate. Somewhat similar in spirit is the approach taken by Sue Savage-Rumbaugh and her colleagues (Savage-Rumbaugh, Romski, Sevcik, & Pate, 1983; Savage-Rumbaugh, Rumbaugh, & Boysen, 1978; Savage-Rumbaugh, Rumbaugh, Smith, & Lawson, 1980). They taught a chimp named Lana and later a bonobo named Kanzi (Savage-Rumbaugh, Shanker, &

Taylor, 1998) a language they called Yerkish, named for the Yerkes primate center where they worked and Lana lived. Lana had 24-hour access to a computer keyboard on which were printed arbitrary symbols, each symbol standing for a concept. Lana could punch the keys to form "sentences." The symbols on the keys she pressed were echoed on a screen, and Yerkish communication from a trainer could appear on the screen. An advantage of having the utterance echoed on a screen was that it reduced the working memory requirements for the speaker; the length of an utterance would not be artificially limited simply because the speaker could not keep a long utterance in mind.

These primates had an opportunity to learn at least two aspects of language that, if they learned them, would represent a remarkable achievement. The first thing they might learn is the symbolic nature of words. We would like to establish what sort of knowledge they have. Can they use the symbol for chocolate in many different contexts, indicating that perhaps they know the abstract relationship between the word and the referent, or do they simply know that they are often given chocolate when they push a key with a particular symbol? The latter may not be very different from what a pigeon can learn. This question concerns the property of language we have called arbitrariness, the notion that a word is a symbol.

A second question we can ask about primate language is whether they understand how to use syntax. As we've discussed, humans are very sensitive to syntax, even to simple aspects of word order. For example, *water bird* is a bird that lives on or near water, whereas *bird water* refers to a particular type of water that is for birds. Can primates appreciate the difference between the two?

The claims made for the learning of primates in these studies ranges from modest to modestly spectacular. The most spectacular of these claims have been made by Patterson about the gorilla Koko, including what is easily the largest vocabulary among the primate speakers, well-formed syntax, spontaneous signing (not simply signing in response to a request to sign), and, most amazingly, puns, jokes, and cunning lies. The problem is that Patterson has not published in scientific journals for a number of years, so her claims would have to be taken at her word. No scientist expects to be believed without a critical review of his or her work by knowledgeable peers. Unfortunately, these interesting claims about primate language cannot be verified.

Many of the other claims fall in a second and considerably less grand group. Washoe acquired 132 signs, Nim acquired 125, and estimates from other groups are in this range. There are some problems with these data, however. The researchers on the Washoe project may well have been too optimistic (or generous) in how they coded signs. Chimps have a limited repertoire of signs that they perform in the wild, without ever being taught. One is a reaching gesture with palm up, which indicates that they want something. Another is shaking the hand, which indicates hurrying. The lion's share of the two-word combinations recorded on the Wahsoe project involved the words *hurry, please, come,* and *more.* Thus about half of the two-word combinations arguably involved signs that were not taught to Washoe. Jane Goodall, upon visiting the Nim Chimpsky project, remarked that she recognized all of Nim's "signs" as gestures that chimps perform in the wild (Pinker, 1994). These data bear on our assessment of whether the ape's language has the characteristic of arbitrariness. This appears to be less of a problem in studies using truly arbitrary symbols for communication instead of hand gestures.

How can we be sure that any of the primates are really using words as symbols? That's another important aspect of arbitrariness. In an operant conditioning paradigm a rat might press a lever for food and receive a reward, but we wouldn't call bar pressing the use of a symbol. When a primate is trained to execute a gesture and receives a food reward or praise for doing so, how does that differ from the bar-pressing rat?

In one experiment, Savage-Rumbaugh and her colleagues (1983) had two chimps engage in a "conversation." The first observed a trainer hide a food item in a container and then pressed the key on a keyboard with the symbol for the food item, thereby telling the second chimp (who never saw the food) what item was hidden. The second chimp was then to request that specific food item, and if it did so correctly, the two split the food.

This result sounds impressive as an example of two chimps communicating, but does it show that chimps are using words as symbols? Robert Epstein and his colleagues didn't think so (Epstein, Lanza, & Skinner, 1980). They got the same behavior from pigeons, named Jack and Jill, housed in adjoining cages with a transparent wall between them. Jack pecked a key labeled "What color?" That was a cue for Jill to look behind a curtain where there were three lights—red, green, and yellow—that were not visible to Jack. After ascertaining which light was illuminated, Jill pecked one of three keys—R, G, or Y—which Jack could see. Jack then pecked a key labeled "Thank you," whereupon Jill was given a food reward. Jack then pecked one of three keys indicating which light was illuminated and received his own reward. Thus we can conclude either that pigeons can use symbolic language or that we need more stringent tests of the symbolic use of language.

What would be a satisfactory demonstration of the use of words as symbols? The key property to look for is transfer to a novel testing situation. Once you know the referent for the word *chocolate* you can use that word in all sorts of situations: you can request chocolate, you can describe chocolate, you can comment on chocolate. If instead you've learned something in a rote manner, as an operantly conditioned response, the behavior is inflexible or is generalizable in predictable and limited ways. Primates in these language studies receive many practice trials and are drilled in the use of these signs and nevertheless speak about a fairly limited range of topics, most of which are requests for things. That said, it's true that at least in some cases they combine signs in ways that they have not been taught to do (Terrace et al., 1979), indicating at least some rudimentary use of words that they have learned as symbols.

There are a few celebrated examples of seeming spontaneity in ape language. One was an instance in which Washoe was near a swan on a pond and the trainer asked, "What that?" Washoe responded, "Water bird," thus appearing to coin a new term for an as yet unnamed object. However, Washoe might have simply been commenting that water was visible, and so was a bird.

What about grammar? Recall that a defining characteristic of language is that it is structured. Also recall that ignoring the importance of grammar in language is a serious mistake; grammar is at the very heart of what makes language language. The truth about primate grammar is that they just don't get it, except in the most rudimentary form. The best analysis of chimp grammar comes from Terrace and his colleagues' analysis of Nim's "sentences." They found that he did seem to understand some basic ideas about word order; for example, he put *more* before another word (*chocolate, tickle*) far more often than by chance. However, analysis of videotapes indicated that Nim's sentences often were full or partial imitations of something his trainer had just finished saying. Finally, we must consider the mind-cracking sameness of primate utterances. Here are the top 10 (in order) four-word "sentences" uttered by Nim.

> Eat drink, eat drink
> Eat Nim eat Nim
> Banana Nim banana Nim
> Drink Nim drink Nim
> Banana eat me Nim
> Banana me eat banana
> Banana me Nim me
> Grape eat Nim eat
> Nim eat Nim eat
> Play me Nim play

Nim's longest utterance, at 16 words, was "Give orange me give eat orange me eat orange give me eat orange give me you."

Bonobos likely have greater linguistic competence than chimps (Brakke & Savage-Rumbaugh, 1995, 1996), and at least one has achieved a vocabulary of several hundred words (Savage-Rumbaugh, 1986). Perhaps the most important difference is that bonobos seem to be more ready to spontaneously learn something about language. Sue Savage-Rumbaugh (1986) notes that her star pupil, Kanzi, initially learned by watching his mother be trained, not by receiving training himself. Further work has shown that bonobos can learn new words through observation (Lyn & Savage-Rumbaugh, 2000). That's important because it undercuts that argument that primates don't learn much about language but really learn what to do to be rewarded. Nevertheless, the learning is rather slow, taking between 6 and 86 exposures to comprehend a word. The average first-grader knows between 8,000 and 14,000 words (Carey, 1978).

The final word on nonhuman primate language is this: it's not close to the language humans use. We began this section by noting that the question of whether nonhuman primates can use language would be interesting because it would tell us something about their mental capabilities. It seems likely that there is some use of words as symbols in the speech of primates and probably some nonrandom ordering of the symbols, showing some primitive understanding of grammar. But the main question posed has been answered: apes cannot learn language or much of anything like language.

Ironically, the opposite conclusion seems to have taken hold in the public imagination. People seem to be under the impression that some apes have been taught to speak to us in a Dr. Doolittle scenario. This "fact" is most often trotted out to humble us, the human species, for being so arrogant as to think that we are special, when in fact other animals have the capability of language, thus proving that we are not that different. Some of the researchers on these projects have reached conclusions in this vein.

As Steve Pinker (1994) eloquently pointed out, the very comparison shows remarkable human arrogance. Why pick language as the metric by which we evaluate whether we are the same as other species? That's a contest humans can't lose, and indeed have not lost, whatever the popular press accounts may say. Why not compare chimps with humans in terms of the ability to climb trees? Why not compare our memories with those of seed-caching birds such as corvids, which can remember thousands of locations in which they've hidden seeds? Why not compare our perceptual abilities with that of honeybees, which can perceive ultraviolet light? The point is that humans are unique, but so are all other species. Each species has abilities and failings. The claim that we should compare our linguistic abilities with those of apes to evaluate their worth is scientifically empty. (For a readable and thought-provoking article on these points, see Povinelli & Bering, 2002.)

Language and Thought

There is little doubt that how and what we think affects what we say and that what we say affects how we think. But is there a deeper relationship between language and thought? It is not the case that each language has the same set of words representing a given number of concepts and that languages differ only in the sound of these words. Instead, languages differ in the concepts for which words exist, and in some languages particular aspects of a concept are highlighted by grammar. Do such differences mean that the speakers of these different languages actually think differently?

The idea that language molds thoughts and molds our perception of reality was advanced by linguist Edward Sapir (1956).

> We see and hear and otherwise experience very largely as we do because the language habits of our community predispose certain choices of interpretation.

This perspective was carried on by one of Sapir's students, a businessman and amateur linguist, Benjamin Whorf (1956). Their position became known as the **Sapir–Whorf hypothesis** or sometimes simply the **Whorfian hypothesis**. The strongest version of the Whorfian hypothesis is that thought is so intimately tied to language that it may be impossible to express the thoughts generated in one language in another language. This strong position has few adherents. It is generally accepted that all languages are flexible enough and powerful enough to express the ideas of other languages. The difference may be one of convenience. For example, in the Kiriwina language of New Guinea, the word *mokita* means "truth that everyone knows but no one speaks about." Americans surely are familiar with this concept and can express it, but it is simpler to express in Kiriwina.

The weak version of the Whorfian hypothesis has received more careful investigation. It states that every language favors some thought processes over others; it's not that your language makes some thoughts impossible, but rather that the language you speak biases you to think in certain ways. This weak version has been tested carefully in a few domains. The Whorfian hypothesis was initially studied in color perception and memory and in counterfactual thinking. In both cases, the data indicated that there was little influence of language on cognition. It turns out, however, that we *can* identify influences of language on cognition; the early conclusions were premature.

EARLY DATA: LANGUAGE DOES NOT INFLUENCE THOUGHT.   One myth about the Whorfian hypothesis should be laid to rest: it is not true that Eskimo languages have a large number of ways to refer to the concept *snow*. Whorf mentions this possible example and claims that there are three words for snow in "Eskimo." The example has been picked up in popular culture and exaggerated to mythic status (Martin, 1986). English has a fair number of words for snow—*snow, slush, sleet, powder*—and may not have any fewer than Inuit languages (Pinker, 1994).

Much of the early systematic work on the Whorfian hypothesis was conducted on color naming. In one of the original studies, Roger Brown and Eric Lenneberg (1954) selected color naming because colors have properties that are objectively describable (wavelength), but different languages divide the color spectrum into different numbers of hues. In their experiment, Brown and Lenneberg showed one group of participants a set of colors. Some were agreed upon as readily namable and these colors were considered codable (that is, linguistically codable). Other participants were then asked to view colors (both codable and not) and were later given a recognition test. Memory was somewhat better for codable colors than noncodable ones, providing weak evidence for the Whorfian hypothesis; the way that participants named colors seemed to affect their memory for them.

[Later research on color memory painted a different picture, however. Eleanor Rosch (then E. R. Heider, 1972), whose categorization research we discussed in chapter 7, examined the color memory of people who speak different languages. Most notably, she went to New Guinea and tested speakers of Dani, a language that has but two color terms: *mola* for lighter colors such as white, yellow, and orange and *mili* for darker colors such as black, purple, and blue. Rosch administered a recognition memory task for colors. There were two key findings. First, the Whorfian hypothesis might lead us to expect that the Dani would easily confuse all *mola* colors, but that's not what happened. Although their scores were lower overall than English speakers, the Dani made the same sorts of mistakes English speakers did, and their performance was best on the same chips on which English speakers excelled (the "reddest" red, for example). The second finding came from a follow-up experiment by Rosch and Donald Oliver (Heider & Oliver, 1972). They administered a recognition test to both Dani and English speakers in which participants were to remember a color chip and then select it from two choices. The crucial comparison was whether the two choices crossed a color line. Sometimes the two chips were similar but one would be called green by most people and the other blue. Other times the two choices were equally similar (the same difference in wavelength) but both would be called blue. Participants performed equally well when the two choices were on the same side or different sides of the color line, and that was true for both Dani and English speakers. These influential results were widely cited as demonstrating that language has little, if any, influence on thought, although some researchers pointed out that there were some problems in the way the experiments were designed (Lucy & Shweder, 1979).

Especially compelling, however, have been a series of experiments showing that there *are* influences of language on color memory. Ian Davies and his colleagues (Roberson, Davies, & Davidoff, 2000) set out to reproduce as closely as possible the results reported by Heider. They tested English speakers and participants from Papua, New Guinea, who speak Berinmo, which has five basic color terms. They found that memory performance matched naming performance; in other words, the sorts of mistakes people made *did* match how they named colors. They also found (unlike Heider) that recognition was easier if the two choices crossed the color line compared to when they did not. Finally, they found that everyone's memory was best for focal colors (the "reddest" red) as Heider reported, but they noted that that was because everyone was biased to pick focal colors when they couldn't remember the color and were just guessing.

Davies and colleagues have examined color memory in a different set of languages: English, Russian, and Setswana, which is spoken in Botswana (Davies, Sowden, Jerrett, Jerrett, & Corbett, 1998). The researchers asked participants to sort color chips into groups, and they dictated to participants the number of categories they should create (between 2 and 12). They predicted that there would be greater agreement among Setswana speakers when they were sorting into a small number of groups, because Setswana has only 6 color names, and greater agreement among the English and Russian speakers when he dictated a large number of groups, because those languages have 11 or 12 color names, respectively. As Davies put it, "The most striking feature of the results was the marked similarity of the [color] groups chosen across the three language groups" (p. 433). However, there were small, reliable differences in expected direction predicted by the Whorfian hypothesis.

Thus the conclusion from the literature on color naming and memory is that there probably *is* an effect of language on thought in this domain. It might not be huge, but it seems to be real.

Another early attempt to test the Whorfian hypothesis concerned counterfactual reasoning in speakers of Mandarin Chinese (henceforth we'll simply call it Chinese). Counterfactual reasoning refers to considering what would happen if something were true that is not true. English speakers use the subjunctive tense: "If we had been on time, we could have made the plane." Chinese does not have a subjunctive tense. If the supposition is obviously false, a Chinese speaker constructs counterfactuals using a normal "if–then" sentence: "If I am a member of the Rolling Stones, I will retire before I embarrass myself." The listener understands that I am not a member of the Rolling Stones and am instead offering advice about what the Stones should do. If the listener cannot be expected to know that the supposition is false, the speaker must explicitly state that fact: "Mrs. Wong not know English. If Mrs. Wong know English, she then can read the *New York Times*" (Au, 1983, p. 157).

Alfred Bloom (1981) presented data indicating that Chinese speakers could not understand a simple story that entailed counterfactual reasoning. Terry Au (1983, 1984) showed in a series of studies that this conclusion was wrong. She attributed Bloom's results to poor translations of the Chinese. Au provided better translations of the stories and reported that her Chinese participants showed normal understanding of counterfactuals, just as English speakers did.

These two early attempts to test the Whorfian hypothesis were plagued by problems, but they are presented here to give a sense of why very little of this work was done until the 1990s. We can list three reasons. First, it looked like language didn't influence thought very much; the few attempts to find such influences had failed (although today we know that language probably *does* influence color memory to some extent). Second, these experiments are difficult and expensive to do; researchers have to find native speakers of two languages that differ in an interesting way, the materials must be translated properly, and so on. Third, researchers were really looking in the wrong place. Color perception is deeply seated in the physiology of the visual system, beginning with the cones in the retina (de Valois & de Valois, 1993). It appears to be a system that will not show much flexibility, whatever one's language is; language would more likely be molded to the inflexible physiology of vision, not the other way around. And it would be strange indeed to propose that all Chinese speakers cannot understand counterfactuals very well. For example, does that mean that Chinese people seldom feel regret? After all, regret requires that one consider a counterfactual ("If I had done X, things would have turned out better").

It is clearly not the case that some thoughts are impossible in other languages or even that some people are unlikely to think in certain ways simply because their language makes the expression of those thoughts a bit awkward. Earl Hunt and Franca Agnoli (1991) emphasized this point in their review of this topic, and they suggested that the right dependent measure is not whether a speaker of a language can have a thought but rather whether there is a processing cost to having a particular type of thought for a speaker of a particular language. That is the metric we usually use in language research, and indeed throughout cognitive psychology. For example, people certainly can process the sentence "The spy saw the cop with a revolver but the cop didn't see him." What's interesting is that there is a small cost of processing that sentence relative to similar sentences. Thus it's wrong to look for catastrophic failures across languages; we're not going to see them. What we might see is small biases in the desired way to process, or slight costs to processing in certain ways, that are associated with a particular language.

RECENT DATA: LANGUAGE INFLUENCES THOUGHT.   More recent work has used better measures to test the Whorfian hypothesis, more often testing whether language influences thought rather than whether language makes thought possible or likely. Much of this work examines the memory representation for objects and how it is used. The expectation is not that certain aspects of the memory representation will be *missing* because of language but that certain aspects of it might be more robust or more likely to be used.

John Lucy has examined the influence of language on memory representations in English and Yucatec Maya. English counting terms serve as a modifier for the noun (as in *one candle*). Yucatec Maya uses classifiers that describe the material of the object counted (for example, *one long thin wax*). We might speculate, therefore, that speakers of this language would be especially sensitive to the materials from which objects are made. In one experiment, Lucy presented participants with three objects (for example, a candle, a stick, and some wax) and asked them to say which two went together. Yucatec speakers tended to classify by material (candle with wax) whereas English speakers tended to classify by shape (candle with stick).

Chinese speakers also use classifiers with numbers, focusing more on the perceptual qualities of objects rather than material. Shi Zhang and Bernd Schmitt (1998) examined whether the use of these classifiers has any impact on the representation of these objects in the memories of Chinese speakers. The experimenters presented pairs of words to English speakers and Chinese speakers and asked them to rate the similarity of the words. They found that the Chinese speakers consistently rated words as more similar if they shared a classifier. (The classifier was not mentioned in the experiment, of course.) So this experiment indicates that Chinese speakers think that a snake is more similar to a river (for example) than English speakers do, and that is true presumably because these two words take the same classifier. A second experiment asked participants to recall words, and the Chinese speakers tended to remember words in clusters, each cluster corresponding to a classifier.

Other languages don't have classifiers but have extensive grammatical gender systems. English codes gender only in some nouns (for example, *girl, boy*) and some pronouns (*he, she*). Spanish marks nouns, pronouns, adjectives, and determiners. The Spanish word for *telescope* (*telescopio*) is masculine, and articles and adjectives follow the noun's gender; hence, to refer to *a telescope* we must use a masculine article (*un telescopio*). Other languages have different grammatical gender systems. German, for example, marks only pronouns and determiners, and it has three categories of gender (masculine, feminine, and neuter). A good deal of work has been devoted to examining whether people think of nouns as following their grammatical gender classification. Most of these studies report support for the Whorfian hypothesis in languages such as Arabic (Clarke, Losoff, McCracken, & Rood, 1984), Hebrew (Guiora, Beit-Halachmi, Fried, & Yoder, 1983), Italian (Ervin, 1962), Spanish (Sera, Reittinger, & del Castillo Pintado, 1991). For example, in one study (Sera, Elieff, Forbes, Burch, Rodriguez, & Dubois, 2002), participants were shown line drawings of objects. They were told that a movie would be made in which objects would come to life, and their job was to say whether they thought a particular object should have a male or female voice. French and Spanish speakers tended to assign voices that matched grammatical gender (although German speakers did not, a finding of some interest that would take us far afield on this subject).

There is reasonable support for a modest version of the Whorfian hypothesis. It is clear that any language spoken by a community will be flexible enough to express most any idea. Different languages do make such expression easier or more difficult. The Whorfian effects that we might expect, therefore, will be modest pluses or minuses in processing speed. Research in the last five or ten years has uncovered such costs and benefits. The next step should be some attempt to systematize these costs and benefits into a theory that integrates language and thought.

Stand-on-One-Foot Questions

15. What key features of language would you want to evaluate if you were investigating the use of language by apes?
16. In the final analysis, can we say that apes use language?
17. Is some version of the Whorfian hypothesis likely to be correct?

Question That Requires Two Feet

18. If the strong version of the Whorfian hypothesis were correct, what would that imply about people who speak more than one language?

KEY TERMS

acquired dyslexia	deep structure	garden path sentence
categorical perception	developmental dyslexia	grammar
competence	dual route models of	language
cross-modal priming	reading	lexical decision

lexicon
McGurk effect
motor theory of speech
   perception
performance
phoneme
phoneme restoration
   effect
phonological dyslexia

phrase structure
   grammars
priming
principle of minimal
   attachment
proposition
recursion
Sapir–Whorf hypothesis
   (Whorfian hypothesis)

situation model
speech stream
surface code
surface dyslexia
surface structure
text
textbase
word-chain grammars

Appendix

SIGNAL DETECTION THEORY

In some areas of cognitive psychology, we conduct experiments in which participants are asked to detect faint signals in spite of background noise. For example, participants might be asked to watch a computer monitor on which a faint light occasionally appears. Such tasks occur in some professions as well. Radar and sonar operators try to detect signals indicative of ships or planes; doctors listen for the sound of a heart murmur; radiologists search for abnormalities on X-ray images.

How can we evaluate whether someone is effective or ineffective at detecting such signals? Take the simple example of detecting a faint visual signal. On each trial of such an experiment, the participant must either say "Yes" or "No," meaning the signal was or was not present. (Sometimes the signal really wasn't there.) It's therefore easy to evaluate the participant's accuracy. Actual signals of possible outcomes on each trial are shown below. Obviously hits and correct rejections represent accurate decisions, and misses and false alarms represent inaccurate decisions.

There are really two factors that go into this decision. One is sensitivity—just how good the participant is at detecting signals—and the other is bias. Bias represents the criterion for saying that a signal is present. If the researcher says, "Whatever you do, don't miss any signals!" participants are likely to be very liberal in saying that they see a signal. If the researcher says, "Whatever you do, don't say that you see a signal when there is not really one there!" participants will be much more conservative. Note that being conservative or liberal in judging whether a signal is present has nothing to do with absolute sensitivity in seeing a signal.

Signal detection theory allows researchers to separate sensitivity and bias. The easiest way to understand how it works is to examine the graphic below.

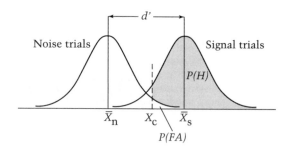

Suppose that the horizontal axis represents the intensity of the signal. You can think of it as the amount of activity in your visual cortex, if you like. The vertical axis is the frequency of a particular type of trial (high means very frequent, low means very infrequent). There are two distributions, labeled "Noise trials" and "Signal trials." "Noise" means background noise—the flicker of the computer monitor, for example. "Signal" really represents the signal and the background noise; thus for most signal trials there is more signal intensity than for most noise trials. The distributions overlap in this example because the perceived intensity of the signal or the background noise can vary from trial to trial, so sometimes it happens that a noise trial is perceived as more intense than a (signal + noise) trial. Although the distributions overlap, their averages (or means, labeled $\bar{X}$) are separate, in the center of the distributions. The distance between the averages is labeled d' ("d-prime"). This is a measure of the participants' sensitivity, their absolute ability to differentiate between the noise and the signal + noise. Here's another way to think about it. Suppose that the task were to detect the sound of someone shouting "Hey!" (signal) amid the background noise of a classroom during a final examination. In that case the intensity of the noise would be very low, and the intensity of the signal would be very high. The noise distribution would be far to the left, and the signal + noise distribution would be far to the right, so the distance between them (d') would be large. If the signal were the sound of someone talking and the background noise a loud rock concert, the two distributions would be very close together, and d' would be small.

Participants will also set a criterion for how intense a signal must be before they will decide that it must contain the signal. That criterion is shown in the figure as X_c. Any stimulus of greater intensity than that will be called signal and any stimulus of lesser intensity will be called no signal. When the two distributions are far apart (as in the examination example), participants could put the criterion anywhere between these distributions and never make a mistake; everything above the criterion is indeed a shout (signal) and everything below the criterion is indeed noise (no shout). When the distributions overlap, however, participants will make some incorrect decisions.

Participant's Decision	Signal Present	Signal Absent
Present	Hit	False alarm
Absent	Miss	Correct rejection

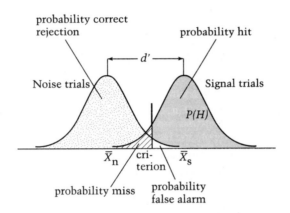

The correct and incorrect decisions can be viewed on this new graph and related to the table above. Consider first what happens when the perceived intensity of the signal is above the criterion. The participant is going to say the signal is present. That will usually be true: as shown by the shaded region of the signal distribution, in most of the trials where the participants say "Yes," the signal is present. Note, however, that one trial of the noise distribution is above the criterion, so there is some chance that a trial above the intensity criterion will actually be a noise trial. That's a false alarm, where the participant says there is a signal but only noise was present.

We can analyze the other decision the same way. When the participant says there is no signal (that is, there is only noise) most of the time that decision is correct; it's a correct rejection. But some signal trials have so little intensity that they fall below the criterion. When that happens, the trial is a miss. The participant calls it a "no signal" trial because the intensity was below criterion, but the signal was actually present.

Note that the proportion of hits, misses, false alarms, and correct rejections will change as the criterion moves to the right or left if the participant changes his or her estimates of how important it is to gain certain accurate judgments or to avoid certain inaccurate ones.

The graph shows you the two values the experimenter really wants to know: the d' or absolute accuracy the participant brings to the task, and the participant's criterion in making the judgments. Again, the participant's sensitivity and criterion shape the number of hits, misses, false alarms, and correct rejections. The technique in signal detection analysis is basically to work backwards from the way we've described it. The experimenter takes the participant's performance (hits, misses, false alarms, correct rejections) as shown in the table above and uses those values to infer the sensitivity and bias. We won't go into the mathematical procedures of how that's done. Thus researchers can take the participant's performance and tease apart the two factors that contribute to his or her decision: the sensitivity and the criterion brought to the detection task.

STATISTICAL SIGNIFICANCE

What if I tell you that I have a trick coin that comes up heads every time it's tossed. You inspect it, and it looks like a normal coin. You toss it and it comes up heads. Are you convinced that it's a trick coin? Probably not, or at least, you shouldn't be. After all, a regular coin comes up heads half the time. Maybe the coin came up heads by chance. What would you do to get a better test of the coin? How many heads in a row would you need to see before you were willing to accept that this was a trick coin? Three? Ten?

There are three steps to note about our thinking here. First, the expected outcome (heads) can occur by chance, and therefore we want to see an outcome that is unlikely to come up by chance—the coin comes up heads three times in a row, for example—before we are convinced. That is the core idea of statistical significance: we look for an outcome that is so improbable, we figure it could not have occurred by chance.

Second, we need to know how rare an event would have to be before we are willing to accept it as improbable. The following table shows the odds of tossing a fair coin a given number of times and having it come up heads each time.

Number of Tosses	Probability of All-Heads (approx.)
1	.5
2	.25
3	.125
4	.063
5	.031
6	.016
7	.008
8	.004
9	.002
10	.001

In psychology, the standard cutoff is a probability of .05. If you know the odds of something occurring by chance and you observe a deviation that would occur with a probability of .05, then you conclude that there are forces other than chance at work; in other words, this must be a trick coin. Thus in the coin example we'd want to see five heads in a row, to take us to a probability smaller than .05, before we'd be convinced that the coin is unfair.

Third, we need to know the odds of the event occurring by chance. To evaluate whether the coin is unfair, we need to know what happens with a fair coin. In the case of the coin, that's easy because it should be heads half the time. For other questions, it's not quite as obvious. For example, suppose we develop a tonic that is supposed to make people feel more energetic. How could we evaluate whether it works? We could give the tonic to someone each day and see whether or not the person feels energetic. But giving it to just one person is rather like tossing the coin only one time; it's too easy for the one person to feel energetic by chance. We could give the tonic to 10 people and see how many of them feel energetic. But what are the odds of feeling energetic by chance, without the tonic? In the case of the coin, we know what should happen by chance. In the case of the tonic, we can't predict what happens by chance, so we need to measure the energy level of a second group of people who don't get the tonic. Then we can compare the self-rated energy levels of people who do and do not get the tonic and ask, "Are the energy ratings of the tonic drinkers higher than the ratings of the people who don't take the tonic?"

Suppose that we find that the tonic drinkers' energy ratings are indeed higher. Isn't it possible that they are a little higher just due to chance? Absolutely. In the case of the coin we demanded that it come up heads many times before we were willing to accept it as a trick coin: there needed to be an extreme difference between what we observed (runs of all-heads) and what would be expected by chance (half heads). The same principle applies to the tonic example. Not just any difference between the groups will do. The difference between the groups needs to be so extreme that it is very unlikely to have occurred by chance. It's easy to calculate the relevant odds for the coin. It's more complicated for the tonic example, but the principle is the same. Statistical significance refers to observing a difference between two groups that is so large that we conclude it is very unlikely to have occurred by chance.

CORRELATION

In psychology, we care deeply about variables. (*Variable* refers to any property that an object can take: hair color is a variable, age is a variable, drug dose, alertness, political affiliation, and so on.) Specifically, we frequently want to know if one variable affects another: for examples, does age affect alertness? We examine this by measuring a number of people for two variables, age and alertness. We can pose our question in terms of statistical significance: does age affect alertness or doesn't it? (Statistical significance is discussed in another section of this appendix.) Statistical significance is critical because it tells us *whether* one thing affects the other. If there is not a statistically significant effect of one variable on the other, then we can't say that age affects alertness.

But even if we know that one variable does affect another, we don't know *how much* of an effect it has. A correlation coefficient is a way of describing this relationship. A correlation coefficient varies between −1 and +1. A correlation of +1 is a perfect positive relationship, which means that increases in one variable are perfectly predictable from increases in the other. For example, suppose I weigh 10 people in pounds, then weigh them all again in kilograms. Now I have two variables—weight in pounds for each person and weight in kilograms for each person. These two variables will show a perfect positive correlation of +1. You virtually never see two variables that are perfectly correlated; it usually happens when you do something silly like correlate the same variable with itself (as we did by measuring weight in two different ways).

A correlation near 0 means that the two variables are not related. For example, we might guess that a person's shoe size is unrelated to his or her memory ability. A negative correlation (approaching −1) means that as the value of one variable gets bigger, the value of the other value gets smaller. For example, we might expect that ratings of job satisfaction and absenteeism are negatively correlated: the happier you are in your job, the fewer days that you are absent from your job.

For the purposes of this book, there are three things you should know about correlations.

1. **Relationship of correlation and statistical significance.** Statistical significance tells you whether two variables are related, and a correlation characterizes that relationship (for example, are increases in one variable associated with increases or decreases in the other variable?). Statistical significance is actually a function of the size of the correlation and the number of observations made. Thus, a correlation of −.42 might be statistically significant or it might not, depending on how many observations went into the calculation. For example, in a small group of people, you might observe only a few small-footed people who are not alert and a few hyperactive bigfoots, so you might think that shoe size is related to alertness.

2. **Size of the correlation.** A correlation near zero—say, −.03—could nevertheless be statistically significant. As a rule of thumb, researchers usually think of correlations of around ±.2 as moderate and ±.4 as sizable.

3. **Correlation and causation.** A correlation tells you that two variables are associated—as one gets bigger, the other gets smaller (or bigger)—but it tells you *nothing* about whether one variable is causing the change in the other. For example, suppose that you observed a positive correlation between attendance at religious services and family income. One person might say, "God takes care of His own. People who go to religious services prosper." But then someone else might say, "No, going to church doesn't cause wealth. Rather, people who are wealthy have more time, and they have greater opportunity to go to church." Thus the first variable may influence the second, or the second might influence the first.

It's also possible that a third variable could drive a correlation. Suppose there is a significant positive correlation between the number of ice cream cones sold in a city and the number of crimes committed. We could imagine public demonstrations demanding that ice cream not be sold anymore—clearly, more ice cream means more crime! Perhaps people get overexcited from the sugar rush. Or perhaps the cause moves in the other direction—people commit crimes, including robberies, so they will have more money, and they blow their ill-gotten gains on ice cream cones. Neither of these hypotheses make much sense, but you could explain the correlation by appealing to a third factor—heat. When the weather is hot, people buy more ice cream cones and also commit more crimes than they do when it's cool. Thus, the correlation between crime and ice cream is really caused by a third variable—heat—that we initially hadn't even considered. The final word is that knowing that two variables are associated means that we know they are associated *and nothing else.* We cannot make any statements about how changes in one variable causes changes in the other.

REPLICATION

To replicate an experiment means to do it again. The motivation for doing an experiment again is to see whether the results are similar the second time the experiment is performed. If so, researchers will say that the results have been replicated. Researchers are more convinced that the results of an experiment are valid if they have been replicated. There are two reasons that's true.

First, there is always some chance that an experimental result was a fluke. For example, suppose I test whether eating raw seafood improves fertility. I take 200 couples and have 100 of the couples eat raw oysters every day, and at the end of six months I compare how many oyster-eating couples and how many no-oyster couples have conceived. I find that more oyster-eaters have conceived. That result could just be a fluke—one group or the other had to be higher (except for the unlikely event of a tie), so how do we know that eating oysters really promotes fertility?

Evaluating the results for statistical significance is supposed to protect against that; the whole point of statistical significance is that it determines whether the difference between two experimental conditions is so great that it is unlikely to have occurred by chance. The logic is this: if eating oysters *didn't* promote fertility, what are the odds there would have been such a big difference between the oyster-eaters and the no-oyster group? The usual cutoff is 0.05, meaning that if the difference you observed in the experiment would only happen 5% of the time by chance, there was really no difference between the two groups. (If this isn't making sense, see the Appendix entry on statistical significance.)

What you have to remember is that *there is a 5% chance that when you get a statistically significant difference, it's a fluke.* That's what the 5% criterion means—you're saying there's just a 5% chance that this result is a fluke. So 95% of the time your result is right, but the other 5% of the time your result is wrong.

If you replicate a result, you are that much more confident that the result is not a fluke. Now the odds are $0.05 \times 0.05 = 0.0025$, or 0.25% that the results are a fluke. So if an experiment replicates, you are more confident that the results are reliable.

Replication brings a second advantage. Suppose that I conducted the oyster study. You might be more convinced of the result if someone else did the study over again. The fact is that research is hard to do well. Mistakes are easy to make. If I made a mistake that influenced the results of the experiment the first time I did it, if I replicate the experiment, won't I also replicate the result? That's another reason people are more confident about the results of an experiment when they see it replicated, especially by a different set of researchers.

Another type of replication is a conceptual replication. Here you don't set out to do an experiment exactly the same way; rather, I want to replicate the basic idea of the experiment. For example, the original hypothesis of the oyster experiment was that eating raw shellfish would help fertility. A conceptual replication might entail eating raw clams instead of oysters.

STUDYING FOR EXAMS

There are some obvious things that you should do to prepare for a test. You should find out what you can from the instructor: What material will be covered and what won't? What is the format (multiple choice, short answer, essay)? You should study the material as you go along during the semester. Don't leave it all for the last day or two before the final exam. You are surely familiar with this advice.

Here are some other pointers that may (or may not) help you get ready for exams.

1. **Recognize the structure of the material.** Class lectures, like text books, are organized hierarchically. (Hierarchical representations of the chapters in this textbook are available at www.prenhall.com/willingham.) Most instructors make between three and seven main points during a lecture. Obviously you should know these points, but they are so basic to the topic (for example, deep processing helps memory) that you're unlikely to be tested on them. The next levels down consist of material that supports the main points—usually experiments—and then one level down from that are the details of the experiments.

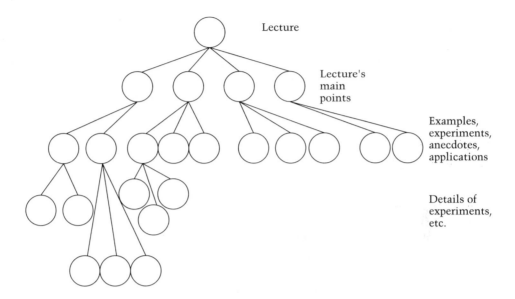

A common mistake in studying is to begin at the bottom level. Students simply start rereading their notes or copying them over. A much better strategy is to think in terms of the lecture organization. What were the main conclusions of the lecture? What supporting evidence was provided for each conclusion? A good study strategy would be to actually create your own outline for each class—that will force you to think about what the main conclusions were and what material supported each conclusion.

Instructors frequently test you on the relationships between levels: Why does a particular study support a conclusion? Why was a particular stimulus crucial to use in an experiment? To answer such questions, you need to consider the relationship between levels of the hierarchy; perhaps you will describe an experiment to support one of the conclusions.

2. **Don't just look over your notes.** This study strategy is the one I hear most often, and it is the worst. By looking over your notes you get a feeling of familiarity for the material—but you're not going to be tested for familiarity. During the test you will not have access to your notes, so you need to study in a way that is as similar as possible to the test conditions. As noted in chapters 5 and 6, retrieval works best when it is as similar as possible to encoding.

3. **Create an outline; then test yourself.** As described above, making an outline is helpful. Once you feel you understand the structure of the material, create flashcards and test yourself. This practice is useful because you will be testing yourself under conditions that are closer to the real test, that is, conditions in which you can't see the answer.

4. **Find a study partner.** After you've already done a fair amount of studying, you are ready to quiz a partner. The advantages of this strategy are that when you're quizzing your partner, you're forced to think of questions that might be on the test, and when your partner is quizzing you, you of course get more practice in answering questions. Even better, your partner may well have noticed the importance of some material that you missed.

Taking an Exam

What should you do when you take a test? I hear three common reasons students don't do as well as they expected on an exam. (I should note that I give only multiple-choice exams.)

1. **I could narrow it down to two choices, but then I had to guess.** A common reason this happens is that students add assumptions or extra information to a question. People are smart and inventive, and we are good at thinking up special conditions under which a wrong answer *could* be correct (if there were no gravity and time moved backwards, for example). If you find yourself thinking, "But if thus and so were the case, then D could be right," then D is not right. Answer only the question; don't add anything. Also, be sure that you are *answering* the question. Answer D may be a true statement, but it may not answer the question. Pick the choice that answers the question, and not simply the one that states something you know to be true.

2. **There was material on the test that I didn't expect.** Clearly in this case, you've studied the wrong material. You need to think more carefully about what is important in the lectures and book and what isn't.

3. **I thought I did well and I still don't understand why I got a low grade.** When this happens, it is often simply a matter of studying 20% harder than you did. What has likely happened is that you confidently picked distractors (wrong answers) that were close to the right answers. The distractors are, of course, written to be difficult. As much as it would be fun to take a test with questions like these:

    Biederman's geon theory is

    a. a feature theory using 3D features

    b. a chapter of *Paradise Lost*

    c. the poorest selling CD by the Beatles

    d. a new burger at McDonalds

    Such questions wouldn't provide much information to your professor about how much Cognitive Psychology you know. Hence, you can expect the distractors to be closely related to the correct answer, and distinguishing them will require detailed knowledge. If you are confidently selecting wrong answers, the reason is most often that you simply didn't know the material well enough.

Answers

CHAPTER 1

1. The first assumption is about what questions should be addressed first. The second type of assumption is something you believe, which may or may not be true, that colors your view of a cognitive process even before you start to study it.

2. For much of this century many psychologists (especially Americans) assumed that any theory of the mind could describe only the environment and people's behaviors. These psychologists were called behaviorists. They assumed that because observation is a critical part of the scientific method and researchers can't observe thought directly, thought cannot be part of a scientific theory. This assumption seems quite solid, but it overlooks the possibility that we can propose ways in which thoughts lead to behaviors. In other words, we can make thoughts indirectly observable if we specify what sort of thoughts lead to what sort of behaviors. That is the approach that cognitive psychologists have used.

3. People believed it probably wouldn't work because that would mean that human behavior was deterministic, which they could not believe was true.

4. They were interested primarily in the origin of knowledge: was knowledge largely innate, or was it acquired through experience? Other psychological questions were addressed during the Renaissance (for example, learning and perception) but usually in service of the larger question of the origin of knowledge.

5. Initially, psychologists sought to explain the contents of consciousness. Behaviorism changed the goal of the discipline to explaining behavior.

6. I would say people don't hold it much at all, given the belief in extrasensory perception (ESP), astrology, and the like. ESP and astrology are exactly the sort of explanations we're talking about; they are unobservable explanations for worldly events. You could gather evidence for or against these phenomena (and there is a great deal of evidence indicating that they are not real), but true believers always have an answer, such as "If you try to gather evidence about it, the ESP goes away" or "Astrology works, but not perfectly every time—it describes only general tendencies of what will happen." Thus, in the end you really *can't* gather evidence that would disprove the existence of these phenomena—whatever happens, there is an explanation—yet many people accept such explanations for things that happen.

7. I think they should, but not in the sense in which introspectionists use them. A great deal of work in cognitive and social psychology has shown that people's introspections on how and why they do things are not always accurate (Nisbett & Wilson, 1977), but there are times when people's descriptions of how they solve problems can be informative. Most importantly, introspections should be part of the data that are to be explained (Marr, 1982). If you are developing a theory of vision, for example, it should explain why a hill over there looks steep even if it isn't. Our introspective experience is part of mental life, and it is worthy of explanation.

8. New data indicated that behaviorism was not completely successful in accounting for animal behavior (for example, fixed action patterns, critical periods) and for some aspects of human behavior (language, apparent strategies in memory retrieval).

9. The heart of the information processing paradigm is the comparison of the brain to a computer. Both process information, in that both take in information, represent it symbolically, manipulate the symbols with different processes, refer to memory, and produce an output. Another important part of the information processing paradigm is that information processing occurs in discrete stages, as shown in the "What is your hometown?" example.

10. Partly by reference to other disciplines. They argued that neuroscience and artificial intelligence researchers used abstract representations in their work with no apparent loss of rigor. They were also successful in arguing that certain problems, such as accounting for human ability in language, seemed to require such representations for an adequate explanation.

11. The answer is very likely to be "Yes." On one hand, you could point to the fact that children seem to reach developmental milestones at around the same time: rolling over, crawling, first steps, first words, and so on. But the critical period idea suggests that if those crucial time windows are missed, it will be difficult to learn the skill later, and the fact that most children learn them at around the same age doesn't speak to that issue. There are only a few examples of children who, because of severe deprivation, seemed not to have the chance to learn to speak, for example, and these cases seem to support the idea of a critical period for language (Itard, 1962).

Other data based on larger numbers of children support the idea of a critical period for language. Children appear to be "programmed" to learn language, learning vocabulary at the unbelievable rate of an average of 9 words per day between the ages of 2 and 9. You may know someone who was raised bilingually. Children can pick up two languages almost as quickly as one (research confirms this observation). This is true only when they are quite young. Once a child is older (and taking a foreign language in school, for example) it is much harder to learn another language.

12. To be honest, I don't even have a very good guess as to the ratio of failures to successes, but I'm confident that the ratio is very low. I bring this question up simply to emphasize that your mind is constantly performing remarkable cognitive feats that you are not aware of. That's part of the point of the "What's your hometown?" analysis: to show that even cognitive processes that appear very simple actually are quite complex when you consider them in information processing terms. One of the ways cognitive psychologists think about this point is to consider what it would take to get a computer to perform the same function. Viewed in that light, it becomes clear that cognitive processes that seem easy to us—recognizing objects, reaching for things—are extremely complex.

13. Yes, absolutely. That is how cognitive psychologists often approach these problems. As I mentioned in that discussion, cognitive psychologists typically work on just one problem (such as memory) rather than trying to figure out how the entire cognitive system works because just one component of the system is dauntingly complicated. If you're trying to figure out how memory works, you could approach it the same way we did in the "What is your hometown?" example. You could figure that memory starts with some information coming in from the environment (someone says "I just saw a quincunx"), and the end product of the memory search is that you conclude that you don't know what a quincunx is. How do you determine that you don't know that? Do you check every single part of your memory, or do you check for a while, and then quit? Wait a minute—what does it mean to "check" memory? How might memories be organized such that you can "check" them? And off you go....

CHAPTER 2

1. Size and distance, shape and orientation, and light source, reflectance, and shadow.

2. You would think that the answer would relate to familiar size. You would assume that the car will be the normal size for a car, so if it looks small it's probably a regular-sized car but far away. To a point, that's true. As we'll see in the next section, however, familiar size helps only a little bit in disambiguating size and distance.

3. No. The earth is much bigger than the moon, so you'd have to move farther away from the earth than the surface of the moon for it to work, or you'd have to move your thumb closer to your eye.

4. Close your textbook and rotate it 45 degrees; it doesn't look like the title is skewed. Why? Because you still see the title relative to the frame of reference of the book cover; relative to the book cover, the title is not skewed—it's still in the same position. Relative to gravity, it is skewed, but vision dominates as a frame of reference in this example.

5. Surfaces are uniformly colored, light sources are above the visual scene, and surface lightness is interpreted depending on the ratios of lightness of areas that are next to one another in the same plane.

6. They show the importance of stereopsis in depth perception. People perceive depth in these displays even though there are no cues to depth except retinal disparity and even though the correspondence problem seems impossibly complex; the two images must be matched up in the left and right retinas so the disparity can be evaluated, but the matching seems very difficult in these stimuli. Nevertheless, the fact that people perceive depth may indicate that our visual systems are good at using stereopsis.

7. The most important difference concerns what we assume is in the environment and what we think is in the mind. The computational point of view assumes that the visual cues in the environment are basically lines; the environment is viewed as an impoverished source of visual information, so a fair amount of computation is necessary for this impoverished input to be made into something sensible. According to the ecological point of view, in contrast, the environment is a wonderfully rich source of information. The psychologist's first job is to discover what these sources of information are and which ones humans use in vision. Ecological psychologists argue that once we do a good job of describing the environment, the job of describing how the mind uses this information will be much easier.

8. Because the day was brilliantly clear, there was no atmospheric perspective. With that cue to distance gone, the city looked oddly like a model.

9. Get low. Strangers may seem scary to toddlers not only because they are strange but also because they appear so big. People (including toddlers) focus on faces, so get your face down to the eyeheight of the toddler.

10. One set of theories says the representation is object centered, meaning that the parts of the objects are located relative to one another. The other set of theories hold that they are viewer centered, meaning that there would be several representations for each object, one for each point of view.

11. There is evidence in both monkeys and humans that different parts of the brain support tasks demanding "what" knowledge and "how" knowledge, namely, the temporal lobe for "what" and the parietal lobe for "how." The second type of evidence comes from humans with intact brains. It is possible to fool the "what" system but not the "how" system with visual illusions.

12. Researchers in this area emphasize that our conscious perception matches not the absolute angle of the hill (obviously) but the difficulty we would have in climbing a particular hill. A difference of a few degrees makes a large difference in terms of the energy it would take to climb the hill. Further, once a hill gets much steeper than 45 degrees it is more or less impossible to climb without equipment, so all hills this steep or steeper look like cliffs.

13. Faces come to mind as an object that we almost always see right side up, and faces are notoriously difficult to recognize when they are inverted. Perhaps you've had this experience when a friend is looking through your photo album. If you're seated across from your friend and are viewing the photos upside down, it's very difficult to recognize the faces of people in the photos—even of yourself! We can't generalize from these particular stimuli to all visual stimuli, but it does seem clear that the representation of faces is biased toward successful recognition when the face is upright.

CHAPTER 3

1. It seems that people can, but it is actually difficult to be certain because it is always possible that people switch attention rapidly between tasks rather than truly dividing attention.

2. It assumes that tasks take a consistent amount of attention, no matter what else the cognitive system is doing. The available evidence is not consistent with that assumption.

3. A multiple resource theory claims that there are multiple pools of attention, perhaps divided by modality (one pool for vision, one for audition, and so on.) Although the idea has some appeal, it has proved difficult to be very specific about how these different pools are set up and when they are called upon.

4. It could be that music with words takes more attention to listen to, but I think another explanation is more likely. It may be that these people cannot help but process the words semantically. Semantic processing of spoken (or sung) words may be automatic. Processing the meaning of the sung words interferes with processing the words that are read. Thus, it's not that music with words takes more attention to listen to; rather, the words are processed whether you want them to be or not, and that interferes with reading.

5. A multiple resources model. The comedian apparently thought that there should be no interference between vision (looking for the house number) and audition (listening to the music). The fact is that we do find the music distracting. As described in the text, even though there is certainly less interference when different modalities are used, there is still some common demand, so people try to minimize the interference.

6. You might guess that because driving is automatic, it doesn't make much difference whether you're talking on a cellular phone; there should be attention to spare while driving. In fact, heavy use of cellular phones (more than 50 min per month) is a risk factor for accidents (Violanti & Marshall, 1996). But you would expect that the expertise of the driver would be a factor, and that seems to be true. Using cellular phones while driving is a greater risk for less experienced drivers, apparently because they are more likely to glance away from the road (usually to dial) for long periods of time and at risky moments when attention to the road is crucial (Wikman, Nieminen, & Summala, 1998). Still other data show that there is a cost to driving—you miss traffic signals and you're slower to react—even using a hands-free phone. Exactly why is not known, but the authors (Strayer & Johnson, 2001) suggest it's because you are imaging a context (the person on the other end of the line) other than the one in which you're driving.

7. The evidence indicates that it's early. A number of studies indicated that the filter might be late, but in those cases it appears that participants might not have been attending solely to the material they were told to attend to; they seem to have been occasionally "sampling" the other channel. Some proposed that the filter is "movable," but this probably means that there is a fixed filter (which is early) and that you can choose to allocate more or less attention to other sources. For example, you can listen closely to your friend at a party and try to ignore other conversations, or you can listen to your friend and simultaneously try to monitor the party around you to see whether anyone is talking about anything interesting.

8. It selects objects for further processing, not locations in space.

9. In a disjunctive search the target differs from the distractors on just one feature (such as color), and the search is easy; in fact, it occurs automatically, meaning that all the elements in the field are evaluated simultaneously, and the participant experiences pop-out. In a conjunctive search, the target is defined by the conjunction of two features (color and shape), and visual search is difficult; the search progresses serially, not in parallel.

10. At the start of the chapter we noted that it is crucial to be able to monitor the environment for things that are not currently attended to see whether attention should be refocused. The heroine apparently is not processing unattended sounds very carefully. Again, it seems as if the filter is early, so to detect the scuffling sound as threatening (and not caused by a tree limb scraping the house, for example), she might need to be focusing attention away from her shower periodically, but the situation she thinks she's in (showering at home) does not warrant frequent sampling of the environment for threatening sounds. You may have noticed the same phenomenon. If you are talking to a friend in your living room at noon, you may not notice the scratching noise of a squirrel on the roof because you have chosen not to allocate much attention to your surroundings. However, a very similar noise may enter awareness if you are talking to your friend while walking down a dark, deserted street at night in a strange New York City neighborhood, because you have allocated more attention to monitoring your surroundings.

11. Any situation in which two objects are intertwined (that is, they spatially overlap) and you successfully attend to just one indicates that you are directing attention to an object, not a location. Another example would be looking at your reflection in the glass of a picture frame and successfully ignoring the picture.

12. Inhibition of return will make it harder to select a recently selected object for attention; ironic processes of mental control will make you select something for attention that you don't want to select; and attending to certain types of stimuli for more than 30 minutes leads to decreased sensitivity in detecting important features of the stimuli (we discussed this as a problem of vigilance).

13. The psychological refractory period and the attentional blink both entail apparent failures of attention, but the tasks are so simple that it seems unlikely that they are due to inadequate attentional resources. Rather, they are likely structural effects, meaning that the decrement in performance is due to competition for cognitive structures other than attention.

14. As you know from reading this chapter, trying not to think about something is ineffective, *if* your cognitive resources are low (as they often are after a breakup). The best strategy would be to tell your friend to go ahead and think about his girlfriend all he wants, perhaps even to the point of forcing himself to think about her. It's hard to predict when thoughts of the girlfriend will subside, but they will likely do so faster if he uses this technique than if he tries not to think about her.

15. Car alarms have a terrible bias: they go off not only for robbers, but for people nudging the car as they walk by, cats jumping on the hood, and sometimes a bystander taking a deep breath nearby. They are like a radar operator who constantly says, "I see a ship!" Car alarms are completely ineffective because they rely on the idea that people will go running to investigate when they hear a car alarm. No one does because alarms go off all the time, just as you would ignore the radar operator who kept claiming to see ships all the time.

16. This is a vigilance task at its worst. These people must watch radar scopes for missiles that never come, yet if they miss the missile on the scope, the results are catastrophic. I would make the shifts of these workers as short as possible (because sensitivity in vigilance tasks declines rapidly).

CHAPTER 4

1. The partial report procedure allows a more accurate estimate than the whole report procedure of how much information people can apprehend with a brief exposure. In partial report, participants are exposed to stimuli and immediately thereafter are given a cue as to which stimuli to report. Because the cue is given after the stimuli have disappeared, the participant cannot know which stimuli he or she will be asked to report, so the percentage of stimuli successfully reported may be taken as a fair estimate of all the stimuli that are reportable. The whole report procedure underestimates the span of apprehension because participants forget some of the stimuli apprehended even as they are reporting others; the partial report procedure avoids that problem.

2. Visual or iconic memory has a large capacity (as many as 15 items or more, depending on conditions), it fades quickly (anywhere from 0.25 to 2 s, depending on conditions), and it can be masked, meaning you can knock the contents of sensory memory out by presenting new stimuli. Echoic memory has similar characteristics, although it is shorter lived (0.25 s).

3. Films typically are shot at 24 frames per second, meaning that each frame of the film would appear for about 42 ms. The shutter of a typical film projector is not open continuously: it is closed more than it is open, so when you watch a film you are looking at a black screen more than you are looking at the movie. Iconic memory carries you over these intervals and makes the visual experience continuous even though the visual stimulation is not.

You may come up with your own examples, but I can tell you about one time I actually used iconic memory. In my old apartment, I didn't have a phone by the bed. If it rang in the middle of the night I had to walk out to the kitchen to answer it. I didn't feel like turning on the light because it was too bright, but I didn't want to crash into furniture on the way to the phone either. I used iconic memory by flipping the lights on for just a moment. That gave me a tachistoscopic flash of the room, and I could read iconic memory to avoid the furniture on the way to the phone.

4. No, retinal afterimages are not the same as iconic memory. Their mechanism is different (they are caused by bleaching of the retinal cells), but your experience wouldn't tell you

that. Two differences that you might notice from your experience are that afterimages have the color opposite to the stimulus (in you stare at something green, the afterimage is red). We said that iconic memory can be cued by color, so it's clearly not an afterimage—if it were you'd pick the wrong color. The other way that afterimages differ is that they move when your eyes move (try it). As we discussed, iconic memory does not move with your eyes.

5. Primary memory was known before the 1950s. In the 1950s it was brought into prominence by Miller's observation that it represented an important bottleneck to processing and by the publication of an easy method to study it (the Brown–Peterson paradigm).

6. Material may be coded acoustically (in terms of sound), semantically (in terms of meaning), or visuospatially (in terms of visual appearance).

7. Forgetting occurs because of proactive interference, retroactive interference, and decay. Proactive interference is the forgetting of new material caused by having learned material earlier. Retroactive interference is the forgetting of previously learned material caused by learning new material. Decay is the spontaneous loss of previously learned material.

8. Not really. That is people's performance on the digit span task, it's true, but it is more accurate to say that the capacity of primary memory depends on how the participant codes the material. The code is important because an acoustic code has a capacity of about 2 s of material. The capacity in visuospatial code is about 4 objects. The capacity in the semantic code depends on the participant's ability to chunk the material.

9. Although this measure can prevent proactive interference from material during the experiment, you can't rule out the possibility of proactive interference from processing just before the experiment. You have no way of knowing what people were doing before they began the experiment, so if some percentage of the participants had just finished studying or thinking about materials similar to those used in the experiment right before they walked in, that could account for the apparent decay effects reported in the experiment. This objection probably is impossible to overcome, and Baddeley and Scott's experiment seems to do about as good a job as possible of ruling out possible proactive interference effects.

10. The best plan is to space your studying so that there are breaks between study sessions. If you can't do that, at least try to study dissimilar subjects back to back because interference is greater when the subjects are similar.

11. Yes, you would expect that to be true because digit span tasks are coded auditorily, and the auditory code depends on time. Thus if digits take longer, on average, to say in one language than another, the average digit span in that language should be smaller. There is evidence supporting that conjecture from bilingual speakers of English and Welsh (Ellis & Hennelly, 1980; Murray & Jones, 2002).

12. *Primary memory* is a generic term that is not tied to any particular theory. *Short-term memory* is a term from a particular theory, the modal model. (Short-term memory was proposed to code material exclusively acoustically, to lose material exclusively through decay, and so on.) *Working memory* is also a term from a particular theory, Baddeley's working memory model. In popular culture, *short-term memory* has taken on the generic meaning. Among psychologists, *short-term memory* usually has the more specific meaning tied to the modal model. However, psychologists do use the term *long-term memory* in the generic sense.

13. The phonological loop is composed of the phonological store, which is the site where 2 s of acoustic material can be stored. The articulatory control process allows us to write acoustic information to the phonological loop through subvocal rehearsal.

14. Working memory capacity correlates with reading comprehension scores and with scores on standardized intelligence tests. Normal aging leads to the decline of a range of cognitive capabilities; some of this decline appears to be rooted in a decline in working memory.

15. This irrelevant verbiage gains obligatory access to the phonological loop, which is where

I'm trying to keep the instructions she just gave me. A nod and a smile would be better.

16. Such patients exist, and their long-term memory is surprisingly good. Remember, the phonological loop is not the only pathway to long-term memory, as evidenced by the fact that people can still encode and rehearse things under articulatory suppression. Vocabulary in their native language doesn't seem impaired in these patients, probably because they have had a lot of practice, but they are impaired in learning vocabulary words in a new language, where the main thing to be learned is the sound of the unfamiliar word (Baddeley, Papagno, & Vallar, 1988).

CHAPTER 5

1. Emotion has an impact, but naturally we remember many things that are not emotional, so it seems likely that this factor affects memory in a limited number of circumstances. Depth of processing—the extent to which material is considered in terms of its meaning—has a profound impact on encoding.

2. Not by itself. But encoding something deeply more times (rather than fewer times) does help.

3. Depth of processing predicts that the extent to which a memory is encoded depends solely on the depth of processing during encoding. It turns out that the match between encoding and retrieval processes also is important. The other problem concerns the levels of processing theory. The theory is not detailed enough to differentiate two different tasks that are shallow.

4. Clearly, the best advice you can offer is to process the material deeply. That means that you have to think about what the material means, and the best way to do that is to generate questions with which to test yourself. Thinking of your own questions has the added advantage of getting you to imagine what your instructor is likely to ask. Regarding remembering names at a party, the advice is more or less the same. If you want to remember names, you have to actually think about the person's name. Most people who don't remember names (including me—I'm horrible) simply don't pay much attention when they first hear the name.

5. Before you give an explanation, verify that this is true. When someone tells me they remember little of their wedding day, I have to curb the desire to narrow my eyes and cock my head in a mask of police-inquisitor suspicion. "Oh really," I want to say. "You don't remember getting dressed that morning? You don't remember the kiss-the-bride part?" One of the first things you learn as a psychologist is that your own experiences and intuitions (and those of your wedding-amnesic friends) can be a terrific source of hypotheses about the human mind, but you shouldn't believe something based on subjective experience alone. Psychology books are full of things that many people believe, yet they are false. (For starters, most people believe in ESP.)

To my knowledge, no one has examined in a rigorous experimental situation whether high emotion can lead to a failure of memory. Let's suppose for a moment that it were true. It might be that emotionality has what is called an inverted-U effect on memory. That means that when emotional levels are low, a bit more emotion improves memory, but that when emotion levels are high, more emotion harms memory. This inverted-U relationship is found in certain types of physical performance tasks, so it might be observed for memory, but this is speculation.

6. I think advertisements that are well remembered, such as jingles, are processed more deeply. It may be that advertisements that are repeated often may become more memorable, despite the result of the Craik and Watkins (1973) experiment. You can think of each repetition of a commercial as another opportunity for you to encode the material deeply. Even if you ignore the ad the first 20 times you see it, perhaps on the next viewing you'll see that the advertised car really does have more leg room, by golly.

7. It reduces what you have to remember by allowing you to chunk, it guides your interpretation of details through the activation of schemas, and it makes unusual things stand out.

8. It ought to be. You can test this hypothesis easily enough. If you're a baseball fan (for example), watch a game (or part of a game) with a nonfan and later see who remembers more of the game.

9. It's easy to guess at what the schemas for these "types" of people would be. Librarians are typically women, they are spinsters, they have glasses and wear their hair in buns, and they are not a lot of fun. Engineers are male, they have little sense of humor and mediocre interpersonal skills, and they wear out-of-date clothes and pocket protectors. It is a sobering thought that our minds may be designed in such a way that we automatically categorize objects (including people) and abstract out schemas (stereotypes) to fit the categories. Naturally, the fact that we know these stereotypes does not mean that we have to act in accordance with them.

10. Here's one way you could do it. There are three main effects of prior knowledge on encoding: it reduces what you have to remember, it guides your interpretation of details, and it makes unusual things stand out. You could chunk those three main points into one image. Take a tour guide (complete with map, camera, and foreign phrase translation book) and reduce him in size. Then put him with a tour group of regular-sized people who are sitting so that he stands out. Silly, yes, but bizarre images are effective for memory.

11. It would make deep processing easier. Recall that deep processing involves connecting new information to information that you already know. If you have more prior knowledge, it will be easier to connect the new information to things you already know.

12. It was "Hey! What did that little monkey leave in my shoe?" This sentence does not fit the schema for a textbook well, and it is therefore likely to be well remembered.

CHAPTER 6

1. Free recall, cued recall, recognition, and savings in relearning are the four measures. They differ in sensitivity in that one measure of memory may indicate that some information has been forgotten, but another measure may show that some part of the memory remains in the storehouse.

2. The most important factor at retrieval is the cues that are provided. Cues that more closely match how the material was encoded are more likely to lead to successful retrieval. Thus if the measure provides more cues, one of the cues is likely to be helpful.

3. The cues are more important, as shown by the recognition failure of recallable words effect.

4. Prior knowledge tells us what usually happens in similar situations. We can use that in two ways. First, we may try harder to retrieve a bit of information because we know from prior knowledge that the event must have happened (as when we struggle to remember the type of cake served at a child's birthday party because we know from prior knowledge that cake must have been served). Second, we may mistake knowledge from prior experience for retrieval of a particular event. For example, we may mistakenly believe that cake was served at a particular child's birthday party because the serving of cake is so consistent with our prior experience of children's birthday parties.

5. He or she might come up with something, but it would be mostly a reconstruction. This date was not picked arbitrarily. In February 1987 Ronald Reagan challenged reporters at a press conference to remember what they were doing August 8, 1985. The reporters were silent. Reagan was trying to make the point that it is hard to remember the events of a specific day 19 months ago, and in a way he was right. Your memory is not designed to answer questions of this sort because it is not indexed according to date. It is indexed by events. If I went to the Metropolitan Museum of Art that day, I may (or may not) be able to recover that fact, but if I did, it would require lots of reasoning about where I was on August 8. However, if you simply ask, "Have you ever been to the Metropolitan Museum of Art?" my answer would be immediate and confident. Cues to the same event can be either very effective or very ineffective in leading you to remember the event.

6. This seems like a straightforward case of recognition failure of a recallable stimulus. Suppose you are walking down the street in your hometown. If someone stopped you and said, "Can you tell me what Peter, that guy in the room down the hall, looks like?" You'd say, "Sure," and you would be able to generate a mental image of Peter and describe him—in short, you recall his face. But when you're walking down the street, you fail to recognize his face. His face is in a context different from the one in which you learned it, just as the word *chair* alone is in a different context from the one in which you learned it if you saw it in the presence of the word *glue*.

7. Decay theory and interference theory. There is little support for decay theory, but it is difficult or impossible to disprove. There is more evidence supporting a role for interference in forgetting, especially for a process of inhibition.

8. This proposal is impossible to disprove, but it is viewed as quite unlikely by memory researchers. The standard observations in support of the idea (hypnosis, Penfield's stimulation studies) are more likely to be reconstructions than real memories.

9. Probably, but it seems to happen very infrequently. It's difficult to obtain convincing evidence of repression because it is always possible that the memory is inaccurate; that the person did not truly forget the event, although he or she may think it forgotten; or that the loss of the memory was caused by a normal forgetting process, not repression.

10. Interference is the big enemy in trying to learn new material. As we've seen, interference can be proactive or retroactive, so long bouts of studying pay diminishing returns. The more you try to learn in a single session, the more difficult learning becomes because of proactive interference, and the more likely you are to forget the material studied earlier because of retroactive interference. Therefore, short, frequent study sessions, broken up by other activities, are the most efficient.

11. The big difference between the ironic processes and the controlled retrieval case is the availability of attention. In the ironic processes experiments, participants get the intrusive "white bear" thoughts *when they are distracted by something else*, or when they are tired, intoxicated, or in some other way impaired. Anderson's participants were not in that state. Thus people get different effects of trying not to think about something depending on what else they are doing at the time.

CHAPTER 7

1. The classical view proposes that people categorize an object by comparing it to a list of necessary and sufficient properties that an object must have to fit a category. Hence, the description of an uncle is "brother of a parent." If a man is the brother of a parent, he is an uncle because he meets the necessary and sufficient conditions for that category. The data indicating that the classical view is either wrong or incomplete concerned participants' ratings of typicality of category exemplars (and other typicality effects). No exemplar of a category should seem more or less typical if we use a list of necessary and sufficient conditions to put items into that category. Either an object meets the category requirements or it doesn't, and an object is therefore either a member of the category or not. Because this seems not to be the case (at least for some categories some of the time) the classical view must be either incorrect or incomplete.

2. Typicality can be measured by asking participants to rate typicality. When asked to verify whether an exemplar is a member of a category (for example, a Dalmatian is a dog), participants are quicker to do so for typical category members. People tend to put more typical exemplars of a category first in a sentence. If a typical instance of a category has a property, people are more willing to guess that this property extends to other members of the category.

3. Prototype theory and exemplar theory both propose that new exemplars are categorized by evaluating the similarity of the exemplar to memory representations; if it is similar, it is

deemed to be a member of the category. The difference is that the exemplar theory proposes that each exemplar of a category is stored in memory, whereas the prototype theory proposes that a prototype is abstracted from many exemplars and then stored.

4. It appears that both types of categorization occur. Studies in the 1980s indicated that at times people categorize on the basis of rules, even if similarity dictates a different categorization. The job now is to determine when one type of categorization is used and when the other is used.

5. This theory seems to require an endlessly large memory store. How big would memory have to be for me to store every instance of a car I look at as a new car? And every dog, and every chair, and so on? This problem has not been overlooked by categorization researchers. One easy solution that some models have taken is to set a criterion for similarity for an individual exemplar to be stored. If the exemplar that you're looking at is similar to an exemplar already in memory, there is no need to store it again (although the fact that you've seen this exemplar again may be stored). This saves you from having 10 million exemplars of your mother stored in memory.

6. The newspapers use the word *grandma* for shock value. Why is it shocking? It's the tension between the classical, rule-driven meaning of *grandma* and the prototypical grandmother. Anyone who is female and the parent of a parent is a grandma. That's the classical categorization definition. The prototypical features of a grandma include much more, such as being sweet, baking cookies, knitting, and sitting quietly at home. Therefore, it's exciting when a grandma does something vigorous or outrageous.

7. First, your memory shows an excellent addressing system in that it can retrieve material very quickly, despite the great volume of material it potentially has available. Second, if the desired information is not in memory, the system makes available information that is either close in meaning or relevant so that you can make an inference that allows you to answer the question.

8. Advantages: It allows the retrieval of object properties, it allows content-addressable storage, typicality is a natural outgrowth of the model, the model creates defaults, and it's resistant to faulty input. Disadvantages: The model has not always been very specific, and it appears that activation spreads to an unreasonable degree.

9. The chief difference is one of representation. In a model with a local representation, a concept is represented by the activity of a single node. In a model with a distributed representation, a concept is represented by the pattern of activation across multiple nodes.

10. You may recall that early empiricist philosophers placed a great deal of emphasis on associations; the building of associations was at the heart of intelligent behavior. Spreading activation models have association at their heart. The links between nodes are nothing more than associations. These models represent an advance over earlier associationist ideas, however, because they are more precise in their predictions. Regarding consciousness, the associationist nature of the model leads to a natural prediction about consciousness. Because activity passes between the nodes in the model, something is always active in the network. We could say that whatever is active is what is in consciousness, so the ebb and flow of activity in the model represents the flow of consciousness.

11. This question is a bit unfair because my hunch is that you would probably say "distributed," and I think the real answer is that neither is very realistic in any important way. On the surface the distributed models look more like networks of neurons. Psychologists are fairly confident that a concept is not represented in a single neuron, and the local representation appears to claim just that, if you take a single node in the network to be a single neuron. But models using the distributed representation still only use hundreds or thousands of "neurons" to represent processes that surely require millions of neurons in the brain. Thus neither model is especially realistic in terms of biological plausibility; both are useful as models of cognitive processes. Other researchers

have worked hard to develop models that take neuroanatomy and neurophysiology quite seriously (e.g., Granger, Wiebe, Taketani, & Lynch, 1996; Levy, 1996), but we haven't discussed those models here.

12. There are a great many of these unbalanced association pairs, in which a strong association (*salt–pepper*) doesn't go the other way (*pepper–salt*). Some researchers have argued that this means each node should be connected by two links, one for each direction. The link from *salt* to *pepper* would be strong, but the link from *pepper* to *salt* would be weak.

13. Most cognitive psychologists agree that the critical feature is different processes and representations that operate on them. Most of the evidence thus far indicates that hypothetical memory systems are separate in terms of the brain structures that support them. Many researchers are willing to bet that anatomic separability goes hand in hand with cognitive differences, but it has been difficult to prove that these anatomically separate systems are also cognitively separate.

14. The proposal that memory systems are separate grew out of the attempt to explain why amnesic patients are able to learn some tasks normally. Initially researchers proposed that some memory process was damaged in amnesia but that certain tasks didn't require that process—those were the tasks that amnesic patients could learn. No one could figure out what that process might be, however, so researchers began to consider the idea that some types of memory were intact in amnesia because they were supported by a separate memory system.

15. At least five: systems supporting declarative memory, repetition priming, motor skill learning, classical conditioning, and emotional conditioning. In fact, some have suggested further fractionation of some of these systems (Keane, Gabrieli, Fennema, Growdon, & Corkin, 1991; Schacter, 1990).

16. It seems likely that these various memory systems all affect behavior simultaneously. For example, when you're learning a new sport, you often acquire information about how to play it through declarative memory, and motor skill processes also contribute. Suppose you

are an experienced tennis player and you want to start playing squash. A squash coach might tell you that your stroke looks too much like a tennis stroke: you keep your wrist locked instead of whipping it, as a squash player would. In this case, the motor skill system is producing behavior consistent with its experience (squash movement), and the declarative system is trying to influence the movement based on the coach's instruction (a declarative memory). Most researchers would agree that these systems may well influence one another directly and that more than one may influence behavior (as in the tennis and squash example), but how this works has not been examined in any detail.

17. The tennis and squash example is a good one. I think another example can be found whenever you are afraid of something but try to control your fear. Suppose I am afraid of snakes but I want to overcome my fear, so I hold a small python (also hoping to impress the friends I'm with). The emotional conditioning system might be telling me to drop the snake and run, whereas the declarative system would be calling up memories that show that this small snake poses no real threat and that I should hang on to it.

CHAPTER 8

1. The three approaches are efficiency theories, which propose setting a criterion of efficiency and selecting the most efficient movement; synergy theories, which propose that because most movements are constrained by synergies of the body, the degrees of freedom problem is not as bad as it first seems; and the mass spring theory, which proposes that because only the endpoints of movements are planned, not the trajectories, the degrees of freedom problem is not as difficult as it first appears.

2. Straight paths in Cartesian space, minimum distance of joint movement, minimum muscle torque, minimum muscle stiffness, minimum jerk of the moving effector.

3. Yes, it's possible. Synergies are biases in which joints or muscles work together. They are not strict rules dictating that joints or muscles must always work together in a particular way.

4. The heart of the degrees of freedom problem is that we can make any movement in more than one way. If there were only one way to move your body to reach a goal (a unique solution) then the degrees of freedom problem wouldn't exist. But the ability to make each movement in more than one way is not a liability. It is what gives you flexibility in making movements, so that you can make effective movements even if the effector is partly disabled (for example, if you have a cast on your wrist).

5. This is a problem, but it can be solved by proposing that in such situations you actually choose more than one endpoint. The first endpoint might be to the side of the obstacle, and the second endpoint would be the target object. In that way, you could reach around obstacles.

6. Movements in a sequence can occur so rapidly that there is not sufficient time for peripheral feedback to reach the brain and initiate the next movement. Studies of monkeys without proprioception indicated that they could execute movements normally.

7. It contains a full set of commands for a movement sequence. The commands can be executed without the need for peripheral feedback. The program can be applied to more than one set of muscles.

8. In a key-pressing task, the time between key presses is well predicted by the number of nodes that need to be traversed in a hierarchical representation of the sequence.

9. The purpose of feedback is to detect error and thereby enable the correction of error. No matter how many times you've practiced a movement, there can always be some error in its execution; perhaps the environment is slightly different than it has been in the past, or perhaps there is always some slight variability in the way the muscles execute commands. Whatever the source, it is sensible to monitor the movement outcome so that it can be corrected if necessary.

10. You should be able to duplicate a piece of the hierarchy and plug it into a new hierarchy with very little change; you simply need to change one control node so that it now includes the imported piece of hierarchy. You can't transfer motor acts so readily in the chaining theory, however, because you run into the problem of two similar chains not being differentiable.

Chain 1: $M_A \rightarrow P_A \rightarrow M_B \rightarrow P_B \rightarrow M_C \rightarrow P_C \rightarrow M_D \rightarrow P_D$

Chain 2: $M_A \rightarrow P_A \rightarrow M_B \rightarrow P_B \rightarrow M_E \rightarrow P_E \rightarrow M_F \rightarrow P_F$

If I want to take the start of Chain 1 and use that as the start of Chain 2, how do I ensure that the end of the chain ends up where I want it? In this example I already know Chain 1, so I want to make use of the link between M_A and M_B, which I already know. But how will I make sure that M_B will lead to M_E as I desire and not M_C as I already know? There is evidence that transferring pieces of hierarchies is possible (Gordon & Meyer, 1987).

11. On the one hand, vision is quite helpful to improving the accuracy of ongoing movements; movements are definitely more accurate with vision than without it. On the other hand, you don't need all that much visual information during an ongoing movement. The exact amount depends on the duration of each visual "snapshot" and on the amount of time these snapshots are separated, but movements can still be quite accurate even if participants have visual information during only 30% of the movement.

12. The two frames of reference are allocentric and egocentric. In allocentric space, objects are located in space relative to other objects. In egocentric space, objects are located relative to part of the body of the observer. It appears that movements are planned in egocentric spatial coordinates. Proprioception is important because you need to know where your body parts are in order to use egocentric space, since egocentric space means locating objects relative to part of the body.

13. Almost all of us have this sensation after sleeping on an arm—we wake up and find that we cannot feel that arm. Indeed, if you try to move it, the arm flops about much as Ian described his limbs working when his problem first developed.

14. As you move, egocentric representations move. If you have located an object relative to your shoulder, for example, and then move your shoulder, the location of the object changes; your shoulder provides the frame of reference, and your shoulder moved. That's why it might be a little confusing to have all objects located in egocentric space; as you moved, all of the locations would change. Instead, it's sensible to localize objects in allocentric space—for example, relative to the walls of the room, which are unlikely to move—so that the locations will be stable. Then you can set up temporary egocentric representations of objects as needed, when you want to act on them in some way.

15. Automaticity seems to occur for all skills (in the neurologically intact person).

16. These conditions are more effective training because the greater variability gives you a more accurate picture of the relationship between the movement parameters that you control and the outcome of the movement.

17. Learning refers to what we think of as underlying ability in a skill. Performance is affected not only by learning (underlying ability) but also by factors that can vary moment to moment, such as fatigue or motivation.

18. Because a program is, by definition, applicable to multiple effectors, it must represent where to move in space (it's not representing the muscle movements to get there). We might guess that some parameters would be the *distance* between the targets (you can make the movements large or small); the *force* of the movements (you can make the movements hard or soft); and the *speed* of the movements (you can move fast or slow). There has been a good deal of experimentation directed at the generalizability of skills, and it confirms what your intuition would tell you; many skills can be generalized along these dimensions.

19. This feature is important because it captures a common practice in the real world. Coaches give verbal instructions to athletes. The knowledge they provide is, of course, conscious knowledge for the athletes; the coach tells a diver that she's arching her back too much as she enters the water, for example. This conscious knowledge can change motor behavior, and what's more interesting, the expectation of both coach and athlete is that with enough practice, this conscious knowledge will become incorporated into the unconscious skill; the diver will not have to think about the position of her back anymore.

20. It would be some indication that attention and awareness are not separable. Normally we think that if we are attending to something, then we are aware of it. The results of these studies have been controversial, but the basic story is that some researchers report that if participants are distracted with a secondary task, learning of the unconscious skill is disrupted, whereas other researchers hold that the learning is not much affected by the secondary task. As of this writing, the issue awaits clarification.

Chapter 9

1. The imageless thought controversy concerned whether it was possible to have thoughts that were not accompanied by images. This debate occurred in the late 19th century and was important because psychologists using introspection examined their own mental images as they solved a problem as a way of learning about thought. If thought could proceed in the absence of images, it meant that at least some thoughts were not open to examination using this method.

2. Paivio pointed out that psychologists were willing to accept participants' verbal reports about purported verbal experience. In other words, when a participant said that he or she remembered some words, the experimenter believed it. Even though there was no assurance that the participant really remembered the words per se, the experimenter used these reports to infer what the cognitive representations were that allowed the participant to remember. Paivio argued that experimenters should be just as willing to accept verbal reports of visual imagery and to use these reports to

make inferences about cognitive processes that allow the participant to remember.

3. The two key results were that mentally rotating an object a greater distance took more time and that mentally rotating an object in depth was not harder than rotating it in the picture plane. This result was important because it was the first study that offered a clear way to study how images are transformed. It was also important because the data were very orderly, implying that a single (perhaps simple) process underlies mental rotation.

4. One problem is that it's hard for me to rate my imagery ability because I don't have anything to which I might compare it. I may think my images are distinct and bright, whereas in reality they may be pale compared to yours. Indeed, in one study Jeffrey Walczyk (1995) correlated participants' ratings of their images with the actual accuracy of the images and found correlations within an individual but not across individuals. That essentially means that I know how clear one of my images is relative to my typical image ("This is a good one" or "This one isn't one of my clearer images"), but I have no idea how my images stack up to yours.

5. This question has been studied frequently, and researchers have found that bizarreness helps memory (Campos, Perez, & Gonzalez, 1997; McDaniel et al., 1995; Sharpe & Markham, 1992; Worthen, 1997, but see Ironsmith & Lutz, 1996; Wollen, Weber, & Lowry, 1972). Why bizarreness helps is not really known. It is always possible that a bit more effort must be put into bizarre images or that they are more distinctive (but see McDaniel et al., 1995). The bizarreness effect was mentioned by the Greeks, but the precise reasons for the memory advantage of bizarre images is still unknown.

6. It depends on the event and on what you're doing, but when you listen to a sporting event, you are likely to engage mental imagery to understand what is happening in the game. For example, if you hear the announcer at a baseball game say, "It's a line drive straight up center field, but the runner at first is going anyway. The ball is caught, and the centerfielder is throwing it back to first to try to tag him up. It's going to be close, but now the runner at third is trying for home." If you're a fan, you're very likely to generate a visual image of this action. We've reviewed data showing that imagery interferes with visual tasks. Thus listening to a sporting event that encourages you to visualize the action may not be a great idea if you are performing a task that is visually demanding, such as driving a car or using power tools.

7. Images might be an epiphenomenon, the results of experiments consistent with the idea that people use images may result from demand characteristics, and the results of imagery experiments can be explained by models of cognition that use propositions alone.

8. Propositions are relational; images do not describe a particular relationship. Propositions have syntax; images do not. Propositions have a truth value; images do not. Propositions are abstract; images are specific. Propositions are not spatial; images are inherently spatial.

9. They showed that demand characteristics are not a factor in imagery experiments. They proposed more specific imagery theories so that more specific predictions could be tested. And, most importantly, they collected data in a variety of paradigms that were easy to account for with an imagery theory but were increasingly difficult to account for with a theory that used only propositions.

10. Here's one way to account for this effect. You need to make two assumptions: details are embedded in larger features, and you can have only a limited number of features active in working memory at one time. For example, suppose you are imaging a rabbit. Now suppose you are asked whether a rabbit has a pink nose. You need more information about the head. This information is embedded in the "head" representation, so you unpack the "head" representation to get more details about it. All the information about the head (including the information about the pink nose) cannot be included when one initially images a rabbit because of working memory limitations. When the question about the nose is asked, the representation is abandoned and another is generated that includes more details

about the head. The creation of this new representation leads to the epiphenomenal feeling of zooming in.

11. Psychologists distrust participants' introspections because in other areas of psychology participants' introspections are wrong at least as often as they are right. First, for many cognitive processes participants have no introspections at all; no one knows how their perceptual processes or motor control processes work. So what reason is there to think that for this particular cognitive function (answering certain types of questions about rabbits' noses and the like) you have reliable introspections? Second, people's introspections often are wrong. For example, participants who are comparing different brands of a product show a bias to select the product on the far right if they are arranged in a line. When asked whether such a factor might have influenced their behavior, however, almost all participants denied it, "usually with a worried glance at the interviewer suggesting that they were dealing with a madman" (Nisbett & Wilson, 1977, p. 244). People's introspections are fine as sources for hypotheses, but they are not trustworthy as data about mechanisms.

12. Images must be generated and maintained. Then they can be inspected and transformed.

13. Visual imagery concerns what objects look like (their color, their basic shape). Spatial imagery concerns objects' locations (where objects are in a scene) and spatial transformations of objects in imagery (for example, mental rotation). Visual imagery is in the ventral visual pathway (the temporal lobe) and spatial imagery is in the dorsal visual pathway (the parietal lobe).

14. The key result was discovered as follows. Participants were asked to image multipart objects on a visible grid. Xs appeared in the grids, and the response time to say whether the Xs would be on the imaged objects depended on the location of the Xs, such that if the Xs were on parts of the object that would be imaged first, response times were short. If the Xs were on parts of the object that would be imaged later, response times were longer. This result was interpreted as showing that participants created the image part by part, and as soon as they imaged the part where the X was, they could answer the question as to whether the X covered the part.

15. Imagery does seem to have some properties in common with Baddeley's visuospatial sketchpad. Imagery is limited in how much it can contain, you can increase its capacity through chunking, and it seems to have dissociable visual and spatial aspects.

16. We've briefly mentioned that imagery might aid perception. If you're imaging an object, it is easier to perceive an object that matches your image, but that situation may be rare in the real world. Imagery may play an important role in certain types of problem solving. For example, a Nobel Prize–winning physicist has said that he often thought of physics problems not in terms of formal proofs but in terms of imaginary physical models of the systems (Feynman & Leighton, 1985). For a brief review of other reports of the importance of imagery in scientific problem solving, see Shepard and Cooper (1986). For a more detailed discussion of the uses of imagery in creativity, see Finke (1996).

17. This broad characterization (or caricature) is not bad. We can think in terms of a rather simple model: low-level perceptual processes can write to a screen of limited spatial extent; this screen is the location of visual experience (where we have the awareness of seeing something). What is written to the screen gets stored in memory in a secondary memory representation. This secondary memory representation is a visual image. We also have the ability to take this representation and write its contents back on the screen. That is visual imagery.

CHAPTER 10

1. Rational models are those in which decisions are internally consistent, that is, in which decisions don't conflict with one another. Normative models of decision making propose a criterion by which choices can be compared and a best choice can be selected.

2. They are similar because they are both criteria that could be used in normative theories of decision making. They differ in that expected value is based solely on the financial return that can be expected from a particular choice, whereas expected utility considers the value a person places on the return and the likelihood that the return will be obtained.

3. Their choices do not show transitivity, and their choices change depending on the problem frame.

4. I doubt it. Utility theory might help in explaining why people play lotteries because the utility of the huge prize is so much greater than the utility of the small amount needed to play. (Although the expected value of a lottery is so abysmally bad, it's still difficult to understand why people play.) That is not true of typical casino games, where the amount bet and the payoff are not very different. Why, then, do people gamble at casinos? As you would guess, the reasons are doubtless many and complex, but a large part of the reason probably results from people believing that they have special knowledge that gives them an edge over the house, if not consistently, than at least at particular moments of play. If you would like to see a cornucopia of these (useless) methods, there are many for sale via the World Wide Web.

5. Suppose you offer a bet to someone with this story: "You're walking down the street in Washington, D.C., and you want to by a soda. You see a sign on a pushcart ahead indicating that sodas cost 75 cents, but you see a pushcart across the street where they cost 70 cents. Would you cross the street to save a nickel?" It's safe to say that some people who would refuse the bet would nevertheless cross the street (incurring a very small risk of being killed) to save a nickel.

6. Representativeness: an event is judged to be more likely to belong to a category if it has the features of the category that are deemed important. Availability: the likelihood of an event is assumed to be proportional to the ease with which examples of the event can be brought to mind. Anchoring and adjustment: The person starts with some initial probability value (anchor) by doing a partial calculation of the problem or by using a probability statement in the problem, then adjusts that initial estimate upward or downward on the basis of other information in the problem.

7. Sample size information, which is important in judging how consistent or stable a probability is. People ignore base rate information (information about the frequency or likelihood of an event in a population) if they get any other information that helps them evaluate a particular event.

8. Gigerenzer argues that people's cognitive systems are biased to use frequencies of events, not probabilities of events. By giving participants problems that describe probabilities, we give them information that is in a format that their cognitive systems cannot readily use.

9. Suppose that people who read lie detector test results are 80% accurate in detecting liars. (I don't think that they are, but let's ignore that for the moment.) Suppose now that I am an employer; some of my employees are stealing from the company, and I want to know who they are. I want all of my employees to submit to a lie detector test. Employee 1 walks in and claims not to have stolen, but the operator of the lie detector equipment says that Employee 1 is lying. What are the chances that Employee 1 has stolen from the company? The fact is that we don't know what the chances are. To figure that out, we would need some base rate information. If 95% of the people in the company aren't stealing, then the chances that this person is stealing is only

40%. When you're administering a lie detector test, you almost never know what the base rate of lying is, and because the lie detector test is imperfect, base rate information is essential to tell you the chances that any one person is lying.

10. When planning a project, researchers probably consider the different components of the project and estimate the time it will take to perform each one. These estimates might be accurate, but people seldom take into account the odds that something will go wrong. The probability of any one thing going wrong is quite low, but there are so many potential things that could go wrong, in aggregate the odds of a problem may be fairly high. People use the total time and fail to adjust adequately.

11. Deductive reasoning allows us to state that a conclusion must be true, given the premises. Inductive reasoning allows us to say only that a conclusion is more or less likely, given the premises.

12. No, familiarity does not seem to be the critical feature. Keep in mind that people can perform well on the problem even if it concerns unfamiliar material (such as tattoos and cassava), and they sometimes don't perform well even if it concerns familiar material (such as what sort of food and drink go together well). The ideas of permission and precaution schemas seem to better describe participants' performance in these tasks.

13. Syntactic models propose that people reason by manipulating the premises with a set of rules. These rules allow conclusions to be drawn from the premises. Semantic models propose that people evaluate the truth of conclusions by determining whether the conclusion is true under all conditions in which the premises are true.

14. Case-based reasoning seems somewhat less interesting than other forms of reasoning, perhaps because it seems as if it is hardly reasoning at all. Nevertheless, it seems likely that we often remember courses of action we pursued in the past if they worked out well. When you see that the time is 10:50 and you know that you have a class in 10 minutes, is it really necessary to reason about your next course of action, or can you rely on your memory of similar situations to guide you? This question is not settled, but my money is on memory.

15. For both conditional statements and syllogisms, the content of the problem is an important factor determining difficulty. Prior experience is likely to be important in solving these problems. Prior experience may suggest possible solutions (as in case-based reasoning models), or it may it suggest how to interpret the meaning of problems (as in semantic reasoning models).

16. No. To draw such a conclusion would actually be a to commit a logical fallacy.

> People don't reason on the Wason card selection task.
>
> The Wason card selection task is a reasoning task.
>
> Therefore, people don't reason on all reasoning tasks.

Chapter 11

1. Heuristics are needed to select operators; most problem spaces are too large for a brute force search, and if the problem is unfamiliar we need some way to reduce the search space.

2. Hill climbing, working backward, and means–ends analysis.

3. First, identify the difference between your current state and the goal state. Second, search for an operator that addresses the largest difference between your current state and goal state. Third, if you cannot apply that operator, set as a subgoal to reach a state where you can apply that operator. Continue until there is no difference between your current state and the goal state.

4. Yes, means–ends analysis would work. Your initial goal is to reach the highest hill. You would first set an operator of moving toward the top of the hill. If you hit an obstacle to moving toward the top of the highest hill (for example, you were at the top of a small hill, or you faced a wall), you would set as a subgoal getting to a state in which you would again be able to move toward the top of the hill (for example, going downhill briefly).

5. Chess has the larger problem space because it has more pieces and each piece can move in more ways. You could reduce the problem space of chess or checkers by reducing the number of pieces or restricting the options for how the pieces move.

6. It seems clear that working backward won't help because you don't know what the goal state is. Hill climbing can't work for the same reason: if you don't know what the goal is, you don't know what constitutes moving toward the goal. Means–ends analysis might work if you could set subgoals that would get you closer to the goal. One possible subgoal might be determining that you have the first number right by feeling a bearing fall in the lock, for example.

7. Background knowledge can help you see the deep structure of the problem, not just the surface features. Background knowledge may also yield automatization of some of the operators, which frees working memory to work on higher-level strategies to address the problem.

8. The key problem appears to be in noticing that an analogy is appropriate in the first place. When people know that an analogy is available, they can usually (but not always) map from the familiar problem to the new problem. Unfortunately, people are too easily distracted by the surface features of a problem rather than the deep features, so they often fail to use analogies.

9. In both cases, you inappropriately apply past knowledge to a new problem. In functional fixedness, you use an object in a way that you have used it in the past; in a set effect, you apply a problem-solving procedure that you have used in the past.

10. This technique is called incubation, and although it sounds plausible, the evidence that it works is far from overwhelming (Goldman, Wolters, & Winograd, 1992; Smith & Blankenship, 1991). It seems plausible because the impasse may be caused by functional fixedness or set effects: you keep retrieving the same nonworkable ideas. If you leave the problem, it seems possible that you would represent the problem differently upon your return, avoiding the impasse.

11. Creativity, although a topic of great intrinsic interest, has been notoriously difficult for psychologists to study. A big part of the problem is that it is hard to study; you can't simply say to someone, "Okay, I've got my equipment all set, the video camera is on, go ahead and be creative NOW!" Nevertheless, we can look at creative behaviors retrospectively and see that they have some of the characteristics of insight problems: creativity involves reformulating components that we are familiar with and making new, greater wholes from the components. The brilliance of a concept such as Ebay is in both its familiarity (a garage sale opportunity to find treasure in someone else's junk) and its exploitation of new technology (you can search through the junk at computer speed). Creativity can also be manifest by seeing underlying similarities where others had not. The operating system of the Macintosh computer is a creative product because it creates an analogy to a desktop, a concept that non-computer users were familiar with and that was readily applicable to computer use. The analogy was so compelling that it became the standard in the personal computer industry.

12. Experts have more domain knowledge than novices, and their knowledge is better organized; *better* in this case means that it is organized according to deep structure, which makes the knowledge more readily applicable to new problems. Experts may well use different procedures in solving problems, but there is no strong evidence supporting that conjecture yet.

13. Practice is not merely engaging in the activity. Deliberate practice implies engaging in the activity to improve proficiency, which means that the person must be motivated, the task must be at the correct level to encourage improvement, there must be immediate corrective feedback, and there must be repetition.

14. A large working memory capacity will make someone a good problem solver, and proficiency in setting subgoals may also be a helpful problem-solving strategy.

15. On the face of it, we almost never see an expert who has not engaged in a great deal of practice. The caveat is that all the data are correlational; the person who did all that practicing did so because he or she wanted to practice

a great deal. So perhaps people who practice a lot are destined to become experts, but if you just took a person at random and made him or her practice the violin 6 hours a day for 10 years, you'd end up with a good violinist but not an expert. In other words, the correlational nature of the evidence may lead us to conclude that practice is a necessary condition for expertise, but it may not be a sufficient condition.

16. I don't think it is. In most insight problems (for example, the candle and radiation problems) we are not struggling to juggle in mind all the different elements of the problem. Rather, the difficulty is restructuring the problem space, and that is not especially demanding of working memory.

17. The first and best advice is simply to practice. The next best advice is to look for the deep structure of problems. Try to avoid simply applying formulas as a series of steps, as though for a recipe. Instead, try to understand what those steps are doing—in other words, try to understand the subgoals that each step or group of steps is achieving. One way to do that may be to compare problems to see how they are similar or different.

CHAPTER 12

1. Definitions of language differ, but most of them include these characteristics of language: language is communicative; the relationship between elements in the language and their meaning is arbitrary; the pattern of elements is structured; language is generative, meaning that the basic elements can be combined in an infinite number of ways; and language is dynamic, meaning it is always evolving.

2. Phonemes are produced differently by different speakers (because of accents, for example), and they are produced differently by individual speakers when the phonemes are in different contexts (a phenomenon called coarticulation).

3. Competence is people's knowledge of grammar (the rules they use to produce sentences).

Performance refers to the sentences people actually produce. Competence is not the same as performance because the sentences people actually produce (performance) are influenced not only by their knowledge of grammar (competence) but by other cognitive factors, such as working memory limitations, or social factors, such as the desire to stop talking when interrupted.

4. They can't capture certain key properties of the way we produce sentences. For example, they cannot explain why we accept as grammatical sentences with words that we never hear together, such as "Color green ideas sleep furiously." Also, the machinery of word-chain grammars cannot produce sentences with remote dependencies (either ... or) with other grammatical structures embedded within them.

5. It's possible because the context and your background knowledge limit the number of interpretations you will entertain as being possible. Because of your past experience with children, you know that the child is saying (roughly), "Let's go get a cookie now" and is unlikely to be saying, "You, me, and the cookie should all leave now." Imagine now that the child says, "Abe, Sarah kick now." You don't know whether Abe kicked Sarah or Sarah kicked Abe because background knowledge doesn't help.

6. One reason song lyrics are difficult to understand is that they are often quite odd ("'Scuse me, while I kiss the sky"). There is simply no telling what the words are going to be. People do use information about what is likely to have been said to understand speech. At the same time, predictability clearly is not the only source of information because we are perfectly able to understand the strangest string of words when they are uttered slowly and clearly. But if other cues are degraded—perhaps the phonemes are slurred and they are uttered as many instruments play—the cues of what the words are likely to mean may be all the more important.

7. Sequences of sounds are not completely random—consonants and vowels tend to alternate—and this is doubtless because such combinations are easier to pronounce, given the musculature of the tongue, lips, and so on. Some researchers (MacNeilage & Davis, 2000) have argued that they have uncovered four sequential sound patterns that are very easy to produce, given these factors. In addition, they claim that these patterns are (1) commonly found in infant babbling, (2) commonly found in languages worldwide, and (3) found in proto-words—that is, hypothetical words from extinct languages that would have given rise to words in today's languages.

8. We can use high-level meaning information to fill in phonemes that are severely degraded (phoneme restoration effect); we perceive phonemes that are slightly degraded as being normal phonemes (categorical perception); and we use visual information to supplement auditory information (McGurk effect).

9. One route is a direct matching process between the spelling of the word and the lexical entry spelling. The other route translates the spelling of the word into a sound and matches this sound to the sound entries in the lexicon.

10. A garden path sentence is one that seems to make no sense toward the end of the sentence because the grammar seems wrong. This occurs because the listener was parsing a sentence and toward the end of the sentence a word was perceived that made it clear that the ongoing parsing scheme was incorrect. Garden path sentences are important because errors in parsing are helpful in determining how parsing is performed and because they show us that the mind parses sentences as words are perceived; we do not wait for the sentence to be completed before we start parsing.

11. People appear to draw inferences when the text they are reading has some information that is missing or inconsistent. The chief debate is over how the cognitive system recognizes that information is missing. Most researchers think that texts are compared with information from long-term memory and with the text itself to find inconsistencies (in one of my favorite examples, Madame Bovary's eyes change color during the course of the novel) or missing information (for example, simple inferences from long-term memory such as that nails are usually driven by hammers).

12. Under normal circumstances, the context of a sentence biases lexical access so that only the appropriate meaning of an ambiguous word becomes active. In the case of a pun, both meanings become active and enter awareness. Note that a simple dual interpretation is not enough for humor ("This is not a very good spring" is not funny). There must be something about the context that makes both meanings potentially applicable, as when a waitress told my table that the only dessert left was pudding, whereupon an acquaintance countered, "You're pudding me on." (The rest of us hid behind our menus.)

13. The text would be criminally boring. The text "Billy walked slowly to the front of the room. The teacher waited for him" would turn into the following:

> Billy—he's a student in the class—was walking toward the front of the room. By "front" of the room, I mean the place where the blackboard is, and the way all the students face when they're sitting. Anyway, he was walking on the floor; I mean, he wasn't walking on top of the desks or anything. And he was walking slowly—not very slowly, to the point that it might take him an hour to reach the front of the room; just an average sort of slow. I think he was walking slowly because he was afraid. I can't be sure of that, because he didn't say so....

This sort of demonstration indicates that not only can we draw inferences as we read texts but doing so is a normal part of reading and saves a good deal of time.

14. This example indicates that sentence processing is sensitive to higher-level concerns. In this case, you would decode the meaning of the sentence, recognize that it was inappropriate given the context, and interpret it as sarcastic.

15. One feature you'd want to evaluate is the extent to which they seem to use words as abstract symbols and not simply as part of a stimulus–response pair. Roughly speaking, that's the difference between knowing that *apple* has the referent of the piece of fruit and being able to use the term *apple* in many different contexts and knowing that if you make a particular hand motion, you often get a piece of apple in return. The second thing you'd want to know is whether they have any appreciation of grammar. As described earlier in the chapter, grammar is central to language because it gives language its flexibility and power.

16. There seems to be some limited evidence for the use of words outside the context in which they were learned, which is evidence for understanding and using words as symbols. There is also evidence for some sensitivity to word order (for example, using *more* before a noun, not after). As you would expect, it's hard to draw a firm line for which the near side definitely is language and the far side definitely is not. Apes can do some of the things that characterize language, and they do them in a rudimentary way. To my way of thinking, that's not really language.

17. Language probably has some influence on thought in terms of the likelihood that you will think in a particular way or the speed with which you can think a particular way. These effects are likely to be small, however. It seems unlikely that the strong version of the Whorfian hypothesis—that language limits our ability to consider certain thoughts—is correct.

18. They should be smarter, on average, than people who speak one language. If certain types of cognition are easier in one language than another, then bilinguals have more types of cognition at their disposal than people who speak just one language. At this point there is no conclusive evidence that being bilingual makes people any smarter than being monolingual (Okoh, 1980; Hakuta, 1986).

Glossary

Abstract word One that does not refer to a physical object.

Abstract construct A theoretical set of processes and representations that you think are useful in explaining some data. An example would be the articulatory loop of working memory.

Accommodation A cue to distance in visual perception. It depends on sensing how much the lens of the eye has changed shape in order to focus the image on the retina; the shape change varies with the distance of the object.

Acoustic confusion effect Errors in primary memory based on sound (e.g., thinking one heard g instead of d). The presence of such errors indicates that participants use an acoustic code in primary memory on the task.

Acquired dyslexia A reading problem caused by brain damage in adults who were normal readers before the injury.

Activation The level of energy or excitement of a node, indicating that the concept the node represents is more accessible for use by the cognitive system.

Addressing system Scheme to organize memories in which each memory is given a unique address that can be used to look it up.

Agnosia A deficit of vision caused by brain damage in which the patient can appreciate shapes but cannot identify objects based on visual cues alone.

Algorithm A formula that can be applied to choice situations. It has the advantage of producing consistent outcomes, but algorithms may be complex and difficult to compute. Algorithms often are compared to heuristics.

Allocentric representation A spatial representation in which objects are located relative to one another. Synonymous with environmental spatial representation.

Analog representation One that has important properties of pictures (e.g., that it occurs in a spatial medium) but is not itself a picture. Mental images are usually referred to as analog representations.

Anatomic dissociation Evidence that two different tasks are supported by different parts of the brain.

Anchoring and adjustment A heuristic used to estimate probabilities in which the person starts with some initial probability value (anchor) by doing a partial calculation of the problem or by using a probability statement in the problem and then adjusting that initial estimate upward or downward based on other information in the problem.

Anterograde amnesia The loss of ability to learn new material after some insult to the brain.

Anticipatory Postural Adjustment Muscle contractions that counteract changes in the center of gravity that occur due to other movements (e.g., reaching movements).

Articulatory control process The process that allows one to enter information into the phonological store; it is literally the process of talking to yourself.

Articulatory suppression Refers to demanding that participants keep the articulatory system busy with nonsense during encoding (usually by saying "thethethethe" or something similar), thereby ensuring that they will not code stimuli in the phonological store.

Atmosphere A situation in which two premises of a syllogism are both either positive or negative or use the same quantifier. People are biased to accept as valid a conclusion that maintains the atmosphere.

Atmospheric perspective A cue to depth. Objects in the distance look less distinct because they are viewed through more dust and water particles in the air that scatter light.

Attention The mechanism for continued cognitive processing. All sensory information receives some cognitive processing; attention ensures continued cognitive processing.

Attentional blink In a rapid serial visual presentation, observers have trouble identifying the second target if it appears anywhere between 100 to 600 ms after the first target.

Auditory suffix effect An extra word presented at the end of a list of to-be-remembered words impairs memory for the last word on the list, even if participants are told to ignore the extra word. It was initially thought to occur by knocking the last word out of echoic memory, but this effect probably occurs in the phonological loop.

Automatic process A process that takes few or no attentional resources and that happens without intention, given the right set of stimuli in the environment.

Availability A heuristic in which the likelihood of an event is evaluated by the ease with which examples of the event can be called to mind.

Base rate The frequency of an event in the general population. When judging the likelihood that an event occurred, people tend to ignore the base rate if they are given any other information about the event.

Basic level category Category that is the most inclusive (i.e., the broadest) of which members still share most of their features.

Behavioral dissociation Evidence that two tasks are affected differently by an independent variable (e.g., declarative memories are much affected by the passage of time, but motor skills are not).

Behaviorism An approach to psychology that claims that the appropriate subject matter of psychology is behavior, not mental processes. It also emphasizes that psychologists should focus on that which is observable (i.e., stimuli in the environment and people's overt behaviors).

Bias In signal detection theory, a measure of the participant's bias to either report or not report the presence of a signal. Bias is measured independently of the participant's actual ability to detect signals.

Binocularly Viewed with two eyes.

Bottom-up processing Processing that starts with unprocessed sensory information and builds toward more conceptual representations.

British Museum algorithm An algorithm that uses very simple processes to derive conclusions. Important in Braine's natural logic theory of deductive reasoning.

Brute force search A problem-solving strategy in which all possible answers are examined until the correct solution is found.

Case-based reasoning theories Theories proposing that we reason by remembering similar problems (cases) that we have encountered in the past.

Categorical perception Refers to the fact that people do not perceive slight variations in how phonemes are pronounced. Phonemes can vary along certain dimensions with no cost in their perceivability.

Category A group of objects that have something in common.

Central executive The cognitive supervisor and scheduler, which integrates information from different sources and decides on strategies to be used in tasks and allocates attention.

Chunk A unit of knowledge that can be decomposed into smaller units of knowledge. Similarly, smaller units of knowledge can be combined ("chunked") into a single unit of knowledge (e.g., chunking the numbers 1, 9, 0, and 0 into a unit to represent the year 1900).

Circular theory   A theory that uses term A to define term B but then also uses term B to define term A, leaving unclear what terms A and B mean.

Classical conditioning   A training procedure that produces a conditioned reflex.

Classical view of categorization   The view that concepts are represented as lists of necessary and sufficient properties.

Cognitive economy   The principle of designing a cognitive system in a way that conserves resources (e.g., memory storage space).

Combinatorial explosion   The phenomenon in which the number of states in the problem space increases very rapidly, even with modest increases in the number of attributes of the problem that might be changed. For example, if one tries to look four moves ahead in a chess game instead of two moves ahead, the number of states in the problem much more than doubles.

Competence   People's knowledge of grammar, that is, the rules that they use to construct sentences. Competence is contrasted with Performance, which refers to the way that people actually talk. Performance is influenced not only by the rules of grammar but by lapses of memory and other factors that make the sentences people utter less grammatical than their competence indicates.

Computational approach   The dominant approach discussed throughout the book, it assumes that the information provided by the environment is impoverished and that the cognitive system must do a lot of computation to derive the richness of environment.

Concepts   The mental representation that allows one to generalize about objects in a category.

Conclusion   A statement of fact derived by logical processes. One may confidently propose that a conclusion is true or false within a problem based on its logical relation to the premises. Whether the conclusion is true in the real world depends on the truth or falseness of the premises.

Concrete word   Concrete words refer to real objects in the word (e.g., pencil, train).

Conditional statements   A logical form composed of three statements. The first premise states, "If condition p is met, then q follows." The second premise states whether p or q is true. The third is a conclusion about p or q.

Conditioned reflex   A reflex that is learned (i.e., that is the product of experience).

Conditioned response   In classical conditioning, the response elicited by a conditioned stimulus after training. It is usually similar but not identical to the unconditioned stimulus.

Conditioned stimulus   In classical conditioning, a stimulus that before training does not elicit a consistent response. During training, its presentation is paired with the unconditioned stimulus.

Conjunctive search   In a visual search task, a search in which the target differs from the distractors on two features, for example, the target is large and red and although some of the distractors are large and some are red, none of the distractors are both large and red. It requires a conjunction of two features (largeness and redness) to identify the target.

Consolidation   A hypothetical process by which memories become more stable over time, even if they are not rehearsed.

Construction   Similar to the idea of reconstruction. Reconstruction is the process by which memories are recalled. Construction is a particular memory that feels to the participant like a real memory but has no basis in fact.

Content-addressable storage   Scheme by which to organize memories in which the content of the memory itself serves as the storage address.

Contention scheduling   The process by which the relative importance of two tasks is weighed if executing the tasks simultaneously is not possible.

Context   Information about the time and place in which a memory was encoded.

Context effect   The idea that memory will be better if the physical environment at encoding matches the physical environment at retrieval.

Continuous task   A task in which there is no obvious beginning and ending to each trial; there is a continuous stream of stimuli and responses (e.g., a pursuit tracking task). Compare with Discrete task.

Control nodes   In a hierarchical sequencing representation, the control nodes tell the movement nodes what to do.

Convergence   A cue to distance. As an object gets closer, an observer crosses his or her eyes more to keep the image of the object on the center of the fovea of each eye. The extent to which the eyes are crossed can be used as a cue to distance.

Conversational implicature   The tendency for people to treat the language of logic as though it has the same meaning as everyday language.

Conversion error   An error in dealing with a syllogism in which a person reverses one of the premises. For example the premise reads "All As are Bs" and the participant believes that it is also true that "All Bs are As."

Correspondence problem   To use binocular parallax as a cue to depth, one must match up the left and right retinal images. The correspondence problem refers to the difficulty of doing that if the images in the retina contain many possible matches.

Critical features   Features of objects that don't change as the object undergoes various transformations (e.g., gets larger or rotates in space).

Critical period   A window of opportunity during which a particular type of learning will be easy for the organism. If the critical period is missed, however, the learning will be difficult or even impossible.

Cross-modal priming   A method of measuring access to the lexicon. In the most frequently used version of cross-modal priming, the participant listens to words and periodically must make a lexical decision about a letter string that appears on a computer screen as quickly as possible. Response times are shorter if the spoken word matches the letter string.

Cue   Some information from the environment (or that the participant is able to generate) as a starting point for retrieval.

Cued recall   A way of testing memory in which the experimenter provides the participant the time and place in which the memory was encoded as well as some hint about the content of the to-be-remembered material (e.g., "Tell me the words I read to you an hour ago. One of them was something to eat.").

Cutaneous receptors   Receptors in and under the skin. Some of these respond when the skin is displaced by pressure. This is important in detecting the pressure exerted by muscle contraction, as when you grip a glass.

Decay theory   Refers to the hypothesis that forgetting results (at least in part) from the spontaneous decomposition of memories over time.

Decision making   A situation in which a person is presented with two or more explicit courses of action, with the requirement that he or she select just one.

Declarative memory   Memory for facts and events, often called "knowing that" memory.

Deductive reasoning   Problems to which one can apply formal logic and derive an objectively correct solution.

Deep processing   Thinking about the meaning of stimulus materials at encoding.

Deep structure   In language, the deep structure is the representation of a sentence constructed according to a basic set of phrase structure rules, without any transformations applied to the resulting representation. If transformations are applied, the sentence might be turned into a question or be phrased in the passive voice, for example.

Default value   A characteristic that is a part of a schema that is assumed to be true in the absence of other information. For example, unless one is told otherwise, one assumes that a dog is furry; furriness is a default characteristic for dogs.

Degrees of Freedom Problem   The problem of how the mind selects which way to execute a movement, given that there are many ways to make any given movement.

Demand characteristics   Anything about the way the experiment is conducted that signals to the participant what the desired, appropriate, or expected behavior is.

Depth of processing A description of how one thinks about material at encoding. Depth refers to the degree of semantic involvement (that is, the word's meaning).

Description invariance A requirement of rational decision making, it is the idea that people will consistently make the same choice irrespective of how the problem is described to them as long as the basic structure of the choices is the same. In fact, description invariance is not met.

Deterministic The view that all acts (including human acts) have antecedent causes in the physical world.

Developmental dyslexia An abnormal development of reading processes in children.

Dichotic listening Task in which participants listen to material on headphones, and each earpiece plays a different message. Participants are to attend to just one message and must Shadow that message to show that they are doing so. The dichotic listening task often is used to study how much the unattended material is processed.

Digit span task Participants hear a list of digits read to them, one digit per second, and must immediately recite the list in the correct order. This task has been used to measure primary memory capacity since the turn of the century.

Direct measure A measure in which one infers something about cognition by directly querying the participant about his or her cognitive processing. For example, a free recall measure directly asks the participant how much of some material they can remember.

Discrete task A task in which each trial has a discrete beginning and ending (e.g., a simple response time task). Compare with Continuous task.

Disjunctive search In a visual search task, a search in which the target differs from the distractors on just one feature (e.g., the target is larger than the distractors or the target is the only stimulus that has a horizontal line in it).

Distractor Items that appear on a visual search experiment trial that are not the target item that the participant is to find. Also used in recognition memory experiments to denote incorrect responses. Synonyms of distractor in memory experiments are *foil* and *lure*.

Distributed representation A representational scheme in which a concept is distributed across multiple units.

Dual-coding hypothesis Paivio's proposal that concepts can be encoded verbally, in terms of mental images, or both.

Dual route models of reading Models that posit two mechanisms for reading. One route uses a direct matchup of the spelling and entries in the lexicon, and the other translates the letters into sounds and then matches the sound to the auditory entry in the lexicon.

Dual task paradigm A method of examining the attentional demands of a task. The target task is performed alone and in the presence of a secondary task; if the target task requires little or no attention, performance should not deteriorate when the secondary task is added.

Early filter A theory proposing that attention acts as a filter early in the processing stream. Implies that all sensory stimuli are analyzed for their physical characteristics, but only those that are attended to are analyzed for their semantic characteristics.

Echoic memory Name given to the auditory variety of sensory memory.

Ecological approach Emphasizes that the environment has rich sources of information in it and that the computations the visual system needs to perform are probably not that extensive.

Effector Part of the body that you use to have an effect on the environment (e.g., the hand, the foot).

Efficiency Theory A solution to the degrees of freedom problem in motor control, which claims that movements are evaluated for their efficiency, and the most efficient movement is selected.

Egocentric representation A spatial representation in which objects are located relative to part of the body.

Elaborative rehearsal A type of encoding in which new material is related to material one already knows.

Emotional conditioning Classical conditioning in which the unconditioned response is an emotion.

Empiricist The view that most of human knowledge is acquired over one's lifetime through experience.

Environmental space A spatial representation in which objects are located relative to one another. Synonymous with allocentric spatial representation.

Epiphenomenon A phenomenon that is not related to the function of a system. Some researchers argued that images are an epiphenomenon; the sensation of "seeing" an image is real, but that doesn't mean that the sensation has anything to do with the actual cognitive task being performed.

Episodic memory Memory that is associated with a particular time and place, with a this-happened-to-me feeling.

Exemplar An instance of a category.

Exemplar model Model of categorization that maintains that all exemplars are stored in memory, and categorization judgments are made by judging the similarity of the new exemplar to all the old exemplars of a category.

Expected utility A normative theory of choice in which the best choice is the one that offers the reward with the greatest personal value to the individual, not necessarily the greatest financial reward. The theory allows that in some situations, it may be more valuable to an individual to be very likely to get a modest reward rather than to have a small probability to get a large reward.

Expected value A normative theory of choice in which the best choice is the one that offers that largest financial payoff.

Eyeheight The height of the observer's eyes from the ground. Can be used as a cue to object size.

Familiar size Using one's knowledge of the typical size of an object as a cue to the likely size and distance of an object. For example, if a child appears larger than an adult, it is likely that the child is closer to the observer.

Feature-matching theory A theory of visual object identification proposing a memory representation of an object's list of features.

Feature singleton An object that has a feature that no other stimulus in the field has.

Fixed-action patterns Complex behaviors in which an animal engages despite very limited opportunities for practice or reward. Usually taken as evidence for innate or inborn learning.

Flanker effect Stimuli (usually words) that appear to the sides of a target and that participants are instructed to ignore, which nevertheless affect participants' behavior.

Flanker task A task in which the participant is asked to respond to one stimulus (typically it's a word to be read) while ignoring a stimulus that appears nearby (the flanker). The typical result is that the to-be-ignored stimulus influences performance.

Flashbulb memories A very rich, very detailed memory that is encoded when something that is emotionally intense happens.

Focus gambling When trying to learn a new category, using the strategy of generating a narrow hypothesis about the necessary and sufficient properties that define a category.

Foil See Distractor.

Fovea The part of the retina that is most accurate in discerning fine details. The fovea is near the center of the retina.

Free recall A way of testing memory in which the experimenter provides no cues other than the time and place in which the memory was encoded (e.g., "Tell me the words I read to you an hour ago.").

Functional fixedness In problem solving, one is fixated on an object serving its typical function, and one fails to think of an alternative use of the object, even though it would be quite useful in the problem.

Functionalism A school of psychology in the late 19th century that held that the functions of mental processes were paramount and that psychologists should therefore focus on describing the function of thought processes.

Galvanic skin response An indirect measure of nervousness that measures how much moisture (perspiration) is on the participant's palms.

Garden path sentence A sentence in which the cognitive system initially builds one phrase structure as the sentence is perceived, but later in the sentence it becomes clear that this in-progress phrase structure is incorrect.

General Problem Solver An artificial intelligence program that uses the means–ends analysis heuristic. The General Problem Solver has been successful in solving a variety of problems.

Generalization Responding to a new stimulus in the way you would respond to an old stimulus that is similar to the new one.

Generalize Usually applied to categories, it means to use information gathered from one exemplar to a different exemplar of the same category. For example, if you learn that a specific dog likes to have its stomach rubbed, you may generalize that knowledge to other dogs and assume that they too like to have their stomachs rubbed.

Generalized motor program A motor program that can produce not just a specific movement, but a whole class of movements.

Generative A property of systems that can produce new, novel output. Language is generative, meaning you can produce and understand completely novel utterances. Generativity seemed difficult to achieve with behaviorist accounts of language, which seemed successful in predicting the likelihood that one would repeat an action, not in describing how a novel action could be generated.

Golgi Tendon Organs Receptors located where the muscles and tendons join that are active when muscles stretch. They are important for proprioception.

Good continuation Points that can be interpreted connecting a straight or smoothly curving line will be interpreted that way rather than as connecting sharply angled lines.

Graceful degradation A property of a model (of memory or of another cognitive process) whereby if the model is partially damaged it is able to continue functioning, although not as accurately. The human brain often shows graceful degradation; if it is damaged, cognitive processes often are compromised, but can still partially function.

Grammar A set of rules that describes the legal sentences that can be constructed in a language.

GSR See Galvanic skin response.

Hemispatial neglect A deficit of attention caused by brain damage in which a patient ignores the half of the visual world opposite the brain damage.

Heuristics Simple cognitive rules that are easy to apply and that usually yield acceptable decisions but can lead to errors.

Hierarchical theory Theory of memory organization in which concepts are organized in a taxonomic hierarchy (e.g., animal is above bird, which is above canary) and characteristic properties are stored at each level.

Hill climbing A heuristic in which one searches for an operator that will take you to a state in the problem space that appears to be closer to the goal than you are now.

Homunculus A small person inside the head who performs cognitive functions such as looking at images on a screen. Proposing a homunculus explains nothing, and no one would ever do it on purpose; accusing someone of having a homunculus in his or her model is a scathing criticism.

Iconic memory Name given to the visual variety of sensory memory.

Illusory correlation People have a bias to judge that two events or characteristics of an event go together if people had a prior belief that they go together or if they are natural associates. Illusory correlation is related to the availability heuristic because you judge that two things are correlated if you can think of many instances in which the two things co-occurred.

Image A representation of knowledge that includes spatial information. Images often are called quasi-pictorial, meaning that they have some of the important qualities of pictures but are not themselves pictures.

Image inspection Processes engaged to better know the visual characteristics of an image.

Imageless thought controversy Debate over whether it is possible to have thoughts that are not accompanied by images. This debate occurred in the late 19th century and was critical to the introspectionist program because they studied imagery as a window into thought processes. If some thought was not accompanied by images, it was not clear how it could be studied.

Imagens Term for representations that support mental images in Paivio's dual-coding hypothesis.

Incidental memory test A memory test in which the participants are not expressly told that their memory will be tested later.

Indirect measure A measure in which you infer something about cognition based on performance. For example, a priming measure does not query participants as to whether they remember having seen particular words presented earlier. Instead, participants are asked to identify briefly presented words to see whether they are more successful in doing so with the words that were presented earlier.

Inductive reasoning Reasoning that allows one to say that a conclusion is more or less likely to be true but does not allow one to say that a conclusion must be true.

Information processing An approach to studying the human mind. It assumes that humans are processors of information, and that representations and processing operating on them underlie cognition. It also assumes that information is processed in stages.

Inhibition A mechanism that suppresses unwanted memories that are triggered by a cue. This suppression takes place to keep these competitors from being retrieved instead of the target memory.

Inhibition of Return A phenomenon of attention. If attention focuses on an object and then moves to another object, it is difficult to return attention to that object for several seconds.

Insight problem A problem in which the solver feels that the answer comes all at once, in an "Aha!" moment of illumination.

Intentional memory test A memory test in which the participants are told that their memory will be tested later.

Interference theory The theory that much or most of forgetting results from retrieval failure caused by interference of other learned material.

Introspectionism A method of studying the mind that became nearly synonymous with structuralism. The method entails observing one's thought processes, but it was deemed important that a more experienced introspectionist train a novice in the method. Researchers using introspection were almost always structuralists, seeking to use introspection to describe the basic components of consciousness.

Intrusion On a memory test, material that is appropriate to another context is inappropriately produced as a response in the wrong context.

Inverse projection problem The problem of recovering three-dimensional shape from a two-dimensional projection, like the projection on the retina.

Isomorph A problem with a different surface story that has a problem space of the same size, number of branches, and minimum solution path as a target problem.

Jerk Rate of acceleration. Used as a measure of efficiency in one theory addressing the Degrees of Freedom Problem.

Joint space In motor control, a representation for planning movements that uses joint angles.

Landmark Task used to test monkeys' ability to appreciate spatial relations.

Language Although definitions vary, key properties of language are often considered to be: communicative, arbitrary, structured, generative, and dynamic.

Late filter A theory proposing that attention acts as a filter late in the processing stream. Implies that all sensory stimuli are analyzed for their physical characteristics and their meaning, but only those that are attended to enter awareness.

Levels of processing framework A framework for understanding memory that proposes that the most important factor determining whether something will be remembered is the depth of processing.

Lexical decision task Task in which the participant sees a letter string on a screen and must decide as quickly as possible whether or not the letter string forms a word.

Lexicon The mental dictionary, which has information stored about all of the words a person knows. The lexicon stores the pronunciation, spelling, and part of speech of each word and has a pointer to another location in which the meaning is stored.

Light source, reflectance, and shadow indeterminacy Refers to the fact that the amount of light hitting the retina from an object depends on the light source, the reflectance of the object, and whether the object is in shadow.

Likelihood principle Suggestion that among the many ways of interpreting an ambiguous visual stimulus, the visual system will interpret it as the stimulus that is most likely to occur in the world.

Limited attention Continued cognitive processing cannot occur for all available sensory stimuli; simply put, you can't pay attention to everything simultaneously.

Linear perspective A cue to depth. Parallel lines converge in the distance, so the closer they are to converging, the farther away the location.

Links Representation of the relationship between concepts. In the hierarchical model the links are labeled (e.g., "has this property"), whereas in spreading activation models the links simply pass activation from one node to another.

Local contrast Dependence of the perceived surface lightness on the ratios of lightness of areas that are next to one another and are in the same plane.

Local representation A representational scheme in which a concept has a single location (e.g., it is represented in one node in a semantic network).

Logogens Term for verbal representation in Paivio's dual-coding hypothesis.

Loss aversion The unpleasantness of a loss is larger than the pleasantness of a similar-sized gain.

Luminance The amount of light your eye receives.

Lure See Distractor.

Maintenance rehearsal A type of encoding in which one repeats new material over and over to oneself.

Mask An array of tiny random black and white squares or a stimulus of randomly oriented squiggles and lines. A mask is used to knock another stimulus out of iconic memory. Mask can also be used as a verb (e.g., "The second stimulus masked the first.").

Mass spring model A model addressing the Degrees of Freedom Problem that capitalizes on a biomechanical property of the way our muscles and limbs are designed. It proposes that endpoints are selected for movements, but trajectories are not planned.

McGurk effect An effect showing that both visual and auditory information are used in phoneme perception.

Means–ends analysis A problem-solving heuristic that uses a set of rules about when to work forward or backward and when and how to set subgoals.

Mediated priming Priming that goes through two links, not just one. For example, if lion primes stripes it is probably because the priming was mediated through tiger (i.e., lion primes tiger, which primes stripes).

Mental model A semantic representation corresponding to a possible configuration of the world. Mental models are the heart of Johnson-Laird's mental models theory of deductive reasoning.

Mnemonic An aid to memory. Mnemonics usually require that you memorize a simple word or set of words. This memorized material then provides cues to the more-difficult-to-memorize material that you want to remember.

Modal model A model composed of the most common features of models of short-term memory in the early 1970s. The modal model turned out to be incorrect in many details.

Monitoring process In Wegner's model of mental control, the monitoring process searches for mental contents that are inconsistent with desired thoughts. The purpose is to serve as a warning system that mental control is failing. This process does not require attentional resources.

Monocularly Viewed with one eye.

Motor control Our ability to plan and execute movements.

Motor program A representation supporting movement that has three key features: it contains a set of commands for movement; peripheral feedback is not needed; the commands can be applied to different effectors.

Motor skill learning Increasing accuracy (either spatial or temporal accuracy) of motor acts that occur as a result of practice.

Motor theory of speech perception A theory positing that speech perception shares processes with or relies on knowledge about how speech is produced.

Movement nodes In a hierarchical sequencing representation, the movement nodes control muscles.

Multiple resources A theory of attention in which attention is thought to be composed of a number of pools of attention, each dedicated to a different type of task.

Multiply determined Term used to emphasize that most behaviors have many factors that influence them. For example, a decision of whether to enter a restaurant may depend on who you're with, your memory of your last trip to the restaurant, how crowded it is, how hungry you are, how much money you have, and other factors.

Muscle spindles Receptors in the fleshy part of muscles that detect muscle stretch. They are important for proprioception.

Nativist The view that much of human knowledge is innate.

Nodes Representation of concepts in hierarchical and spreading activation theories.

Nondeterministic The view that at least some acts have antecedent causes outside the physical world.

Nonmatching to sample Visual recognition task administered to monkeys to test their ability to recognize objects.

Normative theories A theory of choice that describes a set of rules by which some choices are better than others and one choice can be said to be optimal.

Object-centered representation A mental representation of what an object looks like relative to the object itself. The representation can support recognition of the object when it is viewed from any perspective.

Obligatory access Refers to the fact that verbal information (but not all sounds) appear to be entered into the phonological loop by its mere presence, even if the participant does not want it to enter.

Occam's razor The principle that parsimony is important in evaluating scientific theories. Specifically, if two theories account for data equally well, the simpler theory is to be preferred.

Occlusion—in memory A source of forgetting. There is a stronger link from a cue to some undesired memory than to the target, and the cue therefore always calls up the undesired memory.

Occlusion—in perception A cue to depth. An object that occludes another is closer.

Operant conditioning Learning whereby the animal (or person) makes a response that has consequences (e.g., reward or punishment). These consequences change the probability that the response will be made again.

Operating process In Wegner's model of mental control, the operating process seeks mental contents that are consistent with desired thoughts. For example, if one is trying not to think of a white bear, the operating process seeks distractions from that thought. This process requires attentional resources.

Operator A process one can apply to a problem to change to a different state in the problem space.

Parallel distributed processing (PDP) model A model using a distributed representation with nodes and links. The model learns as weights are modified.

Parallel search A visual search in which all of the stimuli in a field are evaluated simultaneously. One can tell that a search is parallel if adding extra distractors to the search does not increase the participant's response time. Participants usually experience pop-out with parallel searches.

Parsimonious A theory is parsimonious if it is the simplest theory possible that accounts for all of the data. The noun is parsimony.

Parsing paradox For some ambiguous figures, it seems impossible to identify the figure without knowing what its parts are, but its parts cannot be identified unless one knows what the figure is.

Partial report procedure Developed by Sperling to examine iconic memory, it's a procedure whereby participants are shown an array of stimuli (usually letters or numbers) very briefly and then are given a cue telling them which subset of the stimuli to report. This method showed that participants perceive most of the stimuli in a complex array.

Performance The grammaticality of the sentences that people utter. Performance is influenced not only by the grammatical rules people know (competence) but by other factors such as lapses of memory and social considerations such as interruptions.

Perkins's laws A set of rules describing how to interpret configurations of line intersections as parts of three-dimensional objects.

Permastore A hypothetical state of memory from which memories are not forgotten.

Phoneme restoration effect Phonemes that are poorly produced are "restored" by higher-level processes so that the perceiver believes that the missing phoneme actually was present. The system can infer what the missing phoneme should have been based on the context.

Phonemes Individual speech sounds.

Phonological dyslexia A pattern of reading difficulty in which the person has difficulty reading nonwords (e.g., slint) but can read irregular words (e.g., yacht).

Phonological loop The part of the working memory model in which auditory information is stored.

Phonological store The part of the phonological loop that can store about 2 s of auditory information.

Phrase structure grammars A grammar that represents sentences hierarchically, with each node of the hierarchy corresponding to a phrase structure.

Pictorial cues Cues to distance that can be used in two-dimensional pictures.

Picture theory of imagery The experience of visual imagery is created by activating a memory representation. This memory representation was created by viewing objects in the real world.

Pop-out A phenomenon in a task in which you are searching for a target among distractors. Subjectively, it feels to the participant as if visual search is unnecessary because the target simply pops out and is instantly recognizable. Objectively, there is very little cost to visual search time if extra distractors are added to the task.

Practice In developing expertise, practice is defined as activity designed to improve skill (as opposed to play or performance) and therefore must include corrective feedback and repetition and must be at the appropriate level of difficulty.

Pragmatic reasoning schemas Sets of rules defined in relation to goals that can be used to evaluate situations such as permissions or obligations. A key aspect of pragmatic reasoning schemas is that they encourage conclusions that are practical in the real world, as opposed to formal logic, which can lead to conclusions that are technically correct but not useful.

Preattentively Refers to processing that occurs whether attention is applied to the stimulus or not.

Premise A statement of fact taken to be true for the purposes of a logical problem.

Primacy effect Refers to the fact that memory for items at the beginning of a list is good (relative to that for items in the middle of the list).

Primary memory Hypothetical buffer in which information may be held briefly. Contrast with Secondary memory.

Priming The facilitation or bias of later processing of a stimulus caused by prior exposure to the stimulus. Usually taken to mean that the representation of the word is in an active state, resulting in easier processing. A word can be primed if a person has seen or heard the word recently or if a word close in meaning has been perceived recently.

Principle of minimal attachment The principle that as the cognitive system parses sentences it is biased to build phrase structures in such a way that it adds new words to existing nodes in the phrase structure hierarchy rather than creating new nodes.

Principle of truth Proposal in Johnson-Laird's model of deductive reasoning that people tend to construct models representing only what is true, not what is false.

Prior beliefs Real-world knowledge that can influence people's evaluation of a syllogism. They are more likely to accept as true a syllogism with a conclusion that they know is true and to reject a syllogism with a conclusion that they know is false.

Proactive interference Earlier learning interferes with new learning.

Probabilistic view of categorization Category membership is proposed to be a matter of probability. Prototype and exemplar models fall within the probabilistic view.

Probability model An approach to studying reasoning, based on the idea that when presented with what experimenters think of as reasoning problems, participants actually treat them as probability problems.

Problem In the study of problem solving, a problem is any situation in which a person has a goal and that goal is not yet accomplished.

Problem behavior graph A representation of the problem space as the participant solved (or attempted to solve) a problem. Problem behavior graphs typically are derived from verbal protocols.

Problem frame The particular way a problem is described. Several problems may offer the same core set of payoffs and probabilities of payoffs, but the problems could vary in terms of how they are described.

Problem space All possible configurations that a problem can take.

Problem state A particular configuration of the elements of the problem.

Procedural memory Memory for skills, often called "knowing how" memory.

Procedure invariance A requirement of rational decision making, it is the idea that people will consistently make the same choice irrespective of how their preference for that choice is measured. In fact, procedure invariance is violated.

Process A process manipulates representations in some way. For example, a computer might have a process for addition to add numbers. The mind might have a process that maintains the activity of a representation in primary memory, thus keeping it in consciousness.

Property inheritance A characteristic of some models of categorization; concepts inherit properties from the concepts that are higher in the hierarchy.

Proposition A verbal representation of knowledge. It is the most basic unit of meaning that has a truth value.

Proprioception A sense of the body's location generated by any of a number of special receptors in the joints, skin, and muscles.

Prototype A prototype has all of the features that are characteristic of a category.

Psychic budget How we mentally categorize money we have spent or are considering spending.

Psychological refractory period A period of time after one response is executed during which a second response cannot be selected.

Random dot stereograms Special stimuli with no cues to depth except binocular parallax.

Rapid Serial Visual Presentation An experimental paradigm in which a series of visual stimuli are presented rapidly, one at a time, typically with the participant required to search for a target somewhere in the series.

Rational In the context of decision making, rational choices are ones that are internally consistent (e.g., that show transitivity).

Rational analysis models of reasoning Models based on the idea that people may answer reasoning problems based on their assessment of the costs and benefits of particular answers.

Recency effect Refers to the fact that memory for items at the end of a list is quite good in a task demanding immediate free recall.

Recognition Method of testing memory in which the experimenter presents the participants with the to-be-remembered material along with other material that was not initially encoded (distractors). The participant must select the to-be-remembered items from among these other items.

Recognition failure of recallable words The effect in which words that were not recognized are nevertheless recalled successfully on a later test.

Reconstruction The idea that memories are not simply pulled out of the storehouse; rather, they are interpreted in terms of prior knowledge to reconstruct what probably happened.

Recursion A process can be recursive if it calls on itself to get its job done. A definition of something is recursive if the definition contains the thing defined. For example, one definition of a sentence is "two sentences joined by the word 'and.' "

Reflex An automatic action by the body that occurs when a particular stimulus is perceived in the environment.

Regression to the mean Statistical phenomenon by which extremely high or low scores on any measure are likely to move toward the mean if they are taken a second time.

Rehearse To practice material in an effort to memorize it.

Relative height A cue to depth. Objects that are higher in the picture plane are farther away.

Release from proactive interference Refers to the effect in which proactive interference dissipates if one changes the stimulus materials.

Repetition priming Effect in which performance of a task is biased by one's having seen the same words or pictures sometime earlier.

Representation A symbol for an entity or concept in the real world. For example, a computer might use a binary code 011 to represent the concept 8.

Representativeness A heuristic that leads you to judge the probability of an event as more likely to belong to a category if it has the features of the category that you deem important.

Repression The active forgetting of an episode that would be too painful or threatening to the self to be remembered.

Response chaining A theory of how sequences are organized in motor control. A movement triggers a proprioceptive feeling of having completed the movement, which triggers the next movement, and so on.

Response competition A source of interference whereby an old response already in memory interferes with a new response that you're trying to learn.

Response selection A hypothetical stage of processing in which a response to a stimulus is selected (e.g., to push a button), but the actual preparation of the motor act (e.g., finger movement) is not yet complete.

Response to stimulus interval The time after the participant has responded but before the next stimulus has appeared.

Restructuring A process emphasized by Gestalt psychologists, applied to a problem whereby one perceives a whole that had not been seen before.

Retina The layer of light-sensitive cells on the back of the eye.

Retinal disparity The disparity in retinal location of the same image for the two eyes.

Retroactive interference Later learning interferes with earlier learning.

Retrograde amnesia The loss of memories encoded before an insult to the brain.

Retrieval induced forgetting The phenomenon whereby retrieving some memories makes you forget other, related memories.

Sample size The number of things in a group that you are evaluating. People mistakenly ignore sample size in judging the reliability or consistency of a measure.

Sapir–Whorf hypothesis Synonymous with Whorfian hypothesis.

Satisfice To select the first choice that is satisfactory (i.e., above some threshold) rather than evaluating every choice and selecting the best of those. Psychologists believe that people must satisfice most of the time because there are usually too many choices to allow evaluation of all of them.

Savings in relearning A way of testing memory in which the participant learns some material (e.g., a list of words) to a criterion (e.g., can recite the list twice without error). After a delay, the participant must relearn the list to criterion again. If the participant can reach criterion in fewer trials the second time, he or she has shown savings in relearning.

Schema   A memory representation containing general information about an object or an event. It contains information representative of a type of event rather than of a single event.

Script   A type of schema that describes a series of events.

Second-order isomorphism   Term used by Shepard and Chipman (1970) to describe the relationship of pictures and mental images. They suggested that the parts of images have the same functional relationship to one another that the parts of pictures have to one another.

Secondary memory   Repository for memories. Contrast with Primary memory.

Selective   The assumption that one is able to disburse the limited resource of attention as desired.

Semantic memory   Memories that are not associated with a particular time and place or with a feeling that the memory happened to you. Semantic memories cover world knowledge (e.g., "frogs are green").

Semantic models of reasoning   Models based on the idea that a conclusion is true if it can be shown to be true under all conditions in which the premises are true.

Semantic network   Name given to all the nodes and links in a spreading activation model.

Semantic priming   Effect in which performance of a task is biased by having seen semantically related words or pictures viewed earlier.

Sensitivity   In signal detection theory, a measure of the participant's absolute ability to detect a signal. Sensitivity is measured independently of any bias the participant might have to report or not report signals. Also, the ability of a test to detect memories that are in the storehouse.

Sensory memory   General term referring to sensory buffers that can hold much information, but only for a second or so.

Serial position   The position of a word (or other stimulus) in a list, usually of to-be-remembered stimuli.

Serial search   A visual search in which each stimulus in a field is evaluated one at a time. One can tell that a search is serial if adding extra distractors to the search increases the participant's response time. Participants do not experience pop-out with serial searches.

Set effects   In problem solving, a set effect occurs when a particular problem-solving procedure is applied because it has been effective in the past, even if it is not appropriate to the current problem.

Shadow   In a dichotic listening task, participants listen to material on headphones, and each earpiece plays a different message. Participants are to attend to just one message and must shadow that message to show that they are doing so. Shadowing means repeating the to-be-attended message aloud as they hear it.

Shallow processing   Thinking about the surface characteristics of stimulus materials (that is, what they look like, sound like, and so on).

Shape and orientation indeterminacy   Refers to the fact that shape and orientation are indeterminate from a two-dimensional projection (e.g., such as a coin that looks like an ellipse if it is turned).

Short-term memory   A particular theory of primary memory. Short-term memory usually is accorded a duration of 30 s (if the material is not rehearsed) and a capacity of about five chunks of information.

Signal detection theory   A method of analyzing data that provides separate measures of sensitivity and bias.

Situation model   A level of representation in text processing. The situation model refers to deep knowledge of a text that represents an integration of information from the text and knowledge the reader had before reading the text.

Size and distance indeterminacy   Refers to the fact that the size of an object on the retina is determined by the actual size of the object and by the distance of the object from the observer.

Source   The information about the context in which something was learned (e.g., from whom one heard it, where one read it).

Span of apprehension The amount of information that can enter consciousness at once.

Spatial imagery Imagery that emphasizes where objects or parts of objects are located. Spatial imagery can be contrasted with visual imagery, which emphasizes what things look like.

Speech stream A term used to refer to spoken speech that emphasizes its continuous nature. Although we perceive speech to be composed of individual words (and therefore to have short breaks between the words), speech sounds are produced fairly continuously.

Spontaneous recovery The sudden uncovering a memory that was thought to be forgotten.

Spreading activation model A model in which memory is conceived of as a network of nodes connected by links, and activation spreads from node to node via the links.

Statistical significance A determination of whether or not a difference (as between two conditions in an experiment) was likely to have occurred by chance. If a difference is not statistically significant, we treat the two conditions as though they are the same.

Stereopsis A cue to distance that depends on the fact that our two eyes get slightly different views of objects.

Strength view of memory The idea that memories vary in how strongly they are represented, and more strongly represented memories are easier to retrieve.

Structural explanation An explanation for the limitation of performing multiple cognitive tasks simultaneously that emphasizes limitations in cognitive structures (e.g., working memory) rather than attentional resources.

Structural similarity Refers to whether two problems share content that allows them to be solved by the same strategy (e.g., if problems can both be solved by Newton's second law, they share structural similarity, even if one involves a falling body and the other an inclined plane).

Structuralism A school of psychology in the late 19th century, the goal of which was to describe the structures that make up thought. Researchers often used the introspective method.

Subordinate level category Defined as a category that is one level less inclusive than the basic level category.

Successive scanning When trying to learn a new category, using the strategy of formulating a hypothesis and making selections based on that hypothesis until it is disconfirmed.

Sunk costs An investment (e.g., of money, time, emotion) that is irretrievably spent and should not affect current decisions about spending but nevertheless often does.

Superordinate level category Defined as a category that is one level more inclusive than the basic level category.

Supervisory attentional system Part of Norman and Shallice's model of attentional control, which Baddeley suggests is a good starting point for a model of the central executive. The SAS selects action when a task must be planned in advance; when automatic processes appear to be having negative or unexpected consequences; when a new, unfamiliar action must be taken; or when or a strong habit must be suppressed.

Supposition Something that one supposes to be true to evaluate the consequences of its being true. Suppositions are important in some theories of deductive reasoning.

Surface code A level of representation in text processing. The surface code refers to the exact wording and syntax of sentences.

Surface dyslexia A pattern of reading difficulty in which the person has difficulty reading irregular words (e.g., yacht) but can read nonwords (e.g., slint).

Surface similarity Refers to whether two problems share similar elements (e.g., if both problems entail inclined planes, the problems have surface similarity even if very different strategies are necessary to solve them).

Surface structure In language, the order in which words are uttered in a sentence. The surface structure is the product of the deep structure plus any transformations that are applied to the deep structure.

Syllogism A logical form composed of three statements of fact: two premises and a conclusion.

Synergy A bias for a set of joints or muscle groups to work together in a particular way

Syntactic models of reasoning Models proposing that humans reason by accepting premises and then applying a set of processes that manipulate the premises in an effort to evaluate a given conclusion or derive a conclusion.

Tacit knowledge In the imagery debate, tacit knowledge is a participant's knowledge of how objects in the real world move. It was suggested by some that participants used this tacit knowledge to simulate real-world movement and thereby produce results in imagery experiments that match real-world phenomena.

Target Term used in visual search experiments for the item that the participant is expected to find. Also used in recognition memory experiments to denote the to-be-remembered material at test.

Template A viewer-centered representation. A simple template matching theory of object recognition says that you compare what you see to templates stored in memory.

Temporal gradient Refers to a characteristic of anterograde amnesia; memories of more recent events are more impaired than memories of events that happened a longer time ago.

Ten-year rule The phenomenon that experts in almost all fields are seldom able to compete at the very highest levels with less than a decade of intense practice.

Text A group of related sentences forming a paragraph or a group of related paragraphs.

Textbase A level of representation in text processing. The textbase represents the ideas of the text but does not preserve the particular wording and syntax.

Texture gradient A cue to depth. A field is assumed to have a uniform texture gradient, so if more detail is visible in part of the field, it is assumed to be closer.

Tip of the tongue phenomenon An effect in which you are certain you know a concept, but cannot think of the proper term for it

Top-down processing Processing in which conceptual knowledge influences the processing or interpretation of lower-level perceptual processes.

Trajectory The path of a movement.

Transfer appropriate processing The idea that memory will be better to the extent that the cognitive processes used at encoding match the cognitive processes used at retrieval.

Transitivity If a relationship holds between the first and second of three elements and it holds between the second and third, it should hold between the first and third. If choices were rational, there would be transitivity of preference between choices. However, transitivity does not always hold.

Typicality The fact that some members of a category are viewed as better (i.e., more typical) exemplars than others (e.g., a golden retriever is a typical dog, whereas a Chihuahua is not).

Unconditioned response In classical conditioning, the response to an unconditioned stimulus (e.g., salivation).

Unconditioned stimulus In classical conditioning, a stimulus that leads to a consistent response from the animal before any training begins (e.g., food).

Unlearning A source of forgetting. Practicing a new association between a cue and a target memory weakens the associative link between the cue and another memory.

Verbal protocol A method of gathering data in problem-solving (or other) experiments. The participant is asked to solve a problem and to simultaneously describe his or her thoughts. These descriptions are assumed to bear some relationship to the cognitive processes that actually support solving the problem and so can be used as a window into these processes.

Viewer-centered representation A mental representation of what an object looks like relative to the observer.

Vigilance The ability to maintain attention to a task in which stimuli appear infrequently.

Visual afterimages If you stare at a stable visual scene for 30 s or so, a visual afterimage appears when you then look at a blank field such as a white wall. The visual afterimage is opposite in color to the image and is caused by cells in the retina becoming "fatigued" from the consistent stimulation.

Visual angle   A measure of the apparent size of things on the retina.

Visual imagery   Sometimes visual imagery refers to any imagery in the visual modality. It also has a more specialized meaning, referring to imagery tasks that emphasize what things look like. Visual imagery can be contrasted with spatial imagery, which emphasizes where things are located.

Visuospatial sketchpad   A buffer on which visual or spatial information can be manipulated and briefly stored. It is thought to be similar to and perhaps synonymous with visual imagery.

What/how hypothesis   Alternative to the what/where hypothesis, this proposal holds that the visual system segregates analysis of what objects are (object recognition and location) and how to manipulate them (visual information dedicated to the motor system).

What/where hypothesis   Hypothesis that the visual system segregates analysis of what objects are (object recognition) and where they are (spatial location).

Whorfian hypothesis   The idea that language influences thought. The strong version of the hypothesis holds that certain thoughts are impossible to entertain in certain languages. The weaker version holds that it may be easier to entertain certain thoughts in certain languages.

Word-chain grammars   A proposal that people construct sentences by chaining one word after another, according to a set of rules about what words would be admissible next in the chain or what words are highly associated with words already in the sentence.

Word length effect   The finding that participants can remember more words if the words can be said quickly.

Working backward   A problem-solving heuristic in which one begins at the goal state of the problem and tries to work back to the starting state.

Working memory   Specific theory of primary memory proposed by Baddeley & Hitch (1974), it has three parts: a phonological loop, a visuospatial sketchpad, and a central executive. Working memory is proposed to be a workspace for cognitive processes, not simply a short-term storage device.

References

Aaronson, D., & Ferres, S. (1986). Reading strategies for children and adults: A quantitative model. *Psychological Review, 93*(1), 89–112.

Adamson, R. E. (1952). Functional fixedness as related to problem solving: A repetition of three experiments. *Journal of Experimental Psychology, 44,* 288–291.

Adelson, E. H. (1998). Illusions and demos [Online]. Available: http://www-bcs.mit.edu/persci/high/gallery/checkershadow_illusion.html.

Aerlemalm, T. (1997). Recognition failure and cue-dependence. *Scandinavian Journal of Psychology, 38,* 183–187.

Aglioti S., DeSouza J. F., & Goodale, M. A. (1995). Size-contrast illusions deceive the eye but not the hand. *Current Biology, 5,* 679–685.

Ahn, W.-K., & Graham, L. M. (1999). The impact of necessity and sufficiency in the Wason four-card selection task. *Psychological Science, 10*(3), 237–242.

Albrecht, J. E., & O'Brien, E. J. (1993). Updating a mental model: Maintaining both local and global coherence. *Journal of Experimental Psychology: Learning, Memory, and Cognition, 19*(5), 1061–1070.

Alivisatos, B., & Petrides, M. (1997). Functional activation of the human brain during mental rotation. *Neuropsychologia, 35*(2), 111–118.

Allard, F., & Starkes, J. L. (1991). Motor-skill experts in sports, dance, and other domains. In K. A. Ericsson & J. Smith (Eds.), *Toward a general theory of expertise: Prospects and limits* (pp. 126–152). New York: Cambridge University Press.

Allen, S. W., & Brooks, L. R. (1991). Specializing the operation of an explicit rule. *Journal of Experimental Psychology: General, 120*(1), 3–19.

Almor, A., & Sloman, S. A. (1996). Is deontic reasoning special? *Psychological Review, 103*(2), 374–380.

Alpert, J. L., Brown, L. S., Ceci, S. J., Courtois, C. A., Loftus, E. G., & Ornstein, P. A. (1996). *Working group on investigation of memories of childhood abuse: Final report.* Washington, DC: American Psychological Association.

Allport, A. (1989). Visual attention. In M. I. Posner (Ed.), *Foundations of Cognitive Science* (pp. 631–682). Cambridge, MA: MIT Press.

Altmann, E. M., & Gray, W. D. (2002). Forgetting to remember: The functional relationship of decay and interference. *Psychological Science, 13,* 27–33.

Altmann, G. T., Garnham, A., & Dennis, Y. (1992). Avoiding the garden path: Eye movements in context. *Journal of Memory & Language, 31*(5), 685–712.

Altmann, G. T. M., Garnham, A., & Henstra, J.-A. (1994). Effects of syntax in human sentence parsing: Evidence against a structure-based proposal mechanism. *Journal of Experimental Psychology: Learning, Memory, and Cognition, 20*(1), 209–216.

Altmann, G., & Steedman, M. (1988). Interaction with context during human sentence processing. *Cognition, 30*(3), 191–238.

Anderson, J. R. (1976). *Language, memory, and thought.* Mahwah, NJ: Erlbaum.

Anderson, J. R. (1983). A spreading activation theory of memory. *Journal of Verbal Learning & Verbal Behavior, 22*(3), 261–295.

Anderson, J. R. (1993). *Rules of the mind.* Mahwah, NJ: Erlbaum.

Anderson, J. R., & Milson, R. (1989). Human memory: An adaptive perspective. *Psychological Review, 96,* 703–719.

Anderson, M. C., Bjork, R. A., & Bjork, E. L. (1994). Remembering can cause forgetting: Retrieval dynamics in long-term memory. *Journal of Experimental Psychology: Learning, Memory, and Cognition, 20,* 1063–1081.

Anderson, M. C., & Green, C. (2001). Suppressing unwanted memories by executive control. *Nature. 410*, 366–369.

Anderson, M. C., & Spellman, B. A. (1995). On the status of inhibitory mechanisms in cognition: Memory retrieval as a model case. *Psychological Review, 102*(1), 68–100.

Anderson, R. C., & Pichert, J. W. (1978). Recall of previously unrecallable information following a shift in perspective. *Journal of Verbal Learning & Verbal Behavior, 17*(1), 1–12.

Arkes, H. R., & Ayton, P. (1999). The sunk cost and Concorde effects: Are humans less rational than lower animals? *Psychological Bulletin, 125*, 591–600.

Arnell, K. M., & Duncan, J. (2002). Separate and shared sources of dual-task cost in stimulus identification and response selection. *Cognitive Psychology, 44*, 105–147.

Arnell, K. M., & Jolicoeur, P. (1999). The attentional blink across stimulus modalities: Evidence for central processing limitations. *Journal of Experimental Psychology: Human Perception & Performance, 25*, 630–648.

Atkinson, R. C., & Shiffrin, R. M. (1968). Human memory: A proposed system and its control processes. In K. W. Spence & J. T. Spence (Eds.). *The psychology of learning and motivation* (Vol. 2). New York: Academic Press.

Attneave, F., & Curlee, T. E. (1983). Locational representation in imagery: A moving spot task. *Journal of Experimental Psychology: Human Perception and Performance, 9*(1), 20–30.

Au, T. K. (1983). Chinese and English counterfactuals: The Sapir–Whorf hypothesis revisited. *Cognition, 15*(1–3), 155–187.

Au, T. K. (1984). Counterfactuals: In reply to Alfred Bloom. *Cognition, 17*(3), 289–302.

Averbach, E., & Sperling, G. (1961). Short term storage of information in vision. In C. Cherry (Ed.), *Information theory*. London: Butterworths.

Baddeley, A. D. (1966). The capacity for generating information by randomization. *Quarterly Journal of Experimental Psychology, 18*(2), 119–129.

Baddeley, A. (1986). *Working memory*. Oxford: Clarendon Press/Oxford University Press.

Baddeley, A. (1996). Exploring the central executive. *Quarterly Journal of Experimental Psychology: Human Experimental Psychology, 49A*, 5–28.

Baddeley, A., Gathercole, S., & Papagno, C. (1998). The phonological loop as a language learning device. *Psychological Review, 105*(1), 158–173.

Baddeley, A. D., Grant, W., Wight, E., & Thomson, N. (1975). Imagery and visual working memory. In P. M. A. Rabbitt & S. Dornic (Eds.). *Attention and performance V* (pp. 205–217). London: Academic Press.

Baddeley, A. D., & Hitch, G. J. (1974). Working memory. In G. Bower (Ed.), *The psychology of learning and motivation* (Vol. 8). New York: Academic Press.

Baddeley, A. D., Lewis, V., & Vallar, G. (1984). Exploring the articulatory loop. *Quarterly Journal of Experimental Psychology: Human Experimental Psychology, 36A*(2), 233–252.

Baddeley, A., & Lieberman, K. (1980). Spatial working memory. In R. Nickerson (Ed.), *Attention and performance VIII* (pp. 521–539). Mahwah, NJ: Erlbaum.

Baddeley, A. D., & Scott, D. (1971). Short term forgetting in the absence of proactive interference. *Quarterly Journal of Experimental Psychology, 23*, 275–283.

Baddeley, A. D., Thomson, N., & Buchanan, M. (1975). Word length and the structure of short-term memory. *Journal of Verbal Learning & Verbal Behavior, 14*(6), 575–589.

Bahrick, H. P. (1984). Semantic memory content in permastore: Fifty years of memory for Spanish learned in school. *Journal of Experimental Psychology: General, 113*(1), 1–29.

Bahrick, H. P. (2000) Long-term maintenance of knowledge. In E. Tulving & F. I. M. Craik (Eds.) *The Oxford handbook of memory* (pp. 347–362). London: Oxford University Press.

Bailenson, J. N., Shum, M. S., Atran, S., Medin, D. L., & Coley, J. D. (2002). A bird's eye view: Biological categorization and reasoning within and across cultures. *Cognition, 84*, 1–53.

Baillet, S. D., & Keenan, J. M. (1986). The role of encoding and retrieval processes in the recall of text. *Discourse Processes, 9*(3), 247–268.

Baizer, J. S., Kralj-Hans, I., & Glickstein, M. (1999). Cerebellar lesions and prism adaptation in Macaque monkeys. *Journal of Neurophysiology, 81*, 1960–1965.

Balakrishnan, J. D., & Ashby, F. G. (1992). Subitizing: Magical numbers or mere superstition? *Psychological Review, 54*, 80–90.

Barclay, J. R., Bransford, J. D., Franks, J. J., McCarrel, N. S., & Nitsch, K. (1974). Comprehension and semantic flexibility. *Journal of Verbal Learning & Verbal Behavior, 13*(4), 471–481.

Bard, C., Fleury, M., & Paillard, J. (1990). Different patterns in aiming accuracy for head-movers and non-head-movers. *Journal of Human Movement Studies, 18*, 37–48.

Barnes, J. M., & Underwood, B. J. (1959). "Fate" of first-list associations in transfer theory. *Journal of Experimental Psychology, 58*, 97–105.

Baron, J., & Strawson, C. (1976). Use of orthographic and word-specific knowledge in reading words aloud. *Journal of Experimental Psychology: Human Perception and Performance, 2*(3), 386–393.

Barrouillet, P. (1996). Transitive inferences from set-inclusion relations and working memory. *Journal of Experimental Psychology: Learning, Memory, and Cognition, 22*(6), 1408–1422.

Bartelt, R., & Darling, W. G. (2002). Opposite effects on perception and action induced by the Ponzo illusion. *Experimental Brain Research, 146*, 433–440.

Bartlett, F. C. (1932). *Remembering: A study in experimental and social psychology.* Cambridge: Cambridge University Press.

Bassok, M. (1990). Transfer of domain-specific problem-solving procedures. *Journal of Experimental Psychology: Learning, Memory, and Cognition, 16*(3), 522–533.

Bassok, M., & Holyoak, K. J. (1989). Interdomain transfer between isomorphic topics in algebra and physics. *Journal of Experimental Psychology: Learning, Memory, and Cognition, 15*(1), 153–166.

Battig, W. F., & Montague, W. E. (1969). Category norms of verbal items in 56 categories: A replication and extension of the Connecticut category norms. *Journal of Experimental Psychology, 80*(3, Pt. 2), 1–46.

Baylis, G. C., & Driver, J. (1993). Visual attention and objects: Evidence for hierarchical coding of location. *Journal of Experimental Psychology: Human Perception and Performance, 19*(3), 451–470.

Beauvois, M. F., & Derouesne, J. (1979). Phonological alexia: Three dissociations. *Journal of Neurology, Neurosurgery, and Psychiatry, 42*, 1115–1124.

Bechara, A., Damasio, A. R., Damasio, H., & Anderson, S. W. (1994). Insensitivity to future consequences following damage to human prefrontal cortex. *Cognition, 50*(1–3), 7–15.

Becker, M. W., Pashler, H., & Anstis, S. M. (2000). The role of iconic memory in change-detection tasks. *Perception, 29*, 273–286.

Bedard, J., & Chi, M. T. (1992). Expertise. *Current Directions in Psychological Science, 1*(4), 135–139.

Begg, I., & Harris, G. (1982). On the interpretation of syllogisms. *Journal of Verbal Learning & Verbal Behavior, 21*(5), 595–620.

Behrmann, M., & Bub, D. (1992). Surface dyslexia and dysgraphia: Dual routes, single lexicon. *Cognitive Neuropsychology, 9*(3), 209–251.

Benvenuti, F., Stanhope, S. J., Thomas, S. L., Panzer, V. P., & Hallett, M. (1997). Flexibility of anticipatory postural adjustments revealed by self-paced and reaction-time arm movements. *Brain Research, 761*, 59–70.

Berardi, N., Pizzorusso, T., & Maffei, L. (2000). Critical periods during sensory development. *Current Opinion in Neurobiology, 10*, 138–145.

Biederman, I. (1981). On the semantics of a glance at a scene. In M. Kubovy & J. Pomerantz (Eds.), *Perceptual organization.* Mahwah, NJ: Erlbaum.

Biederman, I. (1987). Recognition-by-components: A theory of human image understanding. *Psychological Review, 94*(2), 115–117.

Bisiach, E., & Luzzatti, C. (1978). Unilateral neglect of representational space. *Cortex, 14*(1), 129–133.

Bizzi, E., Mussa-Ivaldi, F. A., & Giszter, S. (1991). Computations underlying the execution of movement: A biological perspective. *Science, 253*, 287–291.

Blake, J., & de Boysson-Bardies, B. (1992). Patterns in babbling: A cross-linguistic study. *Journal of Child Language, 19*(1), 51–74.

Bloom, A. H. (1981). *The linguistic shaping of thought: A study in the impact of language on thinking in China and the West.* Mahwah, NJ: Erlbaum.

Bloom, B. S. (1985). Generalizations about talent development. In B. S. Bloom (Ed.), *Developing talent in young people* (pp. 507–549). New York: Ballantine.

Blouin, J., Bard, C., Teasdale, N., Paillard, J., Fleury, M., Forget, R., & Lamarre, Y. (1993). Reference systems for coding spatial information in normal subjects and a deafferented patient. *Experimental Brain Research, 93*, 324–331.

Boland, J. E., & Blodgett, A. (2001). Understanding the constraints on syntactic generation: Lexical bias and discourse congruency effects on eye movements. *Journal of Memory & Language, 45*, 391–411.

Boland, J. E., & Boehm-Jernigan, H. (1998). Lexical constraints and prepositional phrase attachment. *Journal of Memory & Language, 39*(4), 684–719.

Bolhuis, J. J., & Honey, R. C. (1998). Imprinting, learning and development: From behaviour to brain and back. *Trends in Neurosciences, 21*(7), 306–311.

Bouchard, T. J., & McGue, M. (1981). Familial studies of intelligence: A review. *Science, 212*(4498), 1055–1059.

Bousfield, W. A. (1953). The occurrence of clustering in the recall of randomly arranged associates. *Journal of General Psychology, 49,* 229–240.

Bower, G. H. (1972). Mental imagery and associative learning. In L. Gregg (Ed.), *Cognition in learning and memory.* New York: Wiley.

Bower, G. H., Black, J. B., & Turner, T. J. (1979). Scripts in memory for text. *Cognitive Psychology, 11*(2), 177–220.

Bower, G. H., & Springston, F. (1970). Pauses as recoding points in letter series. *Journal of Experimental Psychology, 83,* 421–430.

Bowers, K. S., Regehr, G., Balthazard, C., & Parker, K. (1990). Intuition in the context of discovery. *Cognitive Psychology, 22*(1), 72–110.

Bradshaw, G. L., & Anderson, J. R. (1982). Elaborative encoding as an explanation of levels of processing. *Journal of Verbal Learning & Verbal Behavior, 21*(2), 165–174.

Brakke, K. E., & Savage-Rumbaugh, E. S. (1995). The development of language skills in *pan*: I. Comprehension *Language & Communication, 15,* 121–148.

Brakke, K. E., & Savage-Rumbaugh, E. S. (1996). The development of language skills in *pan*: II. Production. *Language & Communication 17,* 361–380.

Braine, M. D. S. (1990). The "natural logic" aproach to reasoning. In W. F. Overton (Ed.), *Reasoning, necessity, and logic: Developmental perspectives* (pp. 133–157). Mahwah, NJ: Erlbaum.

Braine, M. D. S., & O'Brien, D. P. (1998). The theory of mental-propositional logic: Description and illustration. In M. D. S. Braine & D. P. O'Brien (Eds.), *Mental logic* (pp. 79–89). Mahwah, NJ: Erlbaum.

Braine, M. D. S., Reiser, B. J., & Rumain, B. (1984). Some empirical justification for a theory of natural propositional logic. In G. H. Bower (Ed.), *The psychology of learning and motivation: Advances in research and theory* (Vol. 18). New York: Academic Press.

Braine, M. D. S., & Rumain, B. (1983). Logical reasoning. In J. H. Flavell & E. M. Markman (Eds.), *Handbook of child psychology* (Vol. III, pp. 263–340). New York: Wiley.

Brandon, S., Boakes, J., Glaser, D., & Green, R. (1998). Recovered memories of childhood sexual abuse: Implications for clinical practice. *British Journal of Psychiatry, 172,* 296–307.

Brandt, S. A., & Stark, L. W. (1997). Spontaneous eye movements during visual imagery reflect the content of the visual scene. *Journal of Cognitive Neuroscience, 9*(1), 27–38.

Bransford, J. D., & Johnson, M. K. (1972). Contextual prerequisites for understanding: Some investigations for comprehension and recall. *Journal of Verbal Learning and Verbal Behavior, 11,* 717–726.

Breitmeyer, B. G., & Ganz, L. (1976). Implications of sustained and transient channels for theories of visual pattern masking, saccadic suppression, and information processing. *Psychological Review, 83*(1), 1–36.

Brewer, J. B., Zhao, Z., Desmond, J. E., Glover, G. H., & Gabrieli, J. D. E. (1998). Making memories: Brain activity that predicts how well visual experience will be remembered. *Science, 281*(5380), 1185–1187.

Bridgeman, B., Gemmer, A., Forsman, T., & Huemer, V. (2000). Processing spatial information in the sensorimotor branch of the visual system. *Vision Research, 40,* 3539–3552.

Britt, M. A. (1994). The interaction of referential ambiguity and argument structure in the parsing of prepositional phrases. *Journal of Memory & Language, 33*(2), 251–283.

Britt, M. A., Perfetti, C. A., Garrod, S., & Rayner, K. (1992). Parsing in discourse: Context effects and their limits. *Journal of Memory & Language, 31*(3), 293–314.

Broadbent, D. E. (1958). *Perception and communication.* Oxford: Oxford University Press.

Broadbent, D. E. (1982). Task combination and selective intake of information. *Acta Psychologica, 50*(3), 253–290.

Broadbent, D. E., & Broadbent, M. H. (1987). From detection to identification: Response to multiple targets in rapid serial visual presentation. *Perception & Psychophysics, 42,* 105–113.

Brooks, L. R. (1968). Spatial and verbal components of the act of recall. *Canadian Journal of Psychology, 22*(5), 349–368.

Brown, J. (1958). Some tests of the decay theory of immediate memory. *Quarterly Journal of Experimental Psychology, 10,* 12–21.

Brown, R. (1958). *Words and things.* Glencoe, IL: Free Press.

Brown, R., & Kulik, J. (1977). Flashbulb memories. *Cognition, 5*(1), 73–99.

Brown, R., & McNeill, D. (1966). The "tip of the tongue" phenomenon. *Journal of Verbal Learning & Verbal Behavior, 5*(4), 325–337.

Brown, R. W., & Lenneberg, E. H. (1954). A study in language and cognition. *Journal of Abnormal & Social Psychology, 49,* 454–462.

Bruner, J. S., Goodnow, J. J., & Austin, G. A. (1956). *A study of thinking.* New York: Wiley.

Bryan, W. L., & Harter, N. (1897). Studies in the physiology and psychology of the telegraphic language. *Psychological Review, 4*(1), 27–53.

Bryant, D. J. (1991). Exceptions to recognition failure as a function of the encoded association between cue and target. *Memory & Cognition, 19*, 210–219.

Buchanan, T. W., Denburg, N. L., Tranel, D., & Adolphs, R. (2001). Verbal and nonverbal emotional memory following unilateral amygdala damage. *Learning & Memory, 8*, 326–335.

Buckner, R. L., Kelley, W. M., & Petersen, S. E. (1999). Frontal cortex contributes to human memory formation. *Nature Neuroscience, 2*(4), 311–314.

Buckner, R. L., & Petersen, S. E. (1996). What does neuroimaging tell us about the role of prefrontal cortex in memory retrieval? *Seminars in the Neurosciences, 8*, 47–55.

Bundesen, C., & Larsen, A. (1975). Visual transformation of size. *Journal of Experimental Psychology: Human Perception and Performance, 1*(3), 214–220.

Burgund, E. D., & Marsolek, C. J. (2000). Viewpoint-invariant and viewpoint-dependent object recognition in dissociable neural subsystems. *Psychonomic Bulletin & Review, 7*, 480–489.

Burke, A., Heuer, F., & Reisberg, D. (1992). Remembering emotional events. *Memory & Cognition. 20*, 277–290.

Burke, D. M., MacKay, D. G., Worthley, J. S., & Wade, E. (1991). On the tip of the tongue: What causes word finding failures in young and older adults? *Journal of Memory & Language, 30*, 542–579.

Cabeza, R., & Nyberg, L. (2000). Imaging cognition. II. An empirical review of 275 PET and fMRI studies. *Journal of Cognitive Neuroscience, 12*, 1–47.

Cahill, L., Haier, R. J., Falon, J., Alkire, M. T., Tang, C., Keator, D., Wu, J., & McGaugh, J. L. (1996). Amygdala activity at encoding correlated with long-term, free recall of emotional information. *Proceedings of the National Academy of Sciences, 93*, 8016–8021.

Cahill, L., & McGaugh, J. L. (1995). A novel demonstration of enhanced memory associated with emotional arousal. *Consciousness & Cognition: An International Journal, 4*(4), 410–421.

Calne, D. B. (1999). *Within reason: Rationality and human behavior*. New York: Pantheon.

Caminiti, R., Johnson, P. B., & Urbano, A. (1991). Making arm movements within different parts of space: the premotor and motor cortical representation of a coordinate system for reaching to visual targets. *Journal of Neuroscience, 11*, 1182–1197.

Campos, A., Perez, M. J., & Gonzalez, M. A. (1997). The interactiveness of paired images is affected by bizarreness and image vividness. *Imagination, Cognition & Personality, 16*(3), 301–307.

Canli T., Desmond, J. E., Zhao, Z., & Gabrieli, J. D. (2002) Sex differences in the neural basis of emotional memories. *Proceedings of the National Academy of Sciences of the United States of America. 99*, 10789–10794.

Caplan, D., Alpert, N., & Waters, G. (1998). Effects of syntactic structure and propositional number on patterns of regional cerebral blood flow. *Journal of Cognitive Neuroscience, 10*(4), 541–552.

Caramazza, A., & Shelton, J. R. (1998). Domain-specific knowledge systems in the brain: The animate–inanimate distinction. *Journal of Cognitive Neuroscience, 10*(1), 1–34.

Carlson, B. W. (1990). Anchoring and adjustment in judgments under risk. *Journal of Experimental Psychology: Learning, Memory, and Cognition, 16*(4), 665–676.

Carlton, L. G. (1981a). Processing visual feedback information for movement control. *Journal of Experimental Psychology: Human Perception & Performance, 7*, 1019–1030.

Carlton, L. G. (1981b). Visual information: The control of aiming movements. *Quarterly Journal of Experimental Psychology. A, Human Experimental Psychology, 33A*, 87–93.

Carpenter, P. A., Just, M. A., & Shell, P. (1990). What one intelligence test measures: A theoretical account of the processing in the Raven Progressive Matrices Test. *Psychological Review, 97*(3), 404–431.

Carrozzo, M., Stratta, F., McIntyre, J., & Lacquaniti, F. (2002). Cognitive allocentric representations of visual space shape pointing errors. *Experimental Brain Research, 147*, 426–436.

Castiello, U., & Stelmach, G. E. (1993). Generalized representation of handwriting: Evidence of effector independence. *Acta Psychologica, 82*, 53–68.

Catena, A., Fuentes, L. J., & Tudela, P. (2002). Priming and interference effects can be dissociated in the Stroop task: New evidence in favor of the automaticity of word recognition. *Psychonomic Bulletin & Review, 9*, 113–118.

Catrambone, R. (1994). Improving examples to improve transfer to novel problems. *Memory & Cognition, 22*(5), 606–615.

Catrambone, R. (1995). Aiding subgoal learning: Effects on transfer. *Journal of Educational Psychology, 87*(1), 5–17.

Catrambone, R. (1996). Generalizing solution procedures learned from examples. *Journal of Experimental Psychology: Learning, Memory, and Cognition, 22*(4), 1020–1031.

Catrambone, R. (1998). The subgoal learning model: Creating better examples so that students can solve novel problems. *Journal of Experimental Psychology: General, 127*(4), 355–376.

Catrambone, R. (2002). The effects of surface and structural feature matches on the access of story analogs. *Journal of Experimental Psychology: Learning, Memory, and Cognition, 28*, 318–334.

Catrambone, R., & Holyoak, K. J. (1990). Learning subgoals and methods for solving probability problems. *Memory, and Cognition, 18*(6), 593–603.

Cermak, L. S., & Butters, N. (1972). The role of interference and encoding in the short-term memory deficits of Korsakoff patients. *Neuropsychologia, 10*, 89–96.

Chapman, G. B., & Bornstein, B. H. (1996). The more you ask for, the more you get: Anchoring in personal injury verdicts. *Applied Cognitive Psychology, 10*(6), 519–540.

Charlot, V., Tzourio, N., Zilbovicius, M., Mazoyer, B. M., & Denis, M. (1992). Different mental imagery abilities result in different regional cerebral blood flow activation patterns during cognitive tasks. *Neuropsychologia, 30*(6), 565–580.

Chase, W. G., & Simon, H. A. (1973). Perception in chess. *Cognitive Psychology, 4*(1), 55–81.

Chater, N. (1996). Reconciling simplicity and likelihood principles in perceptual organization. *Psychological Review, 103*(3), 566–581.

Chater, N., & Oaksford, M. (1999). The probability heuristics model of syllogistic reasoning. *Cognitive Psychology, 38*, 191–258.

Chen, W., Kato, T., Zhu, X. H., Ogawa, S., Tank, D. W., & Ugurbil, K. (1998). Human primary visual cortex and lateral geniculate nucleus activation during visual imagery. *Neuroreport, 9*, 3669–3674.

Chen, Z. (1995). Analogical transfer: From schematic pictures to problem solving. *Memory & Cognition, 23*(2), 255–269.

Cheng, P. W., & Holyoak, K. J. (1985). Pragmatic reasoning schemas. *Cognitive Psychology, 17*(4), 391–416.

Cheng, P. W., & Holyoak, K. J. (1989). On the natural selection of reasoning theories. *Cognition, 33*(3), 285–313.

Cheng, P. W., Holyoak, K. J., Nisbett, R. E., & Oliver, L. M. (1986). Pragmatic versus syntactic approaches to training deductive reasoning. *Cognitive Psychology, 18*(3), 293–328.

Cherry, E. C. (1953). Some experiments on the recognition of speech, with one and with two ears. *Journal of the Acoustical Society of America, 25*, 975–979.

Cherubini, P., Garnham, A., & Oakhill, J. (1998). Can any ostrich fly? Some new data on belief bias in syllogistic reasoning. *Cognition, 69*(2), 179–218.

Chi, M. T. H., Feltovich, P., & Glaser, R. (1981). Categorization and representation of physics problems by experts and novices. *Cognitive Science, 5*, 121–152.

Chomsky, N. (1957). *Syntactic structures.* The Hague: Mouton.

Chomsky, N. (1959). A review of B. F. Skinner's verbal behavior. *Language, 35*, 26–58.

Chomsky, N. (1965). *Aspects of the theory of syntax.* Cambridge, MA: MIT Press.

Christianson, S.-A. (1989). Flashbulb memories: Special, but not so special. *Memory & Cognition, 17*, 443.

Christoff, K., Prabhakaran, V., Dorfman, J., Zhao, Z., Kroger, J. K., Holyoak, K. J., & Gabrieli, J. D. (2001). Rostrolateral prefrontal cortex involvement in relational integration during reasoning. *Neuroimage, 14*, 1136–1149.

Clark, F. J., & Burgess, P. R. (1975). Slowly adapting receptors in cat knee joint: Can they signal joint angle? *Journal of Neurophysiology, 38*, 1448–1463.

Clark, H. H., & Clark, E. V. (1977). *Psychology and language: An introduction to psycholinguistics.* New York: Harcourt, Brace, Jovanovich.

Clarke, M., Losoff, A., McCracken, M., & Rood, D. (1984). Linguistic relativity and sex/gender studies: Epistemological and methodological considerations. *Language Learning, 34*, 47–67.

Clarke, V. J., & Lamberts, K. (1997). Strategy shifts and expertise in solving transformation rule problems. *Thinking & Reasoning, 3*(4), 271–290.

Clement, C. A., Mawby, R., & Giles, D. E. (1994). The effects of manifest relational similarity on analog retrieval. *Journal of Memory and Language, 33*, 396–420.

Cohen, N. J., & Squire, L. R. (1980). Preserved learning and pattern-analyzing skill in amnesia: Dissociation of knowing how and knowing what. *Science, 210*, 207–210.

Cole, J. (1995). *Pride and a daily marathon.* Cambridge, MA: MIT Press.

Cole, J., & Paillard, J. (1995). Living without touch and peripheral information about body position and movement: Studies with deafferented subjects. In J. L. M. A. J. Bermudez (Ed.), *The body and the self* (pp. 245–266). Cambridge, MA: MIT Press.

Colle, H. A., & Welsh, A. (1976). Acoustic masking in primary memory. *Journal of Verbal Learning & Verbal Behavior, 15*(1), 17–31.

Collins, A. M., & Loftus, E. F. (1975). A spreading-activation theory of semantic processing. *Psychological Review, 82*(6), 407–428.

Collins, A. M., & Quillian, M. R. (1969). Retrieval time from semantic memory. *Journal of Verbal Learning & Verbal Behavior, 8*(2), 240–247.

Collins, A. M., & Quillian, M. R. (1972). How to make a language user. In E. Tulving & W. Donaldson (Eds.), *Organization of memory* (pp. 309–351). New York: Academic Press.

Coltheart, M., Curtis, B., Atkins, P., & Haller, M. (1993). Models of reading aloud: Dual-route and parallel distributed-processing approaches. *Psychological Review, 100*(4), 589–608.

Coltheart, M., & Rastle, K. (1994). Serial processing in reading aloud: Evidence for dual-route models of reading. *Journal of Experimental Psychology: Human Perception and Performance, 20*(6), 1197–1211.

Conrad, C. (1972). Cognitive economy in semantic memory. *Journal of Experimental Psychology, 92*(2), 149–154.

Conrad, R. (1964). Acoustic confusions in immediate memory. *British Journal of Psychology, 55*(1), 75–84.

Cooper, E. H., & Pantle, A. J. (1967). The total-time hypothesis in verbal learning. *Psychological Bulletin, 68*, 221–234.

Cooper, L. A. (1975). Mental rotation of random two-dimensional shapes. *Cognitive Psychology, 7*(1), 20–43.

Cooper, L. A., Schacter, D. L., Ballesteros, S., & Moore, C. (1992). Priming and recognition of transformed three-dimensional objects: Effects of size and reflection. *Journal of Experimental Psychology: Learning, Memory, and Cognition, 18*, 43–57.

Cooper, L. A., & Shepard, R. N. (1975). Mental transformation in the identification of left and right hands. *Journal of Experimental Psychology: Human Perception and Performance, 1*(1), 48–56.

Corbetta, M., Shulman, G. L., Miezin, F. M., & Petersen, S. E. (1995). Superior parietal cortex activation during spatial attention shifts and visual feature conjunction. *Science, 270*, 802–805.

Corkin, S. (1968). Acquisition of motor skill after bilateral medial temporal lobe excision. *Neuropsychologia, 6*, 255–265.

Corkin, S. (1984). Lasting consequences of bilateral medial temporal lobectomy: Clinical course and experimental findings in H. M. *Seminars in Neurology, 4*, 252–262.

Cornoldi, C., Cortesi, A., & Preti, D. (1991). Individual differences in the capacity limitations of visuospatial short-term memory: Research on sighted and totally congenitally blind people. *Memory & Cognition, 19*(5), 459–468.

Corteen, R. S., & Wood, B. (1972). Autonomic responses to shock-associated words in an unattended channel. *Journal of Experimental Psychology, 94*(3), 308–313.

Cosmides, L. (1989). The logic of social exchange: Has natural selection shaped how humans reason? Studies with the Wason selection task. *Cognition, 31*(3), 187–276.

Cosmides, L., & Tooby, J. (1992). Cognitive adaptations for social exchange. In J. Barkow, L. Cosmides, & J. Tooby (Eds.), *The adapted mind: Evolutionary psychology and the generation of culture* (pp. 163–228). New York: Oxford University Press.

Cosmides, L., & Tooby, J. (1994). Beyond intuition and instinct blindness: Toward an evolutionarily rigorous cognitive science. *Cognition, 50*(1–3), 41–77.

Cosmides, L., & Tooby, J. (1996). Are humans good intuitive statisticians after all? Rethinking some conclusions from the literature on judgment under uncertainty. *Cognition, 58*(1), 1–73.

Cosmides, L., & Tooby, J. (2000). The cognitive neuroscience of social reasoning. In M. Gazzaniga (Ed.), *The cognitive neurosciences* (2nd ed., pp. 1259–1270). Cambridge, MA: MIT Press.

Cowan, N. (1987). Auditory sensory storage in relation to the growth of sensation and acoustic information extraction. *Journal of Experimental Psychology: Human Perception and Performance, 13*(2), 204–215.

Cowan, N. (1995). *Attention and memory: An integrated framework.* New York: Oxford University Press.

Craik, F. I., & Lockhart, R. S. (1972). Levels of processing: A framework for memory research. *Journal of Verbal Learning and Verbal Behavior, 11*, 671–684.

Craik, F. I., & Tulving, E. (1975). Depth of processing and the retention of words in episodic memory. *Journal of Experimental Psychology: General, 104*(3), 268–294.

Craik, F. I., & Watkins, M. J. (1973). The role of rehearsal in short-term memory. *Journal of Verbal Learning & Verbal Behavior, 12*(6), 599–607.

Craver-Lemley, C., & Reeves, A. (1992). How visual imagery interferes with vision. *Psychological Review, 99*(4), 633–649.

Dallas, M., & Merikle, P. M. (1976). Semantic processing of non-attended visual information. *Canadian Journal of Psychology, 30*, 15–21.

Daneman, M., & Carpenter, P. A. (1980). Individual differences in working memory and reading. *Journal of Verbal Learning & Verbal Behavior, 19*(4), 450–466.

Daugman, J. (1990). Brain metaphor and brain theory. In E. Schwartz (Ed.), *Computational neuroscience.* Cambridge, MA: MIT Press.

Davies, I. R. L., Sowden, P. T., Jerrett, D. T., Jerrett, T., & Corbett, G. G. (1998). A cross-cultural study of English and Setswana speakers on a colour triads task: A test of the Sapir–Whorf hypothesis. *British Journal of Psychology, 89*(1), 1–15.

Davis, H. L., Hoch, S. J., & Ragsdale, E. E. (1986). An anchoring and adjustment model of spousal predictions. *Journal of Consumer Research, 13*(1), 25–37.

Dawson, M. E., & Schell, A. M. (1982). Electrodermal responses to attended and nonattended significant stimuli during dichotic listening. *Journal of Experimental Psychology: Human Perception and Performance, 8*(2), 315–324.

De Groot, A. D. (1946/1978). *Thought and choice in chess.* The Hague: Mouton.

de Valois, R. L., & de Valois, K. K. (1993). A multistage color model. *Vision Research, 33*(8), 1053–1065.

Denis, M., & Carfantan, M. (1985). People's knowledge about images. *Cognition, 20*(1), 49–60.

Descartes, R. (1664/1972). *Traite de L'homme* [*Treatise on man*] (T. Hall, Trans.). Cambridge, MA: Harvard University Press.

D'Esposito, M., Postle, B. R., Ballard, D., & Lease, J. (1999) Maintenance versus manipulation of information held in working memory: An event-related fMRI study. *Brain & Cognition, 41*, 66–86.

D'Esposito, M., Postle, B. R., & Rypma, B. (2000). Prefrontal cortical contributions to working memory: Evidence from event-related fMRI studies. *Experimental Brain Research 133*, 3–11.

Deutsch, J. A., & Deutsch, D. (1963). Attention: Some theoretical considerations. *Psychological Review, 70*, 51–61.

di Lollo, V. (1980). Temporal integration in visual memory. *Journal of Experimental Psychology: General, 109*, 75–97.

Dickstein, L. S. (1975). Effects of instructions and premise order on errors in syllogistic reasoning. *Journal of Experimental Psychology: Human Learning & Memory, 1*(4), 376–384.

Dickstein, L. S. (1976). Differential difficulty of categorical syllogisms. *Bulletin of the Psychonomic Society, 8*(4), 330–332.

Dickstein, L. S. (1978). The effect of figure on syllogistic reasoning. *Memory & Cognition, 6*(1), 76–83.

Dinges, D. F., Whitehouse, W. G., Orne, E. C., Powell, J. W., Orne, M. T., & Erdelyi, M. H. (1992). Evaluating hypnotic memory enhancement (hypermnesia and reminiscence) using multitrial forced recall. *Journal of Experimental Psychology: Learning, Memory, and Cognition, 18*, 1139–1147.

Donnelly, C. M., & McDaniel, M. A. (1993). Use of analogy in learning scientific concepts. *Journal of Experimental Psychology: Learning, Memory, and Cognition, 19*(4), 975–987.

Dooling, D. J., & Christiaansen, R. E. (1977). Episodic and semantic aspects of memory for prose. *Journal of Experimental Psychology: Human Learning and Memory, 3*, 428–436.

Downing, P. E., Jiang, Y., Shuman, M., & Kanwisher, N. (2001). A cortical area selective for visual processing of the human body. *Science, 293*, 2470–2473.

Drayna, D., Manichaikul, A., de Lange, M., Snieder, H., & Spector, T. Genetic correlates of musical pitch recognition in humans. *Science, 291*, 1969–1972.

Driver, J., & Spence, C. J. (1994). Spatial synergies between auditory and visual attention. In C. M. M. Umilta (Ed.), *Attention and performance 15: Conscious and nonconscious information processing.* Attention and performance series (pp. 311–331). Cambridge, MA: MIT Press.

Duncker, K. (1945). On problem-solving. *Psychological Monographs, 5*, 113.

Durso, F. T., Rea, C. B., & Dayton, T. (1994). Graph-theoretic confirmation of restructuring during insight. *Psychological Science, 5*(2), 94–98.

Eddy, D. M. (1982). Probabilistic reasoning in clinical medicine: Problems and opportunities. In D. Kahneman, P. Slovic, & A. Tversky (Eds.), *Judgment under uncertainty: Heuristics and biases.* Cambridge: Cambridge University Press.

Efron, R. (1970a). Effect of stimulus duration on perceptual onset and offset latencies. *Perception and Psychophysics, 8*(4), 231–234.

Efron, R. (1970b). The relationship between the duration of a stimulus and the duration of a perception. *Neuropsychologia, 8*(1), 37–55.

Eich, E. (1984). Memory for unattended events: Remembering with and without awareness. *Memory & Cognition, 12*(2), 105–111.

Eich, E., & Macaulay, D. (2000). Are real moods required to reveal mood-congruent and mood-dependent memory? *Psychological Science, 11*, 244–248.

Elliott, D., & Allard, F. (1985). The utilization of visual feedback information during rapid pointing movements. *Quarterly Journal of Experimental Psychology. A, Human Experimental Psychology, 37A*, 407–425.

Elliott, D., Calvert, R., Jaeger, M., & Jones, R. (1990). A visual representation and the control of manual aiming movements. *Journal of Motor Behavior, 22,* 327–346.

Elliott, D., Zuberec, S., & Milgram, P. (1994). The effects of periodic visual occlusion on ball catching. *Journal of Motor Behavior, 26,* 113–122.

Ellis, N. C., & Hennelly, R. A. (1980). A bilingual word-length effect: Implications for intelligence testing and the relative ease of mental calculation in Welsh and English. *British Journal of Psychology, 71,* 43–51.

Engle, R. W., & Bukstel, L. (1978). Memory processes among bridge players of differing expertise. *American Journal of Psychology, 91,* 673–689.

Engle, R. W., Tuholski, S. W., Laughlin, J. E., & Conway, A. R. A. (1999). Working memory, short-term memory, and general fluid intelligence: A latent-variable approach. *Journal of Experimental Psychology: General, 128*(3), 309–331.

Epstein, M. A., & Bottoms, B. L. (2002). Explaining the forgetting and recovery of abuse and trauma memories: Possible mechanisms. *Child Maltreatment, 7,* 210–225.

Epstein, R., DeYoe, E. A., Press, D. Z., Rosen, A. C., & Kanwisher, N. (2001). Neuropsychological evidence for a topographical learning mechanism in parahippocampal cortex. *Cognitive Neuropsychology, 18,* 481–508.

Epstein, R., & Kanwisher, N. (1998). A cortical representation of the local visual environment. *Nature, 392*(6676), 598–601.

Epstein, R., Lanza, R. P., & Skinner, B. F. (1980). Symbolic communication between two pigeons (Columba livia domestica). *Science, 207*(4430), 543–545.

Epstein, W. (1965). Nonrelational judgments of size and distance. *American Journal of Psychology, 78,* 120–123.

Erdelyi, M. H. (1994). Hypnotic hypermnesia: The empty set of hypermnesia. *International Journal of Clinical and Experimental Hypnosis, 42,* 379–390.

Ericsson, K. A. (1996). The acquisition of expert performance: An introduction to some of the issues. In K. A. Ericsson (Ed.), *The road to excellence: The acquisition of expert performance in the arts and sciences, sports, and games* (pp. 1–50). Mahwah, NJ: Erlbaum.

Ericsson, K. A., Krampe, R. T., & Tesch-Roemer, C. (1993). The role of deliberate practice in the acquisition of expert performance. *Psychological Review, 100*(3), 363–406.

Ericsson, K. A., & Simon, H. A. (1993). *Protocol analysis: Verbal reports as data* (Rev. ed.). Cambridge, MA: MIT Press.

Ernst, G. W., & Newell, A. (1969). *GPS: A case study in the generality of problem solving.* New York: Academic Press.

Ervin, S. M. (1962). The connotations of gender. *Word, 18,* 249–261.

Estes, W. K. (1994). *Classification and cognition.* New York: Oxford University Press.

Evans, J. St.-B. T., Barston, J. L., & Pollard, P. (1983). On the conflict between logic and belief in syllogistic reasoning. *Memory & Cognition, 11*(3), 295–306.

Evans, J. St.-B. T., Handley, S. J., Harper, C. N. J., & Johnson-Laird, P. N. (1999). Reasoning about necessity and possibility: A test of the mental model theory of deduction. *Journal of Experimental Psychology, 25,* 1495–1513.

Evans, J. St.-B. T., Newstead, S. E., & Byrne, R. M. J. (1993). *Human reasoning: The psychology of deduction.* Mahwah, NJ: Erlbaum.

Evans, J. St.-B. T. & Over, D. E. (1996). Rationality in the selection task: Epistemic utility versus uncertainty reduction. *Psychological Review, 103,* 356–363.

Fadiga, L, Craighero, L., Buccino, G., & Rizzolatti, G. (2002). Speech listening specifically modulates the excitability of tongue muscles: A TMS study. *European Journal of Neuroscience, 15,* 399–402.

Falmagne, R. J. (199). Language and the acquisition of logical knowledge. In W. F. Overton (Ed.), *Reasoning, necessity, and logic: Developmental perspectives. The Jean Piaget symposium series.* (pp. 111–131). Hillsdale, NJ: Erlbaum.

Farah, M. J. (1985). Psychophysical evidence for a shared representational medium for mental images and percepts. *Journal of Experimental Psychology: General, 114*(1), 91–103.

Farah, M. J. (1990). *Visual agnosia: Disorders of object recognition and what they tell us about normal vision.* Cambridge, MA: MIT Press.

Farah, M. J., Hammond, K. M., Levine, D. N., & Calvanio, R. (1988). Visual and spatial mental imagery: Dissociable systems of representation. *Cognitive Psychology, 20*(4), 439–462.

Feldman, A. G. (1986). Once more on the equilibrium-point hypothesis (1 model) for motor control. *Journal of Motor Behavior, 18,* 17–54.

Femina, D. D., Yeager, C. A., & Lewis, D. O. (1990). Child abuse: Adolescent records vs. adult recall. *Child Abuse and Neglect, 14,* 227–231.

Fernberger, S. W. (1921). A preliminary study of the range of visual apprehension. *American Journal of Psychology, 32,* 121–133.

Ferreira, F., & Clifton, C. (1986). The independence of syntactic processing. *Journal of Memory & Language, 25*(3), 348–368.

Feynman, R. P., & Leighton, R. (1985). *"Surely you're joking, Mr. Feynman!": Adventures of a curious character.* New York: Bantam.

Fiedler, K., Brinkmann, B., Betsch, T., & Wild, B. (2000). A sampling approach to biases in conditional probability judgments: Beyond base rate neglect and statistical format. *Journal of Experimental Psychology: General, 129*, 399–418.

Finke, R. A. (1980). Levels of equivalence in imagery and perception. *Psychological Review, 87*(2), 113–132.

Finke, R. A. (1996). Imagery, creativity, and emergent structure. *Consciousness & Cognition: An International Journal, 5*(3), 381–393.

Finke, R. A., Pinker, S., & Farah, M. J. (1989). Reinterpreting visual patterns in mental imagery. *Cognitive Science, 13*(1), 51–78.

Finke, R. A., & Shepard, R. N. (1986). Visual functions of mental imagery. In K. R. Boff & L. Kaufman (Eds.), *Handbook of perception and human performance* (Vol. 2, pp. 1–55). New York: Wiley.

Finkenauer, C., Luminet, O., Gisle, L., El-Ahmadi, A., Van der Linden, M., & Philippot, P. (1998). Flashbulb memories and the underlying mechanisms of their formation: Toward an emotional-integrative model. *Memory & Cognition, 26*, 516–531.

Flash, T., & Gurevich, I. (1997) Models of motor adaptation and impedance control in human arm movements. In P. Morasso & V. Sanguineti (Eds.) *Self-organization, computational maps and motor control* (pp. 423–481). Amsterdam: Elsevier.

Flash, T., & Hogan, N. (1985). The coordination of arm movements: An experimentally confirmed mathematical model. *The Journal of Neuroscience, 5*, 1688–1703.

Fleishman, E. A., & Parker, J. F. (1962). Factors in the retention and relearning of perceptual motor skill. *Journal of Experimental Psychology, 64*, 215–226.

Fletcher, C. R., & Chrysler, S. T. (1990). Surface forms, textbases, and situation models: Recognition memory for three types of textual information. *Discourse Processes, 13*(2), 175–190.

Fletcher, P. C., Frith, C. D., Baker, S. C., Shallice, T., Frackowiak, R. S., & Dolan, R. J. (1995). The mind's eye: Precuneus activation in memory-related imagery. *Neuroimage, 2*, 195–200.

Fletcher, P. C., & Henson, R. N. A. (2001). Frontal lobes and human memory: Insights from functional neuroimaging. *Brain, 124*, 849–881.

Fleury, M., Bard, C., Teasdale, N., Paillard, J., Cole, J., Lujoie, Y., & Lamarre C. Y. (1995). Weight judgment:

The discrimination capacity of a deafferented subject. *Brain, 118*, 1149–1156.

Fodor, J. A., & Garrett, M. (1967). Some syntactic determinants of sentential complexity. *Perception and Psychophysics, 2*(7), 289–296.

Fodor, J. D. (1995). Comprehending sentence structure. In L. R. Gleitman & M. Liberman (Eds.), *An invitation to cognitive science* (Vol. 1, pp. 209–246). Cambridge, MA: MIT Press.

Forget, R., & Lamarre, Y. (1987). Rapid elbow flexion in the absence of proprioceptive and cutaneous feedback. *Human Neurobiology, 6*, 27–37.

Forster, K. I., & Chambers, S. M. (1973). Lexical access and naming time. *Journal of Verbal Learning & Verbal Behavior, 12*(6), 627–635.

Foulke, E., & Sticht, T. G. (1969). Review of research on the intelligibility and comprehension of accelerated speech. *Psychological Bulletin, 72*(1), 50–62.

Franz, V. H., Gegenfurtner, K. R., Buelthoff, H. H., & Fahle, M. (2000). Grasping visual illusions: No evidence for a dissociation between perception and action. *Psychological Science, 11*, 20–25.

Frazier, L., & Clifton, C. Jr. (1996). *Construal.* Cambridge, MA: MIT Press.

French, R. M., & Chater, N. (2002). Using noise to compute error surfaces in connectionist networks: A novel means of reducing catastrophic forgetting. *Neural Computation, 14*, 1755–1769.

Freyd, J. J. (1987). Dynamic mental representation. *Psychological Review, 94*, 427–438.

Freyd, J. J., & Finke, R. A. (1984). Representational momentum. *Journal of Experimental Psychology: Learning, Memory, and Cognition, 10*(1), 126–132.

Funnell, E. (1983). Phonological processes in reading: New evidence from acquired dyslexia. *British Journal of Psychology, 74*(2), 159–180.

Gabrieli, J. D. E. (1998). Cognitive neuroscience of human memory. *Annual Review of Psychology, 49*, 87–115.

Gabrieli, J. D. E., Fleischman, D. A., Keane, M. M., Reminger, S. L., & Morrell, F. (1995). Double dissociation between memory systems underlying explicit and implicit memory in the human brain. *Psychological Science, 6*, 76–82.

Gallistel, C. R. (1990). *The organization of learning.* Cambridge, MA: MIT Press.

Galton, F. (1883). *Inquiries into human faculty and its development.* London: Macmillan.

Gardner, B. T., & Gardner, R. A. (1967). Teaching sign language to a chimpanzee: II. Demonstrations. *Psychonomic Bulletin, 1*(2), 36.

Gardner, B. T., & Gardner, R. A. (1975). Evidence for sentence constitutents in the early utterances of child and chimpanzee. *Journal of Experimental Psychology: General, 104*(3), 244–267.

Gardner, H. (1976). *The shattered mind.* New York: Vintage.

Gardner, H. (1985). *The mind's new science: A history of the cognitive revolution.* New York: Basic Books.

Gardner, R. A., & Gardner, B. T. (1967). Teaching sign language to a chimpanzee: I. Methodology and preliminary results. *Psychonomic Bulletin, 1*(2), 36.

Gardner, R. A., Gardner, B. T., & Van Cantfort, T. E. (Eds.). (1989). *Teaching sign language to chimpanzees.* Albany: State University of New York Press.

Gaskell, M. G., & Marslen-Wilson, W. D. (1996). Phonological variation and inference in lexical access. *Journal of Experimental Psychology: Human Perception and Performance, 22*(1), 144–158.

Gaskell, M. G., & Marslen-Wilson, W. D. (1998). Mechanisms of phonological inference in speech perception. *Journal of Experimental Psychology: Human Perception and Performance, 24*(2), 380–396.

Gauthier, I., Skudlarski, P., Gore, J. C., & Anderson, A. W. (2000) Expertise for cars and birds recruits brain areas involved in face recognition. *Nature Neuroscience 3,* 191–197.

Gauthier, I., Tarr, M. J., Anderson, A. W., Skudlarski, P., & Gore, J. C. (1999). Activation of the middle fusiform "face area" increases with expertise in recognizing novel objects. *Nature Neuroscience, 2*(6), 568–573.

Gebauer, G., & Laming, D. (1997). Rational choices in Wason's selection task. *Psychological Research, 60*(4), 284–293.

Gentilucci, M., Chieffi, S., Daprati, E., Saetti, M. C., & Toni, I. (1996). Visual illusion and action. *Neuropsychologia, 34,* 369–376.

Gentner, D., Rattermann, M. J., & Forbus, K. D. (1993). The roles of similarity in transfer: Separating retrievability from inferential soundness. *Cognitive Psychology, 25,* 431–467.

Georgopoulos, A. P., Lurito, J. T., Petrides, M., Schwartz, A. B., & Massey, J. T. (1989). Mental rotation of the neuronal population vector. *Science, 243,* 234–236.

German, T. P., & Defeyter, M. A. (2000). Immunity to functional fixedness in young children. *Psychonomic Bulletin and Review, 7,* 707–712.

Gernsbacher, M. A. (Ed.). (1994). *Handbook of psycholinguistics.* San Diego: Academic Press.

Gershberg, F. B., & Shimamura, A. P. (1995). Impaired use of organizational strategies in free recall following frontal lobe damage. *Neuropsychologia, 33*(10), 1305–1333.

Ghez, C., Gordon, J., Ghilardi, M. F., & Sainburg, R. (1995). Contributions of vision and proprioception to accuracy in limb movements. In M. S. Gazzaniga (Ed.), *The cognitive neurosciences* (pp. 549–564). Cambridge, MA: MIT Press.

Gibson, E. (1998). Linguistic complexity: Locality of syntactic dependencies. *Cognition 68,* 1–76.

Gibson, J. J. (1979). *The ecological approach to visual perception.* Boston: Houghton Mifflin.

Gick, M. L., & Holyoak, K. J. (1980). Analogical problem solving. *Cognitive Psychology, 12*(3), 306–355.

Gick, M. L., & Holyoak, K. J. (1983). Schema induction and analogical transfer. *Cognitive Psychology, 15*(1), 1–38.

Gigerenzer, G. (1992). How to make cognitive illusions disappear: Beyond "Heuristics and Biases." *European Review of Social Psychology, 2,* 83–115.

Gigerenzer, G. (2001). Content-blind norms, no norms, or good norms? A reply to Vranas. *Cognition, 81,* 93–103.

Gigerenzer, G., Hell, W., & Blank, H. (1988). Presentation and content: The use of base rates as a continuous variable. *Journal of Experimental Psychology: Human Perception and Performance, 14,* 513–525.

Gigerenzer, G., & Hoffrage, U. (1995). How to improve Bayesian reasoning without instruction: Frequency formats. *Psychological Review, 102*(4), 684–704.

Gigerenzer, G., & Hoffrage, U. (1999). Overcoming difficulties in Bayesian reasoning: A reply to Lewis and Keren (1999) and Mellers and McGraw (1999). *Psychological Review, 106,* 425–430.

Gigerenzer, G., Hoffrage, U., & Ebert, A. (1998). AIDS counselling for low-risk clients. *AIDS CARE, 10,* 197–211.

Gigerenzer, G., Hoffrage, U., & Kleinbölting, H. (1991). Probabilistic mental models: A Brunswikian theory of confidence. *Psychological Review, 98*(4), 506–528.

Gigerenzer, G., & Hug, K. (1992). Domain-specific reasoning: Social contracts, cheating, and perspective change. *Cognition, 43*(2), 127–171.

Gigerenzer, G., & Todd, P. M. (1999). Fast and frugal heuristics: The adaptive toolbox. In G. Gigerenzer, P. Todd, & the ABC Research Group (Eds.), *Simple heuristics that make us smart. Evolution and cognition* (pp. 3–34). New York: Oxford University Press.

Gilchrist, A. L. (1997). Perceived lightness depends on perceived spatial arrangement. In I. Rock (Ed.), *Indirect perception* (pp. 351–356). Cambridge, MA: MIT Press.

Gilhooly, K. J., Logie, R. H., Wetherick, N. E., & Wynn, V. (1993). Working memory and strategies in syllogistic-reasoning tasks. *Memory & Cognition, 21*(1), 115–124.

Gilhooly, K. J., Wood, M., Kinnear, P. R., & Green, C. (1988). Skill in map reading and memory for maps. *Quarterly Journal of Experimental Psychology: Human Experimental Psychology, 40,* 87–107.

Girotto, V., & Gonzalez, M. (2001). Solving probabilistic and statistical problems: A matter of information structure and question form. *Cognition, 78,* 247–276.

Glanville, A. D., & Dallenbach, K. M. (1929). The range of attention. *American Journal of Psychology, 41,* 207–236.

Glanzer, M., & Cunitz, A. R. (1966). Two storage mechanisms in free recall. *Journal of Verbal Learning & Verbal Behavior, 5*(4), 351–360.

Glenberg, A. M. (1997). What memory is for. *Behavioural and Brain Sciences, 20,* 1–55.

Glenberg, A. M., & Langston, W. E. (1992). Comprehension of illustrated text: Pictures help to build mental models. *Journal of Memory & Language, 31*(2), 129–151.

Gobet, F., Lane, P. C. R., Croker, S., Cheng, P. C-H., Jones, G., Oliver, I., & Pine, J.M. (2001). Chunking mechanisms in human learning. *Trends in Cognitive Sciences, 5,* 236–243.

Gobet, F., & Simon, H. A. (1996). The roles of recognition processes and look-ahead search in time-constrained expert problem solving: Evidence from grand-master–level chess. *Psychological Science, 7*(1), 52–55.

Gobet, F., & Simon, H. A. (1998). Expert chess memory: Revisiting the chunking hypothesis. *Memory, 6*(3), 225–255.

Godden, D. R., & Baddeley, A. D. (1975). Context-dependent memory in two natural environments: On land and underwater. *British Journal of Psychology, 66*(3), 325–331.

Goel, V., Gold, B., Kapur, S., & Houle, S. (1997). The seats of reason? An imaging study of deductive and inductive reasoning. *NeuroReport, 8,* 1305–1310.

Goel, V., Gold, B., Kapur, S., & Houle, S. (1998). Neuroanatomical correlates of human reasoning. *Journal of Cognitive Neuroscience, 10*(3), 293–302.

Goldman, W. P., Wolters, N. C., & Winograd, E. (1992). A demonstration of incubation in anagram problem solving. *Bulletin of the Psychonomic Society, 30*(1), 36–38.

Gomi, H., & Kawato, M. (1996). Equilibrium-point control hypothesis examined by measured arm stiffness during multijoint movement. *Science, 272,* 117–120.

Goodale, M. A., & Milner, A. D. (1992). Separate pathways for vision and action. *Trends in Neurosciences, 15,* 20–25.

Gopher, D., Brickner, M., & Navon, D. (1982). Different difficulty manipulations interact differently with task emphasis: Evidence for multiple resources. *Journal of Experimental Psychology: Human Perception and Performance, 8*(1), 146–157.

Gordon, P. C., & Meyer, D. E. (1987). Control of serial order in rapidly spoken syllable sequences. *Journal of Memory and Language, 26,* 300–321.

Graesser, A. C., Millis, K. K., & Zwaan, R. A. (1997). Discourse comprehension. *Annual Review of Psychology, 48,* 163–189.

Graesser, A. C., Singer, M., & Trabasso, T. (1994). Constructing inferences during narrative text comprehension. *Psychological Review, 101*(3), 371–395.

Graf, P., & Schacter, D. L. (1985). Implicit and explicit memory for new associations in normal and amnesic subjects. *Journal of Experimental Psychology: Learning, Memory, & Cognition, 11,* 501–518.

Graf, P., Shimamura, A. P., & Squire, L. R. (1985). Priming across modalities and priming across category levels: Extending the domain of preserved function in amnesia. *Journal of Experimental Psychology: Learning, Memory, and Cognition, 11*(2), 386–396.

Granger, R., Wiebe, S. P., Taketani, M., & Lynch, G. (1996). Distinct memory circuits composing the hippocampal region. *Hippocampus, 6*(6), 567–578.

Graziano, M. S. A., Taylor, C. S. R., & Moore, T. (2002). Complex movements evoked by microstimulation of precentral cortex. *Neuron, 34,* 841–851.

Graziano, M. S. A., Yap, G. S., & Gross, C. G. (1994). Coding of visual space by premotor neurons. *Science, 266,* 1054–1057.

Greeno, J. G. (1974). Hobbits and orcs: Acquisition of a sequential concept. *Cognitive Psychology, 6*(2), 270–292.

Griggs, R. A. (1984). Memory cueing and instructional effects on Wason's selection task. *Current Psychological Research & Reviews, 3*(4), 3–10.

Griggs, R. A., & Cox, J. R. (1982). The elusive thematic-materials effect in Wason's selection task. *British Journal of Psychology, 73*(3), 407–420.

Guiora, A., Beit-Halachmi, B., Fried, R., & Yoder, C. (1983). Language environment and gender identity attainment. *Language Learning, 32,* 289–304.

Gustin, W. C. (1985). The development of exceptional research mathematicians. In B. S. Bloom (Ed.), *Developing talent in young people* (pp. 270–331). New York: Ballantine.

Haber, R. N. (1983). The impending demise of the icon: A critique of the concept of iconic storage in visual information processing. *Behavioral & Brain Sciences, 6*(1), 1–54.

Haffenden, A. M., & Goodale, M. A. (1998). The effect of pictorial illusion on prehension and perception. *Journal of Cognitive Neuroscience, 10*(1), 122–136.

Haffenden, A. M., & Goodale, M. A. (2000). Independent effects of pictorial displays on perception and action. *Vision Research, 40,* 1597–1607.

Hakes, D. T., & Cairns, H. S. (1970). Sentence comprehension and relative pronouns. *Perception and Psychophysics, 8*(1), 5–8.

Hakes, D. T., & Foss, D. J. (1970). Decision processes during sentence comprehension: Effects of surface structure reconsidered. *Perception and Psychophysics, 8*(6), 413–416.

Hakuta, K. (1986). *Mirror of language.* New York: Basic Books.

Hambrick, D. Z., & Engle, R. W. (2002). Effects of domain knowledge, working memory capacity, and age on cognitive performance: An investigation of the knowledge-is-power hypothesis. *Cognitive Psychology, 44,* 339–387.

Hamker, F. H. (2001). Life-long learning cell structures—continuously learning without catastrophic interference. *Neural Networks, 14,* 551–573.

Hampton, J. A. (1995). Testing the prototype theory of concepts. *Journal of Memory & Language, 34*(5), 686–708.

Harris, J. A., Miniussi, C., Harris, I. M., Diamond, M. E. (2002). Transient storage of a tactile memory trace in primary somatosensory cortext. *Journal of Neuroscience, 22,* 8720–8725.

Harris, M., & Coltheart, M. (1986). *Language processing in children and adults.* London: Routledge & Kegan Paul.

Hart, J. T. (1965). Memory and the feeling-of-knowing experience. *Journal of Educational Psychology, 56,* 208–216.

Hart, J. T. (1967). Memory and the memory-monitoring process. *Journal of Verbal Learning & Verbal Behavior, 6*(5), 685–691.

Hasan, Z. (1986). Optimized movement trajectories and joint stiffness in unperturbed, inertially loaded movements. *Biological Cybernetics, 53,* 373–382.

Hassebrock, F., Johnson, P. E., Bullemer, P., Fox, P. W., & Moller, J. H. (1993). When less is more: Representation and selective memory in expert problem solving. *American Journal of Psychology, 106*(2), 155–189.

Haxby, J. V., Gobbini, M. I., Furey, M. L., Ishai, A., Schouten, J. L., & Pietrini, P. (2001) Distributed and overlapping representations of faces and objects in ventral temporal cortex. *Science, 293,* 2425–2430.

Hayes, J. R. (1981). *The complete problem solver.* Philadelphia: Franklin Institute Press.

Hayman, C. A., Macdonald, C. A., & Tulving, E. (1993). The role of repetition and associative interference in new semantic learning in amnesia: A case experiment. *Journal of Cognitive Neuroscience, 5*(4), 375–389.

Hebb, D. O. (1949). *The organization of behavior.* New York: Wiley.

Hebb, D. O. (1968). Concerning imagery. *Psychological Review, 75,* 466–477.

Heider, E. R. (1972). Universals in color naming and memory. *Journal of Experimental Psychology, 93*(1), 10–20.

Heider, E. R., & Oliver, D. C. (1972). The structure of the color space in naming and memory for two languages. *Cognitive Psychology, 3*(2), 337–354.

Helmholtz, H. L. F. von. (1910/1962). *Treatise on physiological optics* (J. P. Southall, Trans., Vol. 3). New York: Dover.

Henry, F. M., & Rogers, D. E. (1960). Increased response latency for complicated movements and a "memory drum" theory of neuromotor reaction. *Research Quarterly of the American Association for Health, Physical Education, & Recreation, 31,* 448–458.

Hess, D. J., Foss, D. J., & Carroll, P. (1995). Effects of global and local context on lexical processing during language comprehension. *Journal of Experimental Psychology: General, 124*(1), 62–82.

Hess, E. H. (1958). "Imprinting" in animals. *Scientific American, 198,* 81–90.

Hikosaka, O., Nakamura, K., Sakai, K., Nakahara, H. (2002). Central mechanisms of motor skill learning. *Current Opinion in Neurobiology, 12,* 217–222.

Hintzman, D. L. (1992). Mathematical constraints and the Tulving–Wiseman law. *Psychological Review, 99*(3), 536–542.

Hoffman, D. D., & Richards, W. A. (1984). Parts of recognition. *Cognition, 18*(1–3), 65–96.

Hoffrage, U., Gigerenzer, G., Krauss, S., & Martignon, L. (2002). Representation facilitates reasoning: What natural frequencies are and what they are not. *Cognition, 84,* 343–352.

Hoffrage, U., Lindsey, S., Hertwig, R., & Gigerenzer, G. (2000). Communicating statistical information. *Science, 290*, 2261–2262.

Holding, D. H. (1976). An approximate transfer surface. *Journal of Motor Behavior, 8*, 1–9.

Holyoak, K. J., & Cheng, P. W. (1995). Pragmatic reasoning about human voluntary action: Evidence from Wason's selection task. In S. E. Newstead & J. St. B. T. Evans (Eds.), *Perspectives on thinking and reasoning: Essays in honour of Peter Wason* (pp. 67–89). Hillsdale, NJ: Erlbaum.

Holyoak, K. J., & Koh, K. (1987). Surface and structural similarity in analogical transfer. *Memory & Cognition, 15*(4), 332–340.

Holyoak, K. J., & Thagard, P. R. (1989). A computational model of analogical problem solving. In S. O. A. Vosniadou (Ed.), *Similarity and analogical reasoning* (pp. 242–266). New York: Cambridge University Press.

Howe, M. L., Rabinowitz, F. M., & Powell, T. L. (1998). Individual differences in working memory and reasoning–remembering relationships in solving class-inclusion problems. *Memory & Cognition, 26*(5), 1089–1101.

Hubel, D. H., & Wiesel, T. N. (1979). Brain mechanisms of vision. *Scientific American, 241*(3), 150–162.

Huber, J., Payne, J. W., & Puto, C. (1982). Adding asymmetrically dominated alternatives: Violations of regularity and the similarity hypothesis. *Journal of Consumer Research, 9*, 90–98.

Hull, C. (1920). Quantitative aspects of the evolution of concepts. *Psychological Monographs* (Whole no. 123).

Hunt, E., & Agnoli, F. (1991). The Whorfian hypothesis: A cognitive psychology perspective. *Psychological Review, 98*(3), 377–389.

Huppert, F. A., & Piercy, M. (1978). Dissociation between learning and remembering in organic amnesia. *Nature, 275*(5678), 317–318.

Hyde, T. S., & Jenkins, J. J. (1973). Recall for words as a function of semantic, graphic, and syntactic orienting tasks. *Journal of Verbal Learning & Verbal Behavior, 12*(5), 471–480.

Intons-Peterson, M. J. (1981). Constructing and using unusual and common images. *Journal of Experimental Psychology: Human Learning & Memory, 7*(2), 133–144.

Ironsmith, M., & Lutz, J. (1996). The effects of bizarreness and self-generation on mnemonic imagery. *Journal of Mental Imagery, 20*(3–4), 113–126.

Irwin, D. E. (1993). Perceiving an integrated visual world. In D. Meyer & S. Kornblum (Eds.), *Attention and performance XIV: Synergies in experimental psychology, artificial intelligence, and cognitive neuroscience* (pp. 121–142). Cambridge, MA: MIT Press.

Irwin, D. E., Yantis, S., & Jonides, J. (1983). Evidence against visual integration across saccadic eye movements. *Perception and Psychophysics, 34*(1), 49–57.

Ishai, A., Ungerleider, L. G., Martin, A., & Haxby, J. V. (2000). The representation of objects in the human occipital and temporal cortex. *Journal of Cognitive Neuroscience, 12 Suppl 2*, 35–51.

Itard, J.-M. G. (1962). *The wild boy of Aveyron*. New York: Appleton-Century-Crofts.

James, W. (1890). *Principles of psychology*. New York: Holt.

Janiszewski, C., & Meyvis, T. (2001). Effects of brand logo complexity, repetition, and spacing on processing fluency and judgment. *Journal of Consumer Research, 28*, 18–32.

Jansma, J. M., Ramsey, N. F., Slagter, H. A., & Kahn, R. S. (2001). Functional anatomical correlates of controlled and automatic processing. *Journal of Cognitive Neuroscience, 13*, 730–743.

Jevons, W. S. (1871). The power of numerical discrimination. *Nature, 3*, 281–282.

Johnson, K. E., & Mervis, C. B. (1997). Effects of varying levels of expertise on the basic level of categorization. *Journal of Experimental Psychology: General, 126*(3), 248–277.

Johnson, M. K., & Hasher, L. (1987). Human learning and memory. *Annual Review of Psychology, 38*, 631–668.

Johnson-Laird, P. N. (1999). Deductive reasoning. *Annual Review of Psychology, 50*, 109–135.

Johnson-Laird, P. N., & Bara, B. G. (1984). Syllogistic inference. *Cognition, 16*(1), 1–61.

Johnson-Laird, P. N., & Byrne, R. M. (1991). *Deduction*. Mahwah, NJ: Erlbaum.

Johnson-Laird, P. N., Byrne, R. M., & Schaeken, W. (1992). Propositional reasoning by model. *Psychological Review, 99*(3), 418–439.

Johnson-Laird, P. N., Legrenzi, P., Girotto, V., Legrenzi, M. S., & Caverni, J.-P. (1999). Naive probability: A mental model theory of extensional reasoning. *Psychological Review, 106*, 62–88.

Johnson-Laird, P. N., Legrenzi, P., Girotto, V., & Legrenzi, M. S. (2000). Illusions in reasoning about consistency. *Science, 288*, 531–532.

Johnson-Laird, P. N., & Savary, F. (1999). Illusory inferences: A novel class of erroneous deductions. *Cognition, 71*(3), 191–229.

Johnston, W. A., & Heinz, S. P. (1978). Flexibility and capacity demands of attention. *Journal of Experimental Psychology: General, 107*(4), 420–435.

Jolicoeur, P. (1990). Identification of disoriented objects: A dual systems theory. *Mind and Language, 5,* 387–410.

Jolicoeur, P. (1998). Modulation of the attentional blink by on-line response selection: Evidence from speeded and unspeeded Task-sub-1 decisions. *Memory & Cognition, 26,* 1014–1032.

Jolicoeur, P., & Kosslyn, S. M. (1985). Is time to scan visual image due to demand characteristics? *Memory & Cognition, 13,* 320–332.

Joseph, J. S., Chun, M. M., Nakayama, K. (1997). Attentional requirements in a "preattentive" feature search task. *Nature, 387,* 805–807.

Julesz, B. (1971). *Foundations of cyclopean perception.* Chicago: University of Chicago Press.

Just, M. A., & Carpenter, P. A. (1992). A capacity theory of comprehension: Individual differences in working memory. *Psychological Review, 99*(1), 122–149.

Kahneman, D. (1973). *Attention and effort.* New York: Prentice Hall.

Kahneman, D., Knetsch, J. L., & Thaler, R. (1990). Experimental tests of the endowment effect and the Coase theorem. *Journal of Political Economy, 98,* 1325–1348.

Kahneman, D., & Tversky, A. (1973). On the psychology of prediction. *Psychological Review, 80*(4), 237–251.

Kako, E. (1999). Elements of syntax in the systems of three language-trained animals. *Animal Learning and Behavior, 27,* 1–14.

Kaplan, C. A., & Simon, H. A. (1990). In search of insight. *Cognitive Psychology, 22*(3), 374–419.

Keane, M. (1987). On retrieving analogues when solving problems. *Quarterly Journal of Experimental Psychology: Human Experimental Psychology, 39*(1-A), 29–41.

Keane, M. M., Gabrieli, J. D. E., Fennema, A. C., Growdon, J. H., & Corkin, S. (1991). Evidence for a dissociation between perceptual and conceptual priming in Alzheimer's disease. *Behavioral Neuroscience, 105,* 326–342.

Keele, S. W. (1981). Behavioral analysis of movement. In J. M. Brookhart, V. B. Mountcastle, & V. B. Brooks (Eds.), *Handbook of Physiology* (Vol. II, Motor Control, pp. 1391–1414). Bethesda, MD: American Physiological Society.

Keele, S. W., Cohen, A., & Ivry, R. (1990). Motor programs: concepts and issues. In M. Jeannerod (Ed.), *Attention and Performance XIII* (pp. 77–110). Hillsdale, NJ: Erlbaum.

Keele, S. W., & Posner, M. I. (1968). Processing visual feedback in rapid movement. *Journal of Experimental Psychology, 77,* 155–178.

Kelly, M. H., Bock, J. K., & Keil, F. C. (1986). Prototypicality in a linguistic context: Effects on sentence structure. *Journal of Memory & Language, 25*(1), 59–74.

Keppel, G., & Underwood, B. J. (1962). Proactive inhibition in short-term retention of single items. *Journal of Verbal Learning & Verbal Behavior, 1*(3), 153–161.

Kerr, N. H. (1987). Locational representation in imagery: The third dimension. *Memory & Cognition, 15*(6), 521–530.

Kerzel, D., & Bekkering, H. (2000). Motor activation from visible speech: Evidence from stimulus response compatibility. *Journal of Experimental Psychology: Human Perception & Performance, 26,* 634–647.

King, J., & Just, M. A. (1991). Individual differences in syntactic processing: The role of working memory. *Journal of Memory & Language, 30*(5), 580–602.

Kintsch, W. (1988). The role of knowledge in discourse comprehension: A construction integration model. *Psychological Review, 95*(2), 163–182.

Kirby, K. N. (1994). Probabilities and utilities of fictional outcomes in Wason's four-card selection task. *Cognition, 51,* 1–28.

Klapp, S. T., Anderson, W. G., & Berrian, R. W. (1973). Implicit speech in reading: Reconsidered. *Journal of Experimental Psychology, 100,* 368–374.

Klauer, K. C., Musch, J., & Naumer, B. (2000). On belief bias in syllogistic reasoning. *Psychological Review, 107,* 852–884.

Klein, R. (1988). Inhibitory tagging system facilitates visual search. *Nature, 334,* 430–431.

Knoblich, G., Ohlsson, S., Haider, H., & Rhemius, D. (1999). Constraint relaxation and chunk decomposition in insight problem solving. *Journal of Experimental Psychology: Learning, Memory, and Cognition, 25*(6), 1534–1536.

Koelega, H. S., Brinkman, J.-A., Hendriks, L., & Verbaten, M. N. (1989). Processing demands, effort, and individual differences in four different vigilance tasks. *Human Factors, 31*(1), 45–62.

Koelsch, S., Schroger, E., & Tervaniemi, M. (1999). Superior pre-attentive auditory processing in musicians. *NeuroReport, 10,* 1309–1313.

Kohler, W. (1929). *Gestalt psychology.* New York: Liveright.

Kolodner, J. L. (1992). An introduction to case-based reasoning. *Artificial Intelligence Review, 6*(1), 3–34.

Kolodner, J. L. (1994). From natural language understanding to case-based reasoning and beyond: A perspective on the cognitive model that ties it all together. In R. C. L. E. Schank (Ed.), *Beliefs, reasoning, and decision making: Psycho-logic in honor of Bob Abelson* (pp. 55–110). Mahwah, NJ: Erlbaum.

Kopelman, M. D. (2002). Disorders of memory. *Brain, 125*, 2152–2190.

Kopferman, H. (1930). Psychologishe Untersuchungen uber die Wirkung Zwei-dimensionaler korperlicher Gibilde. *Psychologicshe Forschung, 13*, 293–364.

Kosslyn, S. M. (1973). Scanning visual images: Some structural implications. *Perception and Psychophysics, 14*(1), 90–94.

Kosslyn, S. M. (1975). Information representation in visual images. *Cognitive Psychology, 7*(3), 341–370.

Kosslyn, S. M. (1976). Using imagery to retrieve semantic information: A developmental study. *Child Development, 47*(2), 434–444.

Kosslyn, S. M. (1980). *Image and mind*. Cambridge, MA: Harvard University Press.

Kosslyn, S. M. (1994). *Image and brain: The resolution of the imagery debate*. Cambridge, MA: MIT Press.

Kosslyn, S. M. (1995). Mental imagery. In S. M. Kosslyn (Ed.), *Visual cognition: An invitation to cognitive science* (Vol. 2, pp. 267–296). Cambridge, MA: MIT Press.

Kosslyn, S. M., Ball, T. M., & Reiser, B. J. (1978). Visual images preserve metric spatial information: Evidence from studies of image scanning. *Journal of Experimental Psychology: Human Perception and Performance, 4*(1), 47–60.

Kosslyn, S. M., Cave, C. B., Provost, D. A., & von Gierke, S. M. (1988). Sequential processes in image generation. *Cognitive Psychology, 20*(3), 319–343.

Kosslyn, S. M., Flynn, R. A., Amsterdam, J. B., & Wang, G. (1990). Components of high-level vision: A cognitive neuroscience analysis and accounts of neurological syndromes. *Cognition, 34*(3), 203–277.

Kosslyn, S. M., & Schwartz, S. P. (1977). A stimulation of visual imagery. *Cognitive Science, 1*, 265–295.

Kosslyn, S. M., Thompson, W. L., & Alpert, N. M. (1997). Neural systems shared by visual imagery and visual perception: A positron emission tomography study. *Neuroimage, 6*, 320–334.

Kotovsky, K., Hayes, J. R., & Simon, H. A. (1985). Why are some problems hard? Evidence from Tower of Hanoi. *Cognitive Psychology, 17*(2), 248–294.

Kotovsky, K., & Simon, H. A. (1990). What makes some problems really hard: Explorations in the problem space of difficulty. *Cognitive Psychology, 22*(2), 143–183.

Kubovy, M. (1983). Mental imagery majestically transforming cognitive psychology. *Contemporary Psychology, 28*, 661–664.

Kubovy, M., Cohen, D. J., & Hollier, J. (1999). Feature integration that routinely occurs without focal attention. *Psychonomic Bulletin & Review, 6*, 183–203.

Kuhl, P. K. (1989). On babies, birds, modules, and mechanisms: A comparative approach to the acquisition of vocal communication. In R. Dooling & S. H. Hulse (Eds.), *The comparative psychology of audition: Perceiving complex sounds* (pp. 379–419). Mahwah, NJ: Erlbaum.

Kwak, H.-W., Dagenbach, D., & Egeth, H. (1991). Further evidence for a time-independent shift of the focus of attention. *Perception and Psychophysics, 49*(5), 473–480.

Kyllonen, P. C., & Christal, R. E. (1990). Reasoning ability is (little more than) working-memory capacity? *Intelligence, 14*(4), 389–433.

Laeng, B., & Teodorescu, D.-S. (2002). Eye scanpaths during visual imagery reenact those of perception of the same visual scene. *Cognitive Science, 26*, 207–231.

Lahiri, A., & Marslen-Wilson, W. (1991). The mental representation of lexical form: A phonological approach to the recognition lexicon. *Cognition, 38*(3), 245–294.

Laming, D. (1996). On the analysis of irrational data selection: A critique of Oaksford and Chater (1994). *Psychological Review, 103*(2), 364–373.

Larkin, J., McDermott, J., Simon, D. P., & Simon, H. A. (1980). Expert and novice performance in solving physics problems. *Science, 208*(4450), 1335–1342.

Lashley, K. S. (1951). The problem of serial order in behavior. In L. A. Jeffress (Ed.), *Cerebral mechanisms in behavior* (pp. 112–131). New York: Wiley.

Le Bihan, D., Turner, R., Zeffiro, T. A., Cuenod, C. A., Jezzard, P., & Bonnerot, V. (1993). Activation of human primary visual cortex during visual recall: A magnetic resonance imaging study. *Proceedings of the National Academy of Sciences of the United States of America, 90*, 11802–11805.

Leake, D. B. (1998). Case-based reasoning. In W. Bechtel & G. Graham (Eds.), *A companion to cognitive science*. Malden, MA: Blackwell.

Leavitt, F. (2002) "The reality of repressed memories" revisited and principles of science. *Journal of Trauma & Dissociation, 3*, 19–35.

Lee, D., & Chun, M. M. (2001). What are the units of visual short-term memory, objects or spatial locations? *Perception & Psychophysics, 63*, 253–257.

Lee-Sammons, W. H., & Whitney, P. (1991). Reading perspectives and memory for text: An individual differences analysis. *Journal of Experimental Psychology: Learning, Memory, and Cognition, 17*(6), 1074–1081.

LeFevre, J.-A., & Dixon, P. (1986). Do written instructions need examples? *Cognition & Instruction,* 3(1), 1–30.

Leopold, R. L., & Dillon, H. (1963). Psycho-anatomy of a disaster: A long term study of post-traumatic neuroses in survivors of a marine explosion. *American Journal of Psychiatry, 119,* 913–921.

Lesgold, A. M. (1984). Acquiring expertise. In J. R. Anderson & S. M. Kosslyn (Eds.), *Tutorials in learning and memory: Essays in honor of Gordon Bower.* New York: Freeman.

Levine, D. N., Warach, J., & Farah, M. J. (1985). Two visual systems in mental imagery: Dissociation of "what" and "where" in imagery disorders due to bilateral posterior cerebral lesions. *Neurology, 35*(7), 1010–1018.

Levy, B. J., & Anderson, M. C. (2002). Inhibitory processes and the control of memory retrieval. *Trends in Cognitive Sciences, 6,* 299–305.

Levy, W. B. (1996). A sequence predicting CA3 is a flexible associator that learns and uses context to solve hippocampal-like tasks. *Hippocampus, 6*(6), 579–590.

Lewandowsky, S., & Li, S.-C. (1995). Catastrophic interference in neural networks: Causes, solutions, and data. In F. N. Dempster & C. J. Brainerd (Eds.), *Interference and inhibition in cognition* (pp. 329–361). San Diego: Academic Press.

Lewis, C., & Keren, G. (1999). On the difficulties underlying Bayesian reasoning: A comment on Gigerenzer and Hoffrage. *Psychological Review, 106*(2), 411–416.

Lezak, M. D. (1995). *Neuropsychological assessment.* New York: Oxford University Press.

Liberman, A. M., Cooper, F. S., & Shankweiler, D. P. (1967). *Human performance in low signal tasks.* Ann Arbor: University of Michigan Press.

Liberman, A. M., Harris, K. S., Hoffman, H. S., & Griffith, B. C. (1957). The discrimination of speech sounds within and across phoneme boundaries. *Journal of Experimental Psychology, 54,* 358–368.

Liberman, A. M., & Mattingly, I. G. (1985). The motor theory of speech perception revised. *Cognition, 21*(1), 1–36.

Light, L. L., & Carter-Sobell, L. (1970). Effects of changed semantic context on recognition memory. *Journal of Verbal Learning and Verbal Behavior, 9,* 1–11.

Loftus, E. F., & Loftus, G. R. (1980). On the permanence of stored information in the human brain. *American Psychologist, 35*(5), 409–420.

Loftus, G. R. (1983). The continuing persistence of the icon. *Behavioral and Brain Sciences, 6,* 28.

Logan, G. D. (1988). Toward an instance theory of automatization. *Psychological Review, 95*(4), 492–527.

Logan, G. D. (2002). An instance theory of attention and memory. *Psychological Review, 109,* 376–400.

Logie, R. H., Gilhooly, K. J., & Wynn, V. (1994). Counting on working memory in arithmetic problem solving. *Memory & Cognition, 22*(4), 395–410.

López, A., Atran, S., Coley, J. D., Medin, D. L., & Smith, E. E. (1997). The tree of life: Universal and cultural features of folkbiological taxonomies and inductions. *Cognitive Psychology, 32,* 251–295.

Lordahl, D. S., & Archer, E. J. (1958). Transfer effects on a rotary pursuit task as a function of first-task difficulty. *Journal of Experimental Psychology, 56,* 421–426.

Lotze, M., Montoya, P., Erb, M., Huelsmann, E., Flor, H., Klose, U., Birbaumer, N., & Grodd, W. (1999). Activation of cortical and cerebellar motor areas during executed and imagined hand movements: An fMRI study. *Journal of Cognitive Neuroscience, 11*(5), 491–501.

Lu, Z. L., Williamson, S. J., & Kaufman, L. (1992). Behavioral lifetime of human auditory sensory memory predicted by physiological measures. *Science, 258*(5088), 1668–1670.

Lubinski, D., Webb, R. M., Morelock, M. J., & Benbow, C. P. (2001). Top 1 in 10,000: A 10-year follow-up of the profoundely gifted. *Journal of Applied Psychology, 86,* 718–729.

Luchins, A. S. (1942). Mechanization in problem solving: The effect of Einstellung. *Psychological Monographs* (6), 95.

Luck, S. J., & Vecera, S. P. (2002). Attention. In S. Yantis (Ed.), *Steven's Handbook of Experimental Psychology* (3rd ed.). Vol. 1, Sensation and Perception (pp. 235–286). New York: Wiley.

Luck, S. J., & Vogel, E. K. (1997). The capacity of visual working memory for features and conjunctions. *Nature, 390,* 279–281.

Lucy, J. A. (1992). *Grammatical categories and cognition: A case study of the linguistic relativity hypothesis.* Cambridge: Cambridge University Press.

Lucy, J. A., & Shweder, R. A. (1979). Whorf and his critics: Linguistic and nonlinguistic influences on color memory. *American Anthropologist, 81,* 581–605.

Lyn, H., & Savage-Rumbaugh, E. S. (2000). Observational word learning in two bonobos (Pan paniscus): Ostensive and non-ostensive contexts. *Language & Communication, 20,* 255–273.

Lyons, J., Fontaine, R., & Elliott, D. (1997). I lost it in the lights: The effects of predictable and variable intermittent vision on unimanual catching. *Journal of Motor Behavior, 29,* 113–118.

Lytle, R. A., & Lundy, R. M. (1988). Hypnosis and the recall of visually presented material: A failure to replicate Stager and Lundy. *International Journal of Clinical and Experimental Hypnosis, 36,* 327–335.

Macchi, L. (2000). Partitive formulation of information in probabilistic problems: Beyond heuristics and frequency format explanations. *Organizational Behavior & Human Decision Processes, 82,* 217–236.

MacDonald, A. W. III, Cohen, J. D., Stenger, V. A., & Carter C. S. (2000). Dissociating the role of the dorsolateral prefrontal and anterior cingulate cortex in cognitive control. *Science, 288,* 1835–1838.

MacDonald, J., Andersen, S., & Bachmann, T. (2000). Hearing by eye: How much spatial degradation can be tolerated? *Perception, 29,* 1155–1168.

MacDonald, J., & McGurk, H. (1978). Visual influences on speech perception processes. *Perception and Psychophysics, 24*(3), 253–257.

MacDonald, M. C., Just, M. A., & Carpenter, P. A. (1992). Working memory constraints on the processing of syntactic ambiguity. *Cognitive Psychology, 24*(1), 56–98.

MacDonald, M. C., Pearlmutter, N. J., & Seidenberg, M. S. (1994). The lexical nature of syntactic ambiguity resolution. Psychological Review, 101(4), 676–703.

MacGregor, J. N., Ormerod, T. C., & Chronicle, E. P. (2001). Information processing and insight: A process model of performance on the nine-dot and related problems. *Journal of Experimental Psychology: Learning, Memory, and Cognition, 27,* 176–201.

MacKay, D. G., & Bowman, R. W., Jr. (1969). On producing the meaning in sentences. *American Journal of Psychology, 82,* 23–39.

Macken, W. J. (2001). Environmental context and recognition: The role of recollection and familiarity. *Journal of Experimental Psychology: Learning, Memory, and Cognition, 28,* 153–161.

MacNeilage, P. F., & Davis, B. L. (2000). On the origin of internal structure of word forms. *Science, 288,* 527–531.

Manktelow, K. I., & Evans, J. S. (1979). Facilitation of reasoning by realism: Effect or non-effect? *British Journal of Psychology, 70*(4), 477–488.

Manktelow, K. I., & Over, D. E. (1990). Deontic thought and the selection task. In K. Gilhooly, M. Keane, R. Logie, & G. Erdos (Eds.), *Lines of thinking: Reflections on the psychology of thought* (Vol. 1). Chichester, UK: Wiley.

Manktelow, K. I., & Over, D. E. (1991). Social roles and utilities in reasoning with deontic conditionals. *Cognition, 39*(2), 85–105.

Marbe, K. (1901). *Experimentelle Untersuchungen uber die psycholgischen Grundlagen der sprachlichen Analogiebildung.* Leipzig: Engellmann.

Mark, L. S. (1987). Eyeheight-scaled information about affordances: A study of sitting and stair climbing. *Journal of Experimental Psychology: Human Perception and Performance, 13*(3), 361–370.

Markman, A. B., & Dietrich, E. (2000). In defense of representation. *Cognitive Psychology, 40,* 138–171.

Marr, D. (1982). *Vision.* San Francisco: W.H. Freeman.

Marshall, J. C. (1984). Toward a ratinal taxonomy of the developmental dyslexias. In R. N. Malatesha & H. A. Whitaker (Eds.), *Dyslexia: A global issue.* Dordrecht, The Netherlands: Martinus Nijhoff.

Marshall, J. C., & Newcombe, F. (1973). Patterns of paralexia: A psycholinguistic approach. *Journal of Psycholinguistic Research, 2*(3), 175–199.

Marslen-Wilson, W., Moss, H. E., & van Halen, S. (1996). Perceptual distance and competition in lexical access. *Journal of Experimental Psychology: Human Perception and Performance, 22*(6), 1376–1392.

Marslen-Wilson, W., & Warren, P. (1994). Levels of perceptual representation and process in lexical access: Words, phonemes, and features. *Psychological Review, 101*(4), 653–675.

Marslen-Wilson, W., & Zwitserlood, P. (1989). Accessing spoken words: The importance of word onsets. *Journal of Experimental Psychology: Human Perception and Performance, 15*(3), 576–585.

Marslen-Wilson, W. D. (1987). Functional parallelism in spoken word-recognition. *Cognition, 25*(1–2), 71–102.

Martin, A., Haxby, J. V., Lalonde, F. M., Wiggs, C. L., & Ungerleider, L. G. (1995). Discrete cortical regions associated with knowledge of color and knowledge of action. *Science, 270*(5233), 102–105.

Martin, A., Ungerleider, L. G., & Haxby, J. V. (2000). Category specificity and the brain. In M. S. Gazzaniga (Ed.), *The new cognitive neurosciences* (2nd ed., pp. 1023–1036). Cambridge, MA: MIT Press.

Martin, L. (1986). "Eskimo words for snow": A case study in the genesis and decay of an anthropological example. *American Anthropologist, 88*(2), 418–423.

Martin, T. A., Keating, J. G., Goodkin, H. P., Bastian, A. J., & Thach, W. T. (1996). Throwing while looking through prisms: I. Focal olivocerebellar lesions impair adaptation. *Brain, 119,* 1183–1198.

Massaro, D. W. (1970). Preperceptual auditory images. *Journal of Experimental Psychology, 85*(3), 411–417.

Massaro, D. W. (1989). Testing between the TRACE model and the fuzzy logical model of speech perception. *Cognitive Psychology, 21*(3), 398–421.

Massaro, D. W., & Loftus, G. R. (1996). Sensory and perceptual storage: Data and theory. In E. L. Bjork, & R. A. Bjork (Eds.), *Memory: Handbook of perception and cognition* (2nd ed., pp. 67–99). San Diego: Academic Press.

Massaro, D. W., & Oden, G. C. (1995). Independence of lexical context and phonological information in speech perception. *Journal of Experimental Psychology: Learning, Memory, and Cognition, 21*(4), 1053–1064.

Massion, J. (1984). Postural changes accompanying voluntary movements: Normal and pathological aspects. *Human Neurobiology, 2*, 261–267.

Mayes, A. R., Meudell, P., & Neat, D. (1980). Do amnesics adopt inefficient encoding strategies with faces and random shapes? *Neuropsychologia, 18*(Suppl. 4, 5), 527–540.

Mayes, A. R., & Montaldi, D. (2001). Exploring the neural bases of episodic and semantic memory: The role of structural and functional neuroimaging. *Neuroscience and Biobehavioral Reviews, 25*, 555–573.

McBeath, M. K., Shaffer, D. M., & Kaiser, M. K. (1995). How baseball outfielders determine where to run to catch fly balls. *Science, 268*(5210), 569–573.

McCarthy, R. A., & Warrington, E. K. (1986). Phonological reading: Phenomena and paradoxes. *Cortex, 22*(3), 359–380.

McClelland, J. L. (1981). *Retrieving general and specific knowledge from stored knowledge of specifics.* Paper presented at the Third Annual Conference of the Cognitive Science Society, Berkeley, CA.

McClelland, J. L., & Elman, J. L. (1986). The TRACE model of speech perception. *Cognitive Psychology, 18*(1), 1–86.

McClelland, J. L., & Rumelhart, D. E. (1981). An interactive activation model of context effects in letter perception: I. An account of basic findings. *Psychological Review, 88*(5), 375–407.

McCloskey, M., & Cohen, N. J. (1989). Catastrophic interference in connectionist networks: The sequential learning problem. In G. H. Bower (Ed.), *The psychology of learning and motivation: Advances in research and theory, 24* (pp. 109–165). San Diego: Academic Press.

McCloskey, M., Wible, C. G., & Cohen, N. J. (1988). Is there a special flashbulb-memory mechanism? *Journal of Experimental Psychology: General, 117*(2), 171–181.

McDaniel, M. A., Einstein, G. O., DeLosh, E. L., May, C. P., & Brady, P. (1995). The bizarreness effect: It's not surprising, it's complex. *Journal of Experimental Psychology: Learning, Memory, and Cognition, 21*(2), 422–435.

McGurk, H., & MacDonald, J. (1976). Hearing lips and seeing voices. *Nature, 264*, 746–748.

McIntyre, J., Stratta, F., & Lacquaniti, F. (1998) Short-term memory for reaching to visual targets: Psychophysical evidence for body-centered reference frames. *Journal of Neuroscience, 18*, 8423–8435.

McKoon, G., & Ratcliff, R. (1992). Inference during reading. *Psychological Review, 99*(3), 440–466.

McKoon, G., & Ratcliff, R. (1998). Memory-based language processing: Psycholinguistic research in the 1990s. *Annual Review of Psychology, 49*, 25–42.

McKoon, G., Ratcliff, R., & Dell, G. S. (1986). A critical evaluation of the semantic–episodic distinction. *Journal of Experimental Psychology: Learning, Memory, and Cognition, 12*(2), 295–306.

McNamara, T. P. (1992). Priming and constraints it places on theories of memory and retrieval. *Psychological Review, 99*(4), 650–662.

McNamara, T. P. (1994). Priming and theories of memory: A reply to Ratcliff and McKoon. *Psychological Review, 101*(1), 185–187.

McNamara, T. P., & Healy, A. F. (1988). Semantic, phonological, and mediated priming in reading and lexical decisions. *Journal of Experimental Psychology: Learning, Memory, and Cognition, 14*(3), 398–409.

McNeil, J. E., & Warrington, E. K. (1993). Prosopagnosia: A face-specific disorder. *Quarterly Journal of Experimental Psychology: Human Experimental Psychology, 46A*(1), 1–10.

McRae, K., Spivey-Knowlton, M. J., & Tanenhaus, M. K. (1998). Modeling the influence of thematic fit (and other constraints) in on-line sentence comprehension. *Journal of Memory & Language, 38*, 283–312.

Medin, D. L., & Schaffer, M. M. (1978). Context theory of classification learning. *Psychological Review, 85*, 207–238.

Meinz, E. J., & Salthouse, T. A. (1998). The effects of age and experience on memory for visually presented music. *Journal of Gerontology: Psychological Sciences, 53B*, P60–P69.

Mellers, B. A., & McGraw, A. P. (1999). How to improve Bayesian reasoning: Comment on Gigerenzer and Hoffrage (1995). *Psychological Review, 106*, 417–424.

Mellet, E., Tzourio, N., Denis, M., & Mazoyer, B. (1998). Cortical anatomy of mental imagery of concrete nouns based on their dictionary definition.

Neuroreport: An international journal for the rapid communication of research in neuroscience, 9(5), 803–808.

Melton, A. W., & Irwin, J. M. (1940). The influence of degree of interpolated learning on retroactive inhibition and the overt transfer of specific responses. *American Journal of Psychology, 53,* 173–203.

Metcalfe, J. (1986a). Feeling of knowing in memory and problem solving. *Journal of Experimental Psychology: Learning, Memory, and Cognition, 12*(2), 288–294.

Metcalfe, J. (1986b). Premonitions of insight predict impending error. *Journal of Experimental Psychology: Learning, Memory, and Cognition, 12*(4), 623–634.

Metcalfe, J., & Wiebe, D. (1987). Intuition in insight and noninsight problem solving. *Memory & Cognition, 15*(3), 238–246.

Meyer, D. E., & Schvaneveldt, R. W. (1971). Facilitation in recognizing pairs of words: Evidence of a dependence between retrieval operations. *Journal of Experimental Psychology, 90*(2), 227–234.

Miller, G. A. (1956). The magical number seven, plus or minus two: Some limits on our capacity for processing information. *Psychological Review, 63,* 81–97.

Millis, K. K., & Just, M. A. (1994). The influence of connectives on sentence comprehension. *Journal of Memory & Language, 33*(1), 128–147.

Mitchell, D. C., Corley, M. M., & Garnham, A. (1992). Effects of context in human sentence parsing: Evidence against a discourse-based proposal mechanism. *Journal of Experimental Psychology: Learning, Memory, and Cognition, 18*(1), 69–88.

Miyake, A., Carpenter, P. A., & Just, M. A. (1994). A capacity approach to syntactic comprehension disorders: Making normal adults perform like aphasic patients. *Cognitive Neuropsychology, 11*(6), 671–717.

Monsaas, J. A. (1985). Learning to be a world-class tennis player. In B. S. Bloom (Ed.), *Developing talent in young people* (pp. 211–269). New York: Ballantine.

Moody, D. B., Stebbins, W. C., & May, B. J. (1990). Auditory perception of communication signals by Japanese monkeys. In W. C. Stebbins & M. A. Berkley (Eds.), *Comparative perception* (Vol. 2, pp. 311–343). New York: Wiley.

Moray, N. (1959). Attention in dichotic listening: Affective cues and the influence of instructions. *Quarterly Journal of Experimental Psychology, 11,* 56–60.

Moray, N. (1967). Where is capacity limited? A survey and a model. *Acta Psychologica, 27,* 84–92.

Morraso, P. (1981). Spatial control of arm movements. *Experimental Brain Research, 42,* 223–227.

Morris, C. D., Bransford, J. D., & Franks, J. J. (1977). Levels of processing versus transfer appropriate processing. *Journal of Verbal Learning & Verbal Behavior, 16*(5), 519–533.

Morton, J. (1969). Interaction of information in word recognition. *Psychological Review, 76*(2), 165–178.

Munger, M. P., Solberg, J. L., & Horrocks, K. K. (1999). The relation between mental rotation and representational momentum. *Journal of Experimental Psychology: Learning, Memory, and Cognition, 25,* 1557–1568.

Murdock, B. B. (1974). *Human memory: Theory and data.* Mahwah, NJ: Erlbaum.

Murray, A., & Jones, D. M. (2002). Articulatory complexity at item boundaries in serial recall: The case of Welsh and English digit span. *Journal of Experimental Psychology: Learning, Memory, & Cognition, 28,* 594–598.

Nairne, J. S. (2002) Remembering over the short-term: The case against the standard model. *Annual Review of Psychology, 53,* 53–81.

Nashner, L. M., Woollacott, M., & Tuma, G. (1979). Organization of rapid responses to postural and locomotor-like perturbations of standing man. *Experimental Brain Research, 36,* 463–476.

Navon, D., & Gopher, D. (1979). On the economy of the human-processing system. *Psychological Review, 86*(3), 214–255.

Neisser, U. (1967). *Cognitive psychology.* New York: Appleton-Century-Crofts.

Neisser, U. (1972). Changing conceptions of imagery. In P. W. Sheehan (Ed.), *The function and nature of imagery.* New York: Academic Press.

Neisser, U. (1984). Interpreting Harry Bahrick's discovery: What confers immunity against forgetting? *Journal of Experimental Psychology: General, 113*(1), 32–35.

Neisser, U., & Becklen, R. (1975). Selective looking: Attending to visually specified events. *Cognitive Psychology, 7*(4), 480–494.

Nelson, K. (1974). Concept, word, and sentence: Interrelations in acquisition and development. *Psychological Review, 81*(4), 267–285.

Neumann, E., & Ammons, R. B. (1957). Acquisition and long-term retention of a simple serial perceptual-motor skill. *Journal of Experimental Psychology, 53,* 159–161.

Newell, A., & Simon, H. A. (1956). The logic theory machine: A complex information processing system. *IRE Transactions on Information Theory,* IT-2, 61–79.

Newell, A., Shaw, J. C., & Simon, H. A. (1962). The process of creative thinking. In H. E. Gruber, G.

Terell, & M. Wertheimer (Eds.), *Contemporary approaches to creative thinking*. New York: Atherton.

Newell, A., & Simon, H. A. (1972). *Human problem solving*. Englewood Cliffs, NJ: Prentice Hall.

Newell, A. M., & Rosenbloom, P. S. (1981). Mechanisms of skill acquisition and the law of practice. In J. R. Anderson (Ed.), *Cognitive skills and their acquisition* (pp. 1–55). Mahwah, NJ: Erlbaum.

Newell, K. M. (1991). Motor skill acquisition. *Annual Review of Psychology, 42*, 213–237.

Newstead, S. E., & Griggs, R. A. (1983). Drawing inferences from quantified statements: A study of the square of opposition. *Journal of Verbal Learning & Verbal Behavior, 22*(5), 535–546.

Newstead, S. E., Pollard, P., & Evans, J. S. (1992). The source of belief bias effects in syllogistic reasoning. *Cognition, 45*(3), 257–284.

Nickerson, R. S., & Adams, M. J. (1979). Long-term memory for a common object. *Cognitive Psychology, 11*(3), 287–307.

Nisbett, R. E., & Wilson, T. D. (1977). Telling more than we can know: Verbal reports on mental processes. *Psychological Review, 84*(3), 231–259.

Nissen, M. J., & Bullemer, P. (1987) Attentional requirements of learning: Evidence from performance measures. *Cognitive Psychology, 19*, 1–32.

Noordman, L. G., Vonk, W., & Kempff, H. J. (1992). Causal inferences during the reading of expository texts. *Journal of Memory & Language, 31*(5), 573–590.

Norman, D. A. (1968). Toward a theory of memory and attention. *Psychological Review, 75*(6), 522–536.

Norman, D. A. (1981). Categorization of action slips. *Psychological Review, 88*(1), 1–15.

Norman, D. A., & Bobrow, D. G. (1975). On data-limited and resource-limited processes. *Cognitive Psychology, 7*(1), 44–64.

Norman, D. A., & Shallice, T. (1986). Attention to action: Willed and automatic control of behavior. In R. J. Davidson, G. E. Schwarts, & D. Shapiro (Eds.), *Consciousness and self-regulation: Advances in research and theory* (Vol. 4, pp. 1–18). New York: Plenum.

Nougier, V., Bard, C., Fleury, M., Teasdale, N., Cole, J., Forget, R., Paillard, J., & Lamarre, Y. (1996). Control of single-joint movements in deafferented patients: evidence for amplitude coding rather than position control. *Experimental Brain Research, 109*, 473–482.

Novick, L. R., & Holyoak, K. J. (1991). Mathematical problem solving by analogy. *Journal of Experimental Psychology: Learning, Memory, and Cognition, 17*(3), 398–415.

Oakhill, J. V., & Johnson-Laird, P. N. (1985). The effects of belief on the spontaneous production of syllogistic conclusions. *Quarterly Journal of Experimental Psychology: Human Experimental Psychology, 37A*(4), 553–569.

Oakhill, J., Johnson-Laird, P. N., & Garnham, A. (1989). Believability and syllogistic reasoning. *Cognition, 31*(2), 117–140.

Oaksford, M., & Chater, N. (1996). Rational explanation of the selection task. *Psychological Review, 103*(2), 381–391.

Oaksford, M., & Chater, N. (1998). A revised rational analysis of the selection task: Exceptions and sequential sampling. In M. Oaksford & N. Chater (Eds.), *Rational models of cognition* (pp. 372–398). Oxford: Oxford University Press.

Oaksford, M., & Chater, N. (2001). The probabilistic approach to human reasoning. *Trends in Cognitive Science, 5*, 349–357.

Oberauer, K., Wilhelm, O., & Diaz, R. R. (1999). Bayesian rationality for the Wason selection task? A test of optimal data selection theory. *Thinking & Reasoning, 5*(2), 115–144.

Oberly, H. S. (1924). The range for visual attention, cognition and apprehension. *American Journal of Psychology, 35*, 332–352.

O'Brien, E. J., & Albrecht, J. E. (1992). Comprehension strategies in the development of a mental model. *Journal of Experimental Psychology: Learning, Memory, and Cognition, 18*(4), 777–784.

O'Craven, K. M., Downing, P. E., & Kanwisher, N. (1999). fMRI evidence for objects as the units of attentional selection. *Nature, 401*(6753), 584–587.

O'Craven, K. M., & Kanwisher, N. (2000). Mental imagery of faces and places activates corresponding stimulus-specific brain regions. *Journal of Cognitive Neuroscience, 12*, 1013–1023.

O'Keefe, J., & Nadel, L. (1978). *The hippocampus and the cognitive map*. Oxford: Oxford University Press.

Okoh, N. (1980). Bilingualism and divergent thinking among Nigerian and Welsh school children. *Journal of Social Psychology, 110*(2), 163–170.

Ormerod, T. C., MacGregor, J. N., & Chronicle, E. P. (2002). Dynamics and constraints in insight problem solving. *Journal of Experimental Psychology: Learning, Memory, and Cognition, 28*, 791–799.

Osherson, D., Smith, E. E., Wilkie, O., López, A., & Shafir, E. (1990). Category-based induction. *Psychological Review, 97*, 185–200.

Osman, A., & Moore, C. M. (1993). The locus of dual-task interference: Psychological refractory effects on movement-related brain potentials. *Journal of Experimental Psychology: Human Perception and Performance, 19*(6), 1292–1312.

Over, D. E., & Evans, J. St.- B. T. (1994). Hits and misses: Kirby on the selection task. *Cognition, 52*, 235–243.

Owen, A. M. (1997). Cognitive planning humans: Neuropsychological, neuroanatomical and neuropharmacological perspectives. *Progress in Neurobiology, 53*, 431–450.

Paap, K. R., & Noel, R. W. (1991). Dual-route models of print to sound: Still a good horse race. *Psychological Research, 53*(1), 13–24.

Paillard, J. (1991). Motor and representational framing of space. In J. Paillard (Ed.), *Brain and space* (pp. 163–182). Oxford: Oxford University Press.

Paivio, A. (1963). Learning of adjective–noun paired associates as a function of adjective–noun word order and noun abstractness. *Canadian Journal of Psychology, 17*(4), 370–379.

Paivio, A. (1965). Abstractness, imagery, and meaningfulness in paired-associate learning. *Journal of Verbal Learning & Verbal Behavior, 4*(1), 32–38.

Paivio, A. (1971). *Imagery and verbal processes*. New York: Holt, Rinehart, & Winston.

Paivio, A. (1986). *Mental representations*. Oxford: Oxford University Press.

Paivio, A. (1991). *Images in mind: The evolution of a theory*. London: Harvester Wheatsheaf.

Paivio, A., & Foth, D. (1970). Imaginal and verbal mediators and noun concreteness in paired-associate learning: The elusive interaction. *Journal of Verbal Learning & Verbal Behavior, 9*(4), 384–390.

Palmer, S. E. (1975). The effects of contextual scenes on the identification of objects. *Memory & Cognition, 3*, 519–526.

Palmer, S. E., Simone, E., & Kube, P. (1988). Reference frame effects on shape perception in two versus three dimensions. *Perception, 17*, 147–163.

Parasuraman, R., & Davies, D. R. (1977). A taxonomic analysis of vigilance perfromance. In R. R. Mackie (Ed.), *Vigilance: Theory, operational performance, and physiological correlates* (pp. 559–574). New York: Plenum.

Parsons, L. M. (1987a). Imagined spatial transformation of one's body. *Journal of Experimental Psychology: General, 116*(2), 172–191.

Parsons, L. M. (1987b). Imagined spatial transformations of one's hands and feet. *Cognitive Psychology, 19*(2), 178–241.

Pashler, H. E. (1998). *The psychology of attention*. Cambridge, MA: MIT Press.

Pashler, H., Carrier, M., & Hoffman, J. (1993). Saccadic eye movements and dual-task interference.

Quarterly Journal of Experimental Psychology: Human Experimental Psychology, 46A(1), 51–82.

Pastore, R. E., Li, X.-F., & Layer, J. K. (1990). Categorical perception of nonspeech chirps and bleats. *Perception and Psychophysics, 48*(2), 151–156.

Patel, V. L., & Groen, G. J. (1991). The general and specific nature of medical expertise: A critical look. In K. A. Ericsson & J. Smith (Eds.), *Toward a general theory of expertise* (pp. 93–125). Cambridge: Cambridge University Press.

Patterson, F. G. (1978). The gesture of a gorilla: Language acquisition in another pongid. *Brain & Language, 5*(1), 72–97.

Patterson, F. G. (1981). Can an ape create a sentence? Some affirmative evidence. *Science, 211*(86–87).

Paulesu, E., Frith, C. D., & Frackowiak, R. S. (1993). The neural correlates of the verbal component of working memory. *Nature, 362*(6418), 342–345.

Pavani F., Boscagli I., Benvenuti F., Rabuffetti M., & Farne A. (1999). Are perception and action affected differently by the Titchener circles illusion? *Experimental Brain Research, 127*, 95–101.

Penfield, W. (1959). *Speech and brain mechanisms*. Princeton, NJ: Princeton University Press.

Petersen, S. E., Fox, P. T., Posner, M. I., Mintun, M., & Raichle, M. E. (1988). Positron emission tomographic studies of the cortical anatomy of single-word processing. *Nature, 331*(6157), 585–589.

Peterson, L., & Peterson, M. J. (1959). Short-term retention of individual verbal items. *Journal of Experimental Psychology, 58*, 193–198.

Petrides M. (1989) Frontal lobes and memory. In F. Boller & J. Grafman (Eds.), *Handbook of neuropsychology* (pp. 601–614). New York: Elsevier.

Phillips, C., & Gibson, E. (1998). On the strength of the local attachment preference. *Journal of Psycholinguistic Research. 26*, 323–346.

Phelps, R. M., & Shanteau, J. (1978). Livestock judges: How much information can an expert use? *Organizational Behavior and Human Performance, 21*, 209–219.

Phillips, L. H., Wynn, V., Gilhooly, K. J., Della Sala, S., & Logie, R. H. (1999). The role of memory in the Tower of London task. *Memory, 7*(2), 209–231.

Piazza, M., Mechelli, A., Butterworth, B., & Price, C. J. (2002). Are subitizing and counting implemented as separate or functionally overlapping processes? *NeuroImage, 15*, 435–446.

Pillemer, D. B. (1984). Flashbulb memories of the assassination attempt on President Reagan. *Cognition, 16*, 63–80.

Pinker, S. (1994). *The language instinct*. New York: William Morrow.

Pinker, S., & Prince, A. (1988). On language and connectionism: Analysis of a parallel distributed processing model of language acquisition. *Cognition, 28*(1–2), 73–193.

Plous, S. (1989). Thinking the unthinkable: The effects of anchoring on likelihood estimates of nuclear war. *Journal of Applied Social Psychology, 19*(1), 67–91.

Podgorny, P., & Shepard, R. N. (1978). Functional representations common to visual perception and imagination. *Journal of Experimental Psychology: Human Perception and Performance, 4*(1), 21–35.

Polit, A., & Bizzi, E. (1978). Processes controlling arm movements in monkeys. *Science, 201,* 1235–1237.

Pomerantz, J. R., & Kubovy, M. (1986). Theoretical approaches to perceptual organization: Simplicity and likelihood principles. In K. R. Boff, & L. Kaufman (Eds.), *Handbook of perception and human performance* (Vol. 2, pp. 1–46). New York: Wiley.

Posner, M. I. (1978), *Chronometric explorations of mind.* Hillsdale, NJ: Erlbaum.

Posner, M. I., & Cohen, Y. A. (1984). Components of visual orienting. In H. Bouma, & D. G. Bouwhuis (Eds.), *Attention & Performance X* (pp. 531–556). Hillsdale, NJ: Erlbaum.

Posner, M. I., & Keele, S. W. (1968). On the genesis of abstract ideas. *Journal of Experimental Psychology, 77*(3, Pt. 1), 353–363.

Posner, M. I., & Keele, S. W. (1970). Retention of abstract ideas. *Journal of Experimental Psychology, 83*(2, Pt. 1), 304–308.

Posner, M. I., & Snyder, C. R. (1975). Attention and cognitive control. In R. L. Solso (Ed.), *Information processing and cognition: The Loyola symposium.* Mahwah, NJ: Erlbaum.

Posner, M. I., Snyder, C. R., & Davidson, B. J. (1980). Attention and the detection of signals. *Journal of Experimental Psychology: General, 109*(2), 160–174.

Povinelli, D. J., & Bering, J. M. (2002) The mentality of apes revisited. *Current Directions in Psychological Science 11,* 115–119.

Premack, D. (1971). Language in chimpanzee? *Science, 172*(3985), 808–822.

Premack, D. (1976a). *Intelligence in ape and man.* Mahwah, NJ: Erlbaum.

Premack, D. (1976b). Language and intelligence in ape and man. *American Scientist, 64*(6), 674–683.

Priest, A. G., & Lindsay, R. O. (1992). New light on novice–expert differences in physics problem solving. *British Journal of Psychology, 83*(3), 389–405.

Proffitt, D. R., Bhalla, M., Gossweiler, R., & Midgett, J. (1995). Perceiving geographical slant. *Psychonomic Bulletin & Review, 2*(4), 409–428.

Proffitt, J. B., Coley, J. D., & Medin, D. L. (2000) Expertise and category-based induction. *Journal of Experimental Psychology: Learning, Memory, and Cognition, 26,* 811–828.

Pylyshyn, Z. W. (1973). What the mind's eye tells the mind's brain: A critique of mental imagery. *Psychological Bulletin, 80*(1), 1–24.

Pylyshyn, Z. W. (1981). The imagery debate: Analogue media versus tacit knowledge. *Psychological Review, 88*(1), 16–45.

Pynoos, R. S., & Nader, K. (1989). Children's memories and proximity to violence. *Journal of the American Academy of Child and Adolescent Psychiatry, 28,* 236–241.

Ratcliff, R., & McKoon, G. (1988). A retrieval theory of priming in memory. *Psychological Review, 95*(3), 385–408.

Ratcliff, R., & McKoon, G. (1994). Retrieving information from memory: Spreading-activation theories versus compound-cue theories. *Psychological Review, 101*(1), 177–184.

Rauschecker, J. P., & Shannon, R. V. (2002). Sending sound to the brain. *Science, 295,* 1025–1029.

Raven, J. C. (1976). *Standard progressive matrices: Sets A, B, C, D, & E.* Oxford: Oxford University Press.

Rayner, K., Carlson, M., & Frazier, L. (1983). The interaction of syntax and semantics during sentence processing: Eye movements in the analysis of semantically biased sentences. *Journal of Verbal Learning & Verbal Behavior, 22*(3), 358–374.

Rayner, K., Garrod, S., & Perfetti, C. A. (1992). Discourse influences during parsing are delayed. *Cognition, 45*(2), 109–139.

Rayner, K., & Pollatsek, A. (1983). Is visual information integrated across saccades? *Perception and Psychophysics, 34*(1), 39–48.

Reber, A. S. (1999). *The new gambler's Bible.* New York: Crown.

Reber, P. J., & Kotovsky, K. (1997). Implicit learning in problem solving: The role of working memory capacity. *Journal of Experimental Psychology: General, 126*(2), 178–203.

Reder, L. M. (1982). Plausibility judgments versus fact retrieval: Alternative strategies for sentence verification. *Psychological Review, 89*(3), 250–280.

Reed, S. K., Ackinclose, C. C., & Voss, A. A. (1990). Selecting analogous problems: Similarity versus inclusiveness. *Memory & Cognition, 18*(1), 83–98.

Reed, S. K., & Bolstad, C. A. (1991). Use of examples and procedures in problem solving. *Journal of Experimental Psychology: Learning, Memory, and Cognition, 17*(4), 753–766.

Register, P. A., & Kihlstrom, J. F. (1987). Hypnotic effects on hypermnesia. *International Journal of Clinical and Experimental Hypnosis, 35,* 155–170.

Reich, S. S., & Ruth, P. (1982). Wason's selection task: Verification, falsification and matching. *British Journal of Psychology, 73*(3), 395–405.

Reingold, E. M., Charness, N., Pomplun, M., & Stampe, D. M. (2001). Visual span in expert chess players: Evidence from eye movements. *Psychological Science, 12,* 48–55.

Reitman, J. S. (1971). Mechanisms of forgetting in short-term memory. *Cognitive Psychology, 2*(2), 185–195.

Revlis, R. (1975). Two models of syllogistic reasoning: Feature selection and conversion. *Journal of Verbal Learning & Verbal Behavior, 14*(2), 180–195.

Richardson-Klavehn, A., & Bjork, R. A. (1988). Measures of memory. *Annual Review of Psychology, 39,* 475–543.

Rips, L. J. (1975). Inductive judgments about natural categories. *Journal of Verbal Learning & Verbal Behavior, 14*(6), 665–681.

Rips, L. J. (1989). Similarity, typicality, and categorization. In S. O. A. Vosniadou (Ed.), *Similarity and analogical reasoning* (pp. 21–59). New York: Cambridge University Press.

Rist, R. S. (1989). Schema creation in programming. *Cognitive Science, 13*(3), 389–414.

Roberson, D., Davies, I., & Davidoff, J. (2000). Color categories are not universal: Replications and new evidence from a stone-age culture. *Journal of Experimental Psychology: General 129,* 369–398.

Robins, S., & Mayer, R. E. (1993). Schema training in analogical reasoning. *Journal of Educational Psychology, 85*(3), 529–538.

Roediger, H. L. III, Wheeler, A., & Rajaram, S. Remembering, knowing, and reconstructing the past. In D. L. Medin (Ed.), *The psychology of learning and motivation: Advances in research and theory, 30* (pp. 97–134).

Rogers, S. (1996). The horizon-ratio relation as information for relative size in pictures. *Perception and Psychophysics, 58*(1), 142–152.

Roll, R., Bard, C., & Paillard, J. (1986). Head orienting contributes to the directional accuracy of aiming at distant targets. *Human Movement Science, 5,* 359–371.

Rosch, E. H. (1973). On the internal structure of perceptual and semantic categories. In T. E. Moore (Ed.), *Cognitive development and the acquisition of language* (pp. 111–144). New York: Academic Press.

Rosch, E., Mervis, C. B., Gray, W. D., Johnson, D. M., & Boyes-Braem, P. (1976). Basic objects in natural categories. *Cognitive Psychology, 8*(3), 382–439.

Rosenbaum, D. A. (2002). Motor Control. In S. Yantis (Ed.), *Steven's Handbook of Experimental Psychology* (3rd ed.). Vol. 1, Sensation and Perception (pp. 315–339). New York: Wiley.

Rosenbaum, D. A., Engelbrecht, S. E., Bushe, M. M., & Loukopoulos, L. D. (1993). Knowledge model for selecting and producing reaching movements. *Journal of Motor Behavior, 25,* 217–227.

Rosenbaum, D. A., Kenny, S., & Derr, M. A. (1983). Hierarchical control of rapid movement sequences. *Journal of Experimental Psychology: Human Perception and Performance, 9,* 86–102.

Rosenbaum, D. A., Loukopoulos, L. D., Meulenbroek, R. G. J., & Vaughan, J. (1995). Planning reaches by evaluating stored postures. *Psychological Review, 102,* 28–67.

Rosenbaum, D. A., Meulenbroek, R. J., Vaughan, J., & Jansen, C. (2001). Posture-based motion planning: Applications to grasping. *Psychological Review. 108,* 709–734.

Rosner, S. R., & Hayes, D. S. (1977). A developmental study of category item production. *Child Development, 48*(3), 1062–1065.

Ross, B. H. (1987). This is like that: The use of earlier problems and the separation of similarity effects. *Journal of Experimental Psychology: Learning, Memory, and Cognition, 13*(4), 629–639.

Ross, B. H. (1989). Distinguishing types of superficial similarities: Different effects on the access and use of earlier problems. *Journal of Experimental Psychology: Learning, Memory, and Cognition, 15*(3), 456–468.

Ross, B. H., & Kennedy, P. T. (1990). Generalizing from the use of earlier examples in problem solving. *Journal of Experimental Psychology: Learning, Memory, and Cognition, 16*(1), 42–55.

Ross, N. E., & Jolicoeur, P. (1999). Attentional blink for color. *Journal of Experimental Psychology: Human Perception & Performance, 25,* 1483–1494.

Rubenstein, H., Lewis, S. S., & Rubenstein, M. A. (1971). Evidence for phonemic recoding in visual word recognition. *Journal of Verbal Learning & Verbal Behavior, 10*(6), 645–657.

Rubin, D. C., & Kozin, M. (1984). Vivid memories. *Cognition, 16*(1), 81–95.

Rumelhart, D. E., Hinton, G. E., & McClelland, J. L. (1986). A general framework for parallel distributed processing. In D. E. Rumelhart, J. L. McClelland, & the PDP Research Group (Eds.), *Parallel distributed processing, Volume 1: Foundations* (pp. 45–76). Cambridge, MA: MIT Press.

Rumelhart, D. E., & McClelland, J. L. (1987). Learning the past tenses of English verbs: Implicit rules or parallel distributed processing? In B. MacWhinney (Ed.), *Mechanisms of language acquisition* (pp. 195–248). Mahwah, NJ: Erlbaum.

Rundus, D., & Atkinson, R. C. (1970). Rehearsal processes in free recall: A procedure for direct observation. *Journal of Verbal Learning & Verbal Behavior, 9*(1), 99–105.

Ruthruff, E., & Pashler, H. E. (2001). Perceptual and central interference in dual-task performance. In K. Shapiro (Ed.), *The limits of attention: Temporal constraints in human information processing* (pp. 100–123). London: Oxford University Press.

Sabbah, P., Simond, G., Levrier, O., Habib, M., Trabaud, V., Murayama, N., Mazoyer, B. M., Briant, J. F., Raybaud, C., & Salamon, G. (1995). Functional magnetic resonance imaging at 1.5 T during sensorimotor and cognitive task. *European Neurology, 35*(3), 131–136.

Sadoski, M., & Paivio, A. (2001). *Imagery and text: A dual coding theory of reading and writing.* Hillsdale, NJ: Erlbaum.

Sagi, D., & Julesz, B. (1985). Fast noninertial shifts of attention. *Spatial Vision, 2,* 141–149.

Salthouse, T. A. (1984). The skill of typing. *Scientific American, 250*(2), 128–135.

Salthouse, T. A. (1993). Influence of working memory on adult age differences in matrix reasoning. *British Journal of Psychology, 84,* 171–199.

Samuel, A. (1996). Phoneme restoration. *Language & Cognitive Processes, 11,* 647–653.

Sanes, J. N., Mauritz, K.-H., Dalakas, M. C., & Evarts, E. V. (1985). Motor control in humans with large-fiber sensory neuropathy. *Human Neurobiology, 4,* 101–114.

Santello, M., Flanders, M., & Soechting, J. F. (1998). Postural hand synergies for tool use. *Journal of Neuroscience, 18,* 10105–10115.

Sapir, E. (1956). *Culture, language and personality.* Los Angeles: University of California Press.

Savage-Rumbaugh, E. S. (1986). *Ape language: From conditioned response to symbol.* New York: Columbia University Press.

Savage-Rumbaugh, E. S., Pate, J. L., Lawson, J., Smith, S. T., & Rosenbaum, S. (1983). Can a chimpanzee make a statement? *Journal of Experimental Psychology: General, 112*(4), 457–492.

Savage-Rumbaugh, E. S., Romski, M. A., Sevcik, R., & Pate, J. L. (1983). Assessing symbol usage versus symbol competency. *Journal of Experimental Psychology: General, 112*(4), 508–512.

Savage-Rumbaugh, E. S., Rumbaugh, D. M., & Boysen, S. (1978). Symbolic communication between two chimpanzees (Pan troglodytes). *Science, 201*(4356), 641–644.

Savage-Rumbaugh, E. S., Rumbaugh, D. M., Smith, S. T., & Lawson, J. (1980). Reference: The linguistic essential. *Science, 210,* 922–925.

Savage-Rumbaugh, S., Shanker, S. G., & Taylor, T. J. (1998). *Apes, language, and the human mind.* New York: Oxford University Press.

Schacter, D. L. (1990). Perceptual representation systems and implicit memory: Toward a resolution of the multiple memory systems debate. *Annals of the New York Academy of Sciences, 608,* 543–571.

Schacter, D. L. (1996). *Searching for memory.* New York: Basic Books.

Schacter, D. L., & Tulving, E. (1994). What are the memory systems of 1994? In D. L. Schacter & E. Tulving (Eds.), *Memory systems 1994* (pp. 1–38). Cambridge, MA: MIT Press.

Schank, R. C., & Abelson, R. P. (1977). *Scripts, plans, goals, and understanding.* Mahwah, NJ: Erlbaum.

Scheerer, M. (1963). Problem-solving. *Scientific American, 208*(4), 118–128.

Schellenberg, E. G., Iverson, P., & McKinnon, M. C. (1999). Name that tune: Identifying popular recordings from brief excerpts. *Psychonomic Bulletin & Review, 6,* 641–646.

Schmalhofer, F., & Glavanov, D. (1986). Three components of understanding a programmer's manual: Verbatim, propositional, and situational representations. *Journal of Memory & Language, 25*(3), 279–294.

Schmid, P. M., & Yeni-Komshian, G. H. (1999). The effects of speaker accent and target predictability on perception of mispronunciations. *Journal of Speech Language & Hearing Research, 42*(1), 56–64.

Schmidt, R. A. (1975). A schema theory of discrete motor skill learning. *Psychological Review, 82,* 225–260.

Schmidt, R. A., & Bjork, R. A. (1992). New conceptualizations of practice: Common principles in three paradigms suggest new concepts for training. *Psychological Science, 3,* 207–217.

Schmidt, R. A., & Lee, T. D. (1999). *Motor control and learning: A behavioral emphasis.* Champaign, IL: Human Kinetics Publishers.

Schmolck, H., Buffalo, E. A., & Squire, L. R. (2000). Memory distortions develop over time: Recollections of the O. J. Simpson trial verdict after 15 and 32 months. *Psychological Science, 11,* 39–45.

Schneider, W., & Shiffrin, R. M. (1977). Controlled and automatic human information processing: I.

Detection, search, and attention. *Psychological Review*, 84(1), 1–66.

Schooler, J. W. (1994). Seeking the core: The issues and evidence surrounding recovered accounts of sexual trauma. *Consciousness & Cognition: An International Journal*, 3(3–4), 452–469.

Schooler, J. W. (2001) Discovering memories of abuse in the light of meta-awareness. *Journal of Aggression, Maltreatment & Trauma*, 4, 105–136.

Schooler, J. W., Bendiksen, M., & Ambadar, Z. (1997). Taking the middle line: Can we accommodate both fabricated and recovered memories of sexual abuse? In M. A. Conway (Ed.), *Recovered memories and false memories. Debates in psychology* (pp. 251–292). Oxford: Oxford University Press.

Schumacher, E. H., Seymour, T. L., Glass, J. M., Fencsik, D. E., Lauber, E. J., Kieras, D. E., & Meyer, D. E. (2001). Virtually perfect time sharing in dual-task performance: Uncorking the central cognitive bottleneck. *Psychological Science*, 121, 101–108.

See, J. E., Howe, S. R., Warm, J. S., & Dember, W. N. (1995). Meta-analysis of the sensitivity decrement in vigilance. *Psychological Bulletin*, 117(2), 230–249.

Seidenberg, M. S., & McClelland, J. L. (1989). A distributed, developmental model of word recognition and naming. *Psychological Review*, 96(4), 523–568.

Seidenberg, M. S., Waters, G. S., Barnes, M. A., & Tanenhaus, M. K. (1984). When does irregular spelling or pronunciation influence word recognition? *Journal of Verbal Learning & Verbal Behavior*, 23, 383–404.

Selfridge, O. G., & Neisser, U. (1960). Pattern recognition by machine. *Scientific American*, 203, 60–68.

Sera, M. D., Elieff, C., Forbes, J., Burch, M. C., Rodriguez, W., & Dubois, D. P. (2002). When language affects cognition and when it does not: An analysis of grammatical gender and classification. *Journal of Experimental Psychology: General*, 131, 377–397.

Sera, M. D., Reittinger, E., & del Castillo Pintado, J. (1991). Developing definitions of objects and events in English and Spanish speakers. *Cognitive Development*, 6, 119–142.

Shaffer, L. H. (1975). Control processes in typing. *Quarterly Journal of Experimental Psychology*. 27, 419–432.

Shaffer, W. O., & LaBerge, D. (1979). Automatic semantic processing of unattended words. *Journal of Verbal Learning & Verbal Behavior*, 18(4), 413–426.

Shafir, E., & Tversky, A. (1995). Decision making. In E. E. Smith & D. N. Osherson (Eds.), *Thinking* (Vol. 3, pp. 77–100). Cambridge, MA: MIT Press.

Shallice, T. (1982). Specific impairments of planning. *Philosophical Transactions of the Royal Society of London*, 298, 199–209.

Shallice, T., & Evans, M. E. (1978). The involvement of the frontal lobes in cognitive estimation. *Cortex*, 14(2), 294–303.

Shanker, S. G., Savage-Rumbaugh, E. S., & Taylor, T. J. (1999). Kanzi: A new beginning. *Animal Learning and Behavior*, 27, 24–25.

Shapiro, D. C., & Schmidt, R. A. (1982). The schema theory: Recent evidence and developmental implications. In J. A. S. Kelso & J. E. Clark (Eds.), *The development of movement control and co-ordination* (pp. 113–150). New York: Wiley.

Shapiro, K. L., Raymond, J. E., & Arnell, K. M. (1994). Attention to visual pattern information produces the attentional blink in rapid serial visual presentation. *Journal of Experimental Psychology: Human Perception & Performance*, 20, 357–371.

Sharpe, L., & Markham, R. (1992). The effect of the distinctiveness of bizarre imagery on immediate and delayed recall. *Journal of Mental Imagery*, 16(3–4), 211–220.

Shepard, R. N., & Chipman, S. (1970). Second-order isomorphism of internal representations: Shapes of states. *Cognitive Psychology*, 1, 1–17.

Shepard, R. N., & Cooper, L. A. (1986). *Mental images and their transformations*. Cambridge, MA: MIT Press.

Shepard, R. N., & Feng, C. (1972). A chronometric study of mental paper folding. *Cognitive Psychology*, 3(2), 228–243.

Shepard, R. N., & Metzler, J. (1971). Mental rotation of three-dimensional objects. *Science*, 171(3972), 701–703.

Sherry, D. F., & Schacter, D. L. (1987). The evolution of multiple memory systems. *Psychological Review*, 94, 439–454.

Shiffrin, R. M., & Schneider, W. (1977). Controlled and automatic human information processing: II. Perceptual learning, automatic attending and a general theory. *Psychological Review*, 84(2), 127–190.

Shih, S.-I., & Sperling, G. (1996). Is there feature-based attentional selection in visual search? *Journal of Experimental Psychology: Human Perception and Performance*, 22(3), 758–779.

Simon, D. P., & Simon, H. A. (1978). Individual differences in solving physics problems. In R. Siegler (Ed.), *Children's thinking: What develops?* Mahwah, NJ: Erlbaum.

Simon, H. A. (1957). *Models of man: Social and rational*. New York: Wiley.

Simon, H. A. (1974). How big is a chunk? *Science, 183*(4124), 482–488.

Simon, H. A., & Chase, W. G. (1973). Skill in chess. *American Scientist, 61*(4), 394–403.

Simon, H. A., & Gilmartin, K. (1973). A simulation of memory for chess positions. *Cognitive Psychology, 5*(1), 29–46.

Simpson, G. B., & Kreuger, M. A. (1991). Selective access of homograph meanings in sentence context. *Journal of Memory & Language, 30*(6), 627–643.

Singer, M., Graesser, A. C., & Trabasso, T. (1994). Minimal or global inference during reading. *Journal of Memory & Language, 33*(4), 421–441.

Skinner, B. F. (1938). *The behavior of organisms: An experimental analysis*. New York: Appleton-Century-Crofts.

Skinner, B. F. (1957). *Verbal behavior*. New York: Appleton-Century-Crofts.

Skinner, B. F. (1984). *The shaping of a behaviorist*. New York: New York University Press.

Skoglund, S. (1956). Anatomical and physiological studies of knee joint innervation in the cat. *Acta Physiologica Scandinavica, 36* (Supplement 124), 1–101.

Slobin, D. I. (1966). Grammatical transformations and sentence comprehension in childhood and adulthood. *Journal of Verbal Learning & Verbal Behavior, 5*(3), 219–227.

Sloman, S. A. (1998). Categorical inference is not a tree: The myth of inheritance hierarchies. *Cognitive Psychology, 35*, 1–33.

Sloman, S. A., & Rumelhart, D. E. (1992). Reducing interference in distributed memories through episodic gating. In A. F. Healy, S. M. Kosslyn, & R. M. Shiffrin (Eds.), *Essays in honor of William K. Estes* (Vol. 1, pp. 227–248). Mahwah, NJ: Erlbaum.

Smith, E. E., & Medin, D. L. (1981). *Categories and concepts*. Cambridge, MA: Harvard University Press.

Smith, E. E., Patalano, A. L., & Jonides, J. (1998). Alternative strategies of categorization. *Cognition, 65*(2–3), 167–196.

Smith, E. E., Shoben, E. J., & Rips, L. J. (1974). Structure and process in semantic memory: A featural model for semantic decisions. *Psychological Review, 81*(3), 214–241.

Smith, E. E., & Sloman, S. A. (1994). Similarity- versus rule-based categorization. *Memory & Cognition, 22*(4), 377–386.

Smith, J. D., & Minda, J. P. (2000). Thirty categorization results in search of a model. *Journal of Experimental Psychology: Learning, Memory, and Cognition, 26*, 3–27.

Smith, S. M. (1988). Environmental context-dependent memory. In G. M. Davies & D. M. Thomson (Eds.), *Memory in context: Context in memory* (pp. 13–44). New York: Wiley.

Smith, S. M., & Blankenship, S. E. (1991). Incubation and the persistence of fixation in problem solving. *American Journal of Psychology, 104*(1), 61–87.

Smith, S. M., Glenberg, A., & Bjork, R. A. (1978). Environmental context and human memory. *Memory & Cognition, 6*(4), 342–353.

Soechting, J. F., Lacquaniti, F., & Terzuolo, C. A. (1986). Coordination of arm movements in three-dimensional space. Sensorimotor mapping during drawing movement. *Neuroscience. 17*, 295–311.

Sosniak, L. A. (1985). Learning to be a concert pianist. In B. S. Bloom (Ed.), *Developing talent in young people* (pp. 19–67). New York: Ballantine.

Spencer, R. M., & Weisberg, R. W. (1986). Context-dependent effects on analogical transfer. *Memory & Cognition, 14*(5), 442–449.

Sperling, G. (1960). The information available in brief visual presentation. *Psychological Monographs, 74*(11, Whole no. 498).

Sperling, G., & Melchner, M. J. (1978). The attention operating characteristic: Example from visual search. *Science, 202*, 315–318.

Sperling, G., & Weichselgartner, E. (1995). Episodic theory of the dynamics of spatial attention. *Psychological Review, 102*(3), 503–532.

Spijkers, W. A. C., & Lochner, P. (1994). Partial visual feedback and spatial end-point accuracy of discrete aiming movements. *Journal of Motor Behavior, 26*, 283–295.

Squire, L. R. (1992). Memory and the hippocampus: A synthesis from findings with rats, monkeys, and humans. *Psychological Review, 99*, 195–231.

Stadler, M. A., & Frensch, P. A. (1998). *Handbook of implicit learning*. Thousand Oaks, CA: Sage.

Stark, L., & Ellis, S. (1981). Scanpaths revisited: Cognitive models direct active looking. In D. Fisher, R. Monty, & J. Senders (Eds.), *Cognition and visual perception* (pp. 193–226). Mahwah, NJ: Erlbaum.

Sternberg, R. J., & Davidson, J. E. (1995). *The nature of insight*. Cambridge, MA: MIT Press.

Sternberg, S., Monsell, S., Knoll, R. L., & Wright, C. E. (1978). The latency and duration of rapid movement sequences: Comparisons of speech and typewriting. In G. E. Stelmach (Ed.), *Information processing in motor control and learning* (pp. 117–152). New York: Academic Press.

Strayer, D. L., & Johnston, W. A. (2001). Driven to distraction: Dual-task studies of simulated driving and conversing on a cellular telephone. *Psychological Science, 12,* 462–466.

Stroop, J. R. (1935). Studies of interference in serial verbal reactions. *Journal of Experimental Psychology,* 18, 643–662.

Swinney, D. A. (1979). Lexical access during sentence comprehension: (Re)consideration of context effects. *Journal of Verbal Learning & Verbal Behavior, 18*(6), 645–659.

Tabossi, P., & Zardon, F. (1993). Processing ambiguous words in context. *Journal of Memory and Language, 32,* 359–372.

Takeuchi, A. H., & Hulse, S. H. (1993). Absolute pitch. *Psychological Bulletin, 113*(2), 345–361.

Talwar, S. K., Xu, S., Hawley, E. S., Weiss, S. A., Moxon, K. A., & Chapin, J. K. (2002). Rat navigation guided by remote control. *Nature, 417,* 37–38.

Tanaka, J. W., & Taylor, M. (1991). Object categories and expertise: Is the basic level in the eye of the beholder? *Cognitive Psychology, 23*(3), 457–482.

Taraban, R., & McClelland, J. L. (1987). Conspiracy effects in word pronunciation. *Journal of Memory & Language, 26*(6), 608–631.

Tarr, M. J. (1995). Rotating objects to recognize them: A case study on the role of viewpoint dependency in the recognition of three-dimensional objects. *Psychonomic Bulletin & Review, 2*(1), 55–82.

Tarr, M. J., & Pinker, S. (1990). When does human object recognition use a viewer-centered reference frame? *Psychological Science, 1,* 253–256.

Tassinari, G., & Berlucchi, G. (1995). Covert orienting to non-informative cues: Reaction time studies. *Behavioural Brain Research, 71,* 101–112.

Taub, E. (1976). Movement in nonhuman primates deprived of somatosensory feedback. *Exercise Sport Science Reviews, 4,* 335–374.

Taub, E., & Berman, A. J. (1968). Movement and learning in the absence of sensory feedback. In S. Freeman (Ed.), *The neuropsychology of spatially oriented behavior* (pp. 173–192). Homewood, IL: Dorsey.

Taub, E., Perrella, P., & Barro, G. (1973). Behavioral development after forelimb deafferentation on day of birth in monkeys with and without blinding. *Science, 181,* 959–960.

Terrace, H. S., Petitto, L. A., Sanders, R. J., & Bever, T. G. (1979). Can an ape create a sentence? *Science, 206*(4421), 891–902.

Tetlock, P. E. (1991). An alternative metaphor in the study of judgment and choice: People as politicians. *Theory & Psychology, 1*(4), 451–475.

Tetlock, P. E. (1992). The impact of accountability on judgment and choice; Toward a social contingency model. *Advances in Experimental Social Psychology, 25,* 331–376.

Tetlock, P. E. (2002). Social functionalist frameworks for judgment and choice: Intuitive politicians, theologians, and prosecutors. *Psychological Review, 109,* 451–471.

Tetlock, P. E., Kristel, O. V., Elson, S. B., Green, M. C., & Lerner, J. S. (2000). The psychology of the unthinkable: Taboo trade-offs, forbidden base rates, and heretical counterfactuals. *Journal of Personality & Social Psychology, 78,* 853–870.

Thaler, R. (1980). Toward a positive theory of consumer choice. *Journal of Economic Behavior and Organization, 1,* 39–60.

Thomas, J. C. (1974). An analysis of behavior in the hobbits–orcs problem. *Cognitive Psychology, 6*(2), 257–269.

Thompson, A. L., & Klatzky, R. L. (1978). Studies of visual synthesis: Integration of fragments into forms. *Journal of Experimental Psychology: Human Perception and Performance, 4*(2), 244–263.

Thorndike, E. L. (1911). *Animal intelligence* (Vol. 2). New York: Macmillan.

Thorndike, E. L., & Woodworth, R. S. (1901). The influence of improvement in one mental function upon the efficiency of other functions. *Psychological Review, 8,* 247–261.

Tinbergen, N. (1952). The curious behavior of the stickleback. *Scientific American, 182,* 22–26.

Tipper, S. P., Driver, J., & Weaver, B. (1991). Object-centred inhibition of return of visual attention. *Quarterly Journal of Experimental Psychology, 43A,* 289–298.

Titchener, E. B. (1909). *Experimental psychology of the thought-processes.* New York: Macmillan.

Todorov, E., & Jordan, M. I. (1998). Smoothness maximization along a predefined path accurately predicts the speed profiles of complex arm movements. *Journal of Neurophysiology, 80,* 696–714.

Toth, J. P., & Hunt, R. R. (1999). Not one versus many, but zero versus any: Structure and function in the context of the multiple-memory systems debate. In J. K. Foster & M. Jelicic (Eds.), *Memory: Structure, function, or process?* (pp. 232–272). London: Oxford University Press.

Tranel, D., Bechara, A., & Damasio, A. R. (2000). Decision making and the somatic marker hypothesis. In M. Gazzaniga (Ed.), *The cognitive neurosciences* (2nd ed., pp. 1259–1270). Cambridge, MA: MIT Press.

Treisman, A. M. (1960). Contextual cues in selective listening. *Quarterly Journal of Experimental Psychology, 12,* 242–248.

Treisman, A., & Gormican, S. (1988). Feature analysis in early vision: Evidence from search asymmetries. *Psychological Review, 95*(1), 15–48.

Trick, L. M., & Pylyshyn, Z. W. (1993). What enumeration studies can show us about spatial attention: Evidence for limited capacity preattentive processing. *Journal of Experimental Psychology: Human Perception & Performance, 19,* 331–351.

Trueswell, J. C., Tanenhaus, M. K., & Garnsey, S. M. (1994). Semantic influences on parsing: Use of thematic role information in syntactic ambiguity resolution. *Journal of Memory & Language, 33*(3), 285–318.

Tulving, E. (1967). The effects of presentation and recall of material in free-recall learning. *Journal of Verbal Learning & Verbal Behavior, 6*(2), 175–184.

Tulving, E. (1972). Episodic and semantic memory. In E. Tulving & W. Donaldson (Eds.), *Organization and memory.* New York: Academic Press.

Tulving, E. (1983). *Elements of episodic memory.* Oxford: Oxford University Press.

Tulving, E. (1986). Episodic and semantic memory: Where should we go from here? *Behavioral & Brain Sciences, 9*(3), 573–577.

Tulving, E., & Pearlstone, Z. (1966). Availability versus accessibility of information in memory for words. *Journal of Verbal Learning & Verbal Behavior, 5,* 381–391.

Tulving, E., Schacter, D. L., McLachlan, D. R., & Moscovitch, M. (1988). Priming of semantic autobiographical knowledge: A case study of retrograde amnesia. *Brain & Cognition, 8*(1), 3–20.

Tulving, E., & Thomson, D. M. (1973). Encoding specificity and retrieval processes in episodic memory. *Psychological Review, 80,* 359–380.

Tulving, Endel. (2002). Episodic memory: From mind to brain. *Annual Review of Psychology, 53,* 1–25.

Turvey, M. T. (1973). On peripheral and central processes in vision: Inferences from an information-processing analysis of masking with patterned stimuli. *Psychological Review, 80*(1), 1–52.

Tversky, A. (1969). Intransitivity of preferences. *Psychological Review, 76*(1), 31–48.

Tversky, A. (1977). Features of similarity. *Psychological Review, 84*(4), 327–352.

Tversky, A., & Kahneman, D. (1973). Availability: A heuristic for judging frequency and probability. *Cognitive Psychology, 5*(2), 207–232.

Tversky, A., & Kahneman, D. (1974). Judgment under uncertainty: Heuristics and biases. *Science, 185*(4157), 1124–1131.

Tversky, A., & Kahneman, D. (1981). The framing of decisions and the psychology of choice. *Science, 211*(4481), 453–458.

Tversky, A., & Kahneman, D. (1983). Extensional versus intuitive reasoning: The conjunction fallacy in probability judgment. *Psychological Review, 90*(4), 293–315.

Tversky, A., & Kahneman, D. (1986). Judgment under uncertainty: Heuristics and biases. In H. R. Arkes & K. R. Hammond (Eds.), *Judgment and decision making: An interdisciplinary reader* (pp. 38–55). Cambridge: Cambridge University Press.

Tversky, A., Sattath, S., & Slovic, P. (1988). Contingent weighting in judgment and choice. *Psychological Review, 95*(3), 371–384.

Tversky, A., & Simonson, I. (1993). Context-dependent preferences. *Management Science, 39,* 1179–1189.

Tversky, A., Slovic, P., & Kahneman, D. (1990). The causes of preference reversal. American *Economic Review, 80,* 204–217.

Ullman, S., & Basri, R. (1991). Recognition by linear combinations of models. *IEEE Transactions on Pattern Analysis and Machine Intelligence, 13,* 992–1006.

Ungerleider, L., & Mishkin, M. (1982). Two cortical visual systems. In D. J. Ingle, M. A. Goodale, & R. J. W. Mansfield (Eds.), *Analysis of visual behavior* (pp. 549–586). Cambridge, MA: MIT Press.

Uno, Y., Kawato, M., & Suzuki, R. (1989). Formation and control of optimal trajectory in human multijoint arm movement: Minimum torque-change model. *Biological Cybernetics, 61,* 89–101.

Valentine, E. R. (1985). The effect of instructions on performance in the Wason selection task. *Current Psychological Research & Reviews, 4*(3), 214–223.

Vallar, G., & Baddeley, A. D. (1984). Phonological short-term store, phonological processing and sentence comprehension: A neuropsychological case study. *Cognitive Neuropsychology, 1*(2), 121–141.

van der Helm, P. A. (2000). Simplicity versus likelihood in visual perception: From surprisals to precisals. *Psychological Bulletin, 126,* 770–800.

van der Kamp, J., Savelsbergh, G., & Smeets, J. (1997). Multiple information sources in interceptive timing. *Human Movement Science, 16*(6), 787–821.

van Dijk, T., & Kintsch, W. (1983). *Strategies of discourse comprehension.* San Diego: Academic Press.

Vargha-Khadem, F., Gadian, D. G., & Mishkin, M. (2002). Dissociations in cognitive memory: The syndrome of developmental amnesia. In A. Baddeley, M. Conway, & J. P. Aggleton, (Eds.), *Episodic memory: New directions in research.* (pp. 153–163). London: Oxford University Press.

Vargha-Khadem, F., Gadian, D. G., Watkins, K. E., Connelly, A., Van Paesschen, W., & Mishkin, M. (1997). Differential effects of early hippocampal pathology on episodic and semantic memory. *Science, 277*(5324), 376–380.

Violanti, J. M., & Marshall, J. R. (1996). Cellular phones and traffic accidents: An epidemiological approach. *Accident Analysis & Prevention, 28*(2), 265–270.

Vishton, P. M., Rea, J. G., Cutting, J. E., & Nunez, L. N. (1999). Comparing effects of the horizontal-vertical illusion on grip scaling and judgment: Relative versus absolute, not perception versus action. *Journal of Experimental Psychology: Human Perception & Performance, 25*, 1659–1672.

Vogel, E. K., Woodman, G. F., & Luck, S. J. (2001). Storage of features, conjunctions, and objects in visual working memory. *Journal of Experimental Psychology: Human Perception and Performance, 27*, 92–114.

von Neumann, J., & Morgenstern, O. (1944). *Theory of games and economic behavior*. Princeton, NJ: Princeton University Press.

Von Wright, J. M. (1968). Selection in visual immediate memory. *Quarterly Journal of Experimental Psychology, 20*(1), 62–68.

Wagner, A. D., Schacter, D. L., Rotte, M., Koutstaal, W., Maril, A., Dale, A. M., Rosen, B. R., & Buckner, R. L. (1998). Building memories: Remembering and forgetting of verbal experiences as predicted by brain activity. *Science, 281*(5380), 1188–1191.

Wallingford, R. (1975). Long distance running. In A. W. Tayler & F. Landry (Eds.), *The scientific aspects of sports training* (pp. 118–130). Springfield, IL: Charles C. Thomas.

Wardlaw, K. A., & Kroll, N. E. (1976). Autonomic responses to shock-associated words in a nonattended message: A failure to replicate. *Journal of Experimental Psychology: Human Perception and Performance, 2*(3), 357–360.

Warren, R. M. (1970). Perceptual restoration of missing speech sounds. *Science, 167*(3917), 392–393.

Warren, R. M., & Sherman, G. L. (1974). Phonemic restorations based on subsequent context. *Perception and Psychophysics, 16*(1), 150–156.

Warren, R. M., & Warren, R. P. (1970). Auditory illusions and confusions. *Scientific American, 223*(6), 30–36.

Warren, W. H. (1984). Perceiving affordances: Visual guidance of stair climbing. *Journal of Experimental Psychology: Human Perception and Performance, 10*(5), 683–703.

Warrington, E., & Weiskrantz, L. (1968). New method of testing long-term retention with special reference to amnesic patients. *Nature, 217*, 972–974.

Warrington, E. K., & Weiskrantz, L. (1979). Conditioning in amnesic patients. *Neuropsychologia, 20*, 233–248.

Wason, P. C. (1968). Reasoning about a rule. *Quarterly Journal of Experimental Psychology, 20*(3), 273–281.

Wason, P. C. (1969). Regression in reasoning? *British Journal of Psychology, 60*(4), 471–480.

Waugh, N. C., & Norman, D. A. (1965). Primary memory. *Psychological Review, 72*(2), 89–104.

Weiskrantz, L., & Warrington, E. K. (1979). Conditioning in amnesic patients. *Neuropsychologia, 17*(2), 187–194.

Wegner, D. M. (1994). Ironic processes of mental control. *Psychological Review, 101*, 34–52.

Wegner, D. M., Schneider, D. J., Carter, S. R., & White, T. L. (1987). Paradoxical effects of thought suppression. *Journal of Personality & Social Psychology, 53*, 5–13.

Weldon, M. S. (1999). The memory chop shop: Issues in the search for memory systems. In J. K. Foster & M. Jelicic (Eds.), *Memory: Structure, Function, or Process?* (pp. 162–204). London: Oxford University Press.

Welford, A. T. (1952). The "psychological refractory period" and the timing of high-speed performance: A review and a theory. *British Journal of Psychology, 43*, 2–19.

Welford, A. T. (1980). The single-channel hypothesis. In A. T. Welford (Ed.), *Reaction time* (pp. 215–252). New York: Academic Press.

Wender K.F., & Rothkegel, R. (2000). Subitizing and its subprocesses. *Psychological Research, 64*, 81–92.

Westheimer, G. (1988). Vision: Space and movement. In R. C. Atkinson, R. J. Herrnstein, G. Lindzey, & R. D. Luce (Eds.), *Steven's handbook of experimental psychology* (2nd ed., Vol. 1, pp. 165–194). New York: Wiley.

Wheeler, M. A., & McMillan, C. T. (2001). Focal retrograde amnesia and the episodic-semantic distinction. *Cognitive, Affective, and Behavioral Neuroscience, 1*, 22–37.

Whitney, P., Ritchie, B. G., & Clark, M. B. (1991). Working-memory capacity and the use of elaborative inferences in text comprehension. *Discourse Processes, 14*(2), 133–145.

Whorf, B. L. (1956). *Language, thought, and reality: Selected writings*. Cambridge, MA: Technology Press of MIT.

Wickelgren, W. (1974). *How to solve problems*. San Francisco: W.H. Freeman.

Wickens, C. D. (1984). Processing resources in attention, dual task performance, and workload assessment. In R. Parasuraman & R. Davies (Eds.), *Varieties of attention* (pp. 63–102). New York: Academic Press.

Wickens, C. D. (1992). *Engineering psychology and human performance* (2nd ed.). New York: Harper-Collins.

Wickens, D., Dalezman, R., Eggemeier, E., & Thomas, F. (1976). Multiple encoding of word attributes in memory. *Memory & Cognition, 4*, 307–310.

Wikman, A.-S., Nieminen, T., & Summala, H. (1998). Driving experience and time-sharing during in-car tasks on roads of different width. *Ergonomics, 41*(3), 358–372.

Wiley, J. (1998). Expertise as mental set: The effects of domain knowledge in creative problem solving. *Memory & Cognition, 26*(4), 716–730.

Williams, L. M. (1995). Recovered memories of abuse in women with documented child sexual victimization histories. *Journal of Traumatic Stress, 8*(4), 649–673.

Willingham, D. B. (1997). Systems of memory in the human brain. *Neuron, 18*, 5–8.

Willingham, D. B. (1998) A neuropsychological theory of motor skill learning. *Psychological Review, 105*, 558–584.

Willingham, D. B., Nissen, M. J., & Bullemer, P. (1989). On the development of procedural knowledge. *Journal of Experimental Psychology: Learning, Memory, and Cognition, 15*, 1047–1060.

Winer, G. A., Cottrell, J. E., Gregg, V., Fournier, J. S., & Bica, L. A. (2002). Fundamentally misunderstanding visual perception: Adults' belief in visual emissions. *American Psychologist, 57*, 417–424.

Wing, A. M. (2000). Motor control: Mechanisms of motor equivalence in handwriting. *Current Biology, 10*, R245–R248.

Winner, E. (2000). Giftedness: Current theory and research. *Current Directions in Psychological Science, 9*(5), 153–156.

Wittgenstein, L. (1953). *Philosophical investigations*. Oxford: Blackwell.

Wollen, K. A., Weber, A., & Lowry, D. H. (1972). Bizarreness versus interaction of mental images as determinants of learning. *Cognitive Psychology, 3*(3), 518–523.

Wong, K. F. E. (2002). The relationship between attentional blink and psychological refractory period. *Journal of Experimental Psychology: Human Perception & Performance, 28*, 54–71.

Wood, N., & Cowan, N. (1995). The cocktail party phenomenon revisited: How frequent are attention shifts to one's name in an irrelevant auditory channel? *Journal of Experimental Psychology: Learning, Memory, and Cognition, 21*(1), 255–260.

Wood, N. L., Stadler, M. A., & Cowan, N. (1997). Is there implicit memory without attention? A reexamination of task demands in Eich's (1984) procedure. *Memory & Cognition, 25*(6), 772–779.

Woodward, A. E., Bjork, R. A., & Jongeward, R. H. (1973). Recall and recognition as a function of primary rehearsal. *Journal of Verbal Learning & Verbal Behavior, 12*, 608–617.

Woodworth, R. (1938). *Experimental psychology*. New York: Henry Holt.

Woodworth, R. S., & Schlosberg, H. (1954). *Experimental psychology* (Rev. ed.). New York: Holt.

Woodworth, R. S., & Sells, S. B. (1935). An atmosphere effect in formal syllogistic reasoning. *Journal of Experimental Psychology, 18*, 451–460.

Worthen, J. B. (1997). Resiliency of bizarreness effects under varying conditions of verbal and imaginal elaboration and list composition. *Journal of Mental Imagery, 21*(1–2), 167–194.

Wraga, M. J. (1999a). The role of eye height in perceiving affordances and object dimensions. *Perception and Psychophysics, 61*, 490–507.

Wraga, M. J. (1999b). Using eye height in different postures to scale the heights of objects. *Journal of Experimental Psychology: Human Perception and Performance, 25*, 518–530.

Wright, C. E. (1990). Generalized motor programs: Reexamining claims of effector independence in writing. In M. Jeannerod (Ed.), *Attention and performance XIII: Motor representation and control* (pp. 294–320). Mahwah, NJ: Erlbaum.

Wulf, G., & Prinz, W. (2001). Directing attention to movement effects enhances learning: A review. *Psychonomic Bulletin & Review, 8*, 648–660.

Wundt, W. (1894). *Lectures on human and animal psychology* (S. E. Creigton and E. B. Tichener, Trans.). New York: Macmillan.

Wyttenbach, R. A., May, M. L., & Hoy, R. R. (1996). Categorical perception of sound frequency by crickets. *Science, 273*, 1542–1544.

Yachanin, S. A. (1986). Facilitation in Wason's selection task: Content and instructions. *Current Psychological Research & Reviews, 5*(1), 20–29.

Yardley, L. (1990). Contribution of somatosensory information to perception of the visual vertical with body tilt and rotating visual field. *Perception and Psychophysics, 42*, 131–134.

Zacks, J. M., Tversky, B., & Iyer, G. (2001). Perceiving, remembering, and communicating structure in events. *Journal of Experimental Psychology: General, 130*, 29–58.

Zelaznik, H. N., Hawkins, B., & Kisselburgh, L. (1983). Rapid visual feedback processing in single-aiming movements. *Journal of Motor Behavior, 15,* 217–236.

Zhang, S., & Schmitt, B. (1998). Language-dependent classification: The mental representation of classifiers in cognition, memory, and ad evaluations. *Journal of Experimental Psychology: Applied, 4*(4), 375–385.

Zwaan, R. A. (1994). Effect of genre expectations on text comprehension. *Journal of Experimental Psychology: Learning, Memory, and Cognition, 20*(4), 920–933.

Zwaan, R. A., & Radvansky, G. A. (1998). Situation models in language comprehension and memory. *Psychological Bulletin, 123,* 162–185.

Credits

Figure 1.7 From *Havanastreet.com*

Figure 1.4 From pp. 108 & 218 from COGNITIVE NEUROSCIENCE: The Biology of the Mind by Michael Gazzaniga et al. Copyright © 1998 by the authors. Reprinted by permission of W. W. Norton & Company.

Figure 1.6a Figure 1-12, p. 13 from R. S. Snell, CLASSICAL NEUROANATOMY FOR STUDENTS, 1980. By permission of Lippincott Williams & Wilkins.

Figure 1.6b From Carlson, Neil R. *Physiology of Behavior 4/e*, 1991. Published by Allyn and Bacon, Boston, MA. Copyright 1991 by Pearson Education. Reprinted by permission of the publisher.

Figure 1.8 From Carlson, Neil R. *Physiology of Behavior 4/e*, 1991. Published by Allyn and Bacon, Boston, MA. Copyright 1991 by Pearson Education. Reprinted by permission of the publisher.

Figure 1.9 From p. 31 in THE HUMAN CENTRAL NERVOUS SYSTEM 3rd edition by R. Nieuwenhuys, J. Voogd, and C. Van Huijzen. Copyright © 1988 by Springer-Verlag. Reprinted by permission.

Figure 2.5 Reproduced from *http://bcs.mit.edu/persci/high/gallery/checkershadowillusion.html*. By permission of Ted Adelson, Massachusetts Institute of Technology.

Figure 2.6 Reprinted from "Perceived Lightness Depends on Perceived Spatial Arrangement" by A. L. Gilchrist, *Science*, 195, January 14, 1977. Copyright © 1977 by American Association for the Advancement of Science. Reprinted by permission.

Figure 2.7 From "Vision: Space and Movement" by G. Westheimer in STEVEN'S HANDBOOK OF EXPERIMENTAL PSYCHOLOGY 2nd edition, Volume 1 by Atkinson et al. Copyright © 1988 by G. Westheimer. Reprinted by permission of John Wiley & Sons, Inc.

Photo 2.2 Copyright Runion des Muses Nationaux/Art Resource, NY.

Photo 2.3 The Kobal Collection/Orion.

Figure 2.16 From *Havanastreet.com*

Figure 2.17 From Human Information Processing 2nd edition by Lindsay/Norman. 1977. Reprinted with permission of Wadsworth, a division of Thomson Learning: *www.thomsonrights.com*.Fax 8007302215

Figure 2.19 Reprinted from COMPUTER VISION, GRAPHICS AND IMAGE PROCESSING, 32, I. Biederman, pp. 29–73, 1985, copyright 1980, with permission from Elsevier.

Figure 2.20 Figure 2, p. 62 from "Rotating Objects to Recognize Them: A Case Study on the Role of View-point Dependency in the Recognition of Three-Dimensional Objects" by M. J. Tarr, *Psychonomic Bulletin & Review*, 2(1), 1995. Copyright © 1991 by the Psychonomic Society, Inc. Reprinted with permission.

Figure 2.22 Figure 3 from "Perceiving Geographical Slant" by D. R. Profitt et al., *Psychonomic Bulletin & Review*, 2(4), 1995. Copyright © 1995 by the Psychonomic Society, Inc. Reprinted by permission.

Association for the n. Advancement of Science. Reprinted by permission.

Figure 5.1 Reprinted from CONSCIOUSNESS AND COGNITION: An International Journal, 4(4), L. Cahill & J. L. McGaugh, "A Novel Demonstration of Enhanced Memory Associated with Emotional Arousal," 1996, with permission of Elsevier.

Figure 5.3 Reprinted from JOURNAL OF MEMORY AND LANGUAGE, 16(5), T. S. Hyde & J. J. Jenkins, "Recall for Words as a Function of Semantic, Graph and Syntactic Orienting Tasks," Copyright 1977, with permission from Elsevier.

Figure 5.4 Reprinted from COGNITIVE PSYCHOLOGY, 11, R. S. Nickerson & M. J. Adams, "Long-Term Memory for a Common Object," Copyright 1979, with permission from Elsevier.

Figure 5.5 Reprinted from JOURNAL OF MEMORY AND LANGUAGE, 16(5), C. D. Morris, J. D. Bransford & J. J. Franks, "Levels of Processing Versus Transfer Appropriate Processing," pp. 519–533, Copyright 1977, with permission from Elsevier.

Figure 5.6 Reprinted from JOURNAL OF MEMORY AND LANGUAGE, 16(5), C. D. Morris, J. D. Bransford & J. J. Franks, "Levels of Processing Versus Transfer Appropriate Processing," pp. 519–533, Copyright 1977, with permission from Elsevier.

Table 5.1 Reprinted from COGNITIVE PSYCHOLOGY, 7(1), G. H. Bower, J. B. Black, and T. J. Turner, "Scripts in Memory for Text," table 2, p. 182, Copyright 1975, with permission from Elsevier.

Figure 6.2 Reprinted from JOURNAL OF MEMORY AND LANGUAGE, 9, L. L. Light & L. Carter-Sobell "Effects of Changed Semantic Context on Recognition Memory," Copyright 1970, with permission from Elsevier.

Figure 6.3 Graph from "Facilitation in Recognizing Pairs of Words: Evidence of a Dependence Between Retrieval Operations" by D. Meyer and R. W. Schvaneveldt, *Journal of Experimental Psychology: General*, 90, 1971. Copyright © 1971 by the American Psychological Association. Reprinted by permission.

Figure 6.5 From *American Journal of Psychology*. Copyright 1940 by Board of Trustees of the University of Illinois. Used with permission of the University of Illinois Press.

Figure 6.6 Reprinted from *Trends in Cognitive Sciences*, 6, B. J. Levy & M. C. Anderson, "Inhibitory processes and the control of memory retrieval," pp. 299–305. Copyright 2002, with permission from Elsevier.

Figure 6.7 Reprinted from *Nature*, 410, M. C. Anderson & C. Green, "Suppressing Unwanted Memories by Executive Control," fig. 1, p. 366, copyright 2001, with permission from *Nature*.

Figure 6.8 & Figure 6.9 Figure 7, p. 17 and sample questions from the Appendix in "Semantic Memory Content in Permastore: Fifty Years of Memory for Spanish Learned in School" by H. P. Bahrick, *Journal of Experimental Psychology*, 113(1), 1984. Copyright © 1984 by the American Psychological Association. Reprinted by permission.

Box 6.2 Adapted from Figure 1, p. 312 from "Frontal Cortex Contributes to Human Memory Formation" by R. L. Buckner, W. M. Kelly, and S. E. Peterson, *Nature Neuroscience*, 2(4), 1999. Copyright © 1999 by Macmillan Magazines Ltd. Reprinted by permission of *Nature*.

Table 6.3 Reprinted from JOURNAL OF MEMORY & LANGUAGE, 28(6), R. J. Gerrig, "Suspense in the Absence of Uncertainty," p. 182, Copyright 1989, with permission from Elsevier.

Figure 7.2 Figure 1, p. 30 from "Perceived Distance and the Classification of Distorted Patterns" by M. E. Posner, R. Goldsmith, and K. E. Welton, Jr., *Journal of Experimental Psychology: General*, 73(1), 1967. Copyright © 1967 by the American Psychological Association. Reprinted by permission.

Figure 7.5 Figure from "Features of Similarity" by A. Tversky, *Psychological Review*, 84(4), 1977. Copyright © 1977 by American Psychological Association. Reprinted by permission.

Figure 7.8 Figure 10, p. 27 from PARALLEL DISTRIBUTED PROCESSING: EXPLORATIONS IN THE MICROSTRUCTURE OF COGNITION Volume I by David E. Rumelhart et al. Copyright © 1986 by the authors. Reprinted by permission of MIT Press.

Table 7.5 Figure 11, p. 27 from PARALLEL DISTRIBUTED PROCESSING: EXPLORATIONS IN THE MICROSTRUCTURE OF

COGNITION Volume 1 by David E. Rumelhart et al. Copyright © 1986 by the authors. Reprinted by permission of MIT Press.

Box 7.1 Box 7.1 From p. 1020 in THE COGNITIVE NEUROSCIENCES 2nd edition by Michael Gazzaniga. Copyright © 2000 by Michael Gazzaniga. Reprinted by permission of MIT Press.

Box 7.3 Figure 1, p. 78 in "Double Dissociation Between Memory Systems Underlying Explicit and Implicit Memory in the Human Brain" by J. D. E. Gabrieli, et al. *Psychological Science*, 6, 1995. Copyright by Blackwell Publishers, Inc. Reprinted by permission.

Figure 8.2 Figure 2, p. 10107 from "Posatural Hand Synergies" by M. Santello, JOURNAL OF NEUROSCIENCE, 18, 1998. Copyright 1998 by the Society for Neuroscience. Reprinted with permission.

Figure 8.4 Figure 1, p. 184 from "Characteristics of Motor Programs Underlying Arm Movements in Monkeys" by A. Polit and E. Bizzi, JOURNAL OF NEUROPHYSIOLOGY, 42, 1978. Copyright 1978 by the Journal of Physiology. Reprinted with permission.

Figure 8.5 Reprinted from HUMAN MOTOR CONTROL, D. A. Rosenbaum, p. 219, Copyright 1991, with permission from Elsevier.

Figure 8.9 From "Hierarchial Control of Rapid Movement Sequences" by D. A. Rosenbaum, S. B. Kenny, M. A. Derr, JOURNAL OF EXPERIMENTAL PSYCHOLOGY: Human Perception and Performance, 9, fig. 3, p. 93, 1983. Copyright 1983 by the American Psychological Association.

Figure 8.10 Adapted from *Journal of Motor Behavior*, 15, fig. 2, p. 229, 1983. Reprinted with permission of the Helen Dwight Reid Educational Foundation. Published by Heldref Publications. Copyright 1983.

Figure 8.11 Adapted from *Journal of Motor Behavior*, 26, fig. 8, p. 120, 1994. Reprinted with permission of the Helen Dwight Reid Educational Foundation. Published by Heldref Publications. Copyright 1994.

Figure 8.14 Figure 1, p. 179 in "The Neural Basis of Motor Skill Learning" by D. B. Willingham. *Current Direction in Psychological Science*, 6, 1995. Copyright 1999 by Blackwell Publishers, Inc. Reprinted by permission.

Box 8.1 Reprinted from "Computations Underlying their Execution of Movement" by Emilio Bizzi et al., SCIENCE, 253, 1991. Copyright 1991 by American Association for the Advancement of Science. Reprinted by permission.

Box 8.3 From *Brain*, 119, "Throwing While Looking Through Prisms" by T. A. Martin, et. al., fig. 1B, page 1185, copyright 1996. Used by permission of Oxford University Press.

Figure 9.2 From MENTAL REPRESENTATIONS: A Dual Coding Approach by Allan Paivio, copyright 1990 by Oxford UNiversity Press, Inc. Used by permission of Oxford University Press, Inc.

Figure 9.4 Reprinted from "Mental Rotation of Three-Dimensional Objects" by R. N. Shepard & J. Metzler, SCIENCE, 171, 1971. Copyright 1971 by American Association for the Advancement of Science.

Figure 9.5 Figure 1, p. 91 from "Scanning Visual Images: Some Structural Implications" by S. M. Kosslyn, *Perception & Psychophysics*, 49(5), 1991. Copyright © 1991 by the Psychonomic Society, Inc. Reprinted by permission.

Figure 9.9 Figure 1, p. 29 from Stephan A. Brandt and Lawrence W. Stark, "Spontaneous Eye Movements During Visual Imagery Reflect the Content of the Visual Scene," *Journal of Cognitive Neuroscience*, 9:1 (January, 1997). Copyright © 1997 by the Massachusetts Institute of Technology. Reprinted by permission.

Figure 9.10 Reprinted from COGNITIVE PSYCHOLOGY, 7(1), L. A. Cooper, "Mental Rotation of Random Two-Dimensional Shapes," Copyright 1975, with permission from Elsevier.

Box 9.1 Reprinted from NEUROLIMAGE, 6, S. M. Kosslyn, W. L. Thompson & N. M. Alpert, "Neural Systems Shared by Visual Imagery and Visual Perception," p. 328, 1997, with permission from Elsevier.

Box 9.2 Reprinted from "Mental Rotation of the Neuronal Population Vector" by A. P. Georgopoulos et al., *Science*, 243, 1989. Copyright 1989 by the American Association for the Advancement of Science. Reprinted by permission.

Author Index

Subject Index